THE

COMMUNIST INTERNATIONAL

AND ITS

FRONT ORGANIZATIONS

HOOVER INSTITUTION BIBLIOGRAPHICAL SERIES: XXI

THE
COMMUNIST INTERNATIONAL
AND ITS
FRONT ORGANIZATIONS

A Research Guide and Checklist of Holdings
In American and European Libraries

By

WITOLD S. SWORAKOWSKI

THE HOOVER INSTITUTION
ON WAR, REVOLUTION, AND PEACE
Stanford, California

1 9 6 5

© 1965 BY THE BOARD OF TRUSTEES OF THE

LELAND STANFORD JUNIOR UNIVERSITY

Library of Congress Catalog Card Number 65–12622

Printed in Germany by Fremdsprachendruckerei Dr. Peter Belej, München 13

To Ela and Michael

PREFACE

The global aims, the open and secret forms of organization, the bizzare methods of operation, and the semiofficial Soviet status of the Communist International characterize this body and its many front organizations as the most anomalous "association" of all time.

The literature published by and on this organizational cobweb is one of the most complicated and troublesome agglomerations of printed material which comes into the hands of scholars, publicists, and students. From the bibliographer's point of view, this is a haphazardly produced group of printed material which, for classification and cataloging purposes, requires a thorough knowledge of the statutes, resolutions, and proceedings of the organizations concerned. Only such knowledge will enable the bibliographer to disentangle the puzzling maze of organizational institutions and their subdivisions, their ever changing names and titles, and their "official" or "authorized" first prints, reprints, and translations. The librarian who attempts to catalog these printed materials certainly faces a difficult task. If he is not particularly exacting and does not want to spend hours in studying the intricacies of these printed materials, he will follow the cataloging procedures of the Library of Congress or the Union List of Periodicals, which, however, cannot always be applied with good results to this type of specific material.

No attempt is known to have been made to compile a comprehensive bibliography of the publications by and on the Communist International and its front organizations. The modest bibliographical contributions to this subject which appeared in past years are discussed later. The present work does not aspire to be such a final bibliography by any means. It is, however, a first attempt to list all books and pamphlets published by and on these organizations that are available in the major libraries of the United States and western Europe. Thus it is a checklist of the holdings of 44 American and four European libraries of books and pamphlets published by and on:

The Communist International
The Red International of Labor Unions
The Communist Youth International
The International Red Aid (MOPR)
The International Peasants' Council (Peasants' International)
The Workers' International Relief
The Communist Women's Organization

These are the principal organizations which, during the time of the operation of the Communist International, from March 1919 to June 1943, promoted, sustained, and directed the communist movement in all corners of the world.

The present checklist does not include a listing of articles published in periodicals and newspapers. Nor does it list the titles of periodicals and newspapers published by these international organizations, with the necessary exception of a few official bulletins published for the participants in congresses and plenums of the Communist International, the Red International of Labor Unions, and the Peasant International. These bulletins contain information about and records of some of these meetings and thus belong here.

The prospective user of materials on the Communist International and its front organizations, even if acquainted with their organizational structure and their general activities and policies, will encounter difficulties in locating the material in most libraries. Deviations in cataloging and in subject classification and headings, together with other peculiarities, are time-consuming stumbling blocks in certain catalogs. All these deviations will be discussed below in order to facilitate search for the material listed in the checklist.

Almost three fourths of the material in this checklist concerns the Communist Internationl, or Comintern, as it is called in abbreviation. The remainder deals with its six most active front organizations. This proportion best indicates the importance of the work of the parent organization as compared with the limited activities of the "auxiliaries." The latter adjusted the timing, intensity, and geographical spread of their work to the needs of the parent organization.

The Communist International, in turn, also had its fluctuations of intensity and fields of concentration of its own work. Its subordination to the vital needs of the Russian Soviet state, the much advertised "fatherland of the proletariat," is obvious even from the preparatory meeting held in Petrograd in December 1918, which preceded the founding of the Comintern, up to its dissolution in May 1943.[1] As long as Lenin was alive, the pretense of joint action of the "world proletariat" was preserved. During the Stalin regime the Communist International itself became an "auxiliary" of Soviet foreign policy.

According to Article 4 of the Statutes of the Communist International, adopted by its second congress, in 1920, the congresses were to be called "not less than once a year." As long as Lenin was in good health, this rule was strictly observed. In 1923 Lenin's health deteriorated considerably and no congress was called that year. Stalin, from the very beginning, evaluated the importance of the Comintern in quite a different manner from Lenin. With disdain he referred to it as the *lavochka* (a small mixed-goods store) and, disregarding statutory requirements, called its congress only three times during the last twenty-one years of the International's existence. Thus, after 1924 the actual work was carried on by the Executive Committee and its Presidium.

The congresses and plenums of the Executive Committee of the Communist International were multinational gatherings of people with at least forty lan-

---

[1] *History of the Communist Party of the Soviet Union,* Moscow, Foreign Languages Publishing House, 1960, pp. 583—584.

guages as their native tongues. After some attempts at restrictions in the beginning, delegates were permitted to use at the meetings any language they chose. Their speeches were translated into Russian, German, French, and English, or digests in these languages were read to the congresses immediately following the speech in another language. Whether a speech was translated verbatim or digested to longer or shorter versions depended upon the importance of the speaker. Only by realizing these time-consuming translating and digesting procedures does it become understandable why some congresses lasted as long as forty-five days.

The number of participants at the congresses grew to considerable proportions. In addition to the official delegates of the member parties, there came to the congresses numerous assistants and advisers to the delegates; "specialists" in various subjects, problems, and areas; "men of confidence" of the the Moscow leadership planted in particular parties; official representatives (the so-called reps) of the Executive Committee of the Comintern residing in some of the more important countries; and a host of contenders for jobs and "special missions" in the Comintern. It is estimated that at some congresses (particularly at the IV-th in 1922 and the VI-th in 1928) the total number of "participants" comprised up to 1,600 persons. To keep these participants informed about the particular phases of a congress, its commissions, and its special bodies, "Bulletins" in two, three, or four languages were published during some congresses. These Bulletins are listed here, together with the material pertaining to the particular congresses and other meetings.

The stenographic records of these meetings grew in volume proportionately with the growth of the communist movement in the world, to its involvement in the internal affairs of the countries concerned, and to the repercussions within the particular member-parties. Especially after Stalin had assumed dictatorial power in the Russian Communist Party and through it in the Comintern, when the purges started in Russia and spread to the member parties, the discussions in the plenary meetings of the congresses and in its commissions expanded considerably. The official Russian minutes of the first congress comprise 682 printed pages. The official Russian record of the controversial VI-th Congress in 1928 fills six volumes ranging in length from 200 to 625 pages.

The increase in the volume of reports, speeches, addresses, resolutions, and theses printed in the official records of the congresses and plenums produced an even greater numerical increase in their reprints and translations into several languages. Some speeches and reports are known to exist in eight languages. As the activities of the Comintern expanded, the number of publications by and about it snowballed to amazing proportions. The scholar and student using these publications should be aware of the peculiarities of their origin.

A few words should be said about the origins of the work on this checklist. The work began with a thorough survey of the catalog and the holdings of the Hoover Institution's library in order to ascertain whether these holdings could support a major research project connected with a documented history of the Communist International. In this early phase it became apparent that the survey should not be limited to the Communist International alone, but should include its principal front organizations. The result was the first draft of a checklist of

Hoover Institution holdings on the Communist International and its six most active front organizations.

In order to obtain a comparative evaluation of these holdings and also to locate important items missing in these holdings, the "Hoover list" was checked against the holdings of four major libraries on the east coast of the United States. The first evaluation, a purely numerical one, showed that Hoover holdings were two to three times larger than the holdings of any of the four major eastern libraries. A comparison of the holdings in relation to their basic importance to research — i. e., minutes of congresses and Executive Committee meetings, collections of documents, memoirs, and reference works — showed that the Hoover holdings contained more of these items than the holdings of any of the other libraries. Some additional key items were, naturally, found in other libraries, but their number was small. Furthermore, most of the items missing in the Hoover Institution's library and held by other libraries were other-language editions of items present in the Hoover holdings.

The availability of the large "Hoover list" and the experience gained during the comparative study of other holdings stimulated the preparation of a joint list of the holdings on this subject of all libraries in the United States which report to the National Union Catalog. This was accomplished by obtaining photographic reproductions of the catalog cards in the National Union Catalog and in the Cyrillic Union Catalog, both located in the Library of Congress. A trip to Europe by the author in 1962 facilitated the inclusion of the major holdings on the Comintern and its front organizations of four European libraries. This is how the survey of the Hoover Institution's holdings reached the extent of the present checklist.

The catalog cards obtained from both Union Catalogs contained the holdings of the Library of Congress and 43 other American libraries whose holdings were reported to the National Union Catalog. A list of these libraries and the European libraries is given in Appendix I. As is generally known, the National Union Catalog does not, by any means, contain cards for all the items held by American libraries. Its completeness depends on the thoroughness of the libraries in report- ting their holdings and acquisitions. The items which have not been reported by the libraries will not be found in the present checklist.

In relying on the catalog cards from 48 libraries in this country and abroad, the checklist developed certain characteristics, of both weakness and strength. Its strength lies in the fact that it indicates the libraries in which a particular listed item can be located. Its weakness reflects the inadequate reporting of libraries of their holdings to the National Union Catalog.

Inadequate reporting may have two causes: first, a certain item might not have been reported to the Union Catalog at all; this may be especially true of a large number of Comintern pamphlets. Some librarians have the mistaken idea that pamphlets are not important. The Union Catalog contains catalog cards from libraries as submitted, and one can find entries such as "15 pamphlets on the Communist International," with no detailed listing of the pamphlets. Presumably, it did not occur to the person who prepared this "simplified" catalog card that some of these pamphlets might be of great research value.

Some libraries do not report pamphlets at all. Thus, should a certain pamphlet be found in a library which is not listed in this checklist as holding this pamphlet, the reason for this would be that it was not reported to the Union Catalog.

The second cause of inadequate reporting is improper subject headings on catalog cards sent to the Union Catalogs. If a library did not insert the Communist International among the subject headings included in the catalog card, there is no entry of its holdings under the subject "Communist International" in the Union Catalog and consequently no reporting of them in this checklist.

As an example, I might mention a few publications by M. N. Roy, the one-time communist leader of India. This prolific writer was delegated by the Comintern to carry out some important missions in China. All his contacts with Chinese communists and communism took place on behalf of the Communist International. His writings on China concern, directly or indirectly, Comintern relations with the Communist Party of China. His principal work on these missions, published first in German *(Revolution und Gegenrevolution in China)*, and later in English *(Revolution and Counter-Revolution in China)*, was cataloged under the subject heading "Communism in China," which is quite correct. But had the catalogers given more attention to the contents, they would have noted that the Communist International was prominently mentioned in the text. A second subject heading — "Communist International" — should have been added. Unfortunately none of the libraries included this second subject heading in their catalog cards even if they had the Roy item. Thus, in their catalogs these items cannot be located under the subject heading "Communist International."

Thus I must repeat that this publication is not an exhausive bibliography, but is merely a joint listing of holdings of 48 American and European libraries cataloged under the author or subject headings of "Communist International" and the six front organizations. In general, items which were not in the available catalog cards did not find their way into the checklist. Some corrections have been made and cataloging errors straightened out, but this could be done only on the basis of the Hoover Institution's holdings. It is possible that during this procedure even some items held by the Institution itself have been overlooked.

About 80 per cent of the material published by and about the Communist International and its front organizations is in languages other than English. Such material cannot be expected to be held by American libraries limiting their foreign-language acquisitions to a certain minimum or to certain fields in the humanities or social sciences. A survey of the reproduced catalog cards from both Union Catalogs clearly indicated which American libraries had multilingual holdings on the Communist International and which libraries limited their acquisitions on this subject to English-language publications only. This survey disclosed that only five American libraries had large multilingual holdings on the subject. They deserve special attention as strong research collections which should be known in their entirety, including not only items reported to the Union Catalogs, but also those which for some reason or other were not reported. From these libraries, photoduplications of pertinent parts of their catalogs were requested and obtained. The five libraries in the United States with major holdings on the Communist International and its front organizations are listed below in the order of their strength of holdings:[2]

	Items	Per cent
Hoover Institution Library	1,251	54.6
New York Public Library	602	26.2
Library of Congress	322	14.0
Harvard University Library	305	13.3
Columbia University Library	289	12.6

Of the other American libraries, only eight hold 25 to 50 items included in this checklist. The remaining 31 libraries have fewer than 25 items, or less than 1 per cent of the total listed here.

The four European libraries included in the checklist are:

	Items	Per cent
International Institute for Social History, Amsterdam	589[3]	25.6
Feltrinelli Institute, Milan	598	26.0
Bibliothèque de Documentation Internationale Contemporaine, Paris	326	14.2
Slavic Institute of the University of Stockholm	143	6.2

It is regrettable that owing to a different cataloging system the holdings of the library of the British Museum in London could not have been included in this checklist. A rather extensive spot survey of its catalog led to an evaluation of its holdings as weaker than the holdings of the New York Public Library, but stronger than those of the Library of Congress.

The West German libraries lost their holdings on international communism partly because of book burning during the Hitler period, and partly as a result of the last war. Among the surviving holdings should be mentioned the collection in the Weltwirtschaftsinstitut in Kiel and in the Weltkriegsbücherei in Stuttgart. In Kiel, a catalog of pertinent articles in periodicals is particularly valuable, but owing to the general exclusion of articles from this checklist, it could not be used. The supposedly strong collections in Geneva, Switzerland, have not been searched and are not included in this checklist. The Labor Relations Institute (Arbetarrörelsens Arkiv) in Stockholm has quite extensive holdings of books, pamphlets, and periodicals published by and on the Communist International and its front organizations. A photographic reproduction of its catalog cards has been obtained, but because of the greatly abbreviated form of the entries, could not be used in this checklist.

The present checklist could have been perhaps more complete, had it been from its inception the outcome of a special project with ample financial backing. As published now, it is the result of my own endeavor to ascertain how much research material on the Communist International and its front organizations

---

[2] These figures have been obtained from a count of location symbols of all items contained in the checklist. The total of 2,300 entries is counted as 100 per cent.

[3] The catalog cards received from the Institute did not include the Red International of Trade Unions. If the Amsterdam holdings on this front organization had been included, the total holdings of this library would have numbered more than 600 items.

is available to scholars, and where the material is located. I hope it establishes facts and dispels myths.

I would like to express here my thanks to the Directors and Librarians of the American and European libraries who provided the photocopies of the catalog cards in their respective libraries, the basic material for the preparation of this checklist. Without their readily given cooperation this volume would not contain the wealth of information which I was able to gather.

Ample technical aid in the preparation of the drafts and the final manuscript has been received from the Hoover Institution and its staff. I owe the Director of the Institution, Dr. W. Glenn Campbell, a debt of gratitude for all his aid toward the completion and publication of this volume. To my colleagues on the Institution's staff, Boris Dubensky and William Boreysza, I would like to extend my thanks for their aid and advice on the editing of the complicated bibliographical entries and on the organization of the entire material. To Karol Maichel, Curator of the East European Collections, who also is in charge of the Institution's publishing operations, I am grateful for bibliographical advice and for seeing the manuscript through the press. To Mrs. Jirina Frisbie, who valiantly struggled with garbled catalog entries and who typed the manuscript, I am expressing my warmest thanks. Finally, I wish to thank Dr. James W. Hulse for his valuable assistance in the early stages of the work, and to Rudolf Lednicky, Slavic Bibliographer in the Library of the University of California at Berkeley, for his editorial help in preparing the final manuscript for print.

WITOLD S. SWORAKOWSKI

Stanford, August 1964

TABLE OF CONTENTS

* Cross references only.

16

---

* Cross references only.

* Cross references only.

18

---

* Cross references only.

PART VIII. OTHER FRONT ORGANIZATIONS OF THE COMMUNIST INTERNATIONAL . . . . 2142 — 2278

---

* Cross references only.

---

* Cross references only.

INTRODUCTION

1. Earlier Bibliographical Contributions

During the early stages of the work on this checklist, a thorough search was undertaken for bibliographical information on the subject. This search confirmed that in the past no broad survey had been made of the literature by or on the Communist International and its front organizations. Even the few bibliographies which were found dealt almost exclusively with the International and neglected the front organizations.

A total of 20 pamphlets and books and a few articles in periodicals were found to contain, in their entirety or in part, bibliographical information on the Comintern. They do far less than cover the subject satisfactorily. The 20 books and pamphlets are included as items 1—20 in this checklist; the articles are discussed below.

Eight of the listed items (nos. 13—20) are, in fact, not bibliographies but catalogs of publications put on the market by the German publisher C. Hoym in Hamburg. This firm was the distributing agency for German-language publications of the Communist International in Moscow and was also the principal communist publisher in Germany in the 1920's. These catalogs were issued in 1920—23 and they list only books and periodicals published by C. Hoym up to the end of 1922. They provide reliable information on the early prints from Hamburg, but do not include German publications produced elsewhere. Thus, their value as source of bibliographic information is limited.

Seven other items (nos. 1, 3, 4, 6, 8, 10, 12) are selective bibliographies, covering short periods, or are lists of publications produced and distributed by certain organizations. They again are of limited value. Two further items, (nos. 5 and 9) were not available for evaluation, being in the possession of only one library, in Paris. Both seem to be of a general character and it is doubtful that they contain any important or significant lists of Comintern publications.

There remain only three of some bibliographical strength which should be discussed individually:

a) *Vsemirnyi kongress Kominterna; ukazatel' literatury* (no. 11). This "guide to the literature" on the VII-th Congress of the Comintern published by a Soviet librarians' organization is a great disappointment. Of the 69 items listed, only 12 refer to the VII-th Congress. The remaining items deal with a variety of other subjects. Taking into consideration that the present checklist contains more that 200 items on the VII-th Congress, this "guide" with is 12 items leads nowhere.

b) Guiliano Procacci's bibliographical essay on the Communist International appeared as an article in the 1958 yearbook of the Feltrinelli Institute in Milan.[1] The reprint of this article is listed here as no. 7. It is the first methodical work in the field of Comintern bibliography. At the same time it is also a checklist of the holdings of the Feltrinelli Institute, listing 140 books and pamphlets and 20 periodicals issued almost exclusively by the Communist International. These were probably the total holdings of the Feltrinelli Institute in 1957 when Procacci prepared his article. Since then the holdings of this rapidly growing library have at least doubled. All items listed in Procacci's essay are contained in this checklist.

c) The latest bibliographical contribution is Günter Herting's *Bibliographie zur Geschichte der Kommunistischen Internationale (1919—1934)* (see no. 2), published in East Berlin in 1960 under the sponsorship of the Institut für Marxismus-Leninismus of the Central Committee of the East German Communist Party (SED). Unfortunately, despite Soviet assertions that this bibliography is widely available,[2] all efforts to obtain this book through several dealers or through a person who intended to buy it directly from the publisher in East Berlin ended in failure. The answer received was: the volume is not for sale, only for official use.

Because of its special contacts, the Institute for Social History in Amsterdam received a copy of the Herting volume. It is listed in the Institute's public catalog, and its title has been entered in the present checklist. A request for a microfilm of the volume, submitted to the Director of the Institute for Social History, has been turned down. Considering the fact that East Germany had not been party to the copyright convention, there must have been other than legal reasons for this refusal. Since this mysterious bibliography was not available for perusal, an annotation of the contents could not be made.

This discussion of bibliographies on the Comintern would not be complete without mentioning two articles contained in Soviet periodicals and dealing with this subject.

1. In the issue no. 2 of 1939 of the periodical *Kniga i proletarskaia revoliutsiia* (pp. 137—139) appeared an anonymous article under the title "On the occasion of the 20-th anniversary of the III-rd Communist International; a short guide to basic literature" *(K 20-letii III Kommunisticheskogo Internatsionala; kratkii ukazatel' osnovnoi literatury)*. It contains 76 entries, of which 25 are of writings by Lenin, 34 by Stalin, and 15 by Dimitrov; of the remaining two, one entry is of the standard history of the Communist Party of the Soviet Union and the other of a pamphlet containing the program and statutes of the Comintern. Of the 25 Lenin entries, four definitely do not pertain to the Comintern. All the Lenin entries are merely references to items in Lenin's *Sochineniia* (Collected Works). The many pamphlets and the few books by Lenin on the Comintern are not mentioned.

Of the 34 Stalin entries, only five concern the Comintern, whereas the remainder deal with a variety of subjects. Of the 34 entries, a total of 30 are, in fact, titles of chapters in four books written by Stalin or by him in collaboration with others. Following a most unusual bibliographical practice, these chapters were made into separate entries, obviously with the intention to pad Stalin's contribution to the literature about the Communist International.

As to Dimitrov's 15 entries, almost all deal with the Communist International; a few concern his trial in Germany after the Reichstag fire.

Thus only a little more than half of the entries listed in this "guide to the basic literature" on the Comintern pertain to the subject. The remainder is a

---

[1] Guiliano Procacci, "L'Internazionale Comunista dal I al VII congresso," in *Annali dell' Istituto Giangiacomo Feltrinelli*, Milan, 1958, pp. 283—313.

[2] *Voprosy istorii KPSS*, Moscow, 1962, no. 9, p. 90.

typical padding designed to impress upon the reader, if he is not acquainted with the subject, how great Stalin's contribution was to Comintern literature. This is the bibliographic aspect of the "cult of personality" practiced in the Soviet Union during Stalin's time. The article is somewhat of a bibliographic curiosity, without real value. It will be worth while to note here that this same article was recently cited in a periodical issued by the Institute of Marxism-Leninism in Moscow as one of the few bibliographical publications recommended for research on the history of the Communist International.[3]

2. Lack of historical studies on the Communist International seems to have been disturbing the Soviet scholarly world lately. In 1963, interest in this deficiency showed up in a bibliographical article by K. S. Trofimov in the periodical published by the Institute of Marxism-Leninism in Moscow, *Voprosy istorii KPSS*.[4] Trofimov mentions that at a meeting of the "Coordination Council for the history of the international workers' and communist movements of the Academy of Sciences of the U.S.S.R. in July 1962" the need for historical studies on the Comintern was discussed and pertinent recommendations were adopted. Unfortunately, Trofimov's information seems to contain some inaccuracies.

The Coordination Council mentioned by Trofimov is an interdepartmental body of the Academy of Sciences of the U.S.S.R. In the official journal of the Academy is a note reporting about a conference of the "Coordination Council of the history of the international workers' and national liberation movements" which took place in Moscow on June 22—25, 1962.[5] Although this report does not mention the Communist International, it is clear that Trofimov has this meeting in mind, because it was the only one which in 1962 dealt with the "international workers' movement." The principal speaker at this conference, B. N. Ponomarev, mentioned the need for historical studies on the efforts of Lenin, of the Communist Party of the Soviet Union, and of the Soviet state for the "development of the revolutionary process in the entire world."[6] The communist agency which fostered this development during the years 1919—43 was none other than the Communist International. Although it is not mentioned by name in the short report on Ponomarev's speech, Trofimov discloses, certainly not without good reason, that in reality the meeting dealt with the history of the Communist International. The report on the next speaker's paper seems to confirm this: V. M. Khvostov spoke about the necessity to cleanse historical studies about the international workers' movement of the "after-effects of the cult of Stalin's personality."[7] Trofimov mentions this, too, hence it is obvious that he has the same meeting in mind. Nevertheless, Trofimov made two mistakes in his article: he says that the meeting took place in July 1962, whereas it was actually held on June 22—25, 1962, and he misquotes the full title of the Coordination Council.

[3] K. S. Trofimov, "Obzor istochnikov i literatury po istorii Kommunisticheskogo Internatsionala," *Voprosy istorii KPSS*, 1963, no. 9, p. 90.

[4] *Ibid.*, pp. 90—99.

[5] *Vestnik Akademii Nauk SSSR*, 1962, no. 10, pp. 101—105.

[6] *Ibid.*, p. 102.

[7] *Ibid.*

Let us return, however, to the contents of Trofimov's bibliographical article. He begins his survey of sources on the history of the Communist International with a general evaluation of the achievements of this organization. In his opinion, the past activities of the Comintern "not only directly influenced world events, but also developed the program and the organizational, strategical, and tactical principles of the world-wide anti-imperialist liberation movement which recently achieved extraordinary successes."[8]

The Soviet author warns that in handling source material and documents of the Comintern originating during the period following the XVI-th Congress of the CPSU — i. e., after June 1930 — one can observe a "growing influence of the cult of Stalin's personality," which "manifested itself not only in the praises of Stalin's individuality, but also in the activities of the Comintern itself, which sometimes took erroneous decisions on Stalin's initiative . . ." The task of the present, he says, is to cleanse the history of the Comintern from the "agglomerated layers of the cult of personality."[9] This warning should be kept in mind by everyone who uses material on the Communist International and its front organizations originating with these same organizations or with any other communist source. It is just as well that this recommendation comes from a Soviet author and that it is printed in an official organ of a learned institution affiliated with the Communist Party of the Soviet Union rather than from an author in the non-communist world, who might be considered biased.

Unfortunately, Trofimov himself does not follow his own recommendations. In listing three bibliographical contributions of the past which should be known to future historians of the Comintern, he begins with the article in the periodical *Kniga i proletarskaia revoliutsiia* of 1939 which was discussed above and which is certainly a typical outgrowth of the cult of Stalin's personality.

As his second bibliographical item of the past, Trofimov lists V. S. Itin's *Kratkii ukazatel' literatury k 20-letiiu Kominterna* (A short guide to literature on the occasion of the 20th anniversary of the Comintern). This item is not included in the present checklist because it has not been located in any of the libraries whose holdings are reported here. But a search in the *Knizhnaia letopis'* for 1939 (no. 10, p. 32) yielded the following information:

[ITIN, V.]

XX let III Kommunisticheskogo Internatsionala; 1919—1939. Kratkii ukazatel' literatury, Moscow, 1939. 1 sheet folded into 6 pages, without cover. (Author not indicated on the title page.)

The above is an exact transcription and translation of the entry in *Knizhnaia letopis'*. It is more than doubtful that this "one sheet" can contain a serious bibliography on a vast subject.

As his third and last bibliographical contribution to the history of the Comintern Trofimov mentions Herting's volume published in East Berlin, which was discussed above. Obviously, the Institute for Marxism-Leninism in Moscow is another place where this mysterious work is held.

---

[8] Trofimov, *op. cit.,* p. 90.
[9] *Ibid.*

Trofimov does not mention Procacci's bibliographical article.

The "historiographic" part of Trofimov's article surveys chronologically the main events concerning the Comintern (congresses, plenums, special conferences) which found their expression in publications. The footnotes contain bibliographic references to books, pamphlets, and articles in periodicals documenting, describing, or discussing a given event. Thus, Trofimov lists the stenographic records of the congresses and plenums and — very incompletely — the reports and speeches presented to these meetings. Furthermore, bibliographic references to the following are included in the footnotes: reference books and collections of documents (both very incomplete), publications (including articles in periodicals) on the occasion of various anniversaries of the Comintern, a selective list of periodicals issued by the Comintern, and a few monographic publications on the history of the Communist International. A total of about 115 books and pamphlets, 33 periodical titles, and 35 articles in periodicals are cited in the footnotes. Of these, at least 90 per cent are in the Russian language; the others are titles in the German, French, English, Spanish, and Czech languages.

Trofimov's article is certainly the first Soviet attempt which may be taken more seriously than the previous limited listings. It suffers, however, from the bad habit adopted by Soviet authors of the Stalin period: namely, it eliminates the writings of latter-day "heretics" such as Trotskii, Bukharin, and Kamenev, who unquestionably contributed to the work and development of the Communist International during their days of glory. Another weak point of Trofimov's bibliographical contribution is that, in listing literature on the history of the Communist International, he limits himself to items dealing exclusively with this organization, to the complete exclusion of items dealing with the Comintern's front organizations. No history of the Communist International can be exhaustive, objective, and historically truthful if it disregards the contributions of its front organizations to the development of the communist movement throughout the world and toward the common goal of communist world-domination. Finally, if the 115 books and pamphlets listed in the Trofimov article are compared with the Hoover Institution's holdings of at least four times as many items on the subject, it seems that his is a very modest contribution to a bibliography on the Communist International. But Trofimov alone should not be blamed for these shortcomings. It is the Soviet system and its control over the work of scholars in the U.S.S.R. which is to be blamed for the bias and incompleteness of their work.

A comparison of the titles of books and pamphlets listed in Trofimov's article with the entries in the present checklist showed that only four items pertinent to the Communist International are missing in this checklist.

2. Collected and Selected Works of Prominent Comintern Leaders

The writings, speeches, letters, and other materials originating with some of the prominent participants in the work of the Communist International and its front organizations were collected and printed in their original language as well as in some translations. Most libraries catalog these collections as single items without subject or cross references to particular subjects. The scholar has to take the initiative himself to search these voluminous primary sources for pertinent information. Owing to the character of the contents of these publications, the librarian has practically no way of pointing out the variety of subjects contained in such "collected" or "selected" works. They are not listed in this checklist, but an attempt is made to include here the most important ones in footnotes.

In most cases, as for instance in the case of Lenin's *Sochineniia*,[10] which are printed in chronological order, it is impossible to make any subject classification of the volumes because the material included refers to a great variety of subjects. Fortunately, there exists a good index to the second and third Russian editions of Lenin's *Sochineniia*.[11] The fourth edition and its German translation are even better indexed than the previous editions.[12] Furthermore, chronological lists of all known writings of Lenin, printed in all Russian editions of his collected and selected works, as well as in various occasional publications, periodicals, and newspapers, are useful research aids.[12a] These abundant indexes facilitate the location of the Lenin items concerning the Communist International. Further, there are special compilations of Lenin's writings and speeches concerning the Communist International[13] which simplify the task of the student and the scholar. Some of these items were published during the period of the "Stalin cult" and the accuracy of reprints in post-1925 editions should be checked against the originals. References to the original sources are indicated at the end of each reprinted item. They can also be checked against the corresponding texts in the second or fifth edition of *Sochineniia,* which seem to be accurate.

---

[10] There are five editions of Lenin's *Sochineniia.* The second edition, of which the third was a reprint, is considered the best. It seems, however, that the fifth edition, begun in 1958 and not yet completed, will be the most complete and valuable. Since these editions are well known and are easy to locate in libraries under the author's name, the inclusion of their full bibliographic entries in this checklist would be superfluous. There are translations also of the second and fourth editions into several languages. The English translation *(Collected Works,* Moscow, 1927—45) is not complete; it includes only vols. 4, 13, 18—21, and 23 of the second / third edition of *Sochineniia.* In 1960 the Moscow Foreign Languages Publishing House started a new English translation of the fourth Russian edition, of which vols. 1—14, 16—20, and 38 have appeared to date. There exist German translations of the second edition, published before 1939, and the fourth edition, published in East Berlin after World War II.
There exist also several editions of selected works of Lenin in Russian and in many other languages. The English edition of *Selected Works* in 12 volumes, published simultaneously in a Moscow and New York printing, has the broadest circulation.
[11] *Spravochnik k II i III izdaniiam Sochinenii V. I. Lenina,* [Moscow,] Partizdat, 1935, vii, 559 p.
[12] Institut Marksa-Engel'sa-Lenina, *Spravochnyi tom k 4 izdaniiu sochinenii V. I. Lenina,* Moscow, Gos. izd-vo polit. lit-ry, 1955—56, 2 vols.
Institut Marksa-Engel'sa Lenina, *Alfavitnyi ukazatel' proizvedenii V. I. Lenina, voshedshikh v 4-e izd. Sochinenii,* [Moscow,] Gos. izd-vo polit. lit-ry, 1951. 136 p.
Vladimir Il'ich Lenin, *Werke. Ins deutsche übertragen nach der 4. russischen Ausgabe. Sachregister,* Hersg. vom Institut für Gesellschaftswissenschaften; Berlin, Dietz, 1957, 2 vols.
Vladimir Il'ich Lenin, *Werke. Ins deutsche übertragen nach der 4. russischen Ausgabe. Inhaltsvergleichsregister* [Hersg. vom Institut für Gesellschaftswissenschaften]; Berlin, Dietz, 1957, 198 p.
[12a] Institut Marksa-Engel'sa-Lenin, *Khronologicheskii ukazatel' proizvedenii V. I. Lenina; v dvukh chastiakh; 1886—1923,* Moscow, Gos. izd-vo polit. lit-ry, 1959. 2 vols.
Institut Marksa-Engel'sa-Lenina, *Vspomogatel'nye ukazateli k khronologicheskomu ukazateliu proizvedenii V. I. Lenina,* Moscow, Izd-vo polit. lit-ry, 1963. x, 490 p.
[13] See items nos. 291—300.

Some material on the Communist International can be found in the *Leninskii Sbornik*,[14] but, again, the scholar has to take the initiative and has to search the volumes and their indexes.

More complicated is the location of the Stalin items concerning the Communist International. Stalin's *Collected Works* and their translations appeared in Moscow only up to Volume XIII, covering the period up to January 1934.[15] Since his death and the raising of accusations against him by Khrushchev at the Party congress in 1956, nothing that Stalin said or wrote has been published in the Soviet Union. Recently, the Hoover Institution announced its intention to continue the publication of Stalin's *Sochineniia*, covering the period from February 1934 to his death in 1953, as well as a volume of texts omitted from the Moscow edition of the thirteen volumes. The first of these continuation volumes should appear early in 1965.

Nevertheless, researchers should not rely on the thirteen volumes of the Moscow edition, because of possible erroneous texts and omissions.[16] The scholar using these volumes will be protected from pitfalls only if he checks the texts of these volumes with the original source indicated at the end of each reprinted item. A welcome aid for the user of the thirteen Stalin volumes is an index prepared by Jack F. Matlock, Jr., and published in the United States.[17]

Much better, although not completely satisfactory, is the situation with regard to Trotskii's writings on the Communist International.[18] One of the volumes of his (incomplete) collected works,[19] deals exclusively with the Communist International and related matters. This volume was published in Moscow in 1926 and is by no means complete. Also an earlier volume, published in Moscow in 1924 and dealing with the first five years of the Comintern (1919—23), is somewhat less complete than its translation into English, issued much later (1945, 1953).[20] A most difficult task is to locate Trotskii's articles dealing directly or marginally with the Communist International, written during the last two years of his life. A complete bibliography of Trotskii's writings and speeches, in preparation by Louis Sinclair, to be published by the Hoover Institution, will facilitate the location of Trotskii's items concerning the Comintern and its front organizations.

The collected and selected works of the former-secretary-general of the Communist International, Georgii Dimitrov, are available in the Bulgarian language

---

[14] *Leninskii Sbornik*, Moscow, 1924——, published irregularly; 36 volumes appeared up to 1959; there is an index for the first 20 volumes.

[15] Iosif Stalin, *Sochineniia*, Moscow, OGIZ, 1946—55, 13 vols.
Iosif Stalin, *Works*, Moscow, Foreign Languages Publishing House, 1953—55, vols. 1—13. There also exist translations of these volumes into other languages.

[16]) Stalin's three speeches given at sessions of the American Commission of the Executive Committee of the Communist International in May 1929 have not been included in Vol. XII of his *Sochineniia*, where they chronologically belong. See annotation to no. 1139.

[17] Jack F. Matlock, Jr., assisted by Fred C. Holling, Jr., *An Index to the Collected Works of J. V. Stalin* [Washington, D. C.], External Research Staff, Office of Intelligence Research, Department of State, 1955, 192 p., mimeographed (items concerning the Communist International are listed on pp. 24—25).

[18] See items nos. 362—376.

[19] *Sochineniia*, Vol. XIII; see no. 366.

[20] See no. 367 for the early Russian edition, and no. 363 for the English translation.

and, in part, in English and French translations.[21] Most of what he wrote and said on the Comintern concerned the new tactical move known as the Popular Front, which he proclaimed at the VII-th Congress of the Communist International in July-August 1935.[22] Of special interest are Dimitrov's publications, mostly small pamphlets, which he wrote in defense of the turn in Soviet foreign policy in 1939, the Hitler-Stalin pact and Nazi-Soviet collaboration.[23] At that time neither the Congress nor the Executive Committee of the Communist International was called by Stalin. Dimitrov's articles in *Pravda*, reprinted in pamphlet form and translated into many languages, were also read over the Moscow radio transmitters in several languages. They became the official Comintern explanation of this reversal of Communist policy and were also authoritative instructions to foreign communist parties as to what policies and tactics to apply in their own countries toward the war, the Nazis, and the Western democracies. After the invasion of the Soviet Union by Hitler these small pamphlets were hastily destroyed by Moscow-faithful communists all over the world.

A collected edition of the writings and speeches of the French wheelhorse of the Comintern, Maurice Thorez, has been in the course of publication since 1950[24] and is not yet complete. Thorez, as a faithful follower of Stalin, went through all the sharp twists and zigzag turns of Moscow's dictates to the Comintern. The reprints in this edition require a careful cross-checking against the originals. A much more modest selection of the articles and speeches of Marcel Cachin contains only a small contribution concerning the Comintern and its French section.[25]

The last of the Comintern's *apparatchiks* (members of party bureaucracy) whose writings and speeches are being published currently is Wilhelm Pieck.[26] He, too, demonstrated "Marxist flexibility" in taking all the zigzag turns in Moscow's Comintern policies and surviving all the purges. The compiler and sponsor of his volumes, the "Marx-Engels-Lenin-Stalin Institut beim ZK der SED," has also adjusted itself to the next zigzag turn, the Khrushchev era, by changing its name to "Institut für Marxismus-Leninismus beim ZK der SED." Not until a full and objective bibliography of all his writings and speeches is

---

[21] Georgii Dimitrov, *Suchineniia*, [Sofia,] Izd-vo na Bulgarskata kommunisticheska partiia, 1951—54, 12 vols.

Georgii, Dimitrov, *Selected Speeches and Articles*, Introduction by Harry Pollitt, London, Lawrence & Wishart, 1951, 275 p.

Georgi Dimitrov, *Oeuvres choisies*, Preface by Maurice Thorez, Paris, Editions sociales, [1952,] xx, 309 p. (This item is only in *BDIC* holdings. Two preceding ones in *Hoover*.)

[22] See nos. 896—1011 and 1530—1565.

[23] See nos. 234 b—236 a.

[24]) Maurice Thorez, *Oeuvres*, Paris, Editions sociales, 1950—, 5 volumes in 20 tomes (up to 1960).

[25] Marcel Cachin, *Marcel Cachin vous parle*, Preface by Etienne Fajon, Introduction by Jean Freville, Paris, Editions sociales, [1959,] 222 p. Included are articles and speeches from the years 1904—57.

[26] Wilhelm Pieck, *Reden und Aufsätze;* Auswahl, Berlin, Dietz, 1952—. At head of title: Marx-Engels-Lenin-Stalin Institut beim ZK der SED.

Wilhelm Pieck, *Ausgewählte Reden und Schriften*, Foreword by Wilhelm Pieck, 2d ed., Berlin, 1955, 2 vols. At head of title: Marx-Engels-Lenin-Stalin Institut beim ZK der SED.

Wilhelm Pieck, *Gesammelte Reden und Schriften*, Foreword by Walter Ulbricht, Berlin, Dietz, 1959—, 3 vols. (to 1960.) At head of title: Institut für Marxismus-Leninismus beim ZK der SED.

compiled would it be possible to judge whether and to what degree the selections published by this institute distort the truth.

To the best of my knowledge, these seem to be all the existing "collected" and "selected" works of the founders of the Comintern and its more prominent *apparatchiks*. The works of Bukharin, Radek, Lozovskii, Pianitskii, and Manuilskii still await their publisher. These prominent leaders wrote extensively and made numerous speeches concerning Comintern matters. Most of these speeches and writings are on record and await the scholar who would collect, edit, and publish them. The writings and speeches of these men on matters related to the Communist International and its front organizations are probably in their great majority contained in publications listed in this checklist. The name index facilitates their location.

3. Arrangement of Material and Entries

The checklist is divided into eight parts. The first part contains items of general character (bibliographies, reference books, biographies, etc.) pertaining to the Communist International and its front organizations jointly. The following four parts deal with the Communist International; separation of the vast material (more than 1,500 items) into divisions will facilitate finding the desired items. The last three parts contain material concerning the six major front organizations of the Comintern.

Each part is subdivided according to subject matter. Where it seemed useful, the entries are organized in chronological order. This organization of the material is the outcome of discussions with scholars and librarians; much attention was given to the opinions and suggestions of scholars who did research on Comintern subjects in the past. This checklist is, after all, intended for their use.

Perhaps the most controversial problem arose from the fact that the listed items are in 22 languages. Theoretically, there were two ways of handling this multi-language material: listing it in strict alphabetical order, disregarding the language of the item, or listing it by languages, retaining the alphabetical order within the particular languages. A compromise solution seemed most advantageous to the user: the alphabetical order, disregarding the language, was adopted in principle, with the exception of those divisions dealing with meetings (congresses, plenums, committee meetings, etc.) where the scholar will be looking for material in that foreign language which he commands most easily. Here he will find first the items in Russian, followed by the German, English, and Fench items. Other languages follow in alphabetical order (Bulgarian, Czech, Hungarian, etc.).

Every item carries a running number. The Index at the end of the volume refers to these numbers. Although the last entry carries the number 2,278, the checklist contains more than 2,300 items. During the proofreading of the galleys some items had to be relocated to other subject divisions and their numbers had to be changed accordingly. In addition, a certain number of items were located after the manuscript went to the printer and these had to be added. The relocated

and added items were given numbers already in use, with the letters a, b, c, ...
added. (See, for example, nos 234, 234a, 234b, 235, 235a.)

Any item listed here may deal prominently with more than one subject.
Thus it may appear in two or more pertinent subject divisions. In order not
to encumber the listing, it was decided that only when the item was listed for
the first time would it carry an entry number. When the item is repeated as
a cross reference in a later subject division, it does not carry a number, but after
the listing of the author or title the number is given under which the full entry
of the item can be found. To the 2,300 numbered entries were added about
400 cross references which carry no number.

The organization of the material dealing with congresses and other meetings
(plenums, presidiums, executive committees, etc.) should be explained here.
Because there may be as many as 140 items referring to a single meeting, it was
necessary to subdivide the material in order to assure easier location of the
desired item. The subdivisions have been set up in the following manner:

a) First listed are the *stenographic records or minutes* of the meeting; in most cases they
contain the full record of all transactions of the meeting and are its most important documentation.

b) Next assembled are all reports, speeches, drafts, memoranda, and other documents *presented to the meeting*. In most cases these are duplications of parts of the stenographic records,
but this is by no means the rule. These prints may contain deviations from the text in the official
record, and if this is the case, these deviations are of importance.

c) In the third place are listed all resolutions, "theses," decisions, and other documents
originating with the meeting. These, again, are mostly reprints of parts of the stenographic
records of the meeting, but important deviations and changes of the text are known to exist.

d) In the fourth place are listed all publications *about the meeting*. These may be general
reports on a given meeting or interpretations of the attitude of the meeting concerning particular
subjects handled by the meeting.

e) In the last place are listed *official bulletins for participants* in the meeting, published by
the Press Bureau of the Communist International in Moscow, acting as the Press Bureau of the
meeting. Such bulletins were published only for a few meetings and they contain important
information on these meetings.

This arrangement of the material on meetings is shown by corresponding
subtitles provided in the listing.

The executive bodies of the Comintern (ECCI) and of some front organizations published, before congresses or before plenary sessions (plenums), reports
about their activities since the preceding congress or plenum. These reports were
distributed to delegates before or at the meeting, and they are important documents listed among the material presented to the meeting (*b*, above). They
can easily be located through the Index.

Only in the case of one congress of the Comintern has an exception been
made in the organization of the material. The prints produced and distributed
as preparatory work for the II-d Congress are listed in a separate subdivision
preceding the stenographic records. This congress, in 1920, was of particular
importance, for which Moscow made special preparations. Details concerning
this material are contained in a note preceding no. 542.

Contrary to this organization, in American libraries the entire material on
a given Comintern meeting (congress, plenum, etc.) is lumped together in the

catalog and organized alphabetically. Hence, if a library has the Russian and English editions of the stenographic records of the meeting, the scholar and student will have to search for them under their title, which in most cases begins with the number of the meeting: "Second Congress . . ." "Third Congress . . ." "Vtoroi kongress . . ." and so on. Some European libraries took the logical step of placing in their catalogs the cards listing the records and minutes of these meetings in front of the other items on the meeting.

4. Languages of Listed Items

The 2,300-odd items in the checklist were published in 22 Western and Slavic languages. About 75 per cent of the items are in four main languages, distributed almost equally as follows:

> English — about 20 per cent
> Russian — about 20 per cent
> German — about 20 per cent
> French — about 15 per cent

The remaining 25 per cent are in 18 other languages, with three of the languages making up between 2 to 5 per cent each and the remaining 15 languages represented by 1 per cent or less. These 18 languages are (in alphabetical order):

Bulgarian	Italian (about 5 per cent)
Czech	Norwegian
Danish	Polish
Dutch (about 2 per cent)	Portuguese
Esperanto	Serbo-Croatian
Estonian	Slovene
Finnish	Spanish (about 3 per cent)
Greek (1 item)	Swedish
Hungarian	Ukrainian

The Hoover Institution's library and other libraries in the United States have materials on the Communist International and its front organizations in the Chinese, Japanese, Turkish, and Arab languages. These holdings were not included in the present checklist. The Hoover Institution, in its Bibliographical Series, has published an annotated bibliography on *The Chinese Communist Movement* which includes publications by and on the Communist International and its front organizations in the Chinese language.[27]

The multilingual publications noted in the checklist were printed during a time span of more than forty years and in at least 75 places scattered over the world. Official changes in orthography were introduced in some countries during this time (particularly in Italy, Poland, and Yugoslavia), and, of course, printing usages differed in various places. This explains the inconsistencies of spelling

---

[27] Hsueh, Chün-tu, *The Chinese Communist Movement 1921—1937: An Annotated Bibliography of Selected Materials in the Chinese Collection of the Hoover Institution on War, Revolution, and Peace* (Stanford, Calif.; Hoover Institution, 1960), viii—131 p.

Hsueh, Chün-tu, *The Chinese Communist Movement 1937—1949: An Annotated Bibliography of Selected Materials in the Chinese Collection of the Hoover Institution on War, Revolution, and Peace* (Stanford, Calif.: Hoover Institution, 1962), x—312 p.

in some of the languages. As a rule, the spelling was left in the entry exactly as it was found on the title page or (when the published item was not available for checking) on the catalog card. As examples may be pointed out *coltura* and *cultura* in Italian and *partja* and *partia* in Polish.

With regard to the transliteration of characters of the Cyrillic alphabets (Russian, Ukrainian, Serbian, and Bulgarian) into Roman equivalents, it seemed appropriate to adopt the transliteration system of the Library of Congress since the checklist will be published in the United States and presumably will have its chief usefulness in this country. Some European scholars and students accustomed to different systems may be disappointed. For their convenience the transliteration table of the Library of Congress is reproduced in Appendix II.[28]

5. Entries of Listed Items

The items in the checklist were cataloged by different American and European libraries, and their catalog cards provided the information for the editing of the bibliographical entries in this volume. These libraries used various cataloging methods, and it therefore became necessary to impose some basic style for the sake of consistency of form and content in the checklist entries. Because the present checklist originated as a list of holdings of the Hoover Institution's library, where, in general, the cataloging rules of the Library of Congress are followed, these rules were adopted for the checklist and, with a few exceptions, were maintained throughout.

To make our system clear, and particularly for the benefit of users who may not be acquainted with cataloging rules, the following is the scheme of a standard entry:

1) Name of the author or authors, as spelled in the author's native language. (Items without author are cataloged under the title.)
2) Full title and subtitle (if any), as found on the title page. (Title on the cover, if different from title page is given at the end of the entry, after the descriptive term: "Cover title.")
3) Place of publication.
4) Name of publisher.
5) Year of publication or year of copyright, if available.
6) Number of pages (pagination).
7) Title of series and current number (if any), if the item belongs to a series.
8) Name of author as printed on the title page, if this spelling is different from the spelling in the author's native language. (See section 7 on spelling and transliteration of authors' names.)

If a publication is a collective work or a collection of materials edited or compiled by a person indicated on the title page, the name of the editor or compiler appears before the title in the same way as the name of an author, with the abbreviation "ed." or "comp." added.

Additions to an entry which did not appear in the title page are enclosed in brackets. If the place or year of publication is missing on the title page, this fact is noted in the entry in the usual abbreviated form (n. p., or n. d.).

---

[28] Minor modifications of the Library of Congress system are indicated in the transliteration table in Appendix II.

Some Comintern publications appeared without a title page and without a cover. In such instances the title from the first printed page is used as the title and this fact is noted at the end of the entry by the term "caption title."

The entries based on catalog cards of libraries which follow different cataloging rules have been adjusted to be consistent in form and content with the style used in the checklist. Wherever this procedure caused difficulties and the published item was not available for checking, the exact content of the catalog card is reproduced in the entry and this fact is mentioned in the annotation; scarcely a dozen items had to be listed in this fashion.

Some discrepancies were found in the libraries' cataloging of speeches and reports, which were sometimes cataloged under the name of the person who made them and sometimes under the title itself. Furthermore, some major libraries were inconsistent in their cataloging of such speeches and reports owing to the fact that they used one form of entry for English-language publications and another — usually the very opposite — for German or Russian. The checklist follows the principle that reports and speeches are listed under the name of the author of the speech or report, on the assumption that a scholar or student will probably search for a certain speech or report under the name of its author rather than under its title.

A change from Library of Congress cataloging rules has been made in the case of corporate entries — that is, of publications sponsored by or published under the imprint of societies, academies, universities, and similar corporate bodies. If such a publication contained in its title page an author's or editor's name, the item has been listed here under that name. A cross reference to the item has also been entered under the name of the corporate body. For example, the useful collection of documents on the Comintern by Bela Kun (no. 121) is better known as the "Bela Kun documents" than as "documents on the Comintern of the Marx-Engels-Lenin Institute in Moscow," which institute, after all, published several other collections of documents on the Comintern. Publications of corporate bodies without an author's or editor's name are listed under the title.

The corporate body is, however, retained as author when the publication contains an official pronouncement of a given society or institution. Here belong the memoranda and declarations of the International Anti-Communist Entente in Geneva, the "Communist Papers" published by the British Parliament, and similar items.

A key to the abbreviations used in the text of the entries will be found in Appendix III.

6. Annotations and Location Symbols

The attention of the user of the checklist should be drawn, first of all, to the subtitles included in the entry when a subtitle was provided by the publisher. In most cases, the subtitle indicates the contents of the item. Thus, in the majority of listed items the title and subtitle are informative about the contents.

The placing of an item within a subject division gives another clue to the contents. A cross reference placed in a certain subject division indicates that the item deals partly with that subject.

Where titles or subtitles do not clearly indicate the contents, annotations have been provided for those items judged to be the more important ones. The annotation gives a concise statement of the contents of the item. In some cases the annotation contains the table of contents taken from the item. Errors in the title and other peculiarities of the item are also brought out in the annotations. About 25 per cent of the entries in the checklist have been annotated.

The location symbols, indicating all libraries which hold a given item, have been placed at the very end of each entry. A key to these symbols can be found in the Location Code in Appendix I. In view of complaints, particularly by foreign scholars, about the difficulties presented by the complicated location symbols used by American libraries, a simplified location code was compiled for this checklist. There is no question that it will be easier to locate Princeton University under the abbreviation "Princ" than under "NjP," or Harvard University under "Harv" rather than "MH." Librarians, it is hoped, will forgive this innovation introduced for the benefit of the uninitiated.

It may be that some libraries are not included in the location symbols at the end of an entry despite the fact that they do possess the given item. Such omissions will be owing to the libraries' having failed to report that item to the National Union Catalog. This question is discussed in section 9.

7. Spelling and Translation of Authors' Names

The books and pamphlets listed in the checklist were published in 22 different languages and printed in about twice as many countries. It must be borne in mind that it was the practice of the multinational publishers to adjust the spelling of the outlandish-sounding names of authors of different nationalities to their own language, transliteration, and orthography. Furthermore, the first names of foreign authors were also "nationalized," that is, they were translated into the language of the particular publication. To illustrate the distortions resulting from adjusting the spelling of foreign names to the language of the publication, a few examples are listed below:

The Russian *Manuilskii* becomes	*Manuilsky* in German
	Manouilsky in French
	Manoeilski in Dutch
The Russian *Chemodanov* becomes	*Tschemodanof* in German
	Tchémodanoff in French
	Czemodanow in Polish
The German *Heckert* becomes	*Gekkert* in Russian
The British *Wallace* becomes	*Valas* or *Ualas* in Russian

The first names of certain authors are also a problem, and their translation into various languages may cause misunderstandings. An example is Lenin himself, who used "Vladimir Ilich" in his publications, or the initials "V.I.", or, in his earlier writings, simply "N." "Clara" and "Klara" Zetkin is another minor problem.

Most American libraries follow the rule of cataloging all translations of the works of a certain author under his name in his native language (transliterated if necessary). The same applies to the catalog cards printed by the Library of Congress. A few American libraries, however, deviate from this rule and prepare cards that can be confusing, as is also true of most European libraries, which have the tendency to catalog translated works under the names of authors as they appear on the title page, in whatever language the item may be printed.

As a rule, this checklist uses the names of authors in their native language. Names in publications printed in the Cyrillic alphabet are transliterated according to Library of Congress rules. All other spellings of these names in translated editions are indicated at the end of the entry ("At head of title: W. E. Tschemodanof") or in the full title entry as it is on the title page ("Bericht an den fünften Kongress der K. J. I. von W. E. Tschemodanof"). All foreign spellings of names are included in the Index with cross references to the spelling of the author's name in his own language.

8. Pseudonyms

Many communist authors have used one or more pseudonyms in their publications. To the researcher their publications are known under the name which appears on the title page. In source references the scholar always uses this name, regardless of whether it is the real name of the author or his pseudonym. Hence the rule followed in this checklist is to use the name on the title page as the author's name in the entry. Thus, Lenin is always "Lenin" and is not listed under his real name, Ulianov; Radek is always "Radek" and not Sobelson, nor is "Zinov'ev" Apfelbaum.

Whenever possible, the problem of pseudonyms is dealt with by inserting in the entry and in the Index an explanation in brackets. The real name is entered in the Index with a reference to the pseudonym. In cases where the author is better known under his pseudonym, explanation is given only in the Index. This refers to such names as Lenin, Radek, Trotskii, Zinov'ev, etc.

There are, however, a few exceptions to this rule. In a few cases when an author used a pseudonym for some time and later resumed his real name, the real name is used throughout the checklist and is adequately cross-indexed. The best known example of such a case is Togliatti, who in the beginning of his communist career used the pseudonym "Ercoli." Later all his speeches and writings appeared under his real name, Togliatti. All of his publications listed here are under Togliatti, and in the listing of his early publications which appeared under the pseudonym "Ercoli" the following note appears at the end of the entry: "At head of title: Ercoli."

The practice of using on catalog cards the author's pseudonomous name as found on the title page is followed by most libraries, with this remarkable exception: Dridzo-Lozovskii's publications appeared under the pseudonym "A. Lozovskii," but most libraries in the United States list these in their catalogs under the real name: "Dridzo, Solomon Abramovich." There is no good reason for this beyond the fact that the catalog cards ordered from the Library of

Congress carry the name of "Dridzo" as author — just enough difference to keep the researcher running from one catalog tray to another.

9. Cataloging Problems

The organization of about 5,200 catalog cards produced by 48 libraries into one systematic checklist was not a simple task. Owing to differences in cataloging rules and methods, and to their broad interpretation by library personnel, the identification of all catalog cards pertaining to the same item was, in certain cases, quite difficult.

Perhaps the most troublesome questions arose from two practices applied by many libraries: (1) the shortening of titles in order to avoid redundancy, and (2) the displacement of the author's name to the end of the entry. These practices are best indicated by examples.

1. *Avoidance of redundancy*. If the subject heading of an item is repeated in the text of the title, the librarian may omit these words in the catalog card as redundant. Thus, while the title of the item in the catalog card is being shortened, at the same time it is being changed. This practice seems logical, but its application works out to the disadvantage of the user of the catalog. Here is an example:

A student may find a reference in a book to an item whose title is:

> Programme of the Communist International, together with the Statutes of the
> Communist International

He consults the catalog of a library and searches for the item under the subject heading "Communist International." He finds the following catalog card:

> Communist International
> Programme, together with the statutes.

If the student does not know (and in most cases he does not) that the librarian was permitted to weed out from the card what was considered redundant and thus eliminated "redundant words" from the title and shortened its text, the student will not know that the item which he knows by its full title is identical with the item cataloged under the shorter title. The subject heading "Communist International" is taken by the librarian as justification for omitting the same words in the catalog entry, without even his having to indicate the fact that the title is shortened by inserting dots (ellipses) in the place where words were omitted.

Now let us see the student's attitude in this matter. For him the title of a book or pamphlet is sacrosanct. He has to quote it in full in any paper or publication which he writes and in which he uses it. He is not permitted to use abbreviations, and he is puzzled if he comes across the abbreviated version of a title in the catalog card. He will lose time in making sure that what he found in the catalog corresponds to the item which he is looking for. From his point of view, a simple question of the title has been complicated. To whose advantage? For what purpose?

From talks with scholars and students who consulted me on library resources on various subjects, I often gathered that they objected to these changes in the

38

established titles of books and pamphlets. In the Hoover Institution this situation does not create a problem, since it is being avoided.

Naturally, users are supposed to know how to use the catalog in a library, and most do. But many scholars, students, free-lance writers, and other users of librariers cannot understand the reasons why a title of a publication should be changed or otherwise garbled. They always bring up the same question: is the library here for the scholar, or the scholar for the library?

Having had to match many catalog cards pertaining to the same item and coming from various libraries during the organization of the material, I had my share of difficulties. Now I have a better understanding of the complaints of the scholars and students. In this checklist I therefore tried to make consistent use of the full titles of items just as they appeared in print on the title page. In some cases, when the item was not available for checking, the shortened titles had to remain.

2. *Displacement of author's name.* In the past, some libraries introduced the practice of cataloging certain items under their titles and then adding at the end of the entry the note: "At head of title: John Doe." This peculiar method serves no good purpose. If John Doe's name precedes the title, it is obvious that John Doe is the author. His name should be placed where it belongs: at the head of the title. At least a hundred cards with displaced authors' names were found during the preparation of this checklist. Here they have all been changed and the entries adjusted to the standard form and contents.

A different procedure was followed in the case of government and society publications for which corporate entries are used. Such publications, if an author is given in addition to the name of the government authority, institution, or society, are listed here under the authors name, with a cross reference to the corporate body.

Another difficulty arose from the fact that some pamphlets were cataloged under the title as given on the cover and not as given on the title page, without placing the note "cover title" on the catalog card. In some cases the difference in the two titles was such that only by perusing the item itself was an identification possible. In the checklist these differences are indicated in the annotation to the item in order to facilitate its location.

10. Erroneous and Misleading Translations

The user of Comintern publications must be aware of the fact that the same item when published in Russian, English, German, French, or any other language, although seemingly identical with its counterparts, is not necessarily so in its content. As mentioned before, in most cases it is practically impossible to establish which item is in the original language and which is a translation.[29] Texts

---

[29] In some stenographic reports of meetings is stated, in parentheses just following the name of the speaker, the language in which he spoke. This is the only way of establishing which is the original of a text and which its translation. Unfortunately, the publishers of stenographic reports seldom gave this informaton.

of the same item, e. g., of the same speech, report, or resolution, may differ in editions in different languages.

These differences might be due to any one of three reasons:

1. Mistakes and inaccuracies in translation.

2. Deliberate omissions, such as the elimination of entire sentences or entire paragraphs, or parts of sentences.

3. Printing errors not corrected during proofreading. Here could be included omissions of single words in the text. The omission of a very important key word, however, leads one to suspect that instead of being an ordinary printing error, the omission may have been intentional.

In support of the above words of caution, a few examples are discussed below.

Perhaps the most striking example of faulty translation and of omissions is the English translation of the *Theses and Statutes of the III Communist International,* listed here as item no. 620. The translation was prepared and the item was published by the "Publishing Office of the Communist International" in Moscow. Hence, this is an official translation and an official publication of the Communist International. Obviously, the text of the English translation has been checked by the publisher, because he inserted into the 83-page pamphlet a loose-leaf "Addendum" containing a corrected text of a paragraph which, as printed in the pamphlet, contained some errors. No other printing errors or other mistakes are mentioned in the "Addendum."

These mistakes and omissions in the Moscow translation were discovered by the leadership of the Communist Party of America. Not afraid to point out a Moscow error (how different from the attitude in later years, during the Stalin era!), the American communists produced and printed their own translation, which is called here the "American edition" (no. 622). In the Preface to this edition the Communist Party of America most officially stated as follows:

> The Theses and Statutes of the Communist International as adopted by the Second World Congress, July 17th—August 7th, 1920, were received by the Communist Party of America in December, 1920, from the Publishing Office of the Communist International at Moscow. Upon examination of this edition, which was translated into English in Moscow, it was found to contain many errors which led the Editorial Committee of the Communist Party to make a careful analysis of the text. It was compared with the German edition and the original Russian text with the result that many omissions and distortions were discovered, and these were of such a nature as to make the Moscow English edition misleading.

The Moscow translation was, indeed, very bad and misleading. The Preface to the corrected "American edition" quotes several of these errors from which it is apparent that entire sentences were omitted, many passages were badly distorted, and the entire translation was unacceptable. A careful comparison of the official Moscow text with the corrected "American" text shows that the Editorial Committee of the Communist Party of America, which made the corrections, introduced more than a hundred major or minor changes in the text. It should be mentioned that the text of this pamphlet contained two very important documents: the first Statute of the Communist International and the seven "theses" on organization, aims, and tactics of the world communist movement which, from then on, became the basic instructions for communists everywhere. Hence, here is an example of a publication of major importance treated with negligence — or, perhaps, it was not negligence, but a purposeful changing of the text; or there could have been both reasons for the discrepancies.

In the winter of 1920/21 there operated in the United States two communist parties: the Communist Party of America and the United Communist Party of America. The former discovered the errors in the Moscow edition of the Statutes and "theses" and issued the above-mentioned corrected "American edition" of this print. The latter party obviously wanted to be first to reissue this important document for distribution among its members. Without rechecking the translation, but with some editorial changes of awkward-sounding English sentences, late in 1920 the United Communist Party of America reprinted the Moscow pamphlet. It is listed here as "Reprint edition" under no. 621 and contains the original Moscow translation with all the omissions and most of the erroneous translations.

The fact that this "Reprint edition" reached the American market and communist membership a few weeks before the corrected "American edition" probably explains the fact that eleven American libraries have the erroneous "Reprint edition," whereas only two libraries have the corrected "American edition." But this fact, in turn, has far-reaching consequences. Almost all writings of American scholars about the first Statute of the Communist International and about the important "theses" of the Second Congress of the Communist International are based on this erroneous "Reprint edition" or its even worse Moscow original. For more details on the three editions of this important item, the reader is advised to consult the annotations to nos. 620—622.

It should be mentioned here that the French translation of this item, prepared and published by the same Comintern office in Moscow, also contains many errors.

The inadequacy of translations in early Comintern publications was also acknowledged by the Marx-Engels-Lenin Institute in Moscow. In 1933 the Institute published a new edition of the Russian text of the protocols of the I-st Congress of the Comintern with ample additions to their first, 1921, Moscow edition.[30] In the Preface to the 1933 edition the editors state that the 1921 edition was based on the German 1920 edition of the protocols.[31] Obviously the editors found the 1921 Russian translation inadequate because they say that now it was "corrected and re-edited after checking it against the original German text." More details on this corrected and enlarged edition are given in the annotation to no. 498.

Another example of errors and distortions in an important text — an abridged English edition of the minutes of the 5-th Plenum of the Executive Committee of the Comintern — is found in item no. 1064, *Bolshevising the Communist International.* A comparison of the English and Russian editions of this item will show that entire speeches which can be found in the Russian edition are missing in the English edition. On the other hand, some passages in

---

[30] The first Moscow edition of these protocols is listed as no. 497, the second edition as no. 498.

[31] Listed here as no. 499.

the English edition contain entire sentences missing in the Russian edition. A typical instance is mentioned in the annotation to this item.

These examples are by no means isolated cases. Many more discrepancies have been found during my work on Comintern documents and publications as well as on the checklist.[32] These should be a warning to scholars, students, and librarians. The scholar and student, in quoting important excerpts from Comintern documents, should compare his text with the corresponding texts in other languages, whenever they exist. If he uses an English, German, or French edition, a comparison with the Russian text is imperative. The librarian should not restrict his holdings to just one edition of the document, on the assumption that the same document published in another language is identical with the one his library holds. In the case of Comintern prints, the librarian must include at least two editions in the holdings of his library, one of them in Russian, if he wants to provide the scholar and student with reliable primary sources.

Another peculiar translation error, distorting the name of one of the Comintern's front organizations, was willingly accepted despite its absurd-sounding name. The organization created in Berlin (November 20—26, 1919) for communist work among young persons was called by the German name *Kommunistische Jugendinternationale* and by the Russian name *Kommunisticheskii Internatsional Molodezhi*. Although the correct translation of this name into English is *Communist Youth International*, the first official publication of this organization in the English language, printed in England early in 1920, appeared under the title *Young Communist International*. From a grammatical point of view this translation is incorrect, and, further, it distorts the true meaning of the name in both the German and the Russian language.

An interesting explanation of how this error occurred was given to me by a former communist who desires to remain unidentified. According to this former communist, a young German communist and his wife arrived in Moscow during the first days of December 1919, bringing with them Willi Münzenberg's typewritten report about the Berlin meeting at which the Communist Youth International was founded. Münzenberg was to publish this report if no advice to the contrary was forthcoming from Moscow via Stockholm. The Secretariat of the Comintern, working at that time under primitive conditions, welcomed the publication of Münzenberg's report in the German language,[33] and decided to publish immediately a French and an English translation of the Manifesto and the Program adopted by the Congress. But no competent English translator could be found in the Comintern who would have had the time to do the work immediately. During a discussion of this matter in Zinov'ev's office, the wife of the German visitor expressed regrets that her high-school English was not adequate for undertaking the work. No one seemed to have taken any notice of her regrets.

The next morning, an unexpected caller appeared at the visitors' hotel room. This was Zinov'ev, who brought the German texts of the Manifesto and the

---

[32] See also section 11. Erroneous Dates, p. 44—45.
[33] For full title see no. 2060.

Program adopted at the founding congress, and a German-English dictionary. He insisted that the young woman undertake the translating of the texts "as well as she could," and said that someone who knew English well would revise her translation. Naturally, "the great Zinov'ev's" request became an order.

While laboring on the translation, the woman came across a German word for which she could not find the English equivalent in the dictionary: *Jugendgenossen*. This was the first word in the second sentence of the text and the woman was desperate to find its English equivalent. She telephoned to Zinov'ev, who had a fast answer: "young comrades." There followed other German word-combinations in the text beginning with *Jugend*, and the woman cheerfully made ample use of Zinov'ev's solution. Thus in her translation the German "revolutionäre Jugendorganisationen" became "revolutionary young organisations," the German "proletarische Jugendorganisationen" became "proletarian young organisations," the German "Jugendinternationale" (referring to the pre-1914 Socialist Youth International) became the "Youth International" in one place and a few lines further the "International Youth" — and again, some lines further, the "Young International." Finally, when in the German text the name "Kommunistische Jugendinternationale" was used for the first time, the woman translated it as "Young Communist International."[34] Nevertheless, some thirty lines further on, at the end of the Manifesto, we find the following slogans: "Young proletarians of all countries! Close your ranks! Unite under the flag of the Communist Youth International! Long live the Communist Youth International!"

It can only be guessed whether this wording of the slogans originated with the translator or with the "someone" who was to revise the translation and who paid special attention to the slogans. It is obvious, however, that some person had to prepare the copy for print and that this person added the titles to the particular items contained in the pamplet. These titles read:

> Manifesto by the First Congress of the Young-Communist-International
> The Programme of the Communist International of Youth
> Message of the E.C. of the IIIrd International to the Young Communist International

In the third item, which obviously was prepared by the Secretariat of the Communist International, the new organization was consistently referred to as the "Communist International of the Youth." Nevertheless, the copy editor provided the pamphlet with the title *The Young Communist International*, and this name was henceforth used for the new organization.

The copy editor made yet another mistake in editing the title page — the subtitle states: *Report of the first international congress held at Berlin from the 20—29th of November 1919*. The actual date of the congress, according to its official record, was November 20—26, 1919.[35]

---

[34] All these examples of erroneous translation are taken from the following sources: the German text from *Unter dem roten Banner: Bericht über den ersten Kongress der Kommunistischen Jugendinternationale*, Berlin, Verlag Junge Garde, [1919], p. 67, (item no. 2060); the English text from *The Young Communist International. Report of the First International Congress held at Berlin from the 20—29th of November 1919*, Glasgow and London, [1920?] pp. 24—26 (item no. 2068).

[35] *Unter dem roten Banner*, p. 75.

American libraries accepted the erroneously translated name, and scholars and students will have to search catalogs for pertinent material under "Young Communist International." In this checklist the correct translation, the Communist Youth International, is used. The somewhat long story about the origin of the erroneous translation will show with what negligence translations of the Comintern texts were made and with what negligence they were published. It supports also the statement, made in the Praface, that the publications of the Comintern and its front organizations are the most complicated and troublesome agglomeration of printed material which comes into the hands of scholars, students, publicists, and librarians.

11. Erroneous Dates

The erroneous translations of important texts in publications of the Communist International and its affiliates are not the only misleading aspects of some of these publications. Errors also occur in the dates of the various meetings of the Comintern and its organs on the title pages and in the texts of their publications. The consistency with which some of these errors apear indicates that they are not printers' errors, but the result of negligence in the preparation, editing, and proofreading of the publication. Quite a number of erroneous dates have been discovered during the compiling of this checklist and are pointed out in the bibliographic entries or in the annotations.

The publication of the protocols of the very first congress of the Communist International appeared with an erroneous date of the congress in the title page and with erroneous dates of the five sessions of the congress. One Russian edition and two German editions, published immediately after the congress in 1920 and 1921, carry on the title pages the date "March 2—19, 1920" although the sessions of the congress took place March 2—6. More details on these erroneous dates are given in the annotation to item no. 498.

The most significant error occurred in twelve publications concerning the II-nd Congress of the Communist International. This congress held its opening session in Petrograd on July 19, 1920, and then adjourned to Moscow for further meetings which continued from July 23 to August 7, 1920. There exist two Moscow editions of the English translation of the minutes of this congress (see nos. 562 and 563). Both state in the subtitle: "Proceedings of the Petrograd session of July 17th and of Moscow sessions of July 19th—August 7th, 1920." The dates July 17 for the Petrograd session and July 19 for the first Moscow ssesion are wrong. In the Moscow edition of the French translation of these minutes only the July 17 date for the Petrograd session is erroneous.

The resolutions and the statute of the Communist International adopted by the II-nd Congress were printed in their Russian version with the correct dates of the congress (see nos. 594 and 595). A reprint of this text, prepared in Prague, carries the wrong date, July 17 (no. 596). Two German translations of the resolutions and statute, prepared and printed in Russia, as well as their two reprints prepared in Germany, have on the title pages the erroneous date of

"July 17th," (nos. 602—607). An English translation of this item prepared and published by the "Publishing Office of the Communist International" in Moscow (no. 620), and its two reprints prepared in the United States (nos. 621 and 622), have the same erroneous date of the opening of the congress, "July 17th," on the title pages. Curiously enough, the French translation of these resolutions and statute (no. 631), prepared and published by the same "Publishing Office," carries the correct date on the title page. Yet, again, a Serbo-Croatian translation of this item, prepared and published in an undisclosed place, carries on the same error of the date (no. 634).

Another confusion in dates occurs in connection with the IV-th Congress of the Comintern, which opened in Petrograd on November 5, 1922, and then adjourned to Moscow, where it met from November 9 to December 5, 1922. A Moscow edition of the Russian text of the minutes of this congress (no. 730), and its English translation published in London (no. 732), both print erroneous dates on the title page.

Other such mistakes in dates were found in the abridged English edition of the minutes of the 5-th Plenum (no. 1064), in the German edition of the minutes (no. 1867), in the resolutions of the III-rd Congress of the Red International of Trade Unions (no. 1879), and in several other publications.

All these errors have been pointed out in detail because the items are important and the erroneous dates, originating in Moscow, have been often repeated by communist and non-communist authors in the United States and in Europe, in serious works whose authors unfortunately did not discover the discrepancies.

12. Fictitious Publishers

When suppressed by the government, local communist parties in certain countries and at certain times operated illegally ("went underground"). In such cases, their publications were produced in Russia or elsewhere and then were smuggled into the country where they were illegally circulated. In order to mislead the police, a fictitious publisher and a fictitious place of publication were put on the title page of the book or pamphlet. The user of this kind of publication may also be misled, and caution is recommended. Sometimes library catalog cards will draw attention to these irregularities, but more often not.

A good example would be the minutes of the II-nd Congress of the Communist International published by the Comintern's Publication Office in Moscow. The English translation appeared first in Moscow in 1920 (no. 562). A second edition of the English translation, in a smaller, pocket-size format, appeared with the following imprint on the title page: "Publishing Office of the Communist International, America, 1921" (no. 563). It is, of course, quite well known that the Moscow "Publishing Office" had no subsidiary in "America" and that there never existed a separate publishing office of the Communist International in the United States or Canada. A careful comparison of this publication with other publications of the Moscow outlet of the Comintern leads one to the conclusion that it was produced in Moscow and then smuggled into the United States for distribution among party members.

Some German-language publications which were produced in France and Switzerland after Hitler came to power in Germany also carry misleading title pages and publication imprints. Wherever such irregularities were found, explanations have been included in the annotation.

13. Different Editions — Identical Contents

The communist parties of Great Britain and the United States cooperated closely in the late twenties and thirties in the printing of materials of the Communist International. Publications issued under the imprint of the Workers Library Publishers in New York carried on the back of the title page the note: "Printed in Gt. Britain." The same item, with "Modern Books" in London as publisher on the title page, would be distributed in Great Britain and the British colonies. Both items would be of the same size, would contain the same number of pages, and would be set in the same type face — in other words, would be identical, except for the publisher on the title page, and the absence of the note "Printed in Gt. Britain" in the London edition. In some cases this note was retained in the London edition.

For bibliographical purposes these prints had to be treated as different editions despite their similarity, owing to the different places of publication. They appear in the checklist as separate entries. For good examples of this procedure see nos. 1207, 1209, 1210; 1212; 1213; 1214, 1215.

14. Postscript

There is no doubt that this checklist includes 97 or 98 per cent of all books and pamphlets published by and on the Comintern and its front organizations. Those not included here were published mostly in the Soviet Union. A survey of the official Soviet bibliographical resource, *Knizhnaia Letopis'*, permits one to surmise that the Russian items not included here are not numerous and that they are mostly of secondary importance.

As to items published outside the Soviet Union, it is possible that some dealing predominantly with communism in particular countries and only partly with the Comintern and its front organizations may not have found their way into this checklist. Their omission may be owing to their having been cataloged by the libraries under the subject heading "Communism in . . ." in the absence of a subject heading for the "Communist International." The catalog cards of such items therefore would not be found among the photoduplicated cards which became the basis of the checklist. In addition, some memoirs and reminiscences of former participants in the work of the Comintern and its front organizations may be missing for the same reason.

Further omissions will have occurred in the case of reports and publications of particular communist parties which belonged to the Comintern, for such items may contain some material dealing with the parties' relationship to the Comintern. In most cases, it can be assumed that passages in these publications touching on the Comintern were so brief or of so abstruse a character in the general text that the publications were not given catalog entries under the Comintern heading.

Finally, the periodicals published by the Comintern and its front organizations should be mentioned as particularly important sources of information, although they are not covered in the checklist. There are about a hundred titles of these periodicals, varying in size form one to about 600 issues. The most important, certainly, are the journal *Communist International*, published in several languages, and the *International Press Correspondence (Inprecor)*, published in three languages. The latter has yearly indexes (at least for several years) and is often used by scholars and students working on Comintern problems. Although both began to appear quite early (in 1919 and 1921 respectively), the *Communist International*, designed for the leadership of the movement, contains more monographic articles than the *Inprecor*, which was intended for the press.

Unfortunately, the *Communist International*, owing to lack of indexes, is far too little exploited by scholars and students. I have talked to many scholars who came to the Hoover Institution searching for material on certain phases or aspects of the activities of the Communist International and its front organizations. When their attention was drawn to this periodical as a primary source for their research, they were eager to make use of the Institution's almost complete sets of editions in four languages. Yet after seeing the amount of material (about 400 bulky issues in each edition) and realizing that they would have to peruse issue after issue in this mass of material, they gave up and left this valuable source untouched. An index to the English-language edition is now in preparation and is planned to be published by the Hoover Institution.

In addition to the periodicals published by the Communist International, there are several excellent files of periodicals published by the particular front organizations. The New York Public Library and the Hoover Institution are particularly strong in this field. These front organizations have been consistently neglected until now. There are no exhaustive studies available in the English language on the Red International of Labor Unions, the Communist Youth International, and the other front organizations. Almost all the published material on these organizations has been written from the communist point of view. This is a broad field, wide open to scholars and students who have knowledge of Russian or German, or preferably of both languages.

The main purpose of my work was to present to the scholar and student a source of information about the kind of material that is available for the study of the Communist International and its front organizations and where it is located. Although the material is spread over two continents, modern technology of reproduction of prints makes it easily available. In my survey of the Hoover Library Collection on Russia, published in 1954,[36] I included a short survey of the material dealing with the Comintern and Cominform. The present check-list is intended to go a step further. I hope the scholar and student will find it useful.

---

[36] Witold S. Sworakowski, *The Hoover Library Collection on Russia* (Collection Survey, No. 1) Stanford, Calif., Stanford University Press, 1954.

THE

COMMUNIST INTERNATIONAL

AND ITS

FRONT ORGANIZATIONS

PART I.

GENERAL

1. Bibliographies

1 EZHEGODNIK leninskoi i istoriko-partiinoi bibliografii. Tom I: Obzor literatury po Leninu i leninizmu, istorii VPK(b) i VLKSM, i istorii Kominterna i KIM'A za 1929 g. Sostavlen Bibliotekoi IMEL. [Moskva] Partiinoe izd-vo, 1932. 210 p. At head of title: Institut Marksa-Engel'sa-Lenina pri TSK VKP(b).

> Chapter 5–"The History of the Comintern and of the Communist Youth International" lists books, pamphlets and articles in periodicals published in the Soviet Union in 1929. *Hoover*

2 HERTING, Günter, comp.
Bibliographie zur Geschichte der Kommunistischen Internationale (1919—1934). Berlin, 1960. ii, 200 p. Institut für Marxismus-Leninismus beim ZK der SED. Bibliothek. *Amst*

3 IUNOVICH, M.
Literatura po mirovomu khoziaistvu i mirovoi politike za 10 let; 1917—1927 gg.; bibliograficheskii ukazatel' knig, vyshedshikh na russkom iazyke v 1917—1927 g. Moskva, Izd-vo Kommunisticheskoi akademii, 1928. 88 p.

> Also contains a short listing of publications by and about the Communist International. *Harv*

4 K 40 [soroka] letiiu osnovaniia Kommunisticheskogo Internatsionala. Moskva, Izd-vo Vsesoiuznoi knizhnoi palaty, 1959. (Letopis' gazetnykh statei, no. 12 and 13 of 1959, 6 pages each.)

> A bibliography of articles in Soviet periodicals. *Hoover, BDIC*

5 KACZANOWSKA, Jadwiga [and] Trzcińska, Maria, comp.
Materjały bibliograficzne do historii Ruchu Robotniczego XIX i XX wieku. Indeks... z udziałem Weroniki Kubickiej. Łódź (Gliwice), Powielarnia Skryptów Politechniki Śląskiej, 1957. 3 vols, mimeographed.

51

(Wydawnictwa Bibliograficzne Biblioteki Uniwersyteckiej w Łodzi, no. 3—5)

Contents of volumes:
Cz. 1: Międzynarodowy Ruch Robotniczy. 396 p.
Cz. 2: Polski Ruch Robotniczy. vi, 287 p.
Cz. 3: Inkes   *BDIC*

6 KOMINTERN; 1919—1929; katalog knig. [Moskva] Gos. izd-vo, 1929. 72 p. On cover: Kommunisticheskii Internatsional. 1919—1929.

A dealer's list of the publishing house Gosudarstvennoe izdateľstvo in Moscow. Includes only those publications of Gos. izd-vo which at the time of the printing of this list were still available. Does not include publications of other publishing houses. Very limited value.   *Hoover, SInSt*

MOSCOW. Institut Marksa-Engel'sa-Lenina. Biblioteka. Ezhegodnik leninskoi i istoriko-partiinoi bibliografii. See no. 1.

7 PROCACCI, Giuliano
L'Internazionale Comunista dal I al VII congresso; 1919—1935. Milano, Istituto Giangiacomo Feltrinelli, 1958. Reprint of pages 283—314 of Annali dell'Istituto Giangiacomo Feltrinelli, 1 (1958)

A listing of books and pamphlets concerning the congresses of the Communist International and the sessions of its Executive Committee available in the library of the Feltrinelli Institute, Milan. Included in this list are some periodicals published by the Communist International. However, since this list's probable date is 1957, it, of course, shows fewer items than a list prepared in 1963 would, 1963 being the basic year for our checklist.

Amst, BDIC, Felt

8 PUBLICATIONS du Bureau Permanent de l'Entente Internationale contre la Troisième Internationale. Genève, 1933—1938. 4 pamphlets, mimeographed.   *BDIC*

9 RALEA, Michel
Révolution et socialisme; essai de bibliographie. Paris, Presses Universitaires de France, 1923. 84 p. (Publications du Centre de documentation sociale. Ecole Normale Supérieure.)   *BDIC*

10 SCHRIFTEN-Verzeichnisse der Kommunistischen Jugendinternationale. Berlin-Schöneberg, 1921.
Heft 1: Drahn, Ernest: Deutsche Schriften zur Sozialisierungsfrage.

This began as a series of bibliographies on subjects recommended for study to members of the Communist Youth International. Although it is a publication of the Youth International, its only known item deals with a broader problem, not directly connected with the activities of the Communist International or its front organizations.   *Hoover, NYPL*

11 VII [sed'moi] Vsemirnyi kongress Kominterna; ukazatel' literatury. Leningrad, Bibliotechnaia metodicheskaia baza Leningradskogo obl. soveta profsoiuzov, 1935. 19 p.

> The title is misleading. This "guide" lists 69 items in the Russian language of which only 12 deal with the VII-th Congress of the Communist International.

Hoover, LC, NYPL

12 VERLAGSVERZEICHNIS mit Grundpreisen für Organisationen. Berlin-Schöneberg, Verlag der Jugendinternationale, 1923. 20 p.

Amst

13 VERÖFFENTLICHUNGEN des Verlages der Kommunistischen Internationale. [n. p., n. d.] 16 p.

Amst

14 VERÖFFENTLICHUNGEN des Verlages der Kommunistischen Internationale. Hamburg, Hoym [n. d.] 12 p.

Amst

15 VERÖFFENTLICHUNGEN des Verlages der Kommunistischen Internationale. Hamburg, Hoym [n. d.] 16 p.

Amst

16 VERÖFFENTLICHUNGEN des Verlages der Kommunistischen Internationale. Verlag der Kommunistischen Internationale; Hamburg, C. Hoym Nachf. L. Cahnbley, 1921. 31 p. Cover-title.

> This seems to be the first edition of the permanent trade catalog of the Hoym publishing house. The next two editions, identified as "2. Auflage" and "3. Auflage", look quite similar to this first edition. As the three preceding items are only in the holdings of the Institute of Social History in Amsterdam and were not available for comparison with the following three editions, their identification is given here as it was found in the Amsterdam catalog.

Hoover, Felt

17 VERÖFFENTLICHUNGEN des Verlages der Kommunistischen Internationale. "2. Aufl." Verlag der Kommunistischen Internationale; Hamburg, C. Hoym Nachf. L. Cahnbley, 1921. 35 p. Cover-title.

Hoover, Harv, Amst

18 VERÖFFENTLICHUNGEN des Verlages der Kommunistischen Internationale. 3. Auflage. Verlag der Kommunistischen Internationale, Auslieferungsstelle für Deutschland, Hamburg, C. Hoym Nachf. L. Cahnbley, 1921. 43 p. plates, ports.

Hoover, Amst

19 VERÖFFENTLICHUNGEN des Verlages der Kommunistischen Internationale 1920 bis 1922. Hamburg, C. Hoym Nachf., 1923, 192 p. plates, ports.

"Dieser Katalog umfasst alle Veröffentlichungen des Verlages der Kommunistischen Internationale (deutsche Abt.) für die Zeit vom 1. Januar 1920 bis 1. Januar 1923."

Contents: Die Kommunistische Internationale. Inhaltsverzeichnis der Hefte 1—23.—Russische Korrespondenz. Inhaltsverzeichnisse der Jahrgänge 1—3.— Alphabetisches Verzeichnis der Veröffentlichungen des Verlages der Kommunistischen Internationale (deutsche Abteilung).

NYPL, Harv, Col, BDIC

20 VERÖFFENTLICHUNGEN des Verlages der Kommunistischen Internationale. Neue Auslandspreise. Gültig ab 1. August 1922. Hamburg, Hoym [n. d.] 16 p. *Amst, BDIC*

2. Reference Books, Yearbooks, Handbooks, Textbooks, Statistics

21 ALMANACH des Verlages der Kommunistischen Internationale. 1921. Verlag der Kommunistischen Internationale, Auslieferungsstelle für Deutschland: Hamburg, Carl Hoym Nachf. Louis Cahnbley, 1921. xi, 331 p. illus. [No more published]

A collection of documentary and propaganda material originating with the Communist International and its front organizations, interspersed with literary contributions of prominent communist and pro-communist writers. Propaganda item intended for German intellectual circles.

Hoover, LC, NYPL, Harv, Col, Duke, JCre, Newb, UTex, Amst, Felt

22 BOCHENSKI, Joseph M. [and] Niemeyer, Gerhart, editors
Handbuch des Weltkommunismus. Freiburg-München, Karl Alber, 1958. 762 p. Subject and person index.

"...das vorliegende Handbuch... beschreibt und erklärt, was der Weltkommunismus während der vierzig Jahre seines Bestehens als politische Macht gewesen ist, was er heute ist und was er kraft seiner Grundprinzipien notwendig sein muss." Foreword. A short sub-chapter of the book contains an outline of the aims and activities of the Communist International, supported by numerous references in the text. En English translation of this item appeared in 1963. *Hoover, LC, NYPL, Harv, Col, Felt, SISt*

23 EHRT, Adolf, ed.
Der Weltbolschewismus; ein internationales Gemeinschaftswerk über die bolschewistische Wühlarbeit und die Umsturzversuche der Komintern in allen Ländern, herausgegeben von der Antikomintern in Verbindung mit den Sachkennnern der ganzen Welt, bearbeitet von Dr.

Adolf Ehrt; mit 400 Bilddokumenten, Karten und Anschauungstafeln. Berlin, Leipzig, Nibelungen-Verlag, 1936. 506 p. illus.

Hoover, LC, NYPL, Col, Felt

24 EHRT, Adolf, ed.
Der Weltbolschewismus; ein internationales Gemeinschaftswerk über die bolschewistische Wühlarbeit . . . [same as above] 2. verbesserte Auflage. Berlin-Leipzig, 1938. 569 p. illus. *Hoover*

25 EZHEGODNIK Kominterna. Spravochnaia kniga po istorii mezhdunarodnogo rabochego, politicheskogo i professional'nogo dvizheniia, statistike i ekonomike vsekh stran mira na 1923. Petrograd-Moskva, Izd-vo Kommunisticheskogo Internatsionala, 1923, xxxiii, 1047 p. tables.

> The first encyclopedic presentation of world affairs from a communist point of view.—Part I deals with the history of the international worker's movement, of the Communist International and the early stage of its front organizations. A compilation of the membership of socialist and communist parties is the first attempt to evaluate the strength of communism on a world wide scale. Broad treatment is given to the trade union movement, social conditions, economic situation, politics, and demography.—Part II deals with the Soviet Union and its autonomous republics.—Part III contains information on the area, population, economic situation, trade union movement, and politics of all "bourgeois states" of the world.—For a somewhat shorter edition and for later years, see the German publication *Jahrbuch für Wirtschaft, Politik und Arbeiterbewegung* (no. 32). See also *Komintern; khoziaistvo, politika i rabochee dvizhenie v kapitalisiticheskikh stranakh za 1924—27 gody* (no. 34).
>
> *Hoover, LC, NYPL, Harv, Col, SInSt*

26 GOPNER, Serafima I., ed.
Ukazatel' 15 let Kominterna 1919—1934. Otv. redaktor S. I. Gopner. Moskva, Vsesoiuznaia spravochnaia kartoteka Ogiz'a, 1934. One leaflet of 14 pages and 227 cards in box. On box: 15 let Kominterna.

> "Kartoteku sostavili tt. IA. I. TSitovich, Sh. TSobel, O. N. Freifeld, pod rukovodstvom t. IA. I. TSitovicha."
> The item consists of a 14-page pamphlet and 227 file cards printed on both sides. Its purpose is explained by the compilers as follows: "The purpose of the cardfile '15 years of the Comintern' is to aid the party-activists, the propagandists and lecturers, in their work to elucidate the basic phases of development of the Comintern, the more important principles concerning its program, tactic and organization, and also the current tasks facing the international communist movement." (p. 3)
> Cards 1–208 are organized by subject, containing excerpts of speeches, writings, resolutions, theses, and similar documentary material, with ample source references. The subjects were handled in chronological sequence. Published in the period of the Stalin cult, the subjects overemphasize his role in the development and work of the Comintern. Conversely, all contributions by Trotskii, Bukharin, Kamenev and other prominent personalities of the early period of the Comintern are completely eliminated.

Cards 209–220 contain a "short chronology of important dates" concerning the Comintern and the international workers' movement. Cards 221–225 contain a list of Comintern congresses, plenums and other meetings, including the number of participating delegates and the agenda of the meetings. Cards 226–227 contain a list of congresses, plenums and meetings of the Red International of Trade Unions, the Communist Youth International, and the international women's meetings. Although the propaganda character of the publication is obvious, it still would be very useful as a reference source, were it not inaccurate and biased because of the Stalin cult and through the elimination of prominent contributions to the development and work of the Comintern by persons purged by Stalin.   *NYPL, Col*

27 INGULOV, Sergei Borisovich
Uchebnik politgramoty; uchebnik dlia kandidatskikh partiinykh shkol. Moskva, Partiinoe izd-vo, 1932. 498 p. incl. front, maps, plates, ports., diagrs.   *Hoover*

28 INTERNATIONAL Anti-Communist Entente
Antibolschewistisches Vade-Mecum; Organisation und Aktivität der Kommunistischen Internationale. Genf, 1939. 271 p. tables. At head of title: Internationale Vereinigung gegen die III. Internationale.
   NYPL

29 INTERNATIONAL Anti-Communist Entente
Anti-Bolshevik vade-mecum. 2d ed. [Geneva, Permanent Bureau] 1927. 191 p. [Published by the society under its earlier name: International Entente against the Third International.]
For 1-st ed see periodical *Vague Rouge*, March 1926.   *Hoover*

30 INTERNATIONAL Anti-Communist Entente
Tableaux des organisations soviétiques travaillant à la révolution dans tous les pays (accompagnés de notes explicatives) [Genève] 1928. 49 p. 1 illus., diagrs. At head of title: Bureau permanent de l'Entente internationale contre la IIIe Internationale. Genève.
   Hoover

31 INTERNATIONAL Anti-Communist Entente
Vade-mecum antibolchévique. [Genève, 1927?] 194 p. diagrs. At head of title: Entente internationale contre la IIIe Internationale. "Bibliographie": p. 123—124.   *Hoover, NYPL*

32 JAHRBUCH für Wirtschaft, Politik und Arbeiterbewegung. Hamburg, Hoym, 1922/23—1925/26. [No more published] illus., charts, tables, maps, index. See annotation to no. 26 and 34.
Hoover: 1922/23, 1923/24, 1925/26; NYPL: 1922/23, 1923/24, 1925/26; Amst: 1922/23

33 KOLESNIKOVA, N. N.

RKP(b) i Komintern. Moskva, Gos. izd-vo, 1925. 230 p. illus., incl. ports. (Uchebnye posobiia dlia shkol I i II stupeni.) [Bibliography at end of each chapter.] *Hoover*

34 KOMINTERN; khoziaistvo, politika, i rabochee dvizhenie v kapitalisti-cheskikh stranakh za 1924—1927 gody. Moskva, Gos. izd-vo, 1928. 1133 p. tables, 2 fold. maps, index.

> Preface signed by: "Redaktsiia russkogo izdaniia: T. L.Akselrod, Kh. Wurm, G. Giunter [Günther]." "The present yearbook of politics and workers move-ment in the Russian language appeared in the German language as Year-book 1925–26" *[Jahrbuch für Wirtschaft, Politik und Arbeiterbewegung].* (From p. 5) The Russian edition eliminated the information on the Soviet Union con-tained in the German edition. The Yearbook is divided into a "General Part" and a second part discussing the economy, politics and workers move-ment in particular countries of the entire world. In the first part should be mentioned short articles on the activities of the Communist International and all its front organizations for the period from "late 1923" to August 1926. According to the Preface, the discussion of the particular countries is broader in the Russian edition than in the German edition. *Hoover*

35 MALAIA entsiklopediia po mezhdunarodnomu profdvizheniiu. Pod red. M. Zelikmana, s predisl. A. Lozovskogo. Pri uchastii Alaz, N. [and others] Moskva, Izd. Profinterna, 1927. ix, 2170 columns, ports.

Hoover, NYPL

36 MIROVOE professional'noe dvizhenie; spravochnik Profinterna pod obshchei red. A. Lozovskogo. Moskva, Gos. izd-vo, 1926—28. 7 vols.

> A description of the economic and social conditions in all countries of the world, including colonies and mandates. Each country is discussed in the same manner. The chapters are entitled as follows:
> 1. Political-economic survey
> 2. The working class
> 3. The Workers' movement (including sub-chapters on "Political parties of the proletariat" and "Trade Unions.")
> A bibliography is added for each country (for the most part somewhat skimpy). Many tables and graphs. Most of the information is now obsolete.
> The particular volumes include the following countries:
> Vol. 1.: Austria, Belgium, Bulgaria, Great Britain
> Vol. 2.: Hungary, Germany, Netherlands, Greece, Denmark, Ireland
> Vol. 3.: Spain, Italy, Latvia, Lithuania, Luxemburg, Norway, Poland, Portu-gal, Rumania, Turkey, Finland
> Vol. 4.: Missing in Hoover
> Vol. 5.: France, Czechoslovakia, Switzerland, Sweden, Yugoslavia, Estonia
> Vol. 6.: Afghanistan, British India, Indo-China, Indonesia, Iraq, China, Korea, Palestine, Persia, Siam, Syria, Philippines, Ceylon, Japan
> Vol. 7.: Australia, New Zealand, Algeria, British possessions and mandates in Africa, Belgian Congo, Egypt, Italian Africa, Madagascar, Morocco, Portuguese Africa, Tunisia, French Africa, Union of South Africa *Hoover (1-3, 5-7), NYPL (1), Col (1)*

37 NOTES et informations sur les organisations internationales para-communistes. Paris, Office National pour la Démocratie Française [n. d.] 24 p. (Les Cahiers de Démocratie Française) *BDIC*

39 PETROVSKII, D., ed.
Partii Kommunisticheskogo Internatsionala; spravochnik propagandista. Sbornik statei o vazhneishikh sektsiiakh Kominterna, pod red. D. Petrovskogo. Moskva, Gos. izd-vo, 1928. xvi, 202 p.

Col, SInSt

40 RED International of Labor Unions. Statistical bureau.
Statisticheskie dannye o polozhenii evropeiskogo proletariata za 1-uiu polovinu 1923 g. Rabota Statisticheschkogo biuro Profinterna, vypolnennaia pod obshchei red. M. Smit. Moskva, Izd. Profinterna, 1924. 38 p. incl. tables, diagrs. *NYPL*

41 SCHWARZ, Salomon
Rote Gewerkschaftsinternationale (R. G. I.). [Berlin, 1932] Photostat copy of an article in *Internationales Handwörterbuch des Gewerkschaftswesens*, vol. 2 p. 1348—1359. *Hoover*

42 SHALAGINOVA, E., ed.
Shest let Kominterna; sbornik posobii dlia massovoi klubnoi raboty. Pod red. E. Shelaginovoi [sic!] Moskva, Gos. izd-vo, 1925. 119 p. At head of title: Glavpolitprosvet. Klubnyi otdel. ["Chto chitat' o Kominterne": p. 117—119.] *Hoover, NYPL*

43 SPRAVOCHNIK derevenskogo kommunista. [Moskva] Partizdat, 1936. 584 p. ["Sostaviteli: Rodinov, M. A., Iosifov, F. M."] *NYPL*

44 TIVEL, A., comp.
5 [piat'] let Kominterna v resheniiakh i tsifrakh. Sostavil Tivel. Moskva [Tip. "Krasnyi Proletarii"] 1924. 123 p. tables. (Prilozhenie k no. 1 zhurnala "Kommunisticheskii Internatsional")

A reference book on the first five years of the activities of the Communist International, its front organizations, and on eleven more important communist parties. The particular chapters of the volume include:

1. The activities of the Comintern.
2. Important international conferences and meetings.
3. Statistical information on the most important communist parties.
4. Information on the Communist Youth International, the Womens' Secretariat, the Co-operative Section, the Red Sport International.
5. Information on arrests and executions of communists.

Hoover, NYPL, BDIC, Felt

45 TIVEL, A. [and] Kheimo, M., comp.
10 [desiat'] let Kominterna v resheniiakh i tsifrakh. Spravochnik po istorii Kominterna. Moskva-Leningrad, Gos. izd-vo, 1929. xvi, 415 p. At head of title: Sostavili A. Tivel i M. Kheimo.

> This is a greatly broadened and improved edition of the preceding item. Contains basic information on all aspects of the work of the Comintern and its front organizations during the first ten years of their activities. The Preface is signed by the Agitation and Propaganda Division of the Executive Committee of the Comintern, thus lending to the publication a semi-official character.
> The first part contains excerpts from appeals and resolutions of the period called "On the Road Toward the Comintern" (1914—1919). The next two parts contain information on the first six congresses and nine meetings of the Executive Committee of the Comintern; excerpts from more important decisions and resolutions of these bodies. The fourth part deals with events that took place during the time between these congresses. The last part contains five groups of "Annexes". The first group lists the "sections" of the Comintern and gives basic information on each of them. The second annex contains information on the Executive Committee and its "apparat". The third group contains information on "international revolutionary organizations" (front organizations). Group four lists and gives information on ten international meetings sponsored by the Communist International. Group five contains a bibliography of publications by and on the Comintern in the Russian language.
> Observed omissions: Not mentioned in part I was the international meeting preparatory to the founding of the Communist International which took place in Moscow on December 19, 1919. Omitted in group three of the "annexes" listing the front organizations was the Young Communist International.
> *Hoover, LC, NYPL, Harv, Felt, SInSt*

46 U. S. Library of Congress. Legislative Reference Service.
World Communist Movement; selective chronology, 1918—1957. Printed for the use of the Committee on Un-American Activities. Washington, D. C., Government Printing Office, 1960. xiv, 232 p.

> The coverage of events concerning the Communist International and its front organizations is spotty and not always accurate. *Hoover, LC, NYPL*

47 VOLIN, Boris
Politgramota; uchebnik dlia kandidatskikh partiinykh shkol. Izd. 2., perer. [Moskva] Partizdat, 1933. 370 p. illus., maps, diagrs.

> Chapter X: "Komintern—shtab mirovoi revoliutsii." A textbook for indoctrination of candidates for party membership exposing Soviet view on tasks and aims of the Comintern. *Hoover*

48 VOLIN, Boris [and] Ingulov, S.
Politgramota. [Moskva] Partizdat TSK VKP(b), 1936. 319 p., illus., maps, diagrs.

> Re-edited edition of preceding item. Chapter X: "Kommunisticheskii Internatsional—shtab mirovoi revoliutsii." The same character as preceding item. *Hoover*

49 VOPROSY prepodavaniia leninizma, istorii VKP(b), Kominterna; steno-
gramma soveshchaniia ... Moskva, Izd-vo Kommunisticheskoi akademii, 1930. 318 p. At head of title: Kommunisticheskaia akademia.
Obshchestvo istorikov-marksistov. *Col*

3. Biographies

50 A la MÉMOIRE de Raymond Lefebvre, Lepetit (François Berthot),
Marcel Vergeat, morts pour la révolution [dans les eaux de l'Ocean
arctique (Mourmansk) vers le 1er octobre 1920. Petrograd, Editions
de l'Internationale Communiste 1921] 109 p. ports. (Editions françaises
de l'Internationale Communiste [65]) *Hoover*

51 ALLES für die Revolution! Aus Leben und Werk der Kämpferin Clara
Zetkin. Berlin, Vereinigung internationaler Verlags-Anstalten, 1927.
71 p.

"Clara Zetkin von Paul Fröhlich": p. 3–17. *Hoover*

52 BALABANOFF, Angelica
Lenin; psychologische Beobachtungen und Betrachtungen. Hannover,
Verlag für Literatur und Zeitgeschichte, 1959. 184 p. [Translation from
Italian. Original title: Lenin visto da vicino.] *Hoover*

53 BLAGOEVA, Stella D.
Dimitrov; a biography. New York, International Publishers, 1934. 124 p.
Hoover

54 BOIARSKAIA, Zinaida S.
Klara TSetkin. Moskva, Izd-vo sots.-ekon. lit-ry, 1959. 113 p. illus.
Hoover

54a BRANDT, Willi and Lowenthal, Richard
Ernst Reuter; ein Leben für die Freiheit. Eine politische Biographie.
München, Kindler Verlag, 1957. 758 p.

Chapters 4–6 contain many references to Comintern actions in Germany in
1919–1921 when Reuter was a leading member of the Communist Party of Germany. Of particular importance is the information on the abortive communist
uprising in Germany in March 1921 and the Comintern's role in this action.
Hoover, NYPL

55 BULGARIA. Ministerstvo na informatsiiata i izkustvata.
Georgi Dimitrov, short biographical notes. [Sofia, 1946] 20 p. ports.

"Edited ... by the Ministry of Information and Arts, Press Department."
Hoover

56 BULGARIA. Ministerstvo na vneshnitie diela i na izpoviedaniiata.
Vassil Kolarov; les dates les plus importantes de sa vie et de son
activité. Sofia [Ministère des Affaires Etrangères] 1948. 53 p. port.
Hoover

57 BULGARSKI Bibliografski Institut
Georgi Dimitrov, 1882—1949; spomenen spravochnik. Sofia, Institut
Khristo Botev, 1949. 122 p.

Chronological record of Dimitrov's political activities and posts. Speech by
V. Chervenkov at Dimitrov's funeral. Select bibliography of Dimitrov's writings. Bibliography of writings about Dimitrov. *Hoover*

58 DEIATELI Kommunisticheskogo Internatsionala. 19 iiulia — 7 avg. 1920.
Petrograd, 15-aia Gos. tip., 1920. 28 p. Various pagings. Text in
Russian and French. On cover: 2-oi Kongress Kommunisticheskogo
Internatsionala.

Reproduction of portraits of prominent participants of the II Congress by
Soviet painters. Excerpts of two manifestoes of the Congress.
Hoover, LC, Col

DIMITROV, Georgi—see no. 53, 55, 57, 61a, 71

59 DORNEMANN, Louise
Clara Zetkin; ein Lebensbild. Hrsg. vom Institut für Marxismus-Leninis-
mus beim ZK der SED. 1. Aufl. Berlin, Dietz, 1957. 439 p.
Hoover

60 DUTT, Rajani Palme
Lenin. London, H. Hamilton [1933] 96 p.

London edition of next item. *Hoover*

61 DUTT, Rajani Palme
Life and Teachings of V. I. Lenin, by R. Palme Dutt. New York, International Publishers [1934] 95 p.

American edition of preceding item. *Hoover, Col*

61a FISCHER, Ernst
Das Fanal; der Kampf Dimitroffs gegen die Kriegsbrandstifter. Wien,
„Neues Österreich", 1946. 275 p. *Hoover*

62 FLYNN, Elizabeth Gurley
Debs, Haywood, Ruthenberg. New York, Workers Library Publishers,
1939. 48 p. *Hoover*

63 HICKS, Granville
John Reed; the making of a revolutionary, by Granville Hicks with the
assistance of John Stuart. New York, Macmillan, 1936. viii, 445 p.
Hoover

HUNT, R. N. Carew
Willi Muenzenberg [An essay in the collective work *International
Communism*] see no. 243.

64 [IBARRURI, Dolores]
Dolores Ibarruri (Passionaria), der Volkstribun Spaniens. Biographie,
Reden, Artikel, Briefe. Strasbourg, Édition Promethée, 1937. 51 p.
Hoover

65 [IBARRURI, Dolores]
Dolores Ibarruri, "Pasionaria," su vida, su lucha; prólogo de Isabel C.
de Diaz de Cossio. Mexico, D. F., Sociedad de Amigos de España,
1938. 31 p. (Colección España, v. 6.) *Hoover*

66 [IBARRURI, Dolores]
Pasionaria; People's Tribune of Spain. New York, Workers Library
Publishers, 1938. 31 p. *Hoover*

67 KOENEN, Wilhelm
Moi vstrechi s Leninym. Moskva, Gos.izd-vo polit. lit-ry, 1960. 53 p.
illus., ports. At head of title: Vil'gelm Koenen. [Translation of "Meine
Begegnungen mit Lenin."] *Hoover*

KOLAROV, Vassil—see no. 56.

LENIN, V. I.—see no. 52, 60, 61, 67—69, 75, 77, 79—81, 84, 85.

LEVINÉ, E.—see no. 82.

LIEBKNECHT, Karl—see no. 70, 82, 83, 88.

68 LOZOVSKII, A.
Le grand stratège de la Guerre de Classes. Paris, Librairie du travail,
1924. 51 p. (Petite Bibliothèque de l'Internationale Syndicale Rouge,
XI.)

A partisan evaluation of Lenin as leader of the international proletariat. (An
essay and an article published in l'Humanité.) *Hoover, Felt*

69 LOZOVSKII, A.
Der grosse Stratege des Klassenkrieges. [Berlin] Verlag der Roten Ge-
werkschafts-Internationale, 1924. 48 p. (At head of title: A. Losowsky.
Bibliothek der Roten Gewerkaschtfs-Internationale, Band 26.)

    For annotation see preceeding item.   *NYPL, Felt*

LUXEMBURG, Rosa—see no. 70, 74, 82, 83, 88.

MEHRING, Franz—see no. 82, 83.

70 Der MEUCHELMORD an Karl Liebknecht und Rosa Luxemburg, Tat-
sachenmaterial. Petrogral, Verlag der Kommunistischen Internationale,
1920, 31 p.   *NYPL*

71 NEDKOV, P.
Dimitroff. [Sofia] 1935. 33 p. diagr. At head of title: P. Nedkoff
                                                  Hoover

72 PIECK, Wilhelm
Clara Zetkin, Leben und Kampf; geboren 5. Juli 1857 / gestorben
20. Juni 1933. Berlin, Dietz [1948] 48 p.   *Hoover*

73 [PÖÖGELMANN, Hans]
Wiktor Kingissepp. Peterburis [Petrograd] 1923. 63 p. port.
(Kommunistlik internatsionaal. Eesti osakonna kirjastus. Töörahwa
kirjandus nr. 58) At head of title: H. P.   *NYPL*

REED, John—see no. 63.

REUTER, Ernst — see no. 54a.

74 ROZA Liuksemburg; sbornik statei K. TSekin, A. Kollontai, IU. Markh-
levskogo i P. Levi. Moskva, Gos. izd-vo, 1921. 41 p. ports.
                                                  Hoover
RUTHENBERG, Charles E.—see no. 62.

75 TONISEV, Mikhail I.
V. I. Lenin—osnovatel' i vozhd' III Kommunisticheskogo Internatsionala.
Moskva, Znanie, 1959. 46 p. (Vsesoiuznoe obshchestvo po rasprostra-
neniiu politicheskikh i nauchnykh znanii. Ser. I: Istoria, 18)
                                       Hoover, Harv, SInSt

76 UNITED STATES. Department of State. Division of Biographic Information. Far Easterners in the Comintern structure. [Washington,

Department of State, Division of Biographic Information, Office of Libraries and Intelligence Acquisition, 1950] 33 p. (OIR Report No. 5226) At head of title: Unclassified. Mimeographed.

Hoover

77 ZBOROVSKII, Isai
Lenin—master revoliutsionnoi propagandy. Moskva, Gos. izd-vo polit. lit-ry, 1958. 287 p. plates, ports.

Hoover

78 ZETKIN, Klara
Bortsy revoliutsii. Peterburg, Gos. izd-vo, 1920. 37 p. port.

Hoover

79 ZETKIN, Klara
Erinnerungen an Lenin. Wien-Berlin, Verlag für Literatur und Politik [c1929] 85 p.

Hoover

80 ZETKIN, Klara
Erinnerungen an Lenin; mit einem Anhang: Aus dem Briefwechsel Clara Zetkins mit W. I. Lenin und N. K. Krupskaia. Berlin, Dietz, 1957. 115 p. ports., facsims.

Hoover

81 ZETKIN, Klara
My recollections of Lenin. Moscow, Foreign Languages Publ. House, 1956. 93 p.

Hoover

82 ZETKIN, Klara
Revolutionäre Kämpfe und revolutionäre Kämpfer 1919; Rosa Luxemburg, Karl Liebknecht, Leo Jogiches, E. Leviné, Franz Mehring und all den treuen, kühnen revolutionären Kämpfern und Kämpferinnen des Jahres 1919 zum Gedächtnis. Stuttgart, Verlag Spartakus, Südd. Arbeiterbuchhandlung [1920] 31 p.

Hoover, LC

83 ZETKIN, Klara
Rosa Luxemburg, Karl Liebknecht, Franz Mehring; den Führern des Spartakusbundes und Gründern der Kommunistischen Partei Deutschlands. Hrsg. von Wilhelm Pieck und Fritz Heckert. Moskau-Leningrad, Verlagsgenossenschaft ausländischer Arbeiter in der UdSSR, 1934. 172 p. ports.

"Die Zusammenstellung des Materials besorgte H. Löwen."

Hoover

84 ZETKIN, Klara
Vospominaniia o Lenine. Moskva, Gos. izd-vo polit. lit-ry, 1955. 70 p. At heat of title: Institut Marksa-Engel'sa-Lenina-Stalina pri TSK KPSS. Klara TSetkin.

Hoover

85 ZETKIN, Klara; Katayama, Sen, and others
Nos rencontres avec Lenine. Moscou, Editions en langues étrangères,
1939. 67 p. plate, ports. *Hoover*

86 [ZETKIN, Klara]
Clara Zetkin. Défense édition. [n. p., 1933] 23 p. ports.
At head of title: En souvenir d'une grande révolutionnaire disparue.
Hoover

87 [ZETKIN, Klara]
Clara Zetkin; ein Sammelband zum Gedächtnis der grossen Kämpferin. Moskau-Leningrad, Verlagsgenossenschaft ausländischer Arbeiter
in der UdSSR, 1934. 131 p. illus.
Brief tributes by well known communists. *Hoover*

ZETKIN, Klara—see nos. 51, 54, 59, 72, 86, 87.

88 ZINOV'EV, Grigorii and Trotskii, L.
Karl Liebknecht und Rosa Luxemburg; Reden von G. Sinowjew und
L. Trotzki auf der Sitzung des Petrograder Sowjets am 18. Januar 1919.
Petrograd, Verlag der Kommunistischen Internationale, 1920. 32 p.
NYPL, LC

4. Collections of documents

89 AKTIONSPROGRAMME der Kommunistischen Internationale. Lodz
[n. d.] 16 p. *BDIC*

90 AM Aufbau; Dokumente des Exekutivkomitees der Kommunistischen
Jugend-Internationale. Berlin, Internationaler Jugendverlag [1921?]
2 vols.

> Heft 1: [covers the period] November 1919–August 1920
> Heft 2: [covers the period] September 1920—Februar 1921
> [Berlin, 1921] 32 p.
> A collection of appeals of the Executive Committee of the Young Communist
> International issued during the above period to its membership and to the
> youth at large. *Hoover* (Heft 2), *NYPL* (Heft 1, 2), *BDIC* (Feft 2)

91 ANTI-Soviet forgeries; a record of some of the forged documents used
at various times against the Soviet government. [London] Workers'
Publications, Ltd., 1927. xiii, 141 p. facsims.

> "The translations from the Russian used in this book were made by Eden
> & Cedar Paul." Foreword by George Lansbury.

65

A Soviet denunciation of allegedly forged documents which attempted to show "first, that the Soviet Government is intimately connected with the Communist International; and secondly, that the Soviet Government makes a practice of interfering in the internal affairs of other countries." (From the Preface, p. v) Among others the famous "Zinoviev letter" and the reaction of the British government to this letter are broadly discussed.

Hoover

92 L'ATTITUDE du prolétariat devant la guerre. Paris, Bureau d'Editions, 1932. 12 p. [error!]

This is the French translation of the next item. See contents in no. 93. The BDIC catalog card indicates "12 p."—which in view of the 80 pages of the English edition, and 115 pages of the Italian edition (no. 133), is probably an error. **BDIC**

93 The ATTITUDE of the proletariat towards war. A collection of documents on a vital question. [London, Modern Books] 1932. 80 p.
Contents: 1) The resolutions of the Berne Conference of the Russian Social-Democratic Labour Party.—2) Lenin's notes on the question of the tasks of our delegation at the Hague Conference.—3) The struggle against imperialist war and the tasks of the communists. Theses, Sixth Congress, 1928.—4) Resolution of the XI Plenum of the E. C. C. I. on the report of comrade Cachin on: the increased danger of interventionist war against the U. S. S. R. and the tasks of the communists. *Felt*

94 BITTELMAN, Alexander, ed.
The advance of the United front; introduction by Alex Bittelman. [New York City, Central Committee, Communist Party of the U. S. A., 1934] 70 p. At head of title: A documentary account.

Hoover

95 BLUEPRINT for world conquest, as outlined by the Communist International, with an introduction by William Henry Chamberlin. Washington, Chicago, Human Events, 1946. 263 p.

Contents: Introduction.—The theses and statutes of the Communist International, as adopted at the second World Congress, July 17 (!) to August 7, 1920. Moscow.—The programme of the Communist International, adopted by the sixth World Congress, September 1, 1928 Moscow.—Constitution and rules of the Communist International. In reprinting the "theses and statutes", Chamberlin repeated the erroneous date "July 17" as it was in the original publication (see no. 622). The correct date of the opening of the II Congress is July 19.

Hoover, LC, NYPL, Harv, Col, BostPL, Duke, Swart, UCal, UChic, UKans, UMich, UPenn, UTenn, UTex, UVirg, Amst, BDIC

96 BOR'BA bol'shevikov za sozdanie Kommunisticheskogo Internatsionala; materialy i dokumenty; 1914—1919 gg. [edited by S. Bantke]

Moskva, Partizdat, 1934. x, 245 p. At head of title: Institut Marksa-Engel'sa-Lenina pri TSK VKP(b)

> "A considerable part of the documents originates with Lenin. Lenin participated in the selection and editing of a large part of remaining documents which have been published. The collection was prepared for print by S. Bantke." Preface. The NYPL cataloged this item whith Lenin's name as author in brackets. *Hoover, NYPL, BDIC, SInSt*

97 Il C[OMITATO] E[secutivo] dell'Internazionale comunista per il Fronte Unico del proletariato. Raccolta di documenti ufficiali a cura del C. E. dell'I. C. Roma, Libreria editrice del Partito Comunista d'Italia, 1922. 85 p. *Felt*

98 The COMMUNIST International, 1919—1943; documents selected and edited by J. Degras. Issued under the auspices of the Royal Institute of International Affairs. London, Oxford University Press, 1956—60. 2 vols.

> Vol. I covers the period 1919—1922; vol. II covers 1923—1928. More to be published. A selection of official texts of Comintern documentation based almost exclusively on *Internationale Presse-Korrespondenz* and German language editions of proceedings of Comintern congresses and Executive Committee meetings. In many cases Russian originals, by having been retranslated from German translations, lost their original distinctive features and intensity. Although the collection is a very convenient research tool, the user is advised to re-check texts against Russian originals and to make sure that *Inprekorr* dates are correct. *Hoover, LC, NYPL, Harv, Col, Amst, BDIC, Felt*

COMMUNIST papers. Documents selected from those obtained on the arrest of communist leaders on the 14th and 21st October 1925. See no. 105.

99 Les COMMUNISTES luttent pour la paix. Paris, Bureau d'Editions, 1936. 111 p.

Contents:
Lenin, Vladimir I.
  Extrait des instructions données à la délégation à la conférence de la paix à la Haye. p. 5—6
Stalin, Josef
  Extrait de son entretien avec M. Roy Howard. p. 7—8
Dimitrov, Georgi
  Le front unique de lutte pour la paix. p. 9—19
Le congrès universel de la paix et la classe ouvrière p. 20—27.
Thorez, Maurice
  Réponse à Hitler. (Discours prononcé à Buffalo le 5 avril 1936.) p. 28—35
Cachin, Marcel
  Pour la sécurité collective. (Discours prononcé au Sénat, le 25 juin 1936.) p. 36—40

Duclos, Jacques
  Le peuple français veut la paix avec tous les peuples. (Déclaration faite le 5 juin 1936, à la Chambre des députés, au nom du groupe communiste) p. 41—42
Pollitt, Harry
  La classe ouvrière anglaise et la paix. p. 43—64
Gallacher, William
  L'anneau de la paix autour de l'Allemagne Hitlerienne. (Discours prononcé le 26 mars 1936 à la Chambre des Communes.) p. 65—67
Gottwald, Clement
  Comment protéger la Tchécoslovaquie contre Hitler. (Discours prononcé à la Chambre des députés tchécoslovaque le 28 avril 1936.) p. 68—77
Front populaire contre la politique de guerre de Hitler, pour le maintien de la paix et pour une Allemagne démocratique. Manifest du Comité central du Parti communiste allemand. p. 78—84
Manifeste du parti communiste d'Italie. p. 85—88
Après Addis-Abéba. p. 89—92
En avant contre les oppresseurs fascistes, traîtres au people et fomentateurs de guerre! (Appel du Comité central du Parti communiste de Pologne) p. 93—101
Browder, Earl
  L'Amérique peut-elle rester neutre? p. 102—107   *Hoover, Felt*

99a 10 [DESIAT] let MOPR v rezoliutsiiakh i dokumentakh. [Moskva] Izd-vo TSK MOPR, 1932. 275 p.

For contents see annotation to English edition, no. 139.   *NYPL*

99b DESIAT let Profinterna v rezoliutsiiakh, dokumentakh i tsifrakh. Sostavil S. Sorbonskii. Pod redaktsiei i s predisloviem A.Lozovskogo. Moskva, VTSSPS, 1930. 276 p.   *NYPL, SInSt*

100 DIEZ años de S.R.I. Barcelona, Ediciones "Combate" [1932] 397 p. At head of title: Socorro Rojo Internacional.

For contents see English edition, no. 139.   *LC, NYPL*

100a DIX années de Secours Rouge International 1922—1932. Paris, Bureau d'Editions, 1933. 240 p. illus.

For contents see English edition, no. 139.   *BDIC*

101 Les DOCUMENTS de l'opposition française et la réponse du parti. [Paris, Bureau d'Editions, 1927] 163 p.

A collection of statements and letters to the Central Committee of the Communist Party of France signed by the following members of the Committee: Henry Barbé, Louis Beors, Marguerite Faussecave, Suzanne Girault, and Albert Treint. These documents, originating with an opposition group in the CPF, are directed against Stalin's policy in the Communist International. They deal with questions taken up by the 8-th Plenum of the Comintern, in particular with the revolutionary events in China, the Austrian uprising, and with the exclusion of Beors and Treint from the Central Committee of the CPF. Included also is an answer of the Central Committee to the opposition group, signed by Semard, Bernard, and Doriot.   *Hoover, NYPL*

102 DOKUMENTE zum Studium des Kommunismus. Hersg. vom Bundes-institut zur Erforschung des Marxismus-Leninismus, Institut für Sowjeto-logie. Köln, Verl. Wissenschaft und Politik, 1962.

Copy was unavailable for fuller listing and annotation.   *BDIC*

103 DRAPER, Harold, ed.
"Out of their own mouths"; a documentary study of the new line of the Comintern on war; edited by Harold Draper. New York, Young People's Socialist League, Greater New York Federation, [1935] 39 p.

An anti-communist exposé showing the "betrayal" of the old socialist anti-war and anti-militarist line by the communists after the signing of the Franco-Soviet Pact of Mutual Aid in May 1935. Draper used 74 excerpts of com-munist statements to prove his point.   *Hoover*

104 GANKIN, Olga (Hess) and Fisher, Harold H., comps.
The Bolsheviks and the World War; the origin of the Third Inter-national. Stanford University, Calif., Stanford University Press, 1940. xviii, 856 p. (The Hoover Library on War, Revolution, and Peace. Publication No. 15.)

"The documents in this volume do not go beyond the autumn of 1918."
Preface.
Contents: The Bolsheviks, the Mensheviks, and the Second International.—The activities of the Bolsheviks abroad, 1914—1916.—International socialist conferences, September 1914—April 1915.— Zimmerwald.— Kienthal.—Tactics and dissensions of the Zimmerwald left.—Stockholm: the Third Zimmerwald conference.—Chronology.—Bibliography.—Biographical notes.
A reprint of this volume by the Stanford University Press appeared in 1960. The only change was that "... a few errata have been corrected and a few easily ascertained death dates added to the biographical notes." Preface to second printing.   *Hoover, LC, NYPL, Harv, Col, Felt, SInSt*

104a GIRINIS, S. V. comp.
Profintern v rezoliutsiiakh. Sostavil i snabdil kommentariami S. Girinis, pod redaktsiei i so vstupitelnoi stat'ei A. Lozovskogo. Moskva, Izd. Profinterna, 1928. 254 p.   *NYPL*

105 GREAT Britain. Parliament.
Communist papers. Documents selected from those obtained on the arrest of the communist leaders on the 14th and 21st October 1925 . . .

London, H. M. Stationery off., 1926. 135 p. facsims. (Gt. Britain. Parliament. Papers by command. Cmd. 2682.)

Contents: 1—22. Relationship of the Communist Party of Great Britain, The Young Communist League and the National Minority Movement to the Third (Communist) International and the Red International of Labour Unions at Moscow.—23. Participation of the Russian trade delegation and of the All-Russian cooperative society (Arcos), London, in the affairs of the Communist Party of Great Britain.—24—30. Finances, including receipts and expenditure, of the Communist Party of Great Britain and of the British Bureau of the Red International of Labour Unions.—31—36. Activities in the United Kingdom of the Communist Party of Great Britain, Red International of Labour Unions and Young Communist League.—37—52. Activities of organizations affiliated to the Communist International including the Communist Party of Great Britain, in British Dominions, colonies and spheres of influences abroad. Appendix: Questionnaire forwarded with document 21.—Glossary. *LC*

106 GREAT Britain. Foreign Office.
Documents illustrating the hostile activities of the Soviet government and Third International against Great Britain. London, H. M. Stationery off., 1927. 31 p. (Russia No. 2 (1927). Papers by command. Cmd. 2874.)

Contents: Part I. Documents found by the police in the course of the search in Soviet House, and referred to by the Prime Minister in his statement on the 24th May, 1927.—Part II. Documents published by the Foreign Office.
Hoover, LC

107 IKKI i VKP(b) po kitaiskomu voprosu; osnovnye resheniia. Moskva "Moskovskii rabochii", 1927. 258 p. *Hoover, LC, SInSt*

108 INDEPENDENT Labor League of America [Communist Party (Opposition)] Where we stand. New York City, the Communist Party (Opposition) [1934—35]. 4 parts. Mimeographed.

Subtitle varies. Hoover Institution has only part 4 with subtitle: Programmatic documents of the Communist Party (Opposition).
Contents: 1. Civil War in Austria; statement of the National Buro.—2. The Present Situation and the Tasks of the Communists; Resolution, July 1934.—3. The San Francisco General Strike.—4. Independent Unionism Today.—5. The Change in Comintern Tactics and the Tasks of the Communist Opposition, resolution September 1934.—6. To the National Executive Committee of the Socialist Party of America; Proposal for United Front by the Communist Party (Opposition).—7. Complete correspondence between the Communist Party, USA and Communist Party, USA (Opposition) in negotiations for Communist unity. *Hoover*

109 L'INTERNATIONALE Communiste et la guerre; documents sur la lutte de l'I.C. contre la guerre impérialiste et pour la défense de l'U.R.S.S. Paris, Bureau d'Editions, 1928. 131 p.

Contents: 1. ptie. Documents antérieurs à l'histoire de l'I.C.—2. ptie. Documents de l'Internationale Communiste. *Hoover, NYPL, Harv, Amst, BDIC, Felt*

110 L'INTERNATIONALE Communiste et sa section française (Recueil de documents). Paris, Librairie de l'Humanité, 1922. 104 p. (Petite bibliothèque communiste)

For annotation see no. 145. *Hoover, BDIC*

111 ITAL'IANSKAIA sotsialisticheskaia partiia i Kommunisticheskii Internatsional (sbornik materialov) Petrograd, Izd. Otdela informatsii Kommunisticheskogo Internatsionala, 1921. 192 p. *Hoover, NYPL*

112 IZ ISTORII mezhdunarodnoi proletarskoi solidarnosti; dokumenty i materialy. At head of title: Glavnoe arkhivnoe upravlenie SSSR.

> Sbornik I: Boevoe sodruzhestvo trudiashchikhsia zarubezhnykh stran s narodami Sovetskoi Rossii (1917—1922). Redaktor G. V. Shumeiko. Moskva, Izd-vo "Sovetskaia Rossiia", 1957. 573 p. illus., facsims., bibliography, pp. 528—[532].
> II: Proletarskaia solidarnost' trudiashchikhsia v bor'be za mir (1927—1924). Redaktor N. V. Matkovskii. Moskva, Izd-vo "Sovetskaia Rossiia", 1958. 559p. illus., facsims.
> III: Mezhdunarodnaia solidarnost' trudiashchikhsia v bor'be s nastupleniem reaktsii i voennoi opasnost'iu (1925—1927). Moskva, Izd-vo "Sovetskaia Rossiia", 1959. 543 p. illus., facsims.
> IV: Mezhdunarodnaia proletarskaia solidarnost' v bor'be s nastupleniem fashizma (1928—1932). Moskva, Izd-vo "Sovetskaia Rossiia", 1960. 589 p. illus., facsims.
> V: Mezhdunarodnaia solidarnost' trudiashchikhsia v bor'be s fashizmom, protiv razviazyvaniia vtoroi mirovoi voiny (1933—1937). Moskva, Izd-vo "Sovetskaia Rossiia", 1961. 549 p. illus., facsims.

Although the great majority of documents contained in these volumes concerns activities of the communist parties all over the world, there are here reprinted also documents originating with the Communist International and its front organizations, and documents concerning the collaboration and relationship of foreign communist parties with these organizations.

Hoover (vols. 1–V), *BDIC* (vols. ?)

113 Der KAMPF um die Kommunistische Internationale; Dokumente der russischen Opposition, nicht veröffentlicht vom Stalin'schen ZK. Veröffentlicht vom Verlag der „Fahne des Kommunismus"... [Berlin, Druckerei für Arbeiter-Literatur Willy Iszdonat, 1928] 176 p.

Contents: Einleitung. — Aus den Thesen des Genossen Sinowjew über die Chinesische Revolution. — Die Chinesische Revolution und die Thesen des Genossen Stalin. — Der Kampf um den Frieden und das Anglo-Russische Komitee. — Zweite Rede zur chinesischen Frage. — Erklärung des Genossen Trotski und Wujowitsch — Zusatzanträge zur Resolution über die Lage in England. — Ist es nicht Zeit zu begreifen. — Hankau und Moskau. — Erklärung der Fünfhundert. — Der sichere Weg. — Anhang: a) Resolution zur chinesischen Frage. — b) Resolution zur Frage des anglo-russischen Komitees. — c) Über die Lösung der Sowjets in China. [This pamphlet relates developments during the 8-th Plenum.] *Hoover, Amst, Felt*

114 KOMINTERN i trudiashchaiasia zhenshchina. Vstup. stat'ia K. Kirsano-
voi. [Leningrad] Partizdat, 1934. 69 p. (Kommunisticheskii Internatsional v dokumentakh). At head of title: Institut Marksa-Engel'sa-
Lenina pri TSK VKP(b).

> See annotation to *Die Komintern und die Werktätige Frau*, no. 117.
>
> *LC, NYPL, BDIC*

115 KOMINTERN i VKP(b) o kitaiskoi revoliutsii. Osnovnye resheniia.
Moskva, Gos. izd., 1927. 88 p.   *SInSt*

116 Die KOMINTERN und der Krieg; Dokumente über den Kampf der
Komintern gegen den imperialistischen Krieg und für die Verteidigung der Sowjetunion; ein Sammelbuch. Hamburg-Berlin, C. Hoym
Nachfolger [c1928] 128 p. (Half-title: Probleme der Weltpolitik und
der Arbeiterbewegung, Bd. 8) „Autorisierte Ausgabe."

> *Hoover, NYPL, Harv, Amst*

117 Die KOMINTERN und die werktätige Frau. Moskau-Leningrad, Verlagsgenossenschaft ausländischer Arbeiter in der UdSSR, 1935. 78 p.
At head of title: Die Kommunistische Internationale in Dokumenten.

> "Enthält die hauptsächlichsten Dokumente der Kommunistischen Internationale
> zur Frage der Arbeit unter den werktätigen Frauen aus der Zeit von 1919 bis
> 1934 ... Den Dokumenten ist eine Einleitung von K. Kirssanowa voraus-
> geschickt." p. [3]   *Hoover, Amst, Felt*

KOMINTERN v rezoliutsiiakh. See no. 120.

KOMMUNISTICHESKAIA akademiia, Moscow. Nauchno-issledovatel-
skii institut po Kitaiu. See no. 138.

118 KOMMUNISTICHESKII Internatsional i voina; dokumenty i materialy
o bor'be Kominterna protiv imperialisticheskoi voiny i v zashchitu
S.S.S.R. Moskva, Gos. izd-vo, 1928. 108 p.

> *Hoover, NYPL, Col, SInSt*

KOMMUNISTICHESKII Internatsional v dokumentakh. [Book by Bela
Kun] See no. 121.

119 KOMMUNISTICHESKII Internatsional v dokumentakh; seriia broshiur
pod red. V. Adoratskogo i drugikh. Moskva, Partizdat, 1933—1934.
At head of title: Institut Marksa-Engel'sa-Lenina pri TSK VKP(b).

> A series of unnumbered pamphlets and small books containing a narration
> on a certain subject supported by documentation originating with the Com-
> munist International. Propaganda material. See the following:

21 [Dvadtsat' odno] uslovie priema v Kommunisticheskii Internatsional. See no. 645.

Komintern i trudiashchaiasia zhenshchina. See no. 114.

O fashistskoi diktature v Germanii. See no. 127.

Protiv belogo terrora. See no. 135.

120 **KUN, Bela, ed.**
Komintern v rezoliutsiiakh. Moskva, Izd-vo Kommunisticheskogo universiteta im. IA. M. Sverdlova, 1926. 241 p.

The above listed item carried the imprint "2nd edition" ("2. izd.") and is identical with a later edition (1927) with imprint "3. izd." These seem to be not new editions but only new printings. A fuller, revised edition of this collection, covering the period 1919—1932, appeared under a somewhat changed title. (See next item.)

Hoover, NYPL, UWash, BDIC

121 **KUN, Bela, ed.**
Kommunisticheskii Internatsional v dokumentakh; resheniia, tezisy i vozzvaniia kongressov Kominterna i plenumov IKKI, 1919—1932. Pod red. Bela Kuna. Moskva, Partiinoe izd-vo, 1933. x, 1007 p. At head of title: Institut Marksa-Engel'sa-Lenina pri TSK VKP(b).

This is a collection of theses and resolutions of the first six Congresses, 12 Plenums and one meeting of the Enlarged Presidium of the Communist International, thus covering the period from March 1919 to September 1932. The reprinted material is not a complete reprint of all the documents which originated at the above mentioned meetings, but only a very broad selection of these. The compiler, Bela Kun, says so himself in the Preface: "The resolutions compiled in this collection reflect only the more important developments in the work of the Communist International." (p. III) A comparison of the contents of this volume with the full list of theses, resolutions, and other documents of the Congresses, Plenums and Presidium meetings contained in Tivel, *10 let Kominterna v resheniakh i tsifrakh* (see no. 45), discloses what is missing. The documentation of each meeting is preceded by some useful general information about the meeting. Source references indicate from where the texts were reprinted. A list of all reprinted items and a name index conclude the volume.   *Hoover, LC, NYPL, Harv, Col, JHop, BDIC, Felt, SInSt*

122 **LENIN, V. I.**
An die Jugend; Reden und Aufsätze. Wien, Verlag der Jugendinternationale, 1925. 61 p. (Bibliothek des jungen Leninisten, Bd. I.)

Hoover

123 **LENIN, V. I.**
Kommunisticheskii Internatsional; stat'i i rechi; predisl. N. N. Popova; primechaniia K. P. Novitskogo. Moskva, Izd-vo "Krasnaia nov'" Glavpolitprosvet, 1924. 344 p. At head of title: N. Lenin.

NYPL, Harv, Col

73

124 LENIN, V. I.
Kommunisticheskii Internatsional; stat'i, rechi, dokumenty 1914—1923,
pod red. V. Knorina. [Moskva] Partizdat, 1934—37. 2 v. facsims. At
head of title: Institut Marksa-Engel'sa-Lenina pri TSK VKP(b).

Hoover, BDIC (vol. I)

125 LENIN, V. I. [and] Zinov'ev, G.
O Kominterne. Stat'i i dokumenty. Moskva, 1924. 175 p.

SInSt

126 LENIN, V. I.
Über den Krieg; Reden und Aufsätze. Berlin-Schöneberg, Verlag der
Jugendinternationale, 1926. 2 vols. (Bibliothek des jungen Leninisten,
Bd. II—III.)

Hoover

127 O FASHISTSKOI diktature v Germanii. Vstup. stat'ia O. Piatnitskogo.
[Moskva] Partizdat, 1934. 245 p. tables. (Kommunisticheskii Inter-
natsional v dokumentakh.) At head of title: Institut Marksa-Engel'sa-
Lenina pri TSK RKP(b).

NYP, BDIC

128 Le PARTI socialiste ilatien et l'Internationale communiste; recueil de
documents. Petrograd, Editions de l'Internationale communiste, 1921.
196 p.

Hoover, Felt

129 POALE Zion
Dokumente des jüdischen kommunistischen Verbandes (Poale Zion)
zur Anschlussaktion an die Kommunistische Internationale. Wien, Verlag "Avantgarde" [1921] 102 p. (On cover: Jüdischer kommunistischer
Verband (Poale Zion) Nr. 1 Sammelhefte "Avantgarde")

"Die dem Verbande angegliederten Parteien und Organisationen": p. [101]—
102.

Hoover, Felt

130 POSLEVOENNYI kapitalizm v osveshchenii Kominterna; sbornik dokumentov i rezoliutsii kongressov i Ispolkoma Kominterna [Podbor materiala proizveden O. N. Freifel'd] Moskva, Partiinoe izd-vo, 1932,
163 p.

Hoover, LC, NYPL, Harv, Col, Duke, Yale

131 PROGRAMMNYE dokumenty kommunisticheskikh partii Vostoka. Pod
red. L. Madiara, P. Mifa, M. Orachevashvili i G. Safarova. Moskva,
Partiinoe izd-vo, 1934. xviii, 293 p.

Hoover, SInSt

132 PROGRAMMNYE dokumenty kommunizma; 1847—1933. Moskva,
Partizdat, 1934. 319 p.

BDIC

133 Il PROLETARIATO di fronte alla guerra. Paris, Edizioni di Stato Operaio, 1932. 115 p.

> Italian translation of *The attitude of the proletariat towards war*. For contents see no. 93. *Felt*

135 PROTIV belogo terrora. Vstup. stat'ia E. Stasovoi. [Moskva] Partizdat, 1934. 79 p. (Kommunisticheskii Internatsional v dokumentakh) At head of title: Institut Marksa-Engel'sa-Lenina pri TSK VKP(b).

> "Broshiura soderzhit riad dokumentov Kommunisticheskogo Internatsionala (rezoliutsii kongressov Kominterna i plenumov IKKI) posviashchennykh bor'be protiv beloga terrora." *Hoover, Harv, BDIC*

136 ROZENFELD, O., ed.
Komintern i profsoiuzy, v resheniiakh kongressov i plenumov i drugikh materialakh Kominterna o profdvizhenii. S predisloviem i pod red. A. Lozovskogo. [Kiev] "Ukrainskii robitnik" [1930] 320 p. At head of title: O. Rozenfeld i I. Zlatopolskii. *Col, Harv, SInSt*

137 SOVIET plot in China. Peking, Metropolitan Police Headquarters, 1928. viii, 162 p.

> Official Chinese publication of 45 documents by the Communist International, Soviet authorities, the Chinese Communist Party, and the Kuomintang, which were found during a police raid on the premises of the Soviet Embassy in Peking on April 6, 1927. Published as the eleventh volume of *Su-lien yin-mou when-cheng hui-pien* (Collection of documentary evidence of the Soviet Russian conspiracy) which contained a total of 324 documents in 10 volumes. For a broader treatment of these documents see C. Martin WILBUR, *Documents on Communism, Nationalism, and Soviet advisers in China, 1918—1927*. no. 143.
> *Hoover, Col*

138 STRATEGIIA i taktika Kominterna v natsional'no-kolonial'noi revoliutsii na primere Kitaia; sbornik dokumentov. Sostavitel' G. Kara-Murza, pod red. P. Mifa. [Moskva] Izd. Instituta MKh i MK, 1934. 394 p. At head of title: Nauchno-issledovatel'skii institut po Kitaiu. Kolonial'nyi sektor IMKh i MP pri Kommunisticheskoi akademii.
> *Hoover, NYPL, Harv, Col, BDIC, Felt, SInSt*

139 TEN years of International Red Aid in resolutions and documents; 1922—1932. [Moscow?, n. d.] 268 p.

> The introductory first chapter states that the volume was compiled to provide information on the I. R. A. to its functionaries. "This book contains the most important documents, accepted in the various fields of I. R. A. activity, and reflects the various stages of development of our organization. The documents are so assorted that every functionary will quickly be able to find those which refer to concrete fields of activity." (p. 9) This chapter is signed: Secretariat of I. R. A.

The titles of the following chapters best explain the contents of the volume:
II. General resolutions
III. Organizational questions
IV. Agitation and propaganda
V. The IRA and the struggle against imperialist war
VI. Political emigration and the right of asylum
VII. Work in the colonies and work among the Negroes
VIII. Relief
IX. The work of patronage and international relations
X. Revolutionary competition
XI. Juridical questions
XII. Financial questions
XIII. The enemies of the I. R. A.
XIV. Record of the most important events in the existence of the I. R. E. [This is a concise but still useful chronology of events concerning the I. R. A; the agenda of more important meetings is included.]
XV. Appendix [Contains the texts of all resolutions of the congresses of the Comintern, the RILU, the CYI, and other front organizations on the I. R. A.]
For editions in other languages see nos. 99 a, 100, 100 a, 144.

Hoover, NYPL, Harv, UMinn, UTex, Felt

140 THÈSES, manifestes et résolutions adoptés par les Ier, IIe, IIIe, et IVe Congrès de l'Internationale Communiste (1919—1923). Textes complets. Paris, Librairie du travail, 1934. xvi, 210 p. (Bibliothèque communiste) *Hoover, LC, NYPL, Harv, Col, UChic, UWash, BDIC, Felt*

141 UNITY will conquer. [New York, Workers Library Publishers, 1936] 47 p.

Contains various documents originating with the Communist International, including Dimitrov's appeals against the Ethiopian war, responses from five European nations, and an article by Klement Gottwald. *NYPL*

142 VSESOIUZNAIA kommunisticheskaia partiia (bol'shevikov).
Partiia i Komintern; o "staroi" i "novoi" oppozitsii; sbornik rezoliutsii i postanovlenii. Izd. 2-e, dop. Moskva, Gos. izd-vo, 1926. 131 p. (Biblioteka zhurnala "Sputnik agitatora") *Hoover, SInSt*

143 WILBUR, C. Martin [and] How, Julie Lien-ying, editors.
Documents on Communism, Nationalism, and Soviet Advisers in China, 1918—1927; papers seized in the 1927 Peking raid. Edited, with Introductory Essays by ... New York, Columbia University Press, 1956. xviii, 617 p. facsims, bibliography: p. 565—594.

American re-translation of 50 documents by the Communist International, Soviet authorities, the Chinese Communist Party and the Kuomintang seized by the Peking police during a raid on the premises of the Soviet Embassy on April 6, 1927. Some of these documents were first published in an official Chinese book, *Soviet Plot in China*. See annotation to no. 137.

Hoover, LC, NYPL, Harv, Col

144 ZEHN Jahre Internationale Rote Hilfe. Resolutionen und Dokumente. Hrsg. vom EK der IRH. Berlin, MOPR, 1932. 268 p.

For contents see English edition, no. 139. *Amst, Felt*

145 ZUR Lage in der Kommunistischen Partei Frankreichs. Hamburg, Hoym 1922. 58 p. (Bibliothek der Kommunistischen Internationale, 32)

"The Executive Committee [of the Communist International] decided to publish the most important documents (letters of the Executive Committee, resolutions, decisions, etc.) concerning the relations of the Communist International with the French Communist Party. The documents gathered here refer to the period from the IIIrd World Congress of the Communist International up to date... Moscow, July, 1922." An interesting collection of documents disclosing also the technical and personal details of the operations of the Communist International. For French edition see no. 110. *Hoover, LC, NYPL, Felt*

5. The Internationals (joint treatment)

146 BACH, I. A. and others.
Les trois Internationales; précis d'histoire. L'Association internationale des travailleurs (1864—1872). La Deuxième Internationale. L'Internationale Communiste (1919—1943). Traduit du russe par Serge Mairey. Paris, Editions sociales, 1955. 94 p.

"Cet ouvrage reproduit trois articles de la Grande encyclopédie soviétique: «La Première Internationale», par I. A. Bach, tome XVIII, p. 283—288; «La Deuxième Internationale», par I. S. Galkine, tome XVIII, p. 288—294; «L'Internationale communiste», par B. N. Ponomarev, tome XXII, p. 258—266."
Hoover, Felt

147 CHICHERIN, Georgii V.
Die internationale Politik zweier Internationalen. Hamburg, Westeuropäisches Sekretariat der Kommunistischen Internationale; in Kommission: C. Hoym Nachf. [1920] 14 p. At head of title: G. Tschitscherin.
Hoover, Amst, Felt

148 CRISPIEN, Arthur
Die Internationale; vom Bund der Kommunisten bis zur Internationale der Weltrevolution. 2. erweiterte Aufl. Berlin, Verlagsgenossenschaft „Freiheit", 1920. 51 p. *Hoover*

149 DALLA seconda alla Terza Internazionale. Milano, "Avanti", 1920. 127 p. (Documenti della rivoluzione, 10.)
BDIC, Felt

150 DUTT, Rajani Palme
The two Interationals. Westminster, The Labour Research Department;
[London] G. Allen & Unwin, 1920. iv, 92 p.

> **Contents:** Foreword.—The origin of the division.—The second International.—
> The foundations of the third International.—The theory of the communists.—
> The proposed Left-wing conference.—The position of the national parties.—
> Appendixes.—Notes on books (p. 91—92)
>
> *Hoover, LC, NYPL, Harv, Col*

151 ESSEN, Aleksandr
Tri Internatsionala. Moskva, Gos. izd-vo, 1926. 252 p.

> *Hoover, NYPL, SInSt*

152 FOSTER, William Zebulon
History of the three Internationals; the world socialist and communist
movements from 1848 to the present. New York, International Publishers [1955] 580 p. Bibliography: p. 559—576.

> *Hoover, LC, NYPL, Col, BDIC, Felt*

153 FOSTER, William Z.
Istoriia trekh Internatsionalov. Mezhdunarodnoe sotsialisticheskoe
i kommunisticheskoe dvizhenie s 1848 goda do nastoiashchego vremeni. Moskva, 1959. 618 p.   *SInSt*

154 GARCIA, Venero Maximiano
Historia de las internacionales en España. [Madrid] Ediciones del
Movimiento, 1956—1957. 3 vols.

> **Contents:** [Vol. 1] 1868—1914.—Vol. 2. De la primera guerra mundial al 18 julio
> de 1936.—Vol. 3. Del 18 julio de 1936 al 1 de abril de 1939.   *Hoover*

155 GUILBEAUX, Henri
Le mouvement socialiste et syndicaliste français pendant la guerre
(esquisse historique) 1914—1918; préface de N. Lenine. Petrograd,
Editions de l'Internationale communiste, 1919. 68 p.   *Hoover*

156 KAUTSKY, Karl
Die Internationale. Wien, Volksbuchhandlung, 1920. 88 p. **Cover-title:**
Vergangenheit und Zukunft der Internationale.   *Hoover, NYPL*

157 KAUTSKY, Karl
Die Internationale und Sowjetrussland. Berlin, J. H. W. Dietz Nachfolger [c1925] 62 p.   *Hoover*

158 LENZ, Josef [pseud. of Joseph Winternitz]
Istoriia Vtorogo Internatsionala. Red. i vstup. stat'ia Karla Radeka.

Perevod s nemetskogo A. V. Vol'skogo [pseud.] i I. B. Rumera. Moskva, "Ogonek", 1931. 285 p. illus., plates, port. groups, facsims.

Hoover

159 LENZ, Josef [pseud. of Joseph Winternitz]
Die II. [zweite] Internationale und ihr Erbe, 1889—1929. Hamburg, Carl Hoym Nachfolger [c1930] 302 p.

Hoover, NYPL

160 MIJUŠKOVIĆ, Milisav, ed.
Prva — Druga — Treća Internacionala; gradja za proučavanje delatnosti triju internacionala. Beograd, Rad, 1950—51. 4 vols. in 1 (Biblioteka istorije medjunarodnog radničkog i socijalističkog pokreta)

Volume I deals with the First International; vol. II with the Second; and vols. III and IV with the Communist International.

Hoover, Col, Felt

161 PERTICONE, Giacomo
Le tre Internazionali. Roma, Atlantica [1944] 374 p. (Materiali per servire alla storia del socialismo italiano)

Hoover, NYPL, Harv

162 POSTGATE, Raymond W.
The Workers' International. London, The Swarthmore Press; New York, Harcourt Brace, 1920. 125 p. On cover: The Swarthmore International Handbooks [6]

A historical essay on the three Internationals, dealing broadly with the First International (83 p.), very briefly with the Second (p. 85—91), and somewhat more broadly with the Third (p. 93—107). Five "Appendixes" contain details on the organization and congresses of all three Internationals. Hoover has also a second printing, dated 1921, identical with 1920 printing. Harvard has only second printing. *Hoover, LC, NYPL, Harv, Col*

163 RADEK, Karl
Tri Internatsionala; lektsii, prochitannye v Sverdlovskom universitete. [Simferopol', Krymgosizdat, 1924] 55 p. *Hoover*

164 RIESCO LARRAIN, J. Luis
La revolución social; de su génesis y de su desarollo. Santiago de Chile, Lagunas & Co., 1924. 693 p. *NYPL*

165 STEIN, Alexander [pseud. of Alexander Rubinstein]
Das Problem der Internationale. Mit Anhang: Resolutionen und Richtlinien der zweiten und dritten Internationale. Berlin, „Freiheit", 1919, 48 p. *Hoover, BDIC, Felt*

166 THAL, Robert
Deuxième ou Troisième Internationale? Préface de Boris Souvarine.
Paris [n. d.] 32 p.   *Amst, Felt*

167 TILAK, K.
Rise and fall of the Comintern; from the First to the Fourth International. [1st ed. n. p., Spark Syndicate, 1947] 157 p.

    "Seeks to recount the principal betrayals of the international working class
    movement by the Third (Communist) International since 1923." Pref.
                                        Hoover, Harv

168 La TROISIÈME Internationale est l'héritière de la première (thèses
pour le 60-e anniversaire de la fondation de la 1-re Internationale).
Paris, Librairie de l'Humanité, 1924. 32 p. (Petite bibliothèque communiste)   *Hoover, Harv, NWest, Amst, BDIC, Felt*

6. Efforts toward the founding of the Third International

a) During World War I

BOR'BA bol'shevikov za sozdanie Kommunisticheskogo Internatsionala; materialy i dokumenty; 1914—1919 gg. See no. 96.

169 FAINSOD, Merle
International socialism and the world war. Cambridge, Mass., Harvard University Press, 1935. xi, 238 p.

    "The present work is intended as the first part of a larger study wich will be
    concerned with the post-war role of the Third International." Pref.
                                Hoover, LC, Harv, Col, Felt

170 FAINSOD, Merle
The origins of the Third International, 1914—1919. Typewritten, 350 p.
(Harvard University Ph. D. dissertation, 1932)   *Harv*

171 FEDORINA, Aleksandra
V. I. Lenin v bor'be za sozdanie Kommunisticheskogo Internatsionala;
materialy k lektsiiam po istorii KPSS. [Moskva] 1959. 47 p.

                                  Hoover, LC, Harv, Col

GANKIN, Olga Hess and Fisher, Harold H.
The Bolsheviks and the World War. See no. 104.

172 MAXE, Jean, pseud.
De Zimmerwald au bolchevisme; ou, Le triumphe du Marxisme pan-germaniste; essai sur les menées internationalistes pendant la guerre, 1914—1920. Paris, Editions Bossard, 1920. 236 p.

Hoover

173 SMIRNOVSKII, V.
Bor'ba Lenina i Stalina za sozdanie Tret'ego Kommunisticheskogo Internatsionala. [Leningrad] Lenizdat, 1940. 71 p.   *Hoover, NYPL*

174 TROTSKII, Lev D.
Voina i revoliutsiia; krushenie Vtorogo Internatsionala i podgotovka Tret'ego. Petrograd, Gos. izd-vo, 1922, 1923. 2 vols. 371, 519 p. maps, ports.

> These volumes present a combination of Trotski's original writings (Intro-duction, "From the Swiss diary," "The war and the International," etc.) and reprints of his articles in newspapers published in Russia and abroad, during the years 1914—1922. They present Trotski's views on international affairs in general, and on the question of the II-nd International in particular, written before and after he joined Lenin and the Bolsheviks.
>
> *Hoover, LC, Col, BDIC*

b) **The International Meeting Preparatory to the Founding of the Communist International, Moscow, December 19, 1918**

175 SOVETSKAIA Rossiia i narody mira; s predisl. Maksima Gor'kogo; rechi, proiznesennye na mezhdunarodnom mitinge v Petrograde. Petrograd, Gos. izd-vo (Petrogradskoe otdelenie), 1919. 48 p. ports.

> This meeting was attended by persons from various countries who happened to be in Russia at that time and who were introduced to the meeting as "representatives" of their respective countries. Among them should be men-tioned: Reinstein (USA), Sadoul (France), Lao (China) Fineberg (Great Britain), Akhmed (India), Halders (USA), Horn (Austria), Sirola (Finland) and Ritters (Netherlands). The meeting was chaired by Maxim Gorky. Zinov'ev, who represented the Petrograd Soviet, said among other things: "I consider our present meeting only as a small prelude to the future great congress of the true third International, which, I am convinced, will also meet in Petrograd..." (p. 11). It should be mentioned that many of the foreign participants of this meeting were also "representatives" of their countries at a second meeting in Moscow on March 2—19, 1919, at which the Communist International was founded.   *Hoover*

176 SOWJETRUSSLAND und die Völker der Welt; Reden auf der Internationalen Versammlung in Petrograd am 19. Dezember 1918; mit einem Vorwort von Maxim Gorki. Petrograd, Verlag der „Kommunistischen Internationale", 1920. 54 p. ports.

    See annotation to no. 175.   *Hoover, Amst*

177 La RUSSIE des Soviets et les peuples du monde; discours prononcés au meeting international de Petrograd, le 19 décembre 1918; avec pref. de Maxime Gorky. Petrograd, Internationale Communiste, 1920. 39 p. ports.

    See annotation to no. 175.   *Amst, Felt*

PART II.

THE COMMUNIST INTERNATIONAL

1. Memoirs and personal accounts

178 BALABANOFF, Angelica

My life as a rebel. New York and London, Harper & Brothers, 1938.
ix, 324 p. ports., facsim. At head of title: Angelica Balabanoff. Il-
lustrated lining-papers. "First edition."   *Hoover*

179 BALABANOFF, Angelica

Ricordi di una socialista. Roma, D.de Luigi, 1946. 387 p.   *Hoover*

179a BUBER-NEUMANN (pseud. of Faust, Margarethe Anna)

Von Potsdam nach Moskau. Stationen eines Irrweges. Stuttgart, Deutsche Verlags-Anstalt [c1957] 477 p.

> Reminiscences of the wife of Heinz Neumann, a prominent German communist
> and "apparatchik" of the Comintern. References to Comintern activities in Ger-
> many, China, and Spain. Details on abortive communist revolt in Canton in
> December 1927.   *Hoover*

180 BUDENZ, Louis F.

This is my story. New York, Whittlesey House, 1947. 379 p. index.

> A personal account of a prominent former member of the Communist Party
> of America. Many references to the activities of the Communist International
> and its representatives in the United States.   *Hoover*

181 CANNON, James P.

The first ten years of American Communism; Report of a Participant.
New York, Lyle Stuart [c1962] 343 p. (Preface by Theodore Draper.)

> Part I contains "Letters to a historian" in which the author answered questions
> of Theodore Draper.—Part II contains an essay on "The Russian Revolution
> and the American Negro Movement."—In Part III the author discusses "The
> Forerunners" of the leftist movement in America: Debs, and the I. W. W.—
> Part IV includes a critical review of Draper's "The Roots of American Com-
> munism" and "American Communism and Soviet Russia."—Throughout the
> book, particularly in Parts I and II, there are many references to the Com-
> munist International.   *Hoover*

182 CASTRO DELGADO, Enrique
Hombres made in Moscú. Para la portada de este libro ha sido utilizado un cuadro del pintor Ramón Ponotones. Mexico, 1960. 737 p. illus. *Hoover*

183 CASTRO DELGADO, Enrique
J'ai perdu la foi à Moscou, traduit et adapté de l'espagnol par Jean Talbot. 6 ed. Paris [Paris] Gallimard [1950] 350 p. *Hoover, BDIC*

184 CASTRO DELGADO, Enrique
La vida secreta de la Komintern; cómo perdí la fé en Moscú. Madrid, Ediciones y Publicaciones Españoles, 1950. 419 p. *Hoover, BDIC*

185 DIOGOT, Vladimir A.
V "svobodnom" podpol'e. Vospominaniia o podpol'noi rabote zagranitsei v 1919—1921 godakh. Moskva, Gos. izd-vo, 1923, 87 p. At head of title: Komissiia po istorii Oktiabr'skoi revoliutsii i R.K.P.(b).

The next two items are enlarged second and third editions of the above item. *Hoover, NYPL*

186 DIOGOT, Vladimir A.
Pod znamenem bol'shevizma; zapiski podpol'shchika. 2-e perer. i dop. izd. Moskva, Izd-vo Vsesoiuznogo ob-va politkatorzhan, 1931. 274 p. illus.

See note to preceding item. *Hoover, NYPL*

187 DIOGOT, Vladimir A.
Pod znamenem bol'shevizma; zapiski podpol'shchika. 3-e perer. i dop. izd. Moskva, Izd-vo Vsesoiuznogo ob-va politkatorzhan, 1933. 416 p. illus.

See note to no. 185. *NYPL*

188 DISCH, M.
Von den Weltkongressen in Moskau 1921. Tagebuchblätter. Hamburg, Verlag der Druck- und Verlagsanstalt Albert Fr. Heil [n. d.] 72 p. *Felt*

189 DUMBADZE, Evgenii V.
Na sluzhbe Cheka i Kominterna; lichnyia vospominaniia. So vstup. stat'ei V. L. Burtseva i s predisl. G. A. Solomona. Paris, Izd-vo "Mishen", 159 p. illus., facsims. *Hoover, NYPL, BDIC*

190 FOSTER, William Z.
From Bryan to Stalin. [New York] International Publishers [c1937] 352 p.

"...the later chapters deal with the period after my affiliation to the Communist party." Preface. Discusses also the early period of the Communist International and the Red International of Trade Unions; the author was very active in both of them.   *Hoover*

191 FOSTER, William Z.
Pages from a worker's life. New York, International Publishers [c1939] 314 p.

"The present book is a sequel to »From Bryan to Stalin«. It contains personal material which did not fit into the scheme of the preceding volume." Foreword.   *Hoover*

192 FROSSARD, Ludovic Oscar
De Jaurès à Lénine; notes et souvenirs d'un militant. Paris, Bibliothèque de documentation sociale, 1930. 309 p. ports.   *Hoover*

193 GITLOW, Benjamin
I confess; the truth about American communism. With an introduction by Max Eastman. New York, Dutton & Co. [1940] viii, 611 p.

A personal account exposing the relations between the Comintern, its representatives in the United States, and the Communist Party of America.
                                                   Hoover, LC, NYPL, Harv

194 GITLOW, Benjamin
The whole of their lives; communism in America, a personal history and intimate portrayal of its leaders. New York, Scribner's Sons, 1948. xvi, 387 p.

A continuation and elaboration of the account listed above.
                                                   Hoover, LC, NYPL, Harv, Col

195 HUMBERT-DROZ, Jules
"L'œil de Moscou" à Paris. (1922—1924) Textes et notes établis avec la collaboration de Annie Kriegel. [Paris Collection Archives Julliard, 1964] 265 p., illus.

Personal notes and correspondence concerning relations between the French C. P. and the Comintern 1921–1928.   *Hoover*

196 KRIVITSKY, Walter G.
In Stalin's Secret Service; an exposé of Russia's secret pulicies by the former chief of the Soviet intelligence in Western Europe. New York, Harper & Bros. 1939. xv, 273 p.

Disclosures about the Comintern's involvement in Soviet intelligence work.
                                                   Hoover

197 KRIVITSKY, Walter G.
Agent de Staline. Paris, Coopération [c1940] 320 p. (Traduit de l'anglais par André Pierre.)

> French translation of preceding item. *Hoover*

197a LEONHARD, Wolfgang
Child of the revolution. Translated by C. M. Woodhouse. Chicago, Regnery, 1958. 447 p.

> Translation of *Die Revolution entlässt ihre Kinder*. For annotation see next item. *Hoover*

197b LEONHARD, Wolfgang
Die Revolution entläßt ihre Kinder. Köln-Berlin, Kiepenheuer & Witsch [c1955] 557 p.

> Several chapters describe the author's expriences as a student of the Comintern school in Kushnarenkovo for future communist party functionaries in various countries, and his participation in the reorganization of the Comintern archives in Ufa. *Hoover*

198 MURPHY, John Thomas
New Horizons. London, John Lane [1941] 352 p. illus.

> An "autobiography". *Hoover, LC, Harv, Felt*

199 ROY, Manabendra Nath
My crime. [Bombay, R. D. Nadkarni, 1937] 19 p. "Reprinted from Independent India dated 27th June 1937."

> Written shortly after the author's expulsion from the Communist International. Cf. p. [1] *Hoover*

200 SERGE, Victor
Mémoires d'un révolutionnaire, 1901—1941. Paris, Editions du Seuil [1951] 416 p. *Hoover*

201 SERGE, Victor
Le tournant obscur. Paris, Iles d'or [1951] 170 p. *Hoover*

201a VALTIN, Jan (pseud. of Krebs, R. J. H.)
Out of the night. New York, Alliance Book Corp. [c1941] 749 p.

> Reminiscences of a Comintern agent who started as a member of the Spartacus Bund. Describes conditions and work of illegal Comintern agencies in many countries. Covers period 1919—1937. *Hoover*

202 WICKS, Harry M.
Eclipse of October. Chicago, Challenge Publishers, 1957. 464 p.

A personal account, published posthumously. The author tries to prove his view that "a Kremlin tyranny arose that was able to obliterate the achievements of the Russian Bolshevik revolution of October 1917, and to turn to its own designs the various parties in other countries that comprised the Communist International." (p. v)   *Hoover, Col*

2. History of the Communist International

203 AKADEMIIA nauk SSSR. Institut istorii.
Sovetskaia Rossiia i kapitalisticheskii mir v 1917—1923 gg. Moskva, Gos. izd-vo polit. lit-ry, 1957. 694 p.

Chapter IX, entitled "The International Communist Movement in 1918—1923" (p. 439—473), of this collective work on Soviet Russia's relations with the non-communist countries deals with the founding and activities of the Communist International up to 1923. It also contains a short account of "The rise and activities of the democratic mass organizations", that is, the Communist Youth International and the Red International of Labor Unions. Chapter IX was written by N. M. Lavrov.

Throughout the entire volume there are many references to the communist parties in the non-communist ("capitalist") countries, to their role in the development of relations between these countries and the Soviet Union, and to the relations of these parties with the Communist International.

The presentation of facts and events is very selective, emphasizing the Soviet point of view.   *Hoover*

205 ALDRED, Guy Alfred
For communism; a communist manifesto defining the workers' struggle and the need of a new Communist International. With a history of the anti-parliamentary movement, 1906—1935. Glasgow, G. A. Aldred, 1935. 120 p.   *Hoover*

206 ARTUSKI, J.
Metamorfozy Kominternu (1929—1935). Z przedmową W. Altera. Warszawa, Wydawnictwo "Myśli Socjalistycznej", 1935. 48 p.   *Amst*

207 BAUMBÖCK, Karl
Deutschlands Sieg im Osten, Grundlage für das neue Europa. Berlin, P. Hochmut, 1942. 87 p.

Nazi propaganda pamphlet against the Soviet Union and the Communist International.   *Hoover*

208 BELIĆ-FRANIĆ, Stevan
Stvaranje treće internacionale. 2., dop. izd. Beograd, Rad, 1959. 31 p.
(Radnički universitet. Medjunarodni radnički pokret. 2. kolo)
Harv, Felt

209 BERZIN, IA.
Partiia bol'shevikov v bor'be za Kommunisticheskii Internatsional. Moskva, Lennigrad, "Moskovskii rabochii", 1931. 127 p. *Hoover*

210 BEWER, O.
L'Internationale communiste et ses sections après le VIe congrès. Paris, Bureau d'Editions, 1932. 102 p. (Les documents de l'Internationale.)
BDIC

211 BOJ o kominternu. [S účast. A. Pollaka, L. Trockého, G. Zinovéva i dr. Praha, 1927] 143 p. *Amst*

212 BORKENAU, Franz
The Communist International. London, Faber and Faber [1938] 442 p.

A rather journalistic report on the history of the C. I. covering the years up to 1937. Written by a former communist, it is well informed but is, at present, dated. "First published in September 1938." "Bibliographical notes": p. 430—436. For 1962 paperback reprint see no. 219.
Hoover, LC, NYPL, Harv, Amst, Felt

213 BORKENAU, Franz
Der europäische Kommunismus; seine Geschichte von 1917 bis zur Gegenwart. München, Lehnen Verlag [c1952] 540 p.

This is a translation from the English (London) orginal of "European Communism" (see no. 215) prepared by the author himself, who states in the Preface that "here and there I added a few words". It is a continuation of Borkenau's earlier book, "The Communist International", the contents of which, in a greatly condensed form, are included in the present volume. Several chapters of the volume deal with the Comintern, containing valuable information on its activities. An important volume for the study of the history of the Communist International. *Hoover, LC, NYPL, Harv, Col, Amst*

214 BORKENAU, Franz
Der europäische Kommunismus; seine Geschichte von 1917 bis zur Gegenwart. Bern, Francke [1952] 540 p.

Swiss edition of preceding item. *Hoover, BDIC, Felt*

215 BORKENAU, Franz
European Communism. London, Faber & Faber [1953] 564 p.

See annotation to no. 213. *LC, NYPL, BDIC, Felt*

216 BORKENAU, Franz
European Communism. New York, Harper [1953] 564 p.

American edition of no. 215.   *Hoover, LC, NYPL, Harv, Col*

217 BORKENAU, Franz
Storia del comunismo europeo (1917—1948). A cura di Salvatore
Francesco Romano. Traduzione di Luisa LaMalfa. Venezia, Neri Pozza
Editore, 1963. 684 p. (Studi politici, no. 10.)   *Felt*

218 BORKENAU, Franz
World communism; a history of the Communist International. New
York, W. W. Norton & Co. [1939] 442 p.

A London reprint of "The Communist International" (see no. 212), produced for
a New York distributor.   *LC, NYPL, Harv*

219 BORKENAU, Franz
World communism; a history of the Communist International. New
introduction by Raymond Aron. [Ann Arbor] University of Michigan
Press [1962] 442 p. Ann Arbor paperbacks, AA67.

"First published in 1938 under title: The Communist International". An American
paperback reprint of the London edition, no. 212.
                              Hoover, LC, NYPL, Col

220 BOUSCAREN, Anthony T.
Imperial Communism. [Washington] Public Affairs Press [1953] 256 p.
                              Hoover

221 BRASLAVSKII, I.
Istoriia mezhdunarodnogo rabochego dvizhenia (1864—1924). [Mos-
kva] "Novaia Moskva", 1925. 281 p.   *Hoover*

222 BRASOL, Boris L.
Mir na pereput'ie. Perevod s angliiskago E. L. Brasola. Belgrad, 1922.
318 p.   *Hoover, NYPL*

223 BRASOL, Boris L.
The World at the Cross Roads. Boston, Small, Maynard & Co. [c1921]
409 p.   *Hoover, LC, NYPL*

224 BUKHARTSEV, Dmitrii
Teoreticheskie oruzhenostsy opportunizma; oshibki pravykh v mezhdu-
narodnykh voprosakh. Moskva, Gos. izd-vo, 1930. 134 p.

A sharp polemic with Bukharin, referring to his activities in the Communist
International.   *NYPL*

225 BULLEJOS, José
Europa entre dos guerras; 1918—1938. Mexico, Ediciones Castilla, 1945. 238 p.

> A political history of Europe written by a prominent Spanish communist who for a few years was a member of the Executive Committee of the Communist International; he was later expelled from the party and jailed in Spain, only to reappear during the civil war as editor of a Communist Party newspaper. The Communist International played a prominent role in the author's history. Dates and facts are often misleadingly inaccurate.
>
> *Hoover*

226 BURMEISTER, Alfred, pseud.
Dissolution and Aftermath of the Comintern: experiences and observations, 1937—1947. New York, Research Program on the USSR, 1955. 43 p. (Mimeographed Series, 77.)
Hoover, LC, NYPL, Col, Amst, BDIC

227 CANNON, James P.
The end of the Comintern, by James P. Cannon; with the Manifesto of the 4th International. New York, Pioneer Publishers [1943] 34 p. "Printed for the Socialist workers party."
Hoover, LC, NYPL, Col

228 CARR, Edward Hallett
A History of Soviet Russia, London, Macmillan; New York, St. Martin's Press, 1951—59. 6 vols.

> Includes bibliographies.
>
> Contents:
> [1—3] The Bolshevik Revolution, 1917—1923 (1951—53)
> [4]　　The Interregnum, 1923—24 (1954)
> [5—6] Socialism in one country, 1924—26 (1958—59)
> Volumes 4—6 contain many references to the Communist International.
> *Hoover, LC, NYPL, Hav, Col*

229 CARVALHO e Souza, Odette de
Komintern. Rio [de Janeiro] J. Olympio, 1938. ix, 379 p.
Hoover, LC, NYPL, Col

230 CATHEREIN, Viktor
Die Dritte Internationale. Freiburg im Breisgau, Herder, 1921. 28 p. (Flugschriften der „Stimmen der Zeit", 23.)
Hoover, Col, Amst, BDIC

CHE cos'e' e che vuole l'Internazionale comunista? See no. 1938.

231 Le CHEMIN de l'Internationale Communiste; guide pour l'histoire de l'I. C. [Les thèses elaborées par la Section d'agitation et de propagande de l'I. C. de l'Internationale Communiste à l'occasion du XVe anniversaire de l'I. C.] Paris, Bureau d'editions, 1934. 53 p. (Les documents de l'Internationale Communiste)

For annotation and English edition see no. 242. For German edition see no. 289. For Russian edition see no. 319. Spanish edition no. 328.

Hoover, BDIC

232 CHTO takoe Tretii Kommunisticheskii Internatsional? Manifest Kommunisticheskoi partii k proletariiam vsego mira. So stat'iami N. Lenina i V. Karpinskogo. Samara, Samarsk. gub. agentstvo Vserossiisk. tsentral'n. isponitel'n. komiteta soveta rab., k. k. i k. deputatov, "TSentropechat'", 1919, 24 p.

A popular propaganda pamphlet containing: an article by V. Karpinskii explaining what the Internationals are; a short description of the founding congress of the Communist International; the text of the Manifesto of this congress; and a short article by Lenin, [Zavoevannoe i zapisannoe] with a very optimistic prophecy of world revolution in the nearest future. *Hoover*

233 CHTO takoe Tretii Kommunisticheskii Internatsional? Manifest Kommunisticheskoi partii k proletariiam vsego mira. So stat'iami N. Lenina i V. Karpinskogo. Moskva, Gos. izd-vo, 1920. 32 p. (Rechi i besedy agitatora No. 7.) At head of title: Rossiiskaia Sotsialisticheskaia Federativnaia Sovetskaia Respublika.

For annotation see preceding item. *Hoover*

234 COLE, G. D. H.
A History of Socialist Thought. London, Macmillan, 1950—1960. 5 vols. in 7 parts.

Vol. IV "Communism and Social Democracy" contains a chapter on "The Rival Internationals, 1919—1921" in which the author stresses the background and main events which led to the founding of the Communist International. There are many references in later chapters of this volume to the Comintern and its relations with the communist parties in various countries.

Hoover, LC, NYPL, Harv, Col, BDIC

234a COMMUNIST International. Amsterdam Sub-Bureau.
New offensive against Soviet Russia; communication of the Amsterdam Sub-Bureau of the third International. [Distributed by the Central Executive Committee of the Communist Party of America, 1920?] [2] p.

Published probably in the spring of 1920 and denouncing an "Entente offensive" against Soviet Russia. Preceding the "Hands off Russia" slogan of the Communist International. Particularly directed against Poland and Japan.

Hoover, LC

234b DIMITROV, G.
Borba protiv imperialisticheskata voina [Sofiia] Izdatelstvo na Bl'gar-skata Komunisticheska Partiia [1949] 42 p.

> This is a belated Bulgarian translation of Dimitrov's article in *Pravda* of May 1, 1940 and of an appeal of the ECCI to the workers of the entire world of the same date. For contents see annotation to no. 235c. It is noteworthy that the Bulgarian translation of two items reflecting Soviet policy during the Nazi-Soviet friendship period were issued by the Communist Party of Bulgaria in 1949.
>
> *Hoover*

235 DIMITROV, Georgii
Communism and the war; together with the manifesto of the Executive Committe of the Communist International, issued November 6th, 1939. [London, Modern Books, 1939] 24 p.

> This pamphlet bearing the printing date November 18, 1939, was published during the Nazi-Soviet friendship period and reflects contemporary Comintern policy. Dimitrov explains Stalin's farsighted policy which led to the conclusion of "the Germano-Soviet 'Amity and Frontier' Treaty" and to the defeat of anti-Soviet war plans of "the capitalist imperialists". He labels the war against Nazi Germany as "an imperialist war, an unjust war", fought in the interest of the capitalist imperialists, — Great Britain, France and the United States. The Secretary General of the E. C. C. I. appeals to the working class of all countries to oppose this "unjust war", to return to the tactic of the united front "from below", and to defeat the Social Democratic leadership which is "openly supporting the imperialist war".
>
> Dimitrov's article is followed by a "Statement issued by the Executive Committee of the Communist International on the twenty-second anniversary of the socialist revolution, November 6, 1939". This statement (called on the cover "manifesto") is in the same vein as Dimitrov's article. Its concluding slogans call for "no support for the policy of the ruling classes aimed at continuing and spreading the imperialist slaughter! Fight for the immediate cessation of the plundering, unjust, imperialist war!"
>
> This pamphlet is at present one of the most unique and rare items, since after the German attack on the Soviet Union, communists everywhere were supposed to have destroyed it.
>
> *Hoover, NYPL, Felt*

235a DIMITROV, G.
La guerra y la clase obrera de los paises capitalistas. Mexico, D. F., Editorial popular, 1939. 22 p.

> For annotation see no. 236 a.
>
> *Hoover*

235b DIMITROV, G.
La guerre et la classe ouvrière des pays capitalistes. Moscou, Editions en langues etrangères, 1939. 23 p.

> For annotation see no. 236 a.
>
> *Hoover*

235c DIMITROV, G.

La lutte contre la guerre imperialiste. Moscou, Éditions en langues étrangères, 1940. 22 p. Cover title.

This pamphlet contains a translation of an article published by Dimitrov in the Moscow *Pravda* of May 1, 1940 and a "May-Day" appeal of the ECCI issued "to the workers of the entire world" on the same day.

Both documents follow an identical political line. They accuse Britain and France for violating the neutrality of "the Scandinavian countries" and excuse the German occupation of Norway and Denmark as its consequence. The Soviet aggression against Finland is also explained as a necessary consequence of the wrongdoings of the "Anglo-Fench war provocateurs". As in the November 1939 Dimitrov article and ECCI appeal (see no. 235), the war against Nazi Germany is qualified as an "imperialist war", and the main attack is now directed against the Social Democrats in the West and their French and British leaders. Both, Dimitrov and the ECCI appeal, recommend to the workers in the "capitalist countries" to oppose the war and to form "a united front of the workers, a popular front of the workers, accomplished from below by the masses".

Hoover

235d DIMITROV, G.

The struggle against the imperialist war. [By Georgi Dimitrov, General Secretary of the Communist International. New York, Workers Library Publishers, May 1940] 23 p. Cover title.

First published as an article in *Pravda* (Moscow) of May 1, 1940. For annotation see no. 235 c.   *Hoover*

236 DIMITROV, Georgii

La Terza Internazionale. Traduzione e nota di Giorgio Karisky. Introduzione di Wolf Giusti. Roma, Edizioni del Secolo O. E. T. [1945] xix, 255 p.

Entry taken from Feltrinelli library catalog. Obviously a selection of Dimitrov's speeches and writings on the Communist International.   *Felt*

236a DIMITROV, G.

The war and the working class. [By Georgi Dimitrov, General Secretary of the Communist International. New York, Workers Library Publishers, October 1939] 23 p. Cover title.

In October 1939, hence after the Nazi aggression against Poland and after the partition of that country by Hitler and Stalin, the General Secretary of the Comintern, Dimitrov, published a pamphlet, in which he conveyed to communists in the entire world the following evaluation of the war of the Allies against Nazi Germany: "In its character and essence, the present war is, on the part of both warring sides, an imperialist, unjust war, despite the fraudulent slogans being employed by the ruling classes of the warring capitalist states..." (p. 4–5) According to Dimitrov, the United States "are aiming to drive their rivals out of the world markets, to strengthen their imperialist positions and to consolidate their domination on the seas and oceans." (p. 6) Nazi Germany is credited with the wisdom to have made "a decisive turn in its foreign policy and to take the path of peaceful relations with the Soviet Union." (p. 9) The Secretary General of the Comintern appeals to "the working class" everywhere for a "courageous struggle against the imperialist war, ... [and to] struggle to end this predatory war." (p. 13) At present this is a very rare pamphlet.   *Hoover*

237 La DISSOLUTION de l'Internationale Communiste. [Vichy] Information de l'Etat Français, juin 1943. 8 p. (Revue de la presse communiste. Juin 1943.)

A short history of the Communist International produced by the Vichy government.   *BDIC*

238 La DISSOLUTION du Komintern. [n. p.] Ed. des Cahiers du Monde Nouveau, 1943. 32 p. (Faits et Documents)

"Collaborationist propaganda pamphlet..." (BDIC)   *BDIC, Felt*

239 DIXIÈME anniversaire de la fondation de la IIIe Internationale; 1919— 1929. Les étapes de l'Internationale communiste. Paris, Bureau d'éditions [1929] 38 p.   *Hoover, Amst, Felt*

239a DRAPER, Theodore
American Communism and Soviet Russia; the formative period. New York, The Viking Press, 1960. 558 p. (A volume in the series: Communism in American Life.)

With a well documented history of the Communist Party of America (1919–1929) as background, the study discusses the relations between this Party and the Comintern, and through it, with Soviet Russia. It describes the role played by the Comintern and its representatives in the United States in the internal factional strife and in the struggle for party leadership. Its documentation exposes the subserviency of the Party to the Communist International and to the interests of the Soviet Union. Extensive source references. Index.   *Hoover, LC*

240 EFWE, pseud.
An alle, gleichviel ob für oder gegen die 21 Bedingungen der Dritten Internationale. [n. p., 1920?] 8 p.   *Hoover, LC, Amst*

241 FEIND im Rücken! Bilder aus der Geschichte der Kommunistischen Internationale. Wien, Verlag Wiener Volksbuchhandlung, 1932. 90 p.
                                                                                      NYPL

241a FERRAT, André
La révolution russe et la IIIe Internationale [Paris, 1947. 28 p.] (*Spartacus*, cahiers mensuels, sér. 1. no. 20.)   *Hoover*

242 15 [FIFTEEN] years of the Communist International; theses for instructors. [New York, Workers Library Publishers, 1934] 51 p.

"Contains the theses of the Agitprop of the Executive Committee of the Communist International prepared in connection with the fifteenth anniversary of the Communist International."
For French text see no. 231. For German text see no. 289. For Russian text see no. 319.   *Hoover, NYPL, Harv, Col, UTex, Amst*

243 FOOTMAN, David, ed.
International communism. London, Chatto & Windus, 1960. 151 p. ("'St. Anthon'y Papers'. Number 9.")

Contents:
Degras, Jane
United front tactics in the Comintern 1921—1928. p. 9—22.
Lowenthal, Richard
The bolshevisation of the Spartacus League. p. 23—71.
Hunt, R. N. Carew
Willi Muenzenberg. p. 72—87.
Browder, Earl
Socialism in America. p. 88—104.
Wint, Guy
Communism in India. p. 105—127.
Leonhard, Wolfgang
International Communism: the Present Phase. p. 128—149.   *Hoover, Felt*

244 FROM revolution to reaction; a history of the 3rd International. [Chicago] Revolutionary Workers League of the U. S. [1942] 31 p.
NYPL

245 FROSSARD, Ludovic Oscar
La décomposition du communisme; Vers l'unité du prolétariat. Paris, Librairie de l'Egalité [1923] 105 p. (Les Cahiers jauresièns [no. 1])
Hoover

246 GAUTHEROT, Gustave
Le monde communiste. Paris, "Spes", 1925. iv, 260 p. maps.   *BDIC*

247 GEGEN die Fälschung der Geschichte der bolschewistischen Partei. Moskau, Verlagsgenossenschaft ausländischer Arbeiter in der UdSSR, 1932. 74 p. On cover: Dokumente und Reden.   *NYPL*

GIUNTER, G.
Shestoi kongress Kominterna. See: Istoriia Kommunisticheskogo Internatsionala v kongressakh; no. 253.

GLAUBAUF, F.
Tretii Kongress Kominterna. See: Istoriia Kommunisticheskogo Internatsionala v kongressakh; no. 253.

248 GORTER, Hermann
Die Moskauer Internationale. [Berlin, n. d.] 16 p.   *BDIC*

249 GUREVICH, A. M.
Zarozhdenie i razvitie Kominterna. Izd. 2. perer. i dop. [Khar'kov?]
Proletarii, 1931. [Pagination not given]   *Harv*

250 HASS, Eric
The Socialist Labor Party and the Internationals. New York, New York
Labor News Co., 1949. 187 p. illus., ports.

> Appendixes: 1. S. L. P. declaration on the dissolution of the Communist Inter-
> national.—2. Report of S. L. P. observers at the "Third International" Congress,
> 1921.—3. The "21 points."   *Hoover, LC, Col*

251 HULSE, James W.
The Forming of the Communist International. Stanford, Stanford University Press, 1964. 275 p.

> A well documented history of the founding and the early activities of the
> Communist International, emphasizing particularly the development of the
> organization during the period between the first and second Congresses.
>   *Hoover*

IABLONSKII, M.
Vtoroi kongress Kominterna. See: Istoriia Kommunisticheskogo Internatsionala v kongressakh; no. 253.

252 INTERNATIONALER Sozialistischer Kampfbund.
Russland und die Komintern. Gedanken für einen internationalen
sozialistischen Neuaufbau. Herausgegeben vom I. S. K. [Intern. Sozial.
Kampfbund, Welwyn Garden City, Herts, "Renaissance" Publishing
Co. 1942?] 64 p.   *LC, Felt*

253 ISTORIIA Kommunisticheskogo Internatsionala v kongressakh; pod red.
A. Lozovskogo. 3. izd. [Kharkov] Izd-vo "Proletarii", 1929—1930,
6 vols.

> Particular volumes:
> 1. Mingulin, I., Pervyi kongress Kominterna. 63 p.
> 2. Iablonskii, M., Vtoroi kongress Kominterna. 59 p.
> 3. Glaubauf, F., Tretii kongress Konminterna. 57 p.
> 4. Tivel, A., Chetvertyi kongress Kominterna. 70 p.
> 5. Vil'iams, B., Piatyi kongress Kominterna. 65 p.
> 6. Giunter, G., Shestoi kongress Kominterna. 69 p.
>
> All items in the Hoover Institution's Library are third editions. Other libraries
> did not indicate the edition, but have the same years of publication. The

Feltrinelli Institute catalog indicates Moscow as the assumed place of publication, placing Moscow in parentheses. This assumption seems to be inaccurate.
Hoover (1–6), *NYPL* (1), *Col* (2–6), *Felt* (1–6), *SInSt* (1–6)

254 IUZEFOVICH, Iosif
Osnovanie Kommunisticheskogo Internatsionala. Moskva, Leningrad, Izd-vo Akademii nauk SSSR, 1940. 274 p. ports. At head of title: Akademiia nauk Soiuza SSR   *Hoover*

255 JAMES, Cyril R.
World revolution, 1917—1936; the rise and fall of the Communist International. London, M. Secker and Warburg, Ltd. [1937] xii, 429 p.

"How much the book owes to the writings of Trotsky, the text can only partially show." p. xii.   *Hoover, Col, Amst, BDIC, Felt*

256 JAMES, Cyril R.
World revolution, 1917—1936; the rise and fall of the Communist International. New York, Pioneer Publishers, 1937. xii, 429 p.

For annotation see preceding item.   *Harv, Felt*

257 JORDI, Hugo
Die Krise der internationalen Arbeiterbewegung. Zürich, Verlag Proletarische Einheit, 1932. 134 p.   *NYPL, Felt*

258 KABAKCHIEV, Khristo St.
Die Entstehung und Entwicklung der Komintern; kurzer Abriss der Geschichte der Komintern. Vorwort von A. Bennet. Hamburg-Berlin, C. Hoym Nachfolger [c1929] 174 p.

Bennet's foreword (p. 5—35) has title: Die Lehren des ersten Jahrzehnts der Komintern. Statt eines Vorwortes.
Hoover, LC, NYPL, Harv, Col, Amst, Felt

259 KABAKCHIEV, Khristo St.
Kak voznik i razvivalsia Kommunisticheskii Internatsional (kratkii istoricheskii ocherk). Moskva [Gos. izd-vo] 1929. 239 p.

Hoover, Col

260 KAMENEV, L.
III [Tretii] Internatsional. Populiarnyi ocherk. Praga, "Pravda", 1920. 27 p. (Rabochaia biblioteka "Pravdy", 3.)

Col, Amst, BDIC

261 KANTOROVICH, Haim
The rise and decline of neo-communism. Baltimore, Md., The Modern Quarterly [1924?] 23 p.   *Hoover*

262 KHITAROV, Rafail M.
Pravaia opasnost' v Kominterne i zadachi KIM. Moskva, Molodaia
gvardiia, 1929. 77 p. (Biblioteka KIM.) *NYPL*

263 KHITAROV, Rafail M.
Die rechte Gefahr in der Komintern und die Aufgaben der KJI. Berlin,
Verlag der Jugendinternationale, 1929, 43 p. *NYPL, Harv*

264 KIN, D.
Liga Natsii i III Internatsional. [n. p., n. d.] 15 p. *BDIC*

265 Le KOMINTERN et la juiverie mondiale. Paris, Editions C. E. A., 1944.
46 p. Cover titler: Essais politiques, no. 3. Running title: Le Komintern
est juif l *LC, NYPL*

266 KOMMUNISTINEN internationali. Stockholm, Fram, 1919. 104 p. At
head of title: Kaikkien maiden koyhälistö, liittykää yhteen!

NYPL

267 KOMOR, I.
10 [deset] let Komunistické Internacionály. [1919—1929] Praha-Karlín,
Komunistické nakladatelství, 1929. 40 p. (Malá knihovna Leninismu.
Sbírka Populárních Přednášek sv. 9.) *Amst*

268 KOMOR, I.
Desiat' let Kominterna. 2. izd. Moskva, Gos. izd-vo, 1929. 60 p.
Harv

269 KOMOR, I.
Dix années d'Internationale Communiste. L'Internationale Communiste,
guide du prolétariat dans sa lutte pour la dictature mondiale. Paris,
Bureau d'Editions [1929] 53 p. 1 illus. *Hoover, NYPL, Amst*

270 KOMOR, I.
Ten years of the Communist International. New York, Workers' Library
[1929] 46 p. (Printed in Great Britain.) *Hoover, NYPL, Felt*

271 KOMOR, I.
Ten years of the Communist International. London, Modern Books,
1929. vi, 46 p. *Col, Amst, Felt*

272 KOMOR, I.
Zehn Jahre Komintern [1919—1929]. Die Komintern, die Führerin im
Kampf um die Weltdiktatur des Proletariats. Hamburg, Hoym [1929]
32 p. illus. *NYPL, Amst*

273 KRUPINSKI, Kurt
De Komintern sedert het uitbreken van den oorlog. Vert. [uit het Duits] door J. Lammertse Lz. Amsterdam, Westland, 1943. 108 p. (Oostland-reeks, 5.) Translation of "Die Komintern seit Kriegsausbruch."

Amst

274 KRUPINSKI, Kurt
Die Komintern seit Kriegsausbruch. [Berlin, O. Stolberg, 1941?] 75 p. (Die Bücherei des Ostraumes.) [First edition?]

NYPPL, Harv

275 KRUPINSKI, Kurt
Die Komintern seit Kriegsausbruch. [Berlin, O. Stolberg, 1941?] 105 p. [Second edition?]   *Hoover, LC, NYPL, Col, Amst*

KUN, Bela, ed.
Komintern v rezoliutsiiakh. [1926 ed.] See no. 120.

KUN, Bela, ed.
Kommunisticheskii Internatsional v dokumentakh; resheniia, tezisy i vozzvaniia kongressov i plenumov IKKI; 1919—1932. See no. 121.

276 KUN, Bela
La social-démocratie contre le Marxisme. Paris, Bureau d'Editions. 1933. 68 p.   *Felt*

277 KUN, Bela
Vragi Kommunisticheskogo Internatsionala. [Moskva] Gos. izd-vo, [1922] 15 p.   *Hoover*

278 KURELLA, Alfred
Vsesoiuznaia kommunisticheskaia partiia(b) i Kommunisticheskii Inter-natsional; o pravom i levom uklone v Kommunisticheskom Internatsio-nale. Moskva, Gos. izd-vo, 1927. 31 p. (Biblioteka rabochego.) At head of title: Chto reshila XV konferentsiia VKP(b).

NYPL

279 KUUSINEN, Otto
Die historische Unwahrheit Sinowjews. Hamburg, C. Hoym Nachfolger [c1928] 103 p. "Die 21 Bedingungen der leninschen Komintern, von G. Sinowjew": p. 81—103.   *Hoover, NYPL*

280 KUUSINEN, Otto
La position de l'Internationale communiste devant la crise, la guerre et le fascisme. Paris, Bureau d'Editions, 1934. 88 p.   *NYPL*

99

281 LANGE, Martin
Was ist die Internationale der kämpfenden Arbeiterklasse? Wien,
Arbeiter-Buchhandlung, 1921. 64 p. *NYPL, Amst, Felt*

282 LANGFELDT, Knut
Moskva-cesene i Norsk politikk. Oslo, Universitetsförlaget [1961] 158 p.
Felt

283 LAPORTE, Maurice
Les mystères du Kremlin. (Dans les coulisses de la IIIe Internationale
et du Parti français.) 2. ed. Paris, Renaissance moderne, 1928. 255 p.
Col, BDIC, SInSt

284 LAUNAY, Jacques de
Fascisme rouge; contribution à la défense de l'Europe. Bruxelles, Editions Montana, 1954. 224 p. illus. *Hoover, Col*

285 LAURAT, Lucien
Du Komintern au Kominform. Paris, Iles d'Or [1951] 102 p.
LC, Col, UWisc, Amst, Felt

286 LAZIĆ, Branko M. [pseud. of Branislav Stranjaković]
Lenine et la IIIe Internationale. Pref. de Raymond Aron. Neuchâtel,
Editions de la Bacconière, 1951. 285 p. (Bibliographie: 273—279)
Hoover, LC, NYPL, Harv, Col, BDIC, Felt

287 LEBEDEV, Nikolai
K istorii Internatsionala. Etapy mezhdunarodnogo ob'edineniia tru-
diashchikhsia. Petersburg-Moskva, Golos truda, 1921. 124 p.
Hoover

288 LEFEBVRE, Raymond
L'Internationale des soviets. Paris, "La Vie ouvrière" [1919]. 14 p.
(Collection de la "Vie ouvrière", II.) *Hoover, BDIC*

289 LEITFADEN der Geschichte der Kommunistischen Internationale.
Moskau-Leningrad, Verlagsgenossenschaft ausländischer Arbeiter in
der UdSSR, 1934. 54 p. At head of title: Agitpropabteilung des EKKI.

"Die vorliegende Broschüre enthält die Thesen, die anlässlich des 15. Jahres-
tages der Gründung der Kommunistischen Internationale von der Agitprop-
abteilung des EKKI ausgearbeitet wurden." For English edition see no. 242.
Hoover, LC, NYPL, Harv, Duke, Amst

290 LEITFADEN der Geschichte der Kommunistischen Internationale. [n. p.,
Strasbourg?] 1934. 36 p. *Amst*

291 LENIN, Vladimir I.
The foundation of the Communist International. New York, International Publishers [c1934] 47 p.

Contains speeches, reports, articles, etc. *Hoover, LC, Amst*

292 LENIN, V. I.
Komintern. S predisl. S. Gopner. [n. p.] 1924. 326 p. At head of title: N. Lenin *SInSt*

LENIN, V. I.
Kommunisticheskii Internatsional; stat'i i rechi; [one volume edition.] See no. 123.

LENIN, V. I.
Kommunisticheskii Internatsional; stat'i, rechi, dokumenty 1914—1923, pod red. V. Knorina. [2 vols.] See no. 124.

LENIN, V. I.
O Kominterne. Stat'i i dokumenty. [1924 edition] See no. 125.

293 LENIN, V. I.
O Kommunisticheskom Internatsionale. Sostavil i snabdil primechaniiami V. Butkovskii. Predisl. V. Kolarova. Moskva, Gos. izd-vo, 1926. 64 p.

Conntains annotations and explanatory footnotes. *NYPL*

294 LENIN, V. I.
O Kommunisticheskom Internatsionale. Moskva, 1934. 296 p.

SInSt

295 LENIN, V. I.
Problems of the Third International; Ramsey [!] Macdonald on the Third International. New York, Contemporary Publishing Association [1919] 24 p.

Lenin's commentary on an article by Ramsay Macdonald, translated in full from an article in l'Humanité of April 14, 1919. *Hoover, NYPL*

296 LENIN, V. I.
III [Tretii] Internatsional i ego mesto v istorii. [n. p.] 1924. 55 p. Bibliotechka lenintsa. *BDIC*

297 LENIN, V. I.
Tretii Internatsional i ioho istorychne znachinnia. Viden-Kyiv, "Nova doba", 1920. 12 p. (On cover: Biblioteka "Novoi dobi", no. 12.)

Hoover, BDIC

298 LENIN, V. I.
Zadachi Kommunisticheskogo Internatsionala. Praga, "Pravda", 1920.
23 p. (Rabochaia biblioteka "Pravdy", no. 2.) *Col, BDIC*

299 LENIN, V. I. [and] Zinov'ev, G.
Za Tretii Internatsional; programma i taktika Kominterna v techenie
pervogo piatiletiia ego deiatel'nosti. Leningrad, Gos. izd-vo, 1924,
519 p. *Harv*

300 LENIN on the historic significance of the Third International. [London,
Martin Lawrence, 1934] 24 p. *Col*

301 LENZNER, N.
Über die rechte Gefahr in der Komintern. Hamburg, Hoym [1929] 56 p.
Amst

302 LORWIN, Lewis L[evitzki]
Labor and Internationalism. New York, MacMillan, 1929. xviii, 192 p.
(The Institute of Economics of the Brookings Institution.)
Hoover, LC, NYPL, Felt

303 LORWIN, Lewis L[evitzki]
L'internationalisme et la classe ouvrière. (Labor and Internationalism.)
Traduit de l'anglais par Frans Longville. Troisième édition. Paris,
Librairie Gallimard, 1933. 435 p. ("Les Documents Bleus", Notre
Temps 10.) *Felt, NYPL*

304 LORWIN, Lewis L[evitzki]
Die Internationale der Arbeit; Geschichte und Ausblick; deutsche Aus-
gabe von Labor and Internationalism. Berlin, Verlag des Institute of
Economics, 1930. 254 p. At head of title: Schriften des Institute of
Economics.

"Die deutsche Übersetzung wurde von Jürgen und Marguerite Kuczynski be-
sorgt." *NYPL*

305 LOUIS, Paul
La crise du socialisme mondial de la IIe à la IIIe Internationale. Paris,
F. Alcan, 1921, 192 p. *Hoover*

LOWENTHAL, Richard
The bolshevization of the Spartacus League; an essay in the collective
work *International Communism;* see no. 243.

306 LOZOVSKII, A.
Amsterdam, Moskau, London. Hamburg, Kommunistische Internationale; Auslieferungsstelle für Deutschland, C. Hoym Nachf., 1921. 29 p.
Hoover, Felt

307 MARTOV, IUlii O.
V bor'be za Internatsional. S predisl. R. Abramovicha. Berlin, "Iskra". 1924. 137 p.

Collection of Martov's articles in "Sotsialisticheskii vestnik" in 1921—22, exposing the failure of the bolshevik-dominated Third International to provide leadership for the entire working class. Martov advocated social-democratic unity, opposed to communism; shortly after his death progress towards this unity was achieved through the unification of the Second and Two-and-a-Half Internationals.
Hoover

308 MARTYNOV, A. [pseud. of Aleksandr Piker]
Bor'ba s opportunizmom v Kominterne. Moskva, Leningrad, Moskovskii rabochii, 1930. 69 p.
Hoover

308a MATSUOKA, Yosuke
Die Bedeutung des deutsch-japanischen Abkommens gegen die Kommunistische Internationale. Tokyo, Nippon Dempo Tsushin-sha, [1938] 63 p.

Preface, two speeches by Yosuke Matsuoka on the subject, texts of the Anti-Comintern Pact of November 17, 1936 and additional Protocol.
Hoover

308b McKENZIE, Kermit E.
Comintern and world revolution. See Addendum.

MINGULIN, I.
Pervyi kongress Kominterna. See: Istoriia Kommunisticheskogo Internatsionala v kongressakh; no. 253.

309 NERMAN, Ture
Kommunisterna; fran Komintern till Kominform. Stockholm, Tidens Förlag [1949] 279 p.
Hoover, SInSt

310 NOLLAU, Günther
Die Internationale; Wurzeln und Erscheinungsformen des proletarischen Internationalismus. Köln, Verlag für Politik und Wirtschaft, 1959. 343 p.

A well documented description of Comintern activities based predominantly on memoirs of former participants in the Comintern bureaucracy. Comintern documentation quoted from various volumes of the "Bibliothek der Kommunisti-schen Internationale" (C. Hoym, Hamburg) without giving titles of volumes. Only part of the volume deals with the Comintern; the remainder concerns the previous Internationals and the Cominform.

Hoover, LC, NYPL, Harv, Col, UWisc, Amst, BDIC, Felt

311 NOLLAU, Günther
International communism and world revolution: history & methods. [Translation by Victor Andersen] With a foreword by Leonard Scha-piro. New York, Praeger [1961] 357 p. (Books that matter)

Translation of preceding item.   *Hoover, NYPL*

312 NOLLAU, Günther
International communism and world revolution: history & methods. [Translation by Victor Andersen] With a foreword by Leonard Scha-piro. London, Hollis & Carter, 1961. xv, 357 p.

Translation of no. 310.   *LC, Col, Felt*

313 OSNOVNYE etapy razvitiia Kominterna. Posobie dlia propagandistov. Moskva & Leningrad, 1929. 144 p.   *SInSt*

314 OUTLINE history of the Communist International. Responsible editor: J. Fineberg. Moscow-Leningrad, Co-operative Publishing Society of Foreign Workers in the USSR., 1934. 51 p. On last page signature: Agitprop of the Executive Committee of the Communist International.

Hoover, UTex

315 PANNEKOEK, Anton
Die Westeuropäische Politik der 3. Internationale. Berlin, Lantzsch [n. d.] 16 p. (Kleine Flugschriften der Kommunistischen Arbeiter-Partei Deutschlands, 3)   *BDIC*

316 PARTIJA sovetskog proletarijata; osnovni momenti iz istorije Komin-terne, 1919—1934. Moskva, Izd. Zadruga Inostranih Radnika u USSR, 1934. 61 p.   *BDIC*

317 PEREYRA, Carlos
La Tercera Internacional; doctrinas y controversias. Madrid, Biblioteca nueva [1933?] 262 p.   *Hoover, NYPL, Col*

318 15 [PIATNADTSAT'] let Kominterna; 1919—1934. Redaktor S. I. Gopner. Moskva-Leningrad, 1934. [Pages not given on catalog card]

The item was unavailable for identification. May be identical with next item.
SInSt

319 PIATNADTSAT' let Kommunisticheskogo Internatsionala; tezisy dlia dokladchikov. Moskva, 1934. 32 p. (Agitprop IKKI)

For English edition see no. 242. *SInSt*

320 PIATNITSKII, Osip A.
The bolshevization of the communist parties by eradicating the social-democratic traditions. 2nd reprint from the "Communist International", revised ... [London, Modern Books, 1932] 87 p.

"Comprises the amended text of the stenographic report of a lecture ... delivered at a conference of International communist party school teachers."

Hoover

321 PIATNITSKII, Osip A.
La crise économique mondiale, l'essor révolutionnaire et les tâches des sections de l'Internationale Communiste. Paris, Bureau d'Editions, 1933. 101 p. *NYPL*

322 PIATNITSKII, Osip A.
Kompartii na puti bol'shevizatsii. 2-e izd., dop. Moskva, Part. izd-vo, 1932. 60 p. (Biblioteka rabochego aktivista.) *Col*

323 PIATNITSKII, Osip A.
V bor'be za mirovuiu sovetskuiu vlast'; 15 let Kommunisticheskogo Internatsionala. [Moskva] Partizdat, 1934. 30 p. *Hoover, BDIC*

324 PIATNITSKII, Osip A. [and] Knorin, V.
Beiträge zur Geschichte der Kommunistischen Internationale. Moskau-Leningrad, Verlagsgenossenschaft ausländischer Arbeiter in der UdSSR, 1934. 59 p. At head of title: O. Pjatnizki, W. Knorin.

For English edition see next item. *Hoover, LC, NYPL, Harv, Col, Amst, Felt*

325 PIATNITSKII, Osip A. [and] Knorin, V.
Leading the world proletariat to new decisive battles. Fifteen years. (By O. Piatnitskii) The struggle for the masses is the struggle for power. (By V. Knorin). Moscow-Leningrad, Co-operative Publishing Society of Foreign Workers in the USSR [1934] 62 p.

English edition of preceding item. *Hoover, NYPL*

326 POUZYNA, I. V.
Bolchevisme. Son histoire, son essence. Préface de S. E. le Cardinal Baudrillart. Paris, Centre d'action anti-communiste [n. d.] 47 p. (Cover title.)

"Collaborationist propaganda of 1940 or 1941." BDIC *BDIC*

327 PROLETARISCHER Internationalismus. Materialien einer Arbeitstagung über Rolle und Bedeutung des proletarischen Internationalismus. Halle, 6./7. November 1959. Zusammengestellt und bearbeitet von Dr. Alfred Anderle und Konrad Hecktheuer. Berlin, Rütten & Loening [1961] 235 p. (Veröffentlichungen des Instituts für Geschichte der Völker der UdSSR an der Martin-Luther-Universität Halle-Wittenberg. Herausgegeben von Alfred Anderle. Reihe B. Abhandlungen, Band I.)

Contents:

Anderle, Alfred
  Lenin-Kämpfer für den proletarischen Internationalismus. p. 13—27.

Zelt, Johannes
  Rote Hilfe, Klassensolidarität und proletarischer Internationalismus. p. 28—43.

[Contents of pages 44—46 omitted in Feltrinelli catalog]

Jauernig, Edmund
  Die Solidarität mit Sowjetrussland — Bindeglied des revolutionären Proletariats über nationale Schranken und Ländergrenzen hinweg. p. 47—57.

Striegnitz, Sonja
  Die aktive Teilnahme ehemaliger deutscher Kriegsgefangener an der Oktoberrevolution 1917 und an den Kämpfen des Bürgerkrieges. p. 58—61.

Lehfeld, Horst
  Die Kommunistische Internationale und der proletarische Internationalismus. p. 62—71.

Krause, Hans
  Die Solidaritätsaktionen des Halleschen Proletariats für Sowjetrussland während der Novemberrevolution und des Jahres 1919. p. 72—78.

Schaaf, Hans-Werner
  Die Aktion "Hände weg von Sowjetrussland" im Industriegebiet von Halle während des 3. Feldzuges der Entente (1920). p. 79—85.

Benkwitz, Max
  Die Rote Hilfe. p. 86—91.

Hofmann, Willy
  Die Aktion "Hände weg von Sowjetrussland" 1919 bis 1920. p. 92—94.

Gebenroth, Otto
  Wie mir die Rote Hilfe geholfen hat. p. 95—97.

Zelt, Johannes
  Zwischenbemerkungen zur Diskussion. p. 98—101.

Müller, Hermann
  Zur Hilfsaktion der deutschen Arbeiterklasse für Sowjetrussland im Jahre 1921. p. 102—115.

Jahn, Gisela
  Die Solidaritätsaktionen der Sowjetischen Arbeiter für das deutsche Proletariat zur Zeit der Ruhrokkupation und der revolutionären Kämpfe im Herbst 1923 in Deutschland. p. 116—128.

Remer, Claus
  Der Besuch von Arbeiterdelegationen in der Sowjetunion — ein Ausdruck des proletarischen Internationalismus und der Solidarität zum Sowjetstaat. p. 129—136.

Kalbe, Ernstgert
Die internationale antifaschistische Solidaritätsbewegung zur Rettung Georgi Dimitroffs im Jahre 1933. p. 137—150.

Basler, Werner
Der Gedanke des proletarischen Internationalismus gegenüber der Sowjetunion in der illegalen antifaschistischen Publizistik 1933—1939. p. 151—160.

Winter, Heinz-Dieter
Der proletarische Internationalismus in der sowjetischen Deutschlandpolitik während des grossen vaterländischen Krieges. p. 161—168.

Schüle, Annerose
Zum Kampf der Sowjetunion für das Zustandekommen des Potsdamer Abkommens. p. 169—174.

Mai, Joachim
Der Kampf der Sowjetunion um einen Friedensvertrag mit Deutschland (1945—1952). p. 175—183.

Heerdegen, Helga
Der Kampf der Sowjetunion um den Abschluss eines gerechten Friedensvertrages mit Deutschland (1954—1959). p. 184—192.

Quilitzsch, Siegmar
Die Rolle der Sowjetunion beim Neuaufbau der Chemieindustrie im Bitterfelder Gebiet 1945 bis 1947, dargestellt am Beispiel der Filmfabrik AGFA Wolfen. p. 193—217.

Schmelzer, Janis
Die Erziehung der Werktätigen und der Jugend der DDR zum proletarischen Internationalismus. p. 218—224.

Morosow, Boris
Über die Zusammenarbeit zwischen dem Komsomol und der FDJ. p. 225—233.

This collective work contains several items which are contributions to the history of the Comintern and some of its front organizations. Other items describe political actions and manifestations undertaken at the initiative of the Comintern. It is obvious that all items are written from the communist point of view. *Felt*

40e [QUARANTIÈME] Anniversaire de la fondation de l'Internationale Communiste. Premier Congrès Moscou, 2—6 mars 1919. (Documents).
See no. 539

328 15 [QUINCE] Años de Internacional Comunista. Guia para la historia de la III Internacional. [Barcelona, Ediciones Europa-Américe, n. d.] 40 p.

Spanish edition of no. 242. *Amst*

329 RADEK, K.
Piat' let Kominterna. Moskva, "Krasnaia nov'" Glavpolit-prosvet, 1924. 2 vols.

Vol. II: Osnovy programmy i taktiki Kominterna. 371 p.
Vol. II: Taktika edinogo fronta. 504 p.
The volumes contain reprints of pamphlets and articles published by Radek
as well as his speeches for the period from September 1918 to June 1924. The
division date between volume I and volume II is January 1921.

Hoover, NYPL (1), Harv (1), Col, SInSt

330 RANSOME, Arthur
Russia in 1919. New York, B. W. Huebsch, 1919. 232 p.   *Hoover*

331 RANSOME, Arthur
Six Semaines en Russie en 1919. Editions de "L'Humanité" Paris, 1919.
188 p.   *Hoover*

332 RANSOME, Arthur
Six weeks in Russia in 1919. London, G. Allen & Unwin, Ltd. [1919]
151 p. American edition has title: Russia in 1919.   *Hoover*

333 REALE, Eugenio
Avec Jacques Duclos au banc des accusés à la réunion constitutive
du Kominform à Szklarska Poreba 22—27 septembre 1947. Traduit de
l'italien par Pierre Bonuzzi. Paris, Librairie Plon, 1958. ix, 203 p.

Col

334 RENNÉ, Baron Raul de
Tainyi smysl nyneshnikh i griadushchikh sobytii. Belgrad, "Nova Shtam-
parija" [1931] 43 p.

Abbreviated translation of a book in French (Bordeaux, 1931). Discusses the
role which the Comintern might play in a future war.   *BDIC*

335 REZANOV, Aleksandr
La travail secret des agents bolchevistes; exposé d'après des docu-
ments authentiques émanent des bolchéviques. Préface de Th. Aubert.
Paris, Editions Bossard, 1926. xviii, 199 p.

Hoover, Harv, BDIC

336 REZANOV, Aleksandr
La troisième Internationale Communiste, le "Komintern"; traduction
du manuscrit russe; illustré de 11 photographies. Paris, Editions Bossard,
1922. 127 p. ports.   *Hoover, NYPL, Harv, Col, Amst, BDIC, Felt*

337 RINDL, Peter
Der internationale Kommunismus. München, Olzog, 1961. 160 p.

Col, Felt

338 RODINEVITCH, Nicolas [and] Comin, Eduardo
La Internacional Comunista o Komintern y sus organizaciones auxiliares. Madrid, Ediciones españolas, 1941. 238 p.   *NYPL, Harv, Col*

339 ROSENBERG, Arthur
A history of bolshevism, from Marx to the first five years' plan. Translated from the German by Ian F. D. Morrow. London, Oxford Univ. Press, 1934. viii, 250 p.   *Hoover, LC, Harv*

340 ROSMER, Alfred
A Mosca al tempo di Lenin. Le origini del comunismo. Firenze, La Nuova Italia [1953] xv, 297 p. ("Documenti della crisi contemporanea", 10.)   *Felt*

341 ROSMER, Alfred
Moscou sous Lenine: les origines du communisme. Pref. par Albert Camus. Paris, P. Horay [1953] 316 p.   *Hoover, Felt*

342 ROY, Manabendra Nath
The Communist International. [Delhi] Radical Democratic Party [1946] 64 p.   *Hoover, NYPL, Harv*

343 ROY, Manabendra Nath
Die internationalen Verbündeten der Opposition in der PKdSU, Hamburg, C. Hoym [1928] 30 p.   *Hoover*

344 RUSSLAND und die Komintern. Gedanken für einen internationalen sozialistischen Neuaufbau. Hrsg. vom Internationalen Sozialistischen Kampf-Bund. [Welwyn Garden City, "Renaissance" Publishing Co., 1942] 64 p.   *Amst*

345 RYS, pseud.
Komintern (Komunistička Internacionala). Zagreb, Mosk, 1934. 32 p. incl. illus., port., diagrs.   *Hoover*

346 SALVADORI, Massimo
The Rise of Modern Communism; a brief history of the communist movement in the twentieth century. New York, Holt, 1952. 118 p. (Berkshire studies in European history)   *Hoover*

346a [SCHIAVI, Alessandro] ed.
Dalla Seconda alla Terza Internazionale. Milano, Società editrice Avanti, 1919. 152 p. (Documenti della rivoluzione)

"Prefazione" signed: A. S. [Alessandro Schiavi]   *Hoover*

347 SEMARD, Pierre
La Situation en U. R. S. S. et les dangers de droite dans L'I. C. [Paris, Imprimerie Centrale, n. d.] xviii, 95 p. *Felt*

348 SERGE, Victor
De Lenine à Staline. Paris, Crapouillot, 1937. 67 p. illus., ports. "Crapouillot, Numéro special, janvier 1937." *Hoover*

349 SERGE, Victor
From Lenin to Stalin; translated from the French by Ralph Manheim. New York, Pioneer Publishers [1937] 112 p. *Hoover*

350 SETON-WATSON, Hugh
From Lenin to Khrushchev; the history of world communism. New York, Praeger, 1960, xv, 432 p.

Revised and extended edition of the author's *From Lenin to Malenkov.* See next item. *Hoover, LC, NYPL, Harv, Col, SInSt*

351 SETON-WATSON, Hugh
From Lenin to Malenkov; the history of world communism. New York, Praeger, 1954. 377 p. *Hoover, LC, NYPL, Harv, Col, BDIC*

352 SETON-WATSON, Hugh
The pattern of communist revolution; a historical analysis. London, Methuen [1953] 377 p.

London edition of preceding item. *Hoover, NYPL, Harv, Col, Felt*

353 SIGNOREL, Jean
Exposé doctrinal du programme du Parti communiste russe, adopté à Moscou, le 18/23 mars 1919. IIIe Internationale. Toulouse, E. Privat, 1921. 78 p. *NYPL*

354 SOUVARINE, Boris
Cauchemar en U. R. S. S. Paris, La Revue de Paris, 1937. 48 p.
Hoover

355 SOUVARINE, Boris
The Third International, London, British Socialist Party [1920?] 22 p. port. *Hoover, NYPL, Col, Amst, BDIC*

356 SOUVARINE, Boris
La troisième Internationale. Paris, Edition "Clarté", 1919. 34 p.

Includes: Sadoul, Jacques: Appel aux Socialistes Français.
Hoover, Col, Amst, Felt

357 Le SOVIET. Numéro special. [n. p.] Comité Communiste Internationaliste pour la construction de la 4-e Internationale, mai 1943. Folio, 2 p. duplicated.

A trotskiist view on the dissolution of the Komintern. Obviously an underground publication. *BDIC*

358 STAKHIV, Matvei
Pro rizhni Internatsional. Lviv [Lwów] Gromadskii golos, 1937. 56 p.
BDIC

359 SVENSSON, Björn
Saadan er Kommunisterne. Copenhagen, 1949. 187 p.

SInSt

360 TATSACHEN zur Geschichte der Komintern. [n. p., n. d.] 94 p.
Felt

TIVEL, A.
Chetvertyi kongress Kominterna. See: Istoriia Kommunisticheskogo Internatsionala v kongressakh; no. 253.

TIVEL, A., comp.
5 [piat'] let Kominterna v resheniiakh i tsifrakh. See no. 44.

TIVEL, A. [and] Kheimo, M.
10 [desiat'] let Kominterna v resheniiakh i tsifrakh. See no. 45.

361 TRACHTENBERG, Jakow
Gegen das Braunbuch; (Rotbuch). Übersetzung von Georg Kandler. Berlin-Grunewald, Jakow Trachtenberg Verlag, 1934. 146 p. illus., maps, facsims.

Anti-Comintern and anti-Soviet propaganda, obviously Nazi-inspired or produced with intention to please the Nazi regime. *Hoover*

362 TROTSKII, Lev
Avant la nouvelle guerre mondiale. Après "la paix" impérialiste de Munich. [Deux articles. Bruxelles] Ed. par le Parti socialiste révolutionnaire, Section belge de la 4-e Internationale [pref. 1939] 51 p.

Two articles written by Trotskii before and after the "Munich Pact", criticizing Stalin's foreign policy, with some remarks on the role of the Comintern in this policy. *Hoover*

363 TROTSKII, Lev
The first five years of the Communist International. Translated from the Russian and edited by John G. Wright. New York, Pioneer Publishers, 1945, 1953. 2 vols. xiii, 373 p. and viii, 384 p.

> The volumes contain speeches, reports, articles, letters and other writings by Trotskii concerning the Communist International, covering the period from the first to the fourth Congress inclusive, i. e., 1919—1922, and a few items published later. Both volumes have annotations and indexes.
> *Hoover, LC, NYPL, Harv, Amst, BDIC, Felt*

364 TROTSKII, Lev
Die Grundfragen der Revolution. Hamburg, Die Kommunistische Internationale, 1923. xiv, 475 p. (Bibliographical footnotes)

> *NYPL*

365 TROTSKII, Lev
L'Internationale communiste après Lenine. (Le grand organisateur de la défaite.) Paris, Rieder, 1930. 438 p.

> French edition of no. 371.   *Hoover, NYPL, Felt*

366 TROTSKII, Lev
Kommunisticheskii Internatsional. Moskva, Leningrad, Gos. izd-vo, 1926. vii, 247 p. (Sochineniia, tom XIII. Seriia IV: Problemy mezhdunarodnoi proletarskoi revoliutsii.)

> "The present volume deals with the activities of the Communist International during the years 1919—1921." ("From the author", p. v) Chapter II "The First Steps of the Communist International", contains Trotskii's speech at the II Congress of the Comintern, four documents originating with the Comintern and one unidentified item about "The unemployed and the trade unions". Chapter III deals with the revolution in Germany and Chapter IV with the creation of a communist party in France. Annotations. Chronology. Index.
> *Hoover, BDIC*

367 TROTSKII, Lev
Piat' let Kominterna. Moskva, Gos. izd-vo [1924] xviii, 612 p.

> For annotation see no. 363.   *Hoover, LC, NYPL, Harv, BDIC, SInSt*

368 TROTSKII, Lev
Problems of the development of the U. S. S. R.; draft of the thesis of the International left opposition on the Russian question. Translated by Morris Lewitt and Max Schachtman. New York, Communist League of America (Opposition), 1931. 47 p. On cover: Russia; problems of the development of the U. S. S. R.
> *Hoover, Harv*

368a TROTSKII, Lev

La Quatrième Internationale et l'U. R. R. S. La nature de classe de l'État soviétique. Paris, Ligue Communiste. Bolcheviks-Léninistes, 1933. 30 p.

See next item. *Hoover, Felt*

369 TROTSKII, Lev

The Soviet Union and the Fourth International; two essays on the class nature of the Soviet state and bolshevik congresses, once and now. Glasgow, G. A. Aldred, 1934, 24 p.

The English translation of the first essay, made by Usick Vanzler (New York, Communist League of America) was originally published under title: *The Class Nature of the Soviet State.* Publisher's foreword. *Hoover, NYPL*

370 TROTSKII, Lev

Stalinism and Bolshevism; concerning the historical and theoretical roots of the Fourth International. New York, 1937. 29 p.

Hoover, SInSt

371 TROTSKII, Lev

The Third International after Lenin. Translated by John G. Wright. [Introduction by Max Schachtman.] New York, Pioneer Publishers [1936] vii, 357 p. (Half title: The selected works of Leon Trotsky.)

"This first edition has been translated from the original Russian manuscripts. None of the material was ever published in the Russian language. A French edition was published under title: *L'Internationale Communiste apres Lenin.* (Introd.) *Hoover, LC, Harv*

372 TROTSKII, Lev

The Third International after Lenin. Translated by John G. Wright. [Introduction by Max Schachtman.] New York, Pioneer Publishers [1957] xii, 400 p. [2nd edition.] (Bibliographical references included in "Notes", p. 311—349.)

For annotation see preceding item. *LC, NYPL, Harv, Col, Felt*

373 TROTSKII, Lev

El triunfo del bolchevismo. Con una semblanza del autor, sus impresiones de España y su actitud respecto a la International (2. ed.) Madrid, Biblioteca nueva [1921?] 268 p. *Hoover*

374 TROTSKII, Lev

La "troisième période" d'erreurs de l'Internationale communiste. Paris, Librairie du travail [1930] 64 p. (Bibliothèque de l'opposition communiste, 2) *Hoover, NYPL*

375 TROTSKII, Lev
La III [terzera] Internationale dopo Lenin. Prefazione, traduzione e note di Livio Maitan. [Milano] Schwarz Editore [1957] 324 p. tables. (Collana di Storia e Cultura. VI.) *Felt*

376 TROTSKII, Lev
Wer leitet heute die Kommunistische Internationale? Berlin-Wilmersdorf, Verlag der Zeitschrift "Die Aktion" (F. Pfemfert) 1930. 59 p. (Kommunistische Aktionsbibliothek [12])

> First written in French and appeared in 1930 as the fourth part of his *L'Internationale Communiste apres Lenine*. Includes annex: "Testament von N. Lenin": p. 48—51. *Hoover, NYPL, Amst*

377 VALLOT, Paul
"Bolchevisme and co." Une entreprise en faillité. Bruxelles, Nouvelle societé d'éditions, 1942. 185 p. (Documents) *Hoover*

VILLIAMS, B.
Piatyi kongress Kominterna. See: Istoriia Kommunisticheskogo Internatsionala v kongressakh; no. 253.

378 VLUGT, E. van der
La Societé des Nations & l'Internationale. Paris, Editions du "Monde Nouveau" [1920] 16 p. Cover title. *NYPL*

379 Der VORSTOSS der "Kommunistischen" Internationale gegen die Gewerkschaften ... Reichenberg, F. Macoun, 1920. 14 p. (Gewerkschaftliche Zeitfragen, no. 1.) *NYPL*

380 VUJOVIĆ, V. D.
Mezhdunarodnoe rabochee dvizhenie i Kommunisticheskii Internatsional. Moskva, Gos. izd-vo, 1926. 79 p. At head of title: V. D. Vuiovich. *Col*

381 WEILENMANN, Friedrich W.
Zur Geschichte der Komintern von der Gründung bis zur "Auflösung." Frankfurt/Main, Welt-Dienst-Verlag, 1944. 15 p. *Hoover*

382 WEISBORD, Albert
For a new Communist International! [New York City, The Communist League of Struggle, 1933] 30 p. *Hoover, Col*

383 WIJNKOOP, D[avid] J.
De tactische stroomingen in de Derde Internationale. Rede geh. in een vergadering van de afd. Amsterdam der C. P. Amsterdam, Brochure-handel der C. P. [n. d.] 16 p. *Amst*

384 YPSILON [pseud. of Johann Rindl and Julian Gumperz]
Pattern for World Revolution. Chicago-New York, Ziff-Davis [c1947] v, 479 p. index.

> "This book attempts to present to the American reader the political psychology of those men and women, who, since the foundation of the Communist International, have fought for its aims in all corners of the globe. The history of this organization and its relationship to the Soviet Republic is treated only as a background for the story of the book." Preface, p. iii.
> *Hoover, LC, NYPL, Harv, Col, BDIC, Felt*

385 YPSILON [pseud. of Johann Rindl and Julian Gumperz]
Stalintern. Paris, La Table Ronde [1948] xiv, 446 p.

> French translation of preceding item. *Hoover, Amst, Felt*

386 ZAMYSLOVA, Zinaida Alekseevna
Kommunisticheskii Internatsional i ego rol' v istorii mezhdunarodnogo rabochego i natsional'no-osvoboditel'nogo dvizheniia; lektsii, prochitannye v Vysshei partiinoi shkole pri TSK KPSS. Moskva, 1957. 106 p. At head of title: Vysshaia partiinaia shkola pri TSK KPSS. Kafedra mezhdunarodnogo rabochego i natsional'no-osvoboditel'nogo dvizheniia. *Hoover, Harv, Felt*

387 ZETKIN, Klara
Von der Internationale des Wortes zur Internationale der Tat. Hamburg, C. Hoym, 1924. 38 p. *Hoover, Amst*

388 ZINOV'EV, G. E.
Die Entstehung der Kommunistischen Internationale und ihre Tätigkeit in den ersten fünf Jahren. Hamburg, C. Hoym Nachf. L. Cahnbley, 1924. 51 p. At head of title: G. Sinowjew. *Hoover*

389 ZINOV'EV, G. E.
Fünf Jahre Kommunistische Internationale. Hamburg, C. Hoym, 1924. ii, 75 p. *Amst, Felt*

390 ZINOV'EV, G. E.
Glavnye etapy v razvitii Kominterna [Moskva] Gos. izd-vo [1922] 14 p. *Hoover*

391 ZINOV'EV, G. E.
Kommunistinen internationaali [n. p., n. d] 35 p. (Suomalaisten kommunisten sarjajulkaisu no. 49.)   *Hoover*

392 ZINOV'EV, G. E.
Die russische Revolution und das internationale Proletariat; zum zweiten Jahrestag der proletarischen Umwälzung in Russland. [Berlin] Kommunistische Internationale, 1920. 15 p. At head of title: G. Sinowjew.
                                                              Hoover, NYPL

393 ZINOV'EV, G. E.
Tretii Kommunisticheskii Internatsional; k istorii mezhdunarodnoi organizatsii proletariata. Peterburg, Gos. izd-vo, 1921. 44 p.   *Hoover*

394 Zum JAHRESTAG der proletarischen Revolution in Russland, 1917--1921 . . . Hamburg, Hoym [1921?] 74 p. illus.
Contributions by Lenin, Trotskii, and Radek.   *NYPL, Harv, Amst*

395 ZURTIAGA, Ramiro A.
Contribuiçao para a historia do Komintern (traduzido do original español por S. L.). Lisboa, Ediçao popular de "Organizaçoes Bloco", 1945. 140 p. ("Documentos do nosso tempo"). "Indice bibliografico": p. 133—140.   *Hoover, Harv*

3. Promotion of world revolution

396 The ACTIVITIES of the Comintern (the Third International) for the sovietization of the world. [n. p., 193-?] 140 p.   *Hoover*

397 Les AGISSEMENTS de la troisième Internationale (Comintern) pour la soviétisation du monde. [Paris? 1935?] 128 p. Cover title   *NYPL, Amst*

398 Les AGISSEMENTS du Comintern pour la soviétisation du monde. (Resumé) [n. p., 1936?] 20 p.
Abbreviated edition of preceding item.   *Hoover*

399 DIX années de lutte pour la révolution mondiale. Edité par la revue "L'Internationale Communiste". Paris, Bureau d'Editions, 1929. 321 p.
                                                              Felt

400 ELIASBERG, George J.
Historische Grundlagen der Kommunistischen Internationale (Der Traum der Weltrevolution). Berlin, Sozialdemokratische Partei Deutschlands [n. d.] 40 p.   *Hoover, Amst*

401 FLORINSKY, Michael T.
World revolution and the U. S. S. R. New York, The Macmillan Company, 1933. xiv, 264 p.   *Hoover, LC, Harv, Col*

402 FISHER, Harold H.
The Communist Revolution; an outline of strategy and tactics. Stanford, Calif., Stanford University Press, 1955. 89 p. (Hoover Institute Studies. Series A.: General Studies No. 2.)   *Hoover*

403 GOPNER, S.
Pid praporom svitovoi proletarskoi revoliutsii; do desiatlittia Kominternu. Kharkiv, Derzh. vidavn. Ukraini, 1929. 201 p. port.   *Col*

404 INTERNATIONAL Anti-Communist Entente.
L'armée rouge, instrument de la révolution mondiale; le monde civilisé en danger. Genève, Bureau Permanent de l'Entente Internationale contre la IIIe Internationale, 1935. 95 p.   *Hoover*

JAMES, Cyril L. R.
World revolution, 1917—1936; the rise and fall of the Communist International. (See no. 254, 255)

405 KOMINTERN et U. R. R. S. La préparation de la révolution communiste. Hier et aujourd'hui. Genève [1948] 80 p. (Bulletin d'information de l'E. J. A. 1948/2.)   *BDIC*

406 KOMMUNISTICHESKII Internatsional o roli partii v revoliutsii. Moskva 1924. 43 p.   *SInSt*

407 KOREY, William
Zinoviev on the problem of world revolution, 1919—27. New York, 1960. 341 p. typescript; thesis, Columbia University. Bibliography: leaves 325—341.   *Hoover, Col*

408 LOVESTONE, Jay
Soviet foreign policy and the world revolution. New York, Workers Age publ. [1935] 31 p.   *Hoover*

409 MARCHENKO, Mitrofan K.
La révolution mondiale. Paris, Valois [1927] 375 p.   *Col.*

McKENZIE, Kermit E.
Comintern and world revolution. See Addendum following no. 2278.

117

410 NORMANN, Alfred
Bolschewistische Weltmachtpolitik; die Pläne der 3. Internationale zur
Revolutionierung der Welt auf Grund authentischer Quellen dargestellt
von Dr. Alfred Normann. Bern, Gotthelf-Verlag, 1935. 287 p. index,
bibliography. [„Vorwort" signed: Théodore Aubert, Vorsitzender der
Internationalen Vereinigung gegen die Dritte Internationale.]
Hoover, NYPL,Harv, Col, BDIC, Felt

PIATNITSKII, Osip A.
V bor'be za mirovuiu sovetskuiu vlast'; 15 let Kommunisticheskogo
Inernatisionala. See no. 323.

411 PILENKO, Aleksandr
La propagande de la guerre civile. (La tactique de la IIIe Internationale). Paris, Imprimérie de Navarre, 1924. 30 p.   *Hoover, BDIC*

412 POSSONY, Stefan, T.
A Century of Conflict; Communist Techniques of World Revolution.
Chicago, H. Regnery, 1953. xx, 439 p.   *Hoover, LC, NYPL*

413 RADEK, Karl
Die Entwicklung der Weltrevolution und die Taktik der kommunistischen
Parteien im Kampfe um die Diktatur des Proletariats. Hrsg. vom West-
europäischen Sekretariat der Kommunistischen Internationale. [Berlin,
Berliner Buch- und Kunstdruckerei, 1920] 66 p.   *Hoover, NYPL, Felt*

414 RADEK, Karl
Die Entwicklung der Welt-Revolution und die Taktik der kommunistischen
Parteien im Kampfe um die Diktatur des Proletariats. Wien, Kommuni-
stische Partei Deutschösterreichs, 1920. 62 p.   *Hoover*

415 RADEK, Karl
Les questions de la révolution mondiale à la lumière du menchevisme
[Petrograd, Editions de l'Internationale communiste, 1921] 39 p. (On
cover: Editions [françaises] de l'Internationale communiste, no. 66.)
Hoover, Amst

416 RADEK, Karl
Razvitie mirovoi revoliutsii i taktika kommunisticheskoi partii v bor'be
za diktaturu proletariata. (Perevod s nemetskogo). Moskva, Gos. izd.,
1920. 88 p.   *Hoover, NYPL*

417 STURM, Robert [pseud. of Rudolf Schricker]
Europa brennt; Moskau am Werk. Bayreuth, Gauverlag Bayerische Ost-
mark. 1936. 184 p. illus., maps.   *LC, Col*

418 TROTSKII, Lev
Die internationale Revolution und die Kommunistische Internationale.
(Autorisierte Übersetzung von A. Müller). Herausgegeben und mit Vorwort versehen von Hans Weber. Berlin, E. Laubsche Verlagsbuchhand-
lung, 1929, 207 p. index.   *Hoover, NYPL, Amst*

TROTSKII, L.
Die neue ökonomische Politik Sowjetrußlands und die Weltrevolution;
Rede gehalten auf dem IV. Weltkongreß der Kommunistischen Inter-
nationale . . . See no. 743.

TROTSKII, L.
La nouvelle politique économique des Soviets et la révolution mondiale. See no. 748.

TROTSKII, L.
Novaia ekonomicheskaia politika Sovetskoi Rossii i perspektivy mirovoi
revoliutsii. See no. 736.

419 TROTSKII, Lev
The strategy of the world revolution. Translated and with an intro-
duction by Max Schachtman. New York, Communist League of America
Opposition, 1930. x, 86 p.   *Hoover, LC, Harv, Col*

420 TROTSKII, Lev
Zapad i Vostok; voprosy mirovoi politiki i mirovoi revoliutsii. Moskva,
Glavpolitprosvet. izd-vo „Krasnaia nov'" 1924. ii, 152 p.   *NYPL*

421 WALSH, Edmund A.
Origine e sviluppo del comunismo mondiale. [Milano] Sperling &
Kupfer, 1951. 319 p. tables.   *Felt*

422 WALSH, Edmund A.
Total Empire; the roots and progress of world communism. Milwaukee,
Bruce, 1951. 293 p. (Science and Culture Series)   *Hoover*

YPSILON [pseud. of Johann Rindl and Julian Gomperz]
Pattern for World Revolution, and its French translation: *Stalintern* —
see nos. 384 and 385.

Het ZEVENDE Wereld-Congres der Comunistische Internationale over
de ontwikkeling der wereldrevolutie. See no. 1031.

423 ZINOV'EV, G. E.
International socialism and the proletarian revolution. Glasgow, The
Socialist Labour Press [1919] 16 p. incl. port.   *Hoover*

424 ZINOV'EV, G. E.
Mirovaia revoliutsiia i Kommunisticheskii Internatsional; perevod rechi
na sezde germanskoi nezavisimoi partii v Galle [Halle] 14 Okt. 1920 g.
[2nd ed.] Petrograd [15-aia gos. tip.] 1921. 97 p.   *Hoover, NYPL, Amst*

425 ZINOV'EV, G. E.
Le prolétariat européen devant la révolution. Discours prononcé au
congrès du Parti Social-Démocrate Independent d'Allemagne, à Halle,
le 14 octobre, 1920. Petrograd, Editions de l'Internationale Communiste,
1921. 96 p. (Editions françaises de l'Internationale Communiste, no. 67.)
                                                                          Felt

426 ZINOV'EV, G. E.
Die Weltrevolution und die III. Kommunistische Internationale; Rede
auf dem Parteitag der USPD in Halle am 14. Oktober 1920. [Berlin?]
Verlag der Kommunistischen Internationale, 1920. 68 p. At head of
title: G. Sinowjew.   *Hoover, NYPL, Amst, BDIC, Felt*

427 ZINOV'EV, G. E.
Die Weltrevolution und die III. Internationale! Rede des Vorsitzenden
vom Exekutivkomitee der III. Internationale auf dem Parteitag der
U. S. P. D. in Halle am 14. Oktober 1920. Halle, Oelssner [n. d.] 47 p.
                                                                     Amst, Felt

428 ZUM Weltprogramm des Kommunismus. Methodische Anleitung zum
Studium des Programms für Zirkel und Kurse. Berlin, Internationaler
Arbeiter-Verlag [n. d.] 32 p.   *Amst*

4. The Relationship Comintern — Soviet Government — CPSU

a) Reports of the Delegation of the CPSU in the ECCI to Party Congresses

Note: The reports of the Delegation of the Communist Party of the Soviet Union
in the Executive Committee of the Communist International are listed here chronologically, starting with the VIII-th Congress of the CPSU in March 1919, and
continuing to the XVIII-th Congress in March 1939, which was the last Congress
before the dissolution of the Comintern in 1943.

In the Hoover Institution's library these reports are cataloged under the following heading:

Kommunisticheskaia Partiia Sovetskogo Soiuza; Delegatsiia v Ispolnitel'nom Komitete Kominterna

This heading is followed by the name of the reporting delegate and/or the title of the report. Some libraries catalog these items only under the name of the reporting delegate or the title of the report.

In the listing below, in order to simplify the entries, the above Russian heading was omitted and the items are listed under the name of the reporting delegate and/or the title of the report.

VIII-th Congress (1919)

429 ZINOV'EV, G. E.
Kommunisticheskii Internatsional; doklad na vos'mom s"ezde R. K. P. [New York] Izd. Tsentrispolkom R. F. K. P. A. [Russian Federation of the Communist Party of Americal] 1920. 32 p. *NYPL, Col*

430 ZINOV'EV, G. E.
Die Kommunistische Internationale. Bericht auf dem achten Kongress der Kommunstischen Partei Russlands. Petrograd, Kommunistische Internationale, 1919. 45 p. (At head of title: G. Sinowjew.) *Amst, BDIC*

431 ZINOV'EV, G. E.
L'Internationale communiste. Petrograd, Éditions de l'Internationale communiste [1919] 48 p. (Editions [françaises] de l'Internationale communiste, no. 22)

"Rapport presenté par le cam. G. Zinov'ev au 8-e congrès du Parti communiste russe, 1919": p. r. *Hoover, NYPL, Felt, SInSt*

XIV-th Congress (1925)

432 ELIZAROV, N. V.
Kommunisticheskii Internatsional i VKP(b). Moskva, Gos. izd-vo, 1926. 79 p. (At head of title: Itogi i resheniia 14-go s"ezda VKP(b). Rabochekrest'ianskaia bibliotechka.) *NYPL*

XV-th Congress (1927)

433 BUKHARIN, N. I.
Otchet delegatsii VKP(b) v IKKI XV s"ezdu VKP(b). [Mezhdunarodnoe polozhenie i zadachi Kommunisticheskogo Internatsionala; doklad

i zakliuchitel'noe slovo, 9—12 dekabria 1927 g.] Moskva, Gos. izd-vo, 1928. 204 p. *Hoover, SInSt*

434 BUKHARIN, N. I.
Die internationale Lage und die Aufgaben der Kommunistischen Internationale. Bericht der Delegation der KPSU(b) beim EKKI an den 15. Parteitag; Referat des Genossen N. Bucharin. Hamburg, Hoym, 1928. 69 p. *NYPL, Amst, Felt*

435 BUKHARIN, N. I.
La situation internationale et les tâches de l'I. C.; rapport au XVe congrès du P. C. de l'URSS. Paris, Bureau d'Editions [n. d.] 104 p.

BDIC, Felt

XVI-th Congress (1930)

436 MOLOTOV, V. M.
Otchet delegatsii VKP(b) v IKKI; Doklad i zakliuchitel'noe slovo na XVI s'ezde VKP(b) 5—7 iiulia 1930 g. Moskva [etc.] Gos. izd-vo, 1930. 69 p. *NYPL*

437 OTCHET TSentral'nogo Komiteta, TSentral'noi Kontrol'noi Komissii i Delegatsii VKP(b) v IKKI XVI s"ezdu VKP(b). Moskva, Gos. izd-vo, 1930. 410 p. At head of title: I. Stalin, L. Kaganovich, S. Ordzhonikidze, V. Molotov

Molotov's report to the XVI-th Congress (Otchet delegatsii VKP(b) v IKKI) is contained on pages 307–373. *Hoover*

438 MOLOTOV, V. M.
Das Anwachsen der Weltkrise des Kapitalismus, der revolutionäre Aufschwung und die Aufgaben der Komintern. Tätigkeitsbericht der EKKI-Delegation der KPdSU auf dem XVI Parteitag der KPdSU, 5. Juli, 1930 [Moskau] Vereinigter Staatsverlag „Der Moskauer Arbeiter", 1931. 77 p. (At head of title: W. Molotoff.) *NYPL*

439 MOLOTOV, V. M.
The developing crisis of world capitalism, the revolutionary crisis and the tasks of the Comintern. [New York, Workers' library 1930] 55 p. (Printed in Great Britain.)

On cover: Report of the delegation of the Communist party of the Soviet Union in the Executive Committee of the Communist International. Report and concluding speech delivered at the XVI-th Congress of the C. P. S. U., Moscow, July 5–7, 1930. *Hoover, Felt*

122

440 MOLOTOV, V. M.
La croissance de la crise mondiale du capitalisme, l'essor révolutionnaire et les tâches de l'Internationale Communiste. Paris, Bureau
d'éditions [n. d.] 77 p. (Rapport sur l'activité de la délégation du P. C.
de l'U. R. S. S. au C. E. de l'I. C., presenté par V. Molotov, au XVIe
congrès du P. C. de l'U. R. S. S., le 5 juillet 1930, suivi du discours
de conclusion prononcé le 7 juillet 1930.)   *Felt*

XVII-th Congress (1934)

441 MANUIL'SKII, D. Z.
Die revolutionäre Krise reift heran. Bericht auf dem 17. Parteitag über
die Tätigkeit der Delegation der KPdSU(B) im Exekutivkomitee der
Kommunistischen Internationale. Moskau-Leningrad, Verlagsgenossenschaft ausländischer Arbeiter in der UdSSR, 1934. 68 p.   *Felt*

442 MANUIL'KII, D. Z.
The revolutionary crisis is maturing; report to the seventeenth Congress
of the Communist party of the Soviet Union on behalf of the delegation
of the C. P. S. U. in the Communist International. New York, Workers
Library Publishers [1934] 48 p.   *Hoover, NYPL*

XVIII-th Congress (1939)

443 MANUIL'SKII, D. Z.
Doklad delegatsii VKP(b) v IKKI na XVIII s"ezde VKP(b). [Moskva]
Gos. izd-vo polit. literatury, 1939. 46. p.   *NYPL*

444 MANUIL'SKII, D. Z.
The world communist movement; report of the delegation of the
Communist party of the Soviet Union (Bolsheviks) in the Executive
Committee of the Communist International to the 18-th Congress of
the C. P. S. U. (b). Delivered March 11, 1939. New York, Workers
Library Publishers [1939] 60 p.   *Hoover*

445 MANUIL'SKII, D. Z.
El frente unico internacional obrero, derrota del fachismo; informe
de la delegación del P. C. (b) de la U. R. S. S. en el Comité ejecutivo
de la Internacional Comunista ante el XVIII congreso del partido.
Mexico, D. F., Editorial Popular, 1939. 48 p.   *Hoover*

b) Reports of members of the Delegation to various Party bodies

In chronological order

1920

446 ZINOV'EV, G. E.
Vtoroi kongress Kommunisticheskogo Internatsionala i ego znachenie. Doklad na zasedanii Petrogradskogo soveta. Moskva, Kommunistiche-skii Internatsional, 1920. 37 p.   *Hoover, Harv*

447 ZINOV'EV, G. E.
Vom Werdegang unserer Partei; Vortrag gehalten in einer Versamm-lung der kommunistischen Parteifunktionäre in Petrograd. Petrograd, Kommunistische Internationale, 1920. 47 p. (Veröffentlichungen, no. 46.)
Hoover, LC, Amst

448 ZINOV'EV, G. E.
Der II. [zweite] Kongress der Kommunistischen Internationale (Bericht in der Sitzung des Petrograder Sowjets am 20. August 1920) Kom-munistische Internationale. Hamburg, Hoym Nachf., 1920. 21 p. At head of title: G. Sinowjew.   *Hoover, Amst, BDIC*

1922

449 ZINOV'EV, G. E.
Komintern i edinyi rabochii front; doklad na vserossiiskoi konferentsii R. K. P. Peterburg, Gos. izd-vo, 1922. 45 p.   *Hoover*

1924

[ZINOV'EV's Report at a meeting of Communist Party functionaries in Leningrad, July 9, 1924.] See item 7 in the annotation to no. 781.

1925

450 ZINOV'EV, G. E.
Zadachi Kominterna i RKP(b). 29 aprelia 1925 goda. Moskva, Gos. izd-vo, 1925. 63 p.

A report tho the XIV-th Conference of the Communist Party of Russia (Bolsheviks), April 29, 1925   *BDIC*

451 ZINOV'EV, G. E.
Les traits essentiels de la période actuelle. Rapport fait à la fraction communiste du IIe Congrès des Soviets de l'U. R. S. S. (20 mai 1925). Paris, Librairie de l'Humanité [n. d.] 56 p. (Petite Bibliothèque Communiste.) *Hoover, Felt*

1927

452 BUKHARIN, N. I.
Itogi plenuma IKKI; doklad tov. N. I. Bukharina na plenume Moskovskogo komiteta VKP(b) 4 iiunia 1927. 2-e izd. Moskva, „Pravda" i „Bednota", 1927. 54 p.

Contents: O borb'e s voinoi. – Bor'ba s voinoi i oppozitsiia. – O kitaiskoi revoliutsii. – Kitaiskaia revoliutsiia i oppozitsiia. *NYPL*

453 RAKHMETOV, V., ed.
Mezhdunarodnoe polozhenie i zadachi Kominterna. Moskva, Gos. izd-vo, 1927. 72 p. illus. At head of title: Seriia posobii po prorabotke reshenii XV konferentsii VKP(b). *NYPL*

1928

454 BUKHARIN, N. I.
Ergebnisse des VI. Kongresses der Kommunistischen Internationale; Rede, gehalten vor dem Parteiaktiv der Moskauer Organisation der KP(B)SU. Anschließend J. Jaroslawski: Kominternkongreß (Mit Wort-Erklärung) Moskau, Zentral-Völker-Verlag, 1929. 66 p. *NYPL*

455 BUKHARIN, N. I.
Die historische Leistung des 6. Weltkongresses der Komintern; Rede vor dem Parteiaktiv der Moskauer Organisation der KPdSU, 5 September 1928 [von] N. Bucharin. Hamburg, C. Hoym Nachfolger [1928] 34 p.
Hoover, NYPL, Harv, Felt

456 MOLOTOV, V. M.
VI [shestoi] kongress i bor'ba za komunizm; doklad na Leningradskom aktive VKP(b) 7 sentiabria 1928 g. Moskva [etc.] Gos. izd-vo, 1928. 63 p. *NYPL*

457 MOLOTOV, V. M. — see Addenum.

1929

458 MOLOTOV, V. M.
Stroitel'stvo sotsializma i protivorechiia rosta; doklad o rabote TSK VKP(b) na I Moskovskoi oblastnoi partiinoi konferentsii 14 sentiabria 1929 goda. Moskva, "Moskovskii rabochii" [1929] 127 p.

Part of this report deals with the political line of the Comintern adopted in its activities in foreign countries. *Hoover*

1935

459 MANUIL'SKII, D. Z.
Itogi VII kongressa Kommunisticheskogo Internatsionala; doklad na Moskovskom i Leningradskom partaktive. Moskva, Partizdat, 1935. 90 p. *Col, SInSt*

460 MANUIL'SKII, D. Z.
Die Ergebnisse des VII. Weltkongresses der Kommunistischen Internationale. Bericht des Genossen Manuilski in der Versammlung des Moskauer und Leningrader Parteiaktivs, September 1935. Moskau-Leningrad, Verlagsgenossenschaft ausländischer Arbeiter in der UdSSR, 1935. 93 p. At head of title: VII. Weltkongreß der Kommunistischen Internationale. D. Manuilski. *Felt*

461 MANUIL'SKII D. Z.
Die Ergebnisse des VII. Kongresses der Kommunistischen Internationale, Referat vor dem Moskauer und Leningrader Parteiaktiv. Strasbourg, Prometheus [1936] 53 p. At head of title: D. Manuilski. [Printed in Switzerland.] *Hoover, NYPL, NWest, Amst*

462 MANUIL'SKII, D. Z.
The work of the seventh Congress of the Communist International. New York, Workers Library Publ. [1936] 80 p.
"Speeches delivered at a meeting of the active members of the Moscow organization of the Communist party of the Soviet Union, September, 1935." p. [4]
See also next item. *Hoover, NYPL, Harv, Amst*

463 MANUIL'SKII, D. Z.
The work of the seventh Congress of the Communist International. a speech delivered at meeting of the active members of the Moscov organization of the C. P. S. U., September 14, 1935. [London, Modern Books, 1935] 63 p.
Identical with New York edition, no. 462. See also no. 968–7. *Hoover, Col, UTex*

464 MANUIL'SKII, D. Z.
Le VIIe congrès est le congrès de l'unité; bilan du VIIe congrès de l'Internationale Communiste. Paris, Bureau d'Editions, 1936. 70 p. At head of title: D. Z. Manouilski.
"Rapport du camarade Manouilski devant les assemblées des militants communistes de Moscou et de Leningrad." *NYPL*

465 MANUIL'SKII, D. Z.
Výsledky VII kongresu Komunistické Internacionály. Referát na moskovském a leningradském aktivu strany. Z ruštiny přeložil J. Svoboda. Překlad přehlédli K. Konečný a V. Prokůpek [Praha, Nedvěda] 1936. 81 p. *Amst*

c) Books and pamphlets on the subject

466 AKHMINOV, G. F.
Die Macht im Hintergrund. Totengräber des Kommunismus. Grenchen/Ulm, Spaten Verlag [1950] 307 p. (At head of title: G. F. Achminow)
Felt

467 AKHMINOV, G. F.
La puissance dans l'ombre; ou le fossoyeur du communisme. Paris, Les Iles d'Or, Diffusion Plon [1952] 371 p. (At head of title: German F. Achminow)
Felt

DRAPER, Theodore
American Communism and Soviet Russia; the formative period. See no. 239a.

DRAPER, Theodore
The Roots of American Communism. See no. 1510.

GITLOW, Benjamin
I confess; the truth about American communism. See no. 194.

GITLOW, Benjamin
The whole of their lives; communism in America, a personal history and intimate portrayal of its leaders. See no. 195.

GREAT Britain. Foreign Office.
Documents illustrating the hostile activities of the Soviet government and Third International against Great Britain. See no. 106.

468 INTERNATIONAL Anti-Communist Entente.
Le Komintern, le gouvernement soviétique et le Parti communiste de l'U. R. S. S.: étude présentée à la 15e Assemblée generale de la Société des Nations. Genève [Imp. du Journal de Genève] 1934. 27 p. At head of title: Bureau permanent de l'Entente internationale contre la IIIe Internationale.
Hoover, NYPL

469 INTERNATIONAL Anti-Communist Entente.
The present policy of the Soviet government and the Third International; memorandum addressed to the governments and to the international institutions by the Permanent Bureau of the International Entente against the Third Inernational . . . [Geneva] 1928. 15 p.
NYPL

IZ ISTORII mezhdunarodnoi proletarskoi solidarnosti; dokumenty i materialy. See no. 112.

470 KAUTSKY, Karl
L'Internationale et la Russie des Soviets. Paris, Librairie populaire, 1925. 48 p. (At head of title: Editions du Parti Socialiste (S. F. I. O.))
NYPL

471 KAUTSKY, Karl
Die Internationale und Sowjetrußland. Berlin, Dietz Nachf. [c1925] 62 p.
Hoover, LC, NYPL, Harv

472 KLOTZ, Henry
La Russie des Soviets; faits et documents. Qu'y a-t-il de vrai dans la formule: Le communisme, voilà l'ennemi. Paris, L. Fournier, 1928. 189 p. fascims.

"Annexe: Instructions générales de la IIIe Internationale aux partis communistes adhérents" – p. 171–181.
LC, NYPL, Col

KRIVITSKY, Walter G.
In Stalin's Secret Service; an exposé of Russia's secret policies ...
See no. 196.

KRIVITSKY, Walter G.
Agent de Staline. See no. 197.

KURELLA, Alfred
Vsesoiuznaia kommunisticheskaia partiia (b) i Kommunisticheskii Internatsional; o pravom i levom uklone v Kommunsticheskom Internatsionale. See no. 278.

473 REITENBACH, Georg
UdSSR. Staatssystem, Parteiaufbau, Komintern. [Berlin, O. Stollberg, 1941] 136 p. diagrs., map. (Die Bücherei des Ostraums.)
Hoover, LC, NYPL, Col

474 RICHARDS, Edward Branson
Soviet control of international communism. Ann Arbor, University Microfilms [1957] ([Univ. microfilms, Ann Arbor, Mich.] Publication No 22,096) Microfilm copy (positive) of typescript. Collation of the original: iv, 2121. Thesis — State University of Iowa. Abstracted in Dissertation abstracts, v. 17 (1957) no. 9, p. 2052—2053. Bibliography: leaves 205—212.
Hoover, Iowa

475 RÜCK, Friedrich
Sovjetunionen och Komintern. Stockholm, Kooperativa förbundets bokforlag, 1943. 180 p.
Hoover, Amst, SInSt

RUSSLAND und die Komintern. Gedanken für einen internationalen sozialistischen Neuaufbau. See no. 344.

476 SHELAVIN, K. I.
Polozhenie v sektsiiakh Kominterna i XVI s"ezd VKP(b). Leningrad, 1930. 80 p.   *SInSt*

477 UNITED States. Department of State. Division of Russian Affairs. The Communist party in Russia and its relations to the Third International and to the Russian soviets. New York, Greenwich, Conn., American Association for International Conciliation [1921] 2 v.   *Hoover, BDIC*

478 UNITED States. Department of State. Division of Russian Affairs. Memorandum on the Bolshevist or Communist Party in Russia and its relations to the Third or Communist International and to the Russian Soviets. Washington, Govt. Printing Office, 1920. 49 p.
Hoover, NYPL, Harv, Col

VSESOIUZNAIA kommunisticheskaia partiia (bolshevikov)
Partiia i Komintern; o "staroi" i "novoi'" oppozitsii; sbornik rezoliutsii i postanovlenii. See no. 142.

5. Organizational Matters

BESCHLÜSSE und Resolutionen angenommen von der 2. Orgkonferenz . . . See no. 1084.

479 BEWER, O.
Le manuel du militant. Paris, Bureau d'Editions, 1931. 90 p.   *Hoover*

COMMUNIST International; Organization Department [For results of two Organization Conferences in 1925 and 1926 see nos. 1060, 1061, 1084, 1085].

La II-e [DEUXIÈME] conférence d'organisation; décisions et résolutions adoptées . . . Se no. 1085.

HOW to organize the Communist Party [Minutes of the Organization Commission of the fifth Congress and instructions] See no. 800.

HVAD er Bolsjevisering? See no. 1083.

480 INSTRUCTION from the Executive Committee to the Mitteleuropäisches Büro in Berlin, signed by Rakosi, Kuusinen, and Lozovskii. Moscow, 1921. Microfilm copy of typewritten original in two parts. Collation of the original 9 and 5 p.   *Hoover*

481 INTERNATIONAL Anti-Communist Entente.
Charts representing the Soviet organizations working for revolution in all countries (with explanatory notes), October 1928 [Geneva, 1928] 49 p. illus., charts. (At head of title: Permanent Bureau of the International Entente against the Third International, Geneva.)   *NYPL, Harv*

482 INTERNATIONAL Anti-Communist Entente.
Organization and activities of the Communist International. English edition. October 1938. Geneva, 1938. 93 leaves, duplicated.

> General information on organization and work of the Comintern together with a description of the organization of the CPSU and of the Soviet State. Contains a long list of prominent Bolshevik leaders who were purged and executed by the Stalin regime. See annotation to next item.   *Hoover*

483 INTERNATIONAL Anti-Communist Entente.
The Red Network; the Communist International at work. London, Duckworth, 1939. 93 p.

> "This book was originally published in French under the title 'Organization and activities of the Communist International'. It was prepared and issued by the International Anti-Communist Entente... A draft English edition was prepared in October 1938, and the present edition has been adapted particularly for readers in this country." The Foreword, signed by J. Baker White. See preceding item.   *Hoover, NYPL, Col, BDIC*

484 INTERNATIONAL Anti-Communist Entente.
Tableaux des organisations soviétiques, travaillant à la révolution dans tous les pays (accompagnés de notes explicatives). Genève, Bureau Permanent de l'Entente contre la IIIe Internationale, 1928. 49 p. illus., diagrs.   *NYPL, Felt*

484a L'I [NTERNATIONALE] C[ommuniste] et les questions d'organisation. Paris, 1925.   *LC*

485 JENKS, M.
The Communist Nucleus; what it is, how it works. New York, Workers Library Publishers [c1928] 61 p. forms. (Workers Library, no. 7.)   *Col*

KUUSINEN, Otto
The international situation and the tasks of the sections of the Comintern. See no. 1209—1211.

KUUSINEN, Otto
Die internationale Lage und die Aufgaben der Sektionen der Kommunistischen Internationale. See no. 1203.

KUUSINEN, Otto
Mezhdunarodnoe polozhenie i zadachi sektsii Kominterna. See no. 1201.

LEITSÄTZE über den organisatorischen Aufbau der Kommunistischen Parteien, über die Methoden und den Inhalt ihrer Arbeit. See no. 697.

486 LENINE et l'organisation [par la Section d'organisation du C. E. de l'I. C.] Paris, Bureau d'Editions, 1928. 178 p.   *Hoover*

487 [NITTI, F.]
Organisation et activité de l'Internationale communiste. Paris, "Les éditions documentaires" [1937] pagination not given.

> See annotation to no. 488.   *Harv*

487a ON the road to bolshevization. New York [c1929] 46 p. (Signed: Executive Committee of the Communist International.)   *NYPL*

O MEZHDUNARODNOM polozhenii i zadachakh sektsii Kommunisticheskogo Internatsionala. Tezisy . . . See no. 1228.

Die ORGANISATION der Betriebszellen; organisatorische Fragen und Beschlüsse des V. Kongresses. See no. 797.

488 ORGANISATION et activité de l'Internationale Communiste. Paris, "Les éditions documentaires" [1938] 223 p. index.

> This item seems to be identical with no. 487. Harvard did not give the number of pages and ascribed the item to F. Nitti.
> NYPL and the other two libraries did not find any reason to ascribe it to Nitti. The item was unavailable for identification.   *NYPL, Amst, Felt*

Der ORGANISATORISCHE Aufbau der Kommunistischen Partei. Organisationsberatung der erweiterten Exekutive (März/April 1925). See no. 1060.

I PARTITI Comunisti e l'organizzazione delle donne. See no. 711.

PIATNITSKII, Osip, A.
Alcuni problemi urgenti. Il movimento dei disocupati. Il lavoro del partito e dei sindacati nelle officine. Le fluttuazioni dei nostri effettivi. See no. 1183.

PIATNITSKII, Osip A.
The bolshevization of the communist parties by eradicating the social-democratic traditions. See no. 320.

PIATNITSKII, Osip A.
Kompartii na puti bol'shevizatsii. See no. 322.

489 PIATNITSKII, Osip A.
The organisation of a world party. London, Communist Party of Great Britain [1928] 94 p.

> On cover: "A Survey of the position of the sections of the Communist International, their achievements, defects and future tasks." Articles reprinted from the "Communist International." *Hoover, LC, NYPL, Harv, Col*

490 PIATNITSKII, Osip A.
Die Organisationsarbeit in den kommunistischen Parteien der kapitalischen Länder. Hamburg, C. Hoym Nachf. [1928] 69 p. *Hoover, NYPL, Felt*

491 PIATNITSKII, Osip A.
Organisatorische Fragen. Berlin, C. Hoym [1925] 64 p. *Felt*

492 PIATNITSKII, Osip, A.
Organizatsionnaia rabota v kompartiiakh kapitalisticheskikh stran. 2 ispr. i dop. izd. Moskva, Gos. izd., 1929. 125 p. *Hoover, SInSt*

PIATNITSKII, Osip A.
Quelques problemes urgents. Le mouvement des chomeurs. Le travail du parti et des syndicats dans les entreprises. La fluctuation de nos effectives. See no. 1180.

493 PIATNITSKII, Osip A.
Questions d'organisation. Paris, Librairie de l'Humanité, 1926. 88, VIII p. diagrs. *Hoover, Felt*

494 PIATNITSKII, Osip A.
Le travail d'organisation dans les partis communistes des pays capitalistes. Paris, Bureau d'Editions [1927] 112 p. (At head of title: O. Piatnitsky) *BDIC*

PIATNITSKII, Osip A.
Urgent questions of the day. Unemployed movement. Factory organization. Fluctuating membership. See no. 1176, 1177.

495 PIATNITSKII, Osip A.
Voprosy partstroitel'stva v sektsiiakh Kominterna. Moskva, Gos. izd-vo,
1926. 64 p.   *NYPL*

Les QUESTIONS d'organisation au Ve Congrès de l'I. C. Cellules
d'entreprises, statuts de l'I. C., directives pour l'organisation, etc. See
no. 804.

La REORGANISATION des partis communistes; rapports et décisions
de la Conférence d'organisation de l'I. C. See no. 1061.

TESIS sobre la estructura y métodos de acción de los partidos comunistas. See no. 715.

THESIS on the propaganda activity of the Communist International
and its sections. See no. 789.

12 [TWELFTH] Plenum E.C.C.I. The international situation and the
tasks of the sections of the Communist International. Theses... See
no. 1233.

496 ÜBER die Bildung der kommunistischen Zellen und Arbeitsgruppen
[Moscow?]. Verlag der Kommunistischen Internationale; Hamburg,
C. Hoym Nachf. L. Cahnbley, 1921. 16 p. (Flugschriften der Kommunistischen Internationale, 11) Signed: Sekretariat des Exekutivkomitees
der Kommunistischen Internationale.   *Hoover, Harv, Amst*

ÜBER die Bolschewisierung der Parteien der Komintern. Thesen...
See no. 1078.

ZINOV'EV, G.
Mezhdunarodnye perspektivy i bol'shevizatsiia kompartii. See no. 1068.

ZINOV'EV, G.
Les perspectives internationales et la bolchevisation. See no. 1075.

ZINOV'EV, G.
Über die Bolschewisierung der Parteien. See no. 1072.

ZINOV'EV, G.
Über die Bolschewisierung der Parteien der Komintern. Thesen. Entwurf... See no. 1073.

PART III.

THE CONGRESSES AND THE EXECUTIVE COMMITTEE

A. The Congresses of the Communist International

1. I-st CONGRESS, Moscow, March 2—6, 1919

a) Protocols

497 PERVYI Kongress Kommunisticheskogo Internatsionala; protokoly zasedanii v Moskve so 2 po 19 marta 1919 goda. Petrograd, Izd. Kommunisticheskogo Internatsionala, 1921. 196 p.

See annotation to no. 498.   *Hoover, LC, Harv*

498 PERVYI Kongress Kominterna; mart 1919 g. Pod redaktsiei E. Korotkogo, B. Kuna i O. Piatnitskogo. Moskva, Partiinoe izd-vo, 1933. vi, 275 p., indexes. (At head of title: Institut Marksa-Engelsa-Lenina pri TSK VKP(b). Protokoly kongressov Kommunisticheskogo Internatsionala.)

This is a revised and enlarged edition of the protocols published in 1921 (see preceding item). In the preface the editors state that the 1921 edition was based on the German text of the protocols published in 1920 (listed here as no. 499). They explain that "as the proceedings of the congress were conducted mainly in the German language, ... the Russian text published in 1921 was a translation from the German [text]; in the present edition [this text] was corrected and re-edited after checking it against the original German text" (p. iv–v). Some speeches were corrected and supplemented on the basis of the original notes taken at the congress and kept in the archives of the Marx-Engels-Lenin Institute in Moscow.

134

Several items have been added to this new edition which have not been included in the German 1920 edition and in the Russian 1921 edition. These items are:

a) A report by V. V. Obolenskii (N. Osinskii) about the international policy of the Entente. This is a reprint of the pamphlet by Obolenskii, *Mezhdunarodnoe polozhenie i politika Soglasiia;* Moscow, Ispolkom Kominterna, 1919.

b) A report by Sirola about the "white terror".

c) Several reports of delegates presented to the congress in writing.

d) Two letters from the Serbian and Hungarian delegates who were unable to come to the congress.

e) Minutes of the Mandate Commission.

f) Six "enclosures", of which the minutes of a "preparatory meeting of delegates" held in Moscow on March 1, 1919, is the most important one.

The editors of the new edition also corrected a few inaccuracies contained in the earlier Russian and German editions. The number of delegates to the congress with voting rights was established at 34 whereas the earlier editions contained the erroneous figure of 35. The number of votes to which these delegates were entitled was established as 49 in the new edition, whereas the earlier editions mentioned 55 votes. Furthermore, the editors settled the dates of the congress as March 2–6, 1919. The earlier Russian and German editions carried in the title pages the eroneous date of March 2–19, 1919, (see nos. 497, 499, 500) and had confusing dates in the text itself.

Finally, the new edition has useful speakers' names and subject indexes.

Hoover, NYPL, BDIC, Felt, SInSt

499 Der I. [Erste] Kongreß der Kommunistischen Internationale; Protokoll der Verhandlungen in Moskau vom 2. bis zum 19. März 1919. Petrograd, Kommunistische Internationale, 1920. 311 p. (Kommunistische Internationale. Publikationen, no. 46)

See annotation to no. 498. *Hoover, NYPL, Harv, Amst*

500 Der I. [ERSTE] Kongreß der Kommunistischen Internationale; Protokoll der Verhandlungen in Moskau vom 2. bis zum 19. März 1919. Verlag der Kommunistischen Internationale; Hamburg, C. Hoym Nachf. L. Cahnbley, 1921. 202 p. (Bibliothek der Kommunistischen Internationale, 7)

See annotation to no. 498.
Hoover, LC, NYPL, Harv, Brown, Duke, JCre, NYUn, Ohio, Amst, Felt

501 PRVI kongres Treće Internacionale; materijali. [Odabiranje materiala, objašnjenja, predgovor i registar Stevanom Belićem-Franićem] Beograd, Rad, 1953. 293 p. (Biblioteka istorije medjunarodnog radničkog i socijalističkog pokreta)

Abridged, stenographic report. *Hoover, Felt*

b) Reports, Speeches, Drafts presented to the Congress

502 LENIN, V. I. [and Bukharin, N.]
Tezisy o burzhuaznoi demokratii i proletarskoi diktature. N. Bukharin.
Diktatura proletariata. [New York] Russkaia federatsiia kommunistich.
partii, 1920. 32 p.

> Lenin's speech at the first Congress of the Communist International adopted as
> thesis. For German edition see no. 504, for English edition see no. 506.   *Hoover*

503 LENIN, V. I.
Die Gründung der Kommunistischen Internationale; Reden, Thesen,
Artikel. Moskau, Verlagsgenossenschaft ausländischer Arbeiter in der
UdSSR, 1934. 70 p. (Kleine Bücherei des Marxismus-Leninismus, Bd. 15)

> Bibliography included in "Anmerkungen", p. 70.   *NYPL*

504 LENIN, V. I.
Thesen über bürgerliche Demokratie und proletarische Diktatur. Stenogramm des Referates und Resolution des Kongresses. Moskau, Verlag
des Exekutivkomitees der Kommunistischen Internationale, 1919. 29 p.
(Kommunistische Bibliothek, no. 2)   *Hoover, Amst*

505 LENIN, V. I.
The foundation of the Communist International. New York, International
Publishers [1934] 47 p.

> Speeches, reports, writings.   *Hoover, Harv, Amst*

506 LENIN, V. I.
Lenin's thesis on bourgeoise [!] democracy and proletarian dictator-
ship. Glasgow, Socialist Labour Press [1919?] 28 p.

> Speech at the first Congress of the Communist International, adopted as thesis.
> *Hoover*

c) Resolutions, Theses, Manifestoes and other documents

LENIN, V. I.
Tezisy o burzhuaznoii demokratii i proletarskoi diktature. See no. 502.

507 MANIFEST Kommunisticheskogo Internatsionala k proletariiam vsego
mira. Tiflis, 1919. 12 p. (Izdatel'stvo "Tretii Internatsional", no. 1)
Hoover

508 MANIFEST Kommunisticheskogo Internatsionala k proletariiam vsego mira. Khar'kov, Vseukr. izd-vo [March] 1920. 20 p. On blue paper.
BDIC

509 PLATFORMA Kommunisticheskogo Internatsionala [priniata na s"ezde III Internatsionala v Moskve v marte 1919 g.] Tiflis, Tip. Ekonomiia, 1919. 15 p. (Izdatel'stvo "Tretii Internatsional" no. 4) *Hoover*

510 REZOLIUTSII i postanovleniia pervogo s"ezda Kommunisticheskogo Internatsionala i vos'mogo s"ezda Rossiiskoi kommunisticheskoi partii. Programma R.K.P. / Ekaterinoslav, 1919. 44, 16 p. (At head of title: Rossiiskaia kommunisticheskaia partiia, Kommunisticheskaia partiia bol'shevikov Ukrainy) *Hoover, LC*

511 Die KOMMUNISTISCHE Internationale (Manifest, Leitsätze und Beschlüsse des Moskauer Kongresses 2.—6. März 1919). Hamburg, Willaschek & Co. [1919?] 56 p. *LC, Col, Amst, BDIC*

512 Die KOMMUNISTISCHE Internationale bis zu ihrem zweiten Kongreß. Manifest, Richtlinien, Beschlüsse des ersten Kongresses, Aufrufe und offene Schreiben des Exekutivkomitees. Petrograd, Die Kommunistische Internationale, 1920. 368 p. *NYPL, UMich*

LENIN, V. I.
Thesen über bürgerliche Demokratie und proletarische Diktatur. Stenogramm des Referates und Resolution des Kongresses. See no. 504.

513 MANIFEST der Kommunistischen Internationale. An das Proletariat der ganzen Welt. Budapest, Volkskommissariat für Unterrichtswesen, 1919. 14 p. (Hungary. Közoktatásügyi népbiztosság. Veröffentlichungen, nr. 10) *Hoover*

514 MANIFEST, Richtlinien, Beschlüsse des ersten Kongresses. Aufrufe und offene Schreiben des Exekutivkomitees bis zum zweiten Kongreß. Kommunistesche Internationale; Auslieferungsstelle, C. Hoym Nachf., Hamburg, 1920. 379 p. (Bibliothek der Kommunistischen Internationale 1)
Hoover, LC, NYPL, Harv, Col, Duke, ULa, Amst, Felt

515 MANIFEST und Richtlinien der Kommunistischen Internationale. [Chicago, Chicago Arbeiterzeitung Publishing Company, 1919] 32 p. Cover title: Manifest der Kommunistischen Internationale. *LC*

516 Das NEUE kommunistische Manifest, Moskau, 1919; mit einem Vorwort von Dr. Heinrich Laufenberg. Hamburg, Willaschek & Co. [1919] 16 p.
Hoover, LC, Amst

517 PROGRAMM der Kommunistischen Internationale. Zürich, Sozialdemo-kratische Partei [1920?] 40 p. (Kampfruf, nr. 5) *Harv, Duke, Amst, Felt*

LENIN, V. I.
Lenin's Thesis on Bourgeoise [!] Democracy and Proletarian Dictator-ship. See no. 506.

518 MANIFESTO and governing rules of the Communist International (adopted by the Congress of the Communist International at Moscow, March 2—6, 1919, and signed by comrades C. Rakovsky, N. Lenin, M. Zinovjev, L. Trotzky, and Fritz Platten) [Chicago, Arbeiter-Zeitung Publ. Co., 1919] 32 p. *Hoover, LC, NYPL, Col, Illin, UMinn*

519 MANIFESTO of the Communist International; Manifesto of the first Congress of the Communist International, held at Moscow, March 2—6, 1919. Issued March 10-th and signed Charles Rakovsky, N. Lenin, G. Zinoview, Leon Trotzky, Fritz Platten. Text received direct from Moscow [n. p., 1919] 2 p. folio. Detached from "Truth" Friday, July 18, 1919. Translated by Ida Ferguson. *Hoover, LC*

520 The MANIFESTO of the Moscow International, signed by Lenin, Trotsky, Platten, Zinoviev and Rakovsky; translated from the "New Yorker Volkszeitung" by H. J. Stenning . . . Manchester, The National Labour Press [1919] 11 p. *Col*

521 The NEW Communist Manifesto of the Third International. With pref. by W[illia]m Paul. Glasgow, Socialist Labour Press [1919] iv, 12 p.
  Amst, Felt

522 L'INTERNATIONALE communiste; manifestes, thèses, résolutions du 1-er congrès de l'I. C., mars 1919 [n. p., n. d.] 51 p. (Publications de la 4-e Internationale, 1) *LC, Harv*

523 MANIFESTE et résolution de l'Internationale Communiste; introduction de Boris Souvarine. Paris, Editions "Clarté", 1919. 35 p. (Collection historique et documentaire) *Hoover, Amst, BDIC, Felt*

THÈSES, manifestes et résolutions adoptés par le Ier, IIe, IIIe et IVe Congrès de l'Internationale Communiste 1919—1923. Textes complets. See no. 140.

524 La III-e [TROISIÈME] Internationale communiste. Thèses adoptées par le 1-er congrès. Documents officiels pour l'année 1919—1920. (Avec collaboration de G. Zinoviev.) Petrograd, Editions de l'Internationale communiste, 1920. 280 p. Cover title. (Editions françaises de l'Inter-nationale communiste, no. 53) *Hoover, UTex, Amst, BDIC*

525 Het PROGRAM van Moskau. Aangenomen op het congres der Communistische Internationale, gehouden van 2 tot 6 Maart 1919 [Het streven der Communistische Internationale. Vert. door G. Vanter] Amsterdam, Bos [n. d.]) 16 p.   *Amst*

526 KOMMUNISTISEN internatsionaalin manifesti koko maailman proletaareille. Hyväksytty Kommunistisen internatsionaalin perustavassa kokouksessa Moskovassa [Helsinki?, 1919?] 16 p.   *Hoover*

527 A KOMMUNISTA Internacionale kiáltványa a világ proletárjaihoz; forditotta Bodó Pál. Budapest, Közoktatsügyi népbiztosság kiadása, 1919. 12 p. (A Közoktatásügyi népbiztosság kiadása 3)   *Hoover*

528 PIERWSZY zjazd Międzynarodówki komunistycznej w Moskwie w marcu 1919 r. ze wstępem W. Mieczyńskiego [n. p.] Wydawnictwo Sekcji polskiej Komunistycznej Partji Niemiec, 1919. iv, 35 p. (Bibljoteka komunistyczna. No. 4)   *Hoover, Amst*

529 PLATFORMA Międzynarodówki komunistycznej, przyjęta na I Kongresie III Międzynarodówki w Moskwie w marcu 1919 roku [n. p.] Wydawnictwo Sekcji polskiej Komunistycznej Partji Niemiec, 1919. 12 p. (Bibljoteka komunistyczna, No. 3)   *Hoover*

530 PLATFORMA Międzynarodówki Komunistycznej, przyjęta na I. kongresie Międzynarodówki w Moskwie w marcu 1919. Wiedeń [Vienna] 1919. 16 p. (Wydawnictwo "Świtu", Nr. 1)   *Hoover*

531 MANIFEST Komunistička Internacijonale. Primljen na prvom zboru medjunarodnih komunista u Moskvi, 6 ožujka 1919. Chicago, Jugosl. medjunarodni soc. savez, 1919. 28 p.   *Hoover*

532 KOMMUNISTINEN internationali. Stockholm, Fram, 1919. 104 p. (At head of title: Kaikkien maiden köyhälistö, liittykää yhteen!)   *NYPL*

533 Den TREDJE internationalen. Manifest, riktlinjer och resolutioner vid den kommunistiska världskongressen i Moskva. Stockholm, Frams förlag, 1919. 82 p. ports. 2 ed. Cover title.   *NYPL*

534 MANIFEST i programa Komunistychnoho Internatsionalu. Vidane Ukrainskoi Federatsii Amerikanskoi Sotsialistichnoi Partii. New York, N. Y., Druk. "Robitnyka", 1919. 29 p.   *Hoover, UChic*

d) Commentaries and writings about the Congress

535 III [TRETII] Internatsional. 6—7 marta 1919 g. . . Moskva, Gos. izd-vo, 1919. 99 p.

> A propaganda pamphlet about the founding of the Communist International for broad circulation in Russia. Contains several resolutions and theses adopted by the first Congress, excerpts from speeches at the Congress, and a few statements about the Congress by some foreign participants. *Hoover, NYPL*

536 Die GRÜNDUNG der Dritten Internationale. Erste Konferenz der Kommunistischen Internationale in Moskau, abgeh. vom 2. bis 6. März 1919. Wien, Kommunistische Partei Deutschösterreichs, 1919. 63 p.

> *Amst, BDIC, Felt*

537 Der I [ERSTE] und II. Kongreß der Kommunistischen Internationale. Dokumente der Kongresse und Reden W. I. Lenins. Berlin, Dietz, 1959. 328 p. (Institut für Marxismus-Leninismus, Berlin)

> This volume was published on the occasion of the 40-th anniversary of the foundation of the Communist International. It contains a descriptive "Preface", p. 7–42, followed by a reprint of 35 items from the stenographic reports on the first and second Congresses, "Annexes" containing three items written by Lenin on the Communist International, and a list of countries represented at these Congresses. The "Preface" mentions only Lenin as the author of the speeches and theses presented to and adopted by the Congresses. The names of Zinov'ev, Trotskii, Bukharin and Radek, who played a considerable role in the drafting of the theses, are eliminated. Even the invitation to the second Congress is reprinted without the signatures of Zinov'ev and Radek. The editors, however, found an occasion to credit Khrushchev with conclusions drawn from the past. *Hoover, NYPL, Harv, Col, Amst, Felt*

538 3-me [TROISIÈME] Internationale; ses principes, son premier congrès . . . [La Chaux-de-Fonds, 1919] 47 p. (Jeunesses socialistes romandes. Bibliothèque, no. 9) *Noover, NYPL, Amst, BDIC, Felt*

539 40-me [QUARANTIÈME] Anniversaire de la fondation de l'Internationale Communiste. Premier Congrès Moscou, 2—6 mars 1919 (Documents) [Avec introd. par Paulette Charbonnel] Les Cahiers du Communisme [n. d.] 48 p. Bibliographia (Contributions à l'Histoire du Parti Communiste français. Supplement aux Cahiers du Communisme (1959) 3) *Amst*

540 La FONDAZIONE della terza Internazionale. Prima conferenza dell'Internazionale comunista (Mosca 2—6 marzo 1919) Milano, Avanti!, 1921. 64 p. (Atti della terza Internazionale 1) *NYPL, Felt*

541 DOBORZYŃSKI, Gustaw

III Międzynarodówka. Drukowane jako manuskrypt. Warszawa, Warszawska druk. wydawnicza, 1919. 122 p. (Wydawnictwa Wydziału prasowego Ministerstwa Spraw Zagranicznych No. 1. "Materjały", p. 57—122)

A description and analysis of the first Congress of the Communist International based on Soviet and foreign press reports. The part "Materjały" contains 23 translated excerpts from *Pravda* and *Izvestiia*. The author concealed the participation of Polish communists in the Congress.   *Hoover, Harv, Amst*

2. II-nd C O N G R E S S, Petrograd, July 19; Moscow,
July 23 — August 7, 1920

a) Preparatory work for the Congress

Note: The Second Congress of the Communist International was prepared by Lenin and his close associates with special care, for their stakes ran high: to transform the hastily created organization from a small propaganda office into a center of revolutionary action on a world-wide scale. Lenin, Zinov'ev, Bukharin and Radek—the Moscow leaders of the movement—undertook the task of preparing the promotional material which was to be distributed before the Congress among foreign communists and sympathizers. This material appeared as pamphlets in the Russian, German, English and French languages. As this was a special preparatory campaign before the Second Congress, not repeated on such a broad scale before any later congresses, the pertinent material has been listed separately, under the title "Prepartory work for the Congress." (See also annotation to no. 571.)

Among these preparatory items the reprint of part of a special issue of the English-language periodical, *Communist International* (No 11/12, June-July 1920) deserves attention. It contained most of the items produced for this promotional campaign (see no. 549). Various combinations of items contained in this reprint were contained in separate pamphlets, with similar or identical titles. In order to facilitate the identification and location of these items, a "Contents Table" has been compiled (see next page).

542 TEZISY ko vtoromu kongressu. Petrograd, Izd-vo Kommunisticheskogo Internatsionala [1920] 107 p.

For contents see *Contents Table* on p. 142.   *Hoover, LC, Harv*

543 TEZISY ko vtoromu kongressu Kommunisticheskogo Internatsionala. Baku, Gos. izd-vo, "Azertsentropechat'", 1920. 99 p.   *Hoover*

Contents Table

"Invitation Print" Abbreviated title of component part: (Item 1–13: see full titles in annotation to no. 549)	Invitation print, no. 549	ZINOVEV, Brennende Tagesfragen (Moscow) no. 546	ZINOVEV, Tagesfragen (Berlin) no. 547	ZINOVEV, Questions les plus pressantes, no. 556	ZINOVEV, Pressing questions, no. 551	THESES presented to II. Congress (Russ. Germ. Engl. French) nos. 542, 545, 550, 553
1. Invitation to Congress	x					
2. ZINOV'EV: The II Congress C.I. and its tasks	x	x	x	x	x	
3. THESES:						
A. Role of CP in revolution	x	x	x			x
B. CP and parliamentarism	x					x
4. ZINOV'EV: Draft – instruction on parliamentarism	x	x	x			x
5. LENIN: Draft Theses on national and colonial question	x					x
6. ZINOV'EV: Theses on Soviets	x	x	x			x
7. THESES on agrarian question	x					x
8. RADEK: Theses on shop committees	x					x
9. LENIN: Theses on fundamental tasks of II Congress	x					x
10. TROTSKII: To forthcoming Congr.	x					
11. KAMENEV: Dictatorship of prolet.	x					
12. [ZINOV'EV]: Theses on conditions of admission to C.I.	x	x	x			x
13. ZINOV'EV: Draft of Constitution	x					
14. ZINOV'EV: The Russian C.P. and the Trade Unions						
A. Speech in Moscow				x[1]		
B. THESES: Party and Trade Unions		x	x	x	x[2]	
15. ZINOV'EV: What the C.I. has been up to now, & what it must become					x[3]	

[1] See annotation to no. 556.

[2] Shorter version of the "Theses". See annotation to no. 551.

[3] English translation of an item which appeared as separate pamphlets in German and French. See nos. 548 and 554. The texts of all three are basically indentical, with slight deviations resulting from the translators' interpretations. The German pamphlet has a long footnote on p. 10–11 reflecting the polemic between the Kommunistische Partei Deutschlands and the Kommunistische Arbeiter Partei Deutschlands.

544 ZINOV'EV, G.

Nabolevshie voprosy mezdunarodnogo rabochego dvizheniia. Petrograd, Izd-vo Kommunisticheskogo Internatsionala [n. d.] 130 p.

Copy was not available for identification of contents. Probably identical with nos. 546 and 547.   *NYPL*

545 LEITSÄTZE zum II. Kongreß der Kommunistischen Internationale. 1920. Petrograd, Verlag der Kommunistischen Internationale, 1920. 111 p.

For contents see *Contents Table* on p. 142.

Hoover, LC, NYPL, Col, UMich, Amst

546 ZINOV'EV, G.

Brennende Tagesfragen der internationalen Arbeiterbewegung. Petrograd [?] Verlag der Kommunistischen Internationale, 1920. 107 p. (At head of title: G. Sinowjew)

For contents see *Contents Table* on p. 142. However, there are some differences in the text of three items included in this pamphlet:

1. "Leitsätze über die Rolle der Kommunistischen Partei in der proletarischen Revolution", is almost identical with item 3, A of the Invitation Print (no. 549), but the German text is more extensive than its English translation. Example: see point 8 on p. 54–55 of this German pamphlet, and column 41 in the Invitation Print.
2. "Wann und unter welchen Bedingungen dürfen Arbeitersowjets geschaffen werden" is also a more extended version than the English translation, which is item 6 of the Invitation Print.
3. „Über die Bedingungen der Aufnahme in die Kommunistische Internationale" seems to be an earlier version of Zinov'ev's draft because it contains only 17 conditions of admission, whereas the English translation in the Invitation Print contains 18.   *Hoover, NYPL, Amst, Felt*

547 ZINOV'EV, G.

Die Tagesfragen der internationalen Arbeiterbewegung. Herausgegeben vom Westeuropäischen Sekretariat der Kommunistischen Internationale. n. p. [Berlin] 1920. 116 p.

For contents see *Contents Table* on p. 142.   *Hoover, NYPL, Amst, Felt*

548 ZINOV'EV G.

Was die Kommunsitische Internationale bisher war und was sie nun werden muß. Hamburg, Verlag der Kommunistischen Internationale (C. Hoym) [1920] 24 p. At head of title: G. Sinowjew.   *Hoover, Amst, Felt*

549 COMMUNIST International; Executive Committee.
Concerning the convocation of the Second World Congress of the Communist International. [Petrograd, 1920] 132 columns. Caption title.

[Reprinted from the periodical "Communist International", no 11/12, June-July, 1920, columns 2101—2232]

This is a reprint of the official invitation to the Second Congress of the Comintern issued and signed by its Executive Committee, which was prepared for circulation among delegates to the Congress. It was not distributed commercially, and is a rare print of the Communist International.

This pamphlet has no title page: on the external cover page is printed in large letters the slogan of the Second Congress: "The Second Congress of the Communist International will show the workers of all the world the shortest way to the victory over the bourgeoisie. Long live the Second Universal Congress of the Third Communist International."

This print has been mentioned later by some participants of the Congress as the "Invitation Print". As parts of this print have been reprinted also separately, herewith is its contents:

1. Concerning the convocation of the second World Congress of the Communist International [Sub-title:] To all Communist Parties and Groups, to all Red Labour Unions, all Organizations of Communist Women, all Unions of Communist Youth, all Workers' Organizations adhering to Communism, and to all honest workers. [Then follows the invitation to the second Congress, signed by G. Zinov'ev as "President of the Executive Committee of the Communist International" and C. Radek as its secretary. Col. 5–8]

2. ZINOV'EV, G., Pressing Questions of the International Labour Movement; The Second Congress of the Communist International and its Tasks. [Col. 9–36 This item is dated "Kursk-Kharkov, May 14, 1920" and was reprinted in several versions, in several languages.]

3. Theses of the Executive Committee of the Communist International for the Second Congress of the Communist International. [Includes:] A. The role of the Communist Party in the Workers' Revolution. B. The Communist Parties and the question of Parliamentarism. [Col. 37–50]

4. ZINOV'EV, G. Draft of Instruction; To Communist members of the bourgeois parliaments and to the Central Committees of Communist Parties... [Col. 51–54]

5. LENIN, N. Preliminary draft of some Theses on the National and Colonial Questions; for the Second Congress of the Communist International. [Col. 55–60]

6. ZINOV'EV, G. When and under what conditions Soviets of Workers' Deputies should be formed. Theses. [Col. 61–64]

7. Theses of the Executive Committee on the agrarian question. [Col. 65–76]

8. RADEK, Karl, The Labour Movement. Shop Committees and the Third International. Theses. [Col. 77–86]

9. LENIN, N. Theses on the Fundamental Tasks of the Second Congress of the Communist International. [Col. 87–102]

10. TROTSKII, To the forthcoming Congress of the Communist International. [Col. 103–112]

11. KAMENEV, L. Dictatorship of the Proletariat. [Col. 113–120]

12. Theses of the Executive Committee of the Communist International for the Second Congress of the Communist International; Conditions for joining the Communist International. [Col. 121–126. This seems to be a second draft of the "conditions of admission". In Zinovev's "Brennende

Tagesfragen der Internationalen Arbeiterbewegung" (see no. 546) there were only 17 points, whereas in this "Invitation Print" are 18. In the end these conditions expanded to the famous "21 conditions".]

    13. ZINOV'EV G. Draft of Constitution of the Communist International. [Col. 127–132]   *Hoover*

550 THESES presented to the second World Congress of the Communist International (Petrograd-Moscow, July 1920) Petrograd, Editions of the Communist International, 1290. 120 p.

    For contents see *Contents Table* on p. 142.   *Hoover, NYPL, Col, JCre, Felt*

551 ZINOV'EV, G.
Pressing questions of the international labour movement. Petrograd, The Communist International, 1920. 105 p.

    Judging from the title, this seems to be an English translation of the French pomphlet: *Les questions les plus pressantes du mouvement ouvrière international* (no. 556) – but, in fact, it is quite different. The first item in this pamphlet, "The party and the Trade Unions" is an abbreviated version of the "Thèses" in the French pamphlet; it contains only 13 points as compared with 17 points in the French edition. The second item in this pamphlet corresponds to item 2 in the Invitation Print (no. 549). The third item (What the Communist International has been up to now, and what it must become) did appear in French and German as separate pamphlets (nos. 548 and 554).   *Hoover*

552 PROJET de statut de l'Internationale communiste. Moscou, typographie de la III-me Internationale [1920?] Cover serves as title page.   *Harv*

553 THÈSES présentées au deuxième congrès de l'Internationale communiste, Petrograd-Moscou, 18 juillet 1920. Petrograd, Edition de l'Internationale communiste [1920] 88 p. Cover serves as title page.

    Contents probably identical with nos. 542, 545, 550.   *Harv, Amst*

554 ZINOV'EV, G.
Ce qui a été jusqu'ici l'Internationale Communiste et ce qu'elle doit être. Petrograd, Editions de l'Internationale Communiste [1920?] 29 p. (Editions françaises de l'Internationale communiste no. 67)   *Hoover*

555 ZINOV'EV, G.
Le deuxième congrès de l'Internationale Communiste et ses buts. Petrograd, Ed. de l'Internationale Communiste, 1920. 39 p.

    Copy was not available for identification. Probably French translation of item 2 in *Contents Table* on p. 142.   *Amst, Felt*

556 ZINOV'EV, G.

Les questions les plus pressantes du mouvement ouvrier international. I. Le Parti Communiste russe et les syndicats. II. Le deuxième congrès de l'Internationale communiste et ses buts. [Petrograd] Editions de l'Internationale Communiste, no. 56 [1920] 163 p.

> The first item in this pamphlet is a speech by Zinov'ev to a party meeting in the "Palace of Labor" in Moscow, early in 1920. It is not reprinted in any publication listed in this checklist. To this speech are attached two annexes: 1. "Theses about the tasks of the party and the trade unions in the field of economy, organization and propaganda at the present time." It is not clear for what body these theses were destined. They consist of 16 points of which 15 deal with the Russian trade union movement, and the last one, "The trade unions and the International," presents the need for the creation of an international labor organization closely connected with the Communist International. These theses were reprinted in two German pamphlets (nos. 546, 547) without changes. The English version of these theses is limited to the first 13 points only (see annotation to 551). The English and German reprints carry the title "The Party and the Trade Union" and do not mention the word "theses". – 2. The second annex is a "draft of resolution". An explanatory note signed by the Secretary of the Central Committee of the Russian Communist Party, Krestinsky, states that this draft was prepared for "the Congress" (obviously the IX-th Congress of the R.C.P.) and that it was in discord with the draft of the Central Committee. The last point of this draft appealed to the R.C.P. to take the initiative in the creation of an International of Trade Unions as a "section" of the Communist International. The second item in this pamphlet corresponds to part 2 of the Invitation Print (see annotation to no. 549, point 2). *Hoover, Felt*

b) Protocols

557 2-oi [VTOROI] kongress Kommunisticheskogo Internatsionala; stenograficheskii otchet. Petrograd, Izd-vo Kommunisticheskogo Internatsionala, 1921. 682 p.

> This is the first edition of the Russian version of the proceedings of the 2-nd Congress. In the preface the editors state that the publication has been produced in haste, and that the translations of some parts into Russian are not perfect. For a second (1934) improved and extended edition see next item.
> *Hoover, LC, NYPL, Harv, Col, Yale, SInSt*

558 VTOROI kongress Kominterna, iiul-avgust 1920 g. Pod redaktsiei O. Piatnitskogo, D. Manuil'skogo, V. Knorina, B. Kuna, i M. Zorkogo. Moskva, Partiinoe izd-vo, 1934, xiv, 754 p. plates, facsim. At head of title: Institut Marksa-Engel'sa-Lenina pri TSK VKP(b).

> Revised and enlarged reprint of the Petrograd 1921 edition with reproduction of the title page of the 1921 edition. Corrected translations of speeches in non-Russian languages. Indexes. *Hoover, LC, NYPL, Harv, Col, BDIC, Felt, SInSt*

559 Der ZWEITE Kongreß der Kommunistischen Internationale; Protokoll der Verhandlungen vom 19. Juli in Petrograd und vom 23. Juli bis 7. August in Moskau. Petrograd, Verlag der Kommunistischen Internationale, 1921. 744 p. Cover title. *UMich, UTex, Felt*

560 Der ZWEITE Kongreß der Kommunistischen Internationale; Protokoll der Verhandlungen vom 19. Juli in Petrograd und vom 23. Juli bis 7. August 1920 in Moskau. Verlag der Kommunistischen Internationale; Auslieferungsstelle für Deutschland: C. Hoym Nachf. L. Cahnbley, Hamburg, 1921. 798 p. (Bibliothek der Kommunistischen Internationale, 22)

> *Hoover, LC, NYPL, Brown, Duke, JCre, NYUn, Ohio, UChic, UMich, UTex, Amst, Felt*

561 Der ZWEITE Kongreß der Kommunistischen Internationale. Wien, Verlag der Arbeiter-Buchhandlung, 1920. 203 p. (Herausgegeben im Auftrage der Kommunistischen Partei Österreichs)

> Anhang: Die kapitalistische Welt und die Kummunistische Internationale; Manifest des zweiten Kongresses der Kommunistischen Internationale: p. 167–195. The first Petrograd meeting of the Congress is erroneously dated July 17 instead of July 19; the date of the Moscow meeting, July 19, should be July 23.
>
> *Hoover, NYPL, Harv, Col, Duke Illin, Princ, UChic, UPenn, UWisc, Amst, BDIC, Felt*

562 The SECOND Congress of the Communist International. Proceedings of Petrograd session of July 17th [!] and of Moscow sessions of July 19th [!] — August 7th, 1920. Moscow, Publishing office of the Communist International, 1920. 500 (i. e., 600 p.; pages 591—600 wrongly numbered 491—500)

> The dates July 17 and 19 are incorrect; should be July 19 for the Petrograd session and July 23 for the Moscow session. *Hoover*

563 The SECOND congress of the Communist International; proceedings of Petrograd session of July 17 [!] and of Moscow sessions of July 19th [!] — August 7th, 1920. Publishing Office of the Communist International, America [sic!] 1921. 234 p. (incompl.)

> Re-edited version of the official Moscow edition (preceding item); cover, typeface and paper indicate that this item was also printed in Moscow. The "America" indicated on the title page as place of publication was intended to mislead U.S. authorities The copy in the library of Northwestern University is incomplete; includes sessions up to July 29 incl., and correspondes to contents of Moscow edition up to p. 222 incl. This obviously refers also to copies in the three remaining libraries. The dates July 17 and 19 in the title and text are incorrect; see annotation to preceding item. *NYPL, NWest, UTex, Felt*

564 II-me [DEUXIÈME] Congrès de la III. Internationale Communiste. Compte-rendu sténographique; Petrograd, 17 juillet [!], Moscou, 23 juillet — 7 août 1920. [Petrograd, n. d.] 628 p.

The date July 17 is incorrect; see annotation to no. 562.   *NWest*

564a DRUGI kongres trece internacionale; materijali. [Odabiranje materijala, objašnjenja, predgovor i register Stevan Belić-Franić] Beograd, Rad, 1956. 381 p. (Biblioteka istorije medjunarodnog radničkog i socijalističkog pokreta)   *Hoover, Harv, Felt*

c) Reports, Speeches, Letters presented to the Congress

565 DOKLADY II [vtoromu] kongressu Kommunisticheskogo Internatsionala. Petrograd, Izd-vo Kommunisticheskogo Internatsionala, 1920. 407 p.

See annotation to no. 573.   *Col, BDIC*

566 LENIN, V. I.
Mezhdunarodnoe polozhenie. (Rech' tov. Lenina na I-m zasedanii II-go kongressa Kommunisticheskogo Internatsionala 19-go iiunia [! should be iiulia] 1920 g.) S prilozheniem tezisov, priniatykh II-ym kongressom Kommunisticheskogo Internatsionala: "Ob osnovnykh zadachakh Kommunisticheskogo Internatsionala" [n. p.] 1920. 32 p.   *BDIC*

567 LENIN, V. I.
Mezhdunarodnoe polozhenie i III Kommunisticheskii Internatsional. (Rech', proiznesennaia na 2-m kongresse) [Moskva] Moskovskii gubernskii soiuz rabochikh poligraficheskogo proizvodstva, 1920. 19 p.   *Hoover, BDIC*

568 LENIN, V. I.
II [Vtoroi] kongress Kommunisticheskogo Internatsionala. [Moskva] Partizdat, 1934. 93 p.

A collection of drafts and final texts of Lenin's theses and resolutions prepared for the II-nd Congress, and his speeches at the Congress. Included are also the theses concerning the conditions of admission to the Communist International which at first were elaborated by Zinov'ev and reworked by Lenin. Zinov'ev's first draft (see no. 546) contained 17 points, whereas Lenin's corrected text contains 19. Finally, there were "21 coditions".   *Hoover, LC, BDIC*

569 LENIN, V. I.
Zadachi Kommunisticheskogo Internatsionala. Rech' na I-m zasedanii II-go kongressa III Internatsionala. Praga, izd-vo "Pravda", 1920. 24 p. (Rabochaia biblioteka "Pravdy", no. 2)   *BDIC*

570 PRIVETSTVIIA vtoromu kongressu III Kommunsiticheskogo Internatsionala. (Prilozhenie k stenograficheskomu otchetu 2-go kongressa, zasedavshemu v Moskve 19 iuliia — 7 avgusta, 1920 g.) Moskva, Izd-vo Kommunisticheskogo Internatsionala, 1920. 107 p.

Hoover, NYPL, Harv, BDIC

571 ZINOV'EV, G.
Otchet Ispolnitel'nogo Komiteta Kommunistecheskogo Internatsionala vtoromu vsemirnomu kongressu Kommunisticheskogo Internatsionala. Petrograd, Kommunisticheskii Internatsional, 1920. 61 p. incl. tables.

Note: A detailed report about the activities of the Executive Committee of the C. I. during the first fifteen months of its existence. In a frank and open manner the chairman of the Committee discusses the beginnings of its work, the difficulties encountered, and the necessity of "interfering" in the internal affairs of the member-parties in order to create a well-disciplined organization which "should work for the overthrow of capitalism." (p. 10) The report mentions that the ECCI has sent its representatives to foreign countries in order to assist the local communist parties in their organizational work and acknowledges that it has given financial support to these parties. Finally, the report mentions the preparatory work accomplished before the calling of the II Congress. (See Note preceding no. 542.) The following annexes are included:

1. A list of statements, addresses, letters, and appeals sent to various foreign parties, organizations, etc.

2. Lists of publications issued by the ECCI in the following languages: in German — 34 items, in French — 48, in English — 49, in Armenian — 2; furthermore, publications of affiliated communist groups in Russia: Czechoslovak — 5 pamphlets, 2 newspapers; Yugoslav — 10 items in Serbian, 8 items in Croatian, 10 items in Slovenian; Hungarian — 30 pamphlets, 10 newspapers, 3 leaflets. Some titles of the publications in these lists are incomplete and incorrect.

3. List of addresses from foreign countries received by the Communist International (about 80 items).

4. List of 39 political parties and organizations which joined the Communist International.

5. Detailed list of donations to the Communist International totaling 47,890,082 Rubles. Expenditures not included. *Hoover*

572 BERICHTE zum zweiten Kongreß der Kommunistischen Internationale. Petrograd, Die Kommunistische Internationale, 1920. 382 p.

Felt has erroneously: "Berichte **des** zweiten Kongreß..." For annotation see next item. *NYPL, Felt*

573 BERICHTE zum zweiten Kongreß der Kommunist. Internationale. Kommunistische Internationale; Auslieferungsstelle C. Hoym Nachf., Hamburg, 1921. 452 p. (Bibliothek der Kommunistischen Internationale, 21)

„Vorliegende Sammlung enthält fast alle Berichte, die dem zweiten Kongreß der Kommunistischen Internationale in schriftlicher Form von den Delegierten überreicht worden sind." Editors note on 3-rd prelim. leaf. Contains also: Zinoviev, G.: Schlußrede auf dem II. Kongreß der Kommunistischen Internationale. Clara Zetkin: Spaa oder Moskau?   *Hoover, LC, NYPL, Harv, Col, Amst, BDIC, Felt*

574 KARSKI, J. (pseud. of Marchlewski, Jan)
Die Agrarfrage und die Weltrevolution von J. Karski (Marchlewski) Anhang: These zur Agrarfrage angenommen vom II. Kongreß der Komm. Internationale. Berlin, A. Seehof [1920] 24 p. Kommunistischer Aufbau, Bd. 3)   *Hoover, Amst, Felt*

Die KOMMUNISTISCHE Internationale bis zu ihrem zweiten Kongreß. Manifest, Richtlinien, Beschlüsse des 1. Kongresses, Aufrufe und offene Schreiben des Exekutivkomitees. See nos. 512, 514.

575 LENIN, V. I.
Die Weltlage und die Aufgaben der Kommunistischen Internationale. Rede auf der ersten Sitzung des II. Weltkongresses der Kommunistischen Internationale in Petrograd am 19. Juli 1920. Moskau, Verlag des Exekutiv-Komitees der Kommunistischen Internationale, 1920. 20 p.
Amst

576 LENIN, V. I.
Die Weltlage und die Aufgaben der Kommunistischen Internationale; Rede in der ersten Sitzung des zweiten Weltkongresses der Kommunistischen Internationale, Petrograd, 19. Juli, 1920. [Hamburg] Verlag der Kommunistischen Internationale [C. Hoym, Nachf.] 1920. 29 p.
Hoover, NYPL

577 LENINS 21 Punkte; der II. Kongreß der III. Internationale in Moskau. Reden und Beschlüsse der Delegierten Lenin, Radek, Dr. Levi, Serrati. Berlin-Fichtenau, Verlag Gesellschaft und Erziehung, 1920. 39 p. ("Einleitung" signed: Arnd H. Stern.)

The pamphlet "contains the full text of the more important resolutions of the [second] Congress, the great speech of Lenin with only omissions of examples and excerpts of the other speeches." (Introduction) The statutes and the 21 conditions of admission to the C.I. are also included. *Hoover, NYPL, Yale, Amst Felt*

578 ZINOV'EV, G.
Bericht des Exekutivkomitees der Kommunistischen Internationale an den zweiten Weltkongreß der Kommunistischen Internationale. Petrograd, Verlag der Kommunistischen Internationale, 1920. 90 p. At head of title: G. Sinowjew   *Harv*

579 ZINOV'EV, G.
Bericht des Exekutivkomitees der Kommunistischen Internationale an den zweiten Weltkongreß der Kommunistischen Internationale. [Berlin] Westeuropäisches Sekretariat der Kommunistischen Internationale, 1920. 39 p. At head of title: G. Sinowjew, Vorsitzender des Exekutivkomitees der Kommunistischen Internationale.

Hoover, NYPL, UMich, Amst, BDIC, Felt

580 ZINOV'EV, G.
Bericht des Exekutivkomitees der Kommunistischen Internationale an den Zweiten Weltkongreß der Kommunistischen Internationale. Petrograd [?] Verlag der Kommunsitischen Internationale, 1920. 40 p. At head of title: G. Sinowjew

Amst

581 ZINOV'EV, G.
Die Rolle der Kommunistischen Partei in der proletarischen Revolution; Rede auf dem zweiten Weltkongreß der Kommunistischen Internationale, Moskau, Juli/August 1920. Mit Resolution des Kongresses. [Berlin] Westeuropäisches Sekretariat der Kommunistischen Internationale, 1920. 54 p.

Hoover, LC, Amst, Felt

582 ZINOV'EV, G. [and] Lenin, V. I.
Die Kommunistische Internationale über die Rolle der Kommunistischen Partei in der Revolution. Reden Sinowjews und Lenins auf dem II. Kongreß der K. I. Leitsätze. Hamburg, C. Hoym Nachf., 1924. 59 p.

NYPL

583 LENIN'S speech at the first session of the second Congress of the Third International [. . .] in Petrograd July 19-it [19th] 1920. Moscow, Executive Committee of the Communist International, 1920. 20.

Amst

584 ZINOV'EV, G.
Report of the Executive Committee of the Communist International to the second world congress of the Communist International. Petrograd, Editions of the Communist International, 1920. 52 p.

Col, Amst

585 ZINOV'EV, G.
Report of the Executive Committee of the Communist International to the Second World Congress of the Communist International. Christiania, Editions of the Communist International in commission by Det Norske Arbeideroartis Forlag, 1920. 23 p.

Hoover

586 FROSSARD, Ludovic Oscar
Le Parti Socialiste et l'Internationale. Rapport sur les négociations conduites à Moscou. Suivi de thèses, présentées au 2-e Congrès de l'International Communiste. Paris, Librairie de l'Humanité et du Parti Socialiste, 1920. 86 p.   *Amst, BDIC, Felt*

587 LENIN, V. I.
La situation internationale et la tâche de la III Internationale. Discours prononcé à la première séance du second Congrès de la Troisième Internationale [. . .] à Petrograd, 19 juillet 1920. Moscou, Comité Exécutif de l'Intrnationale Communiste, 120. 19 p.   *Amst, Felt*

Le MOUVEMENT communiste international, see *Rapports sur le mouvement communiste international,* next item.

588 RAPPORTS sur le mouvement communiste international; présentés au deuxième Congrès de l'Internationale Communiste. Moscou 1920. Petrograd, Editions de l'Internationale Communiste [1921] 439 p. Cover title: Le mouvement communiste internationale.

French translation of no. 573. For contents see annotation to no. 573.
Hoover, NYPL, Col, Amst, Felt

589 ZINOV'EV, G.
Ce que l'Internationale communiste a été, ce qu'elle doit devenir! (Discours prononcé au II-me Congrès mondial de la III-me Internationale sur les condtions d'entrée dans la III-me Internationale)... [La Chaux-de-Fonds, 1921?] 20 p. (Jeunesses socialistes romandes. Bibliothèque. no. 14) At head of title: G. Zinowieff.   *NYPL*

590 ZINOV'EV, G.
Rapport du Comité exécutif au 2-ème Congrès de l'Internationale communiste. Petrograd 1920. Petrograd, Editions de l'Internationale communiste, 1920. 65 p.   *Col, UWisc, Amst, Felt*

591 KOMUNISTYCHNA partiia Ukrainy
Memorandum Ukrainskoi kommunistychnoi partii kongresovi III. Komunistychnogo Internatsionalu. Viden — Kyiv [Drukarnia I. Shtainmana] 1920. 35 p. (Biblioteka "Novi Doby", No. 22)   *Hoover*

d) Resolutions, Theses, Manifestoes and other documents

592 KAPITALISTICHESKII mir i Kommunisticheskii International. Manifest II-go kongressa Kommunisticheskogo (III-go) Internatsionala. Petrograd [1920?] 56 p. *Harv*

593 MANIFEST Kommunisticheskogo Internatsionala k proletariiam vsego mira. Khar'kov, Vseukr. izd-vo [March] 1920. 20 p. On blue paper.
BDIC

594 REZOLIUTSII i ustav Kommunisticheskogo Internatsionala, priniatye vtorym kongressom Kommunisticheskogo Internatsionala, 19-go iiulia — 7-go avgusta 1920 g. Petrograd [1920?] 127 p. *Harv*

595 TEZISY i ustav Kommunisticheskogo Internatsionala, priniatye vtorym kongressom Kommunisticheskogo Internatsionala, 19-go iiulia — 7-go avgusta 1920 g. [N'iu Iork?] Izd. Ob"edinennoi Kommunisticheskoi partii Ameriki, 1921. 62 p. *LC, Harv, Col*

596 USTAV i rezoliutsii Kommunisticheskogo Internatsionala. Priniatye na II kongresse, sostoiavshemsia v Moskve s 17 [!] iiulia po 7 avgusta 1920 g. Praga, "Pravda", 1921. 103 p. (Rabochaia biblioteka "Pravdy")
Amst, BDIC

597 BEDINGUNGEN zur Aufnahme in die Kommunistische Internationale [n. p., n. d.] 46 p. *Amst*

598 Die KAPITALISTISCHE Welt und die Kommunistische Internationale; Manifest des II Kongresses der Kommunistischen Internationale. Kommunistische Internationale; Auslieferungsstelle C. Hoym, Nachf., Hamburg, 1920. 32 p. (Bibliothek der Kommunistischen Internationale, 2)
Hoover, LC, NYPL, Col, Amst, Felt

599 Die KAPITALISTISCHE Welt und die Kommunistische Internationale. Manifest des II. Kongresses der (III.) Kommunistische Internationale. Petrograd, Verlag der Kommunistischen Internationale, 1920. 59 p.
NYPL, Col, Amst

600 Die KAPITALISTISCHE Welt und die Kommunistische Internationale. Manifest des II. Kongresses der Kommunistischen Internationale. [n. p.] Verlag der Kommunistischen Internationale, 1920. 32 p. *Amst, BDIC*

601 Die KAPITALISTISCHE Welt und die Kommunistische Internationale. Manifest des II. Kongresses der III. Kommunistischen Internationale. Moskau, Verlag der III. Kommunistischen Internationale, 1920. 32 p.
Amst

KARSKI, J. (pseud. of Marchlewski, Julian)
Die Agrarfrage und die Weltrevolution. Anhang: Thesen zur Agrarfrage angenommen vom II. Kongreß. See no. 574.

602 LEITSÄTZE und Statuten der Kommunistischen Internationale. Beschlossen auf dem II. Kongreß der Kommunistischen Internationale vom 17. [!] July bis 7. August 1920. Petrograd, Verlag der Kommunistischen Internationale, 1920. 131 p.   *NYPL, Col, Felt*

603 LEITSÄTZE und Statuten der Kommunistischen Internationale. Beschlossen vom II. Kongreß der Kommunistischen Internationale Moskau, vom 17. [!] July — 7. August 1920. [Petrograd] Kommunistische Internationale, 1920. 61 p.   *NYPL, Amst, BDIC*

604 LEITSÄTZE und Statuten der Kommunistischen Internationale (beschlossen vom II. Kongreß der Kommunistischen Internationale, Moskau vom 17. [!] Juli bis 7. August 1920) Hamburg, Kommunistische Internationale, Hoym, 1920. 79 p. (Bibliothek der Kommunistischen Internationale, no. 3)   *Hoover, LC, NYPL, Col, Brown, JCre, UWisc, Amst, Felt*

605 LEITSÄTZE und Statuten der Kommunistischen Internationale. Beschlossen vom II. Kongress der Kommunistischen Internationale Moskau, vom 17. [!] Juli — 7. August 1920. Vollständige Ausgabe. [n. p.] Kommunistische Internationale, 1920. 80 p.

Probably identical with preceding item; cataloged differently.   *Amst, BDIC*

606 LEITSÄTZE und Statuten der Kommunistischen Internationale. Beschlossen vom II. Kongreß der Kommunistischen Internationale Moskau, vom 17. [!] Juli bis 7. August 1920. Halle, Hallische Genossenschafts-Buchdruckerei [n. d.] 80 p.
Amst

LENIN'S 21 Punkte, see no. 577.

MANIFEST, Richtlinien, Beschlüsse des ersten Kongresses. Aufrufe und offene Schreiben des Exekutivkomitees bis zum zweiten Kongreß. See nos. 512. 514.

RICHTLINIEN für die kommunistische Frauenbewegung. Herausgegeben im Auftrag des II. Kongresses der Kommunistischen Internationale vom Exekutivkomitee in Moskau. See no. 2277.

607 STATUTEN und Leitsätze der III. Kommunistischen Internationale, beschlossen auf dem II. Kongreß vom 17. [!] Juli bis 7. August 1920 zu Moskau. Zürich, Propaganda-Ausschuß der Anhänger der III. Internationale der Soz. Partei der Schweiz, 1920. 64 p.   *Hoover, Harv, Amst, Felt*

ZINOV'EV, G.
Die Rolle der Kommunistischen Partei in der proletarischen Revolution; Rede auf dem zweiten Weltkongreß . . . See no. 581.

608 Der ZWEITE Weltkongreß der Kommunistischen Internationale an das französische Proletariat; zur Frage des Anschlusses an die Kommunistische Internationale. [Berlin?] Westeuropäisches Sekretariat der Kommunistischen Internationale, 1920. 18 p.
Hoover, NYPL, Col, Duke, Amst, BDIC, Felt

609 The AGRARIAN question; thesis adopted by the second Congress of the Communist International, Moscow, August, 1920. London, Communist Party of Great Britain [1920] 15 p.   *Hoover, Col*

610 The CAPITALIST world and the Communist International. Manifesto of the II Congress of the III Communist International. Moscow, Publishing office of the III Communist International, 1920. 32 p.   *Hoover, Amst*

611 The CAPITALIST world and the Communist International; manifesto of the second Congress of the third Communist International. [n. p.] The United Communist Party of America [1920?] 32 p.

"Publishing office of the third Communist International. American edition, published by the United Communist Party of America.
LC, NYPL, Harv, Col, UPenn

612 The COMMUNIST International. This pamphlet contains the conditions prescribed by the Second Congress of the Communist International for the admission of parties to the Third International; and also the text of the constitution of a "Red" Trade Union International by the Communist. London, The Indpendent Labour Party, 1920. 15 p. (I.L.P. pamphlets. no. 37)

"Reprinted from the Labour Party Information Bulletin." (Text of catalog card in National Union Catalog.)   *UTex*

613 The FUNDAMENTAL tasks of the Communist International; thesis adopted by the Second Congress, Moscow, August, 1920. London, Communist Party of Great Britain [1920] 15 p.   *Hoover, Col, Duke, Felt*

614 MANIFESTO of the Communist International [adopted by the second Congress of the Communist International] [n. p.] Pub. by the C.E.C. Communist Party of America [1920?] 36 p. Caption title: The capitalist world and the Communist International. See no. 611.   *Hoover, Col, ULa*

615 NATIONAL and colonial questions. (Thesis adopted by the Second Congress of the Communist International, Moscow, August, 1920) With an introduction. London, Communist Party of Great Britain [1920] 14 p.
Hoover, Duke

616 PARLIAMENTARISM, Trade Unionism and the Communist International; theses adopted by the Second Congress, Moscow, August, 1920. London, Communist Party of Great Britain [1920] 15 p.
Hoover, Col, Duke, Felt

617 The ROLE of the Communist party in the proletarian revolution; thesis adopted by the second Congress of the Communist International, Moscow, August, 1920. London, Communist Party of Great Britain [1920] 11. p.

See nos. 581 and 625.   *Hoover, Col, Duke*

618 STATUTES and conditions of affiliation of the Communist International, as adopted at the second Congress, Moscow, August, 1920. London, Communist Party of Great Britain, 1920. 11 p.   *Hoover, Col*

619 THESES and resolutions adopted by the second Congress of the Comintern [Chicago, 1928] Manifold copy. 28 x 22 cm. folio, 32. Paper cover serves as title page   *Harv, UChic*

620 THESES and Statutes of the III Communist International. Adopted by the II Congress July 17th [!] — August 7th, 1920. Moscow, Publishing Office of the Communist International, 1920. 83 p. "Addendum" (loose leaf) ["Moscow edition"]   *Hoover*

> Joint annotation for items nos. 620, 621 and 622.
> There exist three editions of the English translation of the "Theses and Statutes" of the Communist International. The remaining part of the title is different in each edition:
> The first, or *"Moscow edition"*: Theses and Statutes of the III Communist International.
> The second, or *"Reprint edition"*: Theses and Statutes of the Third (Communist) International.

The third, or *"American edition":* The Theses and Statutes of the Communist International.

The sub-titles in all three editions are similar, but not identical. They carry, however, the same date of the II-nd Congress: July 17 to August 7, 1920, and this date is erroneous because the Congress took place from July 19 to August 7, 1920.

The *first edition* was published by the "Publishing Office of the Communist International" in Moscow in 1920. Hence this should be considered as the *official* edition of the Communist International.

The *second edition* was "Reprinted by United Communist Party of America", and printed probably in Chicago. The identical cover and title page state that the original from which the reprint had been prepared comes from the "Publishing Office of the Communist International. Moscow 1920." A publication date is not given, but it is probably 1920.

The *third edition* states on the bottom of the title page: "Issued by the Central Executive Committee of the Communist Party of America, from the original published by the Communist International in Moscow." As the Preface of this edition is dated "February, 1921", there is no doubt that it was published in 1921.

The publisher of the third edition, the Central Executive Committee of the Communist Party of America, states in its signed "Preface to American Edition" the following reasons for preparing and publishing this edition:

"The Theses and Statutes of the Communist International as adopted by the Second World Congress, July 17th — August 7th, 1920, were received by the Communist Party of America in December, 1920, from the Publishing Office of the Communist International at Moscow. Upon examination of this edition, which was translated into English in Moscow, it was found to contain many errors which led the Editorial Committee of the Communist Party to make a careful analysis of the text. It was compared with the German edition and the original Russian text with the result that many omissions and distortions were discovered, and these were of such a nature as to make the Moscow English edition misleading."

Indeed, the Moscow translation was very bad and misleading. The Preface quotes several of these errors from which it becomes apparent that entire sentences were omitted, others badly distorted. A careful comparison of the Moscow text with the corrected "American" text shows that the "Editorial Committee of the Communist Party" introduced more than one hundred major or minor corrections.

It must be stated for the record, that the publishers of the second edition, the United Communist Party of America, also introduced in its reprint quite a number of editorial corrections, but obviously did not trouble to compare the translation with the Russian original. Hence, the "Reprint edition" contains all the omissions and major translation errors prevailing in the Moscow edition. Furthermore, the publishers of the "Reprint edition" disregarded the "Addendum" to the Moscow edition, a small leaf, inserted into the pamphlet, containing a rewording of paragraph 17 on page 23, concerning the Italian Socialist Party.

The contents and the sequence of particular items are almost identical in all three editions. Table of Contents:

Preface (only in third "American" edition)
1. Statutes of the Communist International
2. The Fundamental Tasks of the Communist International
3. Conditions of Admission to the Communist International

4. The Role of the Communist Party in the Proletarian Revolution
5. The Communist Party and Parliamentarism
6. The Trade Union Movement, Factory Committees and the Third International
7. When and under what conditions Soviets of Workers' Deputies should be formed
8. Theses on the National and Colonial Question
   Contents (in first and second edition)
   Addendum (a loose leaf only in Moscow edition)

Individual items of these contents were reprinted in London as separate prints. Item 1 (Statutes of the Communist International) has been reprinted in *Blueprint for World Conquest* (see no. 95). As most American libraries have the "reprint edition", it seemed desirable to draw attention to its erroneous and misleading translation.

621 THESES and Statutes of the Third (Communist) International; Adopted by the Second Congress July 17th [!] — August 7th, 1920. Publishing Office of the Communist International; Moscow, 1920. Reprinted by United Communist Party of America. [Chicago, 1920] 85 p. ["Reprint edition"]

For annotation see preceding item.

Hoover, LC, NYPL, Harv, Col, BrynM, ClevP, UCal, UChic, UVirg, Yale

622 The THESES and Statutes of the Communist International; as adopted at the Second World Congress, July 17 [!] — August 7, 1920, Moscow, Russia. Issued by the Central Executive Committee of the Communist International in Moscow. [n. p.] 1921. 79 p. ["American edition"]

For annotation see no. 620.   *Hoover, IowaAgr*

623 THESES of the Communist International (complete) as adopted by the second Congress held in Moscow, August 1920 ... London, Communist Party of Great Britain [1920] 6 pamphlets in 1 volume. Cover title.
Contents:
1. Statutes and conditions of affiliation of the Communist International. 11 p. Identical with no. 618
2. The fundamental tasks of the Communist International. 15 p. Identical with no. 613
3. Parliamentarism, trade unionism and the Communist International. 14. p. Identical with no. 616
4. The role of the Communist party in the proletarian revolution. 11 p. Identical with no. 617
5. National and colonial questions. 14 p. Identical with no. 615
6. The agrarian question. 15 p. Identical with no. 609

The six items were available as separate pamphlets. The indicated numbers correspond to separate entries for each of them.   *JCre*

624 THESES of the Communist International (complete). As adopted by the second Congress held in Moscow, August 1920. [London] Communist Party of Great Britain [n. d.] 88 p.

> This item, held by the Library of the Institute for Social History in Amsterdam, seems to be identical with the preceding item, but seems to have continous pagination, or the 88 pages were arrived at by adding the numbered and unnumbered pages of the above six items. *Amst*

625 ZINOV'EV, G.
The Role of the Communist Party in the Proletarian Revolution; the historic thesis of the 2nd Congress of the Communist International held in 1920. [London, Marston Printing Co., 1934] 19 p. *Hoover, Amst*

626 Le MONDE capitaliste et l'Internationale Communiste; manifeste du II-e Congrès de l'Internationale Communiste. [Petrograd, ed. de l'Internationale Communiste, 1920] 47 p. *LC, Amst Felt*

628 Le MONDE capitaliste et l'Internationale Communiste; manifeste du II-ème Congrès de la III-ème Internationale Communiste. Paris, Bibliothèque communiste, 1920. 45 p. *Hoover, Harv, NWest, Amst, BDIC*

629 Le MONDE capitaliste et l'Internationale Communiste. Manifeste du II-me Congrès de la III-me Internationale Communiste. [n. p., n. d.] 36 p. (Bibliothèque de jeunesses socialistes romandes, 15) *NYPL, Amst*

630 STATUS & résolutions de l'Internationale Communiste adoptés par le deuxième congrès de l'Internationale Communiste, Petrograd-Moscou 19 juillet — 7 août 1920. Paris, Bibliothèque communiste, 1920. 123 p. *Hoover, Amst, BDIC*

631 STATUTS et résolutions de l'Internationale Communiste. Adoptés par le deuxième Congrès de l'Internationale communiste. Petrograd-Moscou (19 juillet — 7 août 1920). Petrograd, Ed. de l'Internationale Communiste [1920] 118 p. *Hoover, Col, Amst*

632 THÈSES, conditions et statuts de l'Internationale Communiste [adoptés par le deuxième Congrès de l'Internationale Communiste (Petrograd-Moscou, 19 juillet — 7 août 1920) Texte officiel] Avec ills. du 2-me congrès. Chaux-de-Fonds. Le Phare, éducation et documentation communistes, 2 (1920) 15. numéro spécial.

> Probably identical with no. 633 but cataloged differently. *Amst*

633 THÈSES, conditions et statuts de la III-me Internationale; texte officiel voté au deuxième Congrès mondial de l'Internationale Communiste. [Genève? 1921?] 80 p. Cover title. (Bibliothèque communiste romande, no. 16)
See preceding item. *Ohio*

THÈSES, manifestes et résolutions adoptés par le Ier, IIe, IIIe et IVe Congrès de l'Internationale Communiste 1919—1923. Textes complets. See no. 140.

La III-e [TROISIÈME] Internationale communiste. Thèses adoptées par le 1-er congrès. Documents officiel pour l'année 1919—1920. See no. 524.

634 TEZE i statuti III Komunističke internationale; usvojeni na II Kongresu od 17 jula [!] do 7 augusta 1920 god. [n. p., 192-?] 75 p. *NYPL*

635 De COMMUNISTISCHE Internationale. Statuten en stellingen van het tweede Wereldcongres in Moskau 1920. Amsterdam, Brochurehandel der Communistische Partij in Nederland [n. d.] 108 p. *Amst*

636 MANIFEST van de Communistische Internationale. De kapitalistische wereld en de Communistische Internationale [Vert. door W. S. Van Reesema] [n. p.] Communistische Partij, 1921. 48 p. *Amst*

637 The COMMUNIST International. Theses and statutes of the Communist International as voted upon at the II Conference of Petrograd-Moscow. (6—25 July, 1920) Publishing section of Socialist Workers (Communist) Party of Greece, Athens: Printing Office of "Ergatikos Agonas" [Workers' struggle] 1921. 112 p. (Communist books, in Greek language)
NYPL

638 A KAPITALISTA világ és a Kommunista Internacionale; A Kommunista Internatcionale II. világ kongresszusának kiáltványa. Moszkva, Az O.K.P. Magyar osztályai központi irodájának kiadása, 1920. 44 p. (Kommunista könyvtár [30]) *Hoover*

639 A KOMMUNISTA forradalom irányelvei; a III. internacionale 2. kongresszusának kiáltványa és elfogadott tézisei. Wien, Arbeiter-Buchhandlung kiadása, 1920. 92 p. *Hoover, BDIC*

640 TESI e statuto della Internazionale comunista, con aggiuntivi il manifesto della terza Internationale e il discorso di Lenin all'inaugurazione del congresso. Milano, Società editrice Avanti, 1921. 148 p. (Atti della terza Internazionale, 2) *LC, Felt*

641 MOSKVA-tesene; Retningslinjer for den Kommunistiske Internationale. Kristiania [Oslo] 1920. 60 p.   *SInSt*

642 KOMMUNISTIYCZNA Partia Polski
Międzynarodówka Komunistyczna; statut i rezolucje uchwalone na II kongresie Międzynarodówki Komunistycznej. (19-go lipa — 7-go sierpnia 1920 r.) Warszawa, 1921. 75 p.   *Hoover*

643 INTERNACIONAL comunista. Estatutos. Mexico, 1922. [13] p. Cover title. Biblioteca de la Internacional comunista.   *Hoover*

644 Den KAPITALISTISKA världen och kommunistiska internationalen; manifest och teser fran III. Komunistiska internationalens II. kongress. Med en inledning av Otto Grimlund. Stockholm, Fram, 1920. 201 p. At head of title: Proletärer i alla land, förenen er!   *UMinn*

e) Commentaries and writings about the Congress

DEIATELI Kommunisticheskogo Internatsionala. 19 iiulia — 7. avg. 1920. See no. 58.

645 21 [DVADSAT' ODNO] uslovie priema v Kommunisticheskii Internatsional. So vstupitel'noi stat'ei O. Piatnitskogo. Moskva, Partiinoe izd-vo, 1933. 47 p. (Komintern v dokumentakh). At head of title: Institut Marksa-Engel'sa-Lenina pri TSK VKP(b)   *NYPL, Harv, BDIC, SInSt*

646 KAMENEV, L. B.
2-i [vtoroi] s"ezd III Internatsionala. (Posobie dlia agitatorov) Moskva, Gos. izd-vo, 1920. 23 p.   *Hoover, BDIC*

ZINOV'EV, G.
Vtoroi kongress Kommunisticheskogo Internatsionala i ego znachenie. Doklad na zasedanii Petrogradskogo soveta. See no. 466.

647 Der FADEN der Zeit. Beiträge zur historischen Wiederdarstellung der marxistischen Theorie. Der II. Kongreß der III. Internationale und die italienische Linke [n. p., 1962] 46 p. mimeogr.

Contains two articles by A. Bordiga, 2 documents of the II Congress of the Communist International and one document of the P. S. I., Reformist faction.
Felt

648 MÜNZENBERG, W.

Der 2. [zweite] Kongreß der Kommunistischen Internationale und die Kommunistische Jugenditernationale. [Berlin, Druck O. Mickein, n. d.] 19 p. (Flugschriften der Jugend-Internationale. Nr. 9)

NYPL, Amst, BDIC, Felt

649 PIATNITSKII, Osip

Die vom II. Weltkongreß der Komintern angenommenen Aufnahme-bedingugen der Kommunistischen Internationale und die Reinigung der kommunistischen Parteien. Mit einem Anhang: Die 21 Aufnahme-bedingungen der Komintern. Moskau-Leningrad, Verlagsgenossen-schaft Ausländischer Arbeiter in der UdSSR, 1933. 52 p.   *Felt*

650 SCHMID, Arthur

Die Aufnahmebedingungen in die Kommunistische Internationale. Bern, Unionsdruckerei, 1920. 29 p. On cover: „Rote Fackel"   *NYPL, Amst*

651 ZINOV'EV, G.

Die 21 [einundzwanzig] Bedingungen der leninischen Komintern, von G. Sinowjew, Vorsitzendem der Komintern; einstimmig gewählt auf dem 5. Weltkongreß der Kommunistischen Internationale. [Berlin, Verlag der „Fahne des Kommunismus", 1925?] 31 p. (Flugschriften des Ver-Lages „Fahne des Kommunismus")

Hoover, NYPL, Felt

ZINOV'EV, G.

Der II. [zweite] Kongreß der Kommunistischen Internationale (Bericht in der Sitzung des Petrograder Sowjets am 20. August 1920. See no. 448.

652 PIATNITSKII, O. A.

The twenty-one conditions of admission into the Communist International. New York, Workers Library, 1934. 31 p.

Hoover, NYPL, Harv, Col

653 UNITED States. Department of State. Division of Russian Affairs. The 2-nd Congress of the Communist International as reported and inter-preted by the offficial newspapers of Soviet Russia. Petrograd-Moscow, July 19 — August 7, 1920. Washington D. C., Government Printing Office, 1920. 166 p.

Preface signed: Division of Russian Affairs, Department of State.

Hoover, LC, NYPL, Harv, Col, UTex

654 PIATNITSKII, Osip
Les 21 conditions d'admission à l'Internationale Communiste adoptées
au IIe congrès de l'I.C. Précédés d'une étude sur l'épuration des partis
communistes par O. Piatnitski. Paris, Bureau d'Editions, 1933. 43 p.
Hoover, Felt

655 PIERRE, André, ed.
Le 2-e [deuxième] congrès de l'Internationale Communiste 19 juillet —
7 août 1920. Compte rendu des débats d'après les journaux de Moscou.
Paris, Librairie du Parti Socialiste et de l'Humanité, 1920. 68 p.

"Annexe: A tous les membres du P.S. français. A tous les proletaires conscients
de France. Signé: Zinovev, Lenine, Serrati, Rosmer, Levi." *Hoover, Amst, BDIC*

656 2-gi [DRUGI] kongres III-ej Międzynarodówki Komunistycznej (19 lipca
— 7 sierpnia 1920 r.), według źródeł oficjalnych Sowietów. Warszawa,
1920. 67 p. (Biblioteczka wywiadowcza, no. 10)   *NYPL*

f) Bulletins issued for the Congress

657 VESTNIK vtorogo kongressa Kommunisticheskogo Internatsionala.
Petrograd, 1920. Nos. 1—7; Supplements to the daily newspaper
Pravda, July 27—29, August 3, 5, 7, 8; Nos. 164—166, 169, 171, 173,
174.   *Hoover, NYPL*

3. III-rd CONGRESS, Moscow, June 22 — July 12, 1921

a) Protocols

658 TRETII vsemirnyi kongress Kommunisticheskogo Internatsionala; stenograficheskii otchet. Petrograd, Gos. izd-vo, 1922. 500 p.
Hoover, Harv, BDIC

659 III [TRETII] kongress Kommunisticheskogo Internatsionala. (22 iiunia —
12 iiulia, 1921 g.) [Stenograficheskii otchet. Rostov-Don] Gos. izd-vo,
Donskoe otdelenie, 1921. 155 p.

Abbreviated version of stenographic record.   *Harv, Col, BDIC*

660 PROTOKOLL des III. Kongresses der Kommunistischen Internationale (Moskau 22 Juni bis 12. Juli 1921) Verlag der Kommunistischen Internationale; Auslieferungsstelle für Deutschland: C Hoym Nachf. L. Cahnbley, Hamburg, 1921. 1086 p. (Bibliothek der Kommunistischen Internationale, 23

> *Hoover, LC, NYPL, Harv, Duke, Illin, JCre, NYUn, Ohio, UTex, Amst, BDIC, Felt*

661 THIRD Congress of the Communist International. Report of meetings held at Moscow June 22nd — July 12th. [London] Communist Party of Great Britain [1921?] 166 p. "Reprinted from 'Moscow', the special organ of the congress".

> Abbreviated version of Congress records.   *Hoover, Col, ULa, UTex, Felt*

b) Reports, Speeches, Drafts presented to the Congress

662 RADEK, K.
Put' Kommunisticheskogo Internatsionala; rech' proiznesennaia na III kongresse Komunisticheskogo Internatsionala. Leningrad, izd. Kom. Inter., 1921. 51 p.   *BDIC*

663 REVOLIUTSIONNAIA Moskva tret'emu kongressu Kommunisticheskogo Internatsionala. Tekst napisan N. Ovsiannikovym. Moskva, I-aia obraztsovaia tip., 1921. Folio, 10 p. 101 mounted illus.   *BDIC*

664 RUSSIA (1917 — R.S.F.S.R) Narodnyi Komissariat Finansov. Sotsial'-naia revoliutsiia i finansy. Sbornik k III kongressu Kommunisticheskogo Internatsionala. Moskva, Pervaia Moskovskaia fabrika zagotovleniia gos. znkov, 1921. 158 p.   *Hoover*

665 TROTSKII, L.
Novyi etap; mirovoe polozhenie i nashi zadachi. Moskva, Gos. izd-vo, 1921. 160 p.

> **Contents:** Introductory remarks "Instead of a foreword"; – I. The world situation; – II. The school of revolutionary strategy; Annexes: Theses of the III-rd Congress: on the world situation and the tasks of the Communist International; on the question of tactic of the Communist International.   *Hoover, NYPL, BDIC*

666 LENIN, V. I.
Die Politik der Kommunistischen Partei Rußlands (Referat auf dem III. Kongreß der Kommunistischen Internationale, Juni-Juli, 1921) Leipzig [Kommissionsverlag: Frankes Verlag] 1921. 1921. 56 p. (Kleine Bibliothek der Russischen Korrespondenz, Nr. 56—57)   *Hoover*

667 LENIN, V. I.

Thesen zum Referat über Taktik der K.P.R. auf dem III. Kongreß der Kommunistischen Internationale. Moskau, Verlag des Pressebüro der Komintern, 1921. 5 p.

> Before the III-rd Congress started, drafts of theses which were to be submitted to the Congress were circulated among the delegates. The prints contain the names of the persons who had to present the report and the theses to the Congress. Some libraries catalog these proposed theses under the name of the author, and other libraries catalog them under the title. They are listed here consistently under the author's name. *Amst, Felt*

668 RADEK, Karl

Der Weg der Kommunistischen Internationale (Referat über die Taktik der Kommunistischen Internationale, gehalten auf dem III. Weltkongreß, Moskau, Juli 1921). Kommunistische Internationale; Hamburg, C. Hoym, Nachf., 1921. 86 p. (Bibliothek der Kommunistischen Internationale, 18)

Hoover, Harv, Amst, Felt

669 RUSSIA (1917—   R.S.F.S.R.) Narodnyi Komissariat Finansov.

Soziale Revolution und Finanzwesen. Zum III. Kongreß der Kommunistischen Internationale, Sammelwerk hrsg. vom Volkskommissariat der Finanzen der Russischen Sozialistischen Federativen Sowjet Republik. Moskau, Druckerei der Verwaltung der Fabriken für Herstellung der Staatswertzeichen, 1921. 71 p. Graphs and tables.

> See no. 664 and 677. *Amst, Felt*

670 TROTSKII, L.

Die neue Etappe, die Weltlage und unsere Aufgaben. Kommunistische Internationale; Auslieferungsstelle, C. Hoym Nachf., Hamburg, 1921. 167 p. (Bibliothek der Kommunistischen Internationale, 24)

> Anhang: Thesen des dritten Kongresses über die Weltlage und die Aufgaben der Kommunistischen Internationale. Thesen über die Taktik.
> *Hoover, LC, Harv, Col, BDIC, Felt*

671 TROTSKII, L. [and] Varga, E.

Thesen zur Weltlage und die Aufgaben der Kommunistischen Internationale. Moskau, Pressebüro der Komintern, 1921. 15 p.

> See annotation to no. 667. *Felt*

672 VARGA, E.

Die Krise der kapitalistischen Weltwirtschaft. Hamburg, Hoym, 1921. 64 p. tables

> Report at the III Congress of the C.I. For enlarged 2-nd edition see next item. *Hoover, Amst*

673 VARGA, E.

Die Krise der kapitalistischen Weltwirtschaft. 2. verm. und umgerab. Aufl. Hamburg, Hoym, 1922. ii, 147 p. index and tables (Bibliothek der Kommunistischen Internationale, 25)

> See preceeding item. For other editions see E. Varga in Part V (Economic questions; see annotation following no. 1628.) *Hoover, Amst*

674 ZINOV'EV, G.

Die Kämpfe der Kommunistischen Internationale (Bericht über die Tätigkeit der Exekutive, gegeben auf dem III. Weltkongreß der Kommunistischen Internationale, Moskau, Juni 1921). Kommunistische Internationale; Auslieferungsstelle C. Hoym Nachf., Hamburg, 1921. 104 p. (Bibliothek der Kommunistischen Internationale, 19)

> *Hoover, LC, NYPL, Harv, Amst, Felt*

675 CLUNIE, James

The Third (Communist) International; its aims and methods. Glasgow, The Socialist Labour Press [1921 ?] 61 p.

> Cover-title: "A report by James Clunie, delegate of the Socialist Labour Party of Great Britain to the third congress of the Third (Communist) International. Moscow, June–July, 1921. *NYPL*

677 RUSSIA (1917—   R. S. F. S. R.) Narodnyi Komissariat Finansov.

Social revolution and finances. Collection of articles for the III congress of Communist International, edited by the People's Commissariat of Finances of the Russian Socialistic Federative Soviet Republic. Moscow, First Moscow Govt. Currency notes factory, 1921. 65 p. 5 diagr.
> See no. 664 and 669. *Hoover*

678 TROTSKII, L. [and] Varga, E.

The international situation; a study of capitalism in collapse, by L. Trotsky and Prof. E. Varga (presented to the Moscow congress, 1921). London, Communist Party of Great Britain [1921] 20 p.   *Hoover*

679 ZINOV'EV, G.

The report of the Executive Committee of the Communist International; a speech delivered by G. Zinoviev at the III Congress of the Communist International, at Moscow, on June 25th, 1921. Press bureau of the Communist International, 1921. 86 p. port., plates.

> "Supplements": p. 59–86, consist of 3 additional speeches by Zinov'ev and resolution on the report. *Hoover, NYPL*

680 ZINOV'EV, G.
The report of the Executive Committee of the Communist International; a speech delivered by G. Zinoviev at the third congress of the Communist International, at Moscow, on June 25th, 1921. Glasgow, Union Pub. Co., 1921. 91 p. port. *Col*

681 KUUSINEN, O. [and] Koenen, V.
Thèses sur la structure et organisation des parties communistes. Moscou, Section de la Presse de l'Internationale Communiste, 1921. 16 p.

See annotation to no. 667. *Felt*

682 LENIN, V. I.
Thèses sur la tactique du parti communiste de Russie. (Proposées au 3-e Congrès de l'Internationale Communiste.) Moscou, Section de la Presse de l'Internationale Communiste, 1921. 5 p.

See annotation to no. 667. *Felt*

683 THÈSES sur la tactique. Moscou, Section de la Presse de l'Internationale Communiste, 1921. 20 p.

See annotation to no. 667. *Felt*

684 TROTSKII, L.
Nouvelle étape. Paris, l'Humanité, 1922. 142 p. (Bibliothèque communiste) *Hoover, BDIC*

685 TROTSKII, L.
Thèses sur la situation mondiale et nos tâches. Moscou, Section de la Presse de l'Internationale Communiste, 1921. 15 p.

See annotation to no. 667. *Felt*

686 VARGA, E.
La crise de l'économie capitaliste. Moscou, Ed. de l'Internationale Communiste, 1921. 55 p.

"Prepared hurriedly for the use of the members of the 3-rd Congress of the Third Communist International" — Preface. *Hoover, Felt*

687 ZINOV'EV, G.
Compte-rendu de la gestation du Comité exécutif de l'Internationale communiste (1920—1921); discours de Zinov'ev au 3-ème congrès universal (25 juillet 1921) Moscou, Section de la Presse de l'Internationale Communiste, 1921. 69 p. ports.

Includes also 2 speeches by Zinov'ev to the Executive committee of the Communist International during June, 1921, and his final address at the third congress of the Communist International as well as the resolution of the congress on the report of the Executive Comittee.   *Hoover, Amst, Felt*

688 ZINOV'EV, G.
L'Internationale Communiste et l'organisation internationale des syndicats. (La lutte contre l'Internationale Jaune d'Amsterdam.) Moscou, Section de la Presse de l'Internationale Communiste, 1921. 11 p.

The item was not avaiblable for identification. Probably another publication of the kind mentioned in the annotation to no. 667.   *Felt*

689 TROTSKII, L.
De grote congresrede. [Uitgesproken op het 3e wereldcongres der Communistische Internationale te Moskou] De economische wereldcrisis en de nieuwe taak der Communistische Internationale. [Vert. door G. Vanter] A[mster]dam, Brochurenhandel van de Communistische Partij [n. d.] 61 p.   *Amst*

690 LENIN, V. I.
Lenin elvtars elöadasa a burzsoa és proletar demokraciaról a III. Internacionale moszkvai kongresszusan. [Budapest, A Vörös könyvtar kiadóhivatala, 1921?] Cover title. 15 p. (Vörźs könyvtar, 1 sz.)   *Hoover*

691 RADEK, Karl
La via della Internazionale Comunista. Relazione sulla tattica fatta al terzo congresso mondiale di Mosca, Luglio 1921. Roma, Libreria Editrice del Partito Comunista d'Italia, 1921, 92 p. (Biblioteca dell'Internazionale comunista, VIII.)   *BDIC, Felt*

692 ZINOV'EV, G.
Le lotte della Internazionale Comunista. Relazione sull'attività dell'Esecutivo, fatta al terzo congresso mondiale della Internazionale Comunista, Mosca, 1921. Roma, Libreria Editrice del Partito Comunista d'Italia, 1921. 99 p. (Biblioteca dell'Internazionale Comunista, VII.)   *Felt*

693 ZINOV'EV, G.
I. Relazione del Comitato Esecutivo dell'Internazionale Comunista. II. Il passato e l'avvenire dell'Internazionale Comunista. Milano, Società Editrice Avanti!, 1921, 48 p. (Atti della terza Internazionale, 5)   *Felt*

694 ZINOV'EV, G.
La Internacional Communista . . . Mexico, D.-F., Biblioteca internacional [1921?] 18 p.

"Informe del companero G. Zinoviev al III. congreso de la Internacional Communista."   *Hoover, NYPL*

c) Resolutions, Theses, Manifestoes and other documents

695 TEZISY i rezoliutsii III Kongressa Kommunisticheskogo Internatsionala. Moskva, Otdel pechati Kominterna, 1921. 95 p. *NYPL, Amst*

696 TEZISY 3-go kongressa o mirovom polozhenii i zadachakh Kommunisticheskogo Internatsionala. K nedeli Profinterna. Tiflis, Izd. Kavkazskogo biuro Vseros. tsentr. soveta professional'nykh soiuzov, 1922. 22 p. *Hoover, LC, Harv*

697 LEITSÄTZE über den organisatorischen Aufbau der kommunist. Parteien, über die Methoden und den Inhalt ihrer Arbeit. Angenommen in der 24. Sitzung des III. Weltkongressess vom 12. Juli 1921. Verlag der Kommunstischen Internationale; Hamburg, C. Hoym Nachf. L. Cahnbley, 1921. 39 p. (Flugschriften der Kommunistischen Internationale, 5) *Hoover, Amst*

698 THESEN und Resolutionen. Angenommen auf dem III. Kongreß der Kommunistischen Internationale. Moskau, Presse-Büro der Kommunistischen Internationale, 1921. 101 p. *Harv, BostPL, Felt*

699 THESEN und Resolutionen des III. Weltkongresses der Kommunistischen Internationale (Moskau, 22. Juni bis 12. Juli 1921). Kommunistische Internationale; Auslieferungsstelle C. Hoym Nachf., Hamburg, 1921. 191 p. (Bibliothek der Kommunist. Internationale 20) *Hoover, LC, NYPL, Harv, Duke, JCre, UVirg, Amst, Felt*

700 THESEN über die Kommunistische Internationale und die Rote Gewerkschafts-Internationale. (Kampf gegen die gelbe Gewerkschafts-Internationale von Amsterdam) Angenommen in der 24. Sitzung des III. Weltkongressess vom 12. Juli 1921. Hamburg, Hoym, 1921. 19 p. (Flugschriften der Kommunistischen Internationale, 4) *Amst, Felt*

701 THESEN über die Taktik. Angenommen in der 24. Sitzung des III. Weltkongresses vom 12. Juli 1921. Hamburg, Hoym,1921. 34 p. (Flugschriften der Kommunistischen Internationale, 3) *Amst, Felt*

702 THESEN zur Weltlage und die Aufgaben der Kommunistischen Internationale. Angenommen in der 16. Sitzung des III. Weltkongresses vom 4. Juli 1921. Hamburg, Hoym, 1921. 24 p. (Flugschriften der Kommunistischen Internationale, 2) *Amst, Felt*

TROTSKII, L.
Die neue Etappe, die Weltlage und unsere Aufgaben. Anhang: Thesen des dritten Kongresses über die Weltlage und die Aufgaben der Kommunstischen Internationale. Thesen über die Taktik. See no. 670.

703 DECISIONS of the Third Congress of the Communist International held at Moscow, July, 1921. London, Communist Party of Gt. Brit. [1922] 134 p. *Hoover, Col, NWest, UTex*

704 GO to the masses! A manifesto of the third congress of the third International, also the withdrawal statement of the committee for the third International of the Socialist party to the members of the Socialist party. New York City Workers' Council [1921] 20 p.

> This contains two items: 1. An appeal of the E. C. C. I. "to the proletariat of all countries" dated Moscow, July 17, 1921. – 2. "Farewell" to the Socialist Party! by which the Committee for the Third International of the Socialist Party of America announced its leaving the Party and appealed to the membership to follow them. Signed by J. Louis Engdahl and others. *Hoover, LC, Harv*

705 THESES and resolutions adopted at the III World Congress of the Communist International (June 22nd—July 12th, 1921) Moscow, The Press Bureau of the Communist Internat., 1921. 98 p. *NYPL*

706 THESES and Resolutions adopted at the Third World Congress of the Communist International (June 22nd—Joly 12th, 1921) New York City, The Contemporary Publishing Association, 1921. 199 p.
> *Hoover, LC, NYPL, Harv, Col, BrynM, Duke, Illin, JCre, Oberl, Ohio, UMich, UNCar, UPenn, UTex*

707 THÈSES et résolutions. Adoptées au III-ème congrès de l'Internationale Communiste. Moscou, Section de la presse de l'Internationale Communiste, 1921. 100 p.

> The pamphlet contains the theses and resolutions of the III Congress of the C. I. and two additional items: an informative article entitled "The Communist International and the Red International of Trade Unions," (p. 67–75), and a manifesto of the ECCI, entitled "Towards new work, towards new struggles; To the proletariat of the entire world, to men and women" (p. 96–100).
> *Hoover, LC, Ohio, Amst, Felt*

708 THÈSES et résolutions adoptées au III-ème congrès de l'Internationale Communiste. Moscou, Section de la presse de l'Internationale Communister, 1921. 135 p. *Hoover, Amst, BDIC, Felt*

THÈSES, manifestes et résolutions adoptés par le Ier, IIe, IIIe et IVe Congrès de l'Internationale Communiste 1919—1923. Textes complets. See no. 140.

709 De COMMUNISTISCHE Internationale. Stellingen van het Derde Wereld-Congress in Moskou 1921, alsmede de stellingen der Executieve over de Conferentie in Washington. (Vert. door Gerard Vanter) Amsterdam, Brochurehandel der Communistische Partij [n. d.] 67 p.

Amst

710 La NOSTRA tattica (Tesi approvate dal terzo Congresso della I.C. Mosca, 12 luglio 1921). Roma, Libreria Editrice del Partito Comunista d'Italia, 1921. 49 p. (Piccola Biblioteca dell'Internazionale Comunista, VI.)

Felt

711 I PARTITI comunisti e l'organizzazione delle donne. (Tesi approvate dal terzo Congresso della I.C., Mosca, luglio 1921.) Roma, Libreria Editrice del Partito Comunista d'Italia, 1921. 29 p. (Piccola Biblioteca dell'Internazionale Comunista, IX.)

Felt

712 La SITUAZIONE mondiale ed i compiti della Internazionale Comunista. (Tesi approvate al terzo congresso della I.C. Mosca, 4 luglio 1921). Roma, Libreria Editrice del Partito Comunista d'Italia, 1921. 34 p. (Piccola Biblioteca dell'Internazionale Comunista, V.)

Felt

713 TESI e deliberazioni del terzo congresso mondiale della Internazionale Comunista. Mosca, 22 giugno — 12 luglio 1921. Roma, Libreria Editrice del Partito Comunista d'Italia, 1921. 239 p. (Biblioteca dell'Internazionale Comunista, IX.)

Felt

714 Las NUEVAS sendas del comunismo; tesis, acuerdos y resoluciones del III congreso de la Internacional Comunista. Tradución e introduccion de E. Torralva Beci. Madrid: Biblioteca nueva [1921?] 352 p. (Las nuevas doctrinas sociales) At head of title: 1921

NYPL

715 TERCER congreso mundial de la Internacional comunista. Tesis sobre la estructura y métodos de acción de los partidos communistos. Mexico, 1922. 79 p. (Biblioteca de la Internacional comunista)

Col

716 TERCER Congreso Mundial de los partidos comunistas. Tesis sobre la tactica. Mexico [Partido Comunista de Mexico] 1921. 62 p. (Biblioteca de la Internacional Comunista)

Hoover

717 TEZI i rezoliutsii tret'ego kongresu Komunistichnogo Internatsionalu, Moskva, 22 chervnia do 12 lipnia 1921. Viden', vid. Ukrainskoi sektsii Komunistichnoi partii Avstrii, 1922. [160 p.]

Harv

d) Commentaries and writings about the Congress

718 LENIN na III i IV kongressakh Kommunisticheskogo Internatsionala.
Moskva,1934. 110 p. *SInSt*

719 TROTSKII, L.
Mirovoe polozhenie i tretii kongress Kommunisticheskogo Internatsionala. Prilozheniia: I. Taktika Kominterna (rezoliutsiia kongressa Kominterna) 2. Taktika Profinterna (rezoliutsiia I-go kongressa krasnykh
profsoiuzov) Tula, Tul'skoe gubernskoe upravlenie izdatel'skim delom,
1921. 94 p. At head of title: Tul'skii gubernskii komitet Rossiiskoi komm.
partii (bol'shevikov) *Hoover*

720 ZINOV'EV, G.
Taktika Kominterna; posleslovie k rabotam III vsemirnogo kongressa.
Petersburg, Gos. izd-vo, 1921. 69 p. *Hoover*

721 ZINOV'EV, G.
Die Taktik der Kommunistischen Internationale. (Rückblick auf die
Arbeiten des III. Weltkongresses der Kommunist. Internationale.) Kom-
munistische Internationale; Auslieferungsstelle, C. Hoym Nachf. Ham-
burg, 1921. 77 p. (Bibliotek der Kommunistischen Internationale, 26)
Hoover, NYPL, Harv, Col, Amst, BDIC, Felt

722 La QUESTIONE italiana al terzo Congresso della Internazionale Comunista. Roma, Libreria Editrice del Partito Comunista d'Italia, 1921.
viii, 143 p. (Biblioteca dell'Internazionale Comunista, V) *Felt*

e) Bulletins issued for the Congress

723 BIULLETEN' tret'ego kongressa Kommunisticheskogo Internatsionala.
Moskva [Izd. Press-biuro tret'ego kongressa Kominterna] 1921.
LC [holdings unknown]; *Amst,* nos. 6–8, 10–15, 17, 18, 20–22; *BDIC,* nos. 2, 4, 7.

724 BULLETIN des III. Kongresses der Kommunistischen Internationale.
Moskau, Pressebureau des III. Kongresses der Kommunistischen Internationale, 1921. nos. 1—24, June 24—July 20, 1921. 557 p.
Hoover, nos. 1–24; *NYPL,* nos. 1–9; *Amst,* nos. 1–3 (Anhang 1), 10–14; *BDIC*
[holdings unknown]; *Felt,* nos. 15, 18, 23, 24.

725 MOSKAU; Organ des III. Kongresses der Kommunistischen Internationale. Moskau, 1921. [Appeared June 14—July 15, 1921 ?]
BDIC [holding unknown]

726 BULLETIN of the III Congress of the Communist International. Moscow, 1921. nos. 1—41, May 25—July 14, 1921.

NYPL, nos. 1–41; *Amst*, no. 1; *BDIC*, no. 35.

727 MOSCOW; organ of the III Congress of the Communist International. Moscow, 1921. *BDIC* [holdings unknown]

728 BULLETIN du IIIe Congrès de l'Internationale Communiste. Moscou, Section de la Presse de l'Internationale Communiste, 1921. nos. 1—24, June 24—July 20, 1921. *Amst*, nos. 2, 5, 6; *Felt*, nos. 1–22 (missing 15, 18).

729 MOSCOU; organe du 3-e Congrès de l'Internationale Communiste. Moscou, 1921. no. 1—44, May 25—July 17, 1921.

Hoover, nos. 1–44; *NYPL*, nos. 11–12, 16–17; *Amst*, nos. 2, 5, 6; *Felt*, nos. 2–9, 11–15, 19–44.

4. IV-th C O N G R E S S, Petrograd-Moscow, November 5—December 5, 1922

a) Protocols

730 IV [CHETVERTYI] vsemirnyi kongress Kommunisticheskogo Internatsionala, 5 noiabria — 3 dekabria [!] 1922 g. Izbrannye doklady, rechi i rezoliutsii. Moskva, Gos. izd-vo, 1923. 427 p.

Hoover, LC, NYPL, Harv, Col, Illin, Princ, UCal

731 PROTOKOLL des vierten Kongresses der Kommunistischen Internationale, Petrograd--Moskau vom 5. November bis 5. Dezember 1922. Verlag der Kommunistischen Internationale; Auslieferungsstelle: C. Hoym, Nachf. L. Cahnbley, Hamburg, 1923. viii, 1087 p. (Bibliothek der Kommunistischen Internationale, 38)

Hoover, LC, NYPL, Duke, Illin, Ohio NYUn, Amst, Felt

731a BERICH über den IV. Kongreß der Kommunistischen Internationale; Petrograd-Moskau, vom 5. November bis 5. Dezember 1922. Verlag der Kommunistischen Internationale; Hamburg, Auslieferungsstelle: C. Hoym Nachf. L. Cahnbley, 1923. 219 p. (Bibliothek der Kommunistischen Internatinonale, 37)

An abstract of the proceedings of the Congress. A few speeches given in full or verbatim excerpts. *Hoover, LC, NYPL, Harv, Amst, BDIC, Felt*

732 FOURTH Congress of the Communist International; abridged report of meetings held at Petrograd & Moscow, Nov. 7—Dec. 3 (!), 1922. [London] Pub. for the Communist International by the Communist Party of Great Britain [1923?] 296 p.

Hoover, LC, NYPL, Harv, Col, BrynM, Duke, JCre, UPenn, Yale, Felt

b) Reports, Speeches, Drafts presented to the Congress

733 DOKLADY tt. Lenina, Trotskogo, Klary TSetkin i dr. (stenogarficheskii otchet) [Khar'kov] Khar'kovskoe kooperativnoe izd. "Proletarii", 1922. 204 p. *Hoover*

734 LOZOVSKII, A.
Zadachi kommunistov v profdvizhenii; doklad i zakliuchitel'noe slovo na IV kongresse Kominterna, 20—21 noiabria. Moskva, Gos. izd-vo, 1923. 104 p. *Col*

735 RADEK, Karl
Likvidatsiia Versal'skogo mira; doklad IV kongressu Kommunisticheskogo Internatsionala. Petrograd, Kommunisticheskii Internatsional, 1922. 64 p. *Hoover*

736 TROTSKII, L.
Novaia ekonomicheskaia politika Sovetskoi Rossii i perspektivy mirovoi revoliutsii. Moskva, Moskovskii komitet RKP (bol'shevikov) 1923. 70 p. *Hoover*

737 ZINOV'EV, G.
Kommunisticheskii Internatsional za rabotoi; prakticheskie problemy v Kominterne i rabota ego sektsii. Rechi, proiznesennye na IV vsemirnom kongresse Kominterna. Moskva, Gos. izd-vo, 1922. 167 p.

Hoover, NYPL, Harv

738 ZINOV'EV, G.
Kommunisticheskii Internatsional za rabotoi; takticheskie problemy Kominterna i rabota ego sektsii. Rechi, proiznesennye na 4. vsemirnom kongresse Kominterna. 2. izd. Moskva, Gos. izd-vo, 1923. 295 p.

LC, NYPL

739 LOZOVSKII, A.
Die Gewerkschaftsfrage auf dem vierten Kongreß der Kommunistischen Internationale vom 5. Nov. bis 5. Dez. 1922. Referat und Schlußwort von Losowsky sowie die Diskussionsreden von Clark (England), Lansing (Amerika), Heckert (Deutschland) [et al.] Anhang: Richtlinien. Berlin, Verlag der Roten Gewerkschafts-Internationale, 1922, 71 p. (Bibliothek der Roten Gewerkschafts-Internationale, Bd. 15)

Hoover, NYPL, Harv, Amst, BDIC, Felt

740 RADEK, Karl
Die Liquidation des Versailler Friedens. Bericht an den 4. Kongreß der Kommunistischen Internationale. Hrsg. von der Kommunistischen Internationale. Hamburg, Hoym, 1922. 72 p.   *Amst*

741 RADEK, Karl
Die Liquidation des Versailler Friedens. Bericht an den 4. Kongreß der Kommunistischen Internationale. Moskau, Verlag der Kommunistischen Internationale, 1922. 72 p.   *Hoover, Col, Amst, Felt*

742 RADEK, Karl
Die Offensive des Weltkapitals und die Taktik der Kommunistischen Internationale; zwei Reden, gehalten auf dem IV. Weltkongreß der Kommunistischen Internationale im November 1922. Kommunistische Internationale; Auslieferungsstelle, C. Hoym Nachf., Hamburg, 1923. 61 p. (Bibliothek der Kommunsitischen Internationale, 34)

Hoover, LC, NYPL, Amst, Felt

743 TROTSKII, L.
Die neue ökonomische Politik Sowjetrußlands und die Weltrevolution; Rede, gehalten auf dem IV. Weltkongreß der Kommunistischen Internationale am 14. November 1922 zu Moskau. Kommunistische Internationale; Auslieferungsstelle, C. Hoym, Nachf., Hamburg, 1923. 38 p. (Bibliothek der Kommunistischen Internationale, 33)   *Hoover, LC, Felt*

744 ZINOV'EV, G.
Die Kommunistische Internationale auf dem Vormarsch. Kommunistische Internationale; Auslieferungsstelle, C. Hoym Nachf., Hamburg, 1923. 207 p. (Bibliothek der Komm. Internationale, 35)

Hoover, LC, NYPL, Harv, Col, Amst, BDIC, Felt

745 RADEK, Karl
The Winding up of the Versailles Treaty; Raport to the IV Congress of the Communist International. The Communist International, in commission: C. Hoym, Nachf. L. Cahnbley, Hamburg, 1922. 49 p.   *Hoover*

746 VARGA, E.
The process of capitalist decline. Report to the IV congress of the Communist International. Hamburg, Communist International; in commission: C. Hoym Nachf. L. Cahnbley, 1922. 47 p.

See annotation following no. 1628. *Hoover*

747 RADEK, Karl
La tactique communiste & l'offensive du capital. Paris, Librairie de l'Humanité, 1923. 68 p. (Petite bibliothèque communiste)

"Discours au IVe Congrès de l'Internationale Communiste (novembre 1922).
Hoover, Felt

748 TROTSKII, L.
La nouvelle politique économique des Soviets et la révolution mondiale. Paris, Librairie de l'Humanité, 1923. 78 p. (Petite bibliothèque communiste) *Hoover*

749 VARGA, E.
Le déclin du capitalisme; report pour le 4-e congrès mondial de l'Internationale Communiste. Hamburg, Edition de l'Internationale Communiste, à condition C. Hoym Nachf., 1922. 58 p.

See annotation following no. 1628. *Hoover, Felt*

750 ZINOV'EV, G.
L'Internationale Communiste au travail. Paris, Librairie de l'Humanité, 1923. 187 p. At head of title: Bibliothèque communiste. *Harv, BDIC, Felt*

751 RAVESTEYN, W[illem] van
De Oostersche kwestie. Referaat uitgesproken op het Wereldcongres der Kommunistische Internationale gehouden in Nov. 1922 te Moskou. Amsterdam, Brouchurehandel der Kommunistische Partij in Nederlande [n. d.] 44 p. *Amst*

c) Resolutions, Theses, Manifestoes and other documents

752 POSTANOVLENIIA IV vsemirnogo kongressa Kommunisticheskogo Internatsionala. Petrograd, Izd. Kommunisticheskogo Internatsionala, 1923. 188 p.

Contents: Vozzvaniia i privetstviia (10 items); Tezisy i programmy (7 items); Rezoliutsii (22 items). *Hoover, LC*

753 POSTANOVLENIIA IV vsemirnogo kongressa Kommunisticheskogo In-natsionala. Petrograd, Izd-vo Kommunisticheskogo Internatsionala, 1923. 95 p.   *Hoover, LC*

754 THESEN und Resolutionen des IV. Weltkongresses der Kommunistischen Internationale, Moskau, vom 5. November bis 5. Dezember 1922. Verlag der Komm. Internationale; Hamburg, Auslieferungsstelle C. Hoym Nachf. L. Cahnbley, 1923. 121 p. (Bibliothek der Kommunistischen Internationale, 36)   *Hoover, LC, NYPL, JCre, Amst, Felt*

755 RESOLUTIONS & theses of the Fourth Congress of the Communist International, held in Moscow, Nov. 7 [!] to Dec. 3 [!], 1922 [London] Pub. for the Communist International by the Communist Party of Great Britain [1922] 120 p.   *Hoover, LC, NYPL, Harv, Col, Duke, UChic, UTex, Yale, Felt*

756 IV-e [QUARTRIÈME] congrès communiste mondial. Résolutions. Paris, l'Humanité, 1923. 183 p. (Petite bibliothèque communiste)
                                                              Hoover, Harv, ULa, Amst, BDIC

757 RAPPORTS de l'I.S.R. et de l'I.C. [Paris] Librairie du Travail [1923?] 110 p. Cover title. (Petite Bibliothèque de l'Internationale Syndicale Rouge, 9)

> **Contents:** 1) Preface — L. Dudilieux; 2) Statuts de l'Internationale Syndicale Rouge (Rapporteur: A. Lozovsky); 3) Thèses sur l'action communiste dans le mouvement syndical (Adoptées au 4-e Congrès de l'Internationale Communiste); 4) Discours du Camarade Nin (Au nom du Bureau Executif de l'I. S. R.); Discours du Camarade Tresso; Discours du Camarade Zinoviev; Discours de Monmousseau [all preceding speeches at II-nd congress of R. I. L. U]; 5) [Excerpts from the proceedings of the IV-th Congress of the Communist International, 16-th session, Monday November 20, 1922:] Rapport sur le role des communistes dans les syndicats par Lozovsky. Orateurs: Lozovsky, Clark, Lansing. [This last item can be found as a separate print; see nos. 734, 739]
> The NYPL and BDIC have another edition of this item. It is also listed as no. 9 of the Petite Bibliothèque de l'Internationale Syndicale Rouge, but has a somewhat different title. The contents appears in different sequence and the number of pages is different. See next item.   *Hoover*

757a RAPPORTS entre l'Internationale syndicale rouge et l'Internationale communiste. Discours au 2-e congrès et statuts de l'I.S.R. Préface de Dudilieux. Paris, Librairie du travail, 1923. 108 p. (Red International of Labour Unions. Petite bibliothèque de l'Internationale syndicale rouge. [v.] 9) Cover title.

> **Contents:** Discours prononcés au 2e congrès de l'I. S. R. par les camarades Nin, Tresso, Monmousseau et Zinoviev. Discours prononcé au IVe congrès de

l'I. C. par le camarade Losovsky. Annexes: Statuts de l'I. S. R. et Thèses sur l'action communiste dans le mouvement syndical.

This is an exact repetition of the contents of the catalog card in NYPL. It is obviously another edition of the preceding item. *NYPL, BDIC*

THÈSES, manifestes et résolutions adoptés par le Ier, IIe, IIIe et IVe Congrès de l'Internationale Comuniste 1919—1923. Textes complets. See no. 140.

758 ODLUKE IV. Kongresa Komunističke Internacionale. Moskva, od 5. novembra do 5. decembra 1922. Wien, Arbeiterbuchhandlung, 1923. 132 p. Prevedeno sa izdanja Komunističke Internacionale, 36.

Amst

d) Commentaries and writings about the Congress

759 4-yi [CHETVERTYI] kongress Kominterna. Prilozhenie k gazete "Pravda". Moskva, Tip. Krasnyi proletarii [1922] Falio, 16 p. illus.   *BDIC*

LENIN na III i IV kongressakh Kommunisticheskogo Internatsionala. See no. 718.

e) Bulletins issued for the Congress

761 BULLETIN des IV Kongresses der Kommunistischen Internationale. Moskau, Herausgeber: Preßbureau des IV. Kongresses der Komintern, 1922. [30 issues?]
  Amst, nos. 1–4, 6–8, 10, 11, 13–15, 17, 20, 22; *Felt*, nos. 1–6, 9, 10, 12, 13, 17, 23, 24.

762 BULLETIN no. 1—32; Nov. 12—Dec. 12, 1922. Moscow [Press Bureau of the Fourth Congress of the Comintern] 32 nos. in 1 v. irregular. No. 1 issued Nov. 16; no. 32, Dec. 9; no. 14—15 issued together.

This is the exact entry in the catalog card prepared by the Library of Congress and found in the National Union Catalog. Due to abbreviated cataloging used recently in the Library of Congress the title is obviously mutilated. It probably is "Bulletin of the IV Congress..." Judging by the place of publication given as "Moscow", the Bulletin is in the English language. The Union Catalog card indicates also that the item is held by the University of Illinois, but holdings are not indicated. *LC, Illin*

763 BULLETIN du IVe Congrès de l'Internationale Communiste. Moscou, Publication du Bureau de la Presse du IVe Congrès du Comintern, 1922.
Felt, nos. 4, 10–29.

5. V-th CONGRESS, Moscow, June 17—July 8, 1924

a) Protocols

764 PIATYI vsemirnyi kongress Kommunisticheskogo Internatsionala, 17 iiunia — 8 iiulia, 1924 g.; stenograficheskii otchet. Moskva, Gos izd-vo,
1925. 2 vols. 1010 p., 312 p.

> Vol. II, p. 7–22: abridged records of the IV-th Plenum of the Executive Com-
> mittee.   *Hoover, LC, NYPL, Harv, DState, UCal, Yale, BDIC, SInSt*

765 PROTOKOLL; fünfter Kongreß der Kommunistischen Internationale.
[Hamburg] C. Hoym [1924] 2 vols.

> Vol. II, p. 1035–1053: abridged records of the 4-th Plenum of the Executive
> Committee.   *Hoover, Illin, Amst, Felt*

766 FIFTH Congress of the Communist International; abridged report of
meetings held at Moscow June 17th to July 8th, 1924. [London] Published for the Communist International by the Communist Party of
Gt. Britain [1924?] 294 p.

> *Hoover, LC, NYPL, Harv, Col, Duke, Illin, Princ, UCal, UCin, UChic, UNCar,*
> *NYUn, UTex, Yale, Amst, Felt*

767 V-e [CINQUIÈME] congrès de l'Internationale Communiste (17 juin —
8 juillet 1924) Compte rendu analytique. Paris, Librairie del l'Humanité,
1924. 479 p.

> *Hoover, LC, NYPL, Harv, DLab, JCre, Yale, Amst, BDIC (incompl.), Felt*

b) Reports, Speeches, Drafts presented to the Congress

768 DVA goda bor'by i raboty. Obzor deiatel'nosti Ispolkoma i sektsii
Kommunisticheskogo Internatsionala za period s IV po V Kongress.
Moskva, 1924. 135 p.   *SInSt*

769 K voprosu o programme Kommunisticheskogo Internatsionala (materialy) [S uchast. Radeka, Smeralia, Varga i dr.] Moskva, "Krasnaia
Nov'", 1924. 203 p.   *Amst, SInSt*

770 LOZOVSKII, A.
Nasha taktika v profdvizhenii; doklad na V kongresse Kominterna.
Moskva, Izd. Profinterna, 1924. 77 p.   *Hoover*

179

771 ZINOV'EV, G.
Mirovaia partiia leninizma. Leningrad, Gos. izd-vo, 1924. 294 p.

See annotation to no. 781. *Hoover, BDIC*

772 BERICHT über die Tätigkeit der Executive der Kommunistischen Internationale vom IV. bis zum V. Weltkongreß. Hamburg, C. Hoym Nachf., 1924. 111 p. tables.

> Report on the activities of the Executive Committee from December 1922 to May 1924 (estimated period). First report after Lenin's death. Contains: Survey of acitivies of the Ex. Com. and its Divisions ("Abteilungen"); digest of political activities and organizational events of all member parties of the C.I. (including short report on Communist Balkan Federation) emphasizing successes and failures; short presentation of activities of its front organizations (Com. Youth Intern., Red Sport International, International Womens' Secretariat, "Cooperative Section"; short report of activities of the following Divisions: Orient-Abteilung, Propagandaabteilung, Internationale Pressekorrespondenz, Presseabteilung des EKKI, Lenin Kommission, Kommission zum Studium des Faschismus, Proletkino, Budget-Kommission, Internationale Verbindungsabteilung des EKKI; financial report; list of all appeals issued by Ex. Com. during reported period. For English ed. see no. 784. *Hoover, NYPL, Amst, Felt*

773 BUKHARIN, Nikolai [and] Thalheimer, August
Zur Programmfrage der Komm. Internationale. Zwei Reden gehalten am 27. und 28. Juni 1924. Moskau, Herausgegeben vom Pressebüro des Kongresses, 1924. 44 p. At head of title: V. Kongreß der Kommunistischen Internationale. *Felt*

774 MATERIALIEN zum V. Weltkongreß der Komintern. Berlin, Vereinigung Internationaler Verlags-Anstalten [1924] 64 p. („Die Internationale", Ergänzungsheft zum Heft 12, 1924) *Amst*

775 MATERIALIEN zur Frage des Programms der Kommunistischen Internationale. Verlag der Kommunistischen Internationale; Hamburg, C. Hoym Nachf. L. Cahnbley, 1924. 328 p.

> „Die vorliegende Sammlung umfaßt die wichtigsten Materialien zur Frage des Programms der Kommunistischen Internationale aus der Zeit der Vorarbeiten zu dieser Frage für den IV. Weltkongreß der K.I. bis zum heutigen Tage." – p. 5. *Hoover, NYPL, Harv, Felt*

776 [MUENZENBERG, Willi] and Aquila, G.
Bericht über die faschistische Bewegung Frühjahr 1924 unterbreitet dem fünften Kongreß der Kommunistischen Internationale im Auftrage der Komintern Kommission gegen den Faschismus, von M. Willi [pseud.] und G. Aquila. Berlin: Herausgegeben vom Neuen Deutschen Verlag [1924?] 94 p., illus., charts. *NYPL, Amst*

777 RYKOV, A. I. [and] Manuilskii, D. Z.
Bericht über die Wirtschaftslage der Sowjetunion und die Ergebnisse
der Parteidiskussion in der KPR. Manuilsky, Bericht zur National- und
Kolonialfrage. Moskau, Pressebüro des Kongresses, 1924. 68 p. At head
of title: V. Kongreß der Kommunistischen Internationale.   *Amst, Felt*

778 ZINOV'EV, G.
Bericht über die Tätigkeit des Exekutiv-Komitees der Kommunistischen
Internationale, von G. Sinowjew. Moskau: Preßbüro des Kongresses,
1924. 74 p. illus., charts. At head of title: V. Kongreß der Kommunistischen Internationale.   *NYPL, Amst, Felt*

779 ZINOV'EV, G.
Für die Einheit der internationalen Gewerkschaftsbewegung. Reden
gehalten auf dem V. Weltkongreß der Komintern 7. Juli 1924. Hamburg, C. Hoym [1924] 28 p.   *Amst*

780 ZINOV'EV, G.
Schlußwort zum Bericht des Executiv-Komitees der Kommunistischen
Internationale gehalten am 26. Juni 1924, von G. Sinowjew. Anhang:
Resolution zum Bericht. Moskau: Preßbüro des Kongresses, 1924. 79 p.
          NYPL, Felt

781 ZINOV'EV, G.
Die Weltpartei des Leninnismus. Hamburg, C. Hoym Nachf., 1924.
244 p. diagrs.

Contents:
1. Zinov'ev's openig speech at V-th Congress.
2. Zinov'ev's report about the activies of the Executive Committee of the Comintern–which is an extension of the report prepared in advance and
   distributed to the participants. (See no. 768, 772, 784.) Zinov'ev's report also
   printed separately. (See no. 778, 786, 793.)
3. Zinov'ev's closing speech after the discussion of his report. (Published also
   separately; no 780, 787.)
4. Zinov'ev's speech at V-th Congress, July 7, 1924, on "Towards unity of the
   international trade union movement". (Printed also separately; no. 779, 788,
   792, 794.)
5. Speech on the Paris Commune delivered on occasion of the transmittal by
   French communist delegates of a flag to the Moscow proletariat, July 13,
   1924.
6. Zinov'ev's speech at the closing meeting of the V-th Congress "Our achievements".
7. Zinov'ev's report at a meeting of Communist Party functionaries in Leningrad,
   July 9, 1924.
8. Annexes: a) Resolution to the report of the Executive Committee; b) Theses
   to the question of tactics; c) Diagrams illustrating statistics of uneployment,
   of organized trade unionists, of political parties, and of election results in
   England, Germany, France, Italy, Bulgaria and Carpatho-Ruthenia.
          Hoover, Felt

782 BUKHARIN, N. I.
Program of the Communist International; draft submitted as a basis for discussion at the fifth Congress of the Communist International, 1924. [n. p.] 1924. 34 leafs. *Hoover, NYPL*

783 BUKHARIN, N. I.
Report on the program question, by N. Bukharin; with a supplementary report by A. Thalheimer delivered on June 27—28, 1924. Moscow, Press Bureau of the fifth Congress of the Comintern [1924] 43 p. At head of title: Fifth Congress of the Communist International.

Hoover, NYPL

784 FROM the fourth to the fifth World Congress; report of the Executive Committee of the Communist International. London, Published for the Communist International by the Communist Party of Gt. Britain, 1924. 122 p.

"This report has been compiled for the fifth World Congress of the Communist International." For contents see no. 772.
Hoover, LC, NYPL, Harv, Col, Duke Illin, Princ, NYUn, UCal, UVirg, Felt

785 RYKOV, A. I. [and Manuilskii, D. Z.]
Report on the economic position of Soviet Russia and a summary of the discussion in the Russian Communist Party, by comrade Rykov. Report on the national-colonial question, by comrade Manuil'sky. Moscow, Press Bureau of the fifth Congress of the Comintern [1924] 65 p. At head of title: Fifth Congress of the Communist International.
Hoover, NYPL, Col, Amst

786 ZINOV'EV, G.
Report: Work of the Executive Committee of the Communist International. Moscow, Press Bureau of the fifth Congress Comintern, 1924. 72 p. diagrs. At head of title: Fifth Congress of the Communist International. *Hoover, NYPL*

787 ZINOV'EV, G.
Speech in reply to discussion of report on the work of the E.C.C.I. Delivered by G. Zinoviev, June 26th, 1924. Resolution on the report to the E.C.C.I. Moscow, Press Bureau of the fifth Congress of the Comintern [1924] 79 p. At head of title: Fifth Congress of the Communist International. *Hoover, NYPL*

788 ZINOV'EV, G.
Towards trade union unity! [Speech at the fifth Congress of the Communist International] London, Published for the Communist International by the Communist Party of Great Britain [1924] 22 p. *Amst*

789 THESIS on the propaganda activity of the Communist International and its sections. Endorsed by the sub-committee of the Preparations committee composed of Kreibich, Kuusinen, and Bela Kun. [Moscow, Tip. "Red proletary" 1921 ?] 12 p. At head of title: Draft.

Draft of theses later adopted with some changes at the fifth Congress of the Communist International. *Hoover*

790 Le PROGRAMME de l'Internationale Communiste. Projets présentés à la discussion du 5e congrès mondial. [Paris, l'Humanité, 1924] 238 p. Bibliothèque communiste) *Hoover, NYPL, Col, Princ, UChic, Amst, BDIC, Felt*

791 [RYKOV, A. I. and MANUIL'SKII, D. Z.]
Rapport de Rykov sur la question russe. Rapport de Manouilski sur la question nationale et coloniale. Moscou, Bureau de la Presse de l'Internationale Communiste, 1924. [pages?] *Harv*

792 ZINOV'EV, G.
La question syndicale. (Discours au V-e Congrès de l'Internationale Communiste.) Paris, Librairie de l'Humanité, 1924. v, 29 p. (Petite Bibliothèque Communiste) *Amst, Felt*

793 ZINOV'EV, G.
Rapport sur les travaux du Comité Exécutif de l'Internationale Communiste; (19 juin 1924). Moscou, Editions du Bureau de la Presse de l'Internationale Communiste, 1924. 66 p. (V Congrès de l'Internationale Communiste) *Felt*

794 ZINOV'EV, G.
Fagbevaegelsens enhet. Tale paa den 5. Verdenskongres 7. Juli 1924. Utgit ab Norges Kommunistiske Parti. Kristiania, Ny Tid, 1924. 21 p. *Amst*

c) Resolutions, Theses, Manifestoes and other documents

795 K mirovomu proletariatu; manifest piatogo vsemirnogo kongressa Kominterna k desiatiletiiu imperialsticheskoi voiny. Leningrad, Giz, 1924. Folio, 15 p.

See annotations to "Manifest Kominterna k mirovomu proletariatu" (no. 1308) and to "Gegen den Krieg" (no. 1309). *BDIC*

796 V [PIATYI] vsemirnyi kongress Kommunisticheskogo Internatsionala; tezisy, rezoliutsii i postanovleniia. Moskva, Gos. izd-vo, 1924, 206 p.

Contains 28 items originating with the Congress, not including the Manifesto listed as no. 795. *Hoover, LC, Harv*

797 Die ORGANISATION der Betriebszellen; organisatorische Fragen und Beschlüsse des V. Kongresses [Berlin] C. Hoym Nachf. [1924] 78 p.

Minutes of the meeting of the Organization Commission of the V-th Congress, held July 1, 1924, concerning the reorganization of the communist parties on the basis of shop cells; instructions and resolutions on these matters. Prepared by the "Orgabteilung des EK der KI." *Hoover, NYPL, Amst, Felt*

798 Die TAKTIK der Kommunistischen Internationale (Beschlüsse des V. Weltkongresses) Berlin, Vereinigung internationaler Verlagsanstalten, 1924. 47 p.

On cover: Ergänzungsheft zu Heft 19/20, 1924, *Die Internationale.*

Hoover, NWest, Amst

799 THESEN und Resolutionen des V. Weltkongresses der Kommunistischen Internationale, Moskau, vom 17. Juni bis 8. Juli 1924. Hamburg, C. Hoym Nachf., 1924. 189 p. *Hoover, Amst, Felt*

800 HOW to organize the Communist Party. London, Communist Party of Gt. Britain [1924] 130 p.

Minutes of the Organization Commission of the fifth Congress and all instructions and resolutions concerning the question of the re-organization of the Communist parties on the basis of factory nuclei. (Preface, p. 6) *Hoover, Harv*

801 PROGRAMME of the Communist International; draft [by N. I. Bukharin] adopted at the fifth Congress. London, Published for the Communist International by the Communist Party of Great Britain [1924?] 79 p.

Inculdes also a report by A. Thalheimer (p. 66–79). See the discussion of the developments which led to the acceptance of this programme in note to „Program Commission" (following no. 1134). Bukharin's draft is no. 782.

Hoover, NYPL

802 V-e [CINQUIÈME] Congrès Communiste mondial. Résolutions. Paris, Librairie de l'Humanité, 1924. 106 p. (Petite bibliothèque communiste)
Hoover, NYPL, UChic, Yale, Amst, BDIC

803 PROGRAMME de l'Internationale Communiste. Projet adopté par le V-e congrès. Paris, Parti Communiste, Région parisienne, [n. d.] 20 p. duplicated.

See note to „Program Commission" (following no 1134). *BDIC*

804 Les QUESTIONS d'organisation au Ve Congrès de l'I.C. Cellules d'entreprises, statuts de l'I.C., directives pour l'organisation, etc. Paris, Librairie de l'Humanité, 1925. 100 p. (L'I.C. & les questions d'organisation, no. 1)   *Hoover, LC, NYPL, NWest, Yale, Amst, BDIC, Felt*

805 Den KOMMUNISTISKE Internationales taktik. Retningslinjer vedtat paa den 5te Verdenskongres og N.K.P.'s Landsstyres resolution om Kongressens beslutninger. Utgit av N.K.P. Oslo, Ny Tid, 1925. 50.   *Amst*

d) Commentaries and writings about the Congress

806 CHTO postanovil V vsemirnyi kongress Kominterna. Moskva, Gos. izd-vo, 1924. 31 p.

Popular account about the Congress; destined for mass propaganda.

Hoover, UWash, Col

807 PROGRAMNYI vopros na V kongresse Kominterna. Moskva, Gos. izd-vo, 1924. 82 p.

See note to "Program Commission" (following no. 1134).   *Hoover*

808 ZA edinstvo mirovogo profdvizheniia; voporosy profdvizheniia na V kongresse Kominterna. Moskva, Gos. izd-vo, 1924. 159 p.   *Col, Yale*

809 Die ERGEBNISSE des V. Weltkongresses der Komintern. Hamburg, Carl Hoym Nachf., 1924. 29 p.

„Vorbemerkung" signed: Abteilung Agitation und Propaganda der Exekutive der Komintern.   *Hoover, Amst*

810 Die ERGEBNISSE des V. Kongresses der Kommunistischen Internationale und des IV. Kongresses der Kommunistischen Jugendinternationale. Hrsg. vom Exekutivkomitee der KJI. Berlin, Verlag der Jugendinternationale [n. d.] 24 p.   *Amst*

811 REFERENTENMATERIAL zur Berichterstattung über den V. Weltkongreß. [Berlin, Friedrichstadt-Druckerei, 1924] 24 p.   *Amst, Felt*

812 WAS die Arbeiterlinke der Kommunistischen Internationale zu den Beschlüssen des V. Weltkongresses zu sagen hat [n. p., 1924?] 23 p. Als Manuskript gedruckt zur innerparteilichen Diskussion."

A joint statement of the left opposition groups of Germany, Poland and Russia. The item was unavailable for more detailed annotation.   *Amst, Felt*

813 YOUNG Communist International. Executive Committee.
The results of two congresses: the fifth congress of the Communist International and the fourth congress of the Y.C.I. Published by the E. C. of the Y. C. I. [Stockholm, Tr. a/b Fram, 1924] 32 p.

Hoover, NYPL, Harv, Col

814 Le SENS du V-e Congrès mondial. Paris, Librairie de l'Humanité, 1924. 34 p. (Petite bibliothèque communiste)

"Préface" signed: La section d'Agitation et de Propaganda de l'Exécutif de l'I. C.

Hoover, NWest, Amst, Felt

e) Bulletins issued for the Congress

Note. Here are listed the holdings of Hoover and Feltrinelli of the French-language bulletin of the V-th Congress. There also exist bulletins in German and English, but the available information was insufficient for listing. It can be expected that these two bulletins will be included in the checklist of periodicals of the Communist International which this author is preparing for publication.

815 BULLETIN du V-e Congrès de l'Internationale Communiste. Moscou, Bureau de la Presse du V-e Congrès du Comintern, 1924.

Hoover, nos. 1–23; June 14–July 11, 1924; *Felt*, nos. 1–18; June 14–July 5, 1924.

6. VI-th C O N G R E S S, Moscow, July 17—September 1, 1928

a) Protocols

816 STENOGRAFICHESKII otchet VI kongress[a] Konminterna [Moskva, Gos. izd-vo] 1929—30. 6 vols. Cover title.

Contents: Vyp. 1. Mezhdunarodnoe polozhenie i zadachi Kominterna. – Vyp. 2. Protiv imperialisticheskihk voin. – Vyp. 3. Programma mirovoi revoliutsii. – Vyp. 4. Revoliutsionnoe dvizhenie v kolonial'nykh i polukolonial'nykh stranakh. – Vyp. 5. Doklady o SSSR i VKP(b). Zakliuchitel'nye raboty. – Vyp. 6. Tezisy, rezoliutsii, postanovleniia [i] vozzvaniia.

Hoover, LC, [NYPL], Harv, Col (1–4, 6), *[UCal], BDIC* (1, 2, 6), *Felt* (1, 2, 6), *SInSt* (3–6)

817 PROTOKOLL. Sechster Weltkongreß der Kommunistischen Internationale, Moskau, 17. Juli — 1. September 1928. Hamburg, C. Hoym Nachf. [1928—29] 4 vols.

Contents:

v.1. Die internationale Lage und die Aufgaben der Komintern. Der Kampf gegen die imperialistische Kriegsgefahr. (Stenograms of the first 23 sessions of the Congress; indexes. 813 p.)

v.2. (This volume has not been located. It contains the stenograms of sessions 24–28 which dealt with the program of the C.I.)

v.3. Revolutionäre Bewegung in den Kolonien. Lage in der Sowjetunion: a) Wirtschaftliche Lage, b) Lage in der KPdSU. Bericht der Kommissionen. Wahlen. (Stenograms of sessions 29–46; indexes. 643 p.)

v.4. Thesen, Resolutionen, Programm, Statuten. (227 p.)

It is interesting to note that A. Tivel, who for the preparation of his book, *10 let Kominterna v resheniiakh i tsifrakh* (see no. 45), had access to the library and archives of the Comintern, also quotes only vols. 1, 3 and 4 as having been at his disposal. (p. 149) Hence, it is questionable whether volume 2 appeared at all.

vols. 1, 3, 4: *Hoover, NYPL, Harv, Felt*

vols. 1, 4: *Amst*

Holdings unknown: *Illin, Princ, UTex*

818 SIXTH World Congress of the Communist International, July—August 1928. [Vienna, F. Koritschoner, 1928] [632] p. Cover title.

Consists of special numbers 39–92 of v.8 of the English edition of *International Press Correspondence*, Jul. 25–Dec. 31, 1928, issued with special cover title and table of contents. *Hoover, NYPL*

819 VI-e [SIXIÈME] Congrès de l'Internationale Communiste (17 juillet — 1 septembre 1928) Compte rendu sténographique. [Paris] 1928. [*La Correspondance Internationale*. Numéro spécial, 10—13, 15—16, 18—24, 27—39, 41—45, 47—50, July 26—Dec. 11, 1928]

Hoover, NYPL, Harv, Col, UChic, Amst, BDIC, Felt

b) **Reports, Speeches, Drafts presented to the Congress**

820 BUKHARIN, N. I.
Mezhdunarodnoe polozhenie i zadachi Kominterna; otchetnyi doklad Ispolkoma Kominterna i zakliuchitel'noe slovo na VI kongresse Kominterna. Moskva, Leningrad, Gos. izd-vo, 1928. 174 p. At head of title: VI kongress Kominterna. *Hoover, Col, BDIC, Felt*

821 KOMMUNISTICHESKII Internatsional pered shestym vsemirnym kongressom; obzor deiatel'nosti IKKI i sektsii Kominterna mezhdu V i VI kongressami. Moskva, Gos. izd-vo, 1928. 422 p.

See annotation to no. 826. *Hoover, NYPL, SInSt*

822 MANUIL'SKII, D. Z.
Klassy, gosudarstvo, partiia v period proletarskoi diktatury; russkii vopros na VI kongresse Kominterna. Moskva-Leningrad, Gos. izd-vo, 1928. 93 p. *Hoover*

823 PIECK, Wilhelm
Otchet o deiatel'nosti Ispolnitel'nogo Komiteta Kommunisticheskogo Internatsionala 26 iiulia 1935 g. [Moskva] Partizdat, 1935. 97 p. At head of title: VI vsemiryni kongress Kommunisticheskogo Internatsionala. *LC*

824 PROEKT programmy Kommunisticheskogo Internatsionala; priniat programmnoi komissiei IKKI, 25 maia 1928 goda. Moskva, Gos. izd-vo, 1928. 88 p. At head of title: K VI kongressu Kominterna. *Hoover, SInSt*

825 TÄTIGKEITSBERICH der Exekutive der Kommunistischen Internationale für die Zeit vom 5. bis zum 6. Weltkongreß. Die Komintern vor dem 6. Weltkongreß. [Hamburg] C. Hoym Nachf. [1928] 576 p.

NYPL, Duke, Amst, Felt

826 The COMMUNIST International between the fifth and the sixth World Congresses 1924—8. London, Communist Party of Gt. Britain [1928] 508 p.

Oon cover: A report on the position in all sections of the World communist party. "The Reports cover the period up to May 1st, 1928."
Hoover, LC, NYPL, Harv, Col, Duke, DState, UChic, UPenn, UTex, UVirg, Yale, Felt

827 TROTSKII, L.
The draft program of the Communist International; a criticism of fundamentals. Introduction by James P. Cannon. New York, "The Militant", 1929. xi, 139 p.

On cover: Presented to the sixth World Congress of the Communist International. "Part of a larger document sent to the sixth congress of the Communist International." *Hoover, NYPL, Harv*

828 WOLFE, Bertram
Revolution in Latin America, New York, Workers Library Publishers
[c1928] 15 p. illus.

"A reprint of a portion of a speech of comrade Wolfe to the sixth World
Congress of the Communist International." Foreword.   *Hoover*

829 L'ACTIVITÉ de l'I[nternationale] C[ommuniste] du V-e au VI-e Congrès.
Paris, Bureau d'éditions, 1928. 682 p.

See annotation to no. 826.   *Hoover, BDIC, Felt*

830 CLASSE contre classe; la question française au IX-e Exécutif et au
VI-e Congrès de l'I.C. Paris, Bureau d'Editions, 1928? 260 p.

The Preface, signed by P. Semard surveys the developments in the Communist
Party of France concerning the tactic "class against class" promoted by the
E.C.C.I. and rejected by a considerable number of party members in France.
The volume contains: the entire discussion of the French question in the French
Commission of the 9-th Plenum (Feb. 9–25, 1928); the resolution of the 9-th
Plenum in this matter; the entire discussion of the French question by the Latin
Secretariat of the E.C.C.I. during the VI-th Congress of the C.I.; the resolution
of the Presidium of the E.C.C.I. concerning the policies of the Communist
Party of France.
As for the discussion in the French Commission of the 9-th Plenum see also
Klass protiv klassa no. 1131.   *Hoover, BDIC, Felt*

831 PROJET de programme de l'Internationale Communiste; adopté par
la Commission du programme du C.E. d l'I.C., le 25 mai 1928. Paris,
Cahiers du Bolchévisme, juin 1928. 39 p. (Supplément aux Cahiers du
Bolchévisme)   *Amst, BDIC*

832 PROJET de Programme de l'Internationale Communiste; adopté par
la Commission du programme du C.E. de l'I.C., le 25 mai 1928. Paris,
Bureau d'Edition [n.d.] 39 p. (Supplément de l'Internationale Communiste. N. 13 (15 juin 1928)   *Felt*

c) Resolutions, Theses, Manifestoes and other documents

833 PROGRAMMA i ustav Kommunisticheskogo Internatsionala. Priniata
VI kongressom 1 sentiabria 1928 g. v Moskve. Moskva, Gos. izd-vo,
1928. 95 p.   *Hoover, Amst*

834 PROGRAMMA i ustav Kommunisticheskogo Internatsionala. Izd. 4.
Moskva, Gos. izd-vo, 1928. 143 p.   *LC, Harv*

835 PROGRAMMA i ustav Kommunisticheskogo Internatsionala. Izd. 5. Moskva, Gos. izd-vo, 1930. 95 p. *LC, Harv*

836 PROGRAMMA i ustav Kommunisticheskogo Internatsionala. 9. izd. Moskva, Gos. izd-vo, 1931. 190 p. *SInSt*

837 PROGRAMMA i ustav Kominterna. 10. izd., Moskva, Partizdat, 1932. 182 p. *NYPL*

838 PROGRAMMA i ustav Kommunisticheskogo Internatsionala. Leningrad, Lenpartizdat, 1933. 170 p. *Col*

839 PROGRAMMA i ustav Kommunisticheskogo Internatsionala. Moskva, Partizdat, 1934. 112 p. *LC, NYPL, SInSt*

840 PROGRAMMA i ustav Kommunisticheskogo Internatsionala. [Moskva] Partizdat, 1935. 126 p. *Col, DState*

841 PROGRAMMA i ustav Kommunisticheskogo Internatsionala. Moskva, Partizdat, 1936. 216 p.

Harvard has nos. 841 or 842, but due to lack of number of pages in catalog card, identification is impossible. Both items were published in 1936.

LC, Harv [?]

842 PROGRAMMA i ustav Kommunisticheskogo Internatsionala. Moskva, Partizdat, 1936. 191 p.

See annotation to proceeding item. *LC, Harv [?],UChic*

843 PROGRAMMA i ustav. [Moskva] Partizdat, 1937. 79 p. *LC, Harv*

844 PROGRAMMA Kommunisticheskogo Internatsionala (priniata VI kongressom 1 sentiabria 1928 g. v Moskve) [Leningrad] "Leningradskaia Pravda" [1928] 189 p. *LC*

845 PROGRAMMA Kommunisticheskogo Internatsionala, priniataia VI kongressom 1 sentiabria 1928 g. v Moskve. Moskva, Gos. izd-vo, 1928. 122 p.

"This edition is being issued with the text as published in no. 205 of 'Pravda' of September 4, 1928, after correction of printing errors." Publishers note.
Obviously one of the earliest reprints of the program. *Hoover, LC*

846 TEZISY i rezoliutsii VI kongressa Kominterna. Moskva, Gos. izd-vo, 1929. 3 parts.

> Title of part (vypusk) 1 not established. — Vyp. 2. Tezisy o revoliutsionnom dvizhenii v kolonial'nykh i polukolonial'nykh stranakh. — Vyp. 3. Protiv imperialisticheskikh voin.   *Hoover, 2, 3, LC, 2, Harv, 2.*

847 Die KOMMUNISTISCHE Internationale und der Krieg. Thesen des VI. Weltkongresses der Kommunistischen Internationale über den Kampf gegen den imperialistischen Krieg und die Aufgaben der Kommunisten. [n. p.] Herausgegeben vom ZK der KPD [n. d.] 47 p.   *Felt*

848 PROGRAMM der Kommunistischen Internationale, angenommen vom VI. Weltkongreß am 1. September 1928 in Moskau. Anhang: Statuten der Kommunistischen Internationale. Fremdwörterverzeichnis. Hamburg-Berlin, C. Hoym Nachf. [n. d.] 112 p.

> First Hamburg edition. There exist three editions ("Auflage") of this item. The National Union Catalog disregarded these editions and listed all holdings on this first edition card.   *LC, NYPL, Yale, Amst, Felt*

849 PROGRAMM der Kommunistischen Internationale, angenommen vom VI. Weltkongreß am 1. September 1928 in Moskau. Anhang: Statuten der Kommunistischen Internationale; Fremdwörter-Verzeichnis. 2. Aufl. Hamburg-Berlin, C. Hoym Nachf [c1929] 112 p.

> Second Hamburg edition.   *Hoover, Harv*

850 PROGRAMM der Kommunistischen Internationale, angenommen vom VI. Weltkongreß am 1. September 1928 in Moskau. Anhang: Statuten der Kommunistischen Internationale. Fremdwörter-Verzeichnis. 3. Aufl. Hamburg-Berlin, C. Hoym Nachf., 1928. 112 p.

> Third Hamburg edition.   *Hoover, Harv, Amst, Felt*

851 PROGRAMM der Kommunistischen Internationale. Angenommen vom VI. Weltkongreß am 1. September 1928 in Moskau. Moskva, Izdatel'-skoe Tovarishchestvo Inostrannykh Rabochikh v SSSR, 1932. 151 p.
>   *Duke*

852 COMMUNISM and the international situation; theses on the international situation and the tasks of the Communist International, adopted at the sixth World Congress of the Communist International, 1928. New York, Workers' Library [1929] 46 p.

> Printed in Gt. Britain. "Passed ... on the report of N. Bukharin."   *Hoover, Col*

853 COMMUNISM and the international situation; thesis on the international situation and the tasks of the Communist International, adopted at the sixth World Congress of the Communist International, 1928. London, Modern Books, 1929. 46 p.   *LC, Harv, Brown, Illin, ULa, Amst*

854 The PROGRAMME of the Communist International adopted by VI. World Congress on 1st September 1928, in Moscow. [Vienna, International Press Correspondence, 1928] p. 1750—1772. At head of title: Special number. International Press Correspondence. English edition. Vol. 8, no. 92, December 31, 1928.   *Col*

855 PROGRAMME of the Communist International, adopted at the sixth Congress in 1928. [1st Indian ed.] Bombay, People's Pub. Hause, 1948. 72 p.   *Hoover, LC, Harv*

856 PROGRAMME of the Communist International, together with the statutes of the Communist International. New York, Workers' Library Publishers, Inc. [1929] 93 p.

    "First edition—December 1, 1929." For second and third ed. see no. 857 and 858.
    Hoover, NYPL, Harv, Duke, Illin, UConn, UTex, Yale

857 PROGRAM of the Communist International, together with the Statutes of the Communist International; adopted at the forty-sixth session of the sixth World Congress of the Communist International, September 1, 1928. [2d ed.] New York City, Workers' Library Publishers [1933] 96 p.

    For first ed. see no. 856;third ed. no. 858.
    Hoover, NYPL, Harv, Col, Duke, Illin, ULa

858 PROGRAM of the Communist International, together with its constitution. New York, Workers Library Publishers, 1936. 94 p.

    "Third edition, February 1936." For first and second ed. no. 856 and 857.
    Hoover, LC, NYPL, Harv, Col, ClevPL, UCin, ULa, Amst

859 The PROGRAMME of the Communist International; together with the statutes of the Communist International. New York, Workers Library [1929] x, 73 p. Printed in Gt. Britain. Adopted at the forty-sixth session of the sixth World Congress of the Communist International, September 1, 1928.   *Hoover, Harv*

860 The PROGRAMME of the Communist International. Together with the statutes of the Communist Inernational. [2nd pr.] London [Modern Books] 1932. viii, 72 p.   *Amst*

861 PROGRAMME of the Communist International, together with the statutes of the Communist International. Programma i ustav Kommunisticheskogo Internatsionala. Slovar' sostavil M. F. Lor'e. Moskva, Izdatel'skoe t-vo inostrannykh rabochikh v SSSR, 1932. 111 p.

> Text in English, with an English-Russian glossary for language instruction.
>
> *Hoover, LC, BrynM*

862 The REVOLUTIONARY movement in the colonies; thesis adopted by the sixth World Congress of the Communist International. [New York, Workers Library Publishers, 1932] 63 p. [Second printing]

> Lines of main title alternate with those of sub-title. "First printing, January, 1929." "Second printing, December, 1932." p. 63.
>
> *Hoover, NYPL, Harv, Col, Illin, UChic, ULa, UTex*

863 The REVOLUTIONARY movement in the colonies and semi-colonies. Thesis on the revolutionary movement in the colonies and semi-colonies, adopted by the sixth World Congress of th Communist International, 1928. London, Modern Books, 1929. viii, 63 p. *UTex, Amst, Felt*

864 REVOLUTIONARY movement in the colonies and semi-colonies: thesis adopted by the sixth Congress of the Communist International, 1928. [Bombay] People's Pub. House [1928] 67 p. *Hoover*

865 The STRUGGLE against imperialist war and the tasks of the communists; resolution of the VI World Congress of the Communist International, July—August, 1928. New York, City, Workers Library. 1932. 63 p. [First edition]

> *Hoover, LC, NYPL, Col, Brown, Newb, Princ, UChic, UTex, Yale, Amst*

866 The STRUGGLE against imperialist war and the tasks of the communists; resolutions of the 6th World Congress of the Communist International, July—August, 1928. New York City, Workers Library Publishers, 1934. 67 p.

> "First edition, Dec., 1932. Second edition, July, 1934."
>
> *Hoover, Harv, Col, Duke, UCLA, Yale*

867 PROGRAMME de l'Internationale Communiste adopté par le VI-e Congrès mondial le 1-er septembre 1928, a Moscou. [Paris, 1928]. At head of title: Numéro special XLVIII *La Correspondance internationale*, no. 141, 8-e année 23 nov. 1928. *Harv*

868 Le PROGRAMME de l'Internationale Communiste adopté par le VIe congrès mondial, le 1er septembre 1928 à Moscou [Paris, impr. G. Dangan] 1928. 24 p. illus. (Supplément gratuit de *l'Humanité* du 20 décembre 1928)   *BDIC*

869 PROGRAMME de l'Internationale Communiste (adopté par le VI-e congrès mondial le 1-er septembre 1928, à Moscou) suivi des Statuts de l'I. C. Paris, Bureau d'éditions [1928] 85 p.   *Hoover, Amst, BDIC, Felt*

870 PROGRAMME de l'Internationale Communiste. (Adopté par le VIe Congrès mondial le 1-er septembre 1928, à Moscou.) Suivi des statuts de l'I. C. Paris, Bureau d'Edition, 1936. 90 p.   *Harv, Felt*

871 THÈSES et résolutions du VI-e Congrés de l'I. C. Paris, Bureau d'éditions [1928?] 230 p.   *Hoover, Harv, Amst, Felt*

872 THÈSES et résolutions du VI-e Congrès mondial de l'I. C. [Paris, 1928] At head of title: Numéro spécial LI, *La Correspondance internationale*, no. 149, 8-e année 11 déc. 1928   *Harv*

873 MARX, Karl [and] Engels, Friedrich
Het Communistisch Manifest. 1948. Het Program van Moskou, door het zesde wereldcongres van de Communistische Internationale op. 1 september 1928 aangenomen. Vert. door A. Wins, Uitgeg. door de Communstische Partij Holland C.P.H. Centraal Comitee, ter gelegenheid van haar twintigjarig bestaan in April 1929. [Amsterdam] C.P.H. [1929] 127 p.   *Amst*

874 Het PROGRAMM der Communistische Internationale. Aangenomen door het zesde wereldcongres te Moskou. [n. p., n. d.] 48 p.   *Amst*

875 Het PROGRAM der Communistische Internationale. Aangenomen door het zesde wereldcongres te Moskou 1928. Utrecht, "Amstel" [n. d.] 80 p. Met: Statuten van de Kommunistische Internationale en Vreemde woordenlijst.   *Amst*

876 Het PROGRAM der Communistische Internationale. Aangenomen door het zesde wereldcongres te Moskou. Amsterdam, "Amstel" [n. d.] 80 p. Met: Statuten van de Kommunistische Internationale en Vreemde Woordenlijst. (Marxistisch Leninistische Scholing, 3.)   *Hoover*

877 PROGRAMO de komunista Internacio. Akceptita de 1-a 6-a kongreso la 1-an de septembro 1928 en Moskvo [trad. de G. Filipov kaj A.Sissler, kontrol de E. Drezen kaj G. Demidjuk] Moskvo ["Internacional'naja'] 1930. 119 p.   *Amst*

878 LA INTERNAZIONALE comunista e la guerra. (Tesi approvate al VI°
congresso mondiale della Internazionale comunista.) Paris, Edizioni
di Coltura Sociale, 1929. 73 p. (La Internazionale comunista — Dottrina
e movimento, No. 3)   *Felt*

879 PROGRAMMA della Internazionale comunista (approvato dal VI-e
congresso mondiale il 1° settembre 1928, a Mosca) Paris, Edizioni di
Coltura Sociale, 1930. 849 p.   *LC, BDIC, Felt*

880 La SITUAZIONE internazionale comunista e i compiti. Paris, Edizioni
Italiane di Coltura Sociale, 1929. 48 p. (La Internazionale comunista —
Dottrina e movimento, No. 2)   *Felt*

881 Den INTERNASJONALE situasjon og krigsfaren. Kommunistenes opgaver. Den Kommunistiske Internasjonales 6. Verdenskongress' politiske
teser og beslutningen om kampen mot krigsfaren. Oslo, Internasjonal
Arbeiderforlag, 1929. 130 p.   *Amst*

882 PROGRAM i pravila komunistične internacionale. Moskva-Leningrad,
Založniška Zadruga Inozemskih Delavcev v ZSSR, 1924. 117 p.

   The publication date 1924 is certainly a mistake of the printer or cataloger. The
   program and statutes of the Comintern had been adopted by the VIth Congress
   in September 1928, thus they could not have been printed in 1924. Furthermore, the Cooperative Publishing Society of Foreign Workers in the USSR did
   not exist in 1924. Its earliest publications appear only in 1932. Hence probably
   correct publication date is 1934.   *Felt*

883 La LUCHA contra la guerra imperialista y las tareas de los comunistas;
adoptadas por el VI Congreso Mundial de la Internacional Comunista.
Buenos Aires, La Internacional [19 . .] 62 p.   *LC*

884 PROGRAMA y estatutos de la Internacional Comunista Aprobados
en la XLVI sesion del VI Congreso de la Internacional Comunista, el
1 de Septiembre de 1928. Barcelona, Ediciones Europa-America [n. d.]
96 p. (Documentos de la Internacional Comunista)   *Amst*

885 KOMMUNISTISKA internationalens program. Antaget av Kommunistiska internationalens VI världskongress i Moskva den 1 sept. 1928.
Stockholm, Arbetar-kulturs förlag, 1937.   *Harv*

886 Krigsfaran och kommunisternas uppgifter; teser över kampen mot det imperialistiska kriget, antagna av Kominterns sjätte världs-kongress 1928. Stockholm, Fram [1929]   *Harv*

887 PROGRAMMA komunistichnogo internatsionalu, ukhvaliv VI kongres 1 veresnia 1928 r. v Moskvi. Vid. 3. [Kharkiv] 1928. 72 p.   *Harv*

d) Commentaries and writings about the Congress

888 BELL, Tom
Nakanune epokhi novykh voin (Itogi VI Kongressa Kominterna) Pere-vod s angliiskogo V. K. Zhitomirskogo. Moskva [etc.] Moskovskii rabochii [1928] 85 p. incl. tables.   *NYPL*

MOLOTOV, V. M.
VI [Shestoi] kongress i bor'ba za kommunizm; doklad na Leningrad-skom aktive VKP(b) 7 sentiabria 1928 g. See no. 456.

BUKHARIN, N. I.
Ergebnisse des VI. Kongresses der Kommunistischen Internationale; Rede, gehalten vor dem Parteiaktiv der Moskauer Organisation der KP(B) SU. Anschließend J. Jaroslawski: Kominternkongreß. See no. 454.

BUKHARIN, N. I.
Die historische Leistung des 6. Weltkongresses der Komintern; Rede vor dem Parteiaktiv der Moskauer Organisation der KPdSU, 5. September 1928. See no. 455.

MOLTOV, V. M
Der 6. Weltkongreß und der Kampf für den Kommunismus; Rede vor den Leningrader Funktionären der KPdSU 7. September 1928. See no. 457.

889 A la conquête de la jeunesse ouvrière! Les résultats du V-e Congrès mondial de l'I[nternationale] C[ommuniste des] J[eunes] et du VI-e Congrès mondial de l'I[nternationale] C[ommuniste]. Paris, Bureau d'Editions [n. d.] 32 p.   *Amst, BDIC, Felt*

7. VII-th C O N G R E S S, Moscow, July 25—August 21, 1935

Note. The stenographic records of the VII-th Congress have not been published as an entity. However, the reports, speeches, and discussions at the Congress were printed in the Russian language as 21 separate items comprising about 1400 pages (items no. 895–908, 909a–917).

The German, English and French editions (nos. 890–892) of the records appeared only in an "abridged" form, and with considerable delay (1939). But earlier, mostly in 1935, were published the same individual reports, speeches, and discussions in the German, English and French languages (nos. 919–985), containing fuller texts than those published in the "abridged" records.

Furthermore, there were published, and are available, the full texts of the resolutions adopted by the Congress in the Russian, German, English and French languages.

Thus, there seems to be available enough material on this Congress, particularily if one does not take a short cut by using the Moscow-selected "abidged" editions of the records.

a) Protocols

890   VII. [SIEBENTE] Kongreß der Kommunistischen Internationale. Gekürztes stenographisches Protokoll. Moskau, Verlag für Fremdsprachige Literatur, 1939. 599 p.   *Felt*

891   VII [SEVENTH] Congress of the Communist International; abridged stenographic report of proceedings. Moscow, Foreign Languages Publishing House, 1939. vi, 604 p.

Hoover, LC, NYPL, Illin,NYUn, UCal, UMich, UTex, Yale

892   VII-e [SEPTIÈME] Congrès de l'Internationale Communiste. Compte rendu abrégé. Moscou, Editions en langues étrangères, 1939. 562 p.

Amst

893   VII-e [SEPTIÈME] Congrès mondial de l'Internationale Communiste. Paris [1935] 6 fasc., pagination varies. ("La Correspondance Internationale", numéros spéciaux, nos. 64 August 7, 1935, 70, 71, 77, 82, 103 Nov. 3, 1935)   *Felt*

894   El COMMUNISMO al dia; VII congreso de la International comunista; dicursos integros, resoluciones adoptadas; prologo de Jose Bullejos, epilogo de Juan B. Bergua. Madrid, Ediciones Bergua, 1935. xv, 303 p.

LC

b) Reports, Speeches, Drafts presented to Congress

895 CACHIN, Marcel
Kompartiia Frantsii vysoko derzhit boevoe znamia komunizma. [Rech']
27 iiulia 1935 g. Khabarovsk, Dal'giz, 1935. 15 p. At head of title:
VII vsemirnyi kongress Kommunisticheskogo Internatsionala.

Hoover, LC, BDIC

895a CHEMODANOV, V.
Edinyi front molode'zhi protiv fashizma i voiny. (Rech . . . na VII-m
kongresse Kominterna 8 avgusta 1935 g.) [Moskva] 1935. 14 p.

BDIC

896 DIMITROV, G.
Nastuplenie fashizma i zadachi Kommunisticheskogo Internatsionala
v bor'be za edinstvo rabochego klassa protiv fashizma. [Moskva]
Partizdat, 1935. 99 p. At head of title: VII vsemirnyi Kongress Kommunisticheskogo Internatsionala.

Hoover

897 DIMITROV, G.
Nastuplenie fashizma i zadachi Kommunisticheskogo Internatsionala
v bor'be za edinstvo rabochego klassa protiv fashizma; doklad i zakliuchitel'noe slovo [2 avgusta 1935 g. Moskva] Partizdat, 1935. 127 p.
port. At head of title: VII vsemirnyi Kongress Kommunisticheskogo
Internatsionala.

LC, Harv, Col, BDIC

898 DIMITROV, G.
Nastuplenie fashizma i zadachi Kommunisticheskogo Internatsionala
v bor'be za edinstvo rabochego klassa protiv fashizma; doklad na
VII vsemirnom kongresse Kommunisticheskogo Internatsionala, 2. avg.
1935 goda. Politicheskii otchet TSK BRP(k) [Bulgarskoi rabochei partii
(kommunistov)] V s"ezdu partii 19 dek. 1948 g. Moskva, Gospolitizdat,
1948. 223 p. (Bibliotechka po nauchnomu sotsializmu)

Harv, Col

899 DIMITROV, G.
Tepereshnie praviteli kapitalisticheskikh stran — vremennye liudi;
nastoiashchii khoziain mira — proletariat. Moskva, 1935. 20 p.

SInSt

900 GOTWALD, Klement
Kompartiia Chekhoslovakii v bor'be za edinyi front. Moskva, 1935.
24 p.

SInSt

901 KOMMUNISTICHESKAIA partiia Anglii v bor'be za massy i edinyi front proletariata; rechi tt. Kempbella, Kerrigena, Garri Pollita, Palm Datta, Shildsa — delegatov kompartii Anglii. [Moskva] Partizdat, 1935. 111 p. At head of title: VII vsemirnyi kongress Kommunisticheskogo Internatsionala.

> English spelling of above names: Campbell, Corrigan, Harry Pollit, Palm Dutt, Childs. *Hoover, LC, BDIC, SInSt*

902 KOMMUNISTICHESKAIA partiia Avstrii — v bor'be za massy; rechi tt. Kopelinga, Videna, Dopplera, Germana [Hermann] — delegatov avstriiskoi kompartii. [Moskva] Partizdat, 1935. 54 p. At head of title: VII vsemirnyi kongress Kommunisticheskogo Internatsionala.

> *Hoover, LC, NYPL, BDIC, SInSt*

903 KOMMUNISTICHESKAIA partiia Chekhoslovakii v bor'be za edinyi front — protiv voiny i fashizma; rechi tt. Gotval'da, Shverma, Slanskego, Kellera, Zapototskogo, Kopetskogo, Syrovy, Shirokogo — delegatov chekhoslovatskoi kompartii. [Moskva] Partizdat, 1935. 94 p. At head of title: same as no. 902.

> Czech spelling of names: Gottwald, Šverma, Slanský, Keller, Zápotocký, Kopecký, Syrový, Široký. *Hoover, LC, NYPL, BDIC, SInSt*

904 KOMMUNISTICHESKAIA partiia Germanii v bor'be protiv fashizma; rechi Vil'gel'ma Pika [i drugikh. Moskva] Partizdat, 1935. 102 p. At head of title: same as no. 902.

> The item was ont available for identification of all speakers. *LC, BDIC, SInSt*

905 KOMMUNISTICHESKAIA partiia IAponii protiv rezhima voiny, goloda i bezpraviia; rechi tt. Okano, Tanaka, Nisikava — delegatov iaponskoi kompartii. [Moskva] Partizdat, 1935. 47 p. At head of title: same as no. 902. *Hoover, LC, NYPL, Col, BDIC, SInSt*

906 KOMMUNISTICHESKAIA partiia Ispanii v bor'be protiv fashizma; rechi tt. Dolores [Ibarruri], Garsia [Garcia], Khuan [Juan], Ventura, Martines [Martinez], Evaristo — delegatov ispanskoi kompartii. [Moskva] Partizdat, 1935. 85 p. At head of title: same as no. 902.

> *Hoover, LC, BDIC, SInSt*

907 KOMMUNISTICHESKAIA partiia Pol'shi — za antifashistskii front; rechi tt. Lenskogo, Bronkovskogo, Rvalia, Belevskogo, Genrikovskogo — delegatov polskoi kompartii. [Moskva] Partizdat, 1935. 94 p. At head of title: same as no. 902.

> Polish spelling of names: Leński, Bronkowski, Rwal, Bielewski, Henrykowski. *Hoover, LC, BDIC, SInSt*

908 KOMMUNISTICHESKAIA partiia Pribaltiki v bor'be za edinyi front protiv fashizma i voiny; rechi tt. Tuominena (Finlandiia), Mekinena Finlandiia), Lekhtosaari (Finlandiia), Martyna (Latviia), Kuuska (Estoniia), Krumina (Latviia), Angaretisa (Litva) — delegatov kompartii Pribaltiki. [Moskva] Partizdat, 1935. 77 p. At head of title: same as no. 902. *Hoover, LC, BDIC, SIntS*

909 KOMMUNISTICHESKII Internatsional pered VII vsemirnym kongressom; materialy [Moskva] Partizdat, 1935. 605 p.

"Materialy o resheniiakh Ispolkoma Kominterna i ego organov i o deiatel'nosti otdel'nykh sektsii KI v period so vremeni VI kongressa." p. [3]
Hoover, LC, NYPL, Harv, Col, Yale, BDIC, SInSt

909a KUUSINEN, Otto
Dvizhenie molode'zhi i bor'ba protiv fashizma i voennoi opasnosti. Rech na zasedanii 17 avgusta 1935 g. [Moskva] 1935. 31 p., illus. (VII Vsemirnyi kongress Kommunisticheskogo internatsionala)
BDIC

910 MANUIL'SKII, D. Z.
Engel's v bor'be za revoliutsionnyi marksizm. [Moskva] Partizdat, 1935. 42 p. port. At head of title: VII vsemirnyi kongress Kommunisticheskogo Internatsionala. *Hoover, LC, BDIC*

911 MANUIL'SKII, D. Z.
Engel's v bor'be za revoliutsionnyi marksizm. Khabarovsk, Dalgiz, 1935. 31 p. port. At head of title: VII vsemirnyi kongress Kommunisticheskogo Internatsionala. *LC*

912 MANUIL'SKII, D. Z.
Itogi sotsialisticheskogo stroitel'stva v SSSR. [Moskva] Partizdat, 1935. 61 p. inc. port. At head of title: VII vsemirnyi kongress Kommunisticheskogo Internatsionala. *Hoover, LC, NYPL, Harv, Col, BDIC*

913 MARTY, Andre
Vmeste s trudiashchimisia SSSR — na zashchitu mira; iz rechi na zasedanii 14 avgusta 1935 g. [Moskva] Partizdat, 1935. 31 p. port. At head of title: VII vsemirnyi kongress Kommunisticheskogo Internatsionala. *LC, BDIC*

914 PIATNITSKII, O.
Prinuditel'nyi trud, fashizm, i organizatsiia bezrabotnykh na osnove edinogo fronta, 4 avgusta 1935 g. [Moskva] Partizdat, 1935. 38 p. At head of title: VII vsemirnyi kongress Kommunisticheskogo Internatsionala. *Hoover, BDIC*

915 PIECK, Wilhelm
Otchet o deiatel'nosti Ispolnitel'nogo Komiteta Kommunisticheskogo
Internatsionala, 26 iiulia 1935 g. [Moskva] Partizdat, 1935. 97 p. At
head of title: VII vsemirnyi kongress Kommunisticheskogo Internatsionala. *LC, NYPL, Col, BDIC*

916 THOREZ, Maurice
Edinyi i narodnyi front vo Frantsii. 3 avgusta 1935 g. [Moskva] Partizdat, 1935. 61 p. port. At head of title: VII vsemirnyi kongress Kommunisticheskogo Internatsionala. *Hoover, LC, BDIC, SInSt*

917 [TOGLIATTI, P.]
O zadachakh Kommunisticheskogo Internatsionala v sviazi s podgotovkoi imperialistami novoi mirovoi voiny; [doklad] 13—14 avgusta 1935
goda [Moskva] Partizdat, 1935. 92 p. At head of title: VII vsemirnyi
kongress Kommunisticheskogo Internatsionala. M. Erkoli.
Hoover, LC, NYPL, Harv, BDIC

918 VARGA, E.
Mezhdu VI i VII kongressami Kominterna; ekonomika i politika, 1928—
1934. Moskva, Partizdat, 1935. 188 p.

See annotation to no. 973. *Hoover, BDIC*

919 DIMITROV, G. M.
Arbeiterklasse gegen Faschismus. Bericht, erstattet am 2. August 1935
zum 2. Punkt der Tagesordnung des Kongresses: Die Offensive des
Faschismus und die Aufgaben der Kommunistischen Internationale im
Kampf für die Einheit der Arbeiterklasse gegen den Faschismus, Straß-
burg, Prometheus [1935] 140 p. At head of title: VII. Weltkongreß der
Kommunistischen Internationale. *Amt, BDIC*

920 DIMITROV, G. M.
Arbeiterklasse gegen Faschismus. Bericht, erstattet am 2. August 1935
zum 2. Punkt der Tagesordnung des Kongresses: Die Offensive des
Faschismus und die Aufgaben der Kommunistischen Internationale im
Kampf für die Einheit der Arbeiterklasse gegen Faschismus. Straßburg,
Prometheus [1935] 85 p. At head of title: VII. Weltkongreß der Kom-
munistischen Internationale. *Amst*

921 DIMITROV, G. M.
Arbeiterklasse gegen Faschismus. Bericht, erstattet am 2. August 1935
zum 2. Punkt der Tagesordnung des Kongresses: Die Offensive des
Faschismus und die Aufgaben der Kommunistischen Internationale im
Kampf für die Einheit der Arbeiterklasse gegen Faschismus. Prag,
Kreibich [n. d.] 111 p. At head of title: VII. Weltkongreß der Kommunistischen Internationale. *Amst*

922 DIMITROV, G. M.
Arbeiterklasse gegen Faschismus; Bericht und Schlußwort zum 2. Punkt
der Tagesordnung: Die Offensive des Faschismus und die Aufgaben
der Kommunistischen Internationale im Kampfe für die Einheit der
Arbeiterklasse gegen den Faschismus und Ansprache in der Schluß-
sitzung des Kongresses. Moskau-Leningrad, Verlagsgenossenschaft
Ausländischer Arbeiter in der UdSSR, 1935. 176 p. front (port.) At head
of title: VII. Weltkongreß der Kommunistischen Internationale.
Hoover, LC, Amst, SInSt

923 DIMITROV, G. M.
Arbeiterklasse gegen Faschismus. Bericht, erstattet am 2. August 1935
zum 2. Punkt der Tagesordnung des Kongresses: Die Offensive des
Faschismus und die Aufgaben der Kommunistischen Internationale im
Kampfe für die Einheit der Arbeiterklasse gegen Faschismus. Moskau-
Leningrad, Verlagsgenossenschaft Ausländischer Arbeiter in der UdSSR,
1935. 109 p. At head of title: VII. Weltkongreß der Kommunistischen
Internationale. *Felt*

924 [DIMITROV, G.]
Resolutionen und Beschlüsse und Ansprache Dimitrow's auf der Schluß-
sitzung des VII. Weltkongresses. Straßburg, Prometheus Verlag [1935]
56 p. At head of title: VII. Weltkongreß der Kommunistischen Internationale. *Hoover, Amst, Felt*

925 GOTTWALD, K.
Für die Volksfront der Arbeiter, der Freiheit und des Friedens! Rede,
gehalten in der 24. Sitzung des VII. Weltkongresses der Kommunistischen Internationale am 7. August 1935. Moskau, Verlagsgenossenschaft Ausländischer Arbeiter in der UdSSR, 1935. 23 p. illus.   *Amst, SInSt*

926 GOTTWALD, K.
Für die Volksfront der Arbeit, der Freiheit und des Friedens in der
Tschechoslovakei. [Straßburg, Prometheus Verlag, n. d.] 24 p. At head
of title: VII. Weltkongreß der Kommunistischen Internationale. *Harv*

927 Die KOMMUNISTISCHE Internationale vor dem VII. Weltkongreß; Materialien. Moskau, Verlagsgenossenschaft Ausländischer Arbeiter in der UdSSR, 1935. 718 p. tables.

> „Die in diesem Buche enthaltenen Informations-Materialien über die Beschlüsse des Exekutiv-Komitees der Kommunistischen Internationale und seiner Organe sowie über die Tätigkeit der einzelnen Sektionen der Komintern in der seit dem VI. Weltkongreß verflossenen Periode wurden zum Herbst 1934 vorbereitet." p. [5]   *Hoover, LC, NYPL, Harv, Oberl, UMich, Amst, BDIC, Felt*

928 KUUSINEN, Otto
Die Front der jungen Generation. Rede, geh. in der 41. Sitzung des VII. Weltkongresses der Kommunistischen Internationale am 17. August 1935. Straßburg, Prometheus Verlag [n. d.] 27 p.   *Amst*

929 [MANUIL'SKII, D. Z.]
Engels im Kampfe für den revolutionären Marxismus. Rede anläßlich des 40. Todestages von Friedrich Engels, geh. in der 22. Sitzung des VII. Weltkongresses der Kommunistischen Internationale am 5. August 1935. Moskau, Verlagsgenossenschaft Ausländischer Arbeiter in der UdSSR, 1935. 47 p. illus.   *Amst, BDIC, Felt*

930 MANUIL'SKII, D. Z.
Engels im Kampf für den revolutionären Marxismus; Rede anläßlich des 40. Todestages von Friedrich Engels gehalten auf dem VII. Weltkongreß der Kommunistischen Internationale. Straßburg, Prometheus Verlag [1935] 32 p. At head of title: VII. Weltkongreß der Kommunistischen Internationale. D. Manuilski   *Hoover, LC, Amst, Felt*

931 MANUIL'SKI, D. Z.
Der Sieg des Sozialismus in der Sowjetunion und seine weltgeschichtliche Bedeutung. Bericht [an den] VII. Weltkongreß der Kommunistischen Internationale, erstattet am 17. August 1935, zum 4. Punkt der Tagesordnung: „Die Ergebnisse des sozialistischen Aufbaus in der UdSSR", 1935. 68 p. illus.   *Amst, Felt*

932 MANUIL'SKII, D. Z.
Der Sieg des Sozialismus in der Sowjetunion und seine weltgeschichtliche Bedeutung; Bericht, erstattet am 17. August 1935, zum 4. Punkt der Tagesordnung des Kongresses: Die Ergebnisse des sozialistischen Aufbaus in der Sowjetunion. Straßburg, Prometheus Verlag [1936] 54 p. At head of title: VII. Weltkongreß der Kommunistischen Internationale.   *Hoover, LC, NYPL, Amst*

933 PIECK, Wilhelm and others
Die Offensive des Faschismus und die Aufgaben der Kommunisten im
Kampf für die Volksfront gegen Krieg und Faschismus; Referate auf
dem VII. Kongreß der Kommunistischen Internationale (1935) [von]
Wilhelm Pieck, Georgi Dimitroff [und] Palmiro Togliatti. Berlin, Dietz
Verlag, 1957. 295 p.   *NYPL, Harv, UWisc, BDIC, Felt*

934 PIECK, Wilhelm
Der Vormarsch zum Sozialismus; Bericht und Schlußwort zum ersten
Punkt der Tagesordnung des Kongresses: Rechenschaftsbericht über die
Tätigkeit des Exekutivkomitees der Kommunistischen Internationale.
Straßburg, Prometheus Verlag [1936] 95 p. At head of title: VII. Welt-
kongreß der Kommunistischen Internationale.   *Amst, Felt*

935 PIECK, Wilhelm
Der Vormarsch zum Sozialismus. Bericht, Schlußwort und Resolution
zum 1. Punkt der Tagesordnung des Kongresses: Rechenschaftsbericht
über die Tätigkeit des Exekutivkomitees der Kommunistischen Internationale. Moskau-Leningrad, Verlagsgenossenschaft Ausländischer
Arbeiter in der UdSSR, 1935. 131 p. At head of title: VII. Weltkongreß
der Kommunistischen Internationale.   *Felt*

936 THOREZ, Maurice
Die Volksfront für Brot, Freiheit und Frieden. Die Erfolge der antifaschistischen Einheitsfront in Frankreich. Rede, gehalten in der
17. Sitzung des VII. Weltkongresses der Kommunistischen Internationale
(3. August 1935). Straßburg, Prometheus [n. d.] 44 p.   *Amst*

937 [TOGLIATTI, Palmiro]
Kampf gegen Krieg und Faschismus. Bericht zum 3. Punkt der Tagesordnung des VII. Weltkongresses der Kommunistischen Internationale
„Die Vorbereitung des imperialistischen Krieges und die Aufgaben
der Kommunistischen Internationale" (13.—14. August 1935) und Schlußwort (17. August 1935). Moskau, Verlagsgenossenschaft Ausländischer
Arbeiter in der UdSSR, 1935. 124 p. illus. At head of title: M. Ercoli.
                                                      Amst, Felt, SInSt

938 [TOGLIATTI, Palmiro]
Kampf gegen Krieg und Faschismus. Bericht zum 3. Punkt der Tagesordnung des VII. Weltkongresses der Kommunistischen Internationale
„Die Vorbereitung des imperialistischen Krieges und die Aufgaben
der Kommunistischen Internationale" (13.—14. August 1935) und Schlußwort (17. August 1935). Straßburg, Prometheus Verlag [n. d.] 95 p. illus.
At head of title: M. Ercoli.   *Amst, Felt*

939 WANG, Ming
Die revolutionäre Bewegung in den kolonialen und halbkolonialen Ländern und die Taktik der kommunistischen Parteien. Gekürztes Stenogramm der Rede zum 2. Punkt der Tagesordnung: „Die Offensive des Faschismus und die Aufgaben der Kommunistischen Internationale im Kampf für die Einheit der Arbeiterklasse gegen den Faschismus", in der Sitzung vom 7. August 1935. VII. Weltkongreß der Kommunistischen Internationale. Moskau, Verlagsgenossenschaft Ausländischer Arbeiter in der UdSSR, 1935. 64 p. At head of title: Wan Min.   *Amst, Felt*

940 WANG, Ming
Im Zeichen der chinesischen Sowjets; die revolutionäre Bewegung in den kolonialen und halbkolonialen Ländern und die Taktik der kommunistischen Parteien. Umgearbeitetes und ergänztes Stenogramm der Rede in der 23. Sitzung des Kongresses, 7. August 1935. Straßburg, Prometheus Verlag [1935] 61 p. map. At head of title: Wan Min.

Hoover, Harv, Felt

941 CACHIN, Marcel
The fight for the people's front in France [Speech delivered at the] seventh World Congress [of the] Communist International. [London, Modern Books, n. d.] 15 p. Cover title.

Identical with no. 968–10.   *Hoover, Col, Amst*

942 CACHIN, Marcel [and others]
The people's front in France; Speeches by Marcel Cachin, Maurice Thorez, Andre Marty. New York, Workers Library [1935] 95 p. At head of title: Seventh World Congress of the Communist International.

Contents: Marcel Cachin: The Communist Party of France fights for the people's front.
Maurice Thorez: The successes of the anti-fascist united front,.
Andre Morty: For the defense of the Soviet Union.

Hoover, NYPL, Duke, NWest, Amst

943 DIMITROV, G.
The present rulers of the capitalist countries are but temporary, the real master of the world is the proletariat. Concluding address. London, Modern Books [1936] 12 p.

Identical with no. 968–15.   *Hoover, Col, UTex, Amst*

944 [DIMITROV, G.]
Resolutions, including also the closing speech of Georgi Dimitroff. New York, Workers Library [1935] 56 p. At head of title: Seventh World Congress of the Communist International.

Hoover, LC, NYPL, Harv, Amst

205

945 DIMITROV, G.
The united front against fascism; speeches delivered at the seventh World Congress of the Communist International, July 25—August 20, 1935. [5. ed.] New York, New Century Publishers [1945] 144 p. (Marxist pamphlets no. 3) *Hoover*

946 DIMITROV, G.
The united front against fascism and war; the fascist offensive and the tasks of the Communist International in the fight for the unity of the working class against fascism. New York, Workers Library Publishers [1935] 127 p. illus. (port.) At head of title: Seventh World Congress of the Communist International.

On cover: Full report and speech in reply to discussion. "First edition September 1935 ... Third edition, October, 1935." Published also in London and Moscow under title: *The working class against fascism.* *LC, Harv*

947 DIMITROV, G.
The united front against fascism and war. [New York, Workers Library, 1935] 62 p. At head of title: 7th Congress of the Communist International.

Abridged edition compiled from the three speeches of Georgi Dimitroff at the Seventh World Congress of the Communist International. p. 5. See preceding item. Published also in New York under title: *The united front against fascism* (no. 945) *Hoover, NYPL, BDIC, Felt*

948 DIMITROV, G.
The United Front against war and fascism; speeches delivered at the Seventh World Congress of the Communist International. 4-th ed. New York, Workers Library Publishers [1936] 144 p. *Col*

949 DIMITROV, G.
The Working Class against Fascism; Report and Speech in reply to the discussion on the second point of the agenda; The fascist offensive and the tasks of the Communist International in the fight for the unity of the working class against fascism [Also address at close of Congress] Moscow-Leningrad, Cooperative Publishing Society of Foreign Workers in the USSR, 1935. 166 p. At head of title: Seventh World Congress of the Communist International.

"Edited by I. B. Lasker, A. Rothstein and L. Talmy" For London editions see next items. *Hoover, LC, SInSt*

950 DIMITROV, G.

The working class against fascism; report delivered August 2, 1935, on the second point of the agenda: The fascist offensive and the tasks of the Communist International in the fight for the unity of the working class against fascism. [London, Modern Books, 1935] 79 p.

Identical with no. 968–2. *Hoover, Col, UTex, Amst*

951 DIMITROV, G.

The working class against fascism. Speech in reply to discussion. [London, Modern Books, 1936] 32 p.

Identical with no. 968–3. *Hoover, UTex, Amst*

952 DIMITROV, G.

The working class against fascism. London, M. Lawrence [1935] 127 p. port.

"Comprises... the report and the two speeches delivered by G. Dimitrov general secretary of the Communist International, at the body's Seventh World Congress..." *Col*

953 DIMITROV, G.

Working class unity—bulwark against fascism; the fascist offensive and the tasks of the Communist International in the fight for the unity of the working class against fascism, report by Georgi Dimitroff. New York, Workers Library Publishers [1935] 95 p. At head of title: Seventh World Congress of the Communist International.

Hoover, NYPL, Harv, Amst

954 DIMITROV, G.

Working class unity—bulwark against fascism. [New York City, Workers Library Publishers, 1935] 71 p. At head of title: 7th World Congress of the Communist International. "Second edition."

Second edition of preceding item. *LC, NYPL, Col*

955 GOTTWALD, K.

A people's front in defence of labour, freedom and peace; speech delivered at the 24th session, August 7, 1935 [Ed. by F. Johnson] Moscow, Cooperative Publishing Society of Foreign Workers in the U.S.S.R., 1935. 21 p. At head of title: Seventh World Congress of the Communist International.

Published also with title: "The United Front in Czechoslovakia." See next item.
LC, Amst

956 GOTTWALD, K.
The united front in Czechoslovakia; speech by K. Gottwald. New York, Workers Library [1935] 22 p. At head of title: Seventh World Congress of the Communist International.

> Published also with title: A people's front in defence of labour, freedom and peace. See preceding item. *Hoover, NYPL, Col, Amst*

957 GREEN, Gil[ber]
Young communists and the unity of youth. [New York, Youth Publishers, 1935] 15 p. illus. At head of title: 7th World Congress of Communist International.

> "Speech delivered at the seventh World Congress of the Communist International." Discussion of activities of the Young Communist League in the United States. *Hoover, NYPL*

958 KUUSINEN, O. W.
Youth and fascism; the youth movement and the fight against fascism and the war danger; speech by O. Kuusinen. New York, Workers Library Publishers [1935] 30 p. At head of title: Seventh World Congress of the Communist International. *NYPL*

959 MANUIL'SKII, D. Z.
Engels in the struggle for revolutionary Marxism, speech on the fortieth anniversary of the death of Friedrich Engels, delivered at the seventh World Congress of the Communist International, August 5, 1936 New York, Workers Library Publishers [1936] 39 p. At head of title: Seventh World Congress of the Communist International. *LC, NYPL*

960 MANUL'SKII, D. Z.
Results of socialist construction in the U.S.S.R.; report delivered on August 17, 1935. Moscow-Leningrad, Co-operative publishing society of foreign workers in the U.S.S.R., 1935. 65 p. At head of title: Seventh world congress of the Communist International. D. Z. Manuilsky.

> "Edited by J. Fineberg." For abridged New York edition see next item.
> *LC, NYPL*

961 MANUIL'SKII, D. Z.
The results of socialist construction in the USSR. [New York City, City, Workers Library, 1935] 22 p.

> "Abridged stenogram of report delivered to the seventh Congress of the Communist International." – p. 3. For full text see preceding item and no. 968–6.
> *Hoover, Harv, Amst*

962 MANUIL'SKII, D. Z.
The results of socialist construction in the U.S.S.R. Report delivered August 17, 1935. The victory of socialism in the U.S.S.R. The new phase in the development of the world proletarian revolution. Sydney, N.S.W., Modern Publishers [1935?] 61 p. At head of title: The seventh World Congress of the Communist International. *NYPL*

963 MANUIL'SKII, D. Z.
The results of socialist construction in the U.S.S.R. London, Modern Books, 1935. 46 p. Cover title.

"Report delivered to the Seventh World Congress of the Communist International." Identical with no. 968–6. *Hoover, Col, UTex, Amst*

964 MANUIL'SKII, D. Z.
The rise of socialism in the Soviet Union. Report on the results of socialist construction in the U.S.S.R., delivered August 17, 1935 [at the] Seventh World Congress of the Communist International. New York, Workers Library Publishers [1935] 63 p. At head of title: Seventh World Congress of the Communist International. *Amst*

965 PIECK, Wilhelm
Advancing to socialism; report, reply to the discussion, and resolution on the first point of the agenda: the activities of the Executive Committee of the Communist International. Moscow-Leningrad, Cooperative Publishing Society of Foreign Workers in the U.S.S.R., 1935. 123 p. At head of title: Seventh World Congress of the Communist International.

Edited by A. Fineberg. Published also by the Workers Library Publishers New York, under title: *Freedom, peace and bread!* See next item and no. 968–1.
LC, Amst, SInSt

966 PIECK, Wilhelm
Freedom, peace and bread! The activities of the Executive Committee of the Communist International, report by Wilhelm Pieck. New York, Workers Library [1935] 103 p. At head of title: Seventh World Congress of the Communist International.

Published also in Moscow under title: *Advancing to socialism.*
Hoover, LC, NYPL, Harv, Col, Amst

967 POLLITT, Harry
Unity against the national government; Harry Pollitt's speech at the seventh Congress of the Communist International. [London, The Communist Party of Great Britain, 1935] 32 p. *Hoover*

968 REPORT of the seventh World Congress of the Communist International. London, Modern Books [1935] 1 vol. [containing 17 pamphlets; each has special title page and separate paging; the above title is taken from the title page preceding first item.]

This is a *London edition* of the reports and speeches to the VIIth Congress and the resolutions adopted by the Congress. The 17 items are listed below in the sequence as they appear in the volume held by the Library of the Hoover Institution. The catalog cards for this item found in the National Union Catalog indicate that at least seven other libraries have this item. Only two of these libraries listed its contents, Columbia University and the University of Texas. Three other libraries limited themselves to stating "15 v. in 1", and two libraries didn't indicate how many items they have. In the listing of particular items, Columbia University has two slightly different titles which could have resulted from variations of the cover titles. Seven of the 17 items are known as separate publications. They were listed also separately and references have been inserted here.

1. Pieck, W. Report on the activities of the Executive Committee of the Communist International, July 26th, 1935. Verbatim official report. 86 p.

2. Dimitrov, G. The working class against fascism; report delivered August 2, 1935 on the second point of the agenda: The fascist offensiva and the tasks of the Communist International in the fight for the unity of the working class against fascism. 79 p. (See no. 950)

3. Dimitrov, G. The working class against fascism; speech in reply to discussion. 31 p. (See no. 951)

4. [Togliatti, P.] The fight against war and fascism [by] Ercoli [pseud.] 77 p.

5. Manuil'skii, D. Z. Engels in the struggle for revolutionary Marxism; verbatim official text. 29 p.

6. Manuil'skii, D. Z. The results of socialist construction in the U.S.S.R., report delivered August 17, 1935. 46 p. (See no. 963)

7. Manuil'skii, D. Z. The working of the seventh Congress of the Communist International; a speech delivered at a meeting of the active members of the Moscow organization of the C.P.S.U., September 14, 1935. 63 p.

8. Kuusinen, O. The movement of the youth and the struggle against fascism and the danger of war. 15 p.

9. Wang, Ming. The revolutionary movement in the colonial countries; report delivered by Wang Ming [pseud.] August 7, 1935. 47 p. (See no. 975)

10. Cachin, M. The Communist Party of France fights for the People's Front. 14 p. (See no. 941)

11. Thorez, M. The success of the anti-fascist united front. 39 p.

12. Marty, A. For peace! For the defence of the Soviet Union! 19 p.

13. Gottwald, K. For the people's front of labour, freedom and peace. 16 p.

14. Pollitt, H. Unity against the national government. 31 p.

15. Dimitrov, G. The present rulers of the capitalist countries are but temporary; the real master of the world is the proletariat. Concluding address. 12 p. (See no. 943)

16. Full text of the Resolutions adopted at the Seventh Congress. 39 p. (See no. 1018)

17. "Composition of the leading organs of the Communist International": [2] p.

Hoover, 17 items; *Col*, 15 items: no. 1, 2, 4–16; *UTex*, 12 items: no. 1–9, 14–16; *NWest, UChic, UCLA*, 15 items, not specified; *Harv, Princ*, no details cataloged; *Amst*, 7 items: no. 2, 3, 6, 9, 10, 15, 16 (all separately); *Felt* 15 items, no details.

969 RESOLUTIONS, reports, and speeches of the seventh World Congress of the Communist International, held in Moscow from July 25 to August 20, 1935. New York, Workers Library Publishers, 1935—36. 1 vol. various pagings.

This is a listing prepared by the Library of the Louisiana State University, followed by a "Contents" including 12 items. From advertisements of the Workers Library Publishers in New York it results that this *New York edition* contains 16 items. This series is easily identifiable by the globe on the cover, containing inside the inscription: "Seventh World Congress of the Communist International", adorned by a hammer and sickle, and the inscription: "The Congress of struggle for unity of the working class", outside the circle. Obviously, Louisiana State University is the only place which bound these items into one volume or acquired it bound. Other libraries have the particular items as separate pamphlets.

The entire series is listed here in the sequence as it was found in the advertising of the publisher. Each item is identified with the separate entry in this checklist.

1. Dimitrov, G. Working class unity–bulwark against fascism. Full report to seventh World Congress. 95. p. ident. with no. 953.

2. Dimitrov, G. Working class unity–bulwark against fascism. Full report together with speech in reply discussion. 127 p. ident. with no. 946.

3. Dimitrov, G. The united front against fascism and war. Abridged edition compiled from his three speeches. 62 p. ident. with no. 947.

4. Manuil'skii, D. Z. The results of socialist construction in the U.S.S.R. Abridged report. 22 p. ident. with no. 961.

5. Manuil'skii, D. Z. The rise of socialism in the Soviet Union, Full report by... 64 p. ident. with no. 964.

6. Green, Gil. Young communists and unity of the youth. Speech by... ident. with no. 957.

7. Kuusinen, O. W. Youth and fascism; the youth movement and the fight against fascism and war. Speech by... ident. with no. 958.

8. Cachin, M., Thorez, M., Marty, A. The people's front in France. Speeches by ... 95 p. ident. with no. 942.

9. Resolutions of the Seventh World Congress of the C.I., including also the closing speech of Georgi Dimitroff. 56 p. ident. with no. 944.

10. Pieck, W. Freedom, peace and bread! The activities of the Executive Committee of the Communist International. Report by ... 103 p. ident. with no. 966.

11. [Togliatti, P.] The fight for peace. Full Report with speech in reply to discussion, by M. Ercoli [pseud.] ident. with no. 972.

12. Wang, Ming. The revolutionary movement in the colonial countries. Speech by ... 64 p. ident. with no. 974.

13. Browder, Earl. New steps in the united front. Report on the seventh Congress made at Madison Square Garden. 32 p. ident. with no. 1026.

14. Gottwald, K. The united front in Czechoslovakia: speech by ... 22 p. ident. with no. 956.

15. Manuil'skii, D. Z. The Work of the seventh Congress of the Communist International. 80 p. ident. with no. 462.

16. Manuil'skii, D. Z. Engels in the struggle for revolutionary Marxism. 39 p. ident. with no. 959.

ULa, nos. 3, 5, 7–16.
Holdings of other libraries indicated at each item to which reference is given.

970 THESES, Reports, Speeches of the Thirteenth Plenum of the Executive Committee of the Communist International, held in Moscow, December, 1933. New York, Workers Library Publishers [1934] 1 vol. At head of title: Seventh Congress Discussions.

Eight pamphlets with separate title pages and paging, bound in one volume with added title page as listed above. They contain reports, speeches and theses of the 13-th Plenum of Executive Committee, which took place before the VII-th Congress. They served as discussion material for the Congress.

The eight pamphlets are listed here in the sequence in which they are contained in the table of contents of the volume. Particular pamphlets were circulated also separately.

Some of them appeared in second printing. For detailed listing of holdings of particular libraries see 13-th Plenum, nos. 1257–1265.

1. Theses and decisions; Thirteenth Plenum of the E.C.C.I. 23 p.

2. Kuusinen, O. Fascism, the danger of war and the task of the communist parties. 95 p.

3. Piatnitskii, O. The communist parties in the fight for the masses. 95 p.

4. Manuil'skii, D. Z. Revolutionary crisis, fascism and war. 31 p.

5. Knorin, V. Fascism, social-democracy and the communists. 47 p.

6. Pieck, W. We are fighting for a Soviet Germany; report by Wilhelm Pieck. 95 p.

7. Wang Ming and Kang Sin. Revolutionary China today. 95 p.

8. Okano. Revolutionary struggle of the toiling masses of Japan. 31 p.

971 [TOGLIATTI, Palmiro]
The fight against war and fascism; report and speech in reply to the discussion on the third point of the agenda: the preparations for imperialist war and the tasks of the Communist International. Moscow-Leningrad, Cooperative Publishing Society of Foreign Workers in the U.S.S.R., 1935. 115 p. front. (port.) At head of title: Seventh World Congress of the Communist International. Ercoli [pseud.]

> "Edited by F. Johnson." Published also with title: *The fight for peace.* See next item. *Hoover, LC*

972 [TOGLIATTI, Palmiro]
The fight for peace; report on the preparations for imperialist war and the tasks of the Communist International, delivered August 13, 1935, by M. Ercoli [pseud.] New York, Workers Library Publishers [1935] 96 p. At head of title: Seventh World Congress of the Communist International.

> Published also under title: *The fight against war and fascism.* (See preceding item) *LC, NYPL, Amst*

973 VARGA, Eugen
The great crisis and its political consequences; Economics and Politics 1928—1934. [L. E. Mins, editor.] New York, International Publishers [1934]. 175 p. (Printed in Great Britain.)

> "This book is an endeavor to give a brief review of the period between the Sixth and Seventh Congresses of the Communist International. It is not a history but an analysis looking towards the future." Foreword. (Translation of "Mezhdu VI i VII Kongressami Kominterna; ekonomika i politika 1928–1934.) See no. 918. *Hoover*

974 WANG, Ming
The revolutionary movement in the colonial countries; speech revised and augmented, delivered August 7, 1935. New York, Worker Library Publishers [1935] 64 p. At head of title: Seventh World Congress of the Communist International. *Hoover, LC, NYPL, Col, Felt*

975 WANG, Ming
The revolutionary movement in the colonial countries; report delivered by Wang Ming on August 7, 1935. London, Modern Books, 1936. 48 p.

> Identical with no. 968–9. *Hoover, Col, UTex, Amst*

976 CACHIN, Marcel [and Thorez, Maurice]
Du front unique au front populaire, deux discours. Paris, Bureau d'Editions, 1935. 54 p. At head of title: VII-e Congrès Mondial de l'Internationale Communiste. Marcel Cachin. Maurice Thorez.

> Contents: Marcel Cachin. La lutte pour le front populaire. – Maurice Thorez. Le succès du front unique antifasciste. *NYPL, BDIC, Felt*

977 DIMITROV, G.

L'unité de la classe ouvrière dans la lutte contre le fascisme. Paris, Bureau d'Editions, 1935. 2 vol. in 1. front. (port.) At head of title: VII-e Congrès Mondial de l'Internationale Communiste.

> [Vol. 1] Rapport prononcé à la séance du 2 août 1935.
> [Vol. 2] Discours de clôture des débats sur le rapport du camarade Dimitrov, prononcé le 13 août 1935 et discours de clôture du VII-e Congrès, prononcé le 20 août 1935.
> Vol. 2 has cover title: Pour l'unité de la classe ouvrière contre le fascisme.
> *NYPL, BDIC*, vol. 1; *Felt*, one vol.

978 GOTTWALD, K.

La lutte pour le travail, le pain, la paix. Paris, Bureau d'Editions, 1935 16 p. At head of title: VII Congrès Mondial de l'Internationale Communiste. *NYPL, BDIC*

979 KUUSINEN, O. W.

Le front de la jeune génération. Paris, Bureau d'Editions, 1935. 24 p. At head of title: VII-e Congrès Mondial de l'Internationale Communiste.

> "Discours prononcé à la séance du 17 août 1935." *NYPL*

980 MANUILSKII, D. Z.

Le Bilan de l'édification socialiste. Paris, Bureau d'Editions, 1935. 48 p. port. At head of title: VIIe Congrès mondial de l'Internationale Communiste. *BDIC, Felt*

981 MANUIL'SKII, D. Z.

F. Engels dans la lutte pour le marxisme révolutionnaire. Paris, Bureau d'éditions, 1935. 30 p. illus. At head of title: VII-e Congrès Mondial de l'Internationale Communiste. *NYPL, BDIC*

982 MARTY, Andre

Pour la paix, pour la défense de l'U.R.S.S. Paris, Bureau d'Editions, 1935. 23 p. At head of title: VII-e Congrès Mondial de l'Internationale Communiste. *NYPL, BDIC*

983 PIECK, W.

La marche au socialisme. Paris, Bureau d'Editions, 1935. 88 p. At head of title: VII-e Congrès Mondial de l'Internationale Communiste.

> "Rapport sur l'activité du C.E. de l'I.C. et discours de clôture de la discoussion du rapport. 26 juillet — 1-er août, 1935." *Hoover, NYPL, Amst, BDIC*

984 [TOGLIATTI, P.]
La lutte contre la guerre et le fascisme. Paris, Bureau d'Editions, 1935.
86 p. At head of title: VII-e Congrès Mondial de l'Internationale Communiste. M. Ercoli [pseud.]

"Rapport présenté aux séances de 13 et 14 août 1935 et discours de clôture de la discussion du rapport prononcé le 18 août 1935." *NYPL*

985 WANG, Ming
Le front unique dans les pays coloniaux. Paris, Bureau d'Editions, 1935.
48 p. At head of title: VII-e Congrès Mondial de l'Internationale Communiste.

"Sténogramme revu et completé du discours prononcé le 7 août 1935." *NYPL*

986 DIMITROV, G.
Borbata za edinen front protiv fashizma i voinata [Nastuplenieto na fashizma i zadachite na Komunisticheskiia Internatsional v borbata za endinstvoto na rabotnicheskata klasa proti fashizma; doklad pred VII svetoven kongres na Komunisticheskiia Internatsional 2 avgust 1935 godina. [Sofiia] Izd. na Bulgarskata komunisticheska partiia [1949] 116 p. *Hoover*

987 DIMITROV, G.
Za sjednocení milionů proti fašizmu. Praha, Nákl. Nedvěda, 1935. 96 p. At head of title: VII světový kongres Kommunistické Internacionály. *Amst*

988 GOTTWALD, K.
Za správné uplatnění linie VII. kongresu Komunistické Internacionály. Praha-Karlín, Nákl. Nedvěda, 1936. 24 p. At head of title: VII. světový kongres Komunistické Internacionály. *Amst*

989 KU předu k socialismu! Výsledky VII. světového kongresu Komunistické Internacionály. Přel. J. Svoboda. [Praha-Karlín, Nákl. Nedvěda] 1936. 91 p. *Amst*

990 MANUIL'SKII, D. Z.
Socialismus v Sovětském Svazu zvítězil. Přel. J. Svoboda. Praha [Nákl. Nedvěda] 1935. 47 p. At head of title: VII. světový kongres Komunistické Internacionály. *Amst*

991   NAŠE delegace v Moskve. Řeči delegátů komunistické strany Československa na VII. světovém kongresu Komunistické Internacionály
v Moskvě [S účast. K. Gottwalda, J. Švermy, R. Slanského i dr. Praha-
Karlín, Nákl. Nedvěda, 1935] 83 p. At head of title: VII. světový sjezd
Komunistické Internacionály.   **Amst**

992   PIECK, W.
Socialismus — budoucnost světa. Doslovné znění zprávy o činnosti
Exekutivy Komunistické Internacionály, kterou podal v plenu VII. svě-
tového kongresu Komunistické Internacionály dne 26 července 1935,
Vilém Pieck. Z němčiny přeložil Lad. Stoll. [Praha, Nákladem senátora
Františka Nedvěda, 1935] 85 p.   *Amst*

993   [TOGLIATTI, P.]
Boj proti válce a fašizmu. Přel. J. Svoboda. Karlín, Nákl. Nedvěda,
1936. 91 p. At head of title: VII. světový kongres Komunistické Internacionály. M. Ercoli.   *Amst*

994   DIMITROV, G.
Het anti-fascistisch Volksfront. Amsterdam, "Amstel", 1935. 16 p. Het
VII-e wereldcongres van de Kommunistische Internationale.   *Amst*

995   DIMITROV, G.
De arbeidersklasse tegen het fascisme. Het offensief van het fascisme
en de taak van de Kommunistische Internationale in de strijd om de
eenheid van de arbeidersklasse tegen het fascisme. Referaat op het
7e congres der Kommunistische Internationale. [n. p.] 1935 138 p.
                                                                         Amst

996   DIMITROV, G.
De arbeidersklasse tegen het fascisme. Referaat en slotwoord bij het
2e punt van de agenda van het kongres: Het offensief van het fascisme
en de taak van de Kommunistische Internationale in de strijd om de
eenheid van de arbeidersklasse tegen het fascisme. Amsterdam,
Agentschap Amstel, 1935. 138 p. Het VIIe wereldkongres van de Kom-
munstische Internationale.   *Amst*

997   DIMITROV, G.
De arbeidersklasse tegen het fascisme. Referaat, [gehouden in de
15e zitting op de 9e kongresdag van 2 Augustus 1935] en slotwoord
bij het 2e punt van de agenda van het kongres: Het offensief van het
fascisme en de taak van de arbeidersklasse tegen het fascisme.
Amsterdam, "Amstel", 1935. 96 p. port. Het VIIe wereldcongres van
de Kommunistische Internationale.   *Amst*

998 DIMITROV, G.
Eenheidsfront van de arbeidersklasse tegen het fascisme. Amsterdam,
"Amstel", 1936. p. Het VIIe wereldcongres van der Kommunistische
Internationale. *Amst*

999 DIMITROV, G.
De politieke eenheid van het proletariaat. Amsterdam, "Amstel", 1935.
14 p. Het VIIe wereldcongres van de Kommunistische Internaionale.

1000 DIMITROV, G.
Wat het fascisme is. Amsterdam, "Amstel" [n. d.] 16 p. Het VIIe
wereldkongres van de Kommunistische Internationale. *Amst*

1001 DIMITROF heeft het woord. [Amsterdam, Agentschap Amstel, n. d.]
7 p. *Amst*

1002 MANUIL'SKII, D. Z.
De overwinnig van het socialisme in de Sowjet-Unie en haar wereld-
historische beteekenis. [Bericht op] het VIIe wereldkongres van de
Kommunistische Internationale [geh. op 17 Augustus 1935] Antwerpen,
Boekhandel de Nieuwe Tijd, 1936. 70 p. At head of title: D. Z. Ma-
nouilski *Amst*

1003 MANUIL'SKII, D. Z.
De overwinning van het socialisme in de Sowjet-Unie en haar wereld-
historische betekenis. Referaat in het VIIe wereldkongres van de
Kommunistische Internationale op 17 Augustus 1935. Amsterdam,
Agentschap Amstel, 1935. 48 p. illus. At head of title: D. Z. Manoeilski
Amst

1004 De TAAK en de tactiek der Communistische Partijen. Amsterdam,
Agentschap Amstel, 1935. 14 p. (Bibliotheek der Communistische
Internationale, 2) *Amst*

1005 De VERANDERINGEN in de wereldsituatie aan de vooravond v[an]
h[et] zevende wereldkongres. Amsterdam, Agentschap Amstel, 1935.
15 p. (Bibliotheek der Communistische Internationale, 1) *Amst*

1006 DIMITROV, G.
La laborista klaso kontrau la fasismo. Kiev-Kharkov, Ukraina eldonejo
de naci-minoritoj, 193 . 172 p. [In Esperanto] *Hoovevr*

217

1007 DIMITROV, G.
La ofensivo de l'fasismo kaj la taskoj de l'komunista internacio en la batalo por la unueco de la laborista klaso kontrau la fasismo. Raport al VII-a mond-kongreso de l'komunista internacio [n. p., n. d.] 169 p. [In Esperanto]   *Hoover*

1008 DIMITROV, G.
La classe operaia contro il fascismo. Rapporto e discorsi al VII Congresso dell'Internazionale comunista. Bruxelles, Edizioni di Coltura Sociale, 1935. 158 p.   *Felt*

1009 DIMITROV, G.
Il fascismo e la classe operaia. Relazione del compagno D. Dimitrov al VII° Congresso del Comintern. Agosto 1945. [n. p.] Edito dall'Agitprop del Comitato Regionale del Partito Comunista Croato per l'Istria [n. d.] 28 p.   *Felt*

1010 [TOGLIATTI, P.]
La lotta contro la guerra; rapporto al VII Congresso dell'Internazionale comunista. Bruxelles, Edizioni de coltura sociale, 1936. 111 p. At head of title: Ercoli, M.   *Harv*

1011 DIMITROV, G.
Fascismen er fjenden. Beretning aflagt den 2. August 1935 til punkt 2 paa Kongressens dagsorden: fascismens offensiv og den Kommunistiske Internationales opgaver i kampen for arbejderklassens enhed mod fascismen. Kobenhaven, Arbejderfolget, 1935. 84 p.

Hoover

1012 CACHIN, Marcel [and others]
El frente popular contra el fascismo y la guerra en Francia. Discurso de los representantes del partido comunista de Francia, pronunciados en el Congreso. Bancelona [!] Ed. sociales internacionales [1935] 78 p. At head of title: M. Cachin, M. Thorez, A. Marty   *Harv*

1013 MANUIL'SKII, D. Z.
Pidsumki sotsialistichnoho budivnistva v SRSR. [Kiiv] Parvidav TSK KP(b)U, 1935. 54 p. incl. port. At head of title: VII Vsesvitnii kongres komunistychnoho internatsionalu.   *NYPL*

c) Resolutions, Theses, Manifestoes and other documents

1014 REZOLIUTSII VII vsemirnogo kongressa Kommunisticheskogo Internatsionala [Moskva] Partizdat, 1935. 60 p.   *Hoover, LC, NYPL, Harv*

1015 REZOLIUTSII VII vsemirnogo kongressa Kommunisticheskogo Internatsionala. Moskva, Partizdat, 1935. 53 p.   *Hoover, LC, BDIC*

1016 REZOLIUTSII VII vsemirnogo kongressa Kommunisticheskogo Internatsionala. Moskva, 1935. 42 p.   *SInSt*

[DIMITROV, G.]
Resolutionen und Beschlüsse und Ansprache Dimitrov's auf der Schluß-
sitzung des VII Weltkongresses. See no. 924.

1017 VII. [SIEBENTE] Weltkongreß der Kommunistischen Internationale.
Resolutionen und Beschlüsse. Moskau-Leningrad, Verlagsgenossenschaft Ausländischer Arbeiter in der UdSSR, 1935. 63 p.   *Felt*

1018 FULL text of the resolutions adopted at the Seventh Congres. [Lon-
don, Modern Books, 1935?] 39 p. Cover title.

Identical with no. 968–16.   *Hoover, Col, Duke, UTex, Amst*

1019 RESOLUTIONS and decisions. Moscow-Leningrad, Cooperative Publishing society of Foreign Workers in the USSR, 1935. 59 p. At head
of title: Seventh World Congress of Communist International. "Edited
by I. B. Lasker and L. Tamy." [Should be: L. Talmy.]   *Hoover, LC*

1020 CONTRE la guerre et le fascisme: l'unité. Résolutions et décisions.
Paris, Bureau d'Editions, 1935. 47 p.   *NYPL, BDIC*

1021 RESOLUTIES en besluiten [van] het VIIe wereldcongres van de Kom-
munistische Internationale [bij de verslagen van Wilhelm Pieck,
Dimitrof, M. Ercoli [pseud. of Palmiro Togliatti] en Manoeilsky]
Amsterdam, Agentschap Amstel, 1935. 48 p. illus.   *Amst*

1022 CONTRO la guerra e il fascismo: l'unità. (Risoluzioni e decisioni del
VII. Congresso dell'Internazionale comunista) Bruxelles, Edizioni di
Coltura sociale, 1935. 51 p. (Documenti dell'Internazionale.)
                                                          BDIC, Felt

1023 RESOLUCIONES y acuerdos del VII congreso de la Internacional
comunista celebrado en Moscu en el mes de agosto de 1935. Barcelona, Ediciones sociales internacionales [1935?] 47 p. *Hoover*

1024 REZOLIUTSII VII vsesvitn'oho kongresu Komunistychnoho Internatsionalu. [Kyi'v] Partvidav, 1935. 53 p.   *LC*

d) Commentaries and writings about the Congress

MANUIL'SKII, D. Z.
Itogi VII kongressa Kommunisticheskogo Internatsionala; doklad na Moskovskom i Leningradskom partaktive. See no. 459.

VII [SED'MOI] vsemirnyi kongress Kominterna; ukazatel' literatury. See no. 11

1025 VII [SED'MOI] kongress Kommunisticheskogo Internatsionala o molo-dezhi. [Moskva] Molodaia gvardiia, 1935. 129 p.   *Hoover, LC, Harv, SInSt*

MANUIL'SKII, D.
Die Ergebnisse des VII. Weltkongresses der Kommunistischen Inter-nationale. Bericht des Genossen Manuilski in der Versammlung des Moskauer und Leningrader Parteiaktivs, September 1935. See nos. 460 and 461.

1026 BROWDER, Earl
New steps in the United Front. Report on the Seventh Congress of the Communist International made at Madison Square Garden. New York, Workers Library Publishers, 1935. 32 p.   *Hoover*

1027 COMMUNIST Party of Canada.
Canada and the VII World Congress of the Communist International. Outline of Study of the Decisions of the 7th Congress of the Com-munist International and the 9th Plenum of the Central Committee of the Communist Party of Canada. Toronto, Published by Communist Party of Canada [n. d.] 75 p.   *Felt*

1028 GESAMTVERBAND deutscher Anti-Kommunistischer Vereinigungen.
The seventh World Congress of the Communist International, July 25 to August 21, 1935. Edited by the Anti-Comintern (League of German anti-communistic associations) Berlin [Druck: Bibliographisches Institut, Leipzig, 1935?] 56 p.

A compilation of annotated and interpreted excerpts from various Soviet and Comintern publications concerning the history, aims, and activities of the Comintern. Special attention is given to the role of Stalin and the relationship to the CPSU in the work of the Comintern. Also many excerpts from proceed-ings of the VII-th Congress. Although all excerpts are well documented with source references, the Nazi bias of the publication is obvious.   *Hoover, LC, Col*

MANUIL'SKII, D. Z.
The work of the seventh Congress of the Communist International; a speech delivered at meeting of the active members of the Moscow organization of the C.P.S.U., September 14, 1935. See nos. 462 and 463.

1029 The MENACE of New World War. New York, Workers Library Publishers, 1935. 47 p.

> Exerpts from resolutions, reports and speeches delivered to the VII-th Congress of the Communist International. *Hoover, NYPL*

1030 ALEKSINSKII, G.
Moscou et le monde extérieur. A propos du VII-e congrès du Komintern (Reprint from: La Grande Revue, septembre 1935, p. 481—504)
Amst

MANUIL'SKII, D. Z.
Le VII-e congrès est le congrès de l'unité; bilan du VII-e congrès de l'Internationale Communiste. See no. 464.

MANUIL'SKII D. Z.
Výsledky VII kongresu Komunistické Internacionály Referát na moskovském a leningradském aktivu strany. See no. 465.

1031 Het ZEVENDE Wereld-Congres der Comm[unistische]Internationale over de ontwikkeling der wereldrevolutie. Amsterdam, Agentschap Amstel, 1935. 15 p. (Bibliotheek der Communistische Internationale, 3)
Amst

B. The Meetings of the Executive Committee, its Presidium and Commissions

In chronological order

1. Executive Committee (unnumbered), December 27—28, 1921

Note: This meeting of the Executive Committee dealt mainly with the new tactical move of the C. I. proposing a "united front" of the working class and called a first meeting of an enlarged Executive Committee which took place February 24–March 4, 1922. The only known publication resulting from this meeting is listed below.

1032 Die PROLETARISCHE Einheitsfront. Aufruf der Exekutive der Kommunistischen Internationale und der Exekutive der Roten Gewerkschaftsinternationale (Moskau, 1. Januar 1922). Leitsätze über die Einheitsfront (Einstimmig angenommen von der Exekutive der Kommunistischen Internationale am 28. Dezember 1921) [n. p.] Kommunistische Internationale, 1922. ii, 25 p. (Flugschriften der Kommunistischen Internationale 12) *Amst*

2. 1-st Plenum (Enlarged Executive Committee), February 24—March 4, 1922

a) Protocols

1033 Die TAKTIK der Kommunistischen Internationale gegen die Offensive des Kapitals; Bericht über die Konferenz der Erweiterten Exekutive der Kommunistischen Internationale, Moskau, vom 24. Februar bis 4. März 1922. Kommunistische Internationale; Auslieferungsstelle C. Hoym Nachf., Hamburg, 1922. xiii, 175 p. (Bibliothek der Kommunistischen Internationale, 27.)

Official (stenographic?) records of the first session of the Enlarged Executive Committee of the C. I. Additions: List of participants of the session; subject index; names index. *Hoover, LC, NYPL, Amst, Felt*

1034 COMPTE rendu de la conférence de l'Exécutif Elargi de l'Internationale Communiste; Moscou, 24 Février — 4 Mars, 1922. Paris, l'Humanité, 1922. 260 p. (Bibliothèque communiste)

Hoover, Harv, NWest, UVirg, BDIC, Felt

b) Reports, Speeches, Drafts presented to the Plenum

1035 DEIATEL'NOST' Ispolnitel'nogo komiteta i Prezidiuma I. K. Kommunisticheskogo Internatsionala ot 13-go iiulia 1921 g. do 1-go fevralia
1922 g. Petrograd, Izd-vo Kommunisticheskogo Internatsionala, 1922.
464 g.

Contains reprint of the first five issues of *Biulleten' Ispolnite'nogo Komiteta Kommunisticheskogo Internatsionala*, minutes of the meetings of the Executive Committee since its constituent meeting on July 13, 1921; a total of ten meetings
recorded; minutes of 29 meetings of the Presidium and of 12 meetings of the
"Bureau". Also texts of all appeals, letters and other important documents
issued by the Executive Committee and its Presidium. Subject and country index.

Hoover, LC, Amst, SInSt

1036 LOZOVSKII, A. [and] Brandler, Heinrich
Der KAMPF der Kommunisten in den Gewerkschaften. Bericht der
Genossen A. Losowsky und Heinrich Brandler zur Gewerkschaftsfrage
auf der Konferenz der erweiterten Exekutive der Kommunistischen
Internationale vom 24. Februar bis 4. März 1922. Berlin, Verlag der
Roten Gewerkschafts-Internationale, 1922. 35 p. (Bibliothek der Roten
Gewerkschafts-Internationale, Bd. 10)   *Felt*

1037 Die Tätigkeit der Exekutive und des Präsidiums des E. K. der Kom
munistischen Internationale vom 13. Juli 1921 bis 1. Februar 1922.
Petrograd, Verlag der Kommunistischen Internationale, 1922. 410 p.

German edition of no. 1035; contents are identical.   *Hoover, NYPL, Duke, Felt*

1038 TROTSKII, Lev
Die Fragen der Arbeiterbewegung in Frankreich und die Kommunistische Internationale; zwei Reden, gehalten auf der Konferenz
der Erweiterten Exekutive der Kommunistischen Internationale am
26. Februar und 2. März 1922 in Moskau. Kommunistische Internationale; Auslieferungsstelle für Deutschland C. Hoym, Hamburg,
1922. 31 p. (Bibliothek der Kommunistischen Internationale, 30.)

Hoover, LC, Amst, Felt

1039 ZETKIN, Klara
Der Kampf der kommunistischen Parteien gegen Kriegsgefahr und
Krieg; Bericht auf der Konferenz der Erweiterten Exekutive der Kom-

munistischen Internationale, Moskau, 2. März 1922. Kommunistische Internationale; Auslieferungsstelle für Deutschland C. Hoym, Hamburg, 1922. 54 p. (Bibliothek der Kommunistischen Internationale, 29.)

Hoover, LC, Amst, Felt

1040 ZINOV'EV, G.
Die Kommunistische Internationale und die proletar. Einheitsfront; Rede, gehalten in der Konferenz der Erweiterten Exekutive der Kommunistischen Internationale am 24. und 28. Februar 1922 in Moskau. Kommunistische Internationale; Auslieferungsstelle C. Hoym, Hamburg, 1922. 64 p. At head of title: G. Sinowjew. (Bibliothek der Kommunistischen Internationale, 28.) *Hoover, NYPL, Amst, BDIC, Felt*

1041 COMMUNIST Party of the U. S. S. R.(b)
1. Unité du Parti. 2. Tendance anarco-syndicaliste. Lettre du Comité Central du Parti Communiste Russe à la Séance du Comité Exécutif Elargi de l'Internationale Communist. Moscou, Publié par le Département de la Presse du C. E. I. C., 1922. 7 p. *Felt*

1042 ZINOV'EV, G.
La tactique du front unique. Paris, Librairie de l'Humanité, 1922. 48 p. At head of title: G. Zinoviev. (Petite Bibliothèque communiste)

"Discours prononcés à la session du Comité exécutif élargi de l'Internationale communiste, Moscou, 24 [et 28] février 1922." *Hoover, Felt*

3. Executive Committee (unnumbered), May 19, 1922

Note: During the Marseille congress of the French Communist Party (December 1921) strong opposition among the French communists arose against the "democratic centralism" applied by the Communist International and against "the ukazes from Moscow". (See A. Ferrat: *Histoire du Parti Communiste Français,* Paris, 1931, p. 106–108, 117–119.) This opposition led to an internal crisis in the French Communist Party which was discussed during the first Plenum of the E. C. C. I. and was handled later by regular meetings of the Executive Committee. As a result of the discussion of the crisis by a meeting of the Executive Committee on May 19, 1922, the following speech by Trotsky has been published.

1043 TROTSKII, Lev
La crise du Parti Communiste Français. Paris, Librairie de l'Humanité, 1922. 32 p. (Petite Bibliothèque Communiste)

"Deux discours... devant le Comité Exécutif de l'Internationale Communiste séance du 19 mai 1922." *Hoover, Felt*

4. 2-nd P l e n u m (Enlarged Executive Committee), June 7—11, 1922.

a) Protocols

Note: An abstract of the proceedings of this meeting and the adopted resolutions are contained in *Inprecorr*, Nos. 93 and 100 of June 14 and 17, and in the special issue of June 14, 1922.

b) Reports, Speeches, Drafts presented to the Plenum

1044 BERICHT über die Tätigkeit des Präsidiums und der Exekutive der Kommunistischen Internationale für die Zeit vom 6. März bis 11. Juni 1922. Hamburg, Verlag der Kommunsitischen Internationale, C. Hoym Nachf., 1922. 141 p. *Hoover, NYPL, Amst, BDIC, Felt*

1045 RAPPOPORT, Charles
Le Parti Communiste Français au Comité Exécutif de Moscou. Discours du 9 juin 1922, suivi d'une motion pour le Congrès de Paris octobre 1922. Paris, Revue Communiste, 1922. 32 p. *Amst*

5. 3-rd P l e n u m (Enlarged Executive Committee), June 12—23, 1923.

a) Protocols

1046 RASSHIRENNYI plenum Ispolnitel'nogo komiteta Kommunisticheskogo Internatsionala 12—23 iiunia 1923 goda; otchet. Moskva, Izd. "Krasnaia Nov'", 1923. 320 p. *Hoover, LC, NYPL, Col, SInSt*

1047 PROTOKOLL der Konferenz der Erweiterten Exekutive der Kommunistischen Internationale. Moskau, 12.—23. Juni, 1923. Hamburg, C. Hoym Nachf., L. Cahnbley, 1923. vii, 336 p. (Bibliothek der Kommunistischen Internationale 40.) *Hoover, LC, Amst, Felt*

b) Reports, Speeches, Drafts presented to the Plenum

1048 ZINOV'EV, G.
Na plenume Ispolkoma Kominterna. 12. IV. 23. Doklad i zakliuchitel'noe slovo G. Zinov'eva. Moskva, Petrograd, Gos. izd-vo, 1923.
118 p.   *Hoover, LC, BDIC*

1049 BERICHT der Exekutive der Kommunistischen Internationale, 15. Dezember 1922 — 15. Mai 1923. Hrsg. vom Sekretariat des EKKI. Moskau,
Verlag des EKKI, 1923. 80 p. diagrs.

Contains "Der Apparat der Komintern", p. 7–17.   *Hoover, LC, NYPL, Amst, Felt*

1050 Die KOMMUNISTICHEN Parteien Skandinaviens und die Kommunistische Internatonale; die Aussprache mit den skandinavischen Genossen über die Grenzen des Zentralismus in der Konferenz der Erweiterten Exekutive der Kommunistischen Internationale. Moskau, 12—23
Juni 1923. Hamburg, C. Hoym, 1923. v, 193 p. (Bibliothek der Kommunstischen Internationale, 38 [i. e. 39]).   *Hoover, LC, NYPL, Felt*

1051 RADEK, Karl
Der Kampf der Kommunistischen Internationale gegen Versailles und
gegen die Offensive des Kapitals; Bericht erstattet in der Sitzung der
Erweiterten Exekutive der K. I., Moskau, 15. Juni 1923, und in der
Sitzung der Erweiterten Exekutive der Kommunistischen Jugend-Internationale; Moskau, 13. Juli 1923. Kommunistische Internationale; Auslieferung: C. Hoym, Hamburg, 1923. 129 p.   *Hoover, Amst*

1052 RADEK, Karl
Der Kampf der Kommunistischen Internationale gegen Versailles und
gegen die Offensive des Kapitals; Bericht erstattet in der Sitzung der
Erweiterten Exekutive der K. I., Moskau, 15. Juni 1923, und in der
Sitzung der Erweiterten Exekutive der Kommunistischen Jugend-Internationale; Moskau, 13. Juli 1923. 3. Auflage. Kommunsitische Internationale; Auslieferung: C. Hoym, Hamburg, 1923. 77 p.   *Col, Felt*

1053 RADEK, Karl
The international outlook. London, The Communist Party of Great
Britain [1923] 23 p.

"Report to the Enlarged Executive Committee at the sixth session on June 15,
1923."
                                                           Hoover

c) Bulletin issued for the Plenum

1054 BULLETIN der Erweiterten Exekutive der Kommunistischen Internationale. Moskau, „Mospoligraf", 1923. No. 1 (8 Juni 1923) — No. 14 (23 Juni 1923); No. 16 (26 Juni 1923). *Felt*

6. Presidium of E.C.C.I., January 11, 1924.

1055 Die LEHREN der deutschen Ereignisse. Das Präsidium des Exekutivkomitees der Kommunistischen Internationale zur deutschen Frage, Januar 1924. Hamburg, Verlag der Kommunistischen Internationale, Auslieferung: Verlag C. Hoym, Nachf., 1924. 120 p.
LC, NYPL, Harv, Amst, Felt

1056 The LESSONS of the German events. [n. p.] 1924. 83 p. *Col*

1057 Les LEÇONS des événements d'Allemagne; la question allemande au Présidium du C.E. de l'I.C. en janvier 1924. Moscou, 1924. 105 p.
Hoover

7. 4-th Plenum (Enlarged Executive Committee), July 12—13, 1924.

a) Protocols

1058 RASSHIRENNYI plenum Ispolkoma (kratkii protokol). [Contained in volume II of *Piatyi vsemirnyi kongress Kommunisticheskogo Internatsionala*, p. 7—22; see no. 764.]

The minutes of this Plenum have not been printed separately but only as part of the "Annexes" to the stenograms of the Fifth Congress. Location as that of aforementioned volume. *Hoover, LC, NYPL, Harv, DState, UCal, Yale, BDIC*

b) Bulletin issued for the Plenum

1059 BULLETIN de l'Exécutif élargi de l'Internationale Communiste. Moscou, Editions du Bureau de la Presse de l'Internationale Communiste, 1924. no. 1. July 12, 1924.   *Felt:* no. 1, July 12, 1924

8. 1-st Conference on organizational matters, Moscow, March 16—21, 1925

Note: This Conference took place just prior to the 5-th Plenum. Representatives of a majority of member-parties and communist youth organizations participated. It seems that the main purpose of this Conference was the intention of the Russian leadership of the C.I. to mollify the dissatisfaction of several member-parties with some organizational decisions of the V-th Congress. (See nos. 797, 800, 804.) The Conference deliberated about the reorganization of member-parties, the work of factory cells and their influence on factory newspapers, preparation of a model statute for member-parties, creation of communist factions in various elective bodies, and related matters. The following publications dealing with the results of this Conference are available.

1060 Der ORGANISATORISCHE Aufbau der Kommunistischen Partei. [Hamburg] C. Hoym Nachf. [1925] 163 p. diagrs. Ad head of title: Organisationsberatung der Erweiterten Exekutive (März/April 1925)

The date "März/April 1925" is incorrect. The Conference took place March 16–21, and the 5-th Plenum lasted from March 21 to April 6, 1925. Point 7 of the agenda of the Plenum contained a "Report about the Conference on organizational matters" but the Plenum itself did not deal with organizational matters. Not even a Commission for these matters had been appointed by the Plenum.   *Hoover, Amst*

1061 La REORGANISATION des partis communistes; rapports et décisions de la Conférence d'organisation de l'I.C. (16—21 mars 1925). Paris, Librairie de l'Humanité, 1925. 192 p. (L'I.C. et les questions d'organisation, no. 2)   *Hoover, Amst, BDIC*

9. 5-th P l e n u m (Enlarged Executive Committee), March 21—April 6, 1925

a) Protocols

1062 RASSHIRENNYI plenum Ispolkoma Kommunisticheskogo Internatsionala (21 marta — 6 aprelia 1925 g.). Stenograficheskii otchet. Moskva, Gos. izd-vo, 1925. 606 p.

On cover: Protokoly zasedanii. Supplement: Tezisy i rezoliutsii, p. 495–602.
Hoover, NYPL, Harv, Col, Yale, BDIC, SInSt

1063 PROTOKOLL; Erweiterte Exekutive der Kommunsitischen Internationale, Moskau, 21. März — 6. April 1925. [Hamburg] C. Hoym Nachf. [c. 1925] 375 p.   *Hoover, LC, NYPL, Illin, Felt*

1064 BOLSHEVISING the Communist International. Report of the Enlarged Executive of the Communist International, March 21st to April 14th [sic!], 1925. [n. p.] Published for the Communist International by the Communist Party of Great Britain [1925?] 205 p.

An abridged English edition of the minutes of the 5th Plenum. Both the editing and the translation of the minutes considerably damaged and distorted the contents. A comparison of the Russian text and the English edition shows that some speeches have been omitted from the English edition and the speakers not mentioned. Some sentences of the translation were cut or condensed, distorting the meaning of the Russian text. But on the other hand, some of the English texts contain sentences which are missing in the Russian text. (For example, see the speech of Popovich on p. 138 of the English edition and on p. 479 of the Russian text.) The date of the Plenum in the subtitle is erroneous: it should read April 6, and not April 14!   *Hoover, Harv, Col, Duke*

1065 EXECUTIF élargi de l'Internationale Communiste; Compte rendu analytique de la session du 21 mars au 6 avril 1925. Paris, Librairie de l'Humanité, 1925. 323 p.   *Hoover, Harv, Brown, UMinn, Amst, BDIC, Felt*

b) Reports, Speeches, Drafts presented to the Plenum

1066 LOZOVSKII, A.
Za edinstvo mezhdunarodnogo profdvizheniia. Doklad rasshirennomu plenumu IKKI. Moskva, Izd. Profinterna, 1925. 31 p.   *NYPL*

1067 MANUIL'SKII, D.
Pravoe krylo Kominterna i krizis chekho-slovatskoi partii. (Rech' na plenume I.K.K.I.) Moskva, Izd. Kommunisticheskogo universiteta im. IA. M. Sverdlova, 1925. 23 p.   *BDIC*

1068 ZINOV'EV, G.
Mezhdunarodnye perspektivy i bol'shevizatsiia Kompartii. Moskva, Leningrad, Giz., 1925. 112 p.   *BDIC, SInSt*

1069 BUKHARIN, N. I.
Über die Bauernfrage. (Rede vor der Erweiterten Exekutive, April 1925.) [Hamburg] C. Hoym [1925] 57 p.   *Hoover, Felt*

1070 LOZOVSKII, A.
Der Kampf für die Einheit der Weltgewerkschaftsbewegung. Referat auf der Tagung des erweiterten Exekutivkomitees der K[ommunistischen] I[nternationale]. Berlin, Führer-Verlag, 1925. 32 p.   *Amst, Felt*

1071 Der NEUE Kurs. Reden der Genossen Bucharin und Sinowjew. Brief des EKKI. Berlin, Vereinigung Internationaler Verlagsanstalten, 1925. ii, 88 p. [Herausgeber: Zentral Komitee der KPD.]   *Amst*

1072 ZINOV'EV, G.
Über die Bolschewisierung der Parteien. (Reden vor der Erweiterten Exekutive, März-April 1925). Hamburg, Verlag Carl Hoym Nachf., 1925. 130 p.   *Felt*

1073 ZINOV'EV, G.
Über die Bolschewisierung der Parteien der Komintern. Thesen. Entwurf des Gen. Sinowjew gebilligt von den Delegierten der RKP(B), der deutschen und der französischen Kommunistischen Partei. [n. p.] Verlagsabteilung des EKKI, 1925. 27 p. (Erweiterte Exekutive der KI.)
                                                           Felt

1074 BUKHARIN, N.
La question paysanne. I. Discours prononcé au Plenum élargi du C.E. de l'Internationale Communiste, le 2 avril 1925. II. Thèses sur la question paysanne acceptées par l'Exécutif élargi de l'I.C. Paris, Librairie de l'Humanité, 1925. 40 p.   *Hoover, Felt*

1075 ZINOV'EV, G.
Les perspectives internationales et la bolchévisation. La stabilisation du capitalisme et la révolution mondiale. Discours prononcés à l'Exécutif élargi de l'Internationale Communiste, les 25 mars et 4 avril 1925. Suivis des Thèses sur la bolchévisation des partis de l'I.C. adoptées par l'Exécutif élargi de l'I.C. Paris, Librairie de l'Humanité, 1925. 80 p.   *Amst, Felt*

c) Resolutions, Theses, etc. – originating with the Plenum

1076 RASSHIRENNYI Plenum Ispolkoma Kominterna, 21 marta — 6 aprelia 1925 g.; tezisy i rezoliutsii. Moskva, Gos. izd-vo, 1925. 79 p.
Hoover, LC, NYPL, BDIC

1077 ERWEITERTE Exekutive März/April 1925. Thesen und Resolutionen. [Hamburg] C. Hoym Nachf. [c1925] 122 p. Cover title: Thesen und Resolutionen. *Hoover, LC, Harv, Amst, Felt*

1078 Über die Bolschewisierung der Parteien der Komintern; Thesen, einstimmig angenommen von der erweiterten Exekutive der Komintern, Moskau, März/April 1925. Mit Einleitung, Erläuterungen und einem Anhang hrsg. von der Zentrale der KPD [Berlin, Vereinigung Internationaler Verlagsanstalten, 1925] 47 p. (Ergänzungsheft 2 zum Jahrgang 1925] *Die Internationale*) *Hoover*

1079 THESES et résolutions adoptées par l'Exécutif élargi de l'I[nternationale] C[ommuniste] (25 mars — 6 avril 1925). Paris, Librairie de l'Humanité, 1925. 64 p. *Amst, BDIC, Felt*

THÈSES sur la bolchévisation des partis de l'I.C., adoptées par l'Executif élargi de l'I.C. — contained in Zinov'ev, G. E., *Les perspectives internationales et la bolchevisation.* See no. 1075.

THÈSES sur la question paysanne acceptées par l'Executif élargi de l'I.C. — contained in Bukharin, N. I., *La question paysanne;* no. 1074.

d) Commentaries about the Plenum

1080 MANUIL'SKII, D.
K itogam rasshirennogo plenuma Ispolkoma Kominterna. (aprel 1925). Moskva-Leningrad, Gos. izd-vo, 1925. 31 p. *BDIC*

1081 MANUIL'SKII, D.
Uroki cheshskogo krizisa. Moskva-Leningrad, Gos. izd. 1925. 31 p. *BDIC*

1082 Les TRAVAUX et les décisions de l'Exécutif élargi de l'Internationale Communiste (mars—avril 1925). [Avec collab. de Zinoviev, Bukharin, e. a.]. *Cahiers du Bolchévisme*, Numéro Spécial, 22 mai, 1925. *Amst*

1083 HVAD er Bolsjevisering? Oslo, Ny Tid, 1925. 94 p. *Amst*

10. 2-nd Conference on organizational matters, Moscow, February, 1926

Note: This Conference took place simultaneously with the meeting of the 6-th Plenum. Representatives of 17 member-organizations and several communist youth organizations participated. It was a continuation of the 1-st Conference which took place in March 1925. (See Note preceding item no. 1060.) The subjects of this Conference were: a continuation of the discussion about the organization of factory cells, the organization of city and district party committees, the tasks of communist factions in trade unions, peasant organizations, cooperatives, and similar organizations. The following publications containing the decisions and resolutions of this Conference are available.

1084 BESCHLÜSSE und Resolutionen angenommen von der 2. Orgkonferenz der Erweiterten Exekutive und bestätigt vom Orgbüro des EKKI am 26. März 1926. Hamburg, C. Hoym Nachf. [c1926] 134, xii p. At head of title: Zweite Organisationskonferenz. [Inserted page xii: Muster-richtlinien für den Aufbau und die Struktur der kommunistischen Frak-tionen in den Gewerkschaften] *Hoover, NYPL, Harv, Amst*

1085 La II-e [DEUXIEME] conférence d'organisation; décisions et résolu-tions adoptées par la II-e conférence du C.I. de l'I.C. et ratifiées par le Bureau d'organisation du C.E. de l'I.C. le 26 mars 1926. [Préface de J. Piatnitskii] Paris, Librairie de l'Humanité [1926] 98 p. (L'I.C. et les questions d'organisation. No. 3)

Hoover, NYPL, Amst, BDIC, Felt

11. 6-th P l e n u m (Enlarged Executive Committee), February 17—March 15, 1926.

a) Protocols

1086 SHESTOI rasshirennyi plenum Ispolkoma Kominterna (17 fevralia — 15 marta 1926 g.) Stenograficheskii otchet. Moskva-Leningrad, Gos. izd-vo, 1927, vi, 707 p. *Hoover, LC, NYPL, Harv, Col, SInSt*

1087 PROTOKOLL; Erweiterte Exekutive der Kommunistischen Internationale, Moskau, 17. Februar bis 15. März 1926. Hamburg, Hoym [c1926] 672, xviii p.   *Hoover, NYPL, Harv, UCal, UChic, Illin, Yale, Amst, Felt*

1088 SIXTH session of the Enlarged Executive Committee of the Communist International, February—March, 1926, (In *International Press Correspondence*. Vienna, 1926. Vol. 6, p. [253] — 284, [297] — 328, [337] — 367, [377] — 390, [463] — 494, [399] — 414, [423] — 438, [613] — 652). Cover title. "Special number. English edition." Detached copy)   *Hoover, Felt*

1089 COMPTE rendu de la VIe session du Comité exécutif élargi de l'Internationale Communiste, février—mars 1926. Paris, *La Correspondence Internationale*, year VI, no 14 (Febr. 2, 1926) 26, 30, 33, 35, 39, 40, 46, 48, 51, 53, 61, 64, 68 (June 1, 1926, Special issues.)   *Felt*

b) Reports, Speeches, Drafts presented to the Plenum

1090 LOZOVSKII, A.
Komintern i profdvizhenie (doklad na VI rasshirennom plenume IKKI 1-go marta 1926 goda). Moskva, Profintern, 1926. 98 p.   *Hoover*

1091 OTCHET Ispolkoma Kominterna (aprel' 1925 g. — ianvar' 1926 g.) Sostavlen sekretariatom IKKI. Moskva, Gos. izd., 1926. 396 p.
Hoover, LC, NYPL, SInSt

1092 ZINOV'EV, G.
Komintern v bor'be za massy; politicheskii otchet VI rasshirennomu plenumu IKKI (Fevral'—Mart 1926 g. Doklad, zakliuchitel'noe slovo i rezoliutsiia. Moskva [etc.] Gos. izd-vo, 1926. 111 p.   *Hoover*

1093 LOZOVSKII, A.
Kommunisten und Gewerkschaften; Referat und Schlußwort in der VI. Tagung des Erweiterten Exekutiv-Komitees der Kommunistischen Internationale. — Im Anhang Thesen über: Die nächsten Aufgaben der Kommunisten in der Gewerkschaftsbewegung. Berlin, Führer-Verlag, 1926. 132 p.   *NYPL*

1094 TÄTIGKEITSBERICHT der Exekutive der Kommunistischen Internationale, 1925—1926. Ein Jahr Arbeit und Kampf. Hamburg, C. Hoym Nachf., 1926. 368 p.

Contents: Das Exekutivkomitee der Kommunistischen Internationale und seine Abteilungen. – Sektionen der Kommunistischen Internationale in den kapitalistisch Ländern. – Revolutionäre Bewegung in den Orientländern.

Hoover, LC, NYPL, Harv, Illin, Amst, Felt

1095 REPORT on the activities of the Executive Committee of the Communist International. (For the period since the Enlarged Executive March/April 1925 — end of January 1926.) Compiled by the Secretariat of the ECCI. Moscow, 1926. 72, 208, 29 p. [Mimeographed]

Contents:
I. Report on the activities of the ECCI, p. 1–72.
II. Sections of the Communist International in the capitalist countries, p. 1–208.
III. Revolutionary Movement in Eastern Countries, p. 1–28.
IV. Soviet Union. Information on All-Union Communist Party report, p. 29.

Hoover, UChic

1096 Det TYSKE sporsmaal i den Kommunistiske Internasjonale. Debatten paa det utvidede eksekitiv mote i Mars 1926. Oslo, Ny Tid [n. d.] 110 p. *Amst*

c) Resolutions, Theses, etc. originating with the Plenum

1097 VI [SHESTOI] rasshirennyi plenum Ispolkoma Kominterna. Tezisy i rezoliutsii VI rasshirennogo plenuma Ispolkoma Kominterna (17 fevralia — 15 marta 1926 g.). Moskva, Gos. izd-vo, 1926. 139 p.

Hoover, NYPL

ZINOV'EV, G. E.
Komintern v borbe za massy; politicheskii otchet VI rasshirennomu plenumu IKKI (fevral—mart 1926 g.) Doklad, zakliuchitel'noe slovo i rezoliutsiia. See no. 1092.

1098 ERWEITERTE Exekutive (Februar—März 1926). Thesen und Resolutionen. Hamburg, C. Hoym Nachf. [c1926] 203 p. *Hoover, LC, Harv*

THESEN über: Die nächsten Aufgaben der Kommunisten in der Gewerkschaftsbewegung — in Lozowskii, A., *Kommunisten und Gewerkschaften.* See no. 1093.

d) Commentaries about the Plenum

1099 LENTZNER, N.
Novyi etap rabochego dvizheniia; k itogam VI rasshirennogo plenuma IKKI. Moskva, Gos. izd-vo, 1926. 67 p. *NYPL*

12. 7-th P l e n u m (Enlarged Executive Committee)
November 22—December 16, 1926.

a) Protocols

1100 PUTI mirovoi revoliutsii; sed'moi rasshirennyi plenum Ispolnitel'nogo
komiteta Kommunisticheskogo Internatsionala, 22 noiabria — 16 dekabria 1926. Stenograficheskii otchet. Moskva, Gos. izd-vo, 1927.
2 vols.

Subtitles of volumes:
1. Mezhdunarodnoe polozhenie i proletarskaia revoliutsiia. – Angliiskii vopros. –
Puti razvitiia kitaiskoi revoliutsii. – Trestifikatsiia, ratsionalizatsiia i nashi
zadachi v profdvizhenii. viii, 571 p.
2. Vnutripartiinye voprosy VKP(b). – Doklady politicheskoi, kitaiskoi, profsoiuznoi, angliiskoi i dr[ugikh] komissii. – Tezisy i rezoliutsii sed'mogo rasshirennogo plenuma Ispolkoma Kominterna. viii, 467 p.
Hoover, LC, NYPL, Harv, Col, Yale, Felt, SInSt

1101 PROTOKOLL; Erweiterte Exekutive der Kommunistischen Internationale, Moskau, 22. November — 16. Dezember 1926. Hamburg,
C. Hoym Nachf. [c1927] 895 p. *Hoover, LC, NYPL, Harv, Amst, Felt*

1102 COMPTE-rendu de la VIIe session du Comité Exécutif élargi de l'Internationale Communiste; novembre—décembre 1926. Paris, *La Correspondence Internationale*, 1926—1927; year VI, no. 131, 133, 136,
140—142, 144; year VII, no. 1, 4, 6, 8, 11, 12, 15, 18, 20, 22, 25 (Dec.
7, 1926 — Feb. 20, 1927) *Felt*

1103 Le VIIe [SEPTIEME] Exécutif élargi. novembre—décembre 1926. [Paris,
Dagon] 1927. 160 p. *Cahiers du bolchévisme.* Numéro spécial, mars
1927. *Amst, BDIC*

b) Reports, Speeches, etc. presented to the Plenum

1104 BUKHARIN, N.
Kapitalisticheskaia stabilizatsiia i proletarskaia revoliutsiia. Moskva,
Gos. izd-vo, 1927. 347 p. incl. tables. *NYPL, Col*

1105 BUKHARIN, N.
Kapitalisticheskaia stabilizatsiia i proletarskaia revoliutsiia. Moskva
& Leningrad, 1927. 214 p.

This item was unavailable for identification. See preceding item. *SInSt*

1106 RYKOV, A. I.
Rech' na VII rasshirennom plenume Ispolnitel'nogo komiteta Kommunisticheskogo Internatsionala 11 dekabria 1926 g. Moskva, Gos.
izdat., 1927. 31 p. *NYPL, SInSt*

1107 STALIN, Iosif
Eshche raz o sotsial-demokraticheskom uklone v nashei partii. Doklad
i zakliuchitel'noe slovo na VII rasshirennom plenume Ispolnitel'nogo
komiteta Kommunisticheskogo Internatsionala, 7—13 dekabria 1926
goda. Izd. 2. Moskva, Gos. izdat., 1927. 189 p. *Harv*

1108 BUKHARIN, N.
Die kapitalistische Stabilisierung und die proletarische Revolution;
Bericht an das VII. erweiterte Plenum des Exekutivkomitees der
Komintern zum I. Punkt der Tagesordnung: „Die Weltlage und die
Aufgaben der Kommunistischen Internationale." Moskau, EKKI, 1926.
128 p. tables. *NYPL, Felt, SInSt*

1109 LOZOVSKII, A.
Vertrustung, Rationalisierung und unsere Aufgaben in der Gewerkschaftsbewegung; Referat, gehalten am 6 Dezember 1926; [von]
A. Losowsky auf der VII. Tagung der Erweiterten Exekutive der Kommunistischen Internationale. Moskau, Verlag der Roten Gewerkschafts-Internationale, 1927. 46 p. *Hoover, Amst*

1110 TÄTIGKEITSBERICHT der Exekutive der Kommunistischen Internationale, Februar—November 1926. Hamburg, Berlin, C. Hoym Nachfolger [c1926] 176 p.

„Behandelt... die Tätigkeit des EKKI und der einzelnen Sektionen der KI seit
dem letzten Plenum der Erweiterten Exekutive der KI (Februar/März 1926) bis
Mitte Oktober 1926." Einleitende Bemerkung. *Hoover, Amst, Felt*

1111 TAN, Ping-shan
Entwicklungswege der chinesischen Revolution, mit einem Vorwort von K. A. Wittfogel und einem Nachwort von Raskolnikow [pseud.] Hamburg, C. Hoym [1927] 35 p.

„Vorliegende Broschüre enthält in etwas gekürzter Form das Referat des Genossen Tan Ping-shan auf dem 7 Erweiterten Plenum des EKKI."   *Hoover*

1112 BUKHARIN, N.
Capitalist stabilisation and proletarian revolution; report to the VII Enlarged Plenum of the E. C. of the Comintern on point I. on the agenda: "The world situation and the tasks of the Comintern." Moscow, Executive Committee of the Comintern, 1926. 108 p.

Hoover, NYPL

1113 CHINA in revolt. Chicago, Ill., "The Communist" [1927] 64 p.

Speeches on the Chinese question delivered to the 7th Plenum. Contents:
Stalin, I. The prospects of the revolution in China; speech delivered in the Chinese Commission of the Enlarged Executive of the Communist International on November 30, 1926.
Tan, Ping-shan. The situation in China; a speech delivered in the seventh plenary session of the Executive Committee of the Communist International, 1926.
Manuilskii, D. Z. China and the capitalist world.
Bukharin, N. The prerqeuisites and tasks of the Chinese revolution; a speech delivered at the 15th Conference of the KPSU, 1926.
     Hoover, LC, Harv, NWest (Copies in *NWest* and *Hoover* (microfilm) imperfect; p. 5–8 and 11–23 missing.)

1114 MATERIAL on the Russian question. (For the VII Enlarged Executive of the C. I.) Moscow, 1926. 200 sheets. Mimeographed; cover printed. Numeration of sheets supplied; composed of several parts, each separate paging.

"Reports and speeches at the XV-th Conference of the CPSU on the agenda point 'The opposition bloc and the inner party situation'."   *Hoover, Duke*

1115 REPORT on the activities of the Communist International, March— November 1926. [Moscow, Secretariat of the E. C. C. I., 1926] 131 p. Mimeogr.

Contents similar to the March 1925–January 1926 report; see no. 1095.
Hoover, NYPL

1116 STALIN, Iosif
Once more on the social-democratic deviation in our Party; report at the seventh enlarged Plenum of the Executive Committee, Communist International, December 7, 1926. Moscow, Foreign Languages Pub. House, 1952. 206 p. (Library of Marxist-Leninist Classics.)

c) Commentaries on the Plenum

1117 LOZOVSKII, A.
Itogi VII plenuma Ispolkoma Kominterna. Moskva, Gos. izd-vo, 1927.
110 p. *NYPL*

13. 8-th P l e n u m, May 18—30, 1927.

a) Protocols

Note: No protocol of this meeting, published as a separate publication, has been found. Some speeches delivered at this meeting and some of its resolutions have been located in *Inprecorr* nos. 57, 61, 62 ,of 1927 and in the Russian and German editions of the periodical *Communist International*.

b) Reports, Speeches, Drafts presented to the Plenum

1118 PROTIV voiny. Vopros o voine na VIII plenume Ispolkoma Kominterna. Mosva-Leningrad, Gos. izd-vo, 1928. 96 p. *BDIC*

1119 STALIN, I.
Revoliutsiia v Kitae i oshibki oppozitsii. [sub-title:] I. Beseda so studentami universiteta im. Sun-Iat-Sena, 13 maia 1927. g. II. Revoliutsiia v Kitae i zadachi Kominterna. (Rech' na X zasedanii IKKI 24 maia 1927 g.) Moskva, Gos. izd-vo, 1927. 61 p.

Stalin's speech at the meeting of the ECCI on May 24, 1927 is available also in Stalin's collected works: Russian text in *Sochineniia*, vol. ix, p. 282–312; English translation in *Works*, vol. ix, p. 288–318. *Hoover*

1120 Die CHINESISCHE Frage auf dem 8. Plenum der Exekutive der Kommunistischen Internatonale, Mai 1927. Hamburg, C. Hoym [1927] 160 p.

„Der Bericht, der hier veröffentlicht wird, ist kein vollständiges stenographisches Protokoll, sondern eine gekürzte Wiedergabe der Arbeiten des Plenums." (Preface) Contains Bukharin's report "The Chinese Question", and the following discussion with participation of Trotskii and Stalin; report of the Chinese Commission, and resolutions of the 8th Plenum on the Chinese question.
Hoover, Harv, Col, Duke, NYUn, Yale, Felt

c) Resolutions, Theses, etc. originating with the Plenum

1121 VIII [VOS'MOI] plenum Ispolnitel'nogo komiteta Kommunisticheskogo Internatsionala, 18—30 maia 1927 goda. Tezisy, rezoliutsii i vozzvaniia. Moskva, Gos. izd-vo, 1927. 211 p. *Hoover, SInSt*

1122 VIII [VOS'MOI] plenum Ispolnitel'nogo komitete Kommunisticheskogo Internatsionala, 18—30 maia 1927 goda. Tezisy, rezoliutsii i vozzvaniia. Moskva, Gos. izd-vo, 1927. 107 p.

Other edition of preceding item was issued simultaneously. *NYPL, UCal*

1123 COMMUNIST Party of Great Britain.
Resolution of the E.C.C.I. on the situation in Great Britain [Adopted at the VIII Plenum and presented to the IX. Annual Congress of the Communist Party of Great Britain, Oct. 8, 9, 10, 1927.] London, 1927. 12 p. *Hoover*

1124 POSTANOVI chergovogo plenumu vikonkomu Kominternu 19—30 traviia 1927 roku. [Kharkiv] Derzhavne vidavnitstvo Ukrainy, 1927. 112 p. *Col*

d) Commentaries on the Plenum

BUKHARIN, N.
Itogi plenuma IKKI; doklad tov. N. I. Bukharina na plenume Moskovskogo komiteta VKP(b) 4 iiunia 1927. See no. 452.

Der KAMPF um die Kommunistische Internationale; Dokumente der russischen Opposition nicht veröffentlicht vom Stalin'schen ZK. See no. 113.

1125 PETROVSKII, D.
Das Anglo-russische Komitee und die Opposition in der KPSU. Hamburg, Hoym [1927] 56 p. *Amst*

1126 PETROVSKII, D.
Uroki maiskogo plenuma Kominterna. Leningrad [1927?] 77 p. *SInSt*

14. Presidium of E. C., September 27, 1927.

Note: On September 27, 1927, a joint meeting of the Presidium of the E.C.C.I. and the International Control Commission took place in which Stalin delivered a speech containing a sharp polemic with Trotskii and the "Declaration of the Forty-six" (Piatakov, Preobrazhenskii, Serebriakov, etc.) on policies inside the CPSU, and on the Trotskiist political line concerning China. Russian text: Politicheskaia fizionomiia russkoi oppozitsii" – in Stalin, *Sochineniia*, x, 153–167. English translation: Stalin, *Works*, x, 158–172. No other printed material on this meeting has been located.

15. 9-th Plenum, February 9—25, 1928.

Note: No separately printed records of the 9-th Plenum are known to have been published. Broad information about this meeting can be found in *Inprecorr* nos. 17, 18, 20, 26, and 28 of 1928. However, the resolutions and decisions of the Plenum are available in separate pamphlets.

a) Resolutions, Theses, etc. originating with the Plenum

1127 IX [DEVIATYI] Plenum IKKI; rezoliutsii i postanovleniia. 9-25. II. 1928. Moskva, Gos. izd-vo, 1928. 79 p. *SInSt*

1128 NEUNTES Plenum des EKKI, (Februar 1928). Resolutionen und Beschlüsse. Hamburg-Berlin, C. Hoym [c1928] 56 p. *Hoover, Harv, Felt*

1129 RESOLUTIONS adoptées à la IXe session plénière du C.E. de l'I.C. (février 1928). Paris, Bureau d'Editions [1928] 56 p.

Hoover, NYPL, Harv, Col, BDIC

b) Commentaries on the Plenum

1130 BRAUN, P.
At the parting of the ways; the results of the ninth Plenum of the Comintern. London, Communist Party of Great Britain [1928] 130 p.

"The brochure... contains an analysis of the general conspectus provided by the Comintern Plenum and also an analysis of all the definite resolutions."

Introduction, p. 6. **Contents:** The new tactics of the C.P.G.B. – The charter of Social-Reformism and the French Communist Party. – Peace in industry and the trade unions. – The problem of the Chinese revolution. – Appendix: Resolution on the Trotskyist opposition. *Hoover, Harv*

c) French Commission of the 9-th Plenum

1131 KLASS protiv klassa; "natsional'noe edinenie" i Kompartiia Frantsii. Moskva, Gos. izd-vo, 1928. 132 p. At head of title: Deviatyi plenum Ispolkoma Kominterna.

Contains the speeches delivered at the meeting of the French Commission of the 9-th Plenum, and P. Semard's report of this Commission to the Plenum; "Annexes": 1. Resolution of the 9-th Plenum on the French question. – 2. Open letter to the members of the party, adopted by the Central Committee of the Communist Party of France on November 9 and 10, 1927. – 3. Resolution on the economic and political situation, unanimously adopted by the Conference of the Communist Party of France, Jan. 30–Feb. 2, 1928. Other documents concerning the French question at the 9-th Plenum can be found in *Kommunisticheskii Internatsional v dokumentakh, part IV* (see no. 121). The Preface of this volume is signed by Jules Humbert-Droz. The contents of this volume also includes the first half of the volume *Classe contre classe*, listed below. *Hoover, LC, Harv, SInSt*

CLASSE contre classe; la question française au IX-e Exécutif et au VI-e Congrès de l'I.C. See no. 830.

d) British Commission of 9-th Plenum

1132 DEVIATYI plenum Ispolkoma Kominterna. Novaia taktika angliiskoi kompartii; sbornik. Moskva, Gos. izd-vo, 1928. 167 p. *Hoover, SInSt*

1133 COMMUNIST policy in Great Britain. The report of the British commission of the ninth Plenum of the Comintern. London, Communist party of Gt. Brit. [1928] 195 p.

Contents: Part I. Proceedings of the British Commission. – Part II. Report of the British Commission to the Plenum. – Part III. Supplements; they include: 1. Thesis of C.C. CPGB. – 2. Alternative proposals to the thesis of the C.C. – 3. Our Party: its election tactics and its relations to the Labour Party. – 4. Open letter to members of the C.P.G.B. – 5. Resolution of the ninth Plenum of the E.C.C.I. on the British question. *Hoover, Yale*

e) Trade Union Commission of 9-th Plenum

1134 NOVEISHII reformizm, tresty i profsoiuzy. Moskva, Gos. izd-vo, 1928. 172 p. At head of title: Deviatyi plenum Ispolkoma Kominterna.

Abbreviated version of 31 speeches at the meeting of the Trade Union Commission of the 9-th Plenum; report of this Commission to the Plenum; resolutions of the 9-th Plenum on Trade Union problems; excerpts from report of the Trade Union Commission of ECCI to the 9-th Plenum.   *Hoover, Col*

16. Program Commission of E. C. C. I., May 25, 1928.

Note: The IV-the Congress in November 1922 discussed the necessity of elaborating a program of the C. I., and a Program Commission of the Congress prepared a resolution referring all drafts of programs to the E. C. C. I. for consideration. The Congress also urged the E. C. C. I. to publish all drafts for discussion by member-parties.

Before the V-th Congress convened, the E. C. C. I. published "materials" concerning the program (see nos. 769, 775, 782, 790) which were submitted to the Congress for consideration. The V-th Congress again appointed a Program Commission which prepared a draft of a program (see nos. 801, 803). The Congress accepted this draft "as a basis for discussion by the sections [member-parties]". At the same time the Congress decided to form a permanent Program Commission for the elaboration of a draft which should be presented to the VI-th Congress (see no.807). This permanent Commission worked out a draft of a program which was accepted by the Commission on May 25, 1928 and submitted to the VI-th Congress for consideration and approval. This draft was listed among the items presented to the VI-th Congress and is repeated here only for the record. An item by Trotskii concerning this draft is also cross-listed below.

PROEKT programmy Kommunisticheskogo Internatsionala, priniat Programmnoi komissiei IKKI, 25 maia 1928 goda. See no. 824.

PROJET du programme de l'Internationale Communiste; adopté par la Commission du programme du C. E. de l'I. C., le 25 mai 1928. See nos. 831, 832.

TROTSKII, L.
The draft program of the Communist International; a criticism of fundamentals. [Presented to the VI-the World Congress of the Communist International.] See no. 827.

17. Presidium of E.C.C.I., March 13, 1929

Note. There exist seven different editions of the Program of the Communist Youth International adopted by its V-th Congress. They are in six languages: the Czech edition is listed below, whereas the Russian, German, French, Dutch, and two Spanish editions are listed as nos. 2103, 2106, 2107, 2109, 2110 and 2111 among the material pertaining to the V-th Congress of the C. Y. I. No English edition of this important item has been found in the surveyed holdings of American and European libraries.

1138 PROGRAM Komunistične mladinske internacionale. Sprejet na V Kongresu KMI i potrjen na prezidiumu IOKI 14. [!] Marca 1929. Moskva-Leningrad, Zadružna Založba Inozemskih Delavcev v ZSSR, 1933. 106 p. *Felt*

18. American Commission of E.C.C.I., April—May, 1929

1139 STALIN, Iosif
O pravykh fraktsionerakh v amerikanskoi kompartii. Moskva-Leningrad, Gos. izd-vo, 1930. 46 p.

Stalin's speech in the American Commission of the Executive Committee of the C. I. on May 6, 1929, and two speeches at the meeting of the Presidium of the Executive Committee on May 14, 1929, on matters concerning the Communist Party of the United States.
These three speeches have not been reprinted in vol. xii of Stalin's *Sochineniia* which covers the period April 1929 to June 1930, but they are mentioned in the "biographical chronicle" (page 388). *Hoover, LC*

1140 STALIN, Iosif
Stalin's speeches on the American Communist Party; delivered in the American Commission of the Presidium of the Executive Committe of the Communist International. May 6, 1929, and in the Presidium of the Executive Committee of the Communist International on the American question, May 14th, 1929. Published by Central Committee, Communist Party, U. S. A. [New York, Workers Library Publishers, 1931 ?] 39 p.

This is the English translation of the preceding item. According to Theodore Draper, *American Communism and Soviet Russia*, New York, Viking Press, 1960, p. 524, note 6 there exist two English translations of these speeches. One was produced in Moscow immediately following the meetings of the American Commission and of the Presidium; it was published in mimeographed form and distributed to the participants of these meetings; it has been reprinted in a Congressional print, *Investigation of Un-American Propaganda Activities*, vol. xi, p. 7112–7133 and *Appendix — Part 1*, p. 876–897. The second translation is the pamphlet listed here and was published by the Central Committee of the C.P. USA. Draper (ibidem) says that this pamphlet was published in 1929 which seems incorrect because on the back of the title page is advertised a William Z. Forster speech delivered on December 5, 1930. Hence the most probable publication date is early 1931.

This pamphlet contains a Preface (pages 6–10) which is not contained in the Russian edition of the speeches. It condenses the Stalin speeches and presents the viewpoint of the Central Committee of the C.P. USA on the "Lovestone-Gitlow case".   *Hoover*

19. Presidium of E. C., May 14, 1929.

Note: Two Stalin speeches on the American Communist Party are contained in the two items listed under American Commission, just above.

20. 10-th Plenum, July 3—19, 1929

a) Protocols

1141 X [DESIATYI] plenum Ispolkoma Kominterna. Moskva, Gos. izd-vo, 1929. 4 v. (vypusk)

Subtitles of particular volumes:
1. Mezhdunarodnoe polozhenie i zadachi Kommunisticheskogo Internatsionala. 462 p.
2. O mezhdunarodnom krasnom dne. 80 p.
3. Ekonomicheskaia bor'ba i zadachi kompartii. 207 p.
4. Tezisy, rezoliutsii, postanovleniia. 94 p., tables.

These four volumes include the entire record of the 10-th Plenum in the Russian language. They are organized according to the principal subjects of the reports and discussion of the sessions. The 21 sessions are not contained in the volumes in their chronological sequence. Vol. 1 contains the reports presented to the first two sessions and the discussion during sessions 5–16; Kuusinen's report delivered at the first session is also printed separately. (See no. 1144.) Vol. 2 contains the third and fourth sessions; vol. 3 contains sessions 17–21. The fourth volume contains the theses, resolutions and decisions of the Plenum. Another edition of the contents of this fourth volume is known. (See no. 1146.)

The German edition of the record of the 10-th Plenum (see next item) contains the entire material in one volume.

Hoover, compl; *NYPL,* v. 1, 3, 4; *Col,* v. 3; *BDIC,* v. 1; *SInSt,* v. 1, 2.

1142 PROTOKOLL, 10. Plenum des Exekutivkomitees der Kommunistischen Internationale, Moskau, 3. Juli 1929 bis 19. Juli 1929. Hamburg-Berlin, C. Hoym [1929] 953 p. Indexes

Includes "Thesen, Resolutionen, Beschlüsse", p. 887–936. See annotation to no. 1141. *Hoover, NYPL, Harv, Duke, Illin, Amst, Felt*

1143 Xe [DIXIEME] session du Comité Exécutif de l'Internationale Communiste (juillet 1929). Compte rendu sténographique. Numéros spéciaux de *La Correspondance Internationale,* juillet-octobre 1929, p. 853—1148. *Amst, BDIC, Felt*

b) Reports, Speeches, etc. presented to the Plenum

1144 KUUSINEN, O. B.
Mezhdunarodnoe polozhenie i zadachi Kominterna. (Doklad na X-m plenume Kominterna 3 iiulia 1929 g.) Moskva-Leningrad, 1929. 160 p.

This is Kuusinen's report delivered at first session of the 10-th Plenum. Contained also in no. 1141 vol. 1. *BDIC, SInSt*

1145 MOLOTOV, Viacheslav
Komintern i novyi revoliutsionnyi pod"em; rech' na X plenume IKKI 9 iiulia 1929 g. Moskva, Leningrad, Gos. izd-vo, 1929. 75 p.

Molotov's speech delivered during the discussion of the Kuusinen and Manuil'skii reports (in first and second session). Contained also in no. 1141 vol. 1. *Hoover, SInSt*

c) Resolutions, Theses, etc. originating with the Plenum

1146 X [DESIATYI] plenum Ispolkoma Kominterna; tezisy, rezoliutsii, postanovleniia (iiul 1929). Moskva, Gosp. izd-vo., 1929. 80 p.

For other Russian edition of above item see no. 1141, v. 4. For German edition of theses, resolutions and decisions see no. 1142. *Hoover, LC*

1147 The WORLD situation and economic struggle; theses of the tenth plenum E.C.C.I. [London] C.P.G.B. [1929?] 51 p.   *Hoover*

1148 THESES résolutions et décisions adoptées à la Xe session plénière du C.E. de l'I.C. (juillet 1929). Paris, Bureau d'Editions [1929] 67 p.
    Hoover, Amst

1149 Le DECISIONI della X sessione plenaria del C.E. dell'I.C. (luglio 1929) Paris, Edizioni di coltura sociale, 1930. 56 p.   *LC, BDIC*

d) Commentaries on the Plenum

1150 MANUIL'SKII, D.
Itogi X plenuma IKKI. Moskva & Leningrad, 1929. 64 p.   *SInSt*

1151 MANUIL'SKII, D.
Ein Jahr nach dem VI. Weltkongreq der KI. Zum 10. Plenum des Ekki. Hamburg-Berlin, Verlag Carl Hoym Nachf. [1929] 30 p.   *Felt*

1152 SMOL'IANSKII, G. B.
Der neue revolutionäre Aufstieg (Ergebnisse des 10. EKKI-Plenums). Hamburg usw., Hoym [1929] 36 p. At head of title: G. B. Smoljanski.
    Amst, Felt

1153 SMOL'IANSKI, G. B.
La Xe session plénière du Comité Exécutif de l'Internationale Communiste. Paris, Bureau d'Editions, 1929. 40 p.   *Amst, BDIC*

21. Enlarged Presidium of E. C., February 18—28, 1930.

a) Reports, Speeches, Drafts presented to the meeting

1154 MANUIL'SKII, D.
Ekonomicheskii krizis i revoliutsionnyi pod"em; doklad i zakliuchitel'noe slovo na rasshirennom prezidiume Ispolkoma Kommunisticheskogo Internatsionala (ot 18—20 [sic!] fevralia 1930 g.) Moskva, Gos. izd-vo, 1930. 61 p.   *Hoover, BDIC*

1155 MANUIL'SKII, D.
Die Weltwirtschaftskrise und der revolutionäre Aufstieg. Referat auf dem Erweiterten Plenum des Präsidium des EKKI. Hamburg-Berlin, Verlag Carl Hoym Nachf. [1930] 64 p. *Felt*

1156 MOLOTOV, Viacheslav M.
The new phase in the Soviet Union. Report to the Enlarged Presidium of the Executive Committee of the Communist International, February 25, 1930. New York, Workers' Library Publishers [1930?] 55 p.
Hoover, LC, Col.

1157 MANUIL'SKII, D. Z.
La crise économique et l'essor révolutionnaire. Rapport et discours de clôture au Présidium élargi du C[omité] E[xécutif] de l'I[nternationale] C[ommuniste] (18—28 février 1930). Paris, Bureau d'Éditions, 1930. 56 p. *Amst, BDIC, Felt*

1158 MOLOTOV, V. M.
Nová etapa; referát o SSR na rozšířeném presidiu EKI. 25. února 1930. Karlín, Nákladem „Bolševika", 1930. 47 p. (Knihovna Bolševika. Svazek 1) *NYPL*

1159 MOLOTOV, V.
La nuova tappa. (Rapporto sulla situazione dell'U.R.S.S. presentato al Presidium allargato dell'I.C., il 25 febbraio 1930.) Paris, Edizioni di coltura sociale, 1930. 80 p. *BDIC, Felt*

1160 ARBEIDERMASSENE for Kommunismen! Beslutninger pa E.K.K.I.s utvidede presidium februar 1930 samt Manuilskis Molotovs og Losovskis Foredrag. [n. p.] Norges kommunistiske parti [n. d.] 51 p. *Amst*

b) Resolutions, Theses, etc. originating with the meeting

1161 RASSHIRENNYI prezidium Ispolkoma 18—28 fevralia 1930 g. Rezoliutsii. Moskva, 1930. 72 p. *BDIC, SInSt*

1162 ERWEITERTES Presidium des EKKI. (Februar 1930) Thesen und Resolutionen. Hamburg, C. Hoym Nachf., 1930. 61 p.
Hoover, LC, NYPL, Harv, Duke, UWisc, Amst, Felt

1163 RÉSOLUTIONS adoptées par le présidium élargi du C.E.I.C., (18—28 février 1930). Paris, Bureau d'Éditions, 1930. 68 p. *Amst, Felt*

22. 11-th P l e n u m, March 26—April 11, 1931.

a) Protocols

1164 STENOGRAFICHESKII otchet XI plenuma IKKI. Moskva, 1931—32. 2 vols. (vypusk)

Subtitles of particular volumes:

1. Kompartii i krizis kapitalizma. Moskva, Partiinoe izd-vo, 1932. 638 p.
2. Voennaia opasnost' i zadachi Kominterna. Zakliuchitel'nye raboty plenuma. Moskva, Gos. sotsial'no-ekonom. izd-vo, 1931. 254 p.

Hoover, NYPL, Harv, v. 1; SInSt

b) Reports, Speeches, etc. presented to the Plenum

1165 MANUIL'SKII, D.
Kompartii i krizis kapitalizma. Doklad na XI plenume IKKI. Moskva & Leningrad, 1931. 125 p. *SInSt*

1166 CHEMODANOV, V. E.
Unter dem Sturmbanner des leninistischen Komsomol; Bericht und Diskussion über die Lage und Aufgaben der KJI auf dem XI. Plenum des EKKI [von V. E. Tschemodanow. Hamburg] C. Hoym Nachf. [1931] 103 p. At head of title: XI. Plenum des EKKI, 26 März — 11 April 1931.

Hoover

1167 MANUIL'SKII, D.
Die Kommunistischen Parteien und die Krise des Kapitalismus. Bericht vor dem XI. Plenum des EKKI. [Hamburg] Verlag Carl Hoym Nachf. [1931]134 p. At head of title: XI Plenum des EKKI. 26. März—31. April 1931. *Felt*

1168 PIATNITSKII, Osip
Brennende Fragen. Die Arbeit unter den Arbeitslosen. Partei- und Gewerkschaftsarbeit im Betrieb. Die Fluktuation im Mitgliederbestand. Hamburg-Berlin, Verlag Carl Hoym Nachf. [1931] 47 p. (Bücherei des Parteiarbeiters, Band 2) *Felt*

1169 BROWDER, Earl R.
War against workers' Russia! (Issued by the Communist Party, USA)
[New York City, Workers Library Publishers, 1931] 30 p. illus.

> Speech delivered at the eleventh Plenum of the Executive Committee of the
> Communist International in April, 1931.   *Hoover*

1170 CACHIN, Marcel
Preparation for war against the Soviet Union; report to the eleventh
Plenum of the Executive Committee of the Communist International,
April 8, 1931, and discussion on the report. Moscow, Cooperative
Pub. Society of Foreign Workers in the USSR, 1931. 79 p.
                                                   Hoover, LC, Amst

1171 CACHIN, Marcel [and others]
War preparations against the Soviet Union. Report by Marcel Cachin
and speeches by Bratkovsky, Rust, Manner, Schwartz, Browder, Thälmann, Arnot. New York, Workers Library Publishers [1931] 79 p.

> Speeches delivered at the nineteenth session of the 11-th Plenum of the
> Executive Committee of the Communist International. "XIth Plenum Series".
>   *NYPL, Col, Felt*

1172 CO-REPORT of the Young Communist International at the XIth Plenum
of the E[xecutive] C[ommittee] of the C[ommunist] I[nternational]
(March 28, 1931). London, Modern books [n. d.] 77 p.   *Amst*

1173 MANUIL'SKII, D.
The communist parties and the crisis of capitalism. New York, Workers'
Library Publishers [1931] iv, 121 p. Printed in England.

> "Speech delivered on the first item of the agenda of the XI plenum of the
> E. C. C. I. held in March–April 1931, together with the speech in reply to the
> discussion on this subject."   *Hoover, Col*

1174 MANUIL'SKII, D.
The communist parties and the crisis of capitalism. London, Modern
Books [1931 ?] iv, 121 p.   *Amst*

1175 MANUIL'SKII, D.
The communist parties and the crisis of capitalism; report of D. Z.
Manuilsky to the eleventh Plenum of the Executive Committee of the
Communist International, held in March—April, 1931, and speech in
reply to the discussion on the report. Moscow, Co-op. Publ. Soc. of
Foreign Workers in the USSR, 1931. 121 p. On cover: XI Plenum of
the Executive Committee of the Communist International. "Second
edition."   *NYPL, Felt*

1176 PIATNITSKII, Osip
Urgent questions of the day. Unemployed movement. Factory organization. Fluctuating membership. New York, Workers Library Publishers [1931] 42 p. Printed in England.

> Slightly revised and abbreviated report of a speech delivered on the first item of the agenda of the XI plenum of the E. C. C. I. on March 31, 1931.
>
> *Hoover, Amst*

1177 PIATNITSKII, Osip A.
Urgent questions of the day. London, Modern Books [n. d.] 43 p. tables.

> London edition of preceding item. *Amst*

1178 MANUIL'SKII, D.
Les partis communistes et la crise du capitalisme. Rapport à la XIe assemblée plénière du Comité Exécutif de l'Internationale Communiste, [suivi du discours de clôture]. Paris, Bureau d'Éditions, 1931. 144 p. tables. (Les documents de l'Internationale.) At head of title: **D. Z. Manouilski** *NYPL, Amst, BDIC, Felt*

1179 Le PARTI communiste français devant l'Internationale; préface du Bureau politique du P. C. F. — Discours des camarades Manouilski, Thorez, Piatnisky [sic!], Barbé, Vassiliev, Losovski, à le XIe session plénière du Comité éxecutif de l'Internationale Communiste. Paris, Bureau d'Editions, 1931. 86 p. (Les Documents de l'Internationale Communiste) *Hoover, Felt*

1180 PIATNITSKII, Osip
Quelques problèmes urgents. Le mouvement des chômeurs. Le travail du parti et des syndicats dans les entreprises. La fluctuation de nos effectifs. Paris, Bureau d'Editions, 1931. 46 p. (Les Documents de l'Internationale)

> "La brochure est constituée par le sténogramme abrégé du discours prononcé le 31 mars 1931, à la XIe assemblé plénière du C. E. de l'I. C." *Hoover*

1181 CACHIN, Marcel
La preparazione metodica della guerra contro l'Unione dei Soviet. (Rapporto all'XI Plenum dell'I. C.) Bruxelles, Edizioni di Coltura Sociale, 1931. 63 p. *Felt*

1182 MANUIL'SKII, D.
I partiti comunisti e la crisi del capitalismo. (Rapporto del Presidium del C. E. all'XI Plenum dell'I. C.) Bruxelles, Edizioni di Coltura Sociale [1931] 200 p. (Documenti dell Internazionale.) *BDIC, Felt*

1183 PIATNITSKII, O.
Alcuni problemi urgenti. Il movimento dei disocupati. Il lavoro del partito e dei sindicati nelle officine. Le fluttuazioni dei nostri effettivi. Bruxelles, Edizioni di Coltura Sociale, 1931. 72 p. (Documenti della Internazionale.) At head of title: O. Piatniski.

Speech delivered May 31, 1931 to 11-th Plenum. *BDIC, Felt*

1184 MANUIL'SKII, D.
La crisis del capitalismo y los partidos comunistas. Barcelona, Edeya [n. d.] 119 p. index. (Documentos de la Internacional Comunista.)
Amst

c) Resolutions, theses, and other documents originating with the Plenum

1185 TEZISY, rezoliutsii i postanovleniia XI plenuma IKKI. Moskva, Moskovskii rabochii, 1931. 31 p. *Hoover, LC, SInSt*

1186 ELFTES Plenum des EKKI, April 1931. Thesen und Resolutionen. Hamburg, C. Hoym [c. 1931] 36 p. *Harv*

1187 XIth [ELEVENTH] Plenum of the Executive Committee of the Communist International. Theses, resolutions, decisions. Moscow, Co-op. Publ. Soc. of Foreign Workers in the USSR, 1931. 31 p. *Col*

1188 XIth [ELEVENTH] plenum of the Executive Committee of the Communist International; theses, resolutions and decisions. New York, Workers Library Publishers [1931] 32 p. Printed in England *Hoover*

1189 XIth [ELEVENTH] plenum of the Executive Committee of the Communist International; theses, resolutions and decisions. London, Modern Books [1932?] 32 p. Cover-title. *UKans, Amst, Felt*

1190 THESES, décisions, résolutions de la XIe Assemblée plénière du Comité exécutif de l'Internationale Communiste, avril 1931. Paris, Bureau d'Editions, 1931. 42 p. (Les Documents de l'Internationale.)
Hoover

1191 La XIe [ONZIÈME] session plénière du Comité Exécutif de l'Internationale Communiste. L'aggravation de la crise économique mondiale. Les tâches qui en découlent pour les parties communistes. Paris, Impr. G. Dangon [1931] 16 p. (Supplement du journal l'Humanité du 5 mai 1931.)

"Thèses adoptées par la XIe session plénière du C.E de l'I.C." *BDIC, Felt*

1192 TEZE i zaključci XI. plenuma EKKI. Održano u Moskvi početkom aprila 1931. [n. p., n. d.] (Radnička biblioteka 1.) *Amst*

1193 La XI [UNDICESIMA] Sessione plenaria del C. E. della Internazionale Comunista. (Tesi e risoluzioni) Paris, Edizioni di Coltura Sociale, 1931. 36 p. *Felt*

1194 TESIS y resoluciones adoptadas en el XI pleno (abril de 1931). Madrid, Editorial Mundo obrero [1931] 35 p. At head of title: Comité ejecutivo de la Internacional comunista. *NYPL*

d) Commentaries about the Plenum

1195 ALTMAN, M. [and] Ksenofontov, F.
Za diktaturu proletariata. K itogam XI plenuma Ispolnitel'nogo Komiteta Kommunisticheskogo Internatsionala. Moskva, 1931. 93 p. (Seriia: Mezhdunarodnye problemy) *SInSt*

1196 OB itogakh XI plenuma IKKI. Materialy dlia dokladchikov i seti partprosveshcheniia. Moskva-Leningrad, 1931. (APPO IKKI — Kultprop TsKVKP(b)) *SInSt*

1197 ITOGI XI plenuma IKKI. Leningrad, Priboi, 1931. 190 p. At head of title: Sbornik materialov dlia dokladchikov i besedchikov.

> A collection of excerpts of speeches, theses, and resolutions of the 11-th Plenum and of newspaper articles on subjects dealt with by the Plenum. Prepared as a source book for lecturers and propagandists conveying the contemporary party line. *Hoover, LC, UChic, SInSt*

1198 The WORLD crisis and the international class struggle (an outline of the debates and decisions of the XI plenum of the E. C. C. I. held in March—April, 1931) [New York] Workers Library Publishers [1931] 18 p. Printed in England. *Hoover, Harv, Ohio, Yale*

1199 The WORLD crisis and the international class struggle. (An outline of the debates and decisions of the XI Plenum of the E. C. C. I. held in March—April, 1931). London, Modern Books [n. d.] 18 p. *Amst*

23. 12-th P l e n u m, August 27—September 15, 1932.

a) Protocols

1200 XII [DVENADTSATYI] plenum IKKI; stenograficheskii otchet. Moskva, Partizdat, 1933. 3 v.

Contents:
v. 1. Meetings 1–13; 204 p.
v. 2. Meetings 14–24; 261 p.
v. 3. Meetings 25–32; 178 p.

Hoover, LC, NYPL, Harv, v. 1, 2; Duke, Corn, UWash, SInSt

b) Reports, Speeches, Draft presented to the Plenum

1201 KUUSINEN, Otto
Mezhdunarodnoe polozhenie i zadachi sektsii Kominterna. Moskva, Part. izd-vo, 1933. 126 p. On cover: Materialy XII plenuma IKKI.

Harv, SInSt

1202 UZLOVYE voprosy revoliutsionnogo dvizheniia Pol'shi na XII plenume Ispolkoma Kominterna; sbornik rechei, pod red. i s predisl. Io. Bratkovskogo. Moskva, Partiinoe izd-vo, 1933. 127 p. On cover: Materialy XII plenuma IKKI.

A collection of speeches of the delegates of the Communist Party of Poland at the 12-th Plenum containing:
Leński, J. (pseud. of Leszczyński, Juljan) Germany and Poland – key positions of the revolutionary front.
Bronkowski (pseud. of Bortnowski) Against fascism and socialfascism.
Henrykowski (pseud. of Amsterdam, Saul) The fundamental task of the mobilization of the working masses.
Bratkowski J. The defense of the USSR is the task of every worker and peasant of Poland.
Wiktorowicz (pseud.:) The workers youth of Poland in the struggle against imperialist war.
For Polish and Ukrainian editions see nos. 1225, 1227.   *Hoover, LC*

1203 KUUSINEN, O.
Die Internationale Lage und die Aufgaben der Sektionen der Kommunistischen Internationale. Moskau, Verlagsgenossenschaft Ausländischer Arbeiter in der UdSSR, 1933. 112 p.   *Felt*

1204 MANUIL'SKII, D.

Das Ende der kapitalistischen Stabilisierung. Moskau, Verlagsgenossenschaft ausländischer Arbeiter in der UdSSR, 1932. 30 p.

> Title on [p. 4 of] cover: O kontse kapitalicheskoi stabilizatsii. "Diskussionsrede zum Bericht des Genossen Kuusinen auf dem XII. Plenum des Exekutivkomitees der Kommunistischen Internationale (September 1932): Die internationale Lage und die Aufgaben der Sektionen der Komintern."
>
> *Hoover, LC, Col*

1205 MANUIL'SKII, D.

Die Sowjetunion und das Weltproletariat. Moskau, Verlagsgenossenschaft ausländischer Arbeiter in der UdSSR, 1932. 40 p.

> "Bericht auf dem XII. Plenum des Exekutiv-Komitees der Kommunistischen Internationale, (September 1932)."
>
> *Hoover*

1206 PIATNITSKII, O. A.

Die Arbeit der Kommunistischen Parteien Frankreichs und Deutschlands und die Aufgaben der Kommunisten in der Gewerkschaftsbewegung. [Rede auf dem XII. Plenum des Exekutivkomitees der Kommunistischen Internationale (September 1932)] Moskau, Verlagsgenossenschaft Ausländsicher Arbeiter in der UdSSR, 1932. 48 p. At head of title: O. Pjatnizki. *Hoover, LC, Col, Amst, Felt*

1207 XII [TWELFTH] Plenum library.

> **Note:** This is a collective title for a series of seven pamphlets published simultaneously in New York and London. It was taken from the heading of the announcement of the entire series on the last cover page of the *Guide to the XII Plenum E.C.C.I.*, which obviously was the last one to be published in the New York series. The Library of Congress and the New York Public Library indentified some of the seven pamphlets as *"Twelfth Plenum"* series.
>
> Of the New York edition by Workers' Library Publishers the first item *(Capitalist stabilization . . .)* is printed in New York, whereas the remaining six items are identified as "Printed in Great Britain". The London edition is published by Modern Books; the various pamphlets of the New York and London editions are identical with the sole difference in place of publication and publisher.
>
> The items of this series, including also known London edition items, are listed here in the same sequence as on the last cover page of the *Guide to the XII Plenum E.C.C.I.*, New York edition.
>
> In the listing below, the items of the New York edition are numbered at the end of the entry with numbers (1), (2) . . . (7); the London edition with numbers (2a), (3a) . . . (7a). The Kuusinen report has obviously two London editions: nos. 1210 and 1211.

1208 CAPITALIST stabilization has ended; thesis and resolutions of the twelfth Plenum of the Executive Committee of the Communist International. New York, Workers' Library Publishers, 1932. 48 p.   **(1)**

> *Hoover, LC, NYPL, Harv, Col, Duke, Illin, Ohio, Amst*

1209 KUUSINEN, Otto
The international situation and the task of the sections of the Comintern. Report of Comrade Kuusinen at the XIIth Plenum of the Executive Committee of the Communist International. New York, Workers Library Publishers, 1932. 160 p. Printed in Great Britain.   **(2)**   *Hoover, Illin*

1210 KUUSINEN, O.
The international situation and the tasks of the sections of the Comintern. (Report of Comrade Kuusinen at the XIIth Plenum of the Executive Committee of the Communist International) (London) Modern Books Ltd. [n. d.] 159.   **(2a)**   *Felt*

1211 KUUSINEN, Otto
Prepare for power; the international situation and the tasks of the sections of the Comintern; report by O. Kuusinen. [London, printed by Utopia Press, Ltd. 1932?] 159 p. Cover title. At head of title: Twelfth Plenum of the E. C. C. I.   **(2b)**

The Library of Congress gives as publisher: New York, Workers Library Publishers, [1933 ?]   *Hoover, LC, Col*

1212 OKANO
The war in the Far East and the tasks of the Communists in the struggle against imperialist war and military intervention; report of Comrade Okano [pseud. of Sanzo Nosaka] at the XIIth Plenum of the Executive Committee of the Communist International. New York, Workers Library Publishers, 1932. 51 p.   **(3)**   *Hoover, LC, Col, Illin, Felt*

1213 OKANO
The war in the Far East and the tasks of the Communists in the struggle against imperialist war and military intervention. Report at the XII Plenum of the Executive Committee of the Communist International. London, Modern Books [n. d.] 51 p.   **(3a)**   *Amst, Felt*

1214 MANUIL'SKII, D.
The U.S.S.R. and the world proletariat; report at the XII Plenum of the Executive Committee of the Communist International, September 14, 1932. New York, Workers Library Publishers [1932] 48 p. Printed in Great Britain.   **(4)**   *Hoover, NYPL, Illin*

1215 MANUIL'SKII, D.
The U.S.S.R. and the world proletariat. Report at the XII Plenum of Executive Committee of the Communist International, September 14, 1932. London, Modern Books Ltd. [n. d.] 48 p.   **(4a)**   *Felt*

255

1216 MANUIL'SKII, D.
The Soviet Union and the world's workers. Report [at the] XII plenum
E.C.C.I., September 14, 1932. London, Modern Books [n. d.] 48 p. **(4b)**

> This and the preceding pamphlet might be identical; one cataloged from
> title page, the other from the cover title. They were not available for
> identification.   *Amst*

1217 PIATNITSKII, O.
The work of the communist parties of France and Germany and the
tasks of the communists in the trade union movement. Speech by Com.
O. Piatnitsky. New York, Workers' Library Publishers [1932] 79 p. **(5)**
Hoover, LC, Col, Illin

1218 PIATNITSKII, O.
The work of the communist parties of France and Germany and the
tasks of the communists in the trade union movement. Speech by
Com. O. Piatnitsky. London, Modern Books [n. d] 78 p. **(5a)**   *Felt*

1219 The NEXT Step in Britain, America and Ireland; speechs and reports,
XII Plenum E.C.C.I. New York, Workers Library Publishers [1932]
87 p. **(6)**

> **Contents:**
> GUSEV, S. The end of capitalist stabilisation and the basic tasks of the
> British and American sections of the C.I. (Reprinted from No. 19 "Communist
> International".) p. 2–35.
> POLLIT, H. The C.P.G.B. [Communist Party of Great Britain] in the fight for
> the masses. (Reprinted from No. 17–18 "Communist International".) p. 36–66.
> PRINGLE, Jack. The situation in U.S.A. (Reprinted from No. 17–18 "Com-
> munist International".) p. 67–79.
> TROY. For a Communist Party of Ireland. p. 80–[88].
> *Hoover, NYPL, Harv, Col, Illin, Yale*

1220 The NEXT step in Britain, America and Ireland (Speeches and reports
XII plenum E.C.C.I.) London, Modern Books, Ltd. [n. d.] 87 p. **(6a)**

> For annotation see preceding item.   *Felt*

1221 GUIDE to the XII Plenum E.C.C.I.; material for propagandists,
reporters, training classes. New York, Workers Library Publishers
[1932?] 119 p. **(7)**   *Hoover, NYPL, Harv, Col, Illin, Amst*

1222 GUIDE to the XII Plenum E.C.C.I. Material for propagandists,
organisers, reporters, training classes. London, Modern Books [n. d.]
120 p. **(7a)**   *Amst, Felt*

1223 MANUIL'SKII, D.
De Sowjet-Unie en het wreld proletariaat.Rede op het 12de plenum
van het uitvoerend komitee der Kommunistische Internationale, 14 September 1932. Amsterdam, Agentschap Amstel, 1932. 32 p.   *Amst*

1224 MANUIL'SKII, D.
L'Unione dei Soviet e il proletariato mondiale (Rapporto al XII Esecutivo Allargato dell'I.C.). (Settembre 1932) Bruxelles, Edizioni di Coltura Sociale, 1933. 57 p. (Documenti dell'Internazionale, 66.)   *Felt*

1225 XII [DWUNASTE] plenum Komitetu Wykonawczego Międzynarodówki Komunistycznej o Polsce; referat tow. Leńskiego i przemówienia przedstawicieli K.P.P. z przedmową J. Bratkowskiego. Moskwa,
Wydawnictwo partyjne, 1933. 173 p.

For contents see no. 1202.
Hoover, NYPL (pages 33–48 missing in both libraries)

1226 MANUIL'SKII, D.
La Union Sovetica y el proletariado mundial. Informe presentado al
XII pleno del C.E. de la I.C. Barcelona, Publicaciones Edeya [n. d.]
(pages?) (Documentos de la Internacional Comunista.)   *Amst*

1227 VUZLOVI pitaniia revoliutschionogo rukhu Pol'shchi na XII plenumi
Vikonnomu Kominternu. Zbirka promov za red. i z predemovoiu
Io. Bratkovs'kogo. [Kharkiv] Proletar, 1933. 90 p.

See nos. 1202, 1225.   *LC*

c) **Resolutions, theses and other documents originating at the Plenum**

1228 O mezhdunarodnom polozhenii i zadachakh sektsii Kommunisticheskogo Internatsionala. Tezisy po dokladu t. Kuusinena. Moskva,
1932. 16 p.   *SInSt*

1229 TEZISY i rezoliutsii. Moskva, Partizdat, 1933. 32 p. (Materialy XII plenuma IKKI.)   *BDIC*

1230 XII [ZWÖLFTES] Plenum des Exekutivkomitees der Kommunistischen
Internationale (September 1932). Thesen und Resolutionen. Moskau,
Verlagsgenossenschaft ausländischer Arbeiter in der UdSSR, 1932.
46 p.   *Hoover, LC, NYPL, Col, Amst*

CAPITALIST stabilization has ended; thesis and resolutions of the twelfth Plenum etc. — see no. 1208.

1231 XII [TWELFTH] Plenum of the Executive Committee of the Communist International, September 1932. Theses and Resolutions. Moscow, Co-operative Pub. Soc. of Foreign Workers in the USSR, 1933. 36 p.
Hoover, LC, Harv

1232 XII [TWELFTH] Plenum E. C. C. I. Theses and resolutions. London, Modern Books [n. d.] 64 p. *Amst, Felt*

1233 The 12th [TWELFTH] Plenum of the E. C. C. I. The international situation and the tasks of the sections of the Communist International. Theses on the report of comrade Kuusinen (September 1932). Twelfth congress C. P. G. B. London, C. P. G. B. [n. d.] 15 p. *Amst*

1234 THESES, décisions, résolutions de la XIIe Assemblée plènière du Comité exécutif de l'Internationale communiste; septembre 1932. Paris, Bureau d'Éditions, 1933. 44 p. (Les Documents de l'Internationale.) *Hoover, BDIC*

1235 La FINE della stabilizazione del capitalismo e i nostri compiti. (Tesi, risoluzioni e decisioni della XII Sessione plenaria del C. E. dell'I. C.) (Settembre 1932). Bruxelles, Edizioni di Coltura Sociale, 1933. 51 p. (Documenti dell'Internazionale.) *Felt*

1236 TESIS, decisiones y resoluciones. Barcelona, Publicaciones Edeya [1932] 44 p. At head of title: El XII plenum del C. E. de la I. C. (Septiembre de 1932). *NYPL, Felt*

d) Commentaries about the Plenum

1237 CHEMODANOV, V.
Itogi XII plenuma IKKI i zadachi KIM; sokrashchennyi doklad na dekabr'skom plenume IKKIM ob itogakh XII plenuma IKKI i zadachakh sektsii KIM v bor'be za massy trudiashchikhsia molodezhi. [Moskva], Molodaia gvardiia, 1933. 63 p. *Hoover, SInSt*

1238 Det INTERNATIONELLA Läget och Kominternsektionernas uppgifter. Kominterns EK:s XII plenum. Stockholm, Förlagsaktiebolaget arbetarkultur, 1933. 47 p. *Amst, SInSt*

24. Presidium of E. C. C. I., March, 1933.

a) Reports, Speeches, etc. to the meeting

1239 HECKERT, Fritz
Why Hitler in Germany? The report of Fritz Heckert, representative of the Communist party of Germany, to the Executive of the Communist International. With resolution adopted. London, Modern Books [1933?] 47 p.   *Hoover, Amst, Felt*

1240 GERMANY — Hitler or Lenin. New York, Workers' Library Publishers [1933] 31 p. Printed in England. Reprinted from no. 7 of C[*ommunist*] I[*nternational*]   *Hoover*

1241 GERMANY. Hitler or Lenin [The collapse of Weimar Germany and preparation for the German October]. London, Modern Books [1933] 32 p. First publ.: "C.I." 7.   *Amst*

b) Resolutions of the meeting

1242 Die KOMMUNISTISCHE Internationale über die Lage in Deutschland. Moskau-Leningrad, Verlagsgenossenschaft der ausländischen Arbeiter in der UdSSR, 1933. 12 p. Cover-title.

> "Resolution des Präsidiums des EKKI zum Referat des Genossen Heckert über die Lage in Deutschland."   *Hoover, LC, NYPL, Harv, Col, Amst, Felt*

25. 13-th Plenum, November 28—December 12, 1933.

a) Protocols

1243 XIII [TRIDNADTSATYI] Plenum IKKI; stenograficheskii otchet. Moskva, Partizdat, 1934. 597 p.

> The above proceedings of the XIII Plenum are not known to have appeared in any other language than Russian. However, almost the entire contents of

the above Russian volume appeared in 8 pamphlets in the German language
and in 8 pamphlets in English. These pamphlets are listed below.

Hoover, LC, NYPL, Harv, BDIC, SInSt

b) Reports, Speeches, etc. to the Plenum

1244 KOSTANIAN, G.
Nazrevanie revoliutsionnogo krizisa i zadachi sektsii Profinterna.
Moskva, Profizdat, 1934. 55 p.

> Correction slip in Russian added: "In the title of the pamphlet the following
> sub-title is missing: Re-edited stenographic record of speech delivered to the
> XIII Plenum of E.C.C.I."   *Hoover, NYPL*

1245 KUN, Bela [and] Smolianskii, G., ed.
Profsoiuznyi vopros na XIII plenume IKKI, dekabr' 1933 g. Redaktsiia
i predislovie Bela Kuna i G. Smolianskogo. Kharkov, "Ukrainskii
robitnik", 1934. 162 p.   *NYPL*

1246 KUUSINEN, Otto
Fashizm, opasnost' voiny i zadachi kommunisticheskikh partii; doklad
na XIII plenume IKKI. Moskva, Partizdat, 1934. 95 p.   *LC, BDIC, SInSt*

1247 MANUIL'SKII, Dmitrii Z.
Revoliutsionnyi krizis, fashizm i voina; rech' na XIII plenume IKKI
5 dekabria 1933 g. Moskva, Partiinoe izd-vo, 1934. 31 p.   *Hoover*

1248 PIATNITSKII, O.
Kompartii v bor'be za massy; rech' na XIII Plenume IKKI 2-go dekabria
1933 g. Moskva, Partizdat, 1934. 80 p. (XIII plenum IKKI)   *BDIC, SInSt*

1249 WANG, Ming
Revoliutsiia, voina i interventsiia v Kitae i zadachi kompartii; rech' na
XIII plenume IKKI. Moskva, Partizdat, 1934. 77 p. At head of title:
Van Min.   *BDIC, SInSt*

1250 Der FASCHISMUS in Deutschland. Moskau, Verlagsgenossenschaft
ausländischer Arbeiter in der UdSSR, 1934. 282 p. At head of title:
XIII. Plenum des EKKI, Dezember 1933.

> Selections from speeches delivered at the Plenum.
> Contents:
> Der Faschismus in Deutschland und der Kampf des Weltproletariats. — Der
> Kampf der KPD gegen die faschistische Diktatur. — Das Gemeinsame und die
> Besonderheiten der faschistischen Diktatur in Deutschland, Polen und Italien. —

Die Auswirkungen der Errichtung der faschistischen Diktatur in Deutschland auf Österreich und die Tschechoslowakei. — Anhang: Der Faschismus und das Heranreifen der revolutionären Krise.

Hoover, LC, NYPL, Harv (all after p. 256 missing), *Duke, Princ, Yale, Felt*

1251 KNORIN, W.
Faschismus, Sozialdemokratie und Kommunisten. XIII. Plenum des EKKI; Dezember 1933. Moskau, Verlagsgenossenschaft ausländischer Arbeiter in der UdSSR, 1934. 39 p. At head of title: XIII. Plenum des EKKI, Dezember 1933. *Amst, Felt*

1252 KUUSINEN, Otto V.
Faschismus, Kriegsgefahr und die Aufgaben der kommunistischen Parteien; Referat auf dem XIII. Plenum des EKKI. Moskau-Leningrad, Verlagsgenossenschaft ausländischer Arbeiter in der UdSSR, 1934. 86 p. At head of title: XIII. Plenum des EKKI; Dezember 1933
Hoover, LC, Harv, Felt

1253 MANUIL'SKII, D. Z.
Revolutionäre Krise, Faschismus und Krieg. XIII. Plenum des EKKI; Dezember 1933. Moskau, Verlagsgenossenschaft ausländischer Arbeiter in der UdSSR, 1934. 31 p. At head of title: XIII. Plenum des EKKI. Dezember 1933. *Amst, Felt*

1254 PIATNITSKII, Osip A.
Die kommunistischen Parteien im Kampf um die Massen; Rede, gehalten am 2. XII. 1933 auf dem XIII. Plenum des EKKI. Moskau-Leningrad, Verlagsgenossenschaft ausländischer Arbeiter in der UdSSR, 1934. 74 p. At head of title: XIII. Plenum des EKKI; Dezember 1933. O. Pjatnizki. *LC, Harv, Amst, Felt*

1255 PIECK, Wilhelm
Wir kämpfen für ein Räte-Deutschland; der revolutionäre Kampf der deutschen Arbeiterklasse unter Führung der Kommunistischen Partei Deutschlands gegen die faschistische Diktatur. Bericht über die Tätigkeit der Kommunistischen Partei Deutschlands. Moskau-Leningrad, Verlagsgenossenschaft ausländischer Arbeiter in der UdSSR, 1934. 74 p. At head of title: XIII. Plenum des EKKI; Dezember 1933.
LC, NYPL, Col, Felt

1256 WANG, Ming [and Kang, Hsing]
Das revolutionäre China von heute. Moskau-Leningrad, Verlagsgenossenschaft ausländischer Arbeiter in der UdSSR, 1934. 93 p. At head of title: XIII. Plenum des EKKI / Dezember 1933. Wang Ming / Kang Hsing.

Contents: Wang Ming. Revolution und Intervention in China und die Aufgaben der Kommunistischen Partei — Hsing, Kang. Die Entwicklung der revo-

lutionären Bewegung in nicht-Rätechina und die Aufgaben der Kommunistischen Partei.   *LC, Harv, Amst, Felt*

1257 THESES, reports, speeches of the Thirteenth Plenum of the Executive
Committee of the Communist International, held in Moscow, December,
1933. [New York] Workers Library Publishers, 1934. 8 pamphlets in
1 volume. At head of title: Seventh Congress discussion.

Eight pamphlets with separate title pages and pagination each, bound in one
volume, supplied by publisher with cumulative title page as listed above.
They contain reports and speeches, as well as resolutions, theses and decisions
voted on by the Plenum. They are the English version of almost the entire
contents of the stenographic records of the Plenum published in the Russian
language (see no. 1243). The above listed volume is the *New York edition* of
the pamphlets. Some of them appeared as "second printing" with changed
pagination. They were sold as a single volume containing eight pamphlets,
and also as separate pamphlets. The particular pamphlets have on the title
page, at head of title, the following inscription: Thirteenth Plenum of the
Executive Committee of the Communist International – December, 1933.

Seven of these eight pamphlets are known also in a *Moscow edition*, published
by the Co-operative Publishing Society of Foreign Workers in the U.S.S.R.
They appeared only as separate items and are listed following this volume.

The libraries of the Department of State, Washington, D.C., and of the International Institute of Social History in Amsterdam have these pamphlets in
a *London edition* published by Modern Books, Ltd. The Library of the Department of State limited itself to indicating in the catalog card found in the
National Union Catalog "1 v. various pagings", making it impossible to
establish how many and which of the eight pamphlets of the New York
edition are included in this London edition volume. The Amsterdam library
gave a detailed contents of the volume from which it appears that it includes
all but the last (Okano) pamphlets of the New York edition. This London
edition is also listed below.

The cataloging of this unusual series produced some difficulties and several
libraries cataloged it under different titles. The title as listed above is used
by the Library of Congress and six other libraries (L.C. card no. 55–48925).
The libraries of the University of Chicago and of Princeton University use
somewhat different titles. The libraries of the Department of State and of the
International Institute of Social History in Amsterdam, both listing volumes
of the London edition, still use two other different titles. All these titles can
be easily located as parts of the material, pertaining to the 13-th Plenum or
the VII-th Congress. (See no. 970.)

The locations below are indicated first for the *entire* set of pamphlets and
later for each pamphlet separately.

Entire set of pamphlets of the New York edition:

Hoover, LC, Col, Corn, Illin, ULa, UMinn; UChic, Princ "6 v. in 1"

Individual pamphlets of the New York edition:

1258 THESES and decisions. Thirteenth Plenum of the E.C.C.I. 23 p.   (1)
Hoover, LC, Col, Corn, Illin, ULa, UMinn

1259 KUUSINEN, Otto
Fascism, the danger of war and the tasks of the communist parties.
95 p. (2)   *Hoover, LC, NYPL, Col, Corn, Illin, ULa, UMinn, Amst*

1260 PIATNITSKII, O.
The communist parties in the fight for the masses. 95 p. (3)
          Hoover, LC, NYPL, Harv, Col, Corn, Illin, ULa, UMinn

1261 MANUIL'SKII, D. Z.
Revolutionary crisis, fascism and war. 31 p. (4)
          Hoover, LC, Col, Corn, Illin, ULa, UMinn

1262 KNORIN, V.
Fascism, social-democracy and the communists. 47 p. (5)
          Hoover, LC, NYPL, Harv, Col, Illin, ULa, UMinn

1263 PIECK, W.
We are fighting for a Soviet Germany. 95 p. (6)
          Hoover, LC, NYPL, Col, Corn, Illin, ULa, UMinn

1264 WANG, Ming, and Kang, Sin
Revolutionary China today. 95 p. (7)
          Hoover, LC, Col, Corn, Illin, ULa, UMinn, Felt

1265 OKANO, S.
Revolutionary struggle of the toiling masses of Japan. 31 p. (8)
          Hoover, LC, Harv, Col, Corn, Illin, ULa, UMinn, Amst

Moscow edition:

All pamphlets have at head of title: Thirteenth Plenum of the Executive Committee of the Communist International — December 1933. All are published by Co-operative Publishing Society of Foreign Workers in the U.S.S.R. in Moscow in 1934.

1266 THESES and decisions, Thirteenth Plenum of ECCI. 31 p. (1)
          Hoover, NYPL, UTex, Amst, Felt

1267 KUUSINEN, O. W.
Fascism, the danger of war and the tasks of the communist parties;
report by O. W. Kuusinen. 120 p. (2)   *Carn*

1268 PIATNITSKII, O. A.
The communist parties in the fight for the masses; speech by O. Pyatnitsky. 98 p. (3)   *NYPL*

1269 MANUIL'SKII, D. Z.
Revolutionary crisis, fascism and war; speech by D. Z. Manuilsky. (4)
NYPL

1270 KNORIN, V. G.
Fascism, social-democracy and the Communists; speech by V. Knorin.
52 p. (5) *NYPL*

1271 PIECK, W.
We are fighting for a soviet Germany; report by Wilhelm Pieck.
99 p. (6) *NYPL*

1272 WANG, Ming, and Kang, Sin
Revolutionary China today; speeches by Wang Ming and **Kang Sin.**
126 p. (7) *LC, NYPL*

London edition:

The items were unavailable for more detailed identification.

1273 THESES and decisions of the thirteenth plenum of the E. C. C. I. London,
Modern Books Ltd. [1934?] 1 v. various pagings. (Analytical listing
missing.) *DState*

1274 THIRTEENTH Plenum of the E. C. C. I.; theses and decisions. London,
Modern Books [n. d.] 32 p.

> This entry is followed by an enumeration of items belonging to this series;
> they include pamphlets corresponding to items 2–7 of the New York edition.
> Pagination identical with items of Moscow edition. *Amst*

Other languages

1275 KNORIN, V.
Le Fascisme, la Social-Démocratie et les Communistes. Paris, Bureau
d'Editions, 1934. 54 p. "Discours prononcé à la XIIIe Assemblée
plénière du C. E. de l'I. C. (décembre 1933)." *Felt*

1276 KOSTANIAN, G.
La maturation de la crise révolutionnaire et les tâches des sections
de l'I. S. R. Discours prononcé à la XIIIe Session plénière du C. E. de
l'I. C. Paris, C. D. L. P. [1934] 64 p. (Petite Bibliothèque de l'Internationale Syndicale Rouge.) *BDIC*

1277 LOZOVSKII, A.
Luttons pour la majorité de la classe ouvrière; discours prononcé
au XIIIe plenum de l'Exécutif de l'I. C. le 7 décembre 1933 [par
A. Losowsky. Paris, Impr. centrale de la Bourse, 1933] 31 p. (Petite
Bibliothèque de l'Internationale Syndicale Rouge [41])   *Hoover*

1278 MANUIL'SKII, D. Z.
La crise révolutionaire, le fascisme et la guerre. Paris, Bureau d'Editions, 1934. 36 [?] p. (Les Documents de l'Internationale)   *BDIC*

1279 PIATNITSKII, Osip
Les Partis communistes en lutte pour la conquête des masses. Paris,
Bureau d'Editions, 1934. 98 p. couv. illus. (Les Documents de l'Internationale. Discours prononcé à la XIIIe assemblée plénière du C. E.
de l'I. C.)   *Hoover, BDIC*

1281 WANG, Ming, [and] Okano
Sovětská revoluce v Číně. Praha, Nákladem senátora F. Nedvěda
[1933] 51 p. At head of title: Wan Min.

> Speech at XIII-th Plenum of ECCI. Contains also: Okano. Jak bojují japonští
> komunisté proti válce. p. 37–39.   *NYPL*

1283 KOMUNISTYCZNA Partja Polski.
KPP w walce z wojną, faszyzmem i atakiem kapitału. XIII plenum
Komitetu Wykonawczego Międzynarodówki Komunistycznej. Moskwa,
Wydawnictwo partyjne, 1934. 34 p.   *Hoover, NYPL*

1284 KNORIN, W.
Fascismen, socaildemokratin och kommunisterna. Stockholm, 1934.
46 p.   *SInSt*

c) Resolutions, theses, manifestoes and other documents

1285 XIII [TRINADTSATYI] plenum IKKI. Tezisy i postanovleniia. Moskva,
Partiinoe izd-vo, 1934. 32 p.   *Hoover, Amst, BDIC, SInSt*

1286 XIII. [DREIZEHNTES] Plenum des Exekutivkomitees der Kommunistischen Internationale, Dezember 1933: Thesen und Beschlüsse. [Stras-
bourg] Prometheus Verlag, 1933. 23 p.   *LC, Amst, Felt*

1287 THESEN und Beschlüsse. XIII. Plenum des Exekutivkomitees der Kommunistischen Internationale. Moskau, Verlagsgenossenschaft ausländischer Arbeiter in der UdSSR, 1934. 26 p.   *Amst, Felt*

1288 THESEN und Beschlüsse. XIII Plenum des Exekutivkomitees der Kommunistischen Internationale Dezember 1933. [Strasbourg] Prometheus Verlag, 1933. 24 p.   *Amst*

1289 THESEN und Beschlüsse, XIII. Plenum. [München?] 1933.

> This item at Harvard seems to be erroneously catalogued. Lack of number of pages made identification impossible. Probably Strasbourg edition. See preceding item.   *Harv*

1290 EVE of revolutions and wars; resolution of the 13th plenum of the Communist International. [Sydney] Modern Publishers [193-] 8 l. Cover-title.   *NYPL*

1291 THESES and decisions. Thirteenth plenum of the E.C.C.I. New York City, Workers Library Publishers, March, 1934. 23 p. At head of title: 13th Plenum of the Executive committee of the Communist International—December, 1933. "Second printing."

> This is a "second printing" of the item in the New York edition of *Theses and decisions,* listed above under no. 1258.   *Harv, Duke*

THESES and decisions of the thirteenth Plenum of the E.C.C.I. London edition. See no. 1273 and 1274.

THESES and decisions, Thirteenth Plenum of ECCI. Moscow edition. See no. 1266.

1292 THESES and decisions, thirteenth Plenum of the E.C.C.I. Draft resolution, eighth convention of the C.P., U.S.A. New York City, Workers Library Publishers, 1934. 47 p. At head of title: Thirteenth plenum of the Executive committee of the Communist International, December, 1933.   *LC, NYPL, Col, UTex, Yale*

1293 Le FASCISME, le danger de guerre et les tâches des parties communistes. Paris, Bureau d'Editions, 1934. 31 p.

> "Thèses adoptées par la XIIIe Assemblée plénière du C.E. de l'I.C. sur le rapport du camarade Kuusinen."   *Hoover, Felt*

1293a Il FASCISMO, il pericolo di guerra e i compiti dei partiti comunisti. (Tesi, risoluzioni e decisioni della XIII Sessione plenaria del Comitato esecutivo dell'I. C.) (Dicembre 1933). Bruxelles, Edizioni di Coltura Sociale, 1934. 32 p. (Documenti della Internazionale.)   *Felt*

d) Commentaries about the Plenum

1294 KOMPARTII v bor'be za zavoevanie molodezhi. XIII plenum IKKI o rabote sredi molodezhi. Moskva, Partizdat, 1934. 127 p.

> A collection of excerpts from Kuusinen's report on the subject and 11 speeches during the discussion.   *Hoover, LC, Harv, Col, UChic*

1295 LINDEROT, Sven
Komintern visar vägen. Kommunistiska Internatonalens XIII Plenum och Kommunistiska Partiets uppgifter. Stockholm, 1934. 32 p.   *SInSt*

26. Presidium of the E. C. C. I., February, 1934.

1296 SCHÖNAU, Alexander
The February insurrection of the Austrian proletariat. With an appeal signed by the E. C. C. I., the E. B. of the R. I. L. U. and the E. C. of the Y. C. I. Moscow, Cooperative Pub. Society of Foreign Workers in the U. S. S. R., 1934. 74 p.   *Hoover*

27. Executive Committee (unnumbered)
November 6, 1939

DIMITROV, G.
Communism and the war, by G. Dimitrov. Together with the Manifesto of the Executive Committee of the Communist International, issued November 6-th, 1939. See no. 235.

C. Appeals for support of Comintern aims

(Listed in chronological order)

1919

1297 DA ZDRAVSTVUET pervoe maia. Da zdravstvuet kommunizm! Moskva, Izd-vo Kommunisticheskogo Internatsionala, 1919. 16 p. *Hoover, BDIC*

1298 Da ZDRAVSTVUET pervoe maia! Da zdravstvuet kommunizm! Petrograd, Izd-vo Petrogradskogo soveta rabochikh i krasnoarmeiskikh deputatov, 1919. 15 p. *LC, BDIC*

Ein AUFRUF der Kommunistischen Internationalen zum Frieden von Versailles. [Signed by chairman of E.C.C.E. Zinovev, dated: May 13, 1919.] Contained in *Die Kommunisten und der Friede* — see no. 1346.

1299 ON whose side are you? Workers' or Capitalists'? [Leaflet, single page.] Published by the Executive Committee of the Communist International. [n. p., 1919?] *Hoover*

1300 SAY! what are you? Leaflet. Published by the Executive Committee of the Communist International. [Folded to make 8 p.] [n. p., 1919?] *Hoover, NYPL, Amst*

Note: For the Manifesto of the Ist Congress of the Communist International to the workers of the world, see resolutions of this Congress, items nos. 507, 508, 512–516, 518–523, 526, 527, 531, 533, 534.

1920

1301 AUFRUFE des Exekutivkomitees der Kommunistischen Internationale zur polnischen Frage. Berlin, Westeuropäisches Sekretariat der Kommunistischen Internationale, 1920. 15 p. *Hoover, Harv, Col, Amst, Felt*

1302 AUFRUFE des Exekutivkomitees der Kommunistischen Internationale zur polnischen Frage. Moskau, Exekutivkomitee der III. Internationale, 1920. 15 p. *NYPL, Amst*

Der ZWEITE Weltkongreß der Kommunsitischen Internationale an das französische Proletariat; zur Frage des Anschlusses an die Kommunistische Internationale. See no. 608.

1303 The THIRD International to the workers of all countries concerning the Polish question. Moscow, Executive Committee of the III. International, 1920. 14 p. *Hoover, NYPL, Col, UPenn, Amst*

> **Note:** For the Manifesto of the IInd Congress of the Communist International, see the resolutions of this Congress, nos. 592, 593, 598–601, 610, 611, 614, 626–629, 636, 638–640, 644.

1921

1304 AUFRUF des Exekutivkomitees der Kommunistischen Internationale an die Proletarier aller Länder. n. p. [Hamburg?] Kommunistische Internationale, 1921. 10 p. (Flugschriften der Kommunistischen Internationale, 1.) *Amst, Felt*

1305 Die INTERNATIONALE kommunistische Werbewoche vom 3. bis 10. Nov. 1921. Schreiben des Exekutivkomitees der Kommunistischen Internationale. [n. p.], Kommunistische Internationale, 1921. 19 p. (Flugschriften der Kommunistischen Internationale, 8.) *Amst, Felt*

GO to the masses! A manifesto of the third congress of the Third International, also the withdrawal statement of the committee for the Third International of the Socialist party to the members of the Socialist party. See no. 704.

THESES et résolutions. Adoptées au III-ème congrès de l'Internationale communiste. [Contains a manifesto of the ECCI entitled: Towards new work, towards new struggles; To the proletariat of the entire world, to men and women] See no. 707.

1306 OPROEP van de Communistische Internationale, aan de arbeiders van de gehelen wereld. [n. p., 1921?] 8 p. *Amst*

1307 A NUOVO lavoro, a nuove lotte! Appello del C.E. dell'I.C. ai proletari di tutto il mondo; Mosca 12 luglio 1921. Roma, Libr. Editrice del Partito Comunista d'Italia, 1921. 14 p. (Piccola biblioteca dell'I.C., I.) *Felt*

1922

Die PROLETARISCHE Einheitsfront. Aufruf der Exekutive der Kommunistischen Internationale und der Exekutive der Roten Gewerkschaftsinternationale Moskau, 1. January 1922. Leitsätze über die Einheitsfront. See no. 1032.

1924

1308 MANIFEST Kominterna k mirovomu proletariatu. [Moskva] 1924.
xviii p. [Enclosure to *Voennaia mysl' i revoliutsiia*]

> Russian title in BDIC catalog card is incomplete. The French translation of the
> title is more complete: Manifeste de l'Internationale Communiste au proletariat
> mondial, à l'occasion du Xe anniversaire de la guerre imperialiste. See also
> no. 795. *Yale, BDIC*

1309 GEGEN den Krieg! Gegen die Bourgeoisie! Gegen die Sozialverräte-
rei! Für die Weltrevolution! Für die Diktatur des Proletariats! Für den
Kommunismus! Zum 10. Jahrestag des imperialistischen Krieges. Berlin,
Vereinigung Internationaler Verlagsanstalten, 1924. 23 p.

> The E.C.C.I. initiated, and the V-th Congress ordered world-wide demon-
> strations by communists against "counter-revolutionary war" and a "week
> of hate" towards the bourgeoisie and the social-democrats. See nos. 795 and
> item above. *Amst, Felt*

1935

NIEDER mit dem Krieg! [an appeal of October 7, 1935 under this
title, signed by E.C.C.I., is contained in pamphlet *Nieder mit dem
Krieg* — see no. 1597]

1938

MANIFESTO of the Executive Committee of the Communist International, November 7, 1938. (Addition to Dimitrov, G.: *After Munich...*
and *Dopo Monaco...* See nos. 1530, 1532.)

1310 MANIFEST del Comite Executiu de la Internacional Comunista en el
XXI anniversari de la gran revolució socialista. Després del complot
de Munic: Front unic contra el feixisme, per Jordi Dimitrov. [n. p.,
Agitació i propaganda del P.S.U. 1938?] 39 p. (Article publicat a
"Pravda" del Moscou el 7 novembre 1938.) *Amst*

L'APPELLO della Internazionale Communista per il 1 Maggio 1938;
in Dimitrov, G., *Il pegno della vittoria*. See no. 1546.

1939

MANIFESTO issued by the Executive Committee of the Communist International on the twenty-second anniversary of the socialist revolution, November 6, 1939. Contained in G. Dimitrov, *Communism and the war;* see no. 235.

1942

1311 HITLER puede y tiene que ser derrotado en 1942. Llamamiento a los trabajadores de todo el mundo en el primero de mayo. La Habana, 1942. 14 p.

"Published in Moscow for the periodical "The Communist International" on occasion of the first of May." *NYPL*

271

PART IV.

THE COMINTERN IN ACTION

COMINTERN ACTIONS IN THE WORLD

A. General

INTERNATIONAL Anti-Communist Entente.
Charts representing the Soviet organizations working for revolution in all countries (with explanatory notes). See no. 481.

1312 INTERNATIONAL Anti-Communist Entente.
A New World War; "The Bolshevist War"; published on the occasion of the sixth Conference of the International Council of the International Entente Against the Third International. Geneva, October 1929. 64 p. illus.

> The pamphlet attempts to expose contemporary Soviet political maneuverings, undertaken with the Comintern's help, as "a war of a new kind" (p. 8). The Soviet fear of a "capitalist" conspiracy and war against the Soviet Union produced the peculiar Comintern anti-war propaganda, with the Soviet government simultaneously supporting every rebellion and revolutionary movement disturbing peace and order. A short survey of communist internal influences in, and Soviet external relations with over 30 countries concludes the pamphlet.
> *Hoover*

INTERNATIONAL Anti-Communist Entente.
Organization and activities of the Communist International. English Edition. See no. 482.

INTERNATIONAL Anti-Communist Entente.
The Red Network; the Communist International at work. See no. 483.

INTERNATIONAL Anti-Communist Entente.
Tableaux des organisations soviétiques, travaillant à la révolution dans tous les pays. See no. 484.

1313 KOMMUNISTY zagranitsei. Paris, Respubl.-demokrat. biblioteka, 1929. 32 p. On thin paper.

> An account of the activities of the communist parties in various countries in 1928–29 and the role of the Comintern in these activities by the Russian emigré Constitutional-Democratic Party.   *BDIC*

1314 PIATNITSKII, O. A.
Die kommunistischen Parteien in Aktion. Die Konsolidierung der kommunistischen Parteien und die Ursachen der ungenügenden Verankerung des wachsenden politischen Einflusses der K. I. — Sektionen. Hamburg, Hoym [1930] 47 p. tables. Damaged. At head of title: O. Pjatnizki.   *Amst*

1315 PIATNITSKII, O. A.
Le Monde Communiste en Action. Paris, Bureau d'Editions, 1930. 69 p.
                                                                                                          Hoover, Felt

1316 PIATNITSKII, O. A.
World communists in action; the consolidation of the Communist parties and why the growing political influence of the sections of the Comintern is not sufficiently maintained. New York, Workers Library Publishers [1932] 64 p.   *Hoover*

YPSILON
Pattern for World Revolution, and its French translation: Stalintern — See no. 384 and no. 385.

B. Asia

1. General

1317 BRIMMEL, J. H.
Communism in South-East Asia. A political analysis. Issued under the auspices of the Royal Institute of International Affairs. London, Oxford Univ. Press, 1959. 415 p. *Hoover, Felt*

1318 GHAMBASHIDZE, David
Comintern in Asia. Berlin, "Der Neue Orient", c1939. 63 p. illus, map. *NYPL*

1319 HURWICZ, Elias [Gurvich, Il'ia]
Die Orientpolitik der dritten Internationale; an Hand authentischer Quellen dargestellt. Berlin, Deutsche Verlagsgesellschaft für Politik und Geschichte, 1922. 100 p. *Hoover, NYPL, Amst, Felt*

1320 MARTIN, Paul
De quoi comprendre les événements d'Extrême-Orient, les menées du Komintern. Paris, Editions Baudinière [1937] 22 p. fold. map. *Hoover*

PROGRAMMNYE dokumenty kommunisticheskikh partii Vostoka. See no. 131.

1321 PROSTOI, Michel
Tempête d'Asie. Paris, Editions Liberté, 1948. 386 p. *Hoover, Felt*

The REVOLUTIONARY movement in the colonies; theses adopted by the Sixth World Congress of the Communist International. See nos. 862—864.

WANG, Ming
Le front unique dans les pays coloniaux. See no. 985.

WANG, Ming
Im Zeichen der chinesischen Sowjets; die revolutionäre Bewegung in den kolonialen und halbkolonialen Ländern und die Taktik der kommunistischen Parteien. See no. 940.

274

WANG, Ming
Die revolutionäre Bewegung in den kolonialen und halbkolonialen Ländern und die Taktik der kommunistischen Parteien. See no. 939.

WANG, Ming
The revolutionary movement in the colonial countries; report... See nos. 968—9, 969—12, 974, 975.

2. China

1322 AIKHENVALD, A.
O takticheskoi linii Kominterna v Kitae. Moskva, Leningrad, Gos. izd-vo, 1927. 47 p.   *Hoover*

1323 BENNET, A.
Die Kriegsgefahr, die chinesische Revolution und die Kommunistische Internationale. Hamburg, Hoym [1927] 46 p. bibliography.   *Amst*

BUBER-NEUMANN, Margarethe [pseud. of Faust, Margarethe Anna]
Von Potsdam nach Moskau. Stationen eines Irrweges. See no. 179a.

1324 CHINA at Bay [special supplement to *The Communist International*. London, Modern Books, 1936] 79 p. map.   *Hoover*

CHINA in revolt. Speeches at the 7-th Plenum. See no. 1113.

Die CHINESISCHE Frage auf dem 8. Plenum der Exekutive der Kommunistischen Internationale, Mai 1927. See no. 1120.

IKKI i VKP(b) po kitaiskomu voprosu (osnovnye resheniia). See no. 107.

1325 ISAACS, Harold R.
The tragedy of the Chinese revolution. [Revised edition] Stanford, Calif., Stanford University Press [1951] xiii, 382 p. bibliography, index.

> "This book is a history of the defeat of the Chinese revolution of 1925–27. It examines the first intervention of the Soviet Union in China and its consequences." (Preface, p. vii.) As this Soviet intervention was accomplished through agents of the Comintern (Michael Borodin, Heinz Neumann, and others), the volume contains many well documented references to their activities.   *Hoover, LC, NYPL, Harv, Col*

Der KAMPF um die Kommunistische Internationale; Dokumente der russischen Opposition nicht veröffentlicht vom Stalin'schen ZK. See no. 113.

KOMINTERN i VKP(b) o kitaiskoi revoliutsii. Osnovnye resheniia. See no. 115.

1326 LOZOVSKII, A.
Revoliutsiia i kontr-revoliutsiia v Kitae. Moskva, "Moskovskii Rabochii", 1927, 172 p. *Hoover*

1327 LOZOVSKII, A.
Revolution und Konter-Revolution in China. Moskau, Rote Gewerkschafts-Internationale, Auslieferung durch Führer-Verlag, Berlin, 1928. 79 p. *Hoover*

1328 [NAZONOV, N.]
La lettre de Shanghai; document inédit caché par Staline [par N. Nazonof, N. Forkine, A. Albrecht] Paris, l'Unité leniniste [1927?] vii, 24 p. At head of title: L'opposition leniniste. La vérité sur la Chine.

"La lettre de Shanghai... fut expediée, le 17 mars 1927, par la délégation russe envoyée en Chine par Staline lui-même." Pref., signed Albert Treint. See also no. 1335. *Hoover*

1329 NORTH, Robert C.
Moscow and Chinese Communists. Stanford, Stanford University Press, 1952 ix, 306 p. (Hoover Institute Studies.)

A 2-nd edition of this item appeared in 1963. *Hoover, LC, NYPL*

1330 NORTH, Robert C. and Eudin, Xenia J.
M. N. Roy's mission to China; the Communist-Kuomintang split of 1927. Documents translated by Helen J. Powers. Berkeley, University of California Press, 1963. vi, 399 p. bibliography.

Hoover, LC, NYPL, UCal

1331 POKROVSKII, S.
Voprosy kitaiskoi revoliutsii. Leningrad, "Priboi" [1927] 95 p. *Hoover*

1332 ROY, M. N.
Kitaiskaia revoliutsiia i Kommunisticheskii Internatsional; sbornik statei i materialov. Moskva-Leningrad, Gos. izd-vo, 1929. 207 p. *Hoover*

1332a
1332b } ROY, M. N. (for two Roy items see Addendum p. 462.)

SOVIET plot in China. See no. 137.

STALIN, J.
Revoliutsiia v Kitae i oshibki oppozitsii. See no. 1119.

STRATEGIIA i taktika Kominterna v natsional'no-kolonial'noi revoliutsii na primere Kitaia. See no. 138.

TAN, Ping-shan
Entwiąlungswege der chinesischen Revolution, mit einem Vorwort von K. A. Wittfogel und einem Nachwort von Raskolnikow [pseud.]. See no. 1111.

1333 VOPROSY kitaiskoi revoliutsii. Leningrad, Gos. izd-vo, 1927. 239 p.
Hoover

WANG, Ming
Revolutsiia, voina i interventsiia v Kitae i zadachi kompartii; rech' na XIII plenume IKKI. See no. 1249.

WANG, Ming, [and Kang, Hsing]
Das revolutionäre China von heute. See no. 1256.

WANG, Ming, and Kang, Sin
Revolutionary China today. See nos. 1264, 1272.

WANG, Ming [and Okano]
Sovětská revoluce v Číne. See no. 1281.

1334 WHITING, Allen Suess
Soviet policies in China, 1917—1924. New York, Columbia University Press, 1954. [c1953] x, 350 p. (Studies of the Russian Institute of Columbia University) Bibliography: p. [327]—337.   *Hoover, Col*

1335 WIE die chinesische Revolution zugrunde gerichtet wurde; Brief aus Schanghai gerichtet an das Exekutiv-komitee der Kommunistischen Internationale, von Stalin unterschlagen. [Berlin] Verlag der „Fahne des Kommunismus" [1927] 32 p. (On cover: Flugschriften des Verlages „Fahne des Kommunismus") „Herausgeber und verantwortl. Hugo Urbahns."

See also no. 1328.   *Hoover, Harv, Amst, Felt*

WILBUR, C. Martin and How, Julie-Lien-ying, editors.
Documents on Communism, Nationalism, and Soviet Advisers in China, 1918—1927. See no. 143.

1336 WOO, Dick Chong
The Communist International and the revolution in China. [Stanford, Calif.] 1939. iii, 185 leaves. Thesis (M. A.) Stanford University, 1939. Typewritten. Bibliography: 179—185.   *Hoover*

3. India

WINT, Guy
Communism in India. In *International Communism*. See no. 243.

4. Japan

1337 IAPONIIA na russkom Dal'nem Vostoke. Krovavaia epopeia iaponskoi interventsii. (Sostavleno Dal'nevostochnym otdelom I. K. K. I.) Moskva, TS. K. R. K. P., 1922. 72 p.   *Hoover, NYPL*

OKANO, S.
Revolutionary struggle of the toiling masses of Japan. See nos. 970—8, 1265.

OKANO, S. and others.
Kommunisticheskaia partiia Iaponii protiv rezhima voiny, goloda bespraviia; rechi tt. Okano [Tanaka, i Nisikawa]. See no. 905.

5. Manchukuo

1338 The COMINTERN'S activity in Manchuria; a general survey. Hsinking, Manchoukuo, The Manchuria Daily News, 1940. 49 p.   *LC, Harv*

1339 GROZA, B.
Podzhigateli mirovoi revoliutsii za rabotoi. (Zagranichnaia rabota GPU) Harbin,Izd-vo "Nash put'", 1937. iv, 203 p. On cover: Shchupaltsy krasnogo Kominterna.

   Deals with activities of the GPU and Comintern in Manchuria.   *BDIC*

1340 HIDAKA, Noboru, comp.
The Comintern's intrigues in Manchoukuo. [Dairen?] The Manchuria Daily News, 1940. 64 p.   *Hoover, NYPL*

C. Australia

1341 SHARKEY, Laurence, and Kuusinen, O.
History of the Communist Party of Australia; from a lecture by
L. Sharkey. Twenty Years of the Communist International, by O.
Kuusinen. [Sydney?] 1942. 30 p.   *NYPL*

1342 SHARKEY, Laurence, and Kuusinen, O.
An outline history of the Australian Communist Party, by L. L. Sharkey.
Twenty Years of the Communist International, by O. Kuusinen. Sydney,
Australian Communist Party, 1944. 83 p. At head of title: A Marx
School publication.   *LC, Harv*

D. Europe

1. General

BORKENAU, Franz
The Communist International. See no. 212. For other editions see nos.
218, 219.

BORKENAU, Franz
European Communism. See no. 215. For other editions and translations see no. 213, 214, 216, 217.

1343 KABAKCHIEV, Khristo S. and others.
Kommunisticheskie partii Balkanskikh stran. Predisl. V. Kolarova.
Moskva, Gosizdat RSFSR, Moskovskii rabochii, 1930. 239 p. ("Kom-
partii vsekh stran"). At head of title: Khr. Kabakchiev, B. Boshkovich,
Kh. D. Vatis.

> Discusses the Bulgarian, Yugoslav and Greek communist parties and the
> Balkan Communist Federation.   *Hoover*

KRIVITSKY, Walter G.
In Stalin's Secret Service; an exposé of Russia's secret policies by the former chief of the Soviet intelligence in Western Europe. See no. 196.

KRIVITSKY, Walter G.
Agent de Staline. See no. 197.

1344 LAZITCH, Branko
Les partis communistes d'Europe; 1919—1955. Paris, Les Iles d'Or, [1956] 255 p. *Felt*

PANNEKOEK, Anton
Die Westeuropäische Politik der 3. Internationale. See no. 315.

2. Austria

1345 Der ERSTE Mai der Kommunistischen Internationale. Wien, Kommunistische Partei Deutschösterreichs, 1919. 16 p. *Hoover*

1346 Die KOMMUNISTEN und der Friede. Aufruf der Kommunistischen Internationale. Die Versklavung Deutschösterreichs, von Karl Frank. Der Friede für das deutsche Volk, von Otto Ruhle. Wien, Kommunistische Partei Deutschösterreichs [1919?] 32 p. *Hoover, BDIC*

KOPELING, and others.
Kommunisticheskaia partiia Avstrii v bor'be za massu; rechi tt. Kopelinge i dr. See no. 902.

1347 MANUIL'SKII, D. Z.
Der Scheideweg. Faschismus oder Sozialismus Manuilski antwortet Otto Bauer. Hrsg. von der Kommunistischen Partei Österreichs. [Hamburg, Hoym, 1933] 32 p. Sonderdr.: *Rote Fahne*. *Amst*

1348 MANUIL'SKII, D. Z.
Social-Democracy — Stepping-Stone to Fascism, or Otto Bauer's latest discovery. [New York City, Workers Library Publishers, March 1934] 63 p. Cover title.

Contents: Social-Democracy – Stepping Stone to Fascism by D. Z. Manuilskii. – Resolution of Presidium, E.C.C.I., on situation in Germany (April 1st, 1933).

The Fascization of Social-Democracy and the Crisis in the Second International (From the report of comrade Kuusinen to the Thirteenth Plenum of the E.C.C.I.) The first item in this pamphlet is the text of an address delivered by Manuilskii late in 1932 or early 1933, and printed a year later. It accuses Austrian Socialists and their leaders of conduct detrimental to the workers.

Hoover

SCHÖNAU, Alexander
The February insurrection of the Austrian proletariat. See no. 1296.

3. Belgium

1349 LETTRE du C.E. de l'I.C. aux membres du P.C.B. A tous les membres du P.C.B. [n. p., 1928] 8vo, one sheet. *Felt*

1350 PARTI communiste Internationaliste [Belgium]
Que veut l'opposition du Parti bolchevik russe? Que veut le Groupe d'opposition du Parti communiste bèlge? [Bruxelles] Éditions du Groupe de l'opposition du P.C.B. [194-?] 32 p. *Hoover, Felt*

4. Bulgaria

KABAKCHIEV, Khristo and others.
Kommunisticheskie partii Balkanskikh stran. See no. 1343.

5. Czechoslovakia

GOTTWALD, Klement
Kompartiia Chekhoslovakii v bor'be za edinyi front. See no. 900.

KOMMUNISTICHESKAIA partiia Chekhoslovakii v bor'be za edinyi front — protiv voiny i fashizma; rechi tt. Gotval'da, Shvermy, Slanskego, Kellera, Zapototskogo, delegatov chekhoslovatskoi kompartii. See No. 903.

1351 KREIBICH, Karl
Die Weltkrise des Kapitalismus und die Kommunistische Internationale. Das Referat des Genossen Karl Kreibich und die Resolution. 2. Auflage. Reichenberg, Runge & Co., 1921. 46 p. At head of title: Der Reichenbacher Parteitag, 1921.   *NYPL*

MANUIL'SKII, D.
Pravoe krylo Kominterna i krizis chekho-slovatskoi partii. Rech' na plenume I.K.K.I. See no. 1067.

MANUIL'SKII, D.
Uroki cheshskogo krizisa. See no. 1081.

NAŠE delegace v Moskvě. Řeči delegátů komunistické strany Československa na VII. světovém kongresu Komunistické Internacionály v Moskvě. [S účast. K. Gottwalda, J. Švermy, R. Slanského, i dr.] See no. 991.

6. Finland

1352 KUUSINEN, O. W.
The Finnish revolution: a self-criticism. London, Workers' Socialist Federation, 1919. 30 p.   *Hoover*

1353 KUUSINEN, O. W.
Revoliutsiia v Finliandii; samokritika. Petrograd, Kommunisticheskii Internatsional, 1919. 64 p.   *Hoover*

1354 KUUSINEN, O. W.
La révolution en Finlande. Moscou, Editions de l'Internationale Communiste, 1920. ? p.   *NYPL*

1355 KUUSINEN, O. W.
Die Revolution in Finnland. Kommunistische Internationale, Hamburg, Hoym, 1921. 41 p. (Bibliothek der Kommunistischen Internationale, 15.)
                   Hoover, Amst

7. France

1356 BARDOUX, Jacques
J'accuse Moscou... [Paris] Flammarion [1936] 45 p.   *LC, NYPL, SInSt*

1357 BOUGERE, Emile
Histoire du Parti communiste français. Paris, Dompol [1940?] 28 p.
Hoover

CACHIN, Marcel
The fight for the people's front in France; [speech...] See nos. 941, 968—10.

CACHIN, Marcel
Kompartiia Frantsii vysoko derzhit boevoe znamia kommunizma. 27 iiulia 1935 g. See no. 895.

1358 CACHIN, Marcel
Protiv klevety na Sovetskii Soiuz; rech' vo frantsuzskom parlamente 24 dekabria 1929 goda. Moskva [etc.] Gos. izd-vo, 1930. 30 p. 1 illus., part. At head of title: Marsel Kashen.   *Hoover*

1359 CACHIN, Marcel
Zamysly frantsuzskikh imperialistov protiv SSSR (rech' kommunisti-cheskogo deputata vo frantsuzskoi palate deputatov 4 dekabria 1929 g.) Moskva-Leningrad, Gos. izd-vo, 1928. 45 p. At head of title: M. Kashen.   *Hoover*

CACHIN, Marcel and others.
El frente popular contra el fascismo y la guerra en Francia. [Speeches by Cachin, M. Thorez and A. Marty at VII-th Congress] See no. 1012.

CACHIN, Marcel and Thorez, Maurice
Du front unique au front populaire; deux discours. See no. 976.

CACHIN, Marcel and others.
The people's front in France; speeches delivered by Marcel Cachin, Maurice Thorez, André Marty [at VII-th Congress]. See nos. 942, 969—8.

1360 CHAZOFF, Jacques
La C. G. T., colonie soviétique... Paris, Les Editions de France, 1939. vii, 130 p.   *Hoover*

CLASSE contre classe; la question française au IX-e Exécutif et au VI-e Congrès de l'I. C. See no. 830.

1361 COMITÉ de la 3-e Internationale.
La résolution d'adhésion à la 3-e Internationale. [Paris, Impr. G. Dangon, 1920] 8 p.

I-er programme du Parti Communiste Français. Resumé des thèses adoptées par le 2-e congrès de l'I. C. à Moscou et leur adaptation à la situation en France. *BDIC*

1362 COMPÈRE-MOREL, Adeodat
Socialisme et bolchévisme; pourquoi nous n'avons pas adhéré à l'Interntionale dite Communiste des bolchévistes russes. Paris Librairie populaire, 1921. 24 p. On cover: Edition du parti socialiste (S. F. I. O.)
Hoover

1363 DINGLE, Reginald J.
Russia's work in France. London, R. Hale, 1938. 278 p. illus., ports.
Hoover, LC, NYPL

Les DOCUMENTS de l'opposition française et la réponse du parti. See no. 101.

1364 FEDERATION des Syndicats des membres d'Enseignement laique de France, des colonies et protectorats. L'Adhesion à la 3-e Internationale. Brochure de propagande contenant les thèses exposées au Congrès Fédéral de Tours pour et contre l'Adhésion. Marseilles, Coopérative d'Edition et de Librairie de la Fédération. 29 p.
Hoover

1365 FERRAT, A.
Histoire du Parti Communiste Français. Paris, Bureau d'Editions, 1931. 259 p. ("Bibliothèque du Mouvement Ouvrier.") *Hoover*

1366 FRACHON, Benoit, ed.
Les communistes et les syndicats; introduc. de Benoit Frachon. Le travail des fractions syndicales. Résolution du C. E. élargi de l'I. C. Résolution du VII-e congrès du P. F. C. Paris, Bureau d'éditions, 1932. 64 p. (Les documents du Parti communiste (S. F. I. C.)) *Hoover*

1367 FREVILLE, Jean
Né du feu; de la fallité de la II-e Internationale au congrès de Tours. Paris, Editions sociales [1960] 212 p. *Col*

FROSSARD, Ludovic O.
De Jaurès à Lenin; notes et souvenirs d'un militant. See no. 192.

1368 FROSSARD, Ludovic O.
Pour la III-e Internationale. Discours prononcé au XVIII-e Congrès
national du Parti Socialiste, tenu à Tours, du 25 au 30 septembre
1920. Paris, 51 p.   *BDIC*

FROSSARD, Ludovic O.
Le Parti Socialiste et l'Internationale. Rapport sur les négotiations
conduites à Moscou. Suivi de thèses, présentées au 2-e Congrès de
l'Internationale Communiste. See no. 586.

1369 GIRAULT, Ernest
Pourquoi les Anarchistes-Communistes français ont rallié la III-e Internationale. Paris, Librairie de l'Humanité, 1926. 62 p.   *NYPL, Felt*

1370 GUILBEAUX, Henri
La fin des soviets; les soviets partout. Paris. Societé française d'éditions litteraires et techniques, Edgar Malfere, directeur, 1937. 185 p.
                                                                   Hoover

1371 [HERBETTE, Jean]
Ein französischer Diplomat über die bolschewistische Gefahr; Berichte
des Botschafters der französischen Republik in Moskau Jean Herbette
aus den Jahren 1927 bis 1931. Berlin, Deutscher Verlag [c1943] 177 p.
On cover: Die Entstehung des Krieges von 1939; Geheimdokumente
aus europäischen Archiven; herausgegeben von der Archivkommission
des Auswärtigen Amtes; zweite Schrift.

> Reports of the French Ambassador in Moscow, captured and published by
> German authorities during World War II. The reports include information
> on activities of the Communist International and Red International of Trade
> Unions, particularly as referring to France and French affairs. Enclosures
> contain translations of excerpts of various Soviet sources. The volume was
> prepared and edited by Professor Dr. Werner Frauendienst. This information
> results from an autographed copy in possession of W. S. Sworakowski.
>
>   *Hoover*

L'INTERNATIONALE Communiste et sa section française; (Recueil de
documents). See no. 110.

1372 JACOBY, Jean
La guerre rouge est declarée. Paris, Les Editions de France [c1935]
290 p.   *Hoover, LC, NYPL, Harv*

KLASS protiv klassa; "natsional'noe edinenie" i Kompartiia Frantsii.
See no. 1131.

LAPORTE, Maurice
Les mystères du Kremlin. (Dans les coulisses de la II-e Internationale et du Parti français.) See no. 283.

1373 LIGUE Communiste.
Qu'est-ce que l'Opposition communiste de gauche? (Ligue communiste) Paris, 1932. 43 p. *Hoover*

1374 LOZOVSKII, A.
Frankreich und die französische Arbeiterbewegung in der Gegenwart. Eindrücke und Betrachtungen. Verlag der Roten Gewerkschafts-Internationale; Auslieferung für Deutschland durch Phöbus-Verlag, Berlin, 1922. 139 p. (Bibliothek der Roten Gewerkschafts-Internationale, Bd. 13)

> A collection of articles in *Pravda* (Moscow) reporting about conditions and developments in the French workers movement, the socialist political parties and the C.P.F. The author presents quite openly his illegal contacts and is quite outspoken in his observations. Many documentary excerpts in the text. Enclosed are two documents: 1) A letter of the Executive Bureau of the RILU to the Congress of the C.G.T.U. dated June 10, 1922, and 2) A letter of the ECCI to the Central Committee of the C.P.F., dated May 1922.
>
> *Hoover, NYPL, Felt*

1375 LOZOVSKII, A.
Rabochaia Frantsiia (zametki i vpechatleniia). Moskva, Gos. izd-vo, 1923. 139 p.

> For annotation see preceding item. *Hoover*

1376 LOZOVSKII, A.
Réponses du camarade Losovsky aux questions posées par les délégues français en Russie à l'occasion du X-e anniversaire de la Révolution d'octobre. [Paris] Imp. de la Maison des Syndicats, 1928. 63 p. port. (Petite Bibliothèque de l'Internationale Syndicale Rouge, 22.)
Hoover

MARCHAND, René
(Tree items by this author, entered by mistake as nos. 1412–1414, belong here.)

MARTY, André
For peace! For the defense of the Soviet Union! See no. 968—12.

MARTY, André
Pour la paix, pour la défense de l'U.R.S.S. See no 982.

1377 Les ORGANISATIONS du Gouvernement soviétique et du Komintern pour la bolchévisation de la France. [n. p., n. d.] tables, maps. (The maps are reprinted from G. Gautherot: *Le monde communiste*.) *BDIC*

1378 PARTI communiste [français]
Platforme de la gauche; projet de thèses présenté par une groupe de "Gauchistes" (bordiguistes) à l'occasion du V-e congrès du Parti communiste français. Paris, Imp. spéciale de la Librairie du travail, 1926. 56 p.   *Hoover*

Le PARTI communiste français devant l'Internationale; préface du Bureau politique du P.C.F. See no. 1179.

PIATNITSKII, Osip
Die Arbeit der kommunistischen Parteien Frankreichs und Deutschlands und die Aufgaben der Kommunisten in der Gewerkschaftsbewegung. See no. 1206.

PIATNITSKII, Osip
The work of the communist parties of France and Germany and the tasks of the communists in the trade union movement. See nos. 1217, 1218.

RAPPOPORT, Charles
Le Parti Communiste Français au Comité Exécutif de Moscou. Discours... See no. 1045.

1379 RAPPOPORT, Charles
Le Parti socialiste français et la Troisième Internationale. Paris, Ed. de la Revue Communiste, 1920. 15 p.   *BDIC, Felt*

REALE, Eugenio
Avec Jaques Duclos au banc des accusés à la réunion constitutive du Kominform à Szklarska Poreba, 22—27 septembre 1947. See no. 333.

1380 SADOUL, Jacques
Une nouvelle lettre de Jacques Sadoul. Moscou — 17 janvier 1919. [n. p., 1919?] 24 p.   *Felt*

1381 SEVERAC, J. B.
De l'unité d'action à l'unité organique. 2. éd. Paris, Societé d'éditions, "Nouveau Prométhée" [1934] 62 p.

"Appendice: [p. 41–62] Pacte d'unité d'action. — Les vingt-et-une conditions d'admission des parties dans l'Internationale Communiste. — L'U.R.S.S. et la S.D.N. — Le Parti communiste répond à M. Doumergue. — La nouvelle tactique électorale du Parti communiste. — Lettre de l'Internationale ouvrière socialiste à l'Internationale Communiste. — Déclaration des représentants de sept partis à l'exécutif de l'I.O.S."   *Hoover*

1382 SICARD, Maurice Ivan
Doriot contre Moscou. [Paris] Éditions populaires françaises [1941]
53 p. Cover-title. *Hoover*

1383 SOKOLOV, Boris
Le voyage de Cachin et de Frossard dans la Russia des soviets (faits
et documents) Paris, J. Povolozky [1921] 140 p. *Hoover*

THOREZ, Maurice
Edinyi i narodnyi front vo Frantsii. See no. 916.

THOREZ, Maurice
The success of the anti-fascist united front. See no. 968—11.

1384 THOREZ, Maurice
Vive "L'Internationale". Discours de Maurice Thorez le 1-er octobre
1949, à Saint-Denis, en homage à Pierre Degeyter. Paris, I.C.C. [n.d]
15 p. illus. *Felt*

THOREZ, Maurice
Die Volksfront für Brot, Freiheit und Frieden. Die Erfolge der antifaschistischen Einheitsfront in Frankreich; Rede ... See no. 936.

TROTSKII, Lev
La crise du Parti Communiste Français. See no. 1043.

TROTSKII, Lev
Die Fragen der Arbeiterbewegung in Frankreich und die Kommunistische Internationale; zwei Reden... See no. 1038.

1385 TROTSKII, Lev
Le Salut du parti communiste français. Paris, Librairie de "l'Humanité",
1922. 48 p. (Petite Bibliothèque communiste.) *Felt*

1386 WALTER, Gerald (pseud.)
Histoire du Parti Communiste français. Paris, 1948. A. Somogy. 390 p.
Hoover

ZUR Lage in der Kommunistischen Partei Frankreichs. [A collection of
documents.] See no. 145.

Der ZWEITE Weltkongreß der Kommunistischen Internationale an das
französische Proletariat; zur Frage des Anschlusses an die Kommunistische Internationale. See no. 608.

8. Germany

1387 L'ALLEMAGNE et le bolchévisme. [Paris] éd. C.E.A. [1938] 64 p. diagr. Tableau chronologique de concordance entre la politique extérieure de l'URSS et la politique du Komintern de 1917 à 1938. Organisation du Komintern. *BDIC*

1388 AN die Mitglieder der K.A.P.D. Offener Brief des Exekutivkomitees der Kommunistischen Internationale. [n. p.] Kommunistische Internationale, 1921. 16 p. (Flugschriften der Kommunistischen Internationale, 6.) *Amst, Felt*

1389 AUFSTIEG oder Niedergang? Adresse an das Exekutivkomitee und die Sektionen der Kommunistischen Internationale! An die Kommunisten der ganzen Welt! [Berlin, KPD-Opposition, 1931] 16 p. Reprint from *Arbeiterpolitik.* *Amst*

BAUMBÖCK, Karl
Deutschlands Sieg im Osten, Grundlage für das neue Europa. See no. 207.

1390 BRANDLER, Heinrich
Durch die Räte zur Einheit der Arbeiterklasse und zum Kommunismus. Chemnitz, Der Kämpfer [1919] 14 p. (Kommunistische Zeitfragen, No. 1) *Hoover*

BRANDT, Willi, and Lowenthal, Richard
Ernst Reuter; ein Leben für die Freiheit. Eine politische Biographie. See no. 54 a.

BUBER-NEUMANN, Margarethe [pseud. of Faust, Margarethe Anna]
Von Potsdam nach Moskau. Stationen eines Irrweges. See no. 179 a.

1391 CENTRE d'Etudes Anticommuniste, Paris. L'Allemagne et le bolchévisme. [Paris] C.E.A. [1938?] 63 p. diagr. *LC, Col*

1392 CRISPIEN, Arthur
USPD trotz alledem! Rede des Genossen Crispien auf dem Parteitag in Halle. Berlin, Verlagsgenossenschaft „Freiheit" [1920] 40 p.
Hoover

1393 EHRT, Adolf
Communism in Germany; the truth about the communist conspiracy
on the eve of the National Revolution. Published by the General
League of German Anti-Communist Associations. [Berlin, Eckart-
Verlag, c1933] 179 p. illus. (English translation of Ehrt, Adolf, *Révolte
armé*. Inserted page contains: Why Americans should read this book;
signed "For the American Section of the International Committee
to Combat the World Menace of Communism" — preceded by
16 signatures)

This is a Nazi publication containing documentation on communist subversive
activities in Germany and Comintern's involvement in these activities. Discusses
Heinz Neumann's book *Der bewaffnete Aufstand* (for French translation see
no. 1605). Although produced for propaganda purposes, this book still contains much authentic information on persons and actions which later were
discovered as having been directed by the Communist International and its
front organizations.   *Hoover*

1394 EHRT, Adolf
Révolte armée; révélations sur la tentative d'insurrection communiste
à la veille de la Révolution Nationale. Publié par l'Union des associations anticommunistes d'Allemagne. Berlin, Eckart Verlag, 1933. 188 p
illus.

French edition of the preceding item.   *Hoover*

1395 Das EXEKUTIVKOMITEE der 3. Internationale (an die K. A. P.). Offener
Brief an die Mitglieder der K. A. P. [Berlin, Kommunistische Partei
Deutschlands (Spartakusbund)], 1920. 12 p.   *Hoover*

Der FASCHISMUS in Deutschland. [Selections from speeches . . .] See
no. 1250.

O FASHISTSKOI diktature v Germanii. See no. 127.

1396 FISCHER, Ruth
Stalin and German communism; a study in the origins of the state
party. With a preface by Sidney F. Fay. Cambridge, Mass., Harvard
University Press, 1948. xxii, 687 p. illus., map.
                                         Hoover, LC, NYPL, Harv, Col, SInSt

1397 FLECHTHEIM, Osip K.
Die Kommunistische Partei Deutschlands in der Weimarer Republik.
Offenbach a. M., Bollwerk Verlag Karl Drott, 1948. xvi, 294 p. Cover
title: Die K. P. D. in der Weimarer Republik.

This concise history of the KPD contains many references to the relationship
between the Comintern and the KPD. Among the enclosed six documents

should be mentioned the November 1918 proclamation of the Spartakusbund, the statutes of the KPD, and a resolution of a party conference of the KPD concerning the 12th Plenum of the Executive Committee of the Communist International and the tasks of the KPD. Good bibliography.

Hoover, LC, NYPL, Harv, Col

1398 FRANK, Karl
Der Fall Levi in der Dritten Internationale. Wien, Verlag der Arbeiter-Buchhandlung [1921] 15 p.   *Hoover, NYPL*

GERMANY — Hitler or Lenin. See nos. 1240, 1241.

1399 GEYER, Curt
Für die dritte Internationale! Die U.S.P.D. am Scheidewege bei Curt Geyer, nebst Beiträgen von Walter Stöcker und Paul Henning, mit einem Vorwort von Ernst Däumig. Berlin, Verlag „Der Arbeiterrat", 1920. 77 p.   *NYPL*

1400 GEYER, Curt
Za Tretii Internatsional. Nezavisimye na pereput'e. S prilozheniem Valtera Shtekera [Stoecker] i Pavla Genniga [Hennig]. S predisloviem Ernsta Deimiga [Däumig]. Moskva, Kommunisticheskii Internatsional, 1920. 132 p. At head of title: Kurt Geier.   *NYPL, BDIC*

HECKERT, Fritz
Why Hitler in Germany? [Report... to the E.C.C.I., March 1933] See no. 1239.

1401 KOMMUNISTISCHE Arbeiter-Partei Deutschlands.
Das Exekutivkomitee der 3. Internationale und die Kommunistische Arbeiter-Partei Deutschlands. Berlin, Verlag der K.A.P.D. [1920] 15 p.

Contents: Bericht der nach Moskau entsandten Delegation. Offenes Schreiben des Exekutiv-Komitees an die Mitglieder der K.A.P.D. Antwort an das Exekutiv-Komitee.   *Hoover*

1402 [KOMMUNISTISCHE Arbeiter-Partei Deutschlands]
Die Sowjetregierung und die 3. Internationale im Schlepptau der internationalen Bourgeoisie! [n.p.] Kommunistische Arbeiter-Partei Deutschlands [n.d.] 38 p.   *BDIC, Felt*

Die KOMMUNISTISCHE Internationale über die Lage in Deutschland. [March 1933] See no. 1242.

1403 KOMMUNISTISCHE Partei Deutschlands.
Der Weg der Revolution. I. Brief Lenins. II. Rundschreiben des Exekutiv-
Komitees der Kommunistischen Internationale. III. Nachwort. [Berlin,
1920] 20 p.   *Hoover, NYPL, Felt*

1404 KOMMUNISTISCHE Partei Deutschlands. X. Parteitag, Berlin, 1925.
Beschlüsse des X. Parteitages der Kommunistischen Partei Deutsch-
lands, Berlin, 12. bis 17. Juli 1925. Anhang: Brief der Exekutive der
Kommunsitischen Internationale an den Parteitag der KPD. Berlin,
Zentralkomitee der KPD, 1925. 87 p.   *Hoover*

1405 KOMMUNISTISCHE Partei Deutschlands. Zentral-Komitee.
Material für die Parteidiskussion. Berlin, 1926. 29 p. „Nur als Manuskript gedruckt."

> Contents: Sinowjew gegen Trotzki. Kamenew gegen Trotzki. Maslow gegen
> Trotzki. Sinowjew gegen Maslow-Ruth Fischer. Ruth Fischer gegen die deut-
> schen Ultra-linken.   *Hoover*

1406 KOMMUNISTISCHE Partei Deutschlands. Zentral Komitee.
Der neue Kurs; Reden der Genossen Bucharin und Sinowjew; Brief
des EKKI. Berlin, Vereinigung Internationaler Verlags-Anstalten, 1925.
87 p.

> Includes speeches of Bukharin and Zinov'ev to the German Delegation to the
> Communist International Executive Committee, given in Moscow in August,
> 1925, and documents of the Central Committee of the Communist Party of
> Germany.   *Hoover*

1407 KORSCH, Karl
Der Weg der Komintern. Diskussionsrede des Genossen Karl Korsch
auf der Konferenz der politischen [kommunistischen] Partei Deutschlands in Berlin am 16. April 1926 nebst einem Anhang: „Die Platt-
form der Linken". Berlin, H. Schlagewerth [n. d.] 23 p. As Manuskript
gedruckt.   *Felt*

Les LEÇONS des événements d'Allemagne; la question allemande
au Présidium du C.E. de l'I.C. en janvier 1924. See no. 1057.

Die LEHREN der deutschen Ereignisse. Das Präsidium des Exekutivkomitees der Kommunistischen Internationale zur deutschen Frage,
January 1924. See no. 1055.

1408 Der LEIPZIGER Kongreß der U.S.P. und die Kommunistische Internationale. [n. p.] Westeuropäisches Sekretariat der Kommunistischen Internationale, 1920. 19 p.

> Signed: Das Exekutiv-komitee der Kommunistischen Internationale. Vorsitzender: G. Sinowjew.   *Hoover, Col, UCal, Yale, Felt*

The LESSONS of the German events. See no. 1056.

LOWENTHAL, Richard
The bolshevisation of the Spartacus League. In *International Communism*. See no. 243.

1409 LOZOVSKII, A.
Mosca contro Amsterdam. Roma, Libreria Editrice del Partito Comunista d'Italia, 1921. 33 p. At head of title A. Losovskij. (Biblioteca dell'Internazionale dei Sindicati Rossi.)   *Felt*

1410 LOZOVSKII, A.
Moskau oder Amsterdam? Rede des Genossen A. Losowsky gehalten auf dem Parteitag der U.S.P.D. in Halle, Oktober 1920. Mit einem Vorwort und einem Anhang. Leipzig, Frank [1920] 31 p.
>   *Hoover, Felt*

1411 LOZOVSKII, A.
Moskva ili Amsterdam (rech' proiznesennaia na Kongresse nezavisimykh S. D. v Galle [Halle] 14-go noiabria [sic! should be October] 1920 goda). Moskva, Gos. izd-vo, 1921. 29 p. (Biblioteka professional'nogo dvizheniia. Seriia mezhdunarodnaia, No. 3)
>   *Hoover, BDIC*

MANUIL'SKII, D. Z.
Social-Democracy — Stepping Stone to Fascism... See no. 1348.

1412 MARCHAND, René
Pourquoi je me rallié à la formule de la révolution sociale. [Petrograd] Éditions de l'Internationale Communiste, [1919] 78 p.
> The items 1412–1414 concern France and should follow no. 1376.   *Hoover, Felt*

1413 MARCHAND, René
Warum ich Anhänger der sozialen Revolution wurde? Petrograd, Kommunistische Internationale, 1920. 98 p.   *NYPL, Amst*

1414 MARCHAND, René
Why I side with the social revolution. Petrograd, Communist International. 1920. 85 p.   *Hoover, LC*

1415 MARTOV, Iulii O.
Bol'shevizm v Rossii i v Internatsionale; rech' proiznesennaia na s"ezde Nezavisimoi sotsialisticheskoi partii Germanii v Galle [Halle] 15-go oktiabria 1920 goda. S predisloviem i poslesloviem avtora. [Berlin] Izdanie "Sotsialsiticheskogo Vestnika", 1923. 35 p. *Harv, BDIC*

1416 MARTOV, Iulii O.
Das Problem der Internationale u. die russische Revolution; Rede auf dem Parteitag in Halle. [Magdeburg], Magdeburger Volks-Zeitung [1920] 15 p. At head of title: L. Martov.

Speech of Martov as representative of the Social-Democratic Workers Party of Russia to a meeting of the Independent Social Democratic Party of Germany.
Hoover, NYPL, SInSt

O FASHISTSKOI diktature v Germanii. See no. 127.

1417 PANKHURST, E. Sylvia
La grande conspiration contre le socialisme russe et allemand. Petrograd, Editions de l'Internationale Communiste, 1919. 20 p. *Felt*

1418 PANKHURST, E. Sylvia
Die große Verschwörung gegen den russischen und den deutschen Sozialismus. Petrograd, Kommunistische Internationale, 1920. 27 p.
LC, NYPL, Amst

1419 PFAFFENSCHLÄGER, Paul
Moskau oder Amsterdam? Berlin, A. Schlicke & Co. [1921] 46 p. tables.
NYPL

PIATNITSKII, Osip
Die Arbeit der kommunistischen Parteien Frankreichs und Deutschlands und die Aufgaben der Kommunisten in der Gewerkschaftsbewegung. See no. 1206.

PIATNITSKII, Osip
The work of the communist parties of France and Germany and the tasks of the communists in the trade union movement. See nos. 1217, 1218.

PIECK, Wilhelm and others.
Kommunisticheskaia partiia Germanii v bor'be protiv fashizma; rechi Vil'gel'ma Pika [and others]. See no. 904.

PIECK, W.
We are fighting for a Soviet Germany. See nos. 970—6, 1263, 1271.

PIECK, Wilhelm
Wir kämpfen für ein Räte-Deutschland; der revolutionäre Kampf der deutschen Arbeiterklasse unter Führung der Kommunistischen Partei Deutschlands gegen die faschistische Diktatur. Bericht über die Tätigkeit der Kommunistischen Partei Deutschlands. See no. 1255.

PROLETARISCHER Internationalismus. Materialien einer Arbeitstagung über die Rolle und Bedeutung des proletarischen Internationalismus. [This collective work contains several contributions dealing with Comintern-directed actions in Germany.] See no. 327.

1420　RADEK, Karl
In den Reihen der deutschen Revolution, 1909—1919; gesammelte Aufsätze und Abhandlungen. München, L. Wolff [c1921] 463 p.

Hoover

1421　RADEK, Karl
Die Masken sind gefallen; eine Antwort an Crispien, Dittman und Hilferding. [n. p.] Kommunistische Internationale, 1920. 36 p.

Hoover, NYPL, Amst

1422　RADEK, Karl
Na sluzhbe germanskoi revoliutsii (perevod s nemetskogo) [Moskva] Gos. izd-vo, 1921. 269 p.

Hoover

1423　RADEK, Karl
Zur Taktik des Kommunismus; ein Schreiben an den Oktober-Parteitag der K.P.D. Hrsg. im Auftrag der K.P.D. (Spartakusbund) [Berlin, Kommissions Druckerei der K.P.D., 1919] 11 p.

Hoover

1424　REESE, Maria
I accuse Stalinism! An open letter to the C.C. of the Communist Party of Germany and the E.C.C.I. New York, Pioneer Publishers [1933] 16 p.

Hoover

[RESOLUTION of the Presidium, E.C.C.I., on situation in Germany] — contained in Manuilskii, D. Z., *Social-Democracy — Stepping Stone to Fascism...* See no. 1348.

1425　SENDER, Tony
Diktatur über das Proletariat, oder: Diktatur des Proletariats. Das Ergebnis von Moskau. [Frankfurt, Frankfurter Genossenschaftsdruckkerei und Verlag „Volksrecht", 1920] 16 p.

Hoover

1426 THÄLMANN, Ernst
Vorwärts unter dem Banner der Komintern; Rede des Genossen Thälmann auf der Tagung des ZK der KPD am 14. Mai 1931. [Berlin] ZK der KPD [1931] 40 p.   *Hoover*

1427 [TOGLIATTI, Palmiro]
Die antifaschistische Einheitsfront und die nächsten Aufgaben der KPD; Rede des Vertreters des Exekutivkomiteees der Kommunistischen Internationale auf der Brüsseler Konferenz der KPD (Oktober 1935) Strasbourg,Editions Promethée [1935?] 19 p. At head of title: Ercoli.
Hoover

TRACHTENBERG, Jakow
Gegen das Braunbuch; (Rotbuch). See no. 361.

1428 La III-me [TROISIEME] Internationale et les reconstructeurs; réponse de Moscou aux indépendants d'Allemagne concernant la reconstruction de l'Internationale. [La Chaux-de-Fonds, 1920] 16 p. (Jeunesses socialistes romandes. Bibliothèque, no. 11.)   *NYPL, Amst*

1429 TROTSKII, Lev
Problèmes de la révolution allemande. Édité par la Ligue communiste (opposition). Paris [imprim de la Soc. nouv. d'éditions franco-slaves] 1931. 61 p.   *Hoover*

1430 TROTSKII, Lev
The turn in the Communist International and the German situation. [Translated by Morris Lewitt.] New York, Communist League of America (Opposition), 1930. 31 p.   *Hoover*

1431 TROTSKII, Lev
Die Wendung der Komintern und die Lage in Deutschland; hrsg. von der Reichsleitung der Linken Opposition der K.P.D. (Bolschewiki-Leninisten) Berlin, „Der Kommunist" (A. Müller), 1930, 15 p.
Hoover, Amst

1432 UNABHÄNGIGE Sozialdemokratische Partei Deutschlands; Zentralkomitee. Die U.S.P.D. und die 3. Internationale; Bericht des Zentralkomitee über die Ausführung des Leipziger Parteitagsbeschlusses. Remscheid. Gedruckt in der „Bergischen Volksstimme" [1920] 14 p.
Hoover

1433 WACHT auf, Verdammte dieser Erde! An die klassenbewußten sozial-demokratischen Arbeiter Deutschland! Ein offenes Wort von der Kommunistischen Internationale. Hamburg, 1922. 29 p.

> Caption title: An die klassenbewußten Arbeiter Mitglieder der hinübergegangenen, Unabhängigen Sozial demokratischen Partei Deutschlands. Signed: Das Exekutivkomitee der Kommunsitischen Internationale   *Hoover, NYPL, Amst*

1434 WERNER, Paul
Die bayerische Räterepublik; Tatsachen und Kritik, Petrograd, Die Kommunistische Internationale, 1920. 195 p.   *NYPL*

1435 Der ZERSETZUNGSDIENST der K.P.D. [n. p., 1930?] 35 p. Microfilm copy of typescript.   *Hoover*

1436 ZETKIN, Clara
Der Weg nach Moskau [Hamburg?] Kommunistische Internationale, 1920. 31 p.

> A propaganda pamphlet advocating the affiliation of all workers' parties of Germany with the Communist International. Sharp polemic with the U.S.P. and its leaders. Written before the II Congress of the Comintern.
>
> *Hoover, Amst*

1437 Von ZIMMERWALD zu Scheidemann. Ein offenes Wort an die sozial-demokratischen Arbeiter und klassenbewußten Gewerkschaftler. [n.p.] Zentrale der K.P.S [n. d.] 60 p.   *Amst*

1438 ZINOV'EV, G.
Dvenadtsat' dnei v Germanii. Peterburg, Gos. izd-vo, 1920. 119 p.
   Hoover, NYPL

ZINOV'EV, G.
Mirovaia revoliutsiia i Kommunisticheskii Internatsional; perevod rechi na s"ezde germanskoi nezavisimoi partii v Galle [Halle] 14 okt. 1920 g. See no. 424.

1439 ZINOV'EV, G.
Probleme der deutschen Revolution. Hamburg, Hoym, 1923. 109 p.

> Although the author obviously avoids mentioning the Communist International too often, this pamphlet is a discussion of the ways and means toward a proletarian revolution in Germany, consistently advocated since 1919 by the Communist International. The chapter, "The approaching of the German revolution and the tactic of the united front" particularly follows the political line of the Comintern at the time of the publication of this pamphlet, November 1923.   *Hoover*

1440 ZINOV'EV, G.
Les problèmes de la révolution allemande. Paris, Librairie de l'Humanité, 1923. 72 p. (Petite Bibliothèque communiste.)

For annotation see item above. *Hoover*

ZINOV'EV, G.
Le prolétariat européen devant la révolution. Discours prononcé au congrès du Parti Social-Démocrate Independent d'Allemagne, à Halle, le 14 octobre, 1920. See no. 425.

1441 ZINOV'EV, G.
Rurskie sobytiia i zadachi Kominterna. Moskva, "Krasnaia nov'" Glavpolitprosvet, 1923. 38 p. *Hoover*

1442 ZINOV'EV, G.
Twelve days in Germany, by G. Zinoviev. Moscow, Publ. by the Communist International, 1921. 91 p. *Hoover*

ZINOV'EV, G.
Die Weltrevolution und die III. Internationale! Rede des Vorsitzenden vom Exekutvikomitee der III. Internationale auf dem Parteitag der U. S. P. D. in Halle am 14. Oktober 1920. See no. 427.

ZINOV'EV, G.
Die Weltrevolution und die III. Kommunistische Internationale; Rede auf dem Parteitag der U. S. P. D. in Halle am 14. Oktober 1920. See no. 426.

1443 ZINOV'EV, G.
Zwölf Tage in Deutschland. Hamburg, Hoym, 1921. 91 p. At head of title: G. Sinowjew. *NYPL, Harv*

9. Great Britain

1444 ARNOT, Robert Page
Twenty years; the policy of the Communist party of Great Britain from its foundation, July 31st, 1920. [London] Lawrence & Wishart, Ltd. [1940] 79 p. On cover: 1920—1940. *Hoover*

BRAUN, P.
At the parting of the ways; the results of the ninth Plenum of the Comintern. See no. 1130.

CAMPBELL, John, R. and others.
Kommunisticheskaia partiia Anglii v bor'be za massu i edinyi front proletariata; rechi tt. Kembella, Kerrigena. See no. 901.

CLUNIE, James
The Third (Communist) International: its aims and methods. See no. 675.

1445   The COMMUNIST International. London, Independent Labour Party, 1920. 15 p. (I.L.P. Pamphlets; n. s. no. 37)   *Hoover*

1446   The COMMUNIST International and the British Independent Labour Party. Moscow, Executive Committee of the Communist International, 1920. 30 p.   *Hoover, UPenn*

1447   The COMMUNIST International answers the I.L.P. A reprint of a famous document, drafted by Nicolai Lenin. London, Communist Party of Great Britain, 1932. 36 p. First published 1920.   *Amst*

COMMUNIST Party of Great Britain.
Resolution of the E.C.C.I. on the situation in Great Britain. See no. 1123.

COMMUNIST policy in Great Britain. The report of the British commission of the ninth plenum of the Comintern. See no. 1133.

DEVIATYI plenum Ispolkoma Kominterna. Novaia taktika angliiskoi kompartii; sbornik. See no. 1132.

1448   GODDEN, Gertrude M.
The communist attack on Great Britain; international communism at work. London, Burns, Oates & Washbourne Ltd. [1935] 87 p.
    Hoover

1449   GODDEN, Gertrude M.
Communist attack on the people of Great Britain; interntional communism at work. 2d and enlarged ed. London, Burns, Oates & Washbourne, Ltd., 1938. 109 p. "First published 1935". Cover title: Communist attack on Great Britain."   *Hoover*

GREAT Britain. Foreign Office.
Documents illustrating the hostile activities of the Soviet government and Third International against Great Britain. See no. 106.

GREAT Britain. Parliament. Papers by command.
Communist papers. Documents selected from those obtained on the arrest of the communist leaders on the 14th and 21st October 1925...
See no. 105.

1450 INDEPENDENT Labour Party. (Great Britain)
I.L.P. and Comintern with the twenty-one points of the Communist International. London, Independent Labour Party [n. d.] 15 p. "Supplementary Letters"   *Felt*

1451 INDEPENDENT Labour Party. (Great Britain)
I.L.P. and the Communist International. Full text of the correspondence. London, Independent Labour Party [n. d.] 19 p.   *Felt*

1452 INDEPENDENT Labour Party (Great Britain)
The I.L.P. and the Third International; being the questions submitted by the I.L.P. delegation to the Executive of the 3rd International and its reply, with an introductory statement by the National Council of the I.L.P. (issued for the Independent Labour Party) London, Manchester, National Labour Press, 1920. 64 p.

> **Contents:**
> 1. "Introductory Notes" by the National Administrative Council of the I.L.P. containing a summary of the negotiations between the I.L.P. and the Comintern concerning the affiliation of the I.L.P. with the Comintern, and the failure of these negotiations.
> 2. "The Questionnaire" which a delegation of the I.L.P. submitted on May 25, 1920 to the Executive Committee of the Comintern.
> 3. The Comintern's reply.
> The pamphlet "Moscow's reply to the I.L.P." (no. 1457) contains a "Foreword" signed by "The Left Wing Group of the I.L.P." and the items listed above under 2 and 3. The only difference is that the last paragraph in "The I.L.P. and the 3rd International" is entitled "To the Communists *and* the Independent Labour Party", whereas in the pamphlet "Moscow's reply to the I.L.P." this title has the following wording: To the Communists *of* the Independent Labour Party."   *Hoover, Harv, Col*

KOMMUNISTICHESKAIA partiia Anglii v bor'be za massu i edinyi front proletariata; rechi tt. Kembella, Kerrigena [dr.] See no. 901.

1453 LABOUR party (Gt. Brit.)
The communist solar system... London, The Labour Party [1933] 23 p.

> Discusses the branches of the Communist International active in Great Britain.
>   *Hoover, Amst*

1454 LABOUR'S way out; a message to the worker. [n. p.] Educational Bureau of the Third International in Great Britain [n. d.] 15 p.

Amst

1455 LENIN on the I. L. P. With an introduction by William Rust. London, Modern Books Ltd. [1933] 55 p.

> The title of this communist pamphlet is misleading. The reason for its publication was the desire to bring to public attention the exchange of telegrams and letters between the Secretariat of the ECCI and the National Administrative Council of the Independent Labour Party in May–July of 1933 concerning the intended cooperation or affiliation of the I. L. P. with the Comintern. This attempt failed, as it did in 1920. (See "The I. L. P. and the 3rd International", no. 1452 above.) The pamphlet contains five communications exchanged between the Comintern and the I. L. P., followed by Lenin's "Theses for an answer to the German 'Independents' regarding their proposals for negotiations" written in July 1920; Lenin's long essay on "Ramsay McDonald on the Third International", written in July 1920; an excerpt from "Sochineniia", vol. XXV, dealing with Ramsay MacDonald; and an excerpt from Lenin's "Left-wing communism" on the tactic of the communists in Great Britain.

Hoover

LENIN, V. I.
Problems of the Third International; Ramsey [!] Mcdonald on the Third International. See no. 295.

1456 McMANUS, Arthur, ed.
History of the Zinoviev letter; facts about the infamous letter. London, Communist Party of Great Britin, 1925. 47 p.   *Hoover*

1457 MOSCOW'S reply to the I. L. P.; the reply of the E. C. of the Communist International to the questions of the British I. L. P., together with an appeal to the communists inside the party. Glasgow, Pub. on behalf of the Left Wing group of the I. L. P. by H. C. Glass, 1920. 32 p.

> See annotation to nos. 1452, 1455.   *Hoover, NYPL, Col, Amst*

The NEXT step in Britain, America and Ireland; speeches and reports, XII plenum E. C.C. I. See nos. 1219, 1220.

1458 PELLING, Henry
The British Communist Party; a historical profile. London, A. & C. Black [1958] viii, 204 p. illus.

> A general history of the C. P. G. B. with well documented references to its relations to the Communist International and its front organizations.

Hoover

POLLITT, Harry
Unity against the national government; [speech at VII-th Congress]
See nos. 967, 968—14.

1459 TRADES Union Congress General Council (Britain)
The "Zinoviev" letter. Report of investigation by British delegation
to Russia for the Trades Union Congress General Council. November—
December, 1924... [London] The Trades Union Congress General
Council, 1925. 11 p. *Hoover*

1460 WALLHEAD, R. C.
The International (the link to join the workers of the world). London,
I. L. P. Publication Department [1924] 14 p. "Reprinted from the
'Socialist Review' for August, 1924". *Hoover*

10. Hungary

1461 SZANTO, B.
Klassenkämpfe und Diktatur des Proletriats in Ungarn. Petrograd,
Verlag der Kommunistischen Internationale, 1920. 110 p.

Hoover

1462 SZANTO, B.
Klassenkämpfe und Diktatur des Proletariats in Ungarn. Mit Einleitung
von Karl Radek. Herausgegeben vom West-Europäischen Sekretariat
der Kommunsitischen Internationale. [Berlin, Schwarz & Co., 1920] xi,
115 p. *Hoover, LC*

1463 ZINOV'EV G. E.
Mit mond a III. Internacionale a magyarországi proletárforradalom-
ról? Irták G. Zinovjev, Karl Rades és a III. Internacionale nyugat-
európai titkérsága. Az utóhangot Kun Béla irta. Wien, Kommunisták
németausztriai partja, 1920. 48 p. *Hoover*

11. Ireland

The NEXT step in Britain, America and Ireland; (speeches and reports,
XII plenum E. C. C. I.) See nos. 1219, 1220.

12. Italy

Der FADEN der Zeit. Beiträge zur historischen Wiederherstellung der marxistischen Theorie. Der II. Kongreß der III. Internationale und die italienische Linke. See no. 647.

GOTTWALD, Klement
Internationale Aktion gegen Mussolini's Raubkrieg. Der italienische Krieg; die Aktionseinheit der Arbeiterklasse und der Standpunkt der Sozialistischen Arbeiterinternationale. [Part of] no. 1652.

ITAL'IANSKAIA sotsialisticheskaia partiia i Kommunisticheskii Internatsional (sbornik materialov). See no. 111.

1464   KABAKCHIEV, Christo St.
Die Gründung der Kommunistischen Partei Italiens. [n. p.] Kommunistische Internationale, 1921. 56 p.   *Amst*

1465   LETTERE e polemiche fra l'Internazionale comunista, il Partito socialista e la Confederazione generale del lavoro d'Italia. Milano, Soc. Edit. Avanti, 1921. 94 p. ("Atti della Terza Internazionale" no. 4.)
                                                                           NYPL, Felt

1466   NICOLINI, C.
Doklad Ispolkomu Kominterna o raskole v ital'ianskoi sotsialisticheskoi partii. [signed K. Nikolini] Moskva, izd. Otdela pechati Kominterna, 1921. 71 p.   *BDIC*

Le PARTI socialiste italien et l'Internationale communiste; recueil de documents. See no. 128.

La QUESTIONE Italiana al Terzo Congresso della Internazionale Comunista. See no. 722.

REALE, Eugenio
Avec Jacques Duclos au banc de accusés à la réunion constitutive du Kominform à Szklarska Poreba, 22—27 septembre 1947. See no. 333.

1467   ZETKIN, Clara & Walecki, E.
Il Partito Socialista Italiano sulla via del reformismo. Discorsi dei delegati della Internazionale comunista al XVIII Congresso del P. S. I. con un introduzione di C. Zetkin ed una conclusione di E. Walecki. Roma, Libreria Editrice del P. S. I., 1921. 79 p.   *Felt*

1468 ZETKIN, Clara, [and] Walecki, Henri
Dem Reformismus entgegen. Reden auf dem Parteitag der Sozialistischen Partei Italiens in Mailand mit einer Einleitung über die Ergebnisse des Parteitages. [n. p.] Kommunistische Internationale, 1921. 72 p.
Amst

13. Poland

XII [DWUNASTE] Plenum Komitetu Wykonawczego Międzynarodówki Komunistycznej o Polsce; referat tow. Leńskiego i przemówienia
przedstawicieli K. P. P. z przedmową J. Bratkowskiego. See no. 1225.

1469 DZIEWANOWSKI, M. K.
The Communist Party of Poland; an outline of history. Cambridge,
Mass., Harvard Univ. Press, 1959. xvi, 369, p. index.

An outline history of the Communist Party of Poland from its foundation up
to 1957. Many references to the mutual relations between the C. P. P. and the
Comintern.   *Hoover, LC, NYPL, Harv, Col*

KOMMUNISTICHESKAIA partiia Pol'shi — za antifashistskii front;
rechi tt. Lenskogo, Bronkovskogo. See no. 907.

KOMUNISTYCZNA Partja Polski.
KPP w walce z wojną, faszyzmem i atakiem kapitału. [Speech at
13-th Plenum]. See no. 1283.

1470 PETROVSKII, D.
Tretii Internatsional i polskii front. Moskva, Otdel polit. upravl.
Revvoensoveta respubliki, 1920. 14 p.   *BDIC*

PROLETARISCHER Internationalismus. Materialien einer Arbeitstagung
über die Rolle und Bedeutung des proletarischen Internationalismus.
[This collective work contains two contributions concerning the "Hands
off Soviet Russia" policy of the Comintern during the Polish-Soviet
war of 1919—1920.] See no. 327.

1471 REGUŁA, Jan Alfred [pseud. of J. Demant]
Historja Komunistycznej Partji Polski w świetle faktów i dokumentów.
Wydanie drugie, rozszerzone i uzupełnione. Warszawa, 1934. 343 p.
index.

> A well documented, early attempt at writing a history of the Communist Party
> of Poland, with special regard to its relations with the Communist International.
> *Hoover*

UZLOVYE voprosy revolutsionnogo dvizheniia Pol'shi na XII plenume
Ispolkoma Kominterna; sbornik rechei. See no. 1202.

VUZLOVI pitaniia revolutsionnogo rukhu Pol'shchi na XII plenumi
Vikonkomu Kominternu. Zbirka promov za red. i z predmovoiu
Io. Bratkovs'kogo. See no. 1227.

14. Scandinavian Countries

1472 HANSSON, Sigfrid & Andersson, Emil
Moskvateserna och fackföreningsrörelsen, en disputation, mellan
Redaktör Sigfrid Hansson... och Ombusman Emil Andersson. Stock-
holm, Tidens Förlag [1921] 32 p. (Landsorganisationen i Sverge.
Skriftserie. 2.) *NYPL*

1473 KIHLBERG, Leif
Den ryska agenturen i Sverige. Stockholm 1950. 53 p. *SInSt*

Die KOMMUNISTISCHEN Parteien Skandinaviens und die Kommunistische Internationale; die Aussprache mit den skandinavischen
Genossen über die Grenzen des Zentralismus in der Konferenz der
Erweiterten Exekutive der Kommunistischen Internationale. Moskau,
12—23 Juni 1923. See no. 1050.

1474 MERRHEIM, Alphonse
Amsterdam eller Moskva. Oversättning av Allan Vougt. Stockholm,
Tidens Förlag [1921] 58 p. (Landsorganisationen i Sverge. Skrift-
serie. 4.) *NYPL*

15. Spain

Note. For records of consultations between the II-nd and III-rd Internationals on the situation in Spain 1934–1937, see Part V, items no. 1649–1654.

BUBER-NEUMANN, Margarethe [pseud. of Faust, Margarethe Anna] Von Potsdam nach Moskau. Stationen eines Irrweges. See no. 179 a.

1475 CATTELL, David T.
Communism and the Spanish Civil War. Berkeley, University of California Press, 1955. 290 p. (University of California Publications in International Relations, v. 4) *Hoover*

1476 CATTELL, David T.
Soviet Diplomacy and the Spanish Civil War. Berkeley, University of California Press, 1957. 204 p. (University of California Publications in International Relations, v. 5) *Hoover*

1477 DIMITROV, G.
Due anni di lotta eroica del popolo spagnole. Parigi, Edizioni de Coltura Sociale, 1938. 30 p.

See annotation to English edition, no. 1481. *Hoover*

1478 DIMITROV, G.
Ko vtoroi godovshchine geroicheskoi bor'by ispanskogo naroda. Moskva, Gos. izd-vo polit. lit-ry, 1938. 15 p.

See annotation to English edition, no. 1481. *Hoover*

1479 DIMITROV, G.
Spain and the people's front. [New York, Workers Library Publishers, 1937] 37 p.

Extension of an article published in Pravda [Moscow] on November 7, 1937 and in many foreign communist newspapers and periodicals. *Hoover*

1480 DIMITROV, G.
Spain's year of war [New York, Workers Library Publishers, 1937] 14 p. *Hoover*

1481 DIMITROV, G.
Two years of heroic struggle of the Spanish people. [By Georgi Dimitrov; General Secretary of the Communist International. New York, Workers Library Publishers, August 1938] 23 p. Cover title.

> First published as an article in *Pravda*, Moscow, of July 18, 1938. A description of the formation of the People's Front in Spain and a defense of this Front as an example of the advantages resulting from its formation. Attack against the German and Italian intervention and against the non-intervention policy of Britain and France. Discusses Soviet and Comintern policy towards Spain.
> *Hoover*

1482 EXPOSICION del plan secreto para establicir un "soviet" en España. Bilbao [Editorial nacional] 1939. 14 p. illus., facsims.   *Hoover*

GARCIA, Venero Maximiano
Historia de las internacionales en España. See no. 154.

1483 GESAMTVERBAND deutscher anti-kommunistischer Vereinigungen. Denkschrift über die Einmischung des Bolschewismus und der Demokratien in Spanien; ausgewähltes Material und typische Beispiele zusammengestellt von der Anti-Komintern... Berlin-Leipzig, Nibelungen-Verlag, 1939. 31 p. incl. tables. „Bearbeiter: A. Gielen, G. Dohms, P. Wiebe."   *Hoover*

KOMMUNISTICHESKAIA partiia Ispanii v bor'be protiv fashizma; rech tt. Dolores [Ibarruri], Garsia [Garcia, Venero Maximiano], Khuan [Juan], Ventura, Martines [Martinez], Evaristo — delegatov ispanskoi kompartii [at VII-th Congress]. See no. 906.

1484 McGOVERN, John
Terror in Spain, how the Communist International has destroyed working class unity, undermined the fight against Franco, and suppressed the social revolution, by John McGovern... [London, Independent Labor Party, 1938?] 14 p.   *Hoover*

1485 REPORT on the crisis in the C. P. of Spain [Moscow, 1925] 12 sheets. ("Letters of Information from the Secretariat of the ECCI", no. 8, February 28, 1925.) Photo-reproduction from typewritten copy.
   Hoover, NYPL

UNITY for Spain; correspondence between the Communist International and the Labor and Socialist International, June—July 1937. See no. 1654.

16. Switzerland

1486 BRETSCHER, Willi, ed.
Die sozialistische Bewegung in der Schweiz, 1848—1920 ... Hrsg. von
W. Bretscher ... und Dr. E. Steinmann ... Bern, Buchdruckerei G. Iseli,
1923. 160 p. *Hoover*

1487 SCHMID, Arthur
Die Aufnahmebedingungen in die Kommunistische Internationale.
Bern, Soz. Parteibuchhandlung, 1920. 29 p. Rotel Fackel. *Amst*

1488 SCHMID, Jacques
Die Kommunistische Internationale (3. Internationale) und wie stellen
wir uns zu ihr? [n. p., 1919] 154 p. Sonderdr.: Neue Freie Zeitung.
NYPL, Amst, BDIC

1489 SOZIALDEMOKRATISCHE Partei der Schweiz.
Programm der Kommunistischen Internationale. Zürich, Sozialdemo-
kratische Partei der Stadt Zürich [1919] 40 p. (Kampfruf, no. 5.)
NYPL

1490 THESES directrices sur la tactique du prolétariat. [Geneva] Editions
de la "Nouvelle Internationale" [1920?] 16 p.

Communist propaganda pamphlet directed to Swiss workers. *Hoover*

1491 WELTI, Franz
Die III. Internationale und die Schweizerische Sozialdemokratie. Basel,
Buchhandlung des Arbeiterbundes, 1919. 16 p. *Hoover, Amst*

17. Turkey

1492 SHAFIR, Iakov
Die Ermordung der 26 Kommunare in Baku und die Partei der Sozial-
revolutionäre. Hamburg, Verlag der Kommunistischen Internationale,
1922. 46 p. (Beiträge zur Geschichte der Kämpfe des Proletariats in
Rußland 6.) *Hoover*

18. Yugoslavia

1493 BULGARSKA Komunisticheska Partiia.
Krizata v Iugoslavskata Komunisticheska partiia. Sofia [1948?] 28 p.

Includes documents of the Communist International.   *LC*

KABAKCHIEV, Khristo and others.
Kommunisticheskie partii Balkanskikh stran. See no. 1343.

1494 RYS [pseud.]
Komunisti u Hrvatskoj. Zagreb [MOSK] 1936. 40 p. illus.

Hoover

1495 URALSKI
Je li moguće priznati boljsevicku vlast? [Belgrade] Izdanie pistsa,
1924. 58 p.   *Col*

E. Latin America

1. General

WOLFE, Bertram D.
Revolution in Latin America. See no. 828.

2. Chile

1496 FERNANDEZ Larrain, Sergio
Traicion!! Santiago de Chile, Talleres de El Imparcial, 1941. 218 p.
illus. At head of title: Sergio Fernandez L.

Contains the draft of a law for the suppression of communism, the discussion
of this draft in parliament, and discusses communist horrors in Spain during
the civil war.   *LC, Harv*

309

3. Mexico

1497 STRATEGY of the Communists; a letter from the Communist International [Executive Committee] to the Mexican Communist Party. Chicago, Ill., Workers Party of America [1923] 16 p. Cover title.

Hoover, NYPL, Harv, Duke, UChic

F. North America

1. Canada

COMMUNIST Party of Canada.
Canada and the VII World Congress of the Communist International; Outline of study of the decisions of the 7th Congress of the Communist International and the 9th Plenum of the Central Committee of the Communist Party of Canada. See no. 1027.

2. United States of America

1498 ANDERSON, Paul Herbert
The attitude of the American leftist leaders toward the Russian revolution (1917—1923) ... Notre Dame, Ind., 1942. iii, 107 p. Thesis (Ph. D.) University of Notre Dame, 1942. "List of sources and references": p. 99—107.

Hoover

1499 BITTELMAN, Alexander
Milestones in the history of the Communist Party. New York, Workers Library Publishers [1937] 92 p.

"A reprint of ... 'Fifteen years of the Communist party' ... Added is a brief historical survey on the occasion of the eighteenth anniversary of our party."

Hoover

1500 BROWDER, Earl
Build the United People's Front; report to the November Plenum of the Central Committee of the Communist Party of the U.S.A. New York, Workers Library Publishers [1936] 70 p. At head of title: Communist Party of the United States of America; Central Committee.
Hoover

1501 BROWDER, Earl
Communism in the United States. With an Introduction by Alex Bittelman. New York, International Publishers [c1935] xii, 352 p.

> Reprinted in this collection of Browder's speeches, reports and writings from the years 1932–34 are a speech at the XIII-th Plenum of the Comintern and a November 1934 report prepared for the ECCI. This volume was followed by "The Peoples' Front" (see below) *Hoover, LC, NYPL*

BROWDER, Earl
New steps in the United Front. Report on the seventh Congress of the Communist International made at Madison Square Garden. See no. 969—13, 1026.

1502 BROWDER, Earl
The people's front in the United States. London, Lawrence & Wishart, 1938. 354 p. port. "Printed in the U.S.A."

> "This volume is a collection of reports, speeches and articles, written during 1936 and 1937. It is thus a companion volume and continuation of *Communism in the United States*, published in July, 1935." Foreword. *Hoover, LC, NYPL*

1503 BROWDER, Earl
The Second Imperialist War. New York, International Publishers [1940] viii, 309 p.

> "This book gathers the author's writings — speeches, articles, reports — for the period from March, 1939, to the beginning of May, 1940." Foreword, p. v. Besides a chapter dealing with "America and the Communist International", there are many references to this organization throughout the entire volume.
> *Hoover*

BROWDER, Earl
Socialism in America. In *International Communism;* see no. 243.

1504 BROWDER, Earl
Unity for peace and democracy. New York, Workers Library Publishers [1939] 95 p. At head of title: Communist Party of the United States of America.
Hoover

BROWDER, Earl
War against workers' Russia! [Speech at 11-th Plenum]. See no. 1169.

BUDENZ, Louis F.
This is my story. See no. 180.

COMMUNIST International. Amsterdam Sub-Bureau.
New offensive against Soviet Russia; communication of the Amsterdam Sub-Bureau of the third International. Distributed by the Central Executive Committee of the Communist Party of America. See no 234 a.

1505 COMMUNIST International, Executive Committee.
Concerning the tasks of the Communist Party of America [Instructions from the Executive Committee of the Communist International to the Communist Party of America concerning reorganization of the Party. With an accompanying letter signed by Bukharin, Radek and Kuusinen. With many handwritten corrections by Radek. Moscow, 1922]. 10 leaves, (positive photostat)

> Photographic reproduction of original in possession of the U.S. Department of Justice. This document was part of the material seized by the Department of Justice at Bridgeman, Michigan, August 22, 1922, during a raid on a secret convention of the Communist Party of America. See also no. 1526. *Hoover*

1506 COMMUNIST INTERNATIONAL. Executive Committee.
Resolution on the case of Louis C. Fraina [n. p., 1920?] One leaf 29 cm.
LC, Harv

1507 COMMUNIST INTERNATIONAL. Executive Committee.
Vozzwanie Ispolnitel'nogo Komiteta Kommunisticheskogo Internatsionala k Soiuzu industrial'nykh rabochikh mira. [n. p.] Izd. Ts. I. K. R. F. K. P. A. [Central Executive Committee of the Russian Federation of the Communist Party of America] 1920. 24 p. Signed G. Zinov'ev, Predsedatel Tsentr. Ispolnit. Komiteta.

> "Postscript of the editors", p. 21–24. *Hoover, NYPL, Col*

1508 COMMUNIST PARTY of America.
Stenographic report of the "Trial" of Louis C. Fraina. Issued by the Central Executive Committee of the Communist Party of America. [Chicago?] 1920. 48 p.

> "This pamphlet contains the stenographic report of the 'trial' of Louis C. Fraina, International Secretary of the Communist Party, who on the eve of his departure for Europe as a duly accredited delegate to the Third International, was accused of being an 'agent provocateur', by Santeri Nuorteva, Secretary of the Russian Soviet Bureau in this country." *Hoover*

1509 COMMUNIST PARTY of the United States of America. Central Committee.

On the road to bolshevization. New York, Workers' Library Publishers [1929] 46 p. "First edition."

> **Contents:** Introduction, signed: Central Committee C.P.U.S.A. – Excerpts from theses of sixth Congress of the Communist International. – Open letter of the Comintern to the Sixth Convention of the Communist Party of the U.S.A. – Address of the Comintern to the membership of the Communist Party U.S.A. – Decision of the Central Committee of the Communist Party U.S.A. on the address of the Comintern. *Hoover, NYPL*

CANNON, James
The first ten years of American Communism; Report of a Participant. See no. 181.

DRAPER, Theodore
American Communism and Soviet Russia; the formative period. See no. 239 a.

1510 DRAPER, Theodore
The Roots of American Communism. New York, Viking Press, 1957. x, 498 p. illus., ports., facsims.

> A concise and well documented presentation of the beginnings of communism in the United States. Throughout the text there are references to the relationship of the American communist party organizations with the Communist International. *Hoover*

FOSTER, William Z.
From Bryan to Stalin. See no. 190.

FOSTER, William Z.
Pages from a worker's life. See no. 191.

GITLOW, Benjamin
I confess; the truth abouth American communism. See no. 193.

GITLOW, Benjamin
The whole of their lives; communism in America, a personal history and intimate portrayal of its leaders. See no. 194.

GO to the masses! A manifesto of the third Congress of the Third International, also the withdrawal statement of the Committee for the Third International of the Socialist Party to he members of the Socialist Party. See no. 704.

1511 GOLDMAN, Albert
From communism to socialism [Chicago, 1951] 14 p.

Hoover

GREEN, Gil[ber]
Young communists and the unity of the youth. See nos. 957, 969—6.

1512 GREEN, William
Communistic activities in the United States; a report to the President
of the United States. Reprinted from the Congressional Record,
Seventy-Third Congress, Second Session. [San Francisco] The Industrial
Association of San Francisco [1934] 41 p.   *Hoover*

> Communist subversive activities exposed by the chairman of the American
> Federation of Labor. Included is condensation of his memorandum to President
> Roosevelt of Nov. 10, 1933, demanding that the Soviet government, before
> being recognized, give guarantees that such activities will cease.   ***Hoover***

HASS, Eric
The Socialist Labor Party and the Internationals. See no. 250.

1514 LOVESTONE, Jay
Pages from party history. New York City, Workers Library [1929] 36 p.
illus.   *Hoover*

The NEXT step in Britain, America and Ireland; (speeches and reports,
XII plenum E. C. C. I.). See nos. 1219, 1220.

1515 ONEAL, James
"Resolved: that the terms of the Third International are inacceptable
to the revolutionary socialists of the world." Being the report of a
debate, held in Star casino, New York City, Sunday, January sixteenth,
1921. Affirmative, James Oneal ... vs. negative, Robert Minor ...
Temporary chairman George H. Goebel, permanent chairman Benjamin
Glassberg. [N[ew] Y[ork] c[ity, The Academy press 1921] 31 p.

Hoover

1516 OPEN letter of the Comintern to the CEC of the Communist Party of
America for the Finnish members of the Party. [n. p., 1930] 13 p.
(typewritten) Microfilm copy.   *Hoover*

1517 The RED Album. May Day 1921. Cleveland, O., The Toiler, 1921. 16 p.
illus. Cover-title.   *Col*

REDS in America; the present status of the revolutionary movement in the United States... See no. 1526.

1518 SCHACHTMAN, Max
Ten years; history and principles of the Left opposition [New York] Pioneer publishers [1933] 79 p. Printed for the Communist League of America. *Hoover*

1519 SOCIALIST Labor Party [U.S.A.]
Workers of the world, unite! Declaration on the dissolution of the Communist International, adopted May 27, 1943. New York, N.Y., New York Labor News Co., 1943. 31 p. illus., facsim.
Hoover, NYPL

1520 SOCIALIST Labor Party [U.S.A.]
The Socialist Labor Party and the Third International; sociopolitical science vs. revolutionary romanticism. New York, Socialist Labor Party, 1926. 64 p. *Col*

1521 SOCIALIST Labor Party; [U.S.A.] Bulgarian Federation.
Sotsialisticheskata rabotnicheska partiia i Tretiia Internatsional; sotsialno-politicheskata nauka protiv revoliutsionniia romantizm. Granite City, Ill., izd. na Bulgarskiia sotsialist. rab. soiuz v Amerika, 1926. 67 p. *NYPL*

1522 SOCIALIST Labor Party; [U.S.A.] Scandinavian Federation.
Socialist labor party och Tredje internationalen; eller, Socialpolitisk vetenskap i motsats till revolutionśr romantik. En franställning ov Socialist labor party. Översättning fran enelskan av T. B-g. New York, Skandinaviska socialistiska arbetareförbundets förlag, 1926. 63 p.
NYPL

1523 SOCIALIST Labor Party; [U.S.A.] South Slavonian Federation.
Radnici svih zemalja, ujedniti se! Proglas o raspustanju Komunisticke internacionale, usvojen 27. mja 1943. Preveo J. Pirincin. Cleveland, Izdanje Jugoslavenske Federacije S.L.P., 1943. 32 p. *NYPL*

STALIN, Iosif
O pravykh fraktsionerakh v amerikanskoi kompartii. See no. 1139.

STALIN, Iosif
Stalin's speech on the American Communist Party... See no. 1140.

THESES and decisions; thirteenth plenum of the E.C.C.I. Draft resolution, eighth convention of the C.P., U.S.A. See no. 1292.

1524 UNITED Mine Workers of America.
Attempt by communists to seize the American labor movement; a series of six articles prepared by United Mine Workers of America and published in newspapers of the United States. Indianapolis, Ind., International Union, United Mine Workers of America, 1923. 63 p.

>   See annotation to next item.   *Col*

1525 UNITED States Congress. Senate.
Attempt by communists to seize the American labor movement. Prepared by the United Mine Workers of America and published in newspapers of the United States. Presented by Mr. Lodge. Washington, D.C., Government Printing Office, 1924. 43 p. 68-th Congress, 1-st Session, Document No. 14.

> "This series of six articles was prepared by the United Mine Workers of America, disclosing the attempt that is being made by the Red forces, under the direct supervision of Moscow, to seize control of the organized labor movement of America and use it as the base from which to carry on the Communist effort for the overthrow of the American Government. These articles are the result of an independent searching investigation on the part of the United Mine Workers of America which led directly to original sources."
>
> *LC, Harv*

1526 [WHITNEY, Richard Merrill]
Reds in America; the present status of the revolutionary movement in the United States based on documents seized by the authorities in the raid upon the convention of the Communist Party at Bridgman, Michigan, Aug. 22, 1922, . . . New York, Beckwith Press, 1924. 287 p.

> Introduction signed: R. M. Whitney. Contains several Comintern documents and references to Comintern activities in the United States. See also no. 1505.
>
> *Hoover*

1527 WOLFE, Bertram
What is the Communist oposition? 2-nd enlarged edition. New York, Communist Party U.S.A., Opposition [1933] 52 p.   *Harv*

PART V.

APPLICATION OF COMINTERN POLICIES

1. United Front; Tactics and Actions

BITTELMANN, Alexander, ed.
The advance of the United Front. At head of title: A documentary account. See no. 94.

BROWDER, Earl
New steps in the United Front. Report on the seventh Congress made at Madison Square Garden. See nos. 969—13, 1026.

CACHIN, Marcel
Du front unique au front populaire. [Speech at VII-th Congress] See no. 976.

CACHIN, Marcel
The fight for the people's front in France; [speech . . .] See nos 941, 968—10.

CACHIN, Marcel
El frente popular contra el fascismo y la guerra en Francia. [Speech at VII-th Congress] See no. 1012.

CACHIN, Marcel, and others
The people's Front in France; speeches delivered by Marcel Cachin, Maurice Thorez, André Marty [at VII-th Congress] See nos. 942, 969—8.

Il C[OMITATO] E[secutivo] dell'Internazionale comunista per il Fronte Unico del proletariato. Raccolta di documenti officiali a cura del C. E. dell'I. C. See no. 97.

DEGRAS, Jane
United front tractics in the Comintern 1921—1928. An essay in the collective work *International Communism;* see no. 243.

1528 DIETRICH, Paul R.
L'union sacrée antisoviétique. De l'Internationale des armaments à la IIe Internationale. Paris, Bureau d'Editions, 1931. 74 p.

Amst

1529 DIETRICH, Paul R.
The war of intervention against the Soviet Union and the Second International. London, Modern Books, Ltd., 1931. 46 p.

Hoover

DIMITROV, G.
Note: Here are listed only items which appeared as separate publications, collections of speeches, reports, articles, etc., and items written after the VII-th Congress. Separate reports and speeches concerning the United Front are listed with the material pertaining to the VII-th Congress under the Congress. For these items see nos. 896–1011.

1530 DIMITROV, G.
After Munich; the united front of the international proletariat and of the peoples against fascism. Also the Twenty-first anniversary of the great October Socialist Revolution (manifesto of the Executive Committee of the Communist International, November 7, 1938). New York, Workers Library Publishers [1938] 47 p.

Dimitrov's article originally published in *Pravda*, November 7, 1938.

Hoover, Amst

1531 DIMITROV, G.
Dal fronte antifascista alla democrazia popolare. Roma, Edizioni Rinascita, 1950. vii, 264 p. (Biblioteca della democrazia e del movimento operaio. 3)

Felt

1532 DIMITROV, G.
Dopo Monaco; il fronte unico del proletariato internazionale e dei popoli contro il fascismo. Seguito da: L'appello della Internazionale communista per il XXI anniversario della rivoluzione socialista — 7 novembre 1938. Parigi, Edizioni di coltura sociale, 1938. 62 p.

Hoover, Amst

1533 DIMITROV, G.
Edinniat front 1923 goda. [Sofiia] Izd. na Bulgarskata komunisticheska partiia [1949] 115 p.

Hoover

1534 DIMITROV, G.
Edinstvo mezhdunarodnogo proletariata — vysshee velenie perezhivaemogo momenta, [Moskva] Partizdat, 1937.

Harv, SInSt

1535 DIMITROV, G.
Edinyi front mezhdunarodnogo proletariata i narodov protiv fashizma.
Posle Miunkhena. Moskva, Gos. izd-vo polit. lit-ry, 1938   *Harv*

1536 DIMITROV, G.
Die Einheitsfront des Kampfes für den Frieden. Moskau, Verlags-
genossenschaft ausländischer Arbeiter in der UdSSR, 1936. 18 p.
Hoover

1537 DIMITROV, G.
Einheitsfront des Kampfes für den Frieden. Strasbourg, Prométhée
[n. d.] 15 p.   *Amst*

1538 DIMITROV, G.
Die Einheitsfront des Kampfes für den Frieden. Prag, Kreibich [n. d.]
15 p.   *Amst*

1539 DIMITROV, G.
Het front van het volk tegen fascisme en oorlog. Amsterdam, Agentschap "Amstel", 1937. 23 p.   *Amst*

1540 DIMITROV G.
Det internationale proletariats og folkenes enhedsfront mod fascismen, efter sammensvaergelsen i München. Tillaeg: Manifest fra Kom-
munistike Internationales Eksekutiv-komité til 21 — aarsdagen for den
store socialistiske Oktoberrevolution. København, Arbejderforlaget,
1938. 31 p.   *Amst*

1541 DIMITROV, G.
Jednota mezinárodního proletariátu nejvyšším příkazem okamžiku!
[Překladu [sic!] B. Reičina. Praha] 1937. 12 p. At head of title: Jiří
Dimitrov.   *Amst*

1542 DIMITROV G.
Lidová fronta boje proti fašizmu a válce. Z ruštiny přeložil J. Svoboda
[Praha, Hoffmann] 1937. 24 p. At head of title: Jiří Dimitrov.
Amst

DIMITROV, G.
La lutte contre la guerre impérialiste. [1940] See no. 235 c.

1543 DIMITROV, G.
La lutte pour le front unique contre le fascisme et la guerre. Paris,
Editions Sociales Internationales, 1938. 312 p.   *Amst*

1544 DIMITROV, G.
Narodnyi front bor'by protiv fashizma i voiny. Moskva, 1937. 22 p.
SInSt

1545 DIMITROV, G.
Il paese del socialismo e la lotta del proletariato internazionale.
Parigi, Edizioni Italiane di Cultura, 1939. 20 p.
Hoover, Amst

1546 DIMITROV, G.
Il pegno della vittoria. Seguito da: L'Appello della Internazionale
Comunista per il 1 Maggio 1938. Paris, Edizioni di Cultura sociale,
1938. 30 p.
Hoover, Felt

1547 DIMITROV, G.
Problemas del frente único. La Habana, Ediciones sociales [1945]
175 p.

A collection of reports, speeches and articles.
Hoover

1548 DIMITROV, G.
Probleme der Einheits- und Volksfront; Reden und Aufsätze. Moskau,
Verlagsgenossenschaft ausländischer Arbeiter in der UdSSR, 1938.
201 p.

Speeches at the Seventh Congress of the Communist International, Moscow,
1935 and later writings.
Hoover

1549 DIMITROV, G.
Problemite na edinnia front protiv fashizma i voinata; statii i rechi.
Moskva, Izdat. na literatura na chuzhdestranni e'zitsi, 1938. 218 p.
("Perevod ot ruski".)
NYPL

1550 DIMITROV, G.
Problémy jednotné a lidové fronty. Řeči a články. Praha, nákl.
Borecký, 1938. 248 p. port. At head of title: Jiří Dimitrov.
Amst

1551 DIMITROV, G.
Questioni del fronto unico e del fronte popolare; articoli e discorsi.
Paris, Ed. italiane di cultura, 1939. 442 p.

Includes speeches presented at VII Congress of Communist International and
other writings.
Hoover, Amst, Felt

1552 DIMITROV, G.
Sovetskii Soiuz i rabochii klass kapitalisticheskikh stran. [Moskva]
Partizdat, 1937. 15 p. port.
Hoover, Amst

1553 DIMITROV, G.
Sovětský svaz a dělnická třída kapitalistických zemí. [Praha, Nákl., Nedvěda] 1937. 12 p. At head of title: Jiří Dimitrov.   *Amst*

1554 DIMITROV, G.
Die Sowjetunion und die Arbeiterklasse der kapitalistischen Länder. Moskau, Verlagsgenossenschaft Ausländischer Arbeiter in der UdSSR, 1937. 15 p. port.   *Hoover, Amst*

1555 DIMITROV, G.
Tegen het fascisme. Eenheidsfront der internationale arbeidersklasse en der volkeren na het tractaat van München. [Amsterdam, Brochurehandel Communistische Partij van Nederland, 1939] 40 p.
     Amst

1556 DIMITROV, G.
The United Front; the struggle against fascism and war, by Georgi Dimitroff ... New York, International Publishers [c1938] 287 p. front (port.)

> The reports, speeches and articles of Georgii Dimitrov cover all important international developments since 1935. The collection opens with his political report to the Seventh World Congress of the Communist International and runs through the following two years to the end of 1937.   *Hoover*

1557 DIMITROV, G.
The united struggle for peace. New York, Workers Library Publishers, 1936. 22 p.   *Hoover*

1558 DIMITROV, G.
Unity and peace [The united front of the struggle for peace. London, Communist Party of Great Britain, n. d.] 13 p. (The peace library.)
     Hoover, Amst

1559 DIMITROV, G.
L'URSS et le prolétariat international. Paris, Bureau d'Editions, 1939. 24 p.   *BDIC*

1560 DIMITROV, G.
V bor'be za edinyi front protiv fashizma i voiny. Stat'i i rechi; 1935—1937. Leningrad, 1937. 152 p.   *SInSt*

1561 DIMITROV, G.
V bor'be za edinyi front protiv fashizma i voiny; stat'i i rechi, 1935—37. [Moskva] Partizdat, 1937, 169 p.

> Reports, speeches, and articles of Dimitrov covering the years 1935–37; including also his reports and speeches at the VIIth Congress of the Communist International.   *Hoover*

1563 DIMITROV, G.
V bor'be za edinyi front protiv fashizma i voiny; stat'i i rechi, 1935—
1939 g. g. [Leningrad] Gos. izd-vo polit. lit-ry, 1939. 241 p. mounted
port.

New, enlarged edition of previous item, extending coverage up to 1939.
Hoover, LC

1564 DIMITROV, G.
Die Volksfront zum Kampf gegen Faschismus und Krieg. Strasbourg,
Prométhé [1937] 16 p. *Amst*

1565 DIMITROV, G.
Wat moeten de arbeiders doen om de vrede te bewaren? Het eenheidsfront in de strijd voor de vrede. Amsterdam, Agentschap Amstel,
1936. 16 p. *Amst*

1566 EIN Mann ruft, Millionen antworten! Einheit, Einheit, Einheit. [Mit Beiträgen von Franzisco Caballero, Georg Branting, S. Grumbach u. a.]
Basel, Universum [n. d.] 40 p. port. *Amst*

1567 Die EINHEIT wird siegen! Dimitroffs Ruf zur internationalen Aktions-
einheit und die Antwort der sozialistschen Arbeiterinternationale.
[Mit Beiträgen von G. Dimitrov, Georg Branting, Kl. Gottwald u. a.]
Strasbourg, Prometheus [n. d.] 35 p. *Amst*

1568 FIMMEN, Edo
Vers le front unique international (articles et discours); introduction
de Pierre Monatte. Paris, Librairie du travail [1923] 32 p. (Petite bibliothèque de l'internationale syndicale rouge, 6) (Cover title)
NYPL, Felt

1569 FISCHER, Ernst
From people's front to national front. London, Communist Party of
Great Britain, 1942. 12 p. *Hoover*

1570 FISCHER, Ernst
Für oder gegen die Einheitsfront. Strasbourg, Prométhée [1936] 38 p.
Hoover, Amst

Gegen den Krieg! Gegen die Bourgeoisie! Gegen die Sozialverräterei!
Für die Weltrevolution! Für die Diktatur des Proletariats! Für den
Kommunismus. Zum 10. Jahrestag des imperialistischen Krieges. See
no. 1309.

GOTTWALD, K.
Für die Volksfront der Arbeit, der Freiheit und des Friedens in der Tschechoslowakei. [Speech at VII-th Congress] See nos. 925, 926.

GOTTWALD, K.
Kompartiia Chekhoslovakii v bor'be za edinyi front. See no. 900.

GOTTWALD, K.
A people's front in defence of labour, freedom and peace; speech... [VII-th Congress] See nos. 955, 956, 968—13, 969—14.

GOTTWALD, K. and others
Kommunisticheskaia partiia Chekhoslovakii v bor'be za edinyi front — protiv voiny i fashizma; rechi... See no. 903.

1571 HÖGLUND, Z.
Moskva och den proletära enthetsfronten. Eskilstuna [n. d.] 30 p.

SInSt

1572 HOPFFE, Günther
Einigungskomödie oder Einheitsfront. Berlin-Schöneberg, Verlag der Jugendinternationale, 1923. 71 p. *Felt*

1573 KALICKA, Felicja
Problemy jednolitego frontu w międzynarodowym ruchu robotniczym, 1933—1935. Warszawa, Książka i Wiedza, 1962. 471 p. (Zakład Historii Partii przy CK PZPR.) *Hoover, BDIC*

KOMMUNISTICHESKAIA partiia Pol'shi — za antifashistskii front; rechi tt. Lenskogo, Bronkovskogo. See no. 907.

1574 KUN, Bela
Die brennendste Frage — die Aktionseinheit. [Strasbourg?] Prometheus Verlag [1934] 45 p. (On cover: Schriftenreihe der proletarischen Einheit, 2) Printed in Switzerland. *Hoover*

1575 KUN, Bela
The Most Burning Question, Unity of Action. New York, Workers Library Publishers, 1934. 64 p. *Hoover*

1575a KUN, Bela
The Second International in dissolution. Moscow, Cooperative Publishing Society of Foreign Workers in the USSR, 1933. 124 p. *Hoover*

1576 KUN, Bela
Die II. Internationale in Auflösung. Moskau usw., Verlagsgenossenschaft Ausländischer Arbeiter in der UdSSR, 1933. 87 p.   *Amst*

1577 LEDER, Z.
Die Offensive des Kapitals und die Einheitsfront des Proletariats.
[n. p.] Verlag der Kommunistischen Internationale, 1922. 59 p.
                                                          Hoover, Amst

1578 LEDER, Z.
L'Offensive du capital et l'unité du front prolétarien. Paris, Librairie
de l'Humanité, 1922. 86 p. (Petite bibliothèque communiste).
                                                                Hoover

1579 LOVESTONE, Jay
The people's front illusion. From "social fascism" to the "people's
front". New York City, Workers Age Publishers [n. d.] 86 p.
                                                          Hoover, Amst

1580 LOZOVSKII, A.
Mirovoe nastuplenie kapitala i edinyi proletarskii front. Moskva,
Profintern, 1922. 43 p.   *Hoover, NYPL, Felt*

1581 MANUILSKII, D. Z.
Lenin and international labor unity. [New York, Workers Library,
1939.] 31 p. "Reprinted from *The Communist* for March, 1939."
                                                                Hoover

1581a MANUILSKII, D. Z.
Lenin e il movimento operaio internazionale. Parigi, Edizioni Italiane
di Cultura, 1939. 16 p.   *Amst*

De ONDERHANDELINGEN tussen de Socilistische en de Communistische Internationale over het eenheidsfront. Stenografisch verslag . . .
Se no. 1649.

PIATNITSKII, O.
Prinuditel'nyi trud, fashizm, i organizatsiia bezrabotnykh na osnove
edinogo fronta. [Speech' at VII-th Congress] See no. 914.

Die PROLETARISCHE Einheitsfront. Aufruf der Exekutive der Kommunistischen Internationale und der Exekutive der Roten Gewerkschaftsinternationale Moskau, 1. Januar 1922. Leitsätze über die Einheitsfront. See no. 1032.

RADEK, K.
Piat' let Kominterna. [The second volume contains his articles and
speeches promoting the united front movement.] See no. 329.

THOREZ, Maurice
Edinyi i narodnyi front vo Frantsii. See no. 916.

1582 THOREZ, Maurice
Sovremennaia Frantsiia i narodnyi front. Perevod s frantsuzskogo
O. Shargorodskoi. Moskva, 1937. 148 p.   *SInSt*

THOREZ, Maurice
The success of the anti-fascist united front. See no. 968—11.

THOREZ, Maurice
Die Volksfront für Brot, Freiheit und Frieden. Die Erfolge der antifaschistischen Einheitsfront in Frankreich; Rede . . . See no. 936.

La UNIDAD triunfarà. Llamamiento de Dimitrof a la unidad de acción
Internacional. Respuesta de la Internacional Socialista Obrera. See
no 1653.

WANG, Ming
Le front unique dans les pays coloniaux. See no. 985.

1583 WANN Einheitsfront? [Praha, Hellmich, n. d.] 20 p.   *Amst*

1584 ZINOV'EV, G. E.
Alte Ziele, neue Wege über die proletarische Einheitsfront. Hamburg,
Verlag der Kommunistischen Internationale. Auslieferungsstelle: C.
Hoym L. Cahnbley, 1922. 31 p. At head of title: G. Sinowjew.
                                                          Hoover, Amst
ZINOV'EV, G. E.
La tactique du front unique. See no. 1042.

2. Anti-War Propaganda in Defense of the U. S. S. R.

L'ATTITUDE du prolétariat devant la guerre. See no. 92.

The ATTITUDE of the proletariat towards war. A collection of documents on a vital question. See no. 93.

BELL, Tom
Nakanune epokhi novykh voin. (Itogi VI Kongressa Kominterna) See no. 888.

BENNET, A.
Die Kriegsgefahr, die chinesische Revolution und die Kommunistische Internationale. See no. 1323.

BROWDER, Earl
War against Workers' Russia. [Speech at 11-th Plenum] See no. 1169.

BUKHARIN, N. I.
Itogi [8-go] plenuma IKKI. [Deals with the anti-war actions of the C. I.] See no. 452.

CACHIN, Marcel
El frente popular contra el fascismo y la guerra en Francia. Discurso de los representantes del partido comunista de Francia, pronunciados en el VII. Congreso. See no. 1012.

CACHIN, Marcel
Preparation for war against the Soviet Union; report to the eleventh Plenum of the ECCI; April 8, 1931. See nos. 1170, 1171.

CACHIN, Marcel
La Preparazione metodica della guerra contro l'Unione dei Soviet. Rapporto all'XI Plenum dell'I. C. See no. 1181.

Les COMMUNISTES luttent pour la paix. [Collective work] See no. 99.

CONTRE la guerre et le fascisme; l'unité. Résolutions et décisions [du VII-e Congres] See no. 1020.

CONTRO la guerra e il fascismo: l'unità. (Risoluzioni e decisioni del VII. Congresso dell'Internazionale Comunista) See no. 1022.

DIMITROV, G.
Borba protiv imperialisticheskata voina. [1940] See no. 234 b.

DIMITROV, G.
Communism and the war; together with the manifesto of the Executive Committee of the Communist International, issued November 6th, 1939. See no. 235.

DIMITROV, G.
La lutte contre la guerre impérialiste. [1940] See no. 235 c.

DRAPER, Harold, ed.
"Out of their own mouths"; a documentary study of the new line of
the Comintern on war. See no. 103.

EVE of revolutions and wars; resolution of the 13th plenum of the
Communist International. See no. 1290.

Le FASCISME, le danger de guerre et les tâches de parties communistes. "Thèses adoptées par la XIIIe Assemblée plenière du C. E.
de l'I. C." See no. 1293.

Il FASCISMO, il pericolo di guerra e i compiti dei partiti comunisti
(Tesi, risoluzioni e decisioni della XIII Sessione plenaria del Comitato
esecutivo dell'I. C.) See no. 1293 a.

1585   FUNK, Kurt
Soll die Arbeiterklasse vor dem Kriege kapitulieren? Eine Auseinandersetzung mit der Politik der II. Internationale. Paris, Editions Prométhée
[n. d.] 56 p.   *Amst*

1586   GARBIN, N.
L'Internazionale e la guerra. Con prefazione di Filipo Corridoni.
Milano, Impresa Tipogr. Lombarda [n. d.] 31 p.   *Felt*

1587   GEGEN bürgerlichen Militarismus und Sozial-Verräterei. Berlin, Verlag
der Jugendinternationale [1924]. 75 p. (Rüstzeug, Heft 12)

            See next item below.   *Hoover*

GEGEN den Krieg! Gegen die Bourgeoisie! Gegen die Sozialverräterei! Für die Weltrevolution! Für die Diktatur des Proletariats! Für
den Kommunismus. Zum 10. Jahrestag des imperialistischen Krieges.
See no. 1309.

GOTTWALD, Klement
La lutte pour le travail, le pain, la paix. [Speech at VII-th Congress]
See no. 978.

Den INTERNASJONALE situasjon og krigsfaren; Kommunistenes opgaver ... See no. 881.

1588 INTERNATIONAL Anti-Communist Entente.
An aspect of the disarmament problem: the "proletarian war".
Memorandum addressed to governments by the Permanent Bureau
of the International Entente against the Third International. Geneva,
Printed by Sonor Ltd., 1929. 12 p.   *NYPL*

1589 INTERNATIONAL Anti-Communist Entente.
L'URSS, obstacle au désarmament. Genève [1929?] 14 p.
                                                                      Hoover

1590 INTERNATIONAL Anti-Communist Entente.
The U.S.S.R. and disarmament. 2nd ed., revised and extended.
[Geneva] 1932. 17 p.   *Harv*

1591 INTERNATIONAL Red Day (August 1-st 1929). London, Modern Books
Ltd., 1929. 79 p.

> A reprint of articles from the periodical *Communist International* on the
> occasion of an anti-war manifestation initiated by the Comintern. It expressed
> the Comintern's quest for workers' support in preventing a new "imperialist
> war of intervention" against the USSR. Among the contributors are Bela Kun,
> H. Barbé, A. Martynov and several communist leaders from various countries.
> A French translation appeared under the title "La Journée Rouge (1-er aout
> 1929); l'action du proletariat international contre la guerre imperialiste". See
> no. 1594.   *Felt*

1592 INTERNATIONAL Red Day August 1-st 1929. New York, Workers
Library Publishers, 1929. 79 p. "Printed in England"

> New York edition of preceding item.   *Hoover*

L'INTERNATIONALE Communiste et la guerre; documents sur la lutte
de l'I.C. contre la guerre impérialiste et pour la défense de l'U.R.S.S.
See no. 109.

1593 INTERNATIONALE Vereinigung der Kommunistischen Opposition
(IVKO). Der Krieg und die Kommunistische Internationale. Ein offener
Brief der Internationalen Vereinigung der Kommunistischen Opposition
(IVKO). Wolfsheim, Alfred Quiri, 1937. 47 p.   *Felt*

1594 La JOURNÉE rouge (1-er aout 1929); l'action du prolétariat international contre la guerre impérialiste. Paris, Bureau d'Editions, 1929.
122 p.

> For annotation see "International Red Day" no. 1591.   *Hoover, Amst*

328

1595 KHITAROV, R.
Kriegsgefahr, Faschismus und die Aufgaben der K[ommunistischen] J[ugend] — I[nternationale]. Moskau, Zentral-Völker-Verlag, 1931. 23 p. At head of title: R. Chitarow. *Amst, Felt*

K mirovomu proletariatu. Manifest piatogo Vsemirnogo kongressa Kominterna k desiatiletiiu imperialisticheskoi voiny. See no. 795.

Die KOMINTERN und der Krieg; Dokumente über den Kampf der Komintern gegen den imperialistischen Krieg und für die Verteidigung der Sowjetunion; ein Sammelbuch. See no. 116.

KOMMUNISTICHESKII Internatsional i voina; dokumenty i materialy o bor'be Kominterna protiv imperialisticheskoi voiny i v zashchitu S.S.S.R. See no. 118.

Die KOMMUNISTISCHE Internationale und der Krieg. Thesen des VI. Weltkongresses der Kommunistischen Internationale über den Kampf gegen den imperialistischen Krieg und die Aufgaben der Kommunisten. See no. 847.

KOMUNISTYCZNA Partia Polski.
KPP w walce z wojną, faszyzmem i atakiem kapitału. XIII plenum Komitetu Wykonawczego Międzynarodówki Komunistycznej. See no. 1283.

KRIGSFARAN och kommunisternas uppgifter; teser över kampen mot det imperialistiska kriget, antagna av Kominterns sjätte världskongress 1928. See no. 886.

KUUSINEN, Otto
Faschismus, Kriegsgefahr und die Aufgaben der kommunistischen Parteien; Referat auf dem XIII. Plenum des EKKI. See no. 1252.

KUUSINEN, Otto
Fascism, the danger of war and the task of the communist parties. See nos. 970—2, 1259, 1267.

KUUSINEN, Otto
Fashizm, opasnost' voiny i zadachi kommunisticheskikh partii; doklad na XIII plenume IKKI. See no. 1246.

KUUSINEN, Otto
La position de l'Internationale Communiste devant la crise, la guerre et le fascisme. See no. 280.

LENIN, V. I.
Über den Krieg; Reden und Aufsätze. See no. 125.

1596 LISOVSKII, P.
Maski doloi. 2 Internatsional i ugroza voiny. Moskva, 1932. 112 p.
SInSt

LOZOVSKII, A.
Protiv voiny, imperializma i reformizma; doklad i zakliuchitel'noe slovo na Tikhookeanskoi konferentsii profsoiuzov, 16 avgusta, 1929 g. See no. 1789.

La LUCHA contra la guerra imperialista y las tareas de los comunistas; tesis adoptados por el VI Cognreso Mundial... See no. 883.

MANUILSKII, D. Z.
La crise révolutionnaire, le fascisme et la guerre. See no. 1278.

MANUILSKII, D. Z.
Revoliutsionnyi krizis, fashizm i voina; rech' na XIII plenume IKKI 5 dekabria 1933 g. See no. 1247.

MANUILSKII, D. Z.
Revolutionäre Krise, Faschismus und Krieg. XIII. Plenum des EKKI; Dezember 1933. See no. 1253.

MANUILSKII, D. Z.
Revolutionary crisis, fascism and war. See nos. 970—4, 1261, 1269.

MARTY, André
For peace! For the defence of the Soviet Union! See no. 968—12.

MARTY, André
Pour la paix, pour la défense de l'U.R.S.S. [Speech at VII-th Congress] See no. 982.

MARTY, André
Vmeste s trudiashchimisia SSSR — na zashchitu mira; iz rechi na zasedanii 14 avgusta 1935 g. See no. 913.

The MENACE of New World War. Excerpts from resolutions, reports and speeches at VII-th Congress. See no. 1029.

1597 NIEDER mit dem Krieg! Strasbourg, Prometheus Verlag [1935] 43 p.

> **The pamphlet** contains excerpts of Togliatti's (Ercoli) report "The fight against war and fascism" given at the VII-th Congress of the C.I. (see nos. 971, 972) and excerpts from speeches during the discussion of this report. Main emphasis is laid on exposing Nazi Germany and fascist Italy as the instigators of a new world war. Also included are the following documents: the appeal "Down with the war" issued on October 7, 1935 by the ECCI (p. 5–7), and two communications from the ECCI to the Secretariat of the II-nd International concerning the Italian aggression against Abyssinia, dated September 26 (or 25) and October 7, 1935. *Hoover, LC, NYPL, Amst*

1598 L'ŒUVRE des Soviets et la guerre inavouable [par] un communiste. Petrograd, Editions de l'Internationale communiste, 1919. 16 p.

Hoover

OKANO
The war in the Far East and the task of the communists in the struggle against imperialist war and military intervention; report.. at the XIIth Plenum of the ECCI. See nos. 1212, 1213.

PIECK, Wilhelm [and others]
Die Offensive des Faschismus und die Aufgaben der Kommunisten im Kampf für die Volksfront gegen Krieg und Faschismus; Referate auf dem VII. Kongreß der Kommunistischen Internationale. See no. 933.

Il PROLETARIATO di fronte alla guerra. See no. 133.

Iz istorii mezhdunarodnoi proletarskoi solidarnosti; dokumenty i materialy. See vols. ii—v of no. 112.

1599 RUDOLF, N.
Weltkrise — Weltkriegsgefahr. Moskau, Verlagsgenossenschaft Ausländischer Arbeiter in der UdSSR, 1931. 31 p. *Amst*

The STRUGGLE against imperialist war and the tasks of the communists; resolutions of the 6th World Congress... See nos. 865, 866.

TOGLIATTI, Palmiro
Boj proti valce a fašismu. See no. 993.

TOGLIATTI, Palmiro
The fight against war and fascism; report and speech in reply to the discussion on the third point of the agenda: The preparations for imperialist war and the tasks of the Communist International. [VII-th Congress] See nos. 968—4, 971.

TOGLIATTI, Palmiro
The fight for peace; report on the preparations for imperialist war and the tasks of the Communist International at VII-th Congress. See nos. 969—11, 972.

TOGLIATTI, Palmiro
Kampf gegen Krieg und Faschismus. [Report at VII-th Congress] See nos. 936, 937.

TOGLIATTI, Palmiro
La lotta contro la guerra; rapporto al VII Congresso dell'Internazionale Comunista. See no. 1010.

TOGLIATTI, Palmiro
La lutte contre la guerre et le fascisme. [Report at VII-th Congress] See no. 984.

TOGLIATTI, Palmiro
O zadachakh Kommunisticheskogo Internatsionala v sviazi s podgotovkoi imperialistami novoi mirovoi voiny; [report at VII-th Congress] See no. 917.

1600 The WORK of the Soviets and the unconfessable [?] war. Petrograd, Communist International, 1919. 16 p. At head of title: A Communist. (Veröffentlichungen der Kommunistischen Internationale, no. 6)

> The word "unconfessable" seems to be an erroneous translation. The French title (see no. 1598) *"L'oeuvre des Soviets et la guerre inavouable"* would suggest that the English title should read "The work of the Soviets and the unavowable war". The copy was unavailable to verify whether the translation is erroneous or the catalog card wrongly typed. *LC*

ZETKIN, Klara
Der Kampf der Kommunistischen Parteien gegen Kriegsgefahr und Krieg; Bericht auf der Konferenz der Erweiterten Exekutive . . . 2. März 1922. See no. 1039.

3. Armed Uprisings; Riots; Strikes

L'ARMEE Rouge, instrument de la revolution mondiale; le monde civilisé en danger. See no. 404.

1601 ARMIIA Kommunisticheskogo Internatsionala. Petrograd, 1921. 12 p.
LC, Harv

EHRT, Adolf
Communism in Germany; the truth about the communist conspiracy on the eve of the National Revolution. See no. 1393.

EHRT, Adolf
Révolte armée; révélations sur la tentative d'insurrection communiste à la veille de la Révolution Nationale. See no. 1394.

ERFAHRUNGEN, Lehren und Aufgaben in den Wirtschaftskämpfen. Streiktaktik und Streikstrategie. Resolutionen der Straßburger Konferenz. See no. 1790.

INTERNATIONAL Anti-Communist Entente.
A new World War; "The Bolshevist War". See no. 1312.

[INTERNATIONAL Conference on Strike Strategy. Strassburg, January 1929] See nos. 1790—1792.

K voprosu o stachechnoi strategii; iz opyta klassovoi bor'by. Materialy k 3. konkgressu Profinterna. See no. 1869.

KUUSINEN, O. W.
The Finnish revolution; a self-criticism. See no. 1352.

KUUSINEN, O. W.
Revoliutsiia v Finliandii; samokritika. See no. 1353.

KUUSINEN, O. W.
La révolution en Finlande. See no. 1354.

KUUSINEN, O. W.
Die Revolution in Finnland. See no. 1355.

1602 LANGE, Alfred [pseud. of Kippenberger, Hans]
Der Weg zum Sieg. Eine theoretische Erörterung über Marxismus und Aufstand. Herausgegeben von Ernst Schneller. Berlin, 1927. 35 leaves **mimeogr.**

> „Die vorliegende Broschüre versucht, über die Erfahrungen der revolutionären Bewegung der letzten Jahre theoretisch Klarheit zu schaffen und sie zusammenzufassen. In weiten Kreisen des Proletariats und der Werktätigen, selbst unter den mit der Kommunistischen Partei sympatisierenden Arbeitern, bestehen vielfach noch völlig schiefe, kleinbürgerliche Auffassungen über die Revolution und im Besonderen über den bewaffneten Aufstand." "Vorbemerkung" signed by Ernst Schneller, dated: Berlin, March 18, 1927. *Hoover*

1603 LOZOVSKII, A.

La grève est un combat! Essai d'application de la science militaire à la stratégie des grèves. Paris, Impr. Cootypographie, 1931. 93 p. Petite bibliothèque de l'Internationale syndicale rouge, 31)

> This pamphlet contains the text of five lectures and one Annex. The lectures were given at the international Lenin School in Moscow, the Comintern school for revolutionary cadres. They are dated between January 28 and March 26, 1930. According to the preface signed by Lozovskii, the purpose of these lectures was "to state, in a most condensed form, the fundamental problems of our strike tactic, to point out the connexion between economics and politics, the necessity of utilizing the abundant experiences of the economic struggle, the possibility of using in the strike movement many rules established in military science, and to call attention to the bonds existing between the economic and political strikes, the uprising, and the struggle for power". (p. 4) The Annex contains the resolution of the Strassburg Conference on Strike Strategy (see nos. 1790–1792). The text often refers to discussions and resolutions on the economic struggle and strike tactics of the III-th and IV-th Congress of the RILU and the 10-th Plenum of the ECCI. The author stresses on several occasions that the aims and actions of the Communist International and of the Red International of Labor Unions in matters of strikes and the struggle for power are identical and parallel in development. For German editions see nos. 1603a and 1604. *Hoover, Felt*

1603a LOZOVSKII, A.

Der Streik; fünf Vorträge gehalten an der Lenin-Schule zu Moskau. Berlin, Rote Gewerkschafts-Internationale, 1930. 110 p.

> Probably first edition of no. 1604. For contents see no. 1603. *NYPL*

1604 LOZOVSKII, A.

Der Streik als Schlacht; fünf Vorträge gehalten an der Internationalen Lenin-Schule zu Moskau, Januar—März 1930. Berlin, Sefer [1930] 119 p.

> According to the Foreword, this is a second edition of the item. For annotation see no. 1603. *Hoover*

1605 NEUBERG, A. (Pseud. of Neumann, Heinz)

L'Insurrection armée. Paris, Bureau d'Editions, 1931. 278 p. plans, maps, part folded.

> This is a translation of "Der bewaffnete Aufstand" published in 1928. Several sources ascribe authorship to Heinz Neumann (?). A frank discussion of the reasons why several communist uprisings and revolts failed. The following revolts are discussed: Reval (1924); Hamburg (1923); Canton (1927); Shanghai (1926, 1927). Furthermore, the author deals broadly with the organization of "armed forces of the proletariat", and their preparation for insurrection. *Hoover, Felt*

PILENKO, Aleksandre
La propagande de la guerre civile (La tactique de la IIIe Internationale) See no. 411.

PROBLEMS of strike strategy; decisions of the International Conference on Strike Strategy, held in Strassburg, Germany, January 1929. See no. 1791.

PROBLEMY stachechnoi strategii. Doklady i rechi na III kongresse Profinterna. See no. 1873.

1606 REVEL'SKAIA gavan' i bol'sheviki. [n. p., 1921] 48 p. Typescript.
Hoover

SCHÖNAU, Alexander
The February insurrection of the Austrian proletariat. See no. 1296.

1607 SOKOL, I.
La grève des traminots de Varsovie. [Paris, Rédaction de la Revue "L'I.S.R.", 1931?] 20 p. At head of title: Les enseignements d'une grève. (Petite bibliothèque de l'Internationale Syndicale Rouge, 39)
Hoover

STREIK-Strategie. Eine Denkschrift auf Grund der Beratungen auf dem 3 Kongreß der Roten Gewerkschafts-Internationale. See no. 1883.

STRIKE strategy & tactics; the lessons of the industrial struggles. Thesis adopted by the Strassburg Conference, held under the auspices of the Red International of Labor Unions. See no. 1792.

ULBRICHT, Walter
Revolutionäre Streikführung. See no. 1914.

1608 WOLLENBERG, Erich
Der Apparat; Stalins Fünfte Kolonne. Bonn, Bundesministerium für Gesamtdeutsche Fragen [n. d.] 48 p. illus.

> A concise presentation of the different "apparats" of communist and Soviet subversive organizations in Germany since 1919 and their connections with the Comintern, written by a former communist and participant in some of these organizations. *Hoover*

4. The National and Colonial Question

1609 BOERSNER, Demetrio
The Bolsheviks and the national and colonial question (1917—1928)
Genève, E. Droz, 1957. xv, 285 p. (Université de Genève. Institut
universitaire de Hautes Etudes Internationales. Thèse, No. 106)
Hoover, Felt

1610 GAUTHEROT, Gustave
Le bolchévisme aux colonies et l'impérialisme rouge. Avec 36 illustrations. Paris, Librairie de la Revue française, 1930. 446 p. illus., maps,
facsim, diagrs.   *Hoover, LC, Col, Amst* (damaged), *Felt*

1611 INTERNATIONAL Colonial Bureau Hague.
Rapport sur la préparation par le gouvernement soviétique des
révoltes coloniales. [La Haye, 193-?] iv, 68 p. 4 fold. diagr. At head
of title: Edition du Bureau colonial international, La Haye.

"Ouvrages spéciaux sur le bolchévisme dans les colonies nederlandaises,
anglaises et françaises": p. 68.   *Hoover*

MANUIL'SKII, D. Z.
Bericht zur National- und Kolonialfrage. [At V-th Congress.] See
no. 777.

MANUIL'SKII, D. Z.
Rapport de Manouilski sur la question nationale et coloniale. [At
V-th Congress.] See no. 791.

MANUIL'SKII, D. Z.
Report on the national-colonial question. [At V-th Congress.] See
no. 785.

1612 PAVLOVICH-Volonter, M. P. [pseud. of Mikhail VELTMAN]
Voprosy kolonial'noi i natsional'noi politiki i III Internatsional. Sovet-
skaia Rossiia, Azerbaidzhan, Gruziia, Armeniia, Turtsiia. Moskva,
Tip. III Kommunisticheskogo Internatsionala, 1920. 71 p.
NYPL, Harv, Col

1613 Die PRAXIS der bürgerlichen Klassenjustiz im Kampfe gegen die
revolutionären Bewegungen der Werktätigen, nationalen Minderheiten, Kolonial- und Halbkolonialvölker. Hrsg. von der Exekutive
der Internationalen Roten Hilfe. [Mit Einl. von Clara Zetkin.] Berlin,
Mopr [1928] 124 p. Als Manuskript gedruckt.   *Amst*

The REVOLUTIONARY movement in the colonies; theses adopted by the sixth World Congress of the Communist International. See nos. 862, 863, 864.

STRATEGIIA i taktika Kominterna v natsional'no-kolonial'noi revoliutsii na primere Kitaia; sbornik dokumentov. See no. 138.

WANG, Ming
Le front unique dans les pays coloniaux. Speech at VII-th Congress. See no. 985.

WANG, Ming
Im Zeichen der chinesischen Sowjets; die revolutionäre Bewegung in den kolonialen und halbkolonialen Ländern und die Taktik der Kommunistischen Parteien. Speech at VII-th Congress. See nos. 939, 940.

WANG, Ming
The revolutionary movement in colonial countries. Report at VII-th Congress. See nos. 968—9, 969—12, 974, 975.

5. Economic Questions

1614 BARANOV, G. [and] Kogan, M.
Bor'ba Kominterna za revoliutsionnyi vykhod iz mirovogo ekonomicheskogo krizisa. Moscow, 1933. 80 p. *SInSt*

1615 BITTEL, Karl, ed.
Genossenschafts-Thesen der Kommunistischen Internationale. Halle-Merseburg, Verlag Produktiv-Genossenschaft, 1923. 39 p.
Harv, Amst, Felt

1616 INTERNATIONAL Anti-Communist Entente.
Le Commerce avec les Soviets. Genève [Imp. du Journal de Genève] 1931. 19 p. *Felt*

1617 INTERNATIONAL Anti-Communist Entente.
Der Handel mit Sowjet-Rußland 1931. St. Gallen, Buchdruckerei Karl Weiss [n. d.] 20 p. *Felt*

1618 INTERNATIONAL Anti-Communiste Entente, Swiss National Center. La failité du collectivisme en Russie; publication du Centre National Suisse de l'Entente Internationale contre la IIIe Internationale. Genève, Imprimerie Sonor, 1928. 62 p. *Hoover*

1619 KOMMUNISTICHESKAIA Akademiia, Moscow. Institut mirovogo khoziaistva i mirovoi politiki.
Tri goda mirovogo krizisa. Moskva, Part. izd-vo, 1932. [Pagination not given by Harv.]

> Contains chapter "About the international situation and the tasks of the sections of the Communist International", pp. 171–180. *Harv*

MANUIL'SKII, D.
La crise économique et l'essor révolutionnaire. Rapport et discours de clôture au Présidium élargi du CE de l'IC (18—28 février 1930) See no. 1157.

MANUIL'SKII, D.
Ekonomicheskii krizis i revoliutsionnyi pod"em; doklad i zakliuchitel'noe slovo na rasshirennom prezidiume Ispolkoma Kommunisticheskogo Internatsionala (ot 18—20 fevralia 1930 g.) See no. 1154.

MANUILSKII, D. Z.
Das Ende der kapitalistischen Stabilisierung. See no. 1204.

MANUILSKII, D.
Die Weltwirtschaftskrise und der revolutionäre Aufstieg. Referat auf dem erweiterten Plenum des Präsidiums des EKKI. See no. 1155.

1620 MATERIAL supply of the workers. Petrograd, 1922. 14 p. tables.
Hoover, Col, Amst

1621 MINGULIN, I.
Mirovoi ekonomicheskii krizis i bor'ba za proletarskuiu revoliutsiiu. [Moskva] Molodaia gvardiia, 1931. 237 p. *Col*

1622 MIROVOI ekonomicheskii krizis i konets stabilizatsii kapitalizma. Moskva, "Pravda", 1933. 440 p. tables. At head of title: "Bol'shevik". Politiko-ekonomicheskii dvukhnedel'nik TSK VKP(b).

> "The present collective work is composed of articles published in the course of the year 1932 in 'Bol'shevik'". *SInSt*

1623 PIATNITSKII, Osip A.
Mirovoi ekonomicheskii krizis, revoliutsionnyi pod"em i zadachi sektsii Kominterna. Moskva, 1933. 96 p.

> For annotation see no. 1625. *BDIC*

1624 PIATNITSKII, Osip A.
Die Weltwirtschaftskrise, der revolutionäre Aufschwung und die Aufgaben der Sektionen der Kommunistischen Internationale. Moskau-Leningrad, Verlagsgenossenschaft ausländischer Arbeiter in der UdSSR, 1933. 93 p.

> For annotation see next item. *LC, Col*

1625 PIATNITSKII, Osip A.
The world economic crisis; the revolutionary upsurge and the tasks of the communist parties. London, Modern Books Ltd. [n. d., 1933?] 122 p.

> A pamphlet written after the XII Plenum (Sept. 1932), but before the XIII Plenum (December 1933).
> Contents: Introduction: The world Economic Crisis, the end of capitalist stabilization and the danger of imperialist wars. – The capitalist world in the throes of the crisis and the land of socialist construction. – The revolutionary upsurge of the workers' and peasants' movement. – What the communist parties have achieved between the eleventh and twelfth Plenums of the E. C. C. I. – The failure of the communist parties to keep pace with the advance of the revolutionary workers' and peasants' movement. – The tasks of the communist parties. – Postscript: the situation in Germany in connection with the changed conditions, the new tasks of the Communist Party of Germany in the field of party construction and the utilization of legal possibilities in work among the masses. *Hoover, NYPL, Col*

POSLEVOENNYI kapitalizm v osveshchenii Kominterna; sbornik dokumentov i rezoliutsii kongressov i Ispolkoma Kominterna. See no. 130.

1626 RUBINSTEIN, M.
Die Konzentration des Kapitals und die Aufgaben der Arbeiterklasse. Zweite erweiterte Auflage. Verlag der Roten Gewerkschafts-Internationale in Moskau; Auslieferung für Deutschland durch Führer-Verlag, Berlin, 1924. 118 p. (Bibliothek der Roten Gewerkschafts-Internationale, Bd. 29) *Hoover, NYPL, Felt*

1627 SULTAN-ZADE, A. [pseud.]
Krizis mirovogo khoziaistva i novaia voennaia groza. [Moskva] Gos. izd-vo, 1921. viii, 150 p. At head of title: Kommunisticheskii Internatsional. *Hoover*

1628 VARGA, Eugen
The Decline of Capitalism. Published for the Communist International by the Communist Party of Great Britain. London, 1924. 69 p. tables.

Hoover

This pamphlet by Varga may be mistaken for his report to the IV-th Congress of the Communist International, which was printed under the title *The Process of Capitalist Decline* listed as no. 746, and its French edition under the title *Le declin du capitalisme*, listed as no. 749. Footnote 2 to the first chapter of the above listed pamphlet (no. 1628) and to its French translation makes it clear that Varga's report to the IV-th Congress obviously appeared also under the title *The Decline of Capitalism* although it is not identical with the item listed here. This becomes quite clear from Varga's statement on pp. 5–6 of the discussed item.

The existence of at least three pomphlets by Varga, published under the same title: "The Decline of Capitalism", but with completely different texts, requires a complete listing of all publications by Varga printed by or for the Communist International:

1. *Die Krise der kapitalistischen Weltwirtschaft* – a report presented to the III-rd Congress, published by Hoym in Hamburg in 1921. See no. 672.

2. A second, enlarged edition of the above, published by Hoym in Hamburg in the same yar. See no. 673.

3. A French translation of the above, *La crise de l'economie capitaliste*. See no. 686.

4. *The Process of Capitalist Decline* – a report to the IV-th Congress, published by Hoym in Hamburg in 1922. See no. 746.

5. A reprint of the above, published under the title *The Decline of Capitalism* – a copy of which was not located.

6. A French translation of the above report, published under the title *Le declin du capitalisme*. See no. 749.

7. A new pamphlet under the title *The Decline of Capitalism*, published for the Communist International by the Communist Party of Great Britain in 1924. (This is the above listed item no. 1628)

8. A French translation of the above pamphlet, under the title *Essor ou decadence du capitalisme?*. See no. 1630.

9. A third pamphlet under the same title *The Decline of Capitalism* published in August 1928 in London by the Communist Party of Great Britain, similar to the previous item, but certainly not identical. See no. 1635.

10. A small book in Russian for the VII-th Congress of the Communist International under the title *Mezhdu VI i VII Kongressami Kominterna; ekonomika i politika 1928—1934*, published in Moscow in 1935. See no. 918.

11. An English translation of the foregoing item under the title *The Great Crisis and its Political Consequences; Economics and Politics; 1928—1934*, published in New York in 1934. See no. 973.

Of these eleven items the publications presented here under 1, 2 and 3 belong to the III-rd Congress; items 4 and 6 belong to the IV-th Congress; items 10

and 11 belong to the VII-th Congress; items 7, 8 and 9 are not related to any congresses and are listed below; item 5 belongs obviously to the IV-th Congress, but could not be located and is not included in this Checklist.
Other writings of Varga written for or published by the Communist International are listed below.

1629 VARGA, Eugen
De ekonomies-politieke problemen der proletariese diktatuur. Verkorte vertaling door G. Buriks-v. L. v. d. H. [Amsterdam, Bos, 1921] 48 p.

Dutch translation of no. 1633.   *Amst*

1630 VARGA, Eugen
Essor ou décadence du capitalisme? Moscou, Bureau de la Presse de l'Internationale Communiste, 84 p. tables.

Translation of "Decline of Capitalism" 1924 edition. See no. 1628, point 8.
                                                                                    Hoover

1631 VARGA, Eugen
Die Lage der Weltwirtschaft und der Gang der Wirtschaftspolitik in den letzten drei Jahren. [n. p.] Verlag der Kommunistischen Internationale, 1922. 32 p.   *Amst*

1632 VARGA, Eugen
Steuerfrage und Steuerpolitik. [n. p.] Verlag der Kommunistischen Internationale, Hamburg, Hoym [n. d.] 24 p. (Flugschriften der Kommunistischen Internationale, 10)   *Hoover, Amst*

1633 VARGA, Eugen
Die wirtschaftlichen Probleme der proletarischen Diktatur. Wien, „Neue Erde", 1920. 138 p.

Varga's views on the complete re-shaping of the economy of a country under communist rule.   *Hoover, Amst*

1634 VARGA, Eugen
Die wirtschaftlichen Probleme der proletarischen Diktatur. [Second edition] Hamburg, Hoym, 1921. 158 p. (Bibliothek der Kommunistischen Internationale, 8)   *Hoover, Amst*

1635 VARGA, Eugen
The Decline of Capitalism; the Economics of a Period of the Decline of Capitalism after Stabilization. London, Communist Party of Great Britain, 1928. 96 p. Appendix containing 18 tables and graphs without pagination.

See annotation to no. 1628, point 9.   *Hoover*

The WORLD situation and economic struggle; theses of the tenth plenum E. C. C. I. See no. 1147.

1636 [ZINOV'EV, G. E.]
Der Aufbau der Volkswirtschaft und die Sowjetmacht. Rede auf einer allgemeinen Konferenz der Betriebsvertreter. Petrograd, April 1921. [n. p.] Kommunistische Internationale, 1921. 102 p.   *Hoover, Amst*

6. Comintern Reaction to International Conferences

a) Washington Conference on naval armaments and Far Eastern questions, Nov. 12, 1921 – Febr. 6, 1922.

1637 Die KOMMUNISTISCHE Internationale zur Washingtoner Konferenz; Thesen des Exekutiv-komitees der Kommunistischen Internationale [Moscow?] Verlag der Kommunistischen Internationale; Hamburg, C. Hoym Nachf. L. Cahnbley, 1921. 13 p. (Flugschriften der Kommunistischen Internationale, 9)   *Hoover, Amst, Felt*

b) Genoa Conference on general economic questions, Russia and Germany, April 10 – May 19, 1922.

1638 Der KAMPF in Genua: 1. G. Tschitscherin: Rede auf der Konferenz in Genua, am 10. April 1922. 2. Memorandum der russischen Delegation an die Konferenz in Genua. Hamburg, C. Hoym Nachf. L. Cahnbley, 1922. 38 p. (Flugschriften der Kommunistischen Internationale, 13/14)
LC, Felt

1639 PREOBRAZHENSKII, Evgenii A.
Die Ergebnisse der Genueser Konferenz und die wirtschaftlichen Aussichten Europas. Verlag der Kommunistischen Internationale. Hamburg C. Hoym 1922. 51 p. At head of title: E. Preobraschenski.   *Amst*

1640 RADEK, Karl

Genua: die Einheitsfront des Proletariats und die Kommunistische Internationale; Rede auf der Konferenz der Moskauer Organisation der Kommunistischen Partei Rußlands am 9. März 1922. Hamburg, Verlag der Kommunistischen Internationale, 1922. 78 p.

Hoover, Harv, Amst, BDIC, Felt

1641 Les REPRÉSENTANTS de la III-e Internationale membres de la Conférence de Gênes. [n. p., n. d.] 20 p.

A propaganda pomphlet directed against Joffe, Krassin, Litvinov, Radek, Rakovskii, and Zinovev who were members of the Soviet delegation to the Genoa Conference. *Amst, BDIC*

7. The Comintern's Relations with Non-Communist Labor Organizations

Note: In addition to the conferences and meetings listed below, the reader is advised to see the conferences and meetings sponsored by the Red International of Labor Unions (nos. 1776–1796).

a) Conference of the Executive Committees of the Three Internationals; Berlin
April 2, 4, 5, 1922

Note: The Vienna Union, the so-called Two-and-a-Half International, was founded at a socialist conference held in Vienna in February 1921. Its founders were Austrian and German "socialists of the center" who sought a reconciliation between social democracy and communism, and proposed a merger of the II-nd and the III-rd Internationals. On their initiative, representatives of the three Internationals met in Berlin (April 2, 4, 5, 1922) but their discussion led only to the cretaion of a "Committee of Nine" which was instructed to continue negotiations for unification. The trial and conviction of Russian Social Revolutionaries in Moscow in June 1922, caused the withdrawal of the representatives of the II-nd International from the Committee and this put an end to the negotiations. The socialist organizations belonging to the Vienna Union then joined the socialist parties of their respective countries and by May 1923 the Union ceased to exist. (For details see G. D. Cole, *A History of Socialist Thought*, vol. IV, p. 680 ff.) Listed below are the minutes of the Berlin conference, two items containing communist criticisms of the Vienna Union, and a report of the Secretariat of the II-nd International on the subject.

1642 CONFÉRENCE des trois Internationales, tenue à Berlin, les 2, 4 et 5 avril 1922 (Compte-rendu sténographique) Bruxelles, Librairie du Peuple, 1922. 164 p. At head of title: Edition du Comité des Neuf.
Hoover, Felt

1643 MEZHDUNARODNAIA sotsialisticheskaia konferentsiia (Ob"edinennoe zasedanie Ispolkomov trekh Internatsionalov) Stenograficheskii otchet. Moskva, Tip. G.P.U., 67 p.
Hoover

1644 The SECOND and Third Internationals and the Vienna Union; official report of the conference between the Executives, held at the Reichstag, Berlin, on the 2nd April, 1922, and following days. London, The Labour publishing company, 1922. 94 p. Cover title.
Hoover

1645 Die HELDEN der Wiener Konferenz; mit Beiträgen von Lenin, Trotzki, Sinowjew, u. a. Herausg. von der Kommunistischen Partei Österreichs. Wien, Arbeiter-Buchhandlung, 1921. 48 p.

Concerns the founding of the Vienna Union, the so-called Two-and-a-half International.
Felt

1646 LABOUR and socialist International. Secretariat.
Die Einheit der Arbeiterklasse; Bericht über das Organisationsproblem erstattet der Exekutive der Sozialistischen Arbeiter-Internationale, vom Sekretariat der S.A.I. Deutsche Ausgabe, herausgegeben vom Vorstande der S.P.D. Berlin, J.H.W.Dietz Nachfolger, 1926. 15 p.

A memorandum on the possibilities of the union of the Labor and Socialist International and the Communist International.
Hoover

1647 RADEK, Karl
Theorie und Praxis der $2\frac{1}{2}$ Internationale. Kommunistische Internationale; Auslieferungsstelle C. Hoym, Hamburg, 1921. 56 p. (Bibliothek der Kommunistischen Internationale, 5)
Hoover, NYPL, Harv, Col, BDIC, Felt

1648 WARDIN, I. [pseud. of MGELADZE]
Die Sozialrevolutionären Mörder und die sozialdemokratischen Advokaten. (Tatsachen und Beweise) Hamburg, Verlag der Kommunistischen Internationale, C. Hoym, 1922. 40 p. („Beiträge zur Geschichte der Kämpfe des Proletariats in Rußland", no. 5)

Pamphlet issued in connection with the demand of the II-nd International for a fair trial of a group of Russian Social-Revolutionary opponents of the Soviet regime.
Felt

b) Consultations of the II-nd and the III-rd Internationals concerning the situation in Spain, 1934–1937.

Note: In the November 1933 elections in Spain, the republican leftist parties suffered a considerable defeat. The drift of the government toward the right produced a violent reaction on the left. Strikes, riots and local uprisings led to an internal crisis. The communists proposed the formation of a Popular Front and the Comintern supported this proposal. This brought about the Brussels consultation of representatives of the II-nd and III-rd Internationals and the creation of a Popular Front in Spain which in the February 1936 elections obtained a decisive majority in the Cortes. The activities of the Popular Front government led to the Spanish civil war.

aa) Brussels consultation, October 15, 1934.

1649 De ONDERHANDELINGEN tussen de Socialistische en de Communistische Internationale over het eenheidsfront. Stenografisch verslag van de bespreking te Brussel op 15 October 1934, tussen de gedelegeerden van de Socialistische en van de Communistiche Internationale [Marcel Cachin, Maurice Thorez, Emile Vandervelde en Friedrich Adler]. Amsterdam, Agentschap Amstel [n. d.] 19 p.   *Amst*

1650 PROTOKOLL der Verhandlungen zwischen der II. und III. Internationale über die Unterstützung des heldenhaften Kampfes der Werktätigen Spaniens, und ihre Ergebnisse. [Zürich?] Prometheus-Verlag [1935] 50 p.

Stenographic record of the consultations, together with the subsequent documentary material.   *Hoover, NYPL, Amst, Felt*

1651 VERBATIM report of the negotiations between the Second and Third Internationals on the question of supporting the heroic struggle of the Spanish workers. London, Modern Books [1934] 39 p.
Hoover, NYPL, Col, UTex, Amst

bb) Later developments

1652 DIMITROV, G. [and Gottwald, Klement]
Die Einheit wird siegen! Dimitroffs Ruf zur internationalen Aktionseinheit und die Antwort der Sozialistischen Arbeiterinternationale. Strasbourg, Prometheus Verlag [n. d.] 35 p.

The above item contains on pp. 24–34: Klement GOTTWALD: Internationale Aktion gegen Mussolinis Raubkrieg. Der italienische Krieg; die Aktionseinheit der Arbeiterklasse und der Standpunkt der Sozialistischen Arbeiterinternationale   *Felt*

1653 [DIMITROV, G.]
La unidad triunfará. Llamamiento de Dimitrof a la unidad de acción internacional. Respuesta de la International Socialista Obrera. Barcelona, Ediciones Sociales, 1936. 40 p.   *Amst*

1654 UNITY for Spain; correspondence between the Communist International and the Labor and Socialist International, June–July, 1937. [New York, Daily and Sunday Worker, 1937] 15 p.

Letters of the Communist International signed by G. Dimitrov, general secretary.   *Hoover, Harv, Duke*

c) The Frankfurt Conference, March 17–21, 1923

Note: In this conference participated 232 "delegates" representing the Comintern, the Profintern, the Communist Youth International, the Women's Secretariat, the Communist Parties of France, Germany, Great Britain and Italy, Independent Socialist Party of Germany (USPD), and several smaller communist front organizations and German trade unions. According to Soviet sources (Tivel & Kheimo, *10 let Kominterna*, p. 374), 29 of these "delegates" were non-communists. The conference dealt with the following subjects: The situation in France, Germany and Great Britain; the Ruhr problem and the danger of war; the struggle against fascism; the struggle for the united front. The conference created an "Action Committee".

1655 Der INTERNATIONALE Kampf des Proletariats gegen Kriegsgefahr und Fascismus. Protokoll der Verhandlungen der Internationalen Konferenz in Frankfurt am Main vom 17. bis 21. März 1923. Mit einer Einleitung und einem Nachwort. Berlin, Vereinigung Internationaler Verlags-Anstalten, 1923. 45 p.   *Felt*

d) Correspondence with Socialist Youth International.

1656 Die SOZIALISTISCHE Jugendinternationale und die Jungarbeiterdelegationen nach der UdSSR. Ein Briefwechsel zwischen der Sozialistischen Jugendinternationale und der Kommunistischen Internationale. Sonderdruck aus der „Jugendinternationale" Nummer 5/VII. Jhg. Wien, Verlag der Jugendinternationale, 1925? 22 p.   *Hoover*

8. International Meetings initiated by the Communist International

Note: In addition to the conferences and meetings listed below, the reader is advised to see the conferences and meetings sponsored by the Red International of Labor Unions (nos. 1776–1796).

a) Congress of the Peoples of the East, Baku, September 1–8, 1920

Note: According to Soviet sources 1891 "delegates", of whom 1273 were communists, participated in this congress. They supposedly represented 29 "nations of the East". Five reports by Zinov'ev, Radek, Pavlovich, Bela Kun, and Skachko were given to the Congress. The Congress created a Council (Soviet) of Action and Propaganda, composed of 35 communists and 13 non-party members. (Tivel, A. and Kheimo, *10 let Kominterna*, p. 373.)

1657 I-vyi [PERVYI] s"ezd narodov Vostoka, Baku, 1—8 sent. 1920 g.; stenograficheskie otchety. Moskva, izd-vo Kommunisticheskogo Internatsionala, 1920. 232 p. On cover: Kommunisticheskii Internatsional i osvobozhdenie Vostoka. *Hoover, NYPL, UCLA, Amst, BDIC, Felt*

1658 Le PREMIER Congrès des peuples de l'Orient; Bakou, 1—8 sept[embre] 1920. Compte-rendu sténographique. [Pétrograd, Éditions de l'Internationale Communiste, 1921] 229 p. (L'internationale Communiste et la liberation de l'Orient) *Amst, Felt*

1659 SORKIN, Grigorii Z.
Pervyi s"ezd narodov Vostoka. Moskva, Izd-vo vostochnoi literatury, 1961. 78 p. bibliography. *Hoover*

b) Congress of the Toilers of the Far East, Moscow, January 21 – February 1, 1922 and Petrograd, February 2, 1922.

Note: According to Soviet sources, 148 "delegates" participated in this congress, of which 131 had voting powers. They represented the Buriat region, China, the Iakut region, India, Japan, Java, the Kalmyk region, Korea and Mongolia. At this meeting were given 14 reports by Zinov'ev, Katayama, Safarov, Dyn Dyb, and 10 anonymous reporters. (Tivel, A. and Kheimo, M., *10 let Kominterna*, p. 373.)

1660 Der ERSTE Kongreß der kommunistischen und revolutionären Organisationen des Fernen Ostens. Moskau, Januar 1922. Hamburg, Hoym, 1922. x, 140 p. tables. (Vorwort von G. Woitinski) *Amst, Felt*

1661 The FIRST Congress of the Toilers of the Far East; held in Moscow January 21st — February 1st, 1922. Closing session in Petrograd, February 2nd, 1922. [Proceedings] Petrograd, The Communist International, 1922. 248 p. tables.   *Hoover, NYPL, Col*

1662 PERVYI s"ezd revoliutsionnykh organizatsii Dal'nego Vostoka; sbornik. Petrograd, izd. Ispolkoma Kominterna, 1922. 360 p.

Hoover

9. The opposing Elements — Anti-Comintern Organizations and Publications

Note: This part of the Checklist is not a listing of anti-communist publications but includes only items published by organizations whose activities were directed against the Communist International and items which deal with the Communist International from an anticommunist viewpoint.

a) Publication by and about the International Anti-Communist Entente, Geneva.

INTERNATIONAL Anti-Communist Entente.
Antibolschewistisches Vade-Mecum; Organisation und Aktivität der Kommunistischen Internationale. See no. 28.

INTERNATIONAL Anti-Communist Entente.
Anti-Bolshevik vade-mecum. See no. 29.

INTERNATIONAL Anti-Communist Entente.
L'armé rouge, instrument de la révolution mondiale; le monde civilisé en danger. See no. 404.

INTERNATIONAL Anti-Communist Entente.
An aspect of the disarmament problem: the "proletarian war". Memorandum addressed to governments... See no. 1588.

INTERNATIONAL Anti-Communist Entente.
Charts representing the Soviet organizations working for revolution in all countries with explanatory notes. See no. 480.

INTERNATIONAL Anti-Communist Entente.
Le commerce avec les Soviets. See no. 1616.

1663 INTERNATIONAL Anti-Communist Entente.
L'Entente internationale contre la IIIe Internationale. [Geneva] 1925.
13 p. Signed: Theodore Aubert, président du Bureau permanent de
l'Entente internationale contre la IIIe Internationale.   *Hoover*

1664 INTERNATIONAL Anti-Communist Entente.
L'Entente Internationale contre la III-e Internationale. Publié à l'occasion du V-e anniversaire de sa fondation. Genève, Impr. Sonor [1929]
37 p.   *NYPL, Felt*

INTERNATIONAL Anti-Communist Entente. Swiss National Center.
La failité du collectivisme en Russie. See no. 1618.

INTERNATIONAL Anti-Communist Entente.
Der Handel mit Sowjet-Rußland. 1931. See no. 1617.

1665 INTERNATIONAL Anti-Communist Entente.
The International Entente against the Third International, published
on the occasion of the fifth anniversary of its foundation, 1929.
[Geneva, Impr. du Journal de Genève, 1929] 37 p. At head of title:
Permanent bureau of the International Entente against the Third
International.   *Hoover, NYPL, SInSt*

INTERNATIONAL Anti-Communist Entente.
Le Komintern, le gouvernement soviétique et le Parti communiste de
l'U. R. R. S. See no. 468.

1666 INTERNATIONAL Anti-Communist Entente.
La lutte contre le bolchévisme. Genève, 1924. 31 p. At head of title:
Entente internationale contre la IIIe Internationale.   *Hoover*

1667 INTERNATIONAL Anti-Communist Entente.
Mémoire et requête présentés aux gouvernements par l'Entente Internationale contre la III-e Internationale, en vertu de la décision prise
à l'unanimité par son Conseil, composé des représentants de 21 nations
européennes, en sa séance du mardi 26 mai 1925. Genève, Impr.
Sonor, 1925. 11 p.   *NYPL*

1668   INTERNATIONAL Anti-Communist Entente.
Memorandum and petition presented to the governments by the
Entente International against the Third International in accordance
with the unanimous decision of the Council, composed of 21 European
countries, at its meeting on Tuesday, May 26th, 1925. [Geneva, 1925]
11 p.   *Hoover*

1669   INTERNATIONAL Anti-Communist Entente.
Neuf ans de lutte contre le bolchévisme; l'activité de l'Entente Inter-
nationale contre la IIIe Internationale. Genève [Imp. du Journal de
Genève] 1933. 30 p. At head of title: Bureau Permanent de l'Entente
Internationale contre la IIIe Internationale.

Hoover, NYPL, SInSt

INTERNATIONAL Anti-Communist Entente.
A New World War; "The Bolshevist War". See no. 1312.

INTERNATIONAL Anti-Communist Entente.
Organization and activities of the Communist International. See
no. 481.

INTERNATIONAL Anti-Communist Entente.
The present policy of the Soviet government and the Third International; memorandum addressed to the governments and to international institutions... See no. 469.

INTERNATIONAL Anti-Communist Entente.
The Red Network; the Communist International at work. See no. 482.

INTERNATIONAL Anti-Communist Entente.
Die religiösen Verfolgungen in Rußland. Dokumente und Tatsachen.
See no. 1684.

INTERNATIONAL Anti-Communist Entente.
The religious persecutions in Russia. See no. 1685.

1670   INTERNATIONAL Anti-Communist Entente. Russian Section.
The Russian liberation movement. Paris, 1929. 51 p. illust.

NYPL

INTERNATIONAL Anti-Communist Entente.
Tableaux des organisations soviétiques travaillant à la révolution
dans tous les pays accompagnés de note explicatives. See no. 483.

1671 INTERNATIONAL Anti-Communist Entente.
La III-e Internationale contre le christianisme. Faits et documens.
Lettre-préface de S.E. le Cardinal Mercier. Paris, Letouzey et Anée,
1925. 78 p.   *NYPL, BDIC*

INTERNATIONAL Anti-Communist Entente.
The U.S.S.R. and disarmament. See no. 1590.

INTERNATIONAL Anti-Communist Entente.
Vade-mecum antibolchevique. See no. 31.

INTERNATIONALER Verband gegen die III. Internationale. Schweizerischer Landesausschuß.
Der Bankrott des Kollektivismus in Rußland. See no. 1689.

1672 HENTSCH, René
The Soviet offensive. (An appeal to business men) Geneva, 1931.
14 p. (Permanent Bureau of the International Entente against the
Third International)   *SInSt*

[LODYGENSKY, George]
Eine neue Entwicklungsstufe im Kampf der Sowjets gegen die Religion.
[Internationale Vereinigung gegen die III. Internationale, Genf] See
no. 1693.

1673 NOVIK, Dmitri
Théodore Aubert et son œuvre. Le mouvement international contre
le bolchévisme. Geneva, 1932. 46 p.   *SInSt*

**b) Gesamtverband deutscher anti-kommunistischer Vereinigungen
known as Anti-Komintern, Berlin.**

GESAMTVERBAND deutscher Anti-kommunistischer Vereingiungen.
Denkschrift über die Einmischung des Bolschewismus und der Demokratien in Spanien. See no. 1469.

GESAMTVERBAND deutscher Anti-kommunistischer Vereinigungen.
The seventh World Congress of the Communist International. See
no. 1028.

EHRT, Adolf
Communism in Germany; the truth about the communist conspiracy
on the eve of the national revolution. See no. 1386.

EHRT, Adolf
Révolte armée; révélations sur la tentative d'insurrection communiste à la veille de la Révolution Nationale. See no. 1387.

EHRT, Adolf, ed.
Der Weltbolschewismus; ein internationales Gemeinschaftswerk über die bolschewistische Wühlarbeit und die Umsturzversuche der Komintern in allen Ländern, herausgegeben von der Antikomintern... See nos. 23, 24.

c) Centre d'Etudes Anticommuniste, Paris.

CENTRE d'Etudes Anticommuniste, Paris.
L'Allemagne et le bolchévisme. See no. 1384.

POUZYNA, I. V.
Bolchévisme. Son histoire, son essence. See no. 326.

d) Nationalist International.

1674 BERTRAND, Louis [and Keller, Hans]
L'Internationale — ennemie des nations. Hans K. E. L. Keller: Why "the Nationalist International"? Zurich, A. Nauck & Co., 1936. 31 p. Half-title: The Nationalist International.

> Papers delivered at the second International Congress of Nationalists, held in London from the 10th to the 12th of July, 1936.   *LC, Harv*

e) Various authors and publishers

1675 IL FAUT combattre le bolchévisme; livre rouge. Paris, 1942. 114 p. illus.   *Hoover*

KRUPINSKI, Kurt
De Komintern sedert het uitbreken van den oorlog. See no. 273.

KRUPINSKI, Kurt
Die Komintern seit Kriegsausbruch. See nos. 274, 275.

LAUNAY, Jacques de
Fascisme rouge; contribution à la défense de l'Europe. See no. 284.

MATSUOKA, Yosuke
Die Bedeutung des Deutsch-Japanischen Abkommens gegen die Kommunistische Internationale. See no. 308 a.

NORMANN, Alfred
Bolschewistische Weltmachtpolitik; die Pläne der 3. Internationale zur Revolutionisierung der Welt auf Grund authentischer Quellen. [Preface by Théodore Aubert] See no. 410.

1676 VASIL'EV, B.
Komintern i ego vragi. Izd. 2., ispr. i dop. Moskva, Gos. izd-vo, 1930. 61 p. (Chto dolzhen znat' rabochii vstupaiushchii v VKP(b).)

Col

10. Miscellaneous

1677 ALL Power to the workers! Four speeches delivered at the tenth Congress, Russian Communist Party (Bolsheviks) 1921: Radek, Lenin, Krestinsky, and Zinoviev. Petrograd, Information Bureau, Third International [1921] 46 p. *Hoover*

1678 BATAULT, Georges
Les animaux malades de la peste. Avec une préface de Jean de la Fontaine. Genève, Editions du Cheval ailé, 1946. 263 p. On cover: A l'enseigne du cheval ailé.

> According to the annotation in the BDIC catalog, this volume deals with French politics, communism, and the Third International. *BDIC*

1679 BUKHARIN, N. I.
Der Klassenkampf und die Revolution in Rußland. Petrograd, Kommunistische Internationale, 1920. 71 p. *NYPL*

1680 DIMAN, Ia.
Politminimum. [Moskva] "Moskovskii rabochii", 1931. 366 p.

Col

1681 FOGARASI, A.
Der Bankrott der Theorien des Sozialfaschismus am Ende der kapitalistischen Stabilisierung. Moskau, Verlagsgenossenschaft Ausländischer Arbeiter in der UdSSR, 1934. 124 p. *Hoover, Amst*

1682 GONTA, Ivan
Komintern (L'Internationale Communiste). [n.p.] 1936. 27 p. duplicated.
(L'ennemi, no. 1, Nov. 1936) *BDIC*

1683 GUSEV, Sergei I.
Die Lehren des Bürgerkrieges. Kommunistische Internationale. [Hamburg, C. Hoym Nachf.] 1921. 96 p. At head of title: S. I. Gusew.
(Bibliothek der Kommunistischen Internationale, 14.) *Amst*

1684 INTERNATIONAL Anti-Communist Entente.
Die religiösen Verfolgungen in Rußland. Dokumente und Tatsachen. Geneva, Internationale Vereinigung gegen die III. Internationale, 1930. 32 p. *Felt*

1685 INTERNATIONAL Anti-Communist Entente.
The religious persecutions in Russia; documents and facts. Geneva, March 1930. 30 p. *Hoover*

1686 INTERNATIONALE Presse-Korrespondenz. [n.p., n.d.] 40 p. charts and tables.

> Sieben Jahre Inprecor. Mit deutschem, französischem und englischem Titel und Text. (Amst. annotation.) *Amst*

1687 INTERNATIONALE Vereinigung der Kommunistischen Opposition (I.V.K.O.).
Beschlüsse der internationalen Konferenz in Paris, vom 19.—22. Februar 1938, und die Reden der Vertreter der I.V.K.O. [n.p.] Intern. Vereinigung der Kommunistischen Opposition, 1938. 1938. 76 p. *Felt*

1688 INTERNATIONALE Vereinigung der kommunistischen Opposition (IVKO).
Zur Krise in der Sowjetunion. Herausgegeben vom Büro der IVKO. Wolfsheim, A. Quiri, 1937. 81 p. *Felt*

1689 INTERNATIONALER Verband gegen die III. Internationale. Schweizerischer Landesausschuß.
Der Bankrott des Kollektivismus in Rußland. Zürich, Herausg. vom Schweizerischen Landesausschuß des Internationalen Verbandes gegen die III. Internationale, 1928. 56 p. *Felt*

1689a KON, F.
Der kapitalistische Terror. Hamburg, Hoym, 1924. ii, 25 p.   *Amst*

1690 LARIN, Iurii [Pseud. of Lur'e, M. A.] and Kritsman, L. N.
Wirtschaftsleben und wirtschaftlicher Aufbau in Sowjet-Rußland 1917—1920. [n. p.] Kommunistische Internationale, 1921. 198 p. tables. (Bibliothek der Kommunistischen Internationale, 16.)
Hoover, Amst

1691 LASSWELL, Harold D., Leites, Nathan and others
Language of politics; studies in quantitative semantics. [New York, G. W. Stuart, c1949] vii, 398 p. graphs.

> This book on semantics contains also a chapter in which speeches at the congresses of the Communist International and articles in Inprecorr are used as examples of a terminology expressing policy changes.
>
> *Hoover, LC, NYPL, Harv, Col*

1692 LENIN, V. I.
Der "Radikalismus" die Kinderkrankheit des Kommunismus. Leipzig, Westeuropäisches Sekretariat der Kommunistischen Internationale, 1920. 95 p.   *Hoover, Amst*

1693 LODYGENSKY, George
Eine neue Entwicklungsstufe im Kampf der Sowjets gegen die Religion. Vortrag des Herrn Dr. Georg Lodygensky in Genf, January 1930. [n. p., Geneva?] Internationale Vereinigung gegen die III. Internationale [1930] 14 p.   *Felt*

1694 MILIUTIN, Vladimir Pavlovich
Die Organisation der Volkswirtschaft in Sowjet-Rußland. Eine kurze Abhandlung über die Verwaltungsorganisation und die Lage der Industrie in Sowjet-Rußland. [n. p.] Kommunistische Internationale, 1921. 48 p. illus., tables. (Bibliothek der Kommunistischen Internationale, 12.)   *Hoover, Amst*

1695 MOTEIRO, José Getulio
Origens e transformacoes do materialismo historico (de Marx a Stalin). Rio de Janeiro, José Olimpio, 1939. viii, 307 p.   *Col*

1696 [NEVSKII, V. and Ravich, S.]
Arbeiter- und Bauernuniversitäten in Sowjetrußland. Kommunistische Internationale. Hamburg [Hoym Nachf.] 1921. 39 p. tables. At head of title: W. Newski und S. Rawitsch. (Bibliothek der Kommunistischen Internationale, 6.)   *Hoover, Amst*

1697 PAUL, Eden, and, Paul, Cedar
Creative revolution; a study of communist ergatocracy. New York,
T. Seltzer, 1920. 220 p. *LC, NYPL*

1698 PRICE, Morgan Philips
The truth about the Allied intervention in Russia, by M. Philips Price,
correspondent in Russia of the *Manchester Guardian*. 2nd ed. [Moskva,
Gosudarstvennaia tipografiia, 1919] vi, 10 p. (Published by the
Executive Committee of the Communist International) *LC*

1699 RADEK, Karl
Die auswärtige Politik Sowjet-Rußlands. Kommunistische Internationale; Auslieferungsstelle C. Hoym, Hamburg, 1921. 83 p. (Bibliothek
der Kommunistischen Internationale, 11.) *Hoover, Amst*

1700 RADEK, Karl
Pered novoi volnoi revoliutsionnykh potriasenii. (Dve rechi) Moskva,
"Krasnaia Nov," 1923. 83 p. *NYPL*

1701 RADEK, Karl
Programme of socialist construction. Moscow, Executive Committee
of the Communist International, 1920. 22 p. At head of title: Russian
Socialist Federal Soviet Republic. *LC, Col*

1702 VIDOR, John
Spying in Russia. London, J. Long, 1929. 284 p. illus. *Col*

1703 WATON, Harry
Natural dialectics of proletarian internationals and parties, and new
Communist manifesto. [New York] Workers Educational Institute, 1926.
93 p. *Hoover, NYPL*

1704 ZINOV'EV, G. E.
L'armée et le peuple... Petrograd, Éditions de l'Internationale Com-
muniste, 1920. (Éditions françaises de l'Internationale Communiste,
No. 60) *Hoover*

1705 ZINOV'EV, G. E.
Army and people; the Soviet government and the corps of officers
[a lecture delivered in October 1919, to the assembly of military
specialists] Petrograd, Communist International, 1920. 58 p.

Hoover

1706 ZINOV'EV, G. E.

La révolution russe et le prolétariat international. [Chaux-de-Fonds, Le Phare, 1919] 16 p. (Editions des jeunesses socialistes romandes, no. 12)

> Reprint of an article published in the periodical "Communist International" on the occasion of the 2-nd anniversary of the Bolshevik revolution in Russia.
>
> *Hoover*

1707 ZINOV'EV, G. E.

Die russische Revolution und das internationale Proletariat; zum zweiten Jahrestag der proletarischen Umwälzung in Rußland. Petrograd, Kommunistische Internationale, 1919. 31 p.   *Amst*

PART VI.

THE RED INTERNATIONAL OF LABOR UNIONS

(Holdings of the library of the Institute for Social History in Amsterdam not included.)

A. GENERAL

1. Reference Books and Collections of Documents

(Cross references only)

DESIAT' let Profinterna v rezoliutsiiakh, dokumentakh i tsifrakh. Sostavil S. Sorbonski. Pod redaktsiei i s predisloviem A. Lozovskogo. See no. 99 a.

GIRINIS, S. V., comp.
Profintern v rezoliutsiiakh. Sostavil i snabdil kommentariami S. Girinis, pod redaktsiei i so vstuptel'noi stat'ei A. Lozovskogo. See no. 104 a.

GREAT Britain, Parliament.
Communist papers. Documents selected from those obtained on the arrest of the communist leaders on the 14th and 21st October 1925. See no. 105.

MALAIA entsiklopediia po mezhdunarodnomu profdvizheniiu; pod redaktsiei M. Zelikmana, s predisloviem A. Lozovskogo. See no. 35.

MIROVOE professional'noe dvizhenie; spravochnik Profinterna. Pod obshchei redaktsiei A. Lozovskogo. See no. 36.

ROZENFELD, O., ed.
Komintern i profsoiuzy, v resheniiakh kongressov i plenumov i drugikh materialakh Kominterna o profdvizhenii. See no. 136.

SCHWARZ, Salomon

Rote Gewerkschafts-Internationale R. G. I. Berlin, 1922. Photostat copy of an article in the *Internationales Handwörterbuch des Gewerkschaftswesens.* See no. 41

STATISTICHESKIE dannye o polozhenii evropeiskogo proletariata za 1-uiu polovinu 1923 g. Rabota Statisticheskogo biuro Profinterna, vypolnennaia pod obshchei redaktsiei M. Smit. See no. 40.

2. The Trade Union Movement from a Communist Point of View

1708 ARBEITER Offensive gegen Unternehmer Offensive. Berlin, Internationaler Arbeiterverlag [n. d.] 16 p.   *Felt*

1709 BELL, Thomas
The movement for world trade union unity, by Tom Bell. Issued by the Workers (Communist) party. Chicago, Ill., Daily Worker Publishing Co., 1925. 48 p. illus. (port.)   *Hoover*

1710 BRAUN, P.
Les problèmes du mouvement travailliste. Préface de A. J. Cook. Paris, 1925. 29 p. (Petite Bibliothèque de l'Internationale Syndicale Rouge, 17)
Felt

1711 GEGEN den Faschismus, für einheitliche Klassengewerkschaft der Arbeiter. Karlin, A. Zápotocký, 1935. [pagination not given]
Harv

1712 HECKER, T. M.
Der Internationale Kampf um den achtstündigen Maximalarbeitstag. Verlag der Roten Gewerkschafts-Internationale; Auslieferung für Deutschland: Führer-Verlag, Berlin, 1924. [pagination not given] (Bibliothek der Roten Gewerkschafts-Internationale, Bd. 33)
NYPL

JORDI, Hugo
Die Krise der internationalen Arbeiterbewegung. See no. 257.

1713 KOMMUNISTISCHE Zerstörungsarbeit in den Freien Gewerkschaften. Berlin, Verlag Deutscher Bekleidungsarbeiter-Verband, 1921. 46 p.
Felt

1714 LEDER, Z[dislav]
Der Achtstundentag — Sozialreform oder soziale Revolution? Verlag der Roten Gewerkschafts-Internationale; A. f D.: F-V, Berlin, 1923. [pagination not given] (Bibliothek der Roten Gewerkschafts-Internationale, Bd. 25.)   *NYPL*

1715 LEDER, Z[dislav]
Sind die Amsterdamer Gelbe? Zweite erweiterte Auflage. Verlag der Roten Gewerkschafts-Internationale; Auslieferung für Deutschland durch Führer-Verlag, Berlin, 1923. 139 p. (Bibliothek der Roten Gewerkschafts-Internationale, Bd. 14)

> Polemic with the Trade Union International in Amsterdam. The author takes the communist point of view.   *Hoover, NYPL, Felt*

1716 LOZOVSKII, A.
Für die Einheit der Welt-Gewerkschafts-Bewegung. Von A. Losowsky. Berlin, Führer-Verlag, 1924. 15 p.   *Felt*

1717 LOZOVSKII, A.
Grundzüge der Entwicklung der internationalen Gewerkschaftsbewegung. Verlag der Roten Gewerkschafts-Internationale; Auslieferung für Deutschland: Führer-Verlag, Berlin, 1924. 23 p. (Bibliothek der Roten Gewerkschafts-Internationale, Bd. 30)

> *NYPL, Felt*

1718 LOZOVSKII, A.
Die internationale Gewerkschaftsbewegung vor und nach dem Kriege. Berlin, Führer Verlag, 1924. 221 p.

> „Eine Reihe vom Verfasser im August 1923 für verantwortliche Parteifunktionäre beim Zentralkomitee der KPR gehaltene Vorlesungen" Vorwort.
> *Hoover, NYPL, Felt*

1719 LOZOVSKII, A.
Lenin und die Gewerkschaftsbewegung, von A. Losowsky. Berlin, Führer-Verlag, 1924. 19 p. (Bibliothek der Roten Gewerkschafts-Internationale, Bd. 32)   *Hoover, NYPL, Felt*

1720 LOZOVSKII, A.
Le mouvement syndical international avant, pendant et après la guerre [par] A. Losovsky. Paris, l'Internationale syndicale rouge, 1926. 301 p. (Petite bibliothèque de l'Internationale syndicale rouge, no. 20)
> *Hoover, Felt*

1721 LOZOVSKII, A.
Paris, Breslau, Scarborough. Berlin, Führer-Verlag, 1925. 63 p. (At head of title: A. Losovskij)   *Felt*

1722 LOZOVSKII, A.
Parizh, Breslavl, Skarboro. Moskva, Izd. Profinterna, 1925. 71 p.

> *NYPL*

1723 LOZOVSKII, A.
Polozhenie rabochego klassa kapitalisticheskikh stran i bor'ba za edinstvo profdvizheniia. Moskva, Profintern, 1937. 71 p.

Hoover

1724 LOZOVSKII, A.
Les tâches et la tactique des syndicats. Par com. S. [sic!] Lozovsky. Moscou, Edition du Conseil International des syndicats ouvriers, 1921. 23 p.

Felt

1725 MERKER, Paul
Die Spaltung der Arbeiterklasse und der Weg der revolutionären Gewerkschafts-Opposition. Berlin, Internationaler Arbeiter-Verlag, 1929. 55 p.

Hoover

1726 NIN, Andrés
Les anarchistes et le mouvement syndical. Paris, Librairie du Travail [1923?] 21 p. (Petite bibliothèque de l'Internationale syndicale rouge, 10)

Hoover, Felt

1727 NIN, Andrés
El sindicalismo revolucionario y la Internacional. Barcelona, La Batalla [192-?] 15 p.

NYPL

1728 PIATNITSKII, Osip
Die aktuellen Fragen der internationalen Gewerkschaftsbewegung. Hamburg, Carl Hoym Nachf. [1931] 52 p. (Bücherei des Parteiarbeiters, Bd. 1)

Felt

1729 PIATNITSKII, Osip
The immediate tasks of the international trade union movement, by O. Piatnitsky. New York City, Workers' Library [1931?] 40 p. "Printed in England."

Hoover

1730 PIATNITSKII, Osip
Les questions vitales du mouvement syndical révolutionnaire international. Paris, Bureau d'Editions, 1931. 61 p. (Internationale syndicale rouge)

Hoover, Felt

1731 PROLETAIRE sois vigilant! Renforce le front unique! [Paris, 193-] 47 p. (Petite bibliothèque de l'Internationale syndicale rouge, 33)

Hoover, Felt

1732 SMOLIANSKII, Grigorii B.
Etapy mezhdunarodnogo professional'nogo dvizheniia. Moskva, Gos.
izd-vo, 1930. 336 p. *NYPL*

1733 STRASSER, Isa
Arbeiterin und Gewerkschaft. Verlag der Roten Gewerkschafts-Internationale; Auslieferung für Deutschland durch Führer-Verlag, Berlin,
1924. 35 p. (Bibliothek der Roten Gewerkschafts-Internationale, Bd. 28)
Hoover, NYPL, Felt

3. R. I. L. U. History and General

AKADEMIIA Nauk SSSR. Institut istorii.
Sovetskaia Rossiia i kapitalisticheskii mir v 1917—1923 g. [Contains
a chapter on "The rise and activities of the democratic mass organizations" which discusses the R. I. L. U.] See no. 203.

1734 AMSTERDAM o Moscu! Llamamiento de la Internacional sindical roja
a todos obreros y obreras, a todos los sin trabajo, a la juventud
obrera, contra el hambre, la miseria y el paro, contra las maniobras
de la 11° [!] internacional y de la Federación sindical internacional
de Amsterdam. Paris, El Secretariado internacional de la C. G. T. U.
[1930] 15 p. *Hoover*

1735 BRIEFWECHSEL zwischen der Roten Gewerkschafts-Internationale und
dem Internationalen Gewerkschaftsbund über die Herstellung der
Aktionseinheit und der internationalen Gewerkschaftseinheit. [n. p.,
1935] 31 p. On cover: Carl Schutte, Willst du erfahren was sich ziemt?
H. Klaus-Verlag Erlitz, Caputh-Potsdam.

> A clandestine publication issued in Germany during Nazi period. All informa-
> tion from catalog card of BDIC. *BDIC*

1736 HERCLET, Auguste
L'Internationale syndicale rouge et l'unité syndicale. Paris, En vent
à la librairie du travail [1923?] 32 p. (Petite bibliothèque de l'Internationale syndicale rouge, 8) *Hoover, NYPL, BDIC, Felt*

1737 INTERNATIONAL T.U. correspondence course. Issued by the Agitation-propaganda and Workers Education Dept. of the R.I.L.U. [n.p.] 1930. Nos. 1 and 2 of a series of correspondence lessons; 48 and 80 p. (No more published?) *Col* (1), *Jef* (1, 2)

1738 L'INTERNATIONALE rouge des Syndicats. [La Chaux-de-Fonds, 1920?] 23 p. (Jeunesses socialistes romandes. Bibliothèque, no. 13)
NYPL, BDIC

1739 IUZEFOVICH, Iosif
Internatsional professional'nykh soiuzov. Moskva, 1921. 43 p. At head of title: Mezhdunarodnyi sovet professional'nykh i proizvodstvennykh soiuzov. *Hoover*

1740 KERTÉSZ, Miklós
A nemzetköziség utja; öt esztendő a Szakszervezeti internacionale történetéből, irta Kertész Miklós. Budapest, A Népszavakönyvkereskedés kiadása, 1925. 187 p. On cover: Munkáskönyvtár, 45 sz.
Hoover

1741 KRASNAIA Kniga. Kniga 1; god: 1922. Moskva, Izd. Profinterna, 1922. [Pages not given on catalog card] *NYPL*

1742 LOZOVSKII, A.
Chto takoe Profintern. Ko vsem rabochim delegatsiiam, priekhavshim v Moskvu na oktiabr'skie torzhestva. Moskva, Gos. izd-vo, 1927. 48 p.
Hoover

1743 LOZOVSKII, A.
10 [DIEZ] años de vida de la Internacional sindical roja. Resoluciones del Congreso de Estrasburgo sobre los combates buelguisticos. [Montevideo, Confederación sindical latino-americana, 1930] 108 p.
NYPL

1744 LOZOVSKII, A.
Desiaf let Profinterna. Moskva, Izd-vo VTSSPS, 1930. 41 p.
Hoover, SInSt

1745 LOZOVSKII, A.
Fünf Jahre RGI. Berlin, Führer-Verlag, 1925. 31 p. *NYPL, Felt*

1746 LOZOVSKII, A.
The International Council of Trade and Industrial Unions, by A. Losovsky (S. A. Dridzo). New York City, Union Publ. Assoc. [1920 or 1921] 64 p.

"Declaration of principles" of the Council, p. 53–55; Moscow or Amsterdam", p. 61–62. *Hoover, NYPL*

1747 LOZOVSKII, A.
Der Internationale Rat der Fach- und Industrieverbände (Moskau gegen Amsterdam) Herausgegeben im Auftrage des Internationalen Rates der Fach- und Industrieverbände. Berlin, A. Seehof & Co. [1920] 79 p. At head of title: A. Losowski. (Internationale Gewerkschafts-bibliothek, Nr. 1) *Hoover*

1748 LOZOVSKII, A.
Der internationale Rat der Fach- und Industrieverbände (Moskau gegen Amsterdam). Hamburg, C. Hoym Nachf., 1921 64 p. At head of title: A. Losowski. (Bibliothek der Kommunistischen Internationale, Bd. 10) *NYPL, Col, Felt*

1749 LOZOVSKII, A.
Tres años de lucha de la Internacional sindical roja. Barcelona, La Batalla [1923?] 13 p. At head of title: A. Losovsky. (Biblioteca La Batalla) *NYPL*

1750 LOZOVSKII, A.
What is the Red International of labour unions? Moscow, The R. I. L. U., 1927. 35 p. *Hoover, NYPL*

1751 LOZOVSKII, A.
The world's trade union movement. by A. Losovsky [pseud.] With an introduction by Earl R. Browder. Chicago, Ill., The Trade Union Educational League, 1924. 125 p. (Labor Herald Library No. 10)

"Stenographic report of a series of lectures before the school of Russian communist party in Moscow, during July and August, 1923" "Translation by M. A. Skromny." *Hoover, NYPL*

1752 NATIONAL Minority Movement, London.
The 10th anniversary of the Russian Revolution and the R. I. L. U. London [1927] 143 p. [Articles by various authors.] *Hoover*

1753 OLBERG, Paul
Die Rote Gewerkschafts-Internationale und die europäische Gewerk-schaftsbewegung. Stuttgart, Verlagsgesellschaft des deutschen Metall-arbeiter-Verbandes, 1930. 108 p. *Hoover, NYPL*

1754 PADMORE, George
The life and struggles of Negro toilers. London, Published by the
R. I. L. U. magazine for the Internat. Trade Union Committee of Negro
Workers, 1931. 126 p.   *NYPL*

PIATNITSKII, Osip
Alcuni problemi urgenti. Il movimento dei disocupati. Il lavoro del
partito e dei sindicati nelle officine. Le fluttuazioni dei nostri effettivi.
See no. 1183.

1755 PIATNITSKII, Osip
Die Arbeitslosigkeit und die Aufgaben der Kommunisten. Hamburg,
Carl Hoym Nachf. [1931] [pagination not given]   *Felt*

PIATNITSKII, Osip
Brennende Fragen. Die Arbeit unter den Arbeitslosen. Partei- und
Gewerkschaftsarbeit im Betrieb. Die Fluktuation im Mitgliedsbestand.
See no. 1168.

PIATNITSKII, Osip
Quelques problèmes urgents. Le mouvement des chômeurs. Le travail
du parti et des syndicats dans les entreprises. La fluctuation de nos
effectives. See no. 1180.

PIATNITSKII, Osip
Urgent questions of the day. Unemployment movement. Factory
organization. Fluctuating membership. See nos. 1176, 1177.

Die PROLETARISCHE Einheitsfront. Aufruf der Exekutive der Kommunistischen Internationale und der Exekutive der Roten Gewerkschaftsinternationale; Moskau, 1. Januar 1922. See no. 1032.

1756 Les SABOTEURS ou les réformistes à l'œuvre dans l'Internationale
des ouvriers textiles. Edité par le Comité International d'Action et
Propaganda du Textile. [n. p.] 1928. 30 p.   *Felt*

1757 TOMSKII, M.
Principes de l'organisation des syndicats ouvriers. Petrograd, Editions
du Conseil International des Syndicats, 1921. 31 p.   *Hoover, Felt*

4. R. I. L. U. Activities and Propaganda in foreign Countries

a) France

FRACHON, Benoit, ed.
Les communistes et les syndicats; le travail des fractions syndicales.
[Communist work in French trade unions] See no. 1366.

LOZOVSKII, A.
Frankreich und die französische Arbeiterbewegung in der Gegenwart.
Eindrücke und Betrachtungen. See no. 1374.

1758 LOZOVSKII, A.
Nationale und internationale Gewerkschaftseinheit; Rede, gehalten
auf dem Kongreß der Confédération Générale du Travail Unitaire
(CGTU) am 29. August 1925 in Paris. Berlin, Führer-Verlag, 1925. 31 p.
Felt

LOZOVSKII, A.
Réponses du camarade Losovsky aux questions posées par les délé-
gués français en Russie à l'occasion du X-e anniversaire de la
Révolution d'octobre. See no. 1370.

Hoover

1759 Les syndicats et la révolution; discours prononcé par A. Losovsky
[pseud.] au congrès de la C. G. T. U. à Saint Etienne, juin 1922; suivi
du message de l'Internationale syndical rouge. Paris, Librairie du
travail [1922] 61 p. (Petite bibliothèque de l'Internationale syndicale
rouge, 4) *Hoover, Felt*

1760 LOZOVSKII, A.
Zwei Internationalen; eine freundschaftliche Auseinandersetzung mit
den französischen Syndikalisten [von] A. Losowsky. Berlin, Verlag der
Roten Gewerkschafts-Internationale, Bd. 6)

Hoover, NYPL, Felt

PIATNITSKII, Osip
Die Arbeit der Kommunistischen Parteien Frankreichs und Deutschlands
und die Aufgaben der Kommunisten in der Gewerkschaftsbewegung.
[Rede, XII. Plenum EKKI] See no. 1206.

PIATNITSKII, Osip
The work of the communist parties of France and Germany and the tasks of the communists in the trade union movement. See nos. 1217, 1218.

1761 POUR la contre-offensive ouvrière; résolutions du VI-e congrès de la C.G.T.U. Paris, Internationale Syndicale Rouge; Confédération Générale du Travail Unitaire [1930] 64 p. *BDIC*

1762 TRAVAUX du camarade Michel Relenk au Congrès de l'I.S.R. de Moscou reste fidèle à la conception du syndicalisme révolutionnaire français et a son mandat. [Paris, Imprimerie de Coster, n. d.] 23 p.
Felt

b) Germany

1763 LOZOVSKII, A.
Eroberung oder Zerstörung der Gewerkschaften; Rede des Genossen Losowski am 24. September 1920 in Berlin. Leipzig, Frankes Verlag, 1920. 14 p. *Felt*

1764 LOZOVSKII, A.
Aufgaben und Entwicklung der Betriebsräte in Rußland; zwei Reden des Genossen Losowsky auf dem Betriebsräte-Kongreß in Berlin. Leipzig, Frankes Verlag, 1920. 31 p. *Hoover, Felt*

1765 LOZOVSKII, A.
Wie kann die Einheit der Gewerkschaftsbewegung hergestellt werden. Rede des Genossen Losowski, anläßlich des Empfanges der zweiten deutschen Arbeiterdelegation in der Roten Gewerkschafts-Internationale am 12. September 1926, nebst der anschließenden Aussprache mit der Delegation. Im Anhang: Einige Dokumente aus dem Kampfe um die Gewerkschaftseinheit. Moskau, Verlag der Roten Gewerkschafts-Internationale, 1926. 54 p. *Felt*

c) Great Britain

[ANGLO-Russian Trade Union Committee.]
For material on the Anglo-Soviet Trade Union Conference held in London in 1925 and on the Committee created by this conference, see nos. 1781—1787.

GREAT Britain. Parliament.
Communist papers. Documents selected from those obtained on the
arrest of the communist leaders on the 14th and 21st October 1925...
[Contains documents on the relations of the RILU with British communist organizations.] See no. 105.

1766 KANTER, H.
Die Wirtschaftsbilanz des englischen Bergarbeiterstreiks. Moskau,
Verlag der Roten Gewerkschafts-Internationale, 1926. 31 p. Printed
in Germany. *NYPL*

1767 Der STREIK in England und die Arbeiterklasse der Sowjetunion. Mit
einem Vorwort von Fritz Heckert. Moskau, Verlag der Roten Gewerkschafts-Internationale, 1926. 51 p. *Felt*

d) Italy

1768 LOZOVSKII, A.
Offener Brief an die Allgemeine italienische Arbeiter-Konföderation
[von] A. Losowski. Berlin, Internationaler Rat der Fach- und Industrieverbände [1920] 16 p. *Hoover, NYPL*

e) Japan

1769 NOSAKA, J.
A brief review of the labour movement in Japan. [Moscow] Inter-
national Council of Trade and Industrial Unions, 1921. 47 p. tables.
NYPL

f) Spain

1770 MAURIN, J.
L'anarcho-syndicalisme en Espagne. Paris, Librairie du Travail, 1924.
47 p. (Petite bibliothèque de l'Internationale Syndicale Rouge, 13)
Hoover

g) United States

COMMUNIST International. Executive Committee.
Vozzvanie Ispolnitel'nogo komiteta kommunisticheskogo Internatsionala k Soiuzu industrial'nykh rabochikh mira. See no. 1507.

UNITED Mine Workers of America.
Attempt by communists to seize the American labor movement; a series of six articles... See nos. 1524, 1525.

5. The Relations Profintern-Comintern

a) General

1771 GALSEN, S. and Sorbonskii, S.
Komintern i Profintern. Moskva, VTSSPS, 1926. 119 p.   *Hoover*

Der VORSTOSS der „Kommunistischen" Internationale gegen die Gewerkschaften... See no. 379.

VUIOVICH, V. D. [correct name Vujović]
Mezhdunarodnoe rabochee dvizhenie i Kommunisticheskii Internatsional. See no. 380

b) Deliberations and resolutions of Communist International Congresses concerning Profintern.

(Cross-references only)

II-nd Congress, 1920

NIN, Andreas [and others]
Die Rote Gewerkschafts- und die Kommunistische Internationale; die Frage der wechselseitigen Beziehungen zwischen der RGI und der KI. auf dem 2. Kongreß der RGI. See no. 1860.

PARLIAMENTARISM, Trade Unionism and the Communist International; theses adopted by the Second Congress of the C. I. See nos.
616, 623—3.

III-rd Congress, 1921

TROTSKII, L.
Mirovoe polozhenie i tretii kongress Komunisticheskogo Internatsionala [Annexes include the resolution of the I-st Congress of the RILU
on the tactic of the Profintern] See no. 719.

THESEN über die Kommunistische Internationale und die Rote Gewerkschafts-Internationale. (Kampf gegen die gelbe Gewerkschafts-
internationale von Amsterdam.) Angenommen in der 24. Sitzung des
III. Weltkongresses... See no. 700.

THESES et résolutions; adoptées au IIIème congrès de l'Internationale
communiste. [Contains an informative article entitled "The Communist International and the Red International of Trade Unions".]
See no. 707.

ZINOV'EV, G.
L'Internationale Communiste et l'organisation internationale des
syndicats. (La lutte contre l'Internationale Jeaune d'Amsterdam.) See
no. 688.

IV-th Congress, 1922

LOZOVSKII, A.
Die Gewerkschaftsfrage auf dem vierten Kongreß der Kommunistischen
Internationale vom 5. Nov. bis 5. Dez. 1922. Referat und Schlußwort
von Losowsky sowie die Diskussionsreden von Clark, etc. See no. 739.

LOZOVSKII, A.
Zadachi kommunistov v profdvizhenii. Doklad i zkaliuchitel'noe slovo
na IV kongresse Kominterna. See no. 734.

RAPPORTS de l'I. S. R. et de l'I. C. [Contains the statutes of the RILU,
the theses on the communist actions in the trade union movement,
and the discussion in the IV-th Congress of the C. I. of these theses.]
See nos. 757, 757 a.

V-th Congress, 1924

LOZOVSKII, A.
Za edinstvo mirovogo profdvizheniia; voprosy profdvizheniia na V kongresse Kominterna. See no. 808.

ZINOV'EV, G.
Für die Einheit der internationalen Gewerkschaftsbewegung. Rede, gehalten auf dem V. Weltkongreß... See no. 779.

ZINOV'EV, G.
Fagbevaegelsens enhet. Tale paa den 5. Verdenskongres [of the C.I.] See no. 794.

LOZOVSKII, A.
La question syndicale. (Discours au V-e Congrès de Internationale Communiste.) See no. 792.

LOZOVSKII, A.
Towards trade union unity! [Speech at V-th Congress of C.I.] See no. 788.

c) **Deliberations and resolutions of E. C. C. I. Plenums concerning the Profintern**

(Cross-references only)

1-st Plenum, 1922

LOZOVSKII, A., and Brandler, Heinrich
Der Kampf der Kommunisten in den Gewerkschaften. Bericht der Genossen A. Losowsky und Heinrich Brandler zur Gewerkschaftsfrage... [1-st Plenum, Feb.—March 1922.] See no. 1036.

5-th Plenum, 1925

LOZOVSKII, A.
Der Kampf für die Einheit der Weltgewerkschaftsbewegung. Referat auf der [5.] Tagung des erweiterten Exekutivkomitees der K.I. See no. 1070.

LOZOVSKII, A.
Za edinstvo mezhdunarodnogo profdvizheniia. Doklad [5-mu] ras-shirennomu plenumu IKKI. See no. 1066.

6-th Plenum, 1926

LOZOVSKII, A.
Komintern i profdvizheniie (doklad na VI rasshirennom plenume IKKI 1-go marta 1926 goda) See no. 1090.

LOZOVSKII, A.
Kommunisten und Gewerkschaften; Referat und Schlußwort in der VI. Tagung des Erweiterten Exekutiv-Komitees der Kommunistischen Internationale. Im Anhang Thesen über: Die nächsten Aufgaben der Kommunisten in der Gewerkschaftsbewegung. See no. 1093.

7-th Plenum, 1926

LOZOVSKII, A.
Vertrustung, Rationalisierung und unsere Aufgaben in der Gewerkschaftsbewegung; Referat, gehalten am 6. Dezember 1926 auf der VII. Tagung der Erweiterten Exekutive der Kommunistischen International. See no. 1109.

9-th Plenum, 1928

NOVEISHII reformizm, tresty i profsoiuzy. [Abbreviated version of record of Trade Union Commission of the 9-th Plenum including report to Plenum.] See no. 1134.

13-th Plenum, 1933

KOSTANIAN, G.
La maturation de la crise révolutionnaire et les tâches des sections de l'I.S.R. Discours prononcé à la XIIIe Session plénière du C.E. de l'I.C. See no. 1276.

KOSTANIAN, G.
Nazrevanie revoliutsionnogo krizisa i zadachi sektsii Profinterna.
[Speech at 13th Plenum] See no. 1244.

KUN, Bela [and] Smolianskii, G., ed.
Profsoiuznyi vopros na XIII plenume IKKI, dekiabr', 1933 g. See
no. 1245.

LOZOVSKII, A.
Luttons pour la majorité d ela classe ouvrière; discours prononcé
au XIIIe plenum de l'Exécutif de l'I. C. le 7 décembre 1933. See
no. 1277.

6. The Relationship Profintern-Soviet Central Council of Trade Unions

Note: The Soviet Union, as a member of the R. I. L. U., was represented in the Profintern by a delegation of the All-Russian Central Council of Trade Unions. This delegation reported to the congresses of Trade Unions of the Soviet Union.

1772 LOZOVSKII, A.
Ergebnisse und Aussichten der Arbeiter der Roten Gewerkschafts-Internationale. Referat und Schlußwort, gehalten auf dem VIII. Kongreß der Gewerkschaften der Sowjetunion; 15. und 17. Dezember 1928. [von] A. Losowsky. Moskau, Rote Gewerkschafts-Internationale, 1929. 57 p. *Hoover*

1773 LOZOVSKII, A.
Otchet Delegatsii VTSSPS v Profinterne, IX sezdu Profsoiuzov. Moskva, Profizdat, 1932. 61 p. *Hoover*

1774 LOZOVSKII, A.
10 [zehn] Jahre Rote Gewerkschafts-Internationale. Rede gehalten vor dem Moskauer Gewerkschaftsfunktionären am 21. April 1930. Moskau, Verlag der Roten Gewerkschafts-Internationale, 1930. 47 p. *Felt*

1775 L'UNITÉ du mouvement syndical mondial; rapports et discours prononcées au VI-e Congrès des syndicats ouvriers de l'U.R.S.S. Préf. de A. Losovsky. Paris [Bureau de l'Internationale syndicale rouge] 1925. 93 p. (Petite bibliothèque de l'Internationale syndicale rouge, no. 15)

> Lozovski's preface deals with "The formation of the Anglo-Russian Committee of Unity". This is followed by excerpts of speeches at the VI Congress of Soviet Trade Unions by Zinov'ev, Dudilieux (France), Purcell (Britain), Bramley (Britain), Ben Tillet (Britain), Tomskii, Lozovskii, Iuzefovich, Brudno, Geschke and Pollitt (Britain). The last item includes a declaration by the Presidium of the Congress and its resolution concerning the unity of the international trade union movement. *Hoover, BDIC, Felt*

7. Conferences and Meetings sponsored by the R.I.L.U.

a) International Conferences of Revolutionary Transport Workers

Note: These conferences were called by the International Propaganda Committee of Transport Workers, a front organization created by the Red International of Labor Unions, composed of a few communist-dominated transport unions in Western Europe and splinter-organizations which left socialist-controlled transport unions or were expelled from them. At the core of this organization were transport unions from the Soviet Union which, in fact, made up at least 80 per cent of its total membership. (Figures taken from the item below, dealing with the 3-rd Conference.)

3-rd Conference, Moscow, December 5–7, 1922

1776 3 [TRET'IA] Mezhdunarodnaia konferentsiia revoliutsionnykh transportnikov (5—7 dekabria 1922 g.). Otchet, tezisy i rezoliutsii. Moskva, 1923. 84 p. At head of title: Krasnyi Internatsional profsoiuzov. Mezhdunarodnyi komitet propagandy transportnykh rabochikh.

Hoover

5-th Conference, Moscow, April 4–8, 1928

1777 ACHKANOV, Grigorii
Die Aufgaben des Transportproletariats. Bericht des Genossen Atschkanoff auf der 5. Konferenz der revolutionären Transportarbeiter in
Moskau; 4. bis 8. April 1928. Hrsg. vom Internationalen Propaganda-
und Aktionskomitee der revolutionären Transportarbeiter, Moskau,
1928. 23 p.   *Felt*

1778 Die 5. [FÜNFTE] Internationale Konferenz der revolutionären Transportarbeiter; abgehalten in Moskau im April 1928. Hrsg. vom Internationalen Propaganda- und Aktionskomitee der revolutionären
Transportarbeiter, Moskau. Berlin, Führer-Verlag [n. d.] 95 p.

Felt

**b) International Conference of Transport Workers, Berlin,
May 23–24, 1923**

Note: In this conference participated nine delegates of the Fédération Inter-
nationale des Transports (belonging to the non-communist International Federation
of Trade Unions in Amsterdam) and an unknown number of delegates of the
All-Russian Federation of Transport, Railroad and Maritime Workers, representing
all transport workers affiliated with the Red International of Labor Unions. The
RILU had its own transport union front organization, the International Propaganda
Committee of Revolutionary Transport Workers (see point a. above).
The purpose of this conference was to explore the formation of a united front
of transport workers against the danger of war, and to explore the possibilities
of a re-unification of labor unions of transport workers which had been split.
Lozovskii participated in the conference as delegate of the All-Russian Federation,
and not of the RILU. This conference was called at the peak of the Anglo-Soviet
tension, after Great Britain broke off relations with the Soviet Union.

1779 LOZOVSKII, A.
Die Einheitsfront der Transport-Arbeiter. Die Internationale Konferenz
der Transport-Arbeiter vom 28. [sic!] bis 25. Mai 1923 in Berlin. Berlin,
Führer-Verlag, 1923. 14 p.   *Felt*

1780 SEMARD, Pierre
Pour le Front Unique des Transports; avec un recueil de documents.
Paris, Librairie du Travail [1923] 24 p. Cover title.

This pamphlet contains the minutes of the Berlin Conference and documentation on the efforts of French pro-communist labor unions to apply some of the
Berlin resolutions. The French unions affiliated with the Amsterdam Federation
of Transport Workers refused to go along with the Moscow-inspired united
front.   *Hoover*

c) Anglo-Soviet Conference of Trade Unions; London, April 1925.

Note: The Soviet success with the "Hands off Russia" movement among British trade unionists in 1920 and the following years, as well as a visit of British trade unionists to Soviet Russia, resulted in the 1925 conference of British and Soviet Trade Unions. Although the official Soviet delegation was representing the state-controlled trade unions, the Comintern and the Red International of Trade Unions through their British "sections" were active in this venture. The Conference created an "Anglo-Russian Trade Union Committee" which, according to Soviet designs, had to promote the Comintern-sponsored policy of the "united front from below".
Several factors caused the liquidation of this Committee early in 1927.

1781 ANDREEV, Andrei A.
Anglo-russkii komitet. Moskva, Moskovskii rabochii, 1925. 80 p.

BDIC

1782 LONDONSKAIA konferentsiia edinstva. 6—9 aprelia 1925 goda. S predisloviem V. V. Shmidta. Moskva, VTSSPS, 1925. 103 p.

BDIC

1783 LOZOVSKII, A.
Anglo-sovetskaia konferentsiia professional'nykh soiuzov. Moskva, Gos. izd-vo, 1925. 112 p.   *Hoover*

1784 LOZOVSKII, A.
La conférence syndicale anglo-soviétique. Paris, 1925. 96 p. (Petite bibliothèque de l'Internationale Syndicale Rouge, 19)

Hoover

1785 LOZOVSKII, A.
Die englisch-russische Gewerkschaftskonferenz. Berlin, Führer-Verlag, 1925. 111 p.   *Hoover, Felt*

1786 LOZOVSKII, A.
Das Englisch-russische Komitee der Einheit. Moskau, Verlag der Roten Gewerkschafts-Internationale, 1926. 31 p. Printed in Germany. At head of title: A. Losowsky.   *NYPL*

Der KAMPF um die Kommunistische Internationale; Dokumente der russischen Opposition nicht veröffentlicht vom Stalin'schen ZK. [Contains references to the Anglo-Russian Committee] See no. 113.

PETROVSKII, D.
Das anglo-russische Komitee und die Opposition in der KPSU. See no. 1125.

1787 TOMSKII, Mikhail
Getting together; speeches delivered in Russia and England 1924—
1925; with an introduction by R. Page Arnot. London, The Labour
Research Department [1925] 111 p.   *Hoover*

L'UNITÉ du mouvement syndical mondial; rapports et discours prononcées au VI-e Congrès des syndicats ouvriers de l'U.R.S.S. [Impor-
tant discussion of the formation of the Anglo-Russian Committee of
Unity] See no. 1775.

d) Pan-Pacific Trade Union Conference, 1927–1929

1788 LOZOVSKII, A.
The Pan-Pacific Trade Union Conference; Hankow, May 20—26, 1927.
Moscow, The R.I.L.U., 1927. 62 p.   *Hoover, NYPL*

1789 LOZOVSKII, A.
Protiv voiny, imperializma i reformizma; doklad i zakliuchitel'noe
slovo na Tikhookeanskoi konferentsii profsoiuzov 16 avgusta 1929 g.
Moskva, VTSSPS, 1929. 79 p. At head of title: V pomoshch' internatsional'nomu vospitaniiu.   *Hoover*

e) International Conference on Strike Strategy, Strassburg, Germany, January, 1929.

1790 ERFAHRUNGEN, Lehren und Aufgaben in den Wirtschaftskämpfen.
Streiktaktik und Streikstrategie. Resolutionen der Straßburger Kon-
ferenz, mit einem Vorwort von A. Losowsky. Moskau, Verlag der Roten
Gewerkschafts-Internationale [n. d.] 28 p. (Sonderdruck aus der *Roten
Gewerkschaft-Internationale)*   *Felt*

LOZOVSKII, A.
La grève est un combat! Essai d'application de la science militaire
à la stratégie des grèves. [Contains a reprint of the resolution of the
Strassburg Conference.] See no. 1603, 1603a, 1604.

1791 PROBLEMS of strike strategy; decisions of the International conference
on strike strategy held in Strassburg, Germany, January, 1929. Foreword by A. Lozovsky. Preface to American edition by Bill Dunne.
New York City, Published for Trade Union Unity League by Workers
Library [1929] 49 p.   *Hoover*

1792 STRIKE strategy & tactics; the lessons of the industrial struggles. Thesis adopted by the Strassburg Conference held under the auspices of the Red International of Labour Unions. London, Published by the National Minority Movement [n. d.] 28 p.

> Preface signed by Percy Glading. *Felt*

f) International Conference of Negro Workers, 1930.

Note: This conference was formally called by the International Trade Union Committee of Negro Workers, an organization created by the Red International of Labor Unions.

1793 INTERNATIONAL Conference of Negro Workers; Report of proceedings and decisions. Hamburg, 1930.

> This entry is incomplete; it was taken from a NYPL serial catalog card.
> *NYPL*

g) Congress of the Miners of Europe, Saarbrücken, April 16–18, 1932

1794 RAPPPORT et résolutions du Congrès des Mineurs d'Europe; Sarrebruck, les 16/18 avril 1932. Metz, Edité par le Comité International des Mineurs [n. d.] 39 p.

> The item was unavailable for identification. It was placed here on the basis of the catalog entry of the Feltrinelli Library which cataloged this item under the heading "Red International of Labor Unions". *Felt*

h) Meeting of Communists in the R. I. L. U., Moscow, August 2, 1934.

1795 PIATNITSKII, Osip
Probleme der internationalen Gewerkschaftsbewegung. [Strasbourg] Prometheus Verlag [1934] 40 p. Printed in Switzerland. At head of title: O. Pjatnizki.

> „Die vorliegende Broschüre enthält das bearbeitete Stenogramm des Referats O. Pjatnizkis auf der Versammlung der Kommunisten in der GI am 2 August 1934" p. [2] footnote. *Hoover, LC, BDIC*

1796 PIATNITSKII, Osip
Probleme der internationalen Gewerkschaftsbewegung. Bearbeitetes
Stenogramm des Referats auf der Versammlung der Kommunisten in
der RGI am 2. August 1934. Moskau, Verlagsgenossenschaft ausländischer Arbeiter in der UdSSR, 1935. 59 p.

For annotation see preceding item. *Felt*

8. Publications on Conditions in the Soviet Union

Note: The RILU developed, through workers' organizations in various countries
affiliated with it, a broad propaganda of praising the living and working conditions in the Soviet Union. This propaganda material was produced in several
languages and was distributed through communist publishers and bookstores
throughout the world. Pertinent material is listed below.

1797 ACHKANOV, Grigorii
Kampf und Sieg der russischen See- und Binnenschiffer; Material zur
Geschichte des Verbandes der russischen Wassertransportarbeiter.
Verlag der Roten Gewerkschafts-Internationale; Auslieferung für
Deutschland durch Führer-Verlag, Berlin, 1923. 97 p. At head of title:
Gregor Atschkanoff. (Bibliothek der Roten Gewerkschafts-Internatio-
nale, Bd. 24) *Hoover, NYPL, Felt*

1798 ALOUF, A.
Les syndicats et la situation de la classe ouvrière dans l'U.R.R.S.
1921—1925. Préface de A. Losovsky. Paris, 1925. ? p. (Petite bibliothèque de l'Internationale Syndicale Rouge, 2) *NYPL*

1799 ANDREEV, A.
Die russischen Gewerkschaften in den Jahren 1921—22. Verlag der
Roten Gewerkschafts-Internationale; Auslieferung für Deutschland
durch Phöbus-Verlag, Berlin, 1922. 31 p. tables. (Bibliothek der Roten
Gewerkschafts-Internationale, Bd. 11) *Hoover, NYPL, Felt*

1800 ANTOSHKIN, D.
Die Organisation der Angestellten in Rußland. Hrsg. vom Internatio-
nalen Rat der Gewerkschaften und Industrieverbände. Berlin, A. Seehof
& Co. [1920?] 32 p. inc. tables. At head of title: A. Antoschkin.
NYPL

1801 IAROTSKII, Vasili IA
Die Gewerkschaften der U.S.R.R. und der Kampf um die Einheit. Herausgegeben von der Kommission für auswärtige Beziehungen des Zentralrates der Gewerkschaften der USSR. Moskau, 1927. 88 p. At head of title: W. Jarotzki. *NYPL*

1802 KRASNYI soiuz rabochikh i sluzhashchikh pishchevoi promyshlennosti v Sovetskoi Rossii (kratkii istoricheskii ocherk). Moskva, Izd. Krasnogo internatsionala profsoiuzov, 1921. 63 p. *LC*

1803 LINDENAU, Ernst
Die Arbeiter unter der Räte-Republik (Soziale Föderative Sowjet Republik) in Rußland. Nach authentischen Quellen dargestellt von Ernst Lindenau. [Nürenberg, Verlag von Curt Stockhausen, n. d.] 4 leaves. *Felt*

1804 LOZOVSKII, A.
Adónde vamos? Paris, 1930. ? p. (Pequeña biblioteca de la Internacional sindical roja, 27) At head of title: A. Losovski.

This item in Spanish is actually the 27-th item belonging to the Petite bibliothèque de l'Internationale Syndicale Rouge. *NYPL*

1805 LOZOVSKII, A.
Die Russischen Gewerkschaften unter den neuen Verhältnissen. Verlag der Roten Gewerkschafts-Internationale; Auslieferung durch Phöbus-Verlag, Berlin, 1922. 34 p. (Bibliothek der Roten Gewerkschafts-Internationale, Bd. 9) *Hoover, NYPL, Felt*

1806 LOZOVSKII, A.
Les syndicats russes et la nouvelle politique. Paris, 1922. [no pagination given.] At head of title: A. Losovsky. (Petite bibliothèque de l'Internationale Syndicale Rouge, 3) *NYPL*

1807 RESNIKOFF, J.
Die Lage des russischen Arbeiters. Verlag der Roten Gewerkschafts-Internationale; Auslieferung für Deutschland: Führer-Verlag, Berlin, 1923. [no pagination given.] (Bibliothek der Roten Gewerkschafts-Internationale, Bd. 21) *NYPL*

1808 SHAKHNOVSKII, E.
Die Entwicklung des russischen Eisenbahnverbandes. Verlag der Roten Gewerkschafts-Internationale; Auslieferung für Deutschland: Führer-Verlag, Berlin, 1924. [no pagination given.] (Bibliothek der Roten Gewerkschafts-Internationale, Bd. 27) At head of title: E. Schachnowsky. *NYPL*

1809 Die TEXTILARBEITER in Sowjetrußland. Hrsg. vom Internationalen Rat der Gewerkschaften und Industrieverbände. Berlin, A. Seehof & Co. [1920] 20 p. *NYPL*

1810 TOMSKII, M.
Die neuen Aufgaben der russischen Gewerkschaften. Verlag der Roten Gewerkschafts-Internationale; Auslieferung für Deutschland durch Phöbus-Verlag, Berlin, 1922. 33 p. (Bibliothek der Roten Gewerk-schafts-Internationale, Bd. 12) *Hoover, NYPL, Felt*

1811 TSYPEROVICH, Grigorii
Was lehrt die Erfahrung? Der Bekleidungsindustriearbeiterverband [sic!] in Petrograd und seine Teilnahme an der Produktion. Verlag der Roten Gewerkschafts-Internationale; Auslieferung durch A. Wese-mann, Phöbus-Verlag, Berlin, 1922. 48 p. At head of title: G. Zipero-witsch. (Bibliothek der Roten Gewerkschafts-Internationale, Bd. 4) *Hoover, NYPL, Felt*

B. CONGRESSES, CENTRAL COUNCIL AND EXECUTIVE BUREAU SESSIONS

1. I-st Congress, Moscow, July 3—19, 1921

a) Protocols

1812 1-yi [PERVYI] Mezhdunarodnyi kongress revoliutsionnykh profes-sional'nykh i proizvodstvennykh soiuzov. Stenograficheskii otchet. [Moskva, 3—19 iiulia 1921 g.] Moskva, Izd-vo Press-biuro Kongressa [1921] 15 issues, variously paged. Running title: Biulleten' 1-go Mezhdunarodnogo kongressa...

This Bulletin was issued periodically during the congress for the delegates and later reissued as an entity with an added title page. It contains the stenographic records of the congress. NYPL has it cataloged under the above title. BDIC has it cataloged under the title: *Biulleten' pervogo Mezhdunarodnogo kongressa, etc.* NYPL, BDIC

1813 BULLETIN du premier Congrès International des Syndicats Révolutionnaires. Moscow, Bureau de la Presse du I-er Congrès International des Syndicats Ouvriers, 1921. no. 1—16; July 3-?, 1921.

Contains the stenographic record of the meetings. See annotations to nos. 1812 and 1849. *Felt*

1814 DELIBERAZIONI, statuti e appelli del I congresso della Internazionale dei Sindicati Rossi; 3—19 luglio 1921. Roma, Librerie editrice del Partito Comunista d'Italia, 1922. 140 p. (Bibliotheca della Internazionale dei Sindicati Rossi, 1) *Felt*

b) Reports, Speeches, Drafts presented to the Congress

1815 LOZOVSKII, A.
Organizatsionnyi vopros. (Proekt tezisov) Moskva, 1921. 15 p. At head of title: 1-i Mezhdunarodnyi kongress revoliutsionnykh professional'-nykh i proizvodstvennykh soiuzov. *NYPL*

1816 LOZOVSKII, A.
Programa deistvii Krasnogo internatsionala profsoiuzov. Moskva, izd. Otdela pechati Krasnogo internatsionala profsoiuzov, 1921. 102 p. tables. At head of title: Krasnyi internatsional profsoiuzov.

For German edition see no. 1819; for French edition see no. 1828. *NYPL*

1817 OTCHET Mezhdunarodnogo soveta krasnykh professional'nykh i proizvodstvennykh soiuzov za period ot 15 iiulia 1920 goda — 1 iiulia 1921 goda. Moskva, 1921. 195 p. *NYPL*

1818 PROFINTERN i Komintern (vopros o vzaimootnoshenii Profinterna i Kominterna na 1-om Mezhdunarodnom kongresse rev. profsoiuzov) Moskva, 1921. 45 p. At head of title: Krasnyi internatsional profsoiuzov.

Contents: 1) Rech' tov. Rosmera. 2) Rech' Mana. 3) Rech' Lozovskogo. 4) Zakliuchitel'noe slovo Rosmera. 5) Rezoliutsii. *Hoover*

1819 LOZOVSKII, A.
Das Aktionsprogramm der Roten Gewerkschafts-Internationale. 2. Aufl. Verlag der Roten Gewerkschafts-Internationale; Auslieferung durch Phöbus-Verlag, Berlin, 1922. 96 p. (Bibliothek der Roten Gewerkschafts-Internationale, Bd. 5)

> "The purpose of this pamphlet is to explain the program of action adopted by the I-st Congress of Revolutionary Labor Unions and by the III-rd Congress of the Communist International." (Preface to first edition, signed by A. Lozovskii.) This pamphlet was a guide-book of policies and tacties to be followed by "revolutionary trade unions". *Hoover, NYPL, BDIC, Felt*

1820 LOZOVSKII, A.
Aufgaben und Taktik der Roten Gewerkschafts-Internationale. Rede des Genossen Losowsky mit der auf dem Kongreß angenommenen Resolution. Berlin, Verlag der Roten Gewerkschafts-Internationale, 1921. 46 p. (Bibliothek der Roten Gewerkschafts-Internationale, Bd. 2)
BDIC, Felt

1821 LOZOVSKII, A.
Die Thesen. Von A. Losowsky. Die Organisationsfrage. Moskau, 7-a Tipografiia V. S. N. C. [n. d.] 19 p.

> The above listing repeats the contents of the catalog card in the Feltrinelli Library. This is obviously the German edition of item no. 1815. *Felt*

1822 ROSMER, Alfred [and Mann, Tom]
Die Beziehungen zwischen der Roten Gewerkschafts-Internationale und der Kommunist. Internationale; Reden der Genossen Rosmer, Frankreich, und Tom Mann, England, mit der auf dem ersten Kongreß der R. G. I. angenommenen Resolution. Berlin, Verlag der Roten Gewerkschafts-Internationale, 1921. 35 p. (Bibliothek der Roten Gewerkschafts-Internationale, Bd. 3) *Hoover, BDIC, Felt*

1823 TSYPEROVICH, Grigorii V. [and Heckert, Fritz]
Produktionskontrolle und Betriebsräte; Referate der Genossen Ziperowitsch und Heckert auf dem ersten Kongress der Roten Gewerkschafts-Internationale, nebst den angenommenen Resolutionen. Berlin, Verlag der Roten Gewerkschafts-Internationale, 1921. 35 p. (Bibliothek der Roten Gewerkschafts-Internationale, Bd. 7)

Hoover, NYPL, Felt

1824 LOZOVSKII, A.
Aims and tactics of the trade unions. (Drafted by Comrade Losovsky). Moscow, Press Bureau of the International Congress of the Red Trade and Industrial Unions, 1921. 22 p. *NYPL*

1825 LOZOVSKII, A.
The question of organisation. Theses presented by A. Losovsky.
Moscow, Press-Bureau of the International Congress of the Red Trade
and Industrial Unions, 1921. 15 p. *NYPL*

1826 REPORT of the International Council of Red Trade and Industrial
Unions, for the period July 15-th 1920 — July 1-st 1921. Moscow,
Pressbureau of the First International Congress of Red Trade and
Industrial Unions, 1921. 148 p. *NYPL, Harv*

1827 COMPTE-RENDU du Conseil international des syndicats rouges pour
la période de 15 juillet 1920 au 1-r juillet 1921. Moscou, 1921. 160 p.
Hoover

1828 LOZOVSKII, A.
Programme d'action de l'Internationale Syndicale Rouge. Paris,
Librairie du Travail, 1922. 137 p. At head of title: A. Losovsky. (Petite
bibliothèque de l'Internationale Syndicale Rouge, 2)

For annotation see no. 1819. *Hoover, Felt*

1829 LOZOVSKII, A.
Questions d'organisation; thèses du cam. A. Losowsky. Moscou,
Edition du Bureau de la presse du 1-er Congrès international des
syndicats rouges, 1921. 15 p. *Hoover*

1830 TSYPEROVICH, Grigorii [and Heckert, Fritz]
Controllo operario e consigli di fabrica. Roma, Libreria Editrice del
Partito Comunista d'Italia, 1922. 39 p. (Piccola biblioteca dell'Inter-
nazionale dei Sindicati Rossi, 1.)

See no. 1823. *Felt*

1831 CONSTITUTIO ... [Moscow? 192-?] 8 p. Caption title. At head of title:
Project ay comrade A. Lozovsky.

This is an exact copy of the NYPL catalog card. Probably abbreviated cataloging; title seems to be incomplete. *NYPL*

MERRHEIM, Alphonse
Amsterdam eller Moskva. See no. 1404.

c) Resolutions, Theses, Manifestoes and other documents

1832 REZOLIUTSII i postanovleniia pervogo Mezhdunarodnogo kongressa revoliutsionnykh professional'nykh soiuzov. (3—19 iiulia 1921 g., Moskva) S predisloviem A. Lozovskogo. Moskva, 1921. 73 p.

NYPL, Col

1833 REZOLIUTSII i postanovleniia pervogo Mezhdunarodnogo kongressa revoliutsionnykh professional'nykh soiuzov. (3—19 iiulia 1921 g., Moskva). S predisloviem A. Lozovskogo. Tiflis, Izd-vo Kavbiuro VTSSPS, 1921. 79 p.

LC

1834 RESOLUTIONEN, Statuten, Manifeste und Aufrufe des ersten Internationalen Kongresses der Roten Fach- und Industrie-Verbände, 3 Juli bis 19 Juli 1921. Bremen, Verlag der Roten Gewerkschafts-Internationale [1921] 88 p. (Bibliothek der Roten Gewerkschafts-Internationale, **Bd. 1)**

Hoover, NYPL, Felt

1835 SATZUNGEN der Roten Gewerkschafst-Internationale. Bremen, "Phönix-Verlag" [n. d.] 16 p. (Bibliothek der Roten Gewerkschafts-Internationale. Auslieferungsstelle für Mitteleuropa)

BDIC

1836 The CONSTITUTION of the Red International. Chicago, American Labor Union Educational Society [1921] 8 p. Cover title.

NYPL, NWest

1837 RESOLUTIONS and decisions adopted by the first International congress of revolutionary trade and industrial unions. [July 3 to 19th 1921]. With an introduction by A. Losovsky [pseud.] Moscow, 1921. 93 p. At head of title: The Red International of labour unions.

Hoover, NYPL

1838 RESOLUTIONS and decisions of the first International Congress of revolutionary trade and industrial unions. New York, American Labor Union Educational Society, 1921. [pages?] On cover: Published by Lyceum and Literature Department, Workers Party of America.

NYPL

1839 RESOLUTIONS and decisions of the first international congress of Revolutionary trade and industrial unions. [Chicago?] The American labor union educational society [1921] 96 p. "Published by the Voice of labor, November, 1921." On cover: The Red Labor International.

NYPL, Harv, Illin

385

1840 RESOLUTIONS and decisions of the first International Congress of revolutionary trade and industrial unios. [2nd ed. Pub. by the Voice of Labor. Chicago] The American Labor Union Educational Society [Nov. 1921] 96 p. Introduction signed: A. Losovsky. On cover: The Red Labor International. *Hoover, LC, UTex*

1841 RESOLUTIONS and decisions adopted by the First International Congress of Revolutionary Trade and Industrial Unions, 3rd till 19th July, 1921. With an introduction by A. Losovsky. Glasgow, Union Publishing Co., 1922. 121 p. On cover: Labour's new charter.

UMich

1842 RÉSOLUTIONS ET DÉCISIONS DU I-er congrèss international des Syndicats révolutionnaires. Du 3 au 19 juillet 1921, Moscou. Préface de A. Lozovsky. Moscou, Tip. Mosk., 1921. 79 p. *Felt*

1843 RÉSOLUTIONS & status adoptés au I-er congrès international des Syndicats révolutionnaires, Moscou, 3—19 juillet 1921. Préface de Dridzo-Lozovsky. Paris, Librairie du travail, 1921. 87 p. (Petite bibliothèque de l'Internationale syndicale rouge, 1) *Hoover, NYPL, Felt*

1844 STATUTO dell'Internazionale dei Sindicati Rossi. Roma, Libreria Editrice del Partito Comunista d'Italia, 1922. 12 p. (Biblioteca dell'Internazionale dei Sindicati Rossi) *Felt*

d) Commentaries and writings about the Congress

1845 LOZOVSKII, A.
Pervyi Mezhdunarodnyi kongress revoliutsionnykh professional'nykh soiuzov (8-10-vii, [!] 1921) Moskva, Otdel pechati Profinterna [1921] 31 p. At head of title: Krasnyj Internatsional profsoiuzov. *Hoover*

TROTSKII, Lev
Mirovoe polozhenie i tretii kongress Kommunisticheskogo Internatsionala. Prilozheniia: 1. Taktika Kominterna (rezoliutsiia kongressa Kominterna) 2. Taktika Profinterna (rezoliutsiia I-go kongressa Krasnykh Profsoiuzov). See no. 719.

1846 CASCADEN, Gordon
Shall unionism die? "Red" union international congress (meeting in Moscow, Russia) plans division of workers of Canada and United States and destruction of world-wide labor movement; report made by Gordon Cascaden... [Windsor, Ont., 1922] viii, 96 p. *Hoover*

1847 MURPHY, John Thomas
The "Reds" in congress; preliminary report of the first world congress of the Red International of Trade and Industrial Unions [based upon the notes taken by the members of the British Delegation] London, British Bureau, Red International of Trade and Industrial Unions [1921] 28 p.   *Hoover*

1848 WILLIAMS, George
The First congress of the Red trade union international at Moscow, 1921; a report of the proceedings by Geo. Williams, delegate from the I.W.W. Chicago, Ill., Industrial Workers of the World [1922] 59 p. At head of title: Second revised edition.

> "Preliminary report – sent from Berlin has been cut down and contains points not covered in later report." p. 3.   *Hoover, Col, Princ*

e) Bulletins issued for the Congress.

Note: The Bulletins issued for this Congress are listed as nos. 1812 and 1813.

2. II-nd Congress, Moscow, November 19—December 2, 1922

a) Protocols

1849 BIULLETEN' II kongressa Krasnogo Internatsionala Profsoiuzov v Moskve v Kolonnom zale 1-go Doma Soiuzov; 19-go noiabria 1922 goda [— 2-go dekabria 1922 g.] Moskva, Izdanie Krasnogo Profinterna, 1922. 160 p.

> This Bulletin was printed periodically during the Congress and later reprinted as an entity, with current pagination. It contains the stenographic record of the congress.   *Hoover*

1850 II [VTOROI] kongress Krasnogo Internatsionala Profsoiuzov v Moskve, 19 noiabria — 2 dekabria 1922 goda. Moskva, Gos. izd-vo, 1923. 320 p.

> The item was not available for identification. Obviously a later reprint of congress proceedings. *Harv*

b) Reports, Speeches, Drafts presented to the Congress

1851 HECKERT, Fritz [and Pavlik]
Nastuplenie kapitala, raskol'nicheskaia deiatel'nost' Amsterdama i edinyi front. Stenogrammy rechei tov. Gekkerta i Pavlika na II Mezhdunar. kongresse Kr. Internatsionala Profsoiuzov, i rezoliutsiia kongressa. Moskva, Izd. Krasnogo Profinterna, 1923. 51 p. (Malen'-kaia biblioteka Krasnogo Internatsionala Profsoiuzov)
LC, NYPL, Felt

1852 HELLER, Leo
Profsoiuzy na Vostoke; doklad II Mezhdunarodnomu kongressu Krasnogo Internatsionala Profsoiuzov. Moskva, 1923. 32 p. At head of title: L. N. Geller. *Col*

1853 LOZOVSKII, A. [and Hais]
Organizatsionnyi vopros na II kongresse Profinterna. (Stenogrammy.) 1) Doklad t. Lozovskogo; 2) Rech' t. Gais; 3) Zakliuchite'noe slovo t. Lozovskogo. Rezoliutsii kongressa. Moskva, Izd. Krasnogo Profinterna, 1923. 72 p. (Malen'kaia biblioteka Krasnogo Internatsionala Profsoiuzov)
NYPL

1854 NIN, Andreas [and others]
Profintern i Komintern; vopros o vzaimootnosheniiakh Profinterna i Kominterna na 2 Mezhdunarodnom kongresse professional'nykh soiuzov. Stenogrammy rechei Nina, Monmusso Tresso, Zinov'eva; rezoliutsiia kongressa. Moskva, Izd. Krasnogo Profinterna, 1923. 75 p. (Malen'kaia biblioteka Krasnogo Internatsionala Profsoiuzov)
Hoover, LC, NYPL, Harv

1855 OTCHET Ispolnitel'nogo biuro Profinterna [II Mezhdunarodnomu kongressu revoliutsionnykh profsoiuzov] iiul' 1921 — noiabr' 1922 g. Moskva, Krasnyi Internatsional Profsoiuzov [1922] 164 p.
Hoover, NYPL, BDIC

1856 BERICHT des Vollzugsbüros der Roten Gewerkschafts-Internationale an den II Kongreß der revolutionären Gewerkschaften, Moskau, 25. November, 1922. Berlin, 1922. 169 p. *NYPL, BDIC, Felt*

1857 HECKERT, F. [and Pavlik]
Die Einheitsfront, die Spaltungstätigkeit der Amsterdamer und die
Offensive des Kapitals; Stenogramme der Reden der Genossen
Heckert und Pavlik auf dem 2. Kongreß der RGI. Anhang: Die Resolu-
tion des Kongresses. Berlin, 1923. 43 p. (Bibliothek der Roten Gewerk-
schafts-Internationale, Bd. 20)   *NYPL, Felt*

1858 HELLER, Leo
Gewerkschaftliche Bewegung in den Kolonien und Halbkolonien des
Ostens. Rede gehalten auf dem zweiten Kongreß der Roten Gewerkschafts-Internationale. Anhang; Resolution des Zweiten Kongresses
der R.G.I. Berlin, Verlag der Roten Gewerkschafts-Internationale,
1923. 31 p. (Bibliothek der Roten Gewerkschafts-Internationale, Bd. 17)
                                                  Hoover, NYPL, Felt

1859 LOZOVSKII, A. [and Hais]
Die Organisationsfrage auf dem 2. Kongreß der Roten Gewerkschafts-
Internationale; Stenogramm der Reden der Genossen Losowsky und
Hais... Anhang: Resolution. Berlin, Führer-Verlag, 1923. 61 p. (Biblio-
thek der Roten Gewerkschafts-Internationale, Bd. 18)
                                                     NYPL, BDIC, Felt

1860 NIN, Andreas [and others]
Die Rote Gewerkschafts- und die Kommunistische Internationale; die
Frage der wechselseitigen Beziehungen zwischen der RGI. und der
KI. auf dem 2. Kongreß der RGI. Stenogramme der Reden der
Genossen Nin, Monmousseau, Tresso und Sinowjev. Anhang: Die
Resolution des Kongresses. Berlin, Führer-Verlag, 1923. 63 p. (Biblio-
thek der Roten Gewerkschafts-Internationale, Bd. 19)   *NYPL, Felt*

RAPPORTS de l'I.S.R. et de l'I.C. [Important documentation originating with the IV-th Congress of the Communist International and the
II-nd Congress of the Red International of Labor Unions concerning
the relationship between these two organizations] See no. 757.

RAPPORTS entre l'Internationale syndicale rouge et l'Internationale
communiste. [Another edition of the preceding item.] See no. 757a.

c) Resolutions, Theses, Manifestoes and other documents

1861 REZOLIUTSII i postanovleniia II Mezhdunarodnogo kongressa revoliutsionnykh profsoiuzov. 19 noiabria — 2 dekabria 1922 g. Moskva,
Izd. Profinterna, 1922. 61 p. (Malen'kaia biblioteka Krasnogo Internatsionala Profsoiuzov, vyp. 1)   *NYPL*

1862 BESCHLÜSSE und Resolutionen des 2. Internationalen Kongresses der Revolutionären Gewerkschaften vom 19 November bis 2 Dezember 1922 in Moskau. Im Anhang: I. Satzungen der R.G.I. II. Aufrufe und Kundgebungen. Berlin, Verlag der Roten Gewerkschafts-Internationale, Auslieferung für Deutschland durch den Führer-Verlag, 1923. 55 p. (Bibliothek der Roten Gewerkschafts-Internationale, Bd. 16)

Hoover, NYPL, Felt

1863 RESOLUTIONS and decisions, second World congress of the Red International of labor unions held in Moscow, November, 1922. Chicago, Ill., The Trade union educational league [1922] 46 p. (Labor herald library, no. 6) *Hoover, NYPL, Harv, Illin, UChic [1923 ?]*

1864 RESOLUTIONS & decisions of the 2nd world congress of the Red International of Labour Unions, session 19 November to 2 December, 1922. London [1922] 47 p. *Col*

1865 THÈSES et résolutions adoptées au IIme congrès de l'Internationale syndicale rouge, Moscou, novembre, 1922. Préface de Dridzo-Lozovsky, Paris, Librairie du travail [1922] 72 p. (Petite bibliothèque de l'Internationale syndicale rouge, 5) *Hoover, NYPL, BDIC, Felt*

d) Bulletins issued for the Congress

Note: The Bulletin issued for this Congress is listed as no. 1849.

3. III-rd Congress, Moscow, July 8—22, 1924

a) Protocols

1866 III [TRETII] kongress Krasnogo Internatsionala Profsoiuzov, 8—22 iiulia 1924 g. Otchet (po stenogrammam). Moskva, Izd-vo Profinterna, 1924. 404 p.

Contains also the resolutions adopted by the congress (p. 325–392).

Hoover, LC, NYPL, Ohio

1867 PROTOKOLL über den dritten Kongreß der Roten Gewerkschafts-Internationale abgehalten in Moskau vom 8. bis 21. [!] Juli 1924. Berlin, Verlag der Roten Gewerkschafts-Internationale [1924] 431 p.

The date July 21 is an error; the congress lasted until July 22. (See dates on preceding Russian item.)   *Hoover, NYPL, Illin, JHop*

b) Reports, Speeches, Drafts presented to the Congress

1868 FABZAVKOMY i profsoiuzy; Rossiia, Germaniia, Italiia i Frantsiia. (Materialy k III kongressu Profinterna.) Moskva, Izd-vo Profinterna, 1924. 112 p. On cover: Sbornik statei.   *NYPL*

1869 K voprosu o stachechnoi strategii; iz opyta klassovoi bor'by. Materialy k 3. kongressu Profinterna, 1924. 78 p. On cover: Sbornik statei.

LC, NYPL

1870 CHIRKOV, I.
Krest'ianskii Internatsional i soiuzy sel'sko-khoziaistvennykh rabochikh; (materialy k III kongressu Profinterna) Moskva, Izd. Profinterna, 1924. 33 p.   *Hoover, Felt*

1871 O bor'be za 8-chasovoi rabochii den' kak maksimum. (Iz dokladov na III kongresse Profinterna.) Moskva, Izd. Profinterna, 1924. 23 p.

NYPL

1872 MEZHDUNARODNOE profdvizhenie 1923—24 g. Otchet Ispolbiuro III Kongressu Profinterna. Moskva, Izd-vo Profinterna, 1924. 332 p.

NYPL, Col

1873 PROBLEMY stachechnoi strategii. (Doklady i rechi na III kongresse Profinterna.) Moskva, Izd. Profinterna, 1924. 62 p.   *NYPL*

1874 SEMARD [and others]
Mezhdunarodnye komitety propagandy. (Doklady i rechi na III kongresse Profinterna.) Moskva, Izd. Profinterna, 1924. 34 p.
Hoover, LC, NYPL, Harv

1875 BERICHT des Vollzugsbüros der Roten Gewerkschafts-Internationale an den dritten Kongreß der R. G. I. in Moskau am 5. [!] July 1924. Berlin, Verlag der Roten Gewerkschafts-Internationale [1924] 284 p.
NYPL, Felt

1876 SEMARD [and others]
Die internationalen Propaganda-Komitees. Referate und Diskussion auf dem 3. Kongreß der RGI. Berlin, Führer-Verlag, 1924. 36 p. (Bibliothek der Roten Gewerkschafts-Internationale, Bd. 34)   *NYPL*

1877 L'ACTIVITÉ de l'I. S. R. Rapport pour le IIIe congrès de l'Internationale syndicale rouge. Préface de A. Losovsky. Paris, Librairie du travail [1924] 413 p. (Petite bibliothèque de l'Internationale syndicale rouge, No. 12)   *Hoover, BDIC, Felt*

c) Resolutions, Theses, Manifestoes and other documents

1878 REZOLIUTSII III kongressa Profinterna. S predisloviem tov. A. Lozovskogo. Moskva, Izd. Profinterna, 1924. 145 p.   *NYPL*

1879 BESCHLÜSSE, Resolutionen und Aufrufe des 3. Kongresses der Roten Gewerkschafts-Internationale abgehalten in Moskau vom 8 bis 21 Juli [!] 1924. Berlin, Verlag der Roten Gewerkschafts-Internationale, Auslieferung für Deutschland durch Führer-Verlag, 1924. 99 p. (Bibliothek der Roten Gewerkschafts-Internationale, Bd. 31)   *Hoover, NYPL*

1880 RESOLUTIONS and decisions, third World congress of the Red International of labor unions held in Moscow, July, 1924. Chicago, Ill., The Trade Union Educational League [1924] 78 p. (Labor Herald Library No. 12)   *Hoover, NYPL, Col, Duke, Illin, Princ, UChic*

1881 The TASKS of the International trade union movement; being the resolutions and decisions of the Red International of Labour Unions, Moscow, July, 1924. London, The National Minority Movement [1924] 90 p.   *Hoover*

1882 RÉSOLUTIONS adoptées au IIIe congrès de l'I. S. R. (juillet 1924). Préface de Racamond. Paris, Librairie du Travail 1924? 144 p. (Petite biblothèquie de l'Internatonale Syndicale Rouge, No. 14)   *Hoover, NYPL, BDIC, Felt*

d) Commentaries and writings about the Congress

1883 STREIK-Strategie. Eine Denkschrift auf Grund der Beratungen auf dem 3. Kongreß der Roten Gewerkschafts-Internationale. Basel, Druck und Verlag „Union" [n. d.] 48 p.   *Felt*

7

4. IV-th Congress, Moscow, March 17—April 3, 1928

a) Protocols

1884 IV [CHETVERTYI] kongress Profinterna, 17 marta — 3 aprelia 1928 g. Stenograficheskii otchet; rezoliutsii i postanovleniia. Moskva, Izd. Profinterna, 1928. iii, 699 p. *NYPL, Harv, SInSt*

1885 PROTOKOLL über den 4. Kongreß der Roten Gewerkschafts-Internationale, abgehalten in Moskau vom 17. März bis 3. April 1928. Moskau, Verlag der Roten Gewerkschafts-Internationale, 1928. 679 p. *Hoover, NYPL, UChic, Felt*

b) Reports, Speeches, Drafts presented to the Congress

1886 LOZOVSKII, A. Itogi i ocherednye zadachi mezhdunarodnogo profdvizheniia (doklad i zakliuchitel'noe slovo na IV kongresse Profinterna) Moskva, Gos. izd-vo, 1928. 144 p. *Hoover*

1887 MEZHDUNARODNOE profdvizhenie za 1924—27 gg.; otchet Ispolbiuro IV kongressu Profinterna. Moskva, Izd. Profinterna, 1928. 539 p. *NYPL, UWash*

1888 Die INTERNATIONALE Gewerkschafts-Bewegung in den Jahren 1924—1927; Bericht des Vollzugsbüros der Roten Gewerkschafts-Internationale. Moskau; zu beziehen durch: Führer-Verlag, Berlin [1928?] 467 p. *LC, NYPL, Felt*

1889 LOZOVSKII, A. Ergebnisse und Aufgaben der internationalen Gewerkschaftsbewegung. Referat und Schlußwort, gehalten auf dem 4. Kongreß der RGI. Moskau, Verlag der Roten Gewerkschafts-Internationale, 1928. 77 p. At head of title: A. Losowsky. *Felt*

1890 L'INTERNATIONALE syndicale rouge au travail, 1924—1928. [Paris] Impr. de la Maison des syndicats, 1928. 439 p. (Petite bibliothèque de l'Internationale syndicale rouge, 24) *Hoover, Felt*

c) Resolutions, Theses, Manifestoes and other documents

1891 REZOLIUTSII i postanovleniia IV kongressa Profinterna, Moskva, 17. marta — 3. aprelia. Moskva, Izd. Profinterna, 1928. 190 p.

NYPL, Yale

1892 BESCHLÜSSE, Resolutionen und Aufrufe des 4. Kongresses der Roten Gewerkschafts-Internationale, abgehalten in Moskau vom 17. März bis 3. April 1928. Moskau, Verlag der Roten Gewerkschafts-Internationale, 1928. 151 p. *LC, NYPL, Felt*

1893 BESCHLÜSSE und Resolutionen des 4. Kongresses der Roten Gewerkschafts-Internationale, abgehalten in Moskau om 17. März bis 3. April 1928. Zweite, gekürzte Ausgabe. Moskau, Verlag der Roten Gewerkschafts-Internationale, 1929. 95 p. *Felt*

1894 REPORT of the Fourth Congress of the R.I.L.U. London, published in England for the Red International of Labour Unions by the Minority Movement, 1928. 200 p.

Hoover, NYPL, Col, Illin, UChic, Yale, Felt

1895 THESES et résolutions [Pref. de A. Losovsky, [pseud. Paris] Impr. de la maison des syndicats, 1928. 202 p. (Petite bibliothèque de l'I.S.R., 25)

Hoover, NYPL, Felt

d) Commentaries and writings about the Congress

1896 LOZOVSKII, A.
Na novom etape (k IV kongressu Profinterna); sbornik statei. Moskva, Izd. Profinterna, 1928. 65 p. *NYPL*

1897 O IV [CHETVERTOM] kongresse Profinterna. Moskva, Gos. izd-vo, 1928. 121 p. *Hoover*

e) Bulletins issued for the Congress

1898 BULLETIN du IVme congrès de l'ISR. Moscou, 1928. No. 1—22; March 17—April 3. 1928. *Felt (2 issues missing)*

5. V-th Congress, Moscow, August 15—30, 1930

a) Protocols

1899 PIATYI kongress Profinterna, 15—30 avgusta 1930; stenograficheskii otchet; rezoliutsii i postanovleniia. Moskva, Izd-vo VTSSPS, 1930. 724 p. *Yale*

1900 PROTOKOLL des V. Kongresses der Roten Gewerkschafts-Internationale, abgehalten in Moskau vom 15. bis 30. August 1930. Moskau, 1930. 2 vols. Vol. 1 — viii, 543 p.; vol. 2 — viii, 415 p.
NWest, Felt

b) Reports, Speeches, Drafts presented to the Congress

1901 MATERIALY k otchetu Ispolbiuro V kongressu Profinternu. Moskva, Izd-vo VTSSPS, 1930. 3 vols. [with different sub-title]

    v. 1: Not located
    v. 2: Mirovoi krizis; polozhenie i stachechnaia bor'ba mezhdunarodnogo pro-
    letariata. 300 p.
    v. 3: Mirovoe revoliutsionnoe profdvizhenie ot IV do V kongressa Profinterna,
    1928–1930. 244 p.

The Feltrinelli Library, which has vol. 2, and the Library of Congress, which has vol. 3, cataloged the items under the respective subtitles.
LC (v. 3), Felt (v. 2)

1902 LOZOVSKII, A.
Die Rote Gewerkschafts-Internationale im Angriff. Drei Reden, gehatlen auf dem V. Kongress der RGI, mit den Thesen über „Weltkrise, Wirtschaftskampf und Aufgaben der internationalen revolutionären Gewerkschaftsbewegung". Moskau, Verlag der Roten Gewerkschafts-Internationale, 1930. 119 p. On cover: Die RGI im Angriff.
Hoover, LC, NYPL, BDIC, Felt

1903 LOZOVSKII, A.
Der Weg zu den Massen. Die Vorbereitung zum V Kongreß der R[oten] G[ewerkschafts]-I[nternationale] und die Aufgaben der revolutionären Gewerkschaftsopposition. Moskau, Verlag der Roten Gewerkschats-Internationale, 1930. 14 p. At head of title: Losowski, A.
Amst, Felt

1904 LOZOVSKII, A.
The world economic crisis, strike struggles and the tasks of the revotionary trade union movement. Moscow [etc.] State publishers, 1931. 147 p. At head of title: V World Congress RILU.

Hoover, LC, NYPL

1905 SHVERNIK, Nikolai M.
The trade unions of the USSR and their role in building socialism; address and concluding remarks at the V congress of the RILU, 25 August 1930. Moscow, V. TS. S. P. S., 1930. 66 p. Added t.-p.: Rol' professionalnykh soiuzov SSSR.

Hoover

1906 LOZOVSKII, A.
Faisons le point! Crise mondiale, luttes économiques et les tâches du mouvement syndicale révolutionnaire; rapport présenté au Ve congrès de l'International Syndicale Rouge, Moscou, septembre 1930. [Paris, 1930]. 94 p. (Petite bibliothèque de l'Internationale syndicale rouge, 28)

Hoover, Felt

c) Resolutions, Theses, Manifestoes and other documents

1907 K novym boiam; rezoliutsii i postanovleniia V kongressa Krasnogo Internatsionala Profsoiuzov, Moskva, 15—30 avgusta 1930 g. [Moskva] Gos. izdat., 1930. 175 p.

LC, NYPL, Col, SInSt

1908 Die KAMPFBESCHLÜSSE des V. Kongresses der Roten Gewerkschafts-Internationale. Moskau, Verlag der Roten Gewerkschafts-Internationale, 1930. 2 vols. [Vol. 1 — 63 p.; vol. 2 — 88 p.]

Hoover (v. 2); Felt (v. 1, 2)

1909 FÜHRER durch die Beschlüsse des V. RGI-Kongresses; Referentenmaterial herausgegeben durch die Agitprop-Abteilung der RGI. Moskau, Verlag der Roten Gewerkschafts-Internationale, 1930. 63 p.

Felt

1910 RESOLUTIONS of the fifth congress of the R. I. L. U. held in Moscow, August, 1930. London, Pub. for the Red International of Labour Unions by the Minority movement and printed by B. Weinberg, 1931. 173 p. On cover: Resolutions of the World Congress R. I. L. U.

Hoover, NYPL, UTex

1911 RESOLUTIONS on the Minority Movement of Great Britain and the colonial question. Moscow, "The Moscow Worker", 1931. 63 p.

LC

1912 SOCIAL insurance; resolution of the fifth world congress of the R.I.L.U. London, Pub. by the National Minority Movement for the R.I.L.U. [1930] 19 p. *Hoover, Duke*

1913 MÉTHODES et tacticques révolutionaires; thèses et résolutions du 5e congrès de l'I.S.R., Moscou, septembre [!] 1930. [Paris, 1930] 232 p. (Petite bibliothèque de l'Internationale syndicale rouge, 29)

Hoover, BDIC, Felt

d) Comments and writings about the Congress

1914 ULBRICHT, Walter
Revolutionäre Streikführung. Berlin, Verlag Betrieb und Gewerkschaft [1931] 47 p. (Schriften zur Strategie und Taktik des Streiks, Nr. 1)

Discussion of the Berlin metal workers' strike of October 1930 in its relation to the resolutions of the 5th congress of the Red International of Labor Unions.

Hoover

1915 SYNDICATS rouges et Secours Rouge International. Préface de Giovanni Germanetto. Paris, Bureau d'Editions, 1931. 87 p. illus. (Publications du Secours Rouge International)

Deals with the discussion of International Red Aid questions at the V-th Congress of the RILU. *BDIC*

6. Central Council and Executive Bureau Sessions

Note: The first Session of the Central Council took place in July 1921, following the founding of the RILU at the first Congress. No separate prints dealing with this Session were found.

a) 2-nd Session, Moscow, February–March 1922

1916 LOZOVSKII,A.
Mirovoe nastuplenie kapitala i edinyi proletarskii front. [Doklad, prochitannyi na 2. sessii TSentral'nogo Soveta Profinterna.] Moskva, Izd. Profinterna, 1922. 43 p.

"Rezoliutsiia TSentral'nogo Soveta k dokladu A. Lozovskogo i G. Brandlera." (p. 37–43) *Hoover*

1917 LOZOVSKII, A.
Die Weltoffensive des Kapitals und die proletarische Einheitsfront
[von] A. Losowsky Anhang: 1. Beschlüsse des Zentralrats der R.G.I.
zu den Referaten der Genossen Losowsky und Brandler über die Einheitsfront des Proletariats. 2. Telegrammwechsel zwischen der R.G.I
und dem Amsterdamer Internationalen Gewerkschaftsbund. Berlin,
Verlag der Roten Gewerkschafts-Internationale, 1922. 40 p. (Bibliothek
der Roten Gewerkschafts-Internationale, Bd. 8)

Hoover, NYPL, Felt

b) 3-rd Session, Moscow, June 25–July 2, 1923

1918 LOZOVSKII, A.
Die nächsten Aufgaben der Roten Gewerkschafts-Internationale;
Referat in der 3. Sitzung am 27. Juni der dritten Session des Zentralrates der RGI. vom 25. Juni bis zum 2. Juli 1923 und Anhang: Die
beschlossene Resolution. Verlag der Roten Gewerkschafts-Internationale, Auslieferung für Deutschland durch Führer-Verlag, Berlin, 1923.
39 p. (Bibliothek der Roten Gewerkschafts-Internationale Bd. 22)

Hoover, NYPL, Felt

1919 TOMSKII, Mikhail P.
The trade unions, the Party and the state; extracts from speeches by
Comrade Tomsky at a meeting of the III session of the Profintern on
June 29, 1923, and at the joint meetings of the Presidium of the
All-Russian Central Council of Trade Unions with foreign workers
delegations, on August 11 and November 7, 1926. Moscow, Commis-
sion for Foreign Relations of the Central Council of the Trade Unions
of the USSR, 1927. 21 p.   *Hoover*

c) 4-th Session, Moscow, March 9–15, 1926

1920 IV [CHETVERTAIA] Sessiia Tsentral'nogo Soveta Krasnogo Internatsionala Profsoiuzov, 9—15 marta 1926 g.; otchet. Moskva, Izd.
Porfinterna, 1926. 148 p.   *Hoover, NYPL*

1921 PROTOKOLL der vierten Session des Zentralrates der Roten Gewerk-schafts-Internationale; abgehalten in Moskau vom 9. bis 15. März 1926. Moskau, Verlag der Roten Gewerkschafts-Internationale, Auslieferung Berlin, Führer-Verlag, 1926. 155 p. *LC, NYPL, BDIC*

d) 6-th Session, Moscow, December 15–24,1929

1922 PROTOKOLL der sechsten Session des Zentralrates der Roten Ge-werkschafts-Internationale, abgehalten in Moskau vom 15. bis 24. Dezember 1929. Moskau, Verlag der Roten Gewerkschafts-Inter-nationale, 1930. viii, 583 p. *Felt*

1923 IUZEFOVICH, Iosif
Vor dem 5. Kongreß der Roten-Gewerkschafts-Internationale; Referat gehalten auf der VI. Session des Zentralrates der R.G.I. in Moskau, Dezember 1929 [von] I. Jusefowitsch, nebst Diskussion und Resolu-tionen. Moskau, Verlag der Roten Gewerkschafts-Internationale, 1930. 39 p. *Hoover, Felt*

1924 LOZOVSKII, A. [and Merker, Paul]
Lehren und Aussichten der Wirtschaftskämpfe; Referate und Schluß-worte der Genossen A. Losowski und Paul Merker, gehalten auf der VI. Session des Zentralrates der Roten Gewerkschafts-Internationale, Dezember 1929. Moskau, Verlag der Roten Gewerkschafts-Internatio-nale, 1930. 99 p. *Hoover, Felt*

1925 LOZOVSKII, A.
Où allons-nous? Les leçons et les perspectives des luttes économiques. Rapport présenté à la VIe Session du Conseil Central de l'I.S.R. et discours de clôture. [Paris, Bureau d'Editions] 1930. 95 p. (Petite biblio-thèque de l'Internationale Syndicale Rouge, 27.)

Hoover, NYPL

e) Meeting of the Executive Bureau, Moscow, June 1931

1926 LOZOVSKII, A.
Les tâches du mouvement syndical révolutionnaire; discours du cama-rade Losovsky et résolutions adoptées par le Bureau exécutif de l'I.S.R. après discussion avec la délégation de la C.G.T.U. (juin 1931) Paris, Impr. de la Maison des syndicats [1931] 93 p. At head of title: Avant le VIe congrès de la C.G.T.U. *Hoover*

f) Meeting of Executive Bureau, Moscow, August 16, 1931

1927 LOZOVSKII, A.
Les leaders minoritaires sur la sellette [par A. Losovsky, pseud. Paris, 1931] 71 p. (Petite bibliotheque de l'Internationale syndicale rouge, 38)

"Discours prononcé le 16 août 1931 au Bureau executif de l'I.S.R." Polemic with Frossard, Bouville, Rambaud and others from the Parti Socialiste Francais and with the *Cri du Peuple*. *Hoover, Felt*

g) 8-th Session, Moscow, December 7–17, 1931

1928 LOZOVSKII, A.
Za kontrnastuplenie proletariata; doklad i zakliuchitel'noe slovo na VIII sessii Tsentral'nogo Soveta Profinterna, 7—8—17 dekabria 1931 g. Moskva, Profizdat, 1932. 95 p. *Hoover, NYPL*

1929 SHVERNIK, Nikolai M.
Sovetskie profsoiuzy v bor'be za sotsializm (doklad na VIII sessii Tsentral'nogo Soveta Profinterna) Moskva, Profizdat, 1932. 55 p.
Hoover

1930 BESCHLÜSSE der 8. Session des Zentral-Rates der RGI, 7 bis 17 Dezember 1931. [Berlin, Sefer, 1931] 47 p.

English edition has title: The way forward. *Hoover, Felt*

1931 LOZOVSKII, A.
Vorwärts zur Gegenoffensive des Proletariats; Referat und Schlußwort, gehalten auf der VIII. Session des Zentralrats der R.G.I. vom 7, 8 und 17 Dezember 1931 [von] A. Losovsky [Berlin, Sefer, 1932] 140 p.
Hoover, Felt

1932 EVERY factory a fortress. [The tasks of the revolutionary trade union organisations in the work at the factories. Resolution of the VIIIth session of the Central Council of the Red International of Labour Unions. London, The Utopia Press, 1931] 8 p. (R.I.L.U. publications)
Hoover, Duke

1933 SHVERNIK, Nikolai M.
Trade unions under socialism, by J. Shvernik. London, R.I.L.U. publications [1932] 46 p.

"Full text of the speech made... at the Eighth Session of the Central Council of the Red International of Labour Unions", p. [2] Translation of *Sovetskie profsoiuzy v bor'be za sotsializm*. *Hoover*

1934 The WAY forward [position of the R. I. L. U. sections and their role in the leadership of the economic struggles and unemployed movements] theses adopted by the eighth session of the Central Council of the R. I. L. U. London, R. I. L. U. Publications [1931] 25 p.

Hoover, Duke

1935 SHVERNIK, Nikolai M.
Les Syndicats de l'U. R. S. S. au travail; rapport présenté [par] Schwernik à la VIII Session du Conseil central de l'Internationale syndicale rouge, Moscou, décembre 1931. [Paris, Rédaction de la revue "L'I. S. R."] 1932. 67 p. (Petite bibliothèque de l'Internationale syndicale rouge [40])

Translation of his *Sovetskie profsoiuzy v bor'be za sotsializm.* *Hoover, Felt*

PART VII.

THE COMMUNIST YOUTH INTERNATIONAL

Note: Most libraries use the incorrect heading YOUNG COMMUNIST INTER-
NATIONAL. For a discussion of this discrepancy see pages 42–43.

A. GENERAL

1. Bibliographies

(Cross references only)

EZHEGODNIK leninskoi i istoriko-partiinoi bibliografii. Tom I: Obzor
literatury po Leninu i leninizmu, istorii VKP(b) i VLKSM i istorii Kominterna i KIM'A za 1929 g. See no. 1.

SCHRIFTEN-Verzeichnisse der Kommunistischen Jugendinternationale.
See no. 10.

VERLAGSVERZEICHNIS mit Grundpreisen für Organisationen. [Verlag
der Jugendinternationale] See no. 12.

2. General Writings by and about the Communist Youth International

1936 BOBINSKA, Helene
Los pioneros. Madrid Editorial Roja [n. d.] 97 p.   *Hoover*

1937 BOBINSKA, Helene
Les pionniers. Edité par l'Internationale Communiste des Jeunes. Paris,
Bureau d'éditions, 1926. ii, 95 p. Caption title: Les Pionniers au camp.
    NYPL, Amst

1938 CHE cos'e e che vuole l'Internazionale Communista? Milano, Libreria
Editrice Avanti! [1920] 15 p. (Internazionale Giovanile Comunista,
op. 1)   *Felt*

1939 The CHILD of the worker. A collection of facts and the remedy. Compiled and published by the Executive Committee of the Young Communist International. Berlin-Schoeneberg, Publishing House of the Young International, 1923. 61 p. *Harv, Amst*

1940 De COMMUNISTISCHE Jeugd-Internationale. De erfgenaam van de Eerste Socialistische Jeugd-Internationale. [n. p., n. d.] 15 p.

Amst

1941 DIMITROV, G.
Ai giovani! [n. p.] Edizioni "Gioventù" [n. d.] 11 p. *Felt*

DRAHN, Ernst
Deutsche Schriften zur Sozialisierungsfrage. See no. 10.

1942 DUNAEVSKII, V.
Die Frage der sozialistischen Reorganisation der Arbeit. [n. p.] Exekutivkomitee der Kommunistischen Jugend-Internationale [n. d.] 20 p. (Flugschriften der Jugend-Internationale, 8) At head of title: W. Dunajewsky. *NYPL, Amst.*

1943 L'ECHEC des "reconstructeurs" à Vienne. Faits et documents. [n. p.] Editions de l'Internationale Communiste des Jeunes [n. d.] 16 p. (Cahiers de propagande de l'Internationale des Jeunes, 1) *Felt*

1944 EIN Jahr Kommunistische Jugendinternationale, November 1919 — November 1920. [Berlin] Exekutivkomitee der Kommunistischen Jugend-Internationale [1920] 32 p. (Flugschriften der Jugendinternationale, 7)

„Die Veröffentlichungen der Kommunistischen Jugendinternationale im letzten Jahr." p. 25–27. *Hoover, NYPL, Amst, Felt*

1945 The FUNDAMENTAL problems of the Young communist movement. Published by the Executive committee of the Young Communist International. [Berlin, printed by M. Noster] 1922. 91 p.

Hoover, NYPL, Col

1946 GEGEN bürgerlichen Militarismus und Sozialverräterei. Berlin-Schöneberg, Verlag der Jugendinternationale [1924] 75 p. (Rüstzeug, 12)
Hoover, Amst

1947 GRIGORIEV, A.
Für das bolschewistische System der praktischen Arbeit. Im Anhang: Resolution über die Lage und Aufgaben des KJVD. Berlin, Verlag der Jugend-Internationale [n. d.] 24 p. At head of title: A. Grigorjew.

Hoover

1948 Die GRUNDFRAGEN der kommunistischen Jugendbewegung. Aufsätze zum Programm der Kommunistischen Jugend-Internationale. Berlin-Schöneberg, Verlag der Jugendinternationale [1922] 88 p.

Amst, Felt

1949 HEINZ, Karl
Die Aufgaben der sozialistischen Jugendbewegung. Wien, Verband der sozialistischen Arbeiterjugend Deutschösterreichs, 1921. 20 p.

Hoover

1950 Die Entwicklung der Kommunistischen Jugendinternationale. Wien, Verlag der Internationalen Arbeitsgemeinschaft sozialistischer Jugendorganisationen, 1922. 31 p.

Amst, Felt

1951 HISTORIQUE du premier mai. [Paris] Editions de l'Internationale communiste des jeunes, 1923. 22 p. (Mémento du militant, 4)

Hoover

1952 De JEUGD-Internationale en haar program. Den Haag, Communistische Jeugbond "De Zaaier", 1920. 16 p. (Communistische Jeugd Bibliotheek, 1)

Amst

1953 Les JEUNES et la crise. Pour la conquête du pouvoir; pour une seule jeunesse révolutionnaire. Déclaration des Jeunes Bolcheviks-Léninistes. [n. p., n. d.] 2 leaves.

Felt

1954 JUNITAGE; oder, was muß die Arbeiterjugend vom Krieg wissen. Berlin-Schöneberg, Verlag der Jugendinternationale [1922] 11 [1] p.

Hoover

1955 KAMPF gegen die Verelendung der Arbeiterjugend! Schutz gegen die Offensive des Kapitals! Ein Ruf an alle Arbeiter. Berlin-Schöneberg, Jugend Internationale [n. d.] 15 p. Hrsg. vom Exekutiv-Komitee der Kommunistischen Jugend-Internationale.

Amst, Felt

1956 KHITAROV, R.
KIM na grani reshaiushchikh boev. [Moskva] Molodaia gvardiia, 1931. 62 p. (Biblioteka Vsesoiuznogo s"ezda VLKSM, 9)

Hoover

1957 KJI: der Weg der Jugendinternationale: SAJ. [Berlin, Exekutiv-Komitee der Kommunistischen Internationale, 1932?] 22 p.

Hoover

1958 KNITTEL, F.
Chto takoe Kim. [Moskva] Molodaia gvardiia, 1939. 69 p.

NYPL

1959 KOMMUNISTISCHE Jugend-Internationale; Exekutiv Komitee. Offener Brief an alle Sektionen der KJI! An alle Mitglieder der KJI! [Berlin, n. d.] 8 p.

„Verantwortlich für den Inhalt: Konrad Blenke."   *Felt*

1960 Die KOMMUNISTISCHE Jugendinternationale und ihr Programm; Materialien zum Programm der KJI. [Berlin-Schöneberg] Verlag der Jugendinternationale; in Kommission: Arbeiter-Buchhandlung, Wien [1925] 40 p. (Rüstzeug, Hft. 13)

„Vorwort" signed: Exekutivkomitee der Kommunistischen Jugendinternationale.
Hoover, Felt

1961 KUNO
Weltbund der Jugend gegen den Krieg? Eine kommunistische Stimme zur pazifistischen Jugendbewegung. Berlin, Jugendinternationale, 1929. 64 p. tables.   *Amst*

LENIN, V. I.
An die Jugend; Reden und Aufsätze. See no. 122.

1962 LENIN, V. I.
Die Aufgaben der Kommunistischen Jugendorganisation. Rede auf dem 3. allrussischen Kongreß des kommunistischen Jugendverbandes Rußlands am 4 Oktober 1920. [n. p.] Exekutivkomitee der Kommunistischen Jugendinternationale [n. d.] 22 p. (Flugschriften der Jugend-Internationale, 10)   *Hoover, NYPL, Amst*

LENIN, V. I.
Über den Krieg. Reden und Aufsätze. [Verlag der Jugendinternationale] See no. 125.

1963 LENINE et la jeunesse; édité par l'I. C. Paris, Bureau d'Editions [1922] 70 p. illus. (Bibliothèque du Jeune Léniniste, no. 1)   *BDIC*

1964 LEONT'EV, Aleksandr
Proletarskoe iunosheskoe dvizhenie, ego prichiny, kharakter i tseli. [n. p.] 1920. 60 p.   *BDIC*

1965 LUKACZ, G.
Weltreaktion und Weltrevolution. Berlin [1921?] (Flugschriften der Jugend-Internationale, 11)   *NYPL*

1966 LUXEMBURG, Rosa

Briefe aus dem Gefängnis. Berlin, Verlag der Jugendinternationale [c1927] 79 p., illus., facsim. „Herausgegeben vom Exekutiv-Komitee der Kommunistischen Jugendinternationale." *Hoover*

1967 Die MASKEN herunter! Das wahre Gesicht der Schaffer einer gelben Jugend-Internationale. [Berlin] Verlag der Jugend-Internationale [1920] 24 p. (Flugschriften der Jugend-Internationale, 12)

> A violent attack against the Socialist Youth International and its social-democratic founders. *Hoover, NYPL*

1968 MEIN Genosse; ein Buch für die proletarische Jugend, hrsg. vom Exekutivkomitee der Kommunistischen Jugend-Internationale. „2. erweiterte Auflage." Berlin-Schöneberg [1925] 135 p. illus. [Selections from various writers] *Hoover*

1969 Le MOUVEMENT international de la jeunesse. Paris, Fédération des Jeunesses Communistes de France [1925?] 16 p. illus. *BDIC*

1970 NIEDER mit der Intervention. Kampf für den Sozialismus. Hrsg. vom Exekutivkomitee der Kommunistischen Jugendinternationale. Berlin [n. d.] 24 p. *Hoover*

1971 PIATNADTSAT' let KIM. [Seriia broshiur. Moskva] 1934.

> This series contains the following pamphlets (listed incompletely, as found in catalog card of BDIC):
> Drabkina, S. Voina voine...
> Goldberg, A. Pod obshchim znamenem...
> Krasnov, E. Komsomol v Ispanii...
> Tsvetkov, R. Komsomol Bolgarii...
> Stenskii, R. Ne zabudem...
> Iassukami, Komsomol v Iaponii. (See nos. 2002, 2035.) *BDIC*

1972 Les PROBLEMES fondamentaux du mouvement des Jeunesses Communistes. [n. p.] Editions de l'Internationale Communiste des Jeunes, 1922. 73 p. *Amst*

1973 RAKHOMIAGI, P.

Podniat' milliony na bor'bu s kapitalizmom. Moskva, 1933. 68 p. (KIM na boevykh pozitsiakh) *SInSt*

1974 REISST die Grenzpfähle aus! Ein Aufruf zur internationalen Vereinigung aller jugendlichen Arbeiter. [Berlin] Exekutivkomitee der Kommunistischen Jugend-Internationale [1919] 16 p. (Flugschriften der Jugend Internationale, 1) *Hoover, NYPL, Amst*

2976 Die SOZIALISTISCHE Proletarier-Jugend Deutschlands und die Kommunistische Jugend-Internationale. Ein offenes Wort an die Mitglieder der Sozialistischen Proletarierjugend Deutschlands. [n. p.] Exekutivkomitee der Kommunistischen Jugend-Internationale [1920] 16 p. (Flugschriften der Jugend-Internationale, 4) *NYPL, Amst, Felt*

1977 VUJOVIĆ, Vujo
L'I. C. J. en lutte contre l'occupation de la Ruhr et la guerre. Préface: G. Zinov'ev. Moscou, Editions du Bureau de la Presse de l'I. C., 1924. 45 p. illus., facsims. At head of title: V. Vouiovitch. *NYPL*

1978 WARUM Wendung und was bedeutet sie? Berlin, Verlag der Jugendinternationale, 1929. 88 p. *Harv*

1979 WAS ist und was will die Kommunistische Jugendinternationale? Hrsg. vom Exekutivkomitee der Kommunistischen Jugendinternationale. [Berlin-Schöneberg, Internationaler Jugendverlag, n. p.] 16 p. (Flugschriften der Jugendinternationale, 13.) *NYPL, Amst*

1980 Der WEG der Jugendinternationale. SAJ. Berlin, Verlag der Jugendinternationale, F. Reussner [1927?] *Harv*

1981 Ein WORT an alle erwachsenen Arbeiter und Arbeiterinnen; hrsg. vom Exekutiv-Komitee der Kommunistischen Jugendinternationale. Berlin [192-?] 18 p. *NYPL*

1982 ZINOV'EV, G.
Internatsional molodezhi i ego zadachi; rech' na s"ezde molodezhi 16 sentiabria 1919 goda. Petrograd, Gos. izd-vo, 1919. 23 p.
Hoover, BDIC

1983 [ZINOV'EV, G.]
Die Kommunistische Jugendinternationale und ihre Aufgaben. [n. p.] Verlag der Jugendinternationale [n. d.] 48 p. *Col, Amst*

3. The History of the C. Y. I.

1984 AFTER twenty years; the history of the Youth International. [London] Y. C. I. [1927?] 15 p. "Foreword" signed: William Rust.   *Princ*

Am AUFBAU; Dokumente des Exekutivkomitees der Kommunistischen Jugend-Internationale. See no. 90.

1985 CHICHERIN, Georgii
Skizzen aus der Geschichte der Jugend-Internationale. Berlin, Verlag der Jugend-Internationale [1921] 103 p. (Internationale Jugendbibliothek nr. 14) At head of title: Georgij Tschitscherin. "Aus dem russischen übersetzt von Hans Ruoff."   *Hoover, NYPL, Amst, Felt*

1986 DIX années de l'Internationale Communiste des Jeunes; aperçu historique sur l'I. C. J. [Paris, Bureau d'éditions, 1929?] 33 p.

Hoover, Amst

1987 25 [FÜNFUNDZWANZIG] Jahre Jugendinternationale. [Berlin, Verlag der Jugendinternationale, n. d.] 16 p.   *Harv, Amst*

1988 GESCHICHTE der Kommunistischen Jugend-Internationale. Berlin, Verlag der Jugendinternationale [1929—1931] 3 vols. (Editors: R. Schüller, A. Kurella, R. Chitarow)

Particular volumes:
1. Schüler, R., Von den Anfängen der proletarischen Jugendbewegung bis zur Gründung der KJI. [c1931] 224 p.
2. Kurella, Alfred, Gründung und Aufbau der Kommunistischen Jugend-Internationale. [c1929] 256 p.
3. Khitarov, Rafail, Der Kampf um die Massen; vom 2. zum 5. Weltkongreß der KJI. [c1930] 240 p. At head of title: R. Chitarow.

Written by authors who played a leading role in the C. Y. I. at different times, the particular volumes show the influence of the changing political line in world communism under Stalin's influence. Nevertheless, the volumes are a valuable, chronological account of developments and activities of the C. Y. I. and of its relationship to the Communist International and particular communist parties. Many documents and excerpts of documents cited in text and added as annexes. The documents are obviously quoted directly from the archives of the C. Y. I. and carry no source references. The volumes were available separately and also bound in one volume.

Hoover, NYPL, Harv, Amst (v. 3)

1989 GLOBIG, Fritz
. . . aber verbunden sind wir mächtig; aus der Geschichte der Arbeiterjugendbewegung. Berlin,Verl. Neues Leben, 1958. 334 p. illus.

„Dieses Buch entstand unter Mitarbeit des Instituts für Marxismus-Leninismus."
Hoover

1990 ISTORIIA KIM'A. [Leningrad] Molodaia gvardiia [19--] 3 vols. [?]

Particular volumes:
1. [not located]
2. Kurella, Alfred, Ot Berlina do Moskvy (1919–1921 gg.) (2. izd.) 1931. 186 p.
3. [not located]

Volume 2 of this work seems to be a translation of the second volume of *Geschichte der Kommunistischen Jugend-Internationale,* adapted to some extent for the Russian reader. It does not contain the annexed documents which are an important part of the German edition. As Ziegler-Kurella was a German living in the Soviet Union, and as the German edition appeared two years before the Russian one, it can be assumed that the German volume is the original, and the Russian a translation. *Hoover, Col* (both vol. 2 only)

1991 JANUARY fifteenth; the murder of Karl Liebknecht and Rosa Luxemburg. 1919. London, issued by the Young Communist League of Great Britain for the Executive Committee of the Young Communist International [1921] 72 p. illus. (Manuals for proletarian anniversaries, no. 1)
Hoover, Harv

1992 KEMRAD, Semion S.
Vazhneishie daty istorii KIM. 2-e izd., dopoln. Moskva, Molodaia gvardiia, 1930. 156 p.   *NYPL*

KHITAROV, Rafail
Der Kampf um die Massen; vom 2. zum 5. Weltkongreß der KJI. See: *Geschichte der Kommunistischen Jugend-Internationale;* no. 1988.

1993 KHRESTOMATIIA po istorii mezhdunarodnogo iunosheskogo proletarskogo dvizheniia. Sostavil Vl. Miroshevskii. Izd. 2-e, dopoln. [Moskva] Molodaia gvardiia, 1925. 224 p.   *BDIC*

KURELLA, Alfred
Gründung und Aufbau der Kommunistischen Jugend-Internationale. See: *Geschichte der Kommunistischen Jugend-Internationale;* no. 1988.

KURELLA, Alfred
Ot Berlina do Moskvy (1919—1921 gg.) See *Istoriia KIM'A,* no 1990.

409

1994 MÜNZENBERG, Willi
Die dritte Front; Aufzeichnungen aus 15 Jahren proletarischer Jugendbewegung. Berlin, Neuer Deutscher Verlag, 1930. 389 p. illus.

Harv, BDIC

1995 MÜNZENBERG, Willi
Programm und Aufbau der sozialistischen Jugend-Internationale. Stuttgart, Internationaler Jugendverlag [1919] 16 p. (Internationale sozialistische Jugendbibliothek, Heft 2)

Draft of a program and statute for a new international youth organization
("Internationale Verbindung sozialistischer Jugendorganisationen") based on
bolshevik-revolutionary principles and close cooperation with the Communist
International. This pamphlet, written by Münzenberg in a German jail, was
obviously written before the pamphlet listed as no. 1998.

Hoover, NYPL, Amst

1996 MÜNZENBERG, Willi
S Libknekhtom i Leninym; piatnadsat' let v proletarskom iunosheskom
dvizhenii. Perevod s nemetskoi rukopisi B. Gimelfarba. 2. izd. Moskva,
Molodaia gvardiia, 1930. 205 p. illus., facsims.

Bibliography of CYI publications p. 199–203. *Hoover*

1997 MÜNZENBERG, Willi
Den Socialistiske Ungdoms-Internationale. Paa norsk ved A.G.H.
Kristiania, Ungdomsforbundets Forlag, 1919. 24 p. *Amst*

1998 MÜNZENBERG, Willi
Die sozialistische Jugendinternationale. (Foreword by Clara Zetkin)
Berlin, Verlag Junge Garde [1919] 88 p. (Internationale Sozialistische
Jugendbibliothek, Heft 3)

Concise history of the international socialist youth movement before 1914,
during World War I, and shortly after, including the conference in Stuttgart
(1907) and Bern (1915). The pomphlet proposes the creation of a Socialist
Youth International which should unite youth organizations accepting bolshevik principles. It should be borne in mind that the pre-World War I Socialist
Youth International was inactive in 1919. *Hoover, NYPL*

1999 MÜNZENBERG, Willi
Die sozialistischen Jugendorganisationen vor und während des Krieges. Berlin, Verlag Junge Garde, 1919. 243 p.

A biased, but still useful history of the socialist youth organizations. Lead to
background material for the Communist Youth International. *Hoover*

2000 NASONOV, I.
Istoriia KIM (v kratkom izlozhenii) [Moskva] Molodaia gvardiia, 1930.
149 p. incl. tables. *Hoover*

2001 RAKOVSHCHIK, Boris
KIM; ego rozhdenie i razvitie. [Moskva] "Novaia Moskva", 1925.
65 p. illus. At head of title: Armiia KIM. (Biblioteka rabochei molodezhi)   *NYPL*

SCHÜLLER, R.
Von den Anfängen der proletarischen Jugendbewegung bis zur Gründung der KJI. See: *Geschichte der Kommunistischen Jugend-Internationale*, no. 1988.

2002 SEKERSKII,
Komsomol Pol'shi. [Moskva] Molodaia gvardiia, 1934. 45 p. At head
of title: 15 let KIM.
  Obviously belongs to series listed under no. 1971.   *Hoover*

2003 A SHORT history of the Young Communist International. London,
Young Communist League [1929?] 43 p.   *Harv, Amst, Felt*

2004 A SHORT history of the Young Communist International. New York
[193-?] 43 p.
  Obviously New York edition of preceding item.   *UChic*

2005 UNTER dem Banner der 3. Internationale; 10 Jahre KJI. Ein Sammelbuch der Jugendinternationale. [Berlin, Verlag der Jugendinternationale, 1929?] 207 p.   *Felt*

2006 WALLER, Shirley
History of the international socialist youth movement to 1929. Edited
by Tim Wohlforth. New York, "The Young Socialist" [1959] v, 31 p.
(Young Socialist Forum. Educational bulletin, No. 3) Processed.
                                                              Hoover

2007 ZEHN Jahre KJI. Kurzer Abriß der Geschichte der KJI. Berlin, Verlag
der Jugendinternationale [1929?] 59 p.   *Hoover*

2008 10 (ZEHN) Jahre KJI., 1919—1929. Berlin, Verlag der Jugendinternationale [1929] 15 p.   *Hoover*

2009 20 [ZWANZIG] Jahre Jugendinternationale. Material zur Geschichte
der internationalen proletarischen-Jugendbewegung. Hrsg. vom Exekutivkomitee der Kommunistischen Jugendinternationale. Wien, Verlag
der Jugendinternationale Grünberg [1927] 64 p. (Rüstzeug, 16)
                                                                Amst

4. Organization, Instruction, Indoctrination

2010 ARBETARENS politiska grundkunskaper; riktlinjer för de kommunistiska ungdomsförbundens politiska elementarundervisning. Under redaktion av Bernhard Ziegler utgivna av Kommunistiska ungdomsinternationalens exekutivkommitté. Övers. av P. Freudenthal. Stockholm, Fram [1925]

Swedish edition of no. 2020; see it for annotation. *Harv*

2011 FÜRNBERG, F.
Where to begin? How to build a mass Young communist league. [New York, N.Y.] Youth international [192-?] 24 p.

"Distributed in the United States by Young communist league."

Hoover

2012 GORKICH, M., and Limanowski
Opyt podpol'ia; deiatel'nost' i zadachi nelegal'nykh sektskii KIM'A. Moskva, Molodaia gvardiia, 1928. 153 p. At head of title: Biblioteka KIM'A. *NYPL*

2013 GUTSCHKOW, Moritz
Die Grundfragen der illegalen Verbandsarbeit. Wien, Verlag der Jugendinternationale, 1924. 67 p. (Der Verbandsarbeiter, Heft 2)

Hoover

2014 GYPTNER, Richard
From isolation to the masses; textbook for Young Communist Leagues. Berlin, Publishing House of the Young International, 1923. 62 p.

Hoover

2015 GYPTNER, Richard
Vom Verein zur Massenorganisation. Die Betriebszelle der kommunistischen Jugend. Berlin-Schöneberg, Verlag der Jugendinternationale. 1923. 68 p. *Amst, Felt*

2016 HOERNLE, Edwin
Manual for leaders of children's groups. Berlin-Schöneberg, Publishing house of Young International [192-?] 62 p. *Harv*

2017 INSTRUCTIONS on the building up of nuclei and their practical work as the basic units of communist organization. Published by the E.C. of the Y.C.I. [Stockholm, 1924] 36 p. (Young Communist International; The League Worker, no. 1) *NYPL, Princ*

2018 INSTRUKTION über die Betriebszellen und ihre praktische Arbeit als Grundeinheit der Organisation. Berlin-Schöneberg, Verlag der Jugend-internationale [1924?] 39 p. (Der Verbandsarbeiter, Heft 1)

"Vorwort" signed: EK der KJI.   *Hoover, Felt*

MANUALS for proletarian anniversaries. See *January fifteenth;* no. 1991

2019 POLANO, Luigi
Wie weit ist heute eine Autonomie der kommunistischen Jugend-organisation in der kommunistischen Bewegung notwendig und möglich? Von Luigi Polano. Berlin, Verlag der Jugend-Internationale [1921] 23 p. illus. (Internationale Jugendbibliothek, nr. 19)

Hoover, Amst

2020 Das POLITISCHE Grundwissen des jungen Kommunisten; Leitfaden für den politischen Grundunterricht der kommunistischen Jugend-verbände. Unter Redaktion von Bernhard Ziegler; hrsg. vom Exekutiv-komitee der Kommunistischen Jugendinternationale. Berlin-Schöneberg, Jugendinternationale, 1924. 111 p.

"The present textbook for the basic political instruction in communist youth organizations is for the countries outside Russia a first attempt in this direction. For this reason, it shows all the characteristics of such a first attempt ... The predominant part of the text was taken from J. [IU?] Korolenko's *Büchlein des politischen Grundwissens*, which appeared in Russian in immense printings... The methodical part [of this textbook] is based on the experiences of the basic political instruction undertaken by the Communist Party of Russia and by the Russian communist youth organization." (Preface, p. 3–4, signed by B.. Ziegler [the real name of Alfred Kurella] in Moskau, September 15, 1923.) For another, later edition of a similar textbook for political indoctrination see next item.   *Hoover, LC, NYPL, Harv, UMinn, Felt*

2021 Das POLITISCHE Grundwissen des jungen Kommunisten. Wien, Verlag der Jugendinternationale; Egon Grünberg [c1927] 2 vols.

Particular volumes:
1. [Sub-title not known] 200 p.
2. Sub-title: Die Grundfragen der Kommunistischen Jugendinternationale [printed over the collective title *Das politische Grundwissen* etc.] 83 p.
Although these two volumes appeared under the same title as a similar text-book published in 1924 (see preceding item), they do not seem to be related to each other beyond their destination to serve as textbooks for the political indoctrination of members of communist youth organizations. The second volume (the only one which was available for identification), deals with subjects which were not included in the 1924 volume. These subjects are: The role and task of the communist youth organization; History of the Communist Youth

International; The economic struggle and the work of trade unions; The anti-
militarist struggle of the communist youth organization; (titles of chapters
XIV–XVII).   *Hoover* (v. 2), *LC* (?), *NYPL* (2 v.), *Harv* (?), *Felt* (2 v.)

2022 The ROAD to mass organization of proletarian children. [New York]
Youth international publishers [1930] 32 p.

"Decisions of the IV international conference of leaders of Communist Children's Leagues, Moscow, September, 1929, and the resolution of the enlarged
plenum of the Y. C. I., Moscow, December, 1929." "Distributed in the United
States by the Young Communist League."   *Hoover, Harv*

5. Relationship C. Y. I. — Comintern

a) General

KHITAROV, Rafail M.
Pravaia opasnost' v Kominterne i zadachi KIM. See no. 262.

2023 SHATSKIN, L.
Itogi plenumov Kominterna i KIM'A. Moskva, Molodaia gvardiia,
1927. 51 p.   *Hoover*

KHITAROV, Rafail M.
Die rechte Gefahr in der Komintern und die Aufgaben der KJI. See
no. 263.

b) Deliberations and resolutions of Comintern Congresses, Plenums, Presidiums concerning the C. Y. I.

(Cross-references only)

II-nd Congress, 1920

MÜNZENBERG, Willy
Der 2. Kongreß der Kommunistischen Internationale und die Kommunistische Jugendinternationale. See no. 648.

414

V-th Congress, 1924

Die ERGEBNISSE des V. Kongresses der Kommunistischen Internationale und des IV. Kongresses der Kommunistischen Jugendinternationale. See no. 810.

The RESULTS of two congresses: the fifth congress of the Communist International and the fourth congress of the Y. C. I. See no. 813.

VI-th Congress, 1928

A la conquête de la jeunesse ouvrière! Les résultats du V-e Congrès mondial de l'I. C. See no. 889.

VII-th Congress, 1935

CHEMODANOV, V.
Edinyi front molodezhi protiv fashizma i voiny. (Rech' . . . na VII-m kongresse Kominterna 8 avgusta 1935 g.) See no. 895 a.

VII [SED'MOI] kongress Kommunisticheskogo Internatsionala o molodezhi. See no. 1025.

KUUSINEN, O.
Die Front der jungen Generation. Rede, gehalten in der 41. Sitzung des VII. Weltkongresses der Kommunistischen Internationale am 17. August 1935. See no. 928.

GREEN, Gil
Young communists and the unity of the youth. See no. 969—6.

KUUSINEN, O.
Youth and fascism; the youth movement and the fight against fascism and the war danger. See nos. 958, 868—8, 969—7.

KUUSINEN, O.
Le front de la jeune génération [Speech at VII-th Congress] See no. 979.

Presidium of ECCI, March 1929

Note: The program of the C. Y. I. was accepted by the V-th Congress of the C. Y. I. and later confirmed by the Presidium of the ECCI on March 13, 1929. In some items containing this program the date is erroneously given as March 14. The full entries are listed under the V-th Congress of the C. Y. I. (nos. 2103 ff.) No Enlgish text of this program has been located.

PROGRAMMA Kommunisticheskogo internatsionala molodezhi. See no. 2103.

PROGRAMM der Kommunistischen Jugend-Internationale. Angenommen vom 5. Weltkongreß der KJI und bestätigt vom Präsidium des EKKI am 13. März 1929. See no. 2106.

PROGRAMME de l'Internationale Communiste des Jeunes adopté par le Ve congrès de l'I. C. J. et sanctioné par le présidium du C. E. de l'I. C. le 13 mars 1929. See no. 2107.

PROGRAM Komunistične mladinske internacionale. Sprejet na V Kongresu KMI i potrjen na prezidiumu IOKI 14. [sic!] marca 1929. See no. 1138.

PROGRAM van de Kommunistische Jeugdinternationale. Aangenomen op het 5de wereldcongres te Moscou in 1928. See no. 2109.

INTERNACIONAL juvenil comunista. Programa adoptado en el V congreso y sancionado por el presidium del E. C. de la I. C. del 13 de Marzo de 1929. See no. 2110.

PROGRAMMA da Internacional de Juventude comunista. Adoptado pelo V Congresso de I. J. C. e sanccionado pelo Presidium do C. E. da I. C. em 13 der março 1929. See no. 2111.

11-th Plenum, March 1931

CHEMODANOV, V. E.
Unter dem Sturmbanner des leninistischen Komsomol; Bericht und Diskussion über die Lage und Aufgaben der KJI auf dem XI. Plenum des EKKI [von V. E. Tschemodanow. Hamburg] See no. 1166.

CO-REPORT of the Young Communist International at the XIth plenum of the E[xecutive] C[ommittee] of the C[ommunist] I[nternational] (March 28, 1931). See no. 1172.

12-th Plenum, September 1932

CHEMODANOV, V.
Itogi XII plenuma IKKI i zadachi KIM; sokrashchennyi doklad na dekabr'skom plenume IKKIM . . . See no. 1237.

13-th Plenum, December 1933

KOMPARTII v bor'be za zavoevanie molodezhi. XIII plenum IKKI o rabote sredi molodezhi. See no. 1294.

Presidium of ECCI, February 1934

SCHÖNAU, Alexander
The February insurrection of the Austrian proletariat. With an appeal signed by the ECCI, the EB of the RILU and the EC of the YCI. See no. 1296.

6. C.Y.I. Support of United Fronts

2024 CHEMODANOV, V.
We are for the united front. [New York, Youth Publishers, 1934] 16 p.

Hoover, Col, Amst

KHITAROV, R.
Kriegsgefahr, Faschismus und die Aufgaben der K.J.I. See no. 1595.

2025 KIM v bor'be za edinstvo molodezhi. [Moskva] Molodaia gvardiia, 1937. 77 p.

LC

Les TACHES pour la préparation et la tenue du congrès extraordinaire des jeunesses communistes. See no. 2044.

Der VERBAND der sozialist. Arbeiterjugend Deutsch-Österreichs und der Weltkongreß der revolutionären proletarischen Jugend. See no. 2045.

Ein WELTKONGRESS aller proletarischen Jugendorganisationen; hrsg. vom Exekutivkomitee der Kommunistischen Jugendinternationale. See no. 2046.

2026 WOLF, M.
Peredovaia molodezh' v borbe s fashizmom. Moskva, Molodaia gvardiia, 1938. 40 p.

> "Abbreviated stenogram of a report of the Secretary of the Executive Committee of the Y. C. I., May 19, 1938." *BDIC*

7. International "Youth Days"

1920

2027 URKUNDEN-Sammlung von 9 verschiedenen Plakaten, Zeitungen, Flugzetteln vom Internationalen Jugendtag, veranstaltet von der Kommunistischen Jugend-Internationale am 5. 9. 20. [Portfolio in folio size of propaganda material dated 1920. Title from typed slip, inserted at beginning.] *Princ*

1921

2028 GUILLEAU, J. [pseud. of DORIOT, Jacques]
Entre deux guerres. Paris, Libraire de l'Humanité [1921?] 67 p. (Bibliothèque des Jeunesses communistes)

> "Cette brochure a été écrite à Moscou pour servir à la documentation des orateurs participant à la campaigne internationale d'agitation contre le militarisme, organisée du 11 au 18 mars par l'I. C. J." Préface. *Hoover*

1922

2029 SCHONHAAR, Eugen
Der Internationale Jugendtag. Berlin-Schöneberg, Verlag der Jugendinternationale [1922] 30 p. *Amst, BDIC, Felt*

2030 SCHONHAAR, Eugen
La journée internationale des jeunes. [n. p.] Editions de l'Internationale Communiste des Jeunes, 1922. 32 p. *Felt*

1925

2031 Der INTERNATIONALE Jugendtag. Wien, Verlag der Jugendinternationale [1925] 87 p. (Rüstzeug, Hft. 15) On cover: Internationaler Jugendtag. [Issued by the Executive Committee of the Young Communist International.]   *Hoover, Amst*

1930

2032 WELTKAMFTAG der Jugend. [Berlin, Verlag der Jugendinternationale, 1930] 23 p. („Verantwortlich: Hermann Remmele... Herausgeber: Exekutivkomitee der Kommunistischen Jugendinternationale.") Cover title.   *Hoover, NYPL*

1938

2033 XXIV [DVADTSAT' CHETVERTYI] mezhdunarodnyi iunosheskii den' (6 sentiabria 1938 g.) Materialy dlia dokladchikov... Moskva, Molodaia gvardiia, 1938. 88 p.   *BDIC*

8. The Sections of the C.Y.I. (various countries)

2034 Der BLUTIGE Terror gegen die werktätige Jugend Bulgariens. Berlin, Verlag der Jugendinternationale [1925] 47 p.   *NYPL*

2035 IASSUKAMI,
Komsomol v Iaponii. [Moskva] 1934. 30 p. (15 let KIM)

   See no. 1971.   *BDIC, SInSt*

2036 La JEUNESSE avec la révolution chinoise. Paris, Bureau d'éditions, 1927. 60 p. illus. At head of title: Bas les pattes devant la Chine. On cover: Edition spéciale de l'Internationale Communiste des Jeunes.
   NYPL

2037 Die JUGEND der Revolution; drei Jahre proletarische Jugendbewegung, 1918—1920. Verlag der Jugend-Internationale; für Deutschland: Verlag Junge Garde, Berlin [1921] 528 p. illus., maps.

> The first part of the volume (p. 3–67) contains a report of the Executive Committee of the CYI to the second congress (Bericht des Exekutiv-Komitees der Kommunistischen Jugend-Internationale an den Weltkongreß der revolutionären Proletarierjugend) summarizing the activities of the E.C. during the almost two years between the first and second congress. It also includes a list of 49 youth organizations belonging to the International, and a detailed list of all publications (newspapers, periodicals, serial publications) issued by the CYI.
>
> The second part of the volume (p. 71–528) contains reports about the development and activities of communist youth organizations in practically all European countries (Albania omitted), the United States, Mexico, Argentina, China, Korea and Palestine. Particular attention received: Soviet Russia and its Asiatic components, Hungary, Germany and Austria. The propaganda character of these reports is obvious. *Hoover, NYPL, Harv, Felt*

2038 JUNGPROLET wohin? Drittes Reich oder Sowjet-Deutschland. Berlin, Verlag der Jugendinternationale [1930] 24 p. „Für den Inhalt verantwortlich: Hermann Remmele." *Hoover*

2039 KOMSOMOL v tiur'makh. Geroi i mucheniki KIM'A. Sostavil B. Martlin, i Z. Veinberger. [Leningrad] Molodaia gvardiia, 1925. 76 p. illus.
BDIC

2040 KURELLA, Alfred
Noch einmal: Deutsche Volksgemeinschaft; ein Wort an die bürgerliche Jugendbewegung. Berlin-Schöneberg, Verlag der Jugendinternationale, 1923. 40 p. *Hoover*

2041 Das SCHWARZE Buch des weißen Ungarn. Herausgegeben vom Exekutiv-Komitee der Kommunistischen Jugendinternationale. Berlin, Verlag der Jugendinternationale [1920] 19 p. (Internationale Jugendbibliothek, nr. 13) *Hoover, NYPL, Harv, Felt*

2042 WIR kämpfen für ein rotes Preußen im freien sozialistischen Räte-Deutschland. Berlin, Verlag d. Jugendinternationale (Fritz Reussner) [1932] 15 p. Cover title. *Hoover, NYPL*

9. Conferences and Contacts with Non-Communist Youth Organizations

a) Conference of Socialist Youth Organizations from South-Eastern Europe
Vienna, May 16–17, 1920

2043 AM Werk! Protokoll der I. Internationalen Konferenz der sozialistischen Jugendorganisationen Süd-Ost Europas in Wien am 16. und 17. Mai 1920 [Wien] Untersekretariat Süd-Ost der Kommunistischen Jugendinternationale [1920?] 40 p. (Flugschriften der Jugendinternationale, 2)

> This conference was called with the intention to sway some socialist youth organizations in Austria and Czechoslovakia toward the C.Y.I. It is discussed from a communist point of view in *Geschichte der Kommunistischen Jugend-Internationale*, vol. 2, p. 114–117.
>
> *Harv, Amst*

b) Abortive initiative for a World Youth Congress

> **Note:** After the failure of the Berlin Conference of the three Internationals (see nos. 1642–1648), the C.Y.I. attempted to bring about a "united front of the youth". On June 24, 1922, the Executive Committee of the C.Y.I. in an appeal to the socialist youth suggested the calling of a world congress of youth. The purpose of this congress was to formulate some "demands of the youth" and to create an executive body charged with the direction of the struggle for the fulfillment of these demands. The appeal was directed to the youth organizations of the Amsterdam and Vienna (Two-and-a-Half) Internationals and the socialist youth at large. This communist initiative was rejected by the two international organizations, was ignored by their affiliates, and ended in failure. For the C.Y.I.'s viws on this matter see *Geschichte der Kommunistischen Jugend-Internationale*, vol. 2, p. 18 ff.

2044 Les TACHES pour la préparation et la tenue du congrès extraordinaire des jeunesses communistes. Paris, Les Publications Révolutionnaires 1934. 7 p. (Supplement au no. 3 de *Cahiers du Bolchevisme* du 1-er fevrier, 1934.)   *Felt*

2045 Der VERBAND der sozialist. Arbeiterjugend Deutsch-Österreichs und der Weltkongreß der revolutionären proletarischen Jugend. Berlin [1922] (Flugschriften der Jugend-Internationale, 6)

> Entry taken from serial catalog card of NYPL. No more data available.
>
> *Hoover, NYPL*

2046 Ein WELTKONGRESS aller proletarischen Jugendorganisationen; hrsg. vom Exekutivkomitee der Kommunistischen Jugendinternationale. [Berlin, 1922] 20 p.   *NYPL*

c) Exchange of correspondence

2047 IN den Reihen der Gegenrevolution. Briefwechsel des E[xekutiv] K[omitees] der K[ommunistischen] J[ugend] I[nternationale] mit dem E.K. der Internationalen Arbeitsgemeinschaft sozialistischer Jugendorganisationen über die Fragen der Verhaftung jugendlicher Menschewiki. Mit einer Einleitung hrsg. vom Exekutivkomitee der KJI. Berlin-Schöneberg, Verlag der Jugendinternationale, 1923. 82 p.

See also no. 1648.   *Amst*

2048 NICHT wollen oder nicht können? Briefwechsel des Exekutivkomitees der Kommunistischen Jugendinternationale mit dem Vorstande des Verbandes der Sozialist. Arbeiter-Jugend Österreichs. Mit einer Einleitung von Wilh[elm] Münzenberg. [Wien, Verlag der Kommunistischen Jugendinternationale, n. d.] 40 p.   *NYPL, Amst*

10. Publications on Conditions in the Soviet Union

2049 AUS den Erfahrungen des russischen kommunistischen Jugendverbandes. Berlin-Schöneberg, Verlag der Jugendinternationale [n. d.] 52 p. (Rüstzeug, 6)   *Amst*

2050 BLONSKI, Pavel P.
Die Arbeits-Schule. Ins Deutsche übersetzt von Hans Ruoff; mit einem Vorwort herausgegeben von Dr. M. H. Baege. Berlin-Fichtenau, Verlag Gesellschaft und Erziehung, 1921. 2 vols in one. (Schriftenreihe für Theorie und Praxis der Einheits-Arbeits-Schule.) At head of title: P. P. Blonskii. Cover imprint: Berlin-Schöneberg; Verlag der Jugendinternationale. Label on title page of vol. 1: Herausgegeben im Auftrage eds Exekutivkomitees der Kommunistischen Jugendinternationale.

Contains a bibliography in vol. 1, p. 122–126.   *NYPL*

2051 Die JUGEND in der russischen Revolution. Berlin, Verlag der Jugend-internationale [1927] 121 p. diagrs., tables.

„Deutsch bearbeitet von Günther Hopffe." *LC, NYPL*

2052 LENIN, V. I.
La jeunesse communiste et son rôle. Discours prononcé au 3e Congrès Panrusse de la jeunesse communiste. Moscou, Internationale communiste, 1920. 30 p. (Bibliothèque volante, 4) *Hoover*

2053 NAUMOV, I. K.
Les journées d'Octobre. Paris, Bureau d'éditions [1924] 110 p. illus. At head of title: Editions de l'Internationale Communiste des Jeunes. *Hoover, NYPL*

2054 NAUMOV, I. K.
Oktobertage; Erinnerungen aus der Oktoberrevolution 1917. Berlin-Schöneberg, Die Jugendinternationale, 1925. 104 p. *NYPL*

2055 7. [SIEBENTER] November: die russische Revolution. Berlin-Schöneberg, Verlag der Jugendinternationale [1923] 85 p. (Rüstzeug, 8; 1. Sammelbuch über proletarische Gedenktage.) *Harv*

2056 WEGEBEREITER des Kommunismus; 12 Persönlichkeiten aus der Geschichte des Kommunismus. Übersetzt aus dem Russischen von Hans Ruoff-München. Mit einem Vorwort von Hermann Duncker. Berlin-Schöneberg, Verlag der Jugendinternationale, 1923. 103 p. *Felt*

2057 ZIEGLER, B.
Was lehrt uns die russische Arbeiterjugend? [n. p.] Exekutivkomitee der Kommunistischen Jugendinternationale [1919] 19 p. (Flugschriften der Jugend-Internationale, 5) *Hoover, NYPL, Amst*

2058 ZINOV'EV, G. E.
Die Aufgaben der Arbeiter- und Bauern-Jugend. Rede an die Delegierten der Arbeiter- und Bauernjugend am 2. Februar 1919 [n. p.] Exekutiv-Komitee der Kommunistischen Jugend-Internationale [n. d.] 15 p. At head of title: G. Sinowjew. (Flugschriften der Jugend-Internationale, 3) *NYPL, Amst, Felt*

B. CONGRESSES

1. I-st Congress, Berlin, November 20—26, 1919

a) Protocols

2059 PERVYI kongress KIM; stenograficheskaia zapis'; podgotovil k pechati A. Kurella. Moskva, Molodaia gvardiia, 1930. 235 p. (Biblioteka KIM)

LC, UCal

2060 UNTER dem roten Banner; Bericht über den ersten Kongreß der Kommunistischen Jugendinternationale. Herausgegeben vom Exekutiv-Komitee der Kommunistischen Jugendinternationale. Berlin, Verlag Junge Garde [1919] 79 p. (Internationale Jugendbibliothek, Nr. 8)

Hoover, NYPL, Amst, Felt, SInSt

b) Reports, Speeches, Drafts, presented to the Congress

2061 MÜNZENBERG, W.

Unser Programm. Rede über das Programm der Kommunistischen Jugendinternationale, geh. auf dem Gründungskongreß in Berlin. [n.p.] Exekutivkomitee der Kommunistischen Jugend-Internationale [1919?] 20 p. (Flugschriften der Jugend-Internationale, 2)

NYPL, Amst

2062 PAWLOW, W. [pseud. of Shatskin, Lazar] and Kores, B. [pseud.?] Die Aufgaben der kommunistischen Jugendorganisationen nach der Übernahme der Macht durch das Proletariat; aus der Praxis der komm. Jugendorganisationen von Rußland und Ungarn, von W. Pawlow und B. Kores. Herausgegeben v. Exekutiv-Komitee der Kommunistischen Jugendinternationale. Berlin, Verlag Junge Garde [1919] 35 p. (Internationale Jugendbibliothek, Nr. 5)

Speeches given at the First Congress of the Communist Youth International.

Hoover, NYPL, Amst, Felt

c) Resolutions, Theses and other documents

2063 MANIFEST pervogo kongressa Kommunisticheskogo internatsionala molodezhi. Smolensk, Kommunisticheskii soiuz molodezhi Litvy i Belorussii, 1920. 8 p. (Biblioteka kommunisticheskoi molodezhi, 7)

BDIC

2064 BESCHLÜSSE des 1. Weltkongresses der Kommunistischen Jugendinternationale. Berlin [19--? — p.?]

The above entry is taken from a serial catalog entry, with no details.

NYPL

2065 MANIFEST, Programm und Statut der Kommunistischen Jugendinternationale. Berlin, Exekutiv-Komitee der Kommunistischen Jugendinternationale [n. d.] 15 p.   *Hoover, LC, Amst, Felt*

2066 The PROGRAMS of the Y.C.I.; containing the first program, adopted November 1919; the tentative draft for the new program as adopted by the third Congress of the Y.C.I. December 1922, and other material relating thereto. Berlin-Schoeneberg, the Young International, 1923. 56 p.

Preface signed: The Executive committee of the Young Communist International.
Hoover, Princ

d) Commentaries and writings about the Congress

2067 BERLINSKII kongress K.I.M. [Moskva] Molodaia gvardiia, 1925. 104 p.
BDIC

2068 The YOUNG Communist International. Report of the first international congress held at Berlin from the 20—29th [!] of November 1919. Contains manifesto, programme and a report of the actual stand of the Y.C.I. Pub. by the Executive Committee of the Young Communist International. Glasgow, Int. Proletarian School Movement; London, Young Communist League [1920] 32 p. illus.   *Hoover, Amst*

2069 L'INTERNATIONALE Communiste des Jeunes. Compte rendu du premier international congrès tenu le 25—26 novembre 1919 à Berlin; contenant le manifeste à la jeunesse ouvrière de tous les pays, le programme et les statuts d'organisation de l'Internationale Communiste des Jeunes, les rapports des organisations représentées et un article de W. Münzenberg. Puteaux (Seine), Section française de l'Internationale Communiste des Jeunes [1919] 24 p.   *Hoover, Felt*

2. II-nd Congress, Jena and Berlin, April 7—10, 1921
Moscow, July 9, 14—24, 1921

Note: The Berlin-seated Executive Committee called the Congress to Jena, where it was to meet without the permission of local authorities. The Executive Committee of the Communist International insisted, however, that the Congress take place in Moscow where it could function under better conditions. Despite protests of the majority of participants, the ECCI denounced this meeting as an unofficial conference and insisted upon calling the Congress to Moscow. When the German police were about to disband the meeting and perhaps arrest its participants, first in Jena and then in Berlin, the meeting was suspended and a new Congress was called to Moscow.

The dates of the Moscow meetings are confusing. The official history of the CYI mentions that the Congress was officially opened on July 9, and that its proceedings lasted from 14-th to 24-th July. *(Geschichte der Kommunistischen Jugend-Internationale,* vol. II, p. 178) Publications listed below indicate other dates in their titles.

a) Protocols

2070 ZU neuer Arbeit; Bericht vom II. Kongreß der Kommunistischen Jugendinternationale, abgehalten vom 14. bis 21. Juli 1921 in Moskau. Berlin, Verlag der Jugendinternationale für Deutschland [1921] 135 p. (Internationale Jugendbibliothek, Nr. 24) *NYPL, BDIC, Felt*

b) Reports, Speeches, Drafts presented to the Congress

2071 AUFWÄRTS; Bericht des Exekutiv-Komitees der Komm. Jugendinternationale an den Welt-Kongreß der revolutionären Proletarierjugend. Berlin, Verlag der Jugend-Internationale [1921] 67 p. illus., diagr. (Internationale Jugendbibliothek, Nr. 16) Cover title.

„Sonderabdruck aus dem Buche: *Die Jugend der Revolution. Drei Jahre proletarische Jugendbewegung.*" (See no. 2037) *Hoover, NYPL*

2072 THESEN über die Arbeit auf dem Lande. Materialien zum II. Weltkongreß der Kommunistischen Jugendinternationale. Petrograd, Kommunistische Internationale, 1921. 31 p. (Der Kommunistische Jugendverband Rußlands.) *Amst*

2073 THÈSES proposées pour le 2ème congrès de l'Internationale Communiste des Jeunes. [Paris, impr. Dangon, n. d.] 30 p. *BDIC, Felt*

2074 THÈSES sur le travail dans les campagnes. (Materiaux pour le II-e Congrès mondial de l'Internationale Communiste de la Jeunesse) Petrograd, Editions de l'Internationale Communiste, 1921. 32 p.

Felt

c) Resolutions, Theses, and other documents

2075 RESOLUTIONEN und Thesen des II. Kongresses der Kommunistischen Jugendinternationale vom 14. bis 23. Juli 1921 in Moskau. Berlin, Verlag der Jugendinternationale [1921] 49 p. (Internationale Jugendbibliothek, Nr. 23)

Hoover, NYPL, Amst, Felt

d) Commentaries and writings about the Congress

2076 DOSSIER (2) Kongreß d. Jugendinternationale zu Moskau.

This is an exact copy of the card in the catalog of BDIC. No details on contents available.

BDIC

2077 Der VERBAND der Sozialist. Arbeiterjugend Deutsch-Österreichs und der Weltkongreß der revolutionären proletarischen Jugend. Offenes Einladungsschreiben an die Mitglieder des Verbandes der Sozialistischen Arbeiterjugend Deutsch-Österreichs. [Berlin] Exekutivkomitee der Kommunistischen Jugendinternationale [1921] 11 p. (Flugschriften der Jugend-Internationale, nr. 6)

Hoover, Amst

2078 DOCUMENTATION sur le [2e] Congrès mondiale de jeunesse prolétarienne. [Berlin] Internationale Communiste des Jeunes, 1922. 24 p. (Mémento du militant, 2)

BDIC

3. III-rd Congress, Moscow, December 4—16, 1922

a) Protocols

2079 The MINUTES of the Third Congress of the Y.C.I., held in Moscow, December 4th—16th, 1922. Berlin-Schöneberg, Pub. House of the Young International, 1923. 156 p. diagr., 2 maps. "Published by the Executive Committee of the Y.C.I." On cover: Highroads to progress. See no. 2087.

Hoover, Harv

b) Reports, Speeches, Drafts presented to the Congress

2080 Die GRUNDFRAGEN der kommunistischen Jugendbewegung. Auf-
sätze zum Programm der Kommunistischen Jugend-Internationale.
Berlin-Schöneberg, Verlag der Jugendinternationale [1922]. 88 p.
NYPL, Harv, Amst

2081 MATERIAL zum Jungarbeiter-Weltkongreß. Berlin-Schöneberg, Verlag
der Jugendinternationale [1922] 24 p. (Rüstzeug für die Funktionäre
der Kommun. Jugendinternationale, 2) *Amst*

2082 MATERIAL zur Diskussion des Programms der Kommunistischen
Jugendinternationale. Berlin-Schöneberg, Verlag der Jugend-Internationale [1923] 60 p. (Rüstzeug, 4) *Amst*

2083 DOCUMENTATION pour la discussion sur le programme de l'I. C. J.
[Paris] Editions de l'Internationale communiste des jeunes, 1923. 66 p.
(Mémento du militant nr. 5). *Hoover, BDIC*

2084 Les PROBLEMS fondamentaux du mouvement des Jeunesses Communistes. [n. p.] Editions de l'Internationale Communiste des Jeunes,
1922. 73 p. *Amst*

c) Resolutions, Theses, and other documents

2085 IM Zeichen der Arbeit. Resolutionen und Beschlüsse des 3. Kongresses
der Kommunistischen Jugendinternationale. Berlin-Schöneberg, Verlag
der Jugendinternationale, 1923. 61 p. *Amst*

The PROGRAMS of the Y. C. I.; containing the first program, adopted
November 1919; the tentative draft for the new program as adopted
by the third Congress of the Y. C. I. December 1922, and other material
relating thereto. See no. 2066.

2086 RESOLUTIONS and theses adopted by the Third Congress of the
Y. C. I. Berlin, Publishing house of the Young International, 1923. 64 p.
Hoover, UChic

d) Commentaries and writings about the Congress

2087 BERICHT vom 3. Weltkongreß der Kommunistischen Jugendinternationale vom 4.—16. Dezember 1922 in Moskau. Berlin-Schöneberg,
Verlag der Jugendinternationale, 1923. vii, 290 p.

> The item was not available for identification. May contain proceedings of the
> Congress in German.   *Felt*

4. IV.th Congress, Moscow, July 15—24, 1924

a) Reports, Speeches, Drafts presented to the Congress

2088 VOM III. [dritten] zum IV. Weltkongreß der Kommunistischen Jugendinternationale, Bericht des Exekutivkomitees über die Tätigkeit und
die Lage und Entwicklung der KJI. Berlin-Schöneberg, Verlag der
Jugendinternationale [1924?] 75 p. (Rüstzeug, 11)   *NYPL, Amst*

2089 FROM third to fourth; a report on the activities of the Y. C. I. since its
third world congress. [Stockholm] The Executive committee of the
Young Communist International, 1924. 84 p.   *Hoover, NYPL, Harv*

2090 The DRAFT programme of the Young Communist International. [Lon-
don, Young communist International, c/o Young Communist League
of Great Britain, 1924?] 83 p.

> "Foreword" signed: The E. C. of the Y. C. I. "We republish the draft pro-
> gramme of the Y. C. I. together with the report on this question to the *fourth
> congress.*" Foreword.   *Hoover, NYPL, Col, Princ*

2091 DU IIIème [troisième] au IVème congrès de l'Internationale Communiste des Jeunes; rapport du C. E. sur son activité et sur la situation
et le dévelopement de l'I. C. J. [Potsdam, Vereinsdruckerei] 1924. 86 p.
(Young Communist International; Memento du militant, 7)   *NYPL*

b) Resolutions, Theses, and other documents

2092 POSTANOVLENIIA IV Kongressa K.I.M. [Moskva] Molodaia gvardiia,1925. 105 p.   *LC*

2093 Die Beschlüsse des IV. Kongresses der Kommunistischen Jugendinternationale. Berlin-Schöneberg, Verlag der Jugendinternationale [1924]
82 p.   *NYPL, Amst, Felt*

2094 RESOLUTIONS adopted at the fourth Congress of the Young Communist International. Published by the E.C. of the Y.C.I. [Stockholm,
Tryckeriaktiebolaget. Fram, 1924] 120 p.

Hoover, NYPL, Harv, Illin

c) Commentaries and writings about the Congress

Die ERGEBNISSE des V. Kongresses der Kommunistischen Internationale und des IV. Kongresses der Kommunistischen Jugendinternationale. See no. 810.

The RESULTS of two congresses: the fifth congress of the Communist
International and the fourth congress of the Y.C.I. See no. 813.

5. V-th Congress, Moscow, August 20—September 18, 1928

a) Protocols

2095 PROTOKOLL des 5. Weltkongresses der K[ommunistischen] J[ugend]
I[nternationale] 20. August bis 18. September 1928 in Moskau. Berlin,
Verlag der Jugendinternationale, 1929. 475 p. indexes & tables.

Amst gives 475 p. BDIC gives 275 p. Item was not available for identification.
Amst, BDIC

b) Reports, Speeches, Drafts presented to the Congress

2096 KOMMUNISTICHESKII internatsional molodezhi za chetyre goda; obzor deiatel'nosti KIM'A i ego sektsii za period mezhdu IV a V vsemirnymi kongressami. Moskva [etc.] Gos. izd-vo, 1928. 206 p. incl. tables. *Hoover, LC, NYPL*

2097 VOM 4. zum 5. Weltkongreß der Kommunistischen Jugendinternationale; Bericht des Exekutiv-Komitees über Kampf und Arbeit der KJI. Berlin, Verlag der Jugendinternationale, 1928. 184 p. illus. *NYPL*

2098 THESEN und Statut. Entwurf zum 5. Weltkongreß der Kommunistischen Jugendinternationale. Berlin, Verlag der Jugendinternationale, 1928. 483—519 p. (Diskussions-Sonderheft der *Jugend-Internationale*, Juli 1928.) *Amst*

2099 The YOUNG Communist International between the fourth and fifth congresses, 1924—1928. London, Communist Party of Great Britain [1928] 250 p. On cover: The Communist Youth International: report of activity between the 4th and 5th congresses, 1924—1928. New York, Young Workers (communist) League of America.

> Harvard has two copies: one as listed above, the second has on cover: Communist Party of Great Britain.
>
> *Hoover, LC, NYPL, Harv, Duke, NWest, UChic, UMinn, UPenn*

2100 ENTRE deux congrès. Quatre années d'Internationale Communiste des Jeunes. Paris, Bureau d'éditions, de diffusion et de publicité [1929?] 292 p. *Hoover, Felt*

c) Programm Commission of the Congress

2101 PROTOKOLL der Programm-Kommission des 5. Weltkongresses der K[ommunistischen] J[ugend] I[nternationale]. Berlin, Verlag der Jugendinternationale, 1929, 203 p. index. *Harv, Amst*

2102 ENTWURF zum Programm der K[ommunistischen] J[ugend] I[nternationale] als Antrag von der Programmkommission des E[xekutiv] K[omitees] der KJI. [Wien] Verlag der Jugendinternationale [1928] 36 p. Beilage zur *Jugend-Internationale*, IX, 11. *Amst, Felt*

d) Resolutions, Theses, and other documents

2103 PROGRAMMA Kommunisticheskogo internatsionala molodezhi. [Moskva] Molodaia gvardiia, 1929. 127 p.   *LC*

2104 REZOLIUTSII i postanovleniia V Kongressa KIM'A. Moskva. Molodaia gvardiia, 1929. 253 p. (Biblioteka V Kongressa KIM)   *LC*

2105 Die BESCHLÜSSE des 5. Weltkongresses der Kommunistischen Internationale. Berlin, Jugendinternationale, 1928. 216 p.

> Issued in French with title: *Résolutions*. In manuscript on title page: "Beschlagnahmt".   *Hoover, NYPL*

2106 PROGRAMM der Kommunistischen Jugend-Internationale. Angenommen vom 5. Weltkongreß der KJI und bestätigt vom Präsidium des EKKI am 13. März 1929. Berlin, Verlag der Jugend-internationale, 1929. 112 p.   *LC, NYPL, Harv, UVirg, Amst*

2107 PROGRAMME de l'Internationale Communiste des Jeunes adopté par le Ve congrès de l'I.C.J. et sanctionné par le présidium du C.E. de l'I.C. le 13 mars 1929. Paris, Bureau d'éditions, 1929. 83 p. At head of title: I.C.J.   *Hoover, Felt*

2108 RESOLUTIONS du Ve congrès de l'Internationale Communiste des Jeunes. Paris, Bureau d'éditions [1929] 164 p. At head of title: I.C.J.   *Hoover, Col, BDIC, Felt*

PROGRAM Komunistične mladinske internacionale. Sprejet na V Kongresu KMI i potrjen na prezidiumu IOKI 14. [!] Marca 1929. See no. 1138.

2109 PROGRAM van de Kommunistische Jeugdinternationale. Aangenomen op het 5de wereldcongres te Moscou in 1928. Amsterdam, Atalanta [1930] 104 p.   *Amst*

2110 INTERNACIONAL juvenil comunista. Programa adoptado en el V congreso y sanccionado por el presidium del C.E. de la I.C. del 13 de Marzo de 1929. Buenos Aires, "Sudam" [Paris, Impr. Centrale, n. d.] 18 p. (Ediciones proletrias en Portugués)

> Exact copy of the card in the catalog of BDIC.   *BDIC*

2111   PROGRAMMA da International da Juventude comunista. Adoptado
pelo V Congresso da I. J. C. e sanccionado pelo Presidium do C. E.
da I. C. em 13 de Março de 1929. Buenos Aires, "Sudam" [Paris, Impr.
Centrale, n. d.] 116 p. (Ediçaoes proletarias em Portuguez)

Exact copy of the card in the catalog of BDIC.   *BDIC*

e) Commentaries and writings about the Congress

A LA conquête de la jeunesse ouvrière! Les résultats du Ve Congrès
mondial de l'I. C. J. et du VIe Congrès mondial de l'I. C. See no. 889.

6. VI-th Congress, Moscow, September 25—October 10, 1935

a) Reports, Speeches, Drafts presented to the Congress

2112   DIMITROV, G.
Rech' na otkrytii VI kongressa Kommunisticheskogo internatsionala
molodezhi 25 sentiabria 1935 goda. [Moskva] Molodaia gvardiia,
1935. 13 p.   *Hoover, BDIC*

2113   MOLODEZH' v bor'be za edinyi front; materialy VI Vsemirnogo
kongressa Kommunisticheskogo internatsionala molodezhi. [Moskva]
Molodaia gvardiia, 1938. 167 p. illus.

LC, NYPL, Harv, Col, BDIC

2114   WOLF, M.
Opyt raboty i zadachi edinogo fronta molodezhi. Doklad . . .
[Moskva] Molodaia gvardiia, 1935. 39 p. (VI Vsemirnyi kongress
Kommunisticheskogo internatsionala molodezhi)   *BDIC*

2115   CHEMODANOV, V., ed.
Die junge Generation des Sozialismus; Referate auf dem VI. Kongreß
der Kommunistischen Jugendinternationale. Moskau, Verlagsgenossenschaft ausländischer Arbeiter in der UdSSR, 1936. 80 p.   *Col*

2116 WOLF, M.
Youth marches towards socialism. Report to the Sixth World Congress of the Young Communist International. New York, Workers Library Publishers, 1936. 63 p.   *Hoover, BDIC*

2117 WOLF, M.
Unifions les forces de la jeune génération. Rapport du camarade Michel Wolf, membre du Secrétariat de l'I. C. J., au VIe Congrès de l'Internationale Communiste des Jeunes. [Bourges] Editions de la Jeunesse Communiste [n. d.] 54 p.   *Felt*

b) Resolutions, Theses, and other documents

2118 REZOLIUTSII VI Kongressa Kommunisticheskogo internatsionala molodezhi. [Moskva] Molodaia gvardiia, 1935. 29 p.   *LC, BDIC*

2119 The TASK of the United Front of the youth. Resolution unanimously adopted by the sixth world congress of the Young Communist International on Mr. Michael Wolf's report [n. p., n. d.] 8 pages (not numerated); mimeographed.   *Hoover, Harv*

2120 POUR l'union de toutes les organisations non fascistes de la jeunesse. Résolution adoptée à l'unanimité des voix, par le VIe congrès de l'Internationale Communiste des Jeunes, sur le rapport du camarade Michel Wolf. Paris, Maison des Syndicats, Service de l'Imprimerie [n. d.] 4 p.   *Felt*

C. EXECUTIVE COMMITTEE MEETINGS (PLENUMS, PRESIDIUM, BUREAU)

(In chronological order.)

Note: The identification and organization of the material originating in connection with the sessions of the Executive Committee of the C. Y. I. and its organs (Presidium, Bureau), was quite a complicated task. Most of these publications do not exactly identify the particular meetings by a consecutive numeration and/or date on their title pages. In this respect, the youthful publishers were less accurate and consistent than their adult mentors from the Communist International, who carefully numerated their Plenums and provided dates for most of the Presidium meetings.

A consultation of the official history of C.Y.I. *(Geschichte der Kommunistischen Jugend-Internationale,* see no. 1988) did not yield the desired clarification. The authors of these volumes seem themselves confused about the many meetings and conferences called by the Executive Committee. They refer to the same meeting interchangeably as "EK Sitzung" and "Vollsitzung" *(Geschichte,* vol. 2, p. 156–157), or "Erweitertes Plenum" and "Bürositzung". *(Geschichte,* vol. 3, p. 27) The April 1925 "5-th Enlarged Executive Committee session" is called "the first Plenum". *(Geschichte,* vol. 3, p. 80) A new term – "Plenarexekutive" – is also used *(Geschichte,* vol. 3, p. 88).

These meetings are reported here chronologically, on the basis of the imprints on title pages and findings in the official history. Two items are listed without dates because identification was impossible.

1. 1-st Bureau Session, Berlin, June 9—13, 1920

2121 BERICHT über die erste Sitzung des Büros der Kommunistischen Jugendinternationale. Abgehalten am 9. bis 13. Juni 1920 in Berlin. Berlin, Verlag der Jugendinternationale [1920] 39 p. (Internationale Jugendbibliothek, nr. 11)   *Hoover, NYPL, Amst*

2. Enlarged Bureau Session, March 18, 1922

2122 THÈSES et résolutions adoptées à la séance du Bureau élargi de l'Internationale Communiste des Jeunes. [Berlin] Internationale Communiste des Jeunes, 1922. 44 p. (Mémento du militant, no. ?)

BDIC, Felt

3. 4-th Bureau Session, 1923

2123 Die 4. [VIERTE] Bürositzung der K[ommunistischen] J[ugend] I[nternationale] Resolutionen u[nd] Beschlüsse. Berlin-Schöneberg, Jugendinternationale [n. d.] 76 p. (Rüstzeug, 7)   *Amst*

2124 RESOLUTIONS and theses of the fourth Bureau session, pub. by the E.C. of the Young Communist International. Berlin, Publishing House of the Young International, 1923. 109 p.   *Hoover, NYPL*

4. Enlarged Executive Committee, Moscow, July 13, 1923

RADEK, Karl
Der Kampf der Kommunistischen Internationale gegen Versailles und gegen die Offensive des Kapitals; Bericht erstattet in der Sitzung der Erweiterten Exekutive der K.I., Moskau, 15. Juni 1923, und in der Sitzung der Erweiterten Exekutive der Kommunistischen Jugend-Internationale, Moskau, 13. Juli 1923. See nos. 1051, 1052.

5. 5-th Enlarged Executive Committee, April 7—13, 1925

2125 VUJOVIĆ, V.
Die Bolschewisierung der Kommunistischen Jugend-Internationale. Rede des Genossen Vujović auf der 5. Sitzung der Erweiterten Exekutive der KJI. Wien, Verlag der Jugendinternationale [n. d.] 62 p.

Felt

6. Plenum of the Executive Committee, March 1926

2126 VUJOVIĆ V.
Die Lage der Arbeiterjugend und die nächsten Aufgaben der KJI. Rede des Genossen Vujović auf dem Plenum des Exekutiv-Komitees der Kommunistischen Jugendinternationale in Moskau 1926. Wien, Verlag der Jugendinternationale [1926] 24 p. (Beilage zur *Jugend-Internationale*, VII, no. 9)   *Felt*

2127 BESCHLÜSSE und Resolutionen des Plenums des Exekutiv-Komitees der Kommunistischen Jugendinternationale in Moskau, März 1926. Wien, Verlag der Jugendinternationale [1926] 24 p. (Beilage zur *Jugend-Internationale*, VII, 7/8.)   *NYPL, Amst, Felt*

7. 6-th Plenum of the Executive Committee, November-December, 1926

2128 BESCHLÜSSE und Resolutionen des VI. Plenums des Exekutivkomitees der Kommunistischen Jugendinternationale in Moskau, November-December 1926. Organisations-statut der KJI. [n. p., n. d.] 32 p. (Beilage zur *Jugend-Internationale*, VIII, 5.) *Amst, Felt*

2129 RESOLUTIONS of the enlarged Executive of the Young Communist International; November 1926. London, Publ. house of the Young Communist International [1926] 42 p. *NYPL*

8. Plenum of the Executive Committee, Moscow, June 18—27, 1927

2130 BERICHT und Beschlüsse der Vollsitzung der Exekutive der Kommunistischen Jugendinternationale vom 18.—27. Juni [1927] in Moskau. Wien, Verlag der Jugendinternationale, 1927. 40 p. (Sonderheft der *Jugend-Internationale*, VIII, Aug.-September, 1927) *Felt*

9. Presidium of E. C., November 17, 1927

2131 SHATSKIN, [Lazar]
Die Opposition und der Kommunistische Jugend-Verband der Sowjet-Union. Rede des Genossen Schatzkin in der Sitzung des Präsidiums der KJI am 17. November 1927. Berlin, Verlag der Jugend-Internationale [1928] 16 p. (Beilage zur *Jugend-Internationale*, IX, no. 4)
Felt

10. Plenum of the Executive Committee, February 28—March 5, 1928

2132 RESOLUTIONEN der Plenarsitzung des Exekutivkomitees der Kommunistischen Jugendinternationale, 28. Februar, 5. März 1928. Berlin Verlag der Jugendinternationale [1928?] 38 p. *Harv, Felt*

11. Presidium of E. C., 1929

2133 Die WENDUNG. Verkürztes Stenogramm der Diskussion im Präsidium des E[xekutiv] K[omitees] der K[ommunistischen] J[ugend] I[nter-nationale] über Lage und nächste Aufgaben der K. J. I. Berlin, Verlag der Jugendinternationale [1929] 32 p. (Beilage zur *Jugend-Internatio-nale* X, 12
Amst, Felt

12. Enlarged Plenum of Ex. Committee, Moscow, December 1929

The ROAD to mass organization of proletarian children. [Resolution of Enlarged Plenum . . .] See no. 2022.

13. Plenum of the Executive Committee, December 1932

CHEMODANOV, V.
Itogi XII plenuma IKKI i zadachi KIM; sokrashchennyi doklad na dekabr'skom plenume IKKIM ob itogakh XII plenuma IKKI i za-dachakh sektsii KIM v bor'be za massy trudiashchikhsia molodezhi. See no. 1237.

2134 KUN, Bela
Marxism versus social democracy; address delivered at Plenum Executive Committee of the Young Communist International, Decem-ber 1932. New York, Workers Library Publishers [1933?] 73 p. At head of title: Fiftieth anniversary of the death of Karl Marx. By Bela Kun. Printed in Great Britain.
Hoover, BDIC, Felt

2135 CHEMODANOV, V.
Aller où sont les jeunes travailleurs. Discours prononcé à l'Assemblée plénière du Comité exécutif de l'Internationale Communiste des Jeunes en décembre 1932. — Résolution de la session plénière du C[omité] e[xécutif] de l'I[nternationale] C[ommuniste des] J[eunes] sur le rapport de Tchémodanof sur "Le bilan de la XIIème session plénière

du C.E. de l'I.C. et les tâches des sections de l'I.C.J. dans la lutte pour les masses de la jeunesse laborieuse". [Paris, Publications révolutionnaires, Editions de la Fédération des Jeunesses Communistes, 1933] 80 p. At head of title: V. Tchémodanof. On cover: Publications révolutionnaires. *Amst, BDIC*

2136 KNORIN, V.
Luttons pour gagner la jeunesse ouvrière à la révolution. (Discours, prononcé au Comité exècutif de l'Internationale Communiste des jeunes le 22 décembre 1932). Paris, Publications révolutionnaires, Editions du Parti Communiste Français [n. d.] 30 p. At head of title: Knorine, V. *Amst. BDIC*

14. Plenum of Executive Committee, January 1934

2137 CHEMODANOV, V. E.
Komsomol v bor'be protiv fashizatsii i militarizatsii molodezhi; doklad na ianvar'skom [1934] plenume IKKIM 1934 g. Moskva, Molodaia gvardiia, 1934. 70 p. (KIM na boevykh pozitsiiakh) *Hoover*

2138 CHEMODANOV, V. E.
Young communists and the path to Soviet power; report to the January [1934] plenum of the Young Communist International. New York, Youth Publishers [1934] 47 p. *Hoover, Col*

2139 Il FASCISMO, la militarizzazione dei giovani e i compiti della gioventù comunista. Risoluzione del C.E. della I.G.C. Gennaio 1934 sul rapporto del compagno Cemedanov. [n. p.] Edizioni dell' "Avanguardia", 1934. 24 p. (Biblioteca della gioventù proletaria, no. 11) *Felt*

15. Meetings—date not established

2140 RESOLUTIONEN des Präsidium des Exekutive-Komitees der Kommunistischen Jugendinternationale. Zum Bericht des Zentralkomitees des Kommunistischen Jugendverbandes Deutschlands über Lage und Aufgaben des KJV Deutschlands. [Leipzig, Neudruck, 19--?] 16 p. *NYPL, UWisc*

2141 RESOLUTION of the Executive Committee, Young Communist League of the U.S.A., on the immediate tasks in the fight for the working youth. New York, Young Communist League [193-?] 15 p. *Col*

PART VIII.

OTHER FRONT ORGANIZATIONS
OF THE COMMUNIST INTERNATIONAL

A. INTERNATIONAL RED AID (MOPR)

Note: In November 1922, on the initiative of the Association of Old Bolsheviks and the Association of Former Political Prisoners and Deportees, the International Red Aid was created. Its beginnings were obviously not easy. The first "International Conference" of this organization was held in Moscow in July 1924 and was attended by representatives of the I.R.A. chapters from the Soviet Union and Germany. Other "delegations" were made up of visitors from various countries who hapened to be in Moscow on the occasion of the V-th Congress of the Communist International, but actually had nothing in common with the work of the I.R.A. (See no. 2169, Pestkowski, p. 148.)
A second Conference met in Moscow in March–April 1927. Very little is known about this conference. Of the 3,820,000 members which the I.R.A. had in February 1927, almost five years after its creation, 93 per cent belonged to the organization in the Soviet Union, and 7 per cent were spread through eight European countries. (See no. 2154, *5 Jahre*, etc. p. 4.)
It was not till November 1932 that the first and only congress of the I.R.A. assembled in Moscow. At least three Plenums of the Executive Committee of the Executive Committee of the I.R.A. took place in later years, the work being directed by the Presidium and the Secretariat. It ceased to function during World War II.

1. Collections of documents

(Cross-references only)

10 [DESIAT'] let MOPR v rezoliutsiiakh i dokumentakh. See no. 99 a and annotation to no. 139.

2142 ZEHN Jahre Internationale Rote Hilfe. Resolutionen und Dokumente.
See no. 144 and annotation to no. 139.   *Amst, Felt*

TEN years of International red aid in resolutions and documents, 1922—1932. See no. 139.

DIX années de Secours Rouge International, 1922—1932. See no. 100a and annotation to 139.

DIEZ años de S.R.I. Socorro Rojo Internacional. See no. 100 and annotation to no. 139.

2. General Publications by and about the I.R.A.

2143 ARBEJDER contra politi og domstol. [n.p.] Internationale Røde Hjaelp, 1933. 16 p. *Amst*

2144 BAJO el signo del internacionalismo combativo. Momentos fundamentale y proximas; tareas del trabajo de la Mopr en el extanjero. [n.p.] Comité Executivo del Socorro Rojo Internacional [n.d.] 22 p. tables. *Amst*

BENKWITZ, Max
Die Rote Hilfe; in *Proletarischer Internationalismus;* see no. 327.

2145 CONTRE la terreur blanche! Contre le rôle de Judas de la IIème Internationale! Pour la libération des prisonniers révolutionnaires! Pour le Secours Rouge International! [n.p.] Comité Exécutif du S.R.I., 1924. 15 p. *Amst*

2146 CONTRERAS, C[arlos]
Der Matteotti-Fonds ist eine Waffe der Kontrerevolution. Zürich, MOPR Verlag [n.d.] 16 p. *Felt*

2147 DEN' MOPR. 18 marta. Sbornik materialov dlia klubnykh rabotnikov MOPR. [S predisl. E. Davydova i s uchast. V.I. Lenina, L. Leonidova, A. Arnu i dr.] Moskva, MOPR, 1926. 80 p. *Amst*

2148 DEN' Parizhskoi kommuny — den' MOPR [Leningrad] Lenizdat, 1939. 68 p. By A.N. Vigorchik and others *NYPL*

2149 DUTSMAN, V., and Contreras, C.
MOPR za rubezhom; materialy dlia kruzhkov nizovogo aktiva MOPR. Moskva, Izd-vo TSK MOPR SSSR, 1935. 60 [1] p. *Hoover*

2150 FIFTEN years of white terror. Paris, Editions du Secours Rouge Internationale, 1935. 287 p. illus.

> LC or NYPL; location symbol on Union Catalog card was blured in reproduction.

2151 Frauen rufen aus Kerkern. Berlin, MOPR-Verlag, 1930. 15 p. Cover title: Frauen im Kerker und Int. Rote Hilfe.   *Hoover*

2152 FRAUEN unter faschistischen Terror! Frauen in der Solidaritäts- und Kampffront! Material des EK der Internationalen Roten Hilfe für die Delegierten des Internationalen Frauen-Welttreffens gegen Krieg und Faschismus vom 4.—6. August 1934 in Paris. (Bearbeitet von E. Winter.) Zürich, MOPR-Verlag, 1934. 16 p.   *NYPL*

5153 5 [FÜNF] Jahre Internationale Rote Hilfe. Hrsg. von der Exekutive der Internationalen Roten Hilfe. Berlin, MOPR, 1928. 44 p. illus. and tables.   *Amst, Felt*

2154 5 [FÜNF] Jahre Internationale Rote Hilfe! Der Tag der I. R. H. 18 März 1928. Vertrieb: MOPR-Verlag Berlin, February 1928. 14 leaves, lithography of typescript. At head of title: Informations-Material. Attached to this is another publication on orange paper, wih caption title: Zum fünfjährigen Jubiläum der I. R. H.; 8 leaves, lithography of typescript.

> The first publication (*5 Jahre*, etc.) contains a detailed report about the activities of the I. R. A. as an international organization. It presents the "white terror" against communism in various countries as the motive for the creation of the I. R. A. and quotes figures of alleged victims of this terror. It gives an account of the founding of the organization in 1922, its tasks, organization and membership in particular member-countries. It discusses the various forms of aid given by the organization (legal consultants for imprisoned and indicted persons, material help to prisoners and their families, care for children of arrested persons, etc.), and presents statistics and examples of this aid during the past five years. A chapter is dedicated to the necessity of exploiting "leftist intellectuals" in each country for the actions of the I. R. A. and quotes examples of such successful cooperation. A report about the propaganda publications of the I. R. A. in several countries is followed by a detailed account of persecution of I. R. A. functionaries in particular countries.
>
> The annexed circular on orange paper is a detailed instruction on how the propaganda week for the I. R. A. (11–18 March 1928) has to be organized and how the last day has to culminate in public manifestations. Exploitation of the "International Women's Day" (March 8) is recommended, and use of non-communist workers' organizations for a broader propaganda compaign is suggested. A brochure, *"Fünf Jahre IRH"* is announced to appear as propaganda material for this week. The item listed preceding the present publication is probably the announced brochure.   *Hoover*

2155 Die GEFÄHRDETE Staatssicherheit. "MOPR". Der Film "Über die Kinderheime der Roten Hilfe". Hrsg. vom EK der Internationalen Roten Hilfe. [n. p.] 1925. 16 p.   *Felt*

2156 GEGEN den weißen Terror! Gegen die Judasrolle der 2. Internationale! Für die Befreiung der revolutionären Gefangenen! Für die Internationale Rote Hilfe! [n. p.] Exekutivkomitee der IRH., 1924. 16 p. (Flugschriften gegen den weißen Terror! 1)   *Amst, Felt*

2157 GRUNWALD. H.
Ahoi! Seemann! Das geht dich an! [hrsg. vom Exekutivkomitee der Internationalen Roten Hilfe] Moskau, Verlagsgenossenschaft Ausländischer Arbeiter in der UdSSR, 1924. 32 p.   *Hoover*

2158 HELFT den Kindern. Kinderhilfe und Kinderheime der „Roten Hilfe". Hrsg. vom EK der Internationalen Roten Hilfe. [n. p.] 1925 48 p. illus.   *Felt*

2159 HELFT den Kindern der Opfer des Terrors und der Klassenjustiz! Hrsg. vom EK der Internationalen Roten Hilfe [n. p., n. d.] 20 leaves.
                    Felt

2160 KATTEL, B.
15 let MOPR SSSR. Moskva, TSK MOPR, SSSR, 1937. 8 p.   *BDIC*

2161 KHAVKIN, Arthur
Die große Solidarität. Aus der Tätigkeit der Internationalen Roten Hilfe in der Sowjetunion von Arthur Chawkin [With Preface to the Russian edition by P. Lepeshinskii. n. p.] Exekutivkomitee der Internationalen Roten Hilfe [1924] 61 p. illus.   *NYPL, Amst, Felt*

2162 KOLOMAN Wallisch. [Paris, Editions du S. R. I., 1934?] 32 p. Cover title.

Wallisch was a member of the Austrian "Schutzbund" and was tried and condemned to death for participation in the Schutzbund uprising. (See also no. 2178)   *Hoover*

2163 KOROLEV, A.
Den' Parizhskoi kommuny — den' MOPR [Leningrad] Lenoblizdat, 1938. 85 p.   *NYPL*

2164 KROVITSKII, Grigorii A.
Chto takoe MOPR? 3., ispr. i dop. izd. Moskva, Izd-vo TSK MOPR SSSR, 1931. 39 p.   *Hoover*

2165 KROVITSKII, Grigorii A.
Za perestroiku raboty MOPR'a. Moskva, Izd-vo TSK MOPR SSSR, 1930. 47 p. *Hoover*

2166 KUSHNER, M.
Materialy po MOPR; spravochnaia kniga dlia otdelenii, iacheek i aktivnykh rabotnikov MOPR'a Moskva, MOPR, 1925. 208 p. diagrs, tables. *NYPL*

2167 MARTY, André
Qu'est-ce que le Secours Rouge International (S.R.I.) Paris, Edition du S.R.I., 1926. 16 p. *Amst*

2168 MOPR (Mezhdunarodnaia organizatsiia pomoshchi bortsam revoliutsii). Agitsbornik dlia rabochikh klubov pod redaktsiei Nik. Maslenikova. Moskva, 1924. 79 p. (Glavpolitprosvet. Agitatsionnoe otdelenie.) *BDIC*

2169 PESTKOWSKI, Stanisław
Wspomnienia rewolucjonisty. Opracował Korzec. Łódź, Wydawnictwo Łódzkie [1961] 192 p.

> The author was an old Polish revolutionary who after the Bolshevik revolution of 1917 became a high government official. As a prominent member of the Association of Old Bolsheviks and of the Association of Former Political Prisoners, he cooperated in the creation of the MOPR in 1922. He later had various functions in this organization. His memoirs mention many details about the early activities of the I.R.A. *Hoover*

2170 PRISONERS of capitalism. Manifesto of the executive committee of the International Red Aid. London [n. d.] 15 p. *Amst*

2171 QU'EST-CE QUE le Secours Rouge International? Paris, Secours Rouge International, 1924. 32 p. (Brochure 1) *Amst*

2172 RODE Hjaelp Opgaver og virksomhed. Udgivet af Internationale Røde Hjaelp. Arbejderforlaget, [n. p.] 1935. 32 p. *Amst*

2173 SCHAFFT Rote Hilfe! Richtlinien für die Arbeit in der Roten Hilfe. Berlin, Vereinigung Internationaler Verlagsanstalten, 1925. 59 p.
Hoover

2174 Le SECOURS Rouge Internationale et la Fédération Internationale des Ligues pour la Défense des Droits de l'Homme et du Citoyen. Paris, Imprimerie Cooperative Etoile [n. d.] 12 leaves. *Felt*

2175 SHIRVINDT, Evsei
Russian prisons, with an introduction by J. T. Murphy. London, International class war prisoners' aid [1928] 31 p. *Hoover*

2176 SPIRU, Vasile
Vopreki belomu terroru. Moskva, TSK MORP SSSR, 1936. 46 p.
Hoover, BDIC

SYNDICATS rouges et Secours Rouge International. See no. 1915.

2177 V boiakh za mirovoi oktiabr'; literaturno-khudozhestvennyi sbornik k desiatiletiiu MORP. [Moskva] Izd-vo TSK MOPR SSSR, 1932. 127 p.
LC

2178 WALLISCH, Koloman, das Leben und Sterben eines Revolutionärs. [Zürich, MOPR-Verlag, n. d.] 16 p. (See no. 2162)
See annotation to no. 2162. *Amst*

2179 WAS ist und was will die Internationale Hilfe? [n. p.] Exekutivkomitee der Internationalen Roten Hilfe [n. d.] 72 p. illus.
Amst, Felt

2180 WAS ist und was will die Internationale Rote Hilfe? Referenten-Material für Referenten der IRH. [Berlin, Gutnoff, n. d.] 28 p. tables.
Amst, Felt

2181 ZELT, Johannes
Rote Hilfe, Klassensolidarität und proletarischer Internationalismus; in *Proletarischer Internationalismus;* see no. 327.

2181a ZELT, Johannes
... und nicht vergessen die Solidarität! Aus der Geschichte der Internationalen Roten Hilfe und der Roten Hilfe Deutschlands. Berlin, Rütten & Loening [1960] 159 p. illus. „Verwendete Literatur und Dokumente" p. 155—159. *Hoover, Felt*

2182 ZETKIN, Klara
Werk und Weg der Internationalen Roten Hilfe; 10 Jahre Kampf und Solidarität. Berlin, Tribunal-Verlag W. Pieck [1932] 32 p. *Hoover*
[ZETKIN, Clara]
Clara Zetkin. See no. 86.

[ZETKIN, Clara]
Clara Zetkin; ein Sammelband zum Gedächtnis der großen Kämpferin. See no. 87.

2182a [ZETKIN, Clara]
Clara Zetkin's Ruf zur internationalen Solidarität. [Mit Vorw. von E. D. Stassova] Zürich, MOPR [1933] 24 p. illus. *Amst*

3. Denunciations of "Class Justice" in Non-Communist Countries

2183 HALLE, Felix
Anklage gegen Justiz und Polizei zur Abwehr der Verfolgungen gegen das proletarische Hilfswerk für die politischen Gefangenen und deren Familien. Anhang: Äußerungen führender Künstler, Gelehrter und Schriftsteller. Berlin, MOPR Verlag, 1926. 98 p. *NYPL*

2184 The PRACTICE of bourgeois class-justice in the struggle against the revolutionary movement of the workers, the national minorities and the colonial and semi-colonial peoples. Berlin, The Executive Committee of the International class war prisoners aid in the MOPR publishing house [1928] 116 p. At head of title: Printed as manuscript.

"International class war prisoners aid is identical with the International Red Aid." – p. 5 Report of a Conference organized by jurists in the Soviet Union, November, 1927. *Hoover*

2185 Die PRAXIS der bürgerlichen Klassenjustiz im Kampfe gegen die revolutionären Bewegungen der Werktätigen, nationalen Minderheiten, Kolonial- und Halbkolonialvölker. Hrsg. von der Exekutive der Internationalen Roten Hilfe. [Mit Einl. von Clara Zetkin]. Berlin, MOPR [1928] 124 p. [Printed as manuscript] *Amst*

2186 FRANTZ
Vor der Justiz des Feindes. Die juristische Hilfe der IRH. Zürich, MOPR Verlag [n. d.] 15 p. *NYPL, Amst*

4. The I. R. A. and Events in various Countries

a) Austria

2187 Les MEMBRES du Schutzbund sur les combats de février et sur la solidarité internationale. Paris, Editions du S. R. I., 1934. 39 p. On cover: Les Schutzbundler d'Autriche sur leurs combats de février. *NYPL*

2188 [TROSTEL, Willy, ed.]
Schutzbündler über die Februarkämpfe und das internationale Solidaritätswerk der Internationalen Roten Hilfe. [Unter Mitwirkung von Hertha Müller, Heinz Roscher, Dörnberger, u. a.] Zürich, MOPR-Verlag [n. d.] 23 p. *Hoover, Amst, Felt*

b) Bulgaria

2189 KOLAROV, Vasil
Im Lande der Galgen. Hrsg. vom Exekutivkomitee der Internationalen Roten Hilfe. [Zürich, Gedruckt von der Unionsdruckerei] 1926. 80 p. illus. At head of title: W. Kolaroff. *Hoover, NYPL*

2190 Der WEISSE Tod in Bulgarien; ein Hilferuf. [Halle a. d. Saale] Exekutivkomitee der Internat. Roten Hilfe, 1925. 16 p. illus.

Hoover, Amst

c) China

2191 DENG-Bao-Siang
Das blutende China. Berlin, MOPR-Verlag, 1928. 40 p. *Amst*

d) France

2192 ZHERTVY frantsuzskogo militarizma; sbornik. Moskva, Izd-vo TSK MOPR SSSR, 1931. 30 p. *Hoover*

e) Germany

2193 ANGEKLAGTER Hitler. Protokolle, Augenzeugen- und Tatsachenberichte aus den faschistischen Folterhöllen Deutschlands. Zürich, MOPR-Verlag, [n. d.] 16 p. *Amst*

2194 Die INTERNATIONALE Solidarität mit dem deutschen Proletariat. Die Hilfsaktion der Internationalen Roten Hilfe. [Zürich, MOPR-Verlag, n. d.] 8 p. *Amst*

2195 MÜLLER, Hertha
Die Werktätigen der Welt verteidigen die Arbeiterklasse Deutschlands. Zürich, MOPR Verlag [n. d.] 8 p. *Hoover*

2196 PIECK, Wilhelm
Geroi proletarskoi solidarnosti. Moskva, TSK MOPR SSSR, 1936. 63 p.

Concerns the work of MOPR in Germany. *BDIC*

2197 WINKEL, Emil
Gestapo. Aus der Tätigkeit der Geheimen Staatspolizei Deutschlands. Zürich, MOPR-Verlag, 1934. 16 p. *Amst*

f) Great Britain

2198 WRIGHT, Ada
De Vara rede; wat de Negermoeder in het Engelsch sprak, en wat de Vara er van heeft vertaald. [Amsterdam, I.R.H., 1931] 7 p. Dutch and English) *NYPL*

g) Hungary

2199 GREINER, I.
Arest i begstvo (iz epokhi padeniia proletarskoi diktatury v Vengrii) Vospominaniia polit-emigranta. Perevod s vengerskogo Emilii Greiner-Gekk. Moskva, TSK MOPR SSSR, 1927. 21 p. *Hoover*

h) Netherlands

2200 FRIESLAND in dwangbuis. Rode Hulp. [Amsterdam, Uitgeverij "Introhulp", 1934?] 15 p. illus. *NYPL*

i) Poland

2201 AKADEMIIA navuk B.S.S.R., Minsk.
Kraina shybenits i karnykh ekspedytsyi; da 10-godz'dzia MOPR'u. Mensk, 1932. 72 p. illus., tables. At head of title: Belaruskaia akademiia navuk. Kamisiia na vyvuchen'niu zakhodniai Belarusi. *NYPL*

2202   KIARINI, A., ed.
       Desiat' let belogo terrora; sbornik statei s predisl. Klary Tsetkin. Pod
       redaktsiei A. Kiarini. Moskva, Zdat. TSK MOPR SSSR, 1929. x, 110 p.
       illus.   *NYPL*

2203   MARX, Magdaleine
       La Pologne est un enfer. Paris, Secours Rouge International, 1924.
       31 p. (Brochure, 2)   *Amst*

2204   Das POLEN Pilsudskis. [Berlin?] Exekutiv-Komitee der IRH, 1926. 32 p.
                                                                         NYPL

2205   SELDT, R.
       Le procès des torturés de Luck; scènes de sanglante oppresion en
       Ukraine occidentale. [Paris, Soc. nouvelle d'imprimerie et d'édition,
       1933?] 16 p. At head of title: Editions du S. R. I. (Cover title.)
                                                                         NYPL

2206   WIDELSKI, Kazimierz
       Der Bombenfabrikant; eine wahre Geschichte aus dem Polen Pilsud-
       skis. [Berlin?] Hrsg. vom EK der IRH, 1926. 24 p. On cover: Eine wahre
       Geschichte aus dem Polen Pilsudskis.   *Hoover, NYPL*

j) Rumania

2207   GRIGORESCU, N.
       Le procès des cheminots de Bucarest. [Paris, Soc. nouvelle d'imprimerie
       et d'éditions, 1933?] 31 p. illus. At head of title: Les éditions du S.R.I.
                                                                         NYPL

2208   SPIRU, Vasile
       Aus den Totenhäusern Groß-Rumäniens; Vorwort von Henri Barbusse.
       [Berlin] Exekutivkomitee der IRH, 1926. 32 p. illus.   *Hoover*

k) Spain

2209   BLACHE, Robert
       Der Zusammenstoß zweier Welten in Spanien und die internationale
       Solidaritätsaktion der IRH für das revolutionäre Spanien. Zürich, Paris,
       MOPR-Verlag, 1935. 20 p.   *Hoover, NYPL*

2210 ERENBURG, Il'ia
Estampas de España. [Madrid, 1937?] 55 p. (Ediciones S. R. I.)

NYPL

l) United States of America

2211 MARKOSCH, F.
Die Neger in den Vereinigten Staaten von Nordamerika; hrsg. vom
Exekutivkomitee der Internationalen Roten Hilfe. Berlin, MOPR-Verlag,
1930. 47 p. Hoover, NYPL

5. Conferences, Congresses, Plenums of I. R. A.

a) 1-st International Conference of I. R. A., Moscow, July 14–16, 1924

2212 PERVAIA mezhdunarodnaia konferentsiia MOPR, 14—16 iiulia 1924 g.;
stenograficheskii otchet. Moskva, Izd. I. K. MOPR, 1924. 127 p. *LC*

2213 Die INTERNATIONALE Rote Hilfe. Ihre Tätigkeit und Aufgaben (Bericht
des Z.-K. der I. R. H. für die Zeit vom 1. Januar 1923 bis zum 1. Mai
1924.) Moskau, Zentralkomitee der I. R. H., 1924, 47 p. tables

Amst

b) 1-st Congress of I. R. A., Moscow, November 11–24, 1932

2214 PROTOKOLL des ersten Weltkongresses der Internationalen Roten
Hilfe; der 1. Weltkongreß der IRH fand vom 10—24 November 1932
in Moskau statt. Moskau-Leningrad, Verlagsgenossenschaft ausländischer Arbeiter in der UdSSR, 1933. 265 p. index. „Herausgegeben
unter Redaktion des EK der IRH." Hoover, NYPL, Duke

2215 MANUIL'SKII, Dmitrii
Der Kampf um die klassenlose Gesellschaft (Erfolge und Schwierig-
keiten des sozialistischen Aufbaus in der USSR.) Rede gehalten auf
dem 1. Weltkongreß der Internationalen Roten Hilfe in Moskau am
21 November 1932. Berlin, Tribunal Verlag W. Pieck [1933] 31 p.

Hoover

2216 MANUIL'SKII, D.
La lotta per la societá senza classi (Estratto dal rapporto presentato
il 21 Novembre 1932 al Congresso Mondiale del S. R. I.) [n. p.] Edizioni
del Partito Communista d'Italia, 1933. 29 p. (Piccola Biblioteca Proletaria, 15)

Felt

2217 RÜSTET zum Weltkongreß der Internationalen Roten Hilfe; 10 Jahre
IRH. Berlin, Tribuna Verlag W. Pieck [1931] 23 p. tables.

Hoover, Amst

2218 10 [ZEHN] Jahre Kampf gegen den weißen Terror, den Faschismus,
den Krieg. [Resolutionen des Weltkongresses der IRH]. Moskau,
November 1932. Paris, Verlag der I. R. H. [n. d.] 71 p.   *Amst, Felt*

2219 RESOLUTIONS of the World congress of the International Red Aid
(November 1932). New York, National Educational Dept., International
Labor Defense [1932?] 3 parts in 1 vol. (Reproduced from typewritten
copy)

NYPL

2220 10 [DIX] ans de lutte contre la terreur blanche, le fascisme [et] la
guerre; résolutions du Congrès mondial du Secours Rouge International. Moscou, novembre 1932. Paris, Editions du S. R. I. [1933?]
97 p.

Col

2221 RESOLUCIONES del congreso mundial del Socorro Rojo Internacional.
Madrid, etc., Combate [n. d.] 96 p.   *Amst*

2222 II CONGRESSO Mondiale del Socorro Rosso. [n. p., n. d.] 24 p.

Felt

c) 2-nd Plenum of E. C. of I. R. A., Moscow, August 26–30, 1928

2223 MARTY, André
Für Rettung aller Opfer der Reaktion und des Faschismus. Reden auf
der II. Plenartagung des Exekutiv-Komitees der Internationalen Roten
Hilfe. Anhang: Begrüßung des Plenums. [Zürich, MOPR, 1935] 24 p.

Amst

d) 3-rd Plenum of E. C. of I. R. A., Moscow, April 12–15, 1931

2224 KORD'E, M., and Franz, G.
Na boevom postu revoliutsii; k itogam 3-go plenuma IK MOPR.
Moskva, Izd-vo TSK MOPR SSSR, 1931. 29 p.   *LC*

6. Reports on I. R. A. Activities to I. R. A. of USSR Meetings

(In chronological order)

2225 STASOVA, Elena
MOPR's banners abroad; report to the third MOPR Congress of the
Soviet Union, by H. Stassova. Moscow, Executive Committee of I. R. A.,
1931. 39 p. At head of title: International Red Aid (MOPR)
Hoover, LC, NYPL, Col

2226 STASOVA, Elena
Unter dem Banner der Internationalen Roten Hilfe; Bericht auf dem
3. Kongreß der Roten Hilfe der Sowjet-Union. Moskau, Verlag der
Exekutive der Internationalen Roten Hilfe, 1931. 35 p. At head of
title: Internationale Rote Hilfe.   *NYPL*

2227 STASOVA, Elena
Die IRH. Zum zehnjährigen Bestehen am Vorabend ihres Weltkongres-
ses. Bearbeitetes Referat, gehalten auf dem II. Plenum des Z. K. der
RH USSR, April 1932. Berlin, Tribunal-Verlag [1932] 47 p.
Hoover

2228 STASOVA, Elena
Za edinyi front solidarnosti i pomoshchi (doklad na IV plenume TSK
MOPR SSSR, 17 noiabria 1935 g.) Moskva, izd-vo TSK MOPR SSSR,
1935. 47 p.   *Hoover*

B. THE INTERNATIONAL PEASANTS' COUNCIL
(PEASANTS' INTERNATIONAL)

1. International Conferences

a) 1-st International Peasants' Conference, Moscow, Oct. 10–15, 1923

Note: The first two meetings of the International Peasants' Council are defined as "international conferences". The German texts use the term "Bauernkongress" and "Weltkongress der Bauern". The present listing will use the translation of the Russian term, hence "International Peasants' Conferences".

Also the date of the first Conference is given differenty in German and in the Russian and French sources. Here again, the date accepted was from the Russian and French sources: October 10–15, 1923.

2229 PROTOKOLL vom ersten Internationalen Bauernkongreß vom 10 bis 16 [!] Oktober, 1923, in Moskau. Berlin, Verlag Neues Dorf, 1924. 170 p. (Bibliothek des Internationalen Bauern-Rates, 7) On cover: Der erste Weltkongreß der Bauern. *Hoover, LC*

2230 Ire [PREMIÈRE] Conférence internationale paysanne, tenue à Moscou, dans la riche salle du trône du palais du Kremlin, les 10, 11, 12, 13, 14 et 15 otctobre 1923. Thèses, messages & addresses. Paris, Bibliothèque paysanne [1923] 120 p. At head of title: C.P.I. [Conseil paysan international] *Hoover, Amst, BDIC, Felt*

2231 RED peasant international; a minor item in the forgotten byways of recent history. [Washington, D.C., International Peasant Union, n.d.] vi, 57 p. mimeogr. (International Peasant Union documents, no. 19.)

Translation of *1re Conference internationale paysanne, tenue à Moscou...*
Hoover, Amst, BDIC

2232 WELCHE Genossenschaften können uns helfen? Zwei Referate mit Diskussion vom Ersten Weltkongreß der Bauern in Moskau vom 10.—16. [!] Oktober 1923. Vorwort von Heinrich Rau. Berlin, Verlag Neues Dorf, 1924. 30 p. (Der Erste Weltkongreß der Bauern, 3)

Felt

b) 2-nd International Peasants' Conference, Moscow, November 1927

2233 CONFERENCE paysanne internationale (sténogramme et résolution); Moscou, novembre 1927. Conseil paysan international. Berlin, Verlag Neues Dorf, 1928. 39 p. illus.   *Hoover*

c) 1-st European Peasants' Cnogress, Berlin, March 26–29, 1930

2234 BULLETIN zum Europäischen Bauern-Kongreß. Hrsg. vom Komitee zur Vorbereitung des Europäischen Bauern-Kongresses in Berlin. Berlin [Thomas] 1930. No. 1—3.   *Amst*

2235 Het EERSTE Europeesche Congres van werkende boeren; geh. te Berlijn 26—29 Maart 1930. Amsterdam, Nederl. boerencomité [n. d.] 32 p.   *Amst*

2. Books and Pamphlets dealing with the Peasants International

BUKHARIN, N. I.
La question paysanne. I. Discours prononcé au Plenum Elargi du C.E. de l'Internationale Communiste, le 2 avril 1925. II. Thèses sur la question paysanne acceptées par l'Exécutif élargi ge l'I.C. See no. 1047.

BUKHARIN, N. I.
Über die Bauernfrage. (Rede vor der Erweiterten Exekutive, April, 1925) See no. 1069.

CHIRKOV, I.
Krest'ianskii Internatsional i soiuzy sel'sko-khoziaistvennykh rabochikh; (materialy k III kongressu Profinterna). See no. 1870.

2236 DINGLEY, S.
Bor'ba krest'ianstva Indonezii; perevod s frantsuzskoi rukopisi V. D. Ustinovicha. Moskva, Gos. izdat, 1927. 112 p. At head of title: S. Dingli. (Biblioteka: Revoliutsionnoe krest'ianskoe dvizhenie, 2)
                                      Hoover

2237 DINGLEY, S.
The peasant movement in Indonesia. Berlin, R. L. Präger, 1927. 59 p.
At head of title: Farmers and Peasants' International. (Library of the
revolutionary farmers and peasants' movements, 2)

Hoover, NYPL

2238 DOMBAL, Ch., [and others]
Bor'ba za krest'ianstvo. Moskva, Kommunisticheskaia Akademiia,
1926. 80 p. (As co-authors are listed: Dombal, Ch., Boshkovich, V.,
Kheveshi, A., [Hevesi, A.] and Gorov, A.)

A collection of articles published by a meeting of the international peasant
press. Annotation from BDIC catalog card. *BDIC*

2239 HEVESI, A.
Vengerskoe krest'ianstvo i ego bor'ba. Perevel s vengerskoi rukopisi
Teodor Mali. Podgotovil k pechati Vl. D. Ustinovich. Moskva, Gos.
izd., 1927. 175 p. illus., diagrs., tables. (Biblioteka: Revoliutsionnoe
krest'ianskoe dvizhenie, 5) *Hoover*

2240 JACKSON, George D.
The Green International and the Red Peasant International; a study
of Comintern policy towards the peasant political movement in Eastern
Europe, 1919—1930. New York, 1961. x, 427 leaves. Reproduction of
typescript. Thesis, Columbia University. Bibliography: p. 396—427.

Col

2241 MESHCHERIAKOV, Nikolai
The peasantry and the revolution. Berlin, R. L. Präger, 1927. 67 p.
At head of title: N. L. Mecheriakov. Bibliographical footnotes. (Farmers
and peasants international Library, 1) *Hoover, Amst*

2242 Le PAYSAN russe. Paris, Bureau d'éditions, 1928. 96 p. (Correspon-
dant paysan international.) *Hoover*

2243 Der WELTBUND der Bauern; die Gründung des Internationalen Bauern-
Rates. Vorwort von Heinrich Rau. Berlin, Verlag Neues Dorf, 1924.
55 p. (Der erste Weltkongreß der Bauern, 4) *LC, Felt*

C. WORKERS INTERNATIONAL RELIEF

Note: This front organization was founded on orders from the Executive Committee of the Communist International, at a meeting in Berlin, in September 1921. An official Comintern publication gives the following explanation of its aims and activities: "In the beginning, the W.I.R. was founded for the organization of aid to the starving people of Soviet Russia by the international proletariat. Later, the W.I.R. set its goal to: aid the strikers, the victims of an act of nature, and children of workers; [to give] social aid to women, invalids and the aged; [to foster the] organization of Friends of Soviet Russia; [to organize] expositions of Soviet industrial products and art abroad; [and] antifascist propaganda.
"A special field of activity of the W.I.R. is the production of proletarian movie pictures. For this purpose the W.I.R. has its own movie picture organizations in the U.S.S.R., Germany, Italy, Norway, America, France, Sweden and other countries. The W.I.R. has national sections [affiliated organizations] in almost all countries." (Tivel, *10 let Kominterna*, p. 370)
International congresses of the W.I.R., took place in 1923 (twice), 1925, 1927 and 1931. The Executive offices were located in Berlin, where Willi Münzenberg played a leading role as Secretary General of the organization.

1. Congresses and Conferences

a) 1-st Congress, Berlin, December 1923

2244 FIMMEN, Edo
Die Gewerkschaften und die Internationale Arbeiterhilfe. Rede geh. auf dem Weltkongreß der I.A.H. in Berlin am 9. Dezember 1923. Wien, Moderner Verlag [n. d.] 11 p.　　　*Amst*

b) Conference, Berlin, November 1927

2245 PROTOKOLL der internationalen IAH-Konferenz in Berlin am 20. November 1927 mit Erläuterungen und Ergänzungen. [Unter Mitw. von Willi Münzenberg, Meta Krauss-Fessel, H. Galm u. a.] Berlin, Verlag der Internationalen Arbeiterhilfe [n. d.] 84 p. On cover: Dein Urteil.
　　　Amst

c) 8-th [?] Congress, Berlin, October 1931

2246 MIT neuer Kraft für neue Aufgaben. Dokumente, Resolutionen u[nd] Entschließungen des 8. Weltkongresses der Internationalen Arbeiter-Hilfe vom 9.—15. Oktober 1931 in Berlin. Mit einer Einleitung von Willi Münzeberg. [Berlin, Zentralkomitee der Internationalen Arbeiter-Hilfe, n. d.] 32 p. *Amst*

2. Books and Pamphlets by and about the W. I. R.

2247 CAPTIVES of capitalism. [n. p.] Committee for International Workers Aid [n. d.] 16 p. illus. *Amst*

2248 CHILDREN's Relief and the children's homes of the Workers International Relief. [Berlin, Central Committee of the Workers' International Relief, n. d.] 33 p. illus. *Amst*

2249 Die DRITTE Säule der kommunistischen Politik. I. A. H. „Internationale Arbeiterhilfe." Dargestellt nach authentischem Material. Berlin, Verlagsgesellschaft des Allgemeinen Deutschen Gewerkschaftsbundes, 1924. 24 p. *Amst*

2250 Die 1. [ERSTE] internationale Arbeiteranleihe der Internationalen Arbeiterhilfe für Sowjet-Rußland zur Finanzierung gemeinwirtschaftlicher Produktions-Unternehmungen in Landwirtschaft, Industrie, Bergbau, Fischerei und Forstwirtschaft der Russischen Sozialitischen Föderativen Sowjet-Republik (R. S. F. S. R.). 2. Aufl. Berlin, Auslandskomitee der Internationalen Arbeiterhilfe für Sowjet-Rußland [n. d.] 24 p. illus. On cover: Bruder hilf! *Amst*

2251 FRIEDRICH, Walter
Die Jugend darbt, die Jugend kämpft! Berlin, Jugendbüro beim Zentralkomitee der Internationalen Arbeiter-Hilfe [n. d.] 24 p. (Flugschriftenreihe des Jugendaktivs der Internationalen Arbeiter-Hilfe, no. 1.) *Amst*

2252 GLOBIG, F[ritz]
Millionen im Kampfe gegen Faschismus und imperialistischen Krieg. Amsterdam, Zentralkomitee der IAH [n. d.] 48 p. illus. *Amst*

2253 GUILBEAUX, Henri
La reconstruction économique de la Russie et le Secours Ouvrier
International. Paris, Librairie du Travail, 1924. 39 p.

Hoover, Amst

2254 KINDERHILFE und Kinderheime der Internationalen Arbeiter-Hilfe
[Berlin, Zentralkomitee der Internationalen Arbeiterhilfe, n. d.] 33 p.
illus. [Captions under illustrations in: German, French, English and
Czech.]
Amst

2255 KOMMUNISTIK politik under välgörenhetens mask. "Internationell
arbetarehjälp" belyst medelst autentiska dokument. Stockholm, Tidens
Förlag, 1924. 36 p. (Landsorganisationens Skriftserie, 10)

NYPL, Amst

2256 MIT Pflug und Traktor. [Mit Vorw. von Willi Münzenberg. Berlin, Zentralkomitee der Internationalen Arbeiterhilfe, n. d.] 16 p. illus.

Amst

2257 MÜNZENBERG, Willi
Brot und Maschinen für Sowjet-Rußland. Ein Jahr proletarischer Hilfs-
arbeit. Berlin, Auslandskomitee der Internationalen Arbeiterhilfe für
Sowjet-Rußland [1922] 39 p. tables
Amst

2258 MÜNZENBERG, Willi
Die dritte Säule der kommunistischen Weltpolitik I[nternationale]
A[rbeiter] H[ilfe]. [Berlin-Schöneberg, Sieber, 1924] 20 p.
Amst

2259 MÜNZENBERG, Willi
Erobert den Film! Winke aus der Praxis für die Praxis proletarischer
Filmpropaganda. Berlin, Neuer Deutscher Verlag, 1925. 28 p. illus.

Hoover

2260 MÜNZENBERG, Willi
Fünf Jahre Internationale Arbeiterhilfe. Berlin, Neuer Deutscher Verlag
W. Münzenberg, 1926. 183 p. plates, ports. Bibliography: p. 181—183.

Hoover, Amst

2261 MÜNZENBERG, Willi
Für Brot und Freiheit; die Aufgaben und das Ziel der Internationalen
Arbeiterhilfe. [Vortrag, gehalten vor den Delegierten der Landes-
konferenz der I.A.H. am Freitag, den 28. November 1930] Frankfurt
am Main, 1930. 20 p. (Heft 1 einer Serie von Broschüren im Auftrage
des Zentralkomitees der I.A.H.)
Hoover

2262 MÜNZENBERG, Willi
Für Brot und Freiheit. Vortrag, geh. vor den Delegierten der Landes-
konferenz der IAH und mehreren Tausend Frankfurter Arbeitern am
Freitag, dem 28. November 1930 in Frankfurt/M. auf einstimmigen
Beschluß der Versammlung als Broschüre gedruckt. 6. Auflage. Berlin,
Verlag des Zentralkomitees der Internationalen Arbeiterhilfe, 1931.
39 p.   *Amst*

2263 MÜNZENBERG, Willi
Solidarität; zehn Jahre Internationale Arbeiterhilfe, 1921—1931. Berlin,
Neuer Deutscher Verlag, 1931. 527 p. illus., tables, facsims., graphs.
On cover: Solidarität.

   A detailed report about the activities of the W.I.R. for ten years prepared
   for the anniversary congress (Berlin, October 2–15, 1931). In the chapter
   dealing with organizational matters and the congresses of the W.I.R. the
   author discloses the real aims of this front organization: "From the very
   beginning the campaign had a pronounced political outlook. It was more
   than a charitable aid to the starving, it was an active support for the first
   workers' state of the world" (p. 158) Throughout the volume are names of
   prominent scholars, writers, artists and other notable noncommunists who
   sponsored or supported various actions of the W.I.R. All major actions –
   including the relief for starving Soviet Russia – are discussed in detail. The
   activities of affiliated organizations in over 30 countries are discussed. A graph
   on p. 522 shows the distribution of the total expenditures of 118.5 million marks
   to particular actions of the organization. Of this total 21 million marks were
   spent for the famine relief in Soviet Russia, 37.5 million marks for the support
   of strikes, 29.8 million marks for the production of "proletarian movie pictures",
   21.5 million marks for publications (propaganda). The total of expenditures
   (118.5 million marks) does not correspond with the total of over 330 million
   marks which were paid to the organization by offiliated organizations all over
   the world (table on p. 204–207), in addition to incomes from the films (31.7 million marks) and from the sale of publications (25.5 million marks, the two last
   figures taken from graph on p. 522). A list of W.I.R. publications, including
   140 entries (books, pamphlets, leaflets, periodicals, newspapers, bulletins)
   concludes the volume. This is a basic source for the study of the activities
   of this front organization, created on orders of the Executive Committee of
   the Communist International.   *Hoover, Amst*

2264 MÜNZENBERG, Willi
Die Tätigkeit des internationalen Proletariats in der Hilfsaktion für
die Hungernden in Rußland. Berlin [n. d.] 19 p. Separatdruck aus der
Kommunistischen Internationale.   *Hoover*

2265 NANSEN, Fridtjof
An das Gewissen der Völker! Rede vor der Konferenz des „Internationalen Arbeitsamts beim Völkerbund" in Genf am 12. November
1921. [Berlin] Auslandskomitee zur Organisierung der Arbeiterhilfe
für die Hungernden in Rußland [n. d.] 24 p. illus.   *Amst*

2266 OEHRING, Richard
Die Großfischerei der I. A. H. in Sowjetrußland. Der erste vollständige
Bericht mit Bilanz, Statistik, Plänen und Photos. Berlin, Zentralkomitee
der Internationalen Arbeiterhilfe [n. d.] 36 p. (Schriften über die pro-
duktive Wirtschaftshilfe, 2) *Amst*

2267 QUELQUES Documents sur le Secours Ouvrier International. Orga-
nisme de propaganda de l'Internationale Communiste. Namur, Imprimerie du peuple, 1926. 60 p. *Amst*

2268 REICHSARBEITSKONFERENZ des Bundes der Freunde der I. A. H.
27 Juli 1924 im Berliner Rathaus. [Berlin, n. d.] 8 p. *Amst*

2269 REPORT of the English and French delegation of the Workers International Relief on productive enterprises of the W. I. R. in the USSR,
August—September 1925. [London, Co-operative Printing Society,
1925] 35 p. illus. On cover: The Workers' Red Cross. *Hoover*

2270 Die SÄULE der proletarischen Selbsthilfe I. A. H. Eine Antwort auf die
Broschüre des A. D. G. B. [Berlin, Zentralkomitee der Internationalen
Arbeiterhilfe, n. d.] 63 p. *Amst*

2271 The SONNENBURG concentration camp, by an escaped prisoner.
[New York City, Workers International Relief and International Labor
Defense, 1934] 38 p. *Hoover*

2272 WAS ist es mit der IAH? Warum wir nicht mehr in der Internationalen
Arbeiter Hilfe arbeiten. Zwickau, Bezirksvorstand der Sozialdemokratischen Partei Deutschland [n. d.] 24 p. *Amst*

D. COMMUNIST WOMEN'S ORGANIZATIONS AND CONFERENCE

Note: The Communist International, from its founding congress on, deliberated
during each congress about "work through women," i. e. the exploitation of
women for spreading communist influence. During the congresses, women-
delegates held their own "consultations" and „conferences", but they never
created a separate women's international. Rather, they infiltrated various international women's organizations at different times and used them, with varying
success, as communist fronts. The directing organ was always a "women's
secretariat" or "women's section" in the Secretariat of the ECCI.

Comintern records reveal that an international women's "consultation" took place during the founding Congress in 1919, and three international conferences of communist women took place in 1921, 1924, and 1926 (Tivel, *10 let Kominterna*, p. 376). Only one printed report about the 1920 conference was located. A few pamphlets add scarce information on these activities. More information is available in scattered articles and notes in the periodical *The Communist International*.

1. 1-st International Conference of Communist Women, Moscow, July 30—August 3, 1920

2273 OTCHET o pervoi Mezhdunarodnoi konferentsii kommunistok; so vstup. stat'ei A. Kollontai; s predisl. P. Vinogradskoi. [Moskva] Gos. izd-vo, 1921. 128 p. illus.

The volume contains an account about the conference and texts of speeches and reports to the conference. Annexed: theses adopted by the conference, a list of participants and texts of greetings received by the conerence.

Hoover, BDIC

2. International Women's Conference against War and Fascism, Paris, August 4—6, 1934

See: *Frauen unter faschistischen Terror;* no. 2152.

3. Books and Pamphlets concerning Women's Activities in the Communist International

2274 BLONINA, El.
Rabotnitsy v Internatsionale. Moskva, Gos. izd-vo, 1920. 46 p.
Hoover, BDIC

2275 BOIARSKAIA, Z.
Mezhdunarodnoe zhenskoe rabochee dvizhenie. Moskva, Gos. izd-vo, 1926. 46 p. (Biblioteka rabotnitsy i krest'ianki; seriia "Mezhdunarodnoe zhenskoe dvizhenie", no. 1)
Col

2276 KOLLONTAI, Alexandra M.
Rabotnitsa i krest'ianka v Sovetskoi Rossii. Petrograd, Izd. Kommunisticheskogo Internatsionala, 1921. 48 p. In place of imprint: Mezhdunarodnyi sekretariat po rabote sredi zhenshchin pri Ispolkome Kominterna.
NYPL

KOMINTERN i trudiashchaiasia zhenshchina. See no. 114.

Die KOMINTERN und die werktätige Frau. See no. 117.

2277 RICHTLINIEN für die kommunistische Frauenbewegung. Herausgegeben im Auftrag des II. Kongresses der Kommunistischen Internationale vom Exekutivkomitee in Moskau. Anhang: Einleitung zur
russischen Ausgabe der Richtlinien. Leipzig, Frankes Verlag, 1920. 31 p.
Felt

2278 ZHENSKOE mezhdunarodnoe dvizhenie; sbornik statei. Podarok
krest'ianke ot moskovskoi pechatnitsy. Moskva, Moskovskii gub. soiuz
rabochikh poligraficheskogo proizvodstva, 1920. 16 p. *BDIC*

ADDENDUM

308b McKENZIE, Kermit E.
Comintern and world revolution, 1928—1934; the shaping of doctrine.
London, New York, Columbia University Press, 1963 [c1964] 368 p.
(Columbia Unviersity. Studies of the Russian Institute) *Hoover*

457 MOLOTOV, V. M.
Der 6. Weltkongreß und der Kampf für den Kommunismus; Rede vor
den Leningrader Funktionären der KPdSU 7. September 1928. Hamburg,
C. Hoym Nachf. [c1928] 27 p. *Hoover, NYPL, Amst, Felt*

1332a ROY, M. N.
My experiences in China [2. ed.] Calcutta, Renaissance Publishers,
1945. 70 p.

"A summary of the chapters of 'Revolution and counterrevolution in China'
setting forth the march of events during the years 1926–27, ... written in 1930
and published only in German." (Introduction.) See annotation to next item.
Hoover

1332b ROY, M. N.
Revolution and counter revolution in China. Calcutta, Renaissance
Publishers [1946] viii, 689 p.

„This book was written ... in 1930. It was published in German in the following
year ... The closing chapters are based on ... *The Chinese revolution*, published
in Russian by the State Publishing Department." (p. vi) The author obviously
refers here to the Russian item listed above as no. 1332. The English edition is
a translation of the German volume *Revolution und Gegenrevolution in China*
which appeared in 1931. This German edition is not held by the Hoover Institution and was not reported by any other library. *Hoover*

APPENDIXES

APPENDIX I

Location Code

Amst	International Institute for Social History, Amsterdam, Netherlands
BDIC	Bibliotheque de Documentation Internationale Contemporaine, Paris, France
BostPL	Boston Public Library, Boston, Mass.
Brown	Brown University, Providence, R. I.
BrynM	Bryn Mawr College, Bryn Mawr, Pa.
Carn	Carnegie Endowment for International Peace, New York, N.Y.
ClevP	Cleveland Public Library, Cleveland, Ohio
Col	Columbia University Library, New York, N.Y.
Corn	Cornell University, Ithaca, N.Y.
DLab	Department of Labor, Library, Washington D. C.
DState	Department of State, Library, Washington, D. C.
Duke	Duke University, Durham, N. C.
Felt	Feltrinelli Institute, Milan, Italy
Harv	Harvard University Library, Cambridge, Mass.
Hoover	Hoover Institution, Stanford, Calif.
Illin	University of Illinois, Urbana, Ill.
Iowa	State University of Iowa, Iowa City, Iowa
IowaAgr	Iowa State College of Agriculture, Ames, Iowa
JCre	John Crerar Library, Chicago, Ill.
Jeff	Jefferson School of Social Science, New York, N.Y.
JHop	Johns Hopkins University, Baltimore, Md.
LC	Library of Congress, Washington, D. C.
Newb	Newberry Library, Chicago, Ill.
NWest	Northwestern University, Evanston, Ill.
NYPL	New York Public Library, New York, N.Y.
NYUn	New York University, New York, N.Y.
Oberl	Oberlin College, Oberlin, Ohio
Ohio	Ohio State University, Columbus, Ohio
Princ	Princeton University, Princeton. N.J.
SInSt	Slavic Institute of the University of Stockholm, Stockholm, Sweden
Swart	Swarthmore College, Swarthmore, Pa.
UCal	University of California, Berkeley, Calif.
UChic	University of Chicago, Chicago, Ill.
UCin	University of Cincinati, Cincinati, Ohio
UCLA	University of California at Los Angeles, Los Angeles, Calif.
UCon	University of Connecticut, Storrs, Conn.
UKans	University of Kansas, Lawrence, Kans.

ULa	Luoisiana State University, Baton Rouge, La.
UMich	University of Michigan, Ann Arbor, Mich.
UMinn	University of Minnesota, Minneapolis, Minn.
UNCar	University of North Carolina, Chapel Hill, N. C.
UPenn	University of Pennsylvania, Philadelphia, Pa.
UTenn	University of Tennessee, Knoxville, Tenn.
UTex	University of Texas, Austin, Tex.
UVirg	University of Virginia, Charlottesville, Va.
UWash	University of Washington, Seattle, Wash.
UWisc	University of Wisconsin, Madison, Wisc.
Yale	Yale University, New Haven, Conn.

APPENDIX II

Transliteration Table

Russian Letters		Transliteration	
А	а	A	a
Б	б	B	b
В	в	V	v
Г	г	G	g
Д	д	D	d
Е	е	E	e
Ж	ж	Zh	zh
З	з	Z	z
И	и	I	i
Й	й	I	i
К	к	K	k
Л	л	L	l
М	м	M	m
Н	н	N	n
О	о	O	o
П	п	P	p
Р	р	R	r
С	с	S	s
Т	т	T	t
У	у	U	u
Ф	ф	F	f
Х	х	Kh	kh
Ц	ц	TS	ts
Ч	ч	Ch	ch
Ш	ш	Sh	sh
Щ	щ	Shch	shch
Ъ	ъ[1]	ʺ	ʺ
Ы	ы	Y	y
Ь	ь	ʹ	ʹ
Э	э	E	e
Ю	ю	IU	iu
Я	я	IA	ia

[1] Transliterated when in the middle of word, disregarded when final.

APPENDIX III

Key to Abbreviations

[c]	copyright (taken from copyright page)
C. E. or CE	Comité Executif
CEIC	Comité Executif de l'Internationale Communiste
CGTU	Confédération Générale du Travail Unitaire
C. I. or CI	Communist International
comp.	compiled or compiler
CPF	Communist Party of France
CPGB	Communist Party of Great Britain
CPH	Communist Party of the Netherlands
CPSU	Communist Party of the Soviet Union
CYI	Communist Youth International
diagrs.	diagrams
dop.	dopolnennoe or dopolnitelnoe
dr.	i drugie (and others)
E. B. or EB	Executive Bureau
E. C. or EC	Executive Committee
ECCI	Executive Committee of the Communist International
ed.	edited or editor
EK	Exekutiv Komitee
EKKI	Exekutiv Komitee der Kommunistischen Internationale (in Serbo-Croatian prints: the same in Serbo-Croatian)
facsim.	facsimile
G. I. or GI	Gewerkschafts Internationale
Gos.	
Gos. izd-vo	} Gosudarstvennoe izdatelstvo
Gosizdat	
hrsg. Hrsg.	herausgegeben bei, or Herausgeber
I. C. or IC	Internationale Communiste
ICJ or IJC	Internationale Communiste des Jeunes
IKKI	Ispolnitelnyi komitet Kommunisticheskogo Internationala
IKKIM	Ispolnitelyi komitet Kommunisticheskogo Internationala Molodezhi
illus.	illustrations
ILP	Independent Labour Party (Great Britain)
IMEL	Institut Marksa-Engelsa-Lenina in Moscow
IRA	International Red Aid
IRH	Internationale Rote Hilfe

ISR	Internationale Syndicale Rouge
KAPD	Kommunistische Arbeiter Partei Deutschlands
KIM	Kommunisticheskii Internatsional Molodezhi
KJ or KJI	Kommunistische Jugendinternationale (Jugend-Internationale)
KP(b)SU	Kommunistische Partei (bolschewiki) der Sowjet Union
KP(b)U	Komunistychna partia (bolshevikiv) Ukrainy
KPD	Kommunistische Partei Deutschlands
KPP	Komunistyczna Partia Polski
KPR	Kommunistische Partei Rußlands
KPSU	Kommunistische Partei der Sowjet Union
mimeogr.	mimeographed
MOPR	Mezhdunarodnaia Organizatsiia Pomoshchi Bortsam Revoliutsii
n. d.	no date (on title page)
n. p.	no place of publication (on title page)
Partizdat	Partiinoe izdatel'stvo
P. C. or PC	Parti Communiste
PCB	Parti Communiste Belge
PCF or PFC	Parti Communiste Français
pererab.	pererabotanoe
polit. lit-ry	politicheskii literatury
ports.	portraits in text
predisl.	predislove
red.	redaktsiia or redaktor
RGI	Rote Gewerkschafts Internationale
RILU	Red International of Labor Unions
RKP(b)	Rossiiskaia Kommunisticheskaia Partiia (bolsheviki)
sots. ekon. lit.	sotsialno ekonomicheskoi literatury (izdatelstvo)
SRI	Secours Rouge Internationale, and Soccoro Rojo Internacional
t., tt.	tovarishch, or tovarishii
tip.	tipografiia
TS. K. or TSK	Tsentralnyi komitet
UdSSR	Union der Sozialistischen Sowjet Republiken
USSR	Union of Socialist Soviet Republics
VKP(b)	Vsesoiuznaia Kommunisticheskaia Partiia (bolshevikov)
VLKSM	Vsesoiuznyi Leninskii Kommunisticheskii Soiuz Molodezhi
stup.	vstupitelnaia (statia)
V. TS. S. S. P. S.	Vsesoiznyi tsentralnyi sov'et professionalnykh soiuzov
W. I. R.	Workers International Relief
Y. C. I. or YCI	Young Communist International (Communist Youth International)
ZK	Zentral Komitee

INDEX

The numerals refer to current entry numbers of the Checklist.

The Preface and Introduction have not been indexed.

Abbreviations used in the Index: n. aft. — note after; n. bef. — note before.

For other abbreviations see p. 469.

A

Abramovich, R., 307
Achkanov, Grigorii, 1777, 1797
Achminov, G. F., **see** Akhminov
Adler, Friedrich, 1649
Adoratskii, V., 119
Agrarian problems, 549, 574, 609
Aikhenvald, A., 1322
Akademiia nauk SSSR, Institut istorii, 203;
    see also Kommunisticheskaia akademiia
Akhmed, 175
Akhminov, G. F., 466–67
Akselrod, T. L., 34
Alaz, N., 35
Albrecht, A., 1328
Aldred, Guy Alfred, 205
Aleksinskii, G. (French: Alexinsky), 1030
All-Russian Central Council of Trade
    Unions (Vserossiiskii TSentralnyi Sovet
    Professionalnykh Soiuzov), 1905, 1929,
    1933, 1935; its relationship to R.I.L.U.,
    1772–75
All-Russian Cooperative Society (London
    office, known as Arcos), 105
Allied Intervention in Russia, 1337, 1698
Alouf, A., 1798
Alter, Wiktor, 206
Altman, M., 1195
American left and Russian Revolution, 1498
American Section of the International
    Committee to Combat the World
    Menace of Communism, 1393
Amsterdam, Saul (pseud.: Henrykowski;
    Russian: Genrikovskii), 907, 1202
Anarchists, 1726, 1770
Anderle, Alfred, 327
Andersen, Victor, 311, 312
Anderson, Paul Herbert, 1498
Andersson, Emil, 1472
Andreev, Andrei A., 1781, 1799
Angaretis, 908

Anglo-Russian Trade Union Conference,
    1781–87; (It created the:) Anglo-Russian
    Trade Union Committee, 113, 1125,
    1781–87, 1775, 1781
Anti-Comintern Pact (1936), 308a
Antikomintern (Gesamtverband deutscher
    Anti-Kommunistischer Verbände), Berlin,
    23, 24, 1028, 1386, 1387, 1393, 1394, 1469,
    1483
Anti-war propaganda and actions of
    Comintern and its member-sections (also
    pacifist propaganda), 93, 99, 103, 109,
    112, 116, 118, 125, 280, 452, 795, 816–819,
    846, 847, 865, 866, 878, 881, 883, 886, 888,
    913, 917, 933, 936–38, 968, 970–72, 978,
    982, 984, 993, 1010, 1012, 1020, 1022,
    1029, 1039, 1118, 1134, 1164, 1169–71,
    1181, 1212, 1213, 1246, 1247, 1252, 1253,
    1259, 1261, 1267–69, 1278, 1283, 1290,
    1293, 1293a, 1309, 1323, 1585–1600, 1627,
    1789; **see also** World War II, Comintern
    attitude; Fascism as a war danger
Antoshkin, D., 1800
Aquila, G. (pseud. of Sas [Schasch],
    Gyula), 776
"Arcos" **see** All-Russian Cooperative
    Society
Armed uprisings, communist theory and
    tactic, 404, 1602–05, 1869; in particular
    countries, **see** Revolution
Armenia, 1612
Arnot, Robert Page, 1171, 1444, 1787
Arnu, A., 2147
Aron, Raymond, 219, 286
Artuski, J., 206
Asia, 1317–21
Aubert, Theodore, 335, 410, 1663, 1673
Australia, 1341, 1342
Austria, 108, 902, 1296, 1345–48, 2187, 2188
Autonomous tendencies in C.Y.I., 1050,
    2019
Axelrod, T. L., **see** Akselrod
Azerbaijan, 1612

471

of "class justice", 2185–86; general publications by and about I.R.A., 2143–2182a; reports to Soviet I.R.A., 2225–28

Conference, congresses, plenums:
  Conference (1924), 2212, 2213
  1-st Congress (1932), 2212
  2-nd Plenum (1928), 2223
  3-rd Plenum (1931), 2224

International situation (in communist evaluation), 566–69, 575, 576, 665, 670–673, 678, 684, 685, 696, 702, 712, 719, 735, 736, 740–43, 745–48, 816–20, 852, 853, 880, 881, 1005, 1051–53, 1068, 1075, 1100, 1104, 1105, 1108, 1112, 1114, 1144, 1147, 1164, 1165, 1167, 1173–75, 1178, 1182, 1184, 1198, 1199, 1201, 1203, 1209–1213, 1228, 1233, 1235, 1323

International Trade Union Committee of Negro Workers, 1754

International Trade Union Federation (Also called Trade Union International), Amsterdam, 700, 1715, 1734, 1746, 1851, 1857

International trade union movement, 36, 688, 1708–33, 1753, 1795, 1796; task of, 1881, 1886, 1889, 1902–04, 1906; task of communists in, 734, 739, 757, 757a, 1036, 1090, 1093, 1100, 1109, 1117, 1168, 1176, 1177, 1180, 1183, 1206, 1244; C.I. tactic in, 770, 771, 779, 781, 788, 792, 794, 808; struggle for unity under C.I. leadership, 1066, 1070, 1775; at 13-th Plenum, 1245

Internationale Arbeitsgemeinschaft sozialistischer Jugendorganisationen, 2047

Internationale Presse-Korrespondenz, 1686

Internationale Vereinigung der Kommunistischen Opposition (I.V.K.O.), 1593, 1687, 1688

Internationaler Sozialistischer Kampf-Bund, 344

Internationals, joint treatment of First, Second, and Third, 146, 148, 151, 152–54, 156, 160–63, 167; First and Third, 168; Second and Third, 147, 149, 150, 159, 165, 166; Second, see Socialist International; Third, see Communist International

Iosifov, F.M., 43
Ireland, 1219, 1220
Isaacs, Harold R., 1325
Istituto Giangiacomo Feltrinelli, Milan, 7

Italy, 111, 128, 647, 722, 1464–68, 1768; the Italian "Left" and the C.I., 647
IUnovich, M., 3
IUzefovich, IOsif (German: Jusefowitsch, J.), 254, 1739, 1775, 1923

J

Jackson, George D., 2240
Jacoby, Jean, 1372
Jahn, Gisela, 327
James, Cyril R., 255, 256
Japan, 308a, 905, 970(8), 1265, 1337, 1769, 1971, 2035
Jaroslawski, J., see IAroslavskii, I.
Jauernig, Edmund, 327
Jaurès, Jean Léon, 193
Jenks, M., 485
Jews in Comintern, 129, 265
Joffe, A.A., 1641
Jogiches, Leo, 82
Johnson, F., 955, 971
Jordi, Hugo, 257
Juan (Russian: Khuan), 906
Jusefowitsch, I., see IUzefovich, IOsif
Jürgen, **304**

K

Kabakchiev, Khristo St., 258, 259, 1343
Kaczanowska, Jadwiga, 5
Kaganovich, L., 437
Kalbe, Ernestgert, 327
Kalicka, Felicja, 1573
Kamenev, Lev Borisovich (pseud. of Rosenfeld), 26, 260, 546, 646, 1405
Kandler, Georg, 361
Kang, Sheng (**also** Kang, Sin, Hsing, Kang), 970, 1256, 1264, 1272
Kanter, H., 1766
Kantorovich, Haim, 261
Kara-Murza, G., 138
Karisky, Giorgio, 236
Karpinski, V.A., 232, 233
Karski, J., see Marchlewski, Julian
Kashen, M., see Cachin, Marcel
Katayama, Sen, 85, n. bef. 1660
Kattel, B., 2160
Kautsky, Karl, 157, 470–71

M

Madiar, L., 131

Mai, Joachim, 327

Mairey, Serge, 146

Maitan, Livio, 375

Malenkov, Georgii Maksimilianovich, 350, 351

Malfere, Edgar, 1370

Mali, Teodor, 2239

Manchukuo, 1338–40

Manheim, Ralph, 349

Manifestoes of the Communist International, 140, 235, 507, 508, 510–16, 518–24,
526–28, 531–34, 592, 593, 598–601, 610,
611, 614, 626–29, 636, 638–40, 644, 795,
1308, 1310, 1530, 1532, 1540

Mann, Tom, 1818, 1822

Manner, Kullervo, 1171

Manuilskii, Dmitrii Z. (also Manoeilski, or
Manouilski or Manuilsky), 441–45, 459–
465, 559, 777, 785, 791, 822, 910–12,
929–32, 959–64, 968–70, 980, 981, 990,
1002, 1003, 1013, 1021, 1067, 1080, 1081,
1113, 1145, 1150, 1151, 1154, 1155, 1157,
1160, 1165, 1167, 1173, 1174, 1175, 1178,
1179, 1182, 1184, 1204, 1205, 1214–16,
1223, 1224, 1226, 1247, 1253, 1261, 1269,
1278, 1347, 1348, 1581a, 2215, 2216

Marchand, René, 1412, 1413, 1414

Marchenko, Mitrofan K., 409

Marchlewski, Julian (pseud.: Karski, J.;
Russian: Markhlevskii, IU.), 74, 574

Markosch, F., 2211

Martin, Paul, 1320

Martinez, 906

Martlin, **see** Matlin

Martov, L. (Tsederbaum, YUlii Osipovich;
pseudonyms: Martov, YU., Egorov), 307,
1415, 1416

Marty, André, 913, 942, 968, 969, 982, 1012,
2167, 2223

Martyn, 908

Martynov, A. (pseud. of Piker, Aleksandr),
308, 1591

Marx, Karl, 339, 873, 1695, 2134

Marx, Magdaleine, 2203

Marx-Engels-Lenin Institute, Moscow, **see**
Institut Marksa-Engelsa-Lenina

Maslenikov, Nik., 2168

Maslow, P., 1405

Matkovskii, N. V., 112

Matlin, B., 2039

Matsuoka, Yosuke, 308a

Matteotti, Giacomo, 2146

Maurin, J., 1770

Maxe, Jean, 172

May first celebration, history of, 1951

Mecheriakov, N. L., **see** Meshcheriakov, N.

Mehring, Franz, 82, 83

Mekinen, 908

Memoirs, 178–202

Mercier, Cardinal, 1671

Merker, Paul, 1725, 1924

Merrheim, Alphonse, 1474

Meshcheriakov, Nikolai, 2241

Mexico, 1497

Mezhdunarodnaia Organizatsiia Pomoshchi Bortsam Revolliutsii (MOPR),
see International Red Aid

Mezhdunarodaia Organizatsiia Rabochei
Pomoshchi (Mezhrabpom), **see** Workers
International Relief

Mgeladze, **see** Wardin, I. (pseud.)

Mieczyński, W., 528

Mif, P., 131, 138

Mijusković, Milisav, 160

Miliutin, Vladimir Pavlovich, 1694

Mingulin, I., 253, 1621

Ming Wang, **see** Wang Ming

Minor, Robert, 1515

Mins, L. E., 973

Miroshevskii, Vl., 1993

Mitteleuropäisches Büro der Kommunistischen Internationale, Berlin, instructions
from ECCI, 480

Molotov, Viacheslav M., 436, 437, 438, 439,
440, 456–58, 1145, 1156, 1158, 1159, 1160.

Monatte, Pierre, 1568

Monmousseau, Gaston (Russian: Monmusso), 757, 757a, 1854, 1860

Morosow, Boris, 327

Morrow, F. D., 339

Moscow extends greetings to III-rd
congress, 663

Moteiro, Jose Getulio, 1695

Müller, A., 418

Müller, Hermann, 327

Müller, Hertha, 2188, 2195

Münzenberg, Willi (pseud.: M., Willi), 243,
648, 776, 1994–99, 2048, 2061, 2069,
n. bef. 2244–46, 2256–59, 2261–64

Munich pact (1938), 1310, 1530, 1532, 1540

Murphy, John Tohams, 198, 1847, 2175

Mussolini, Benito, 1652